Basic Guide to
Data Communications

McGRAW-HILL/DATA COMMUNICATIONS BOOK SERIES EDITION **2**

Basic Guide to Data Communications

EDITED BY RAY SARCH

Data Communications BOOK SERIES

McGraw-Hill, Inc.
1221 Avenue of the Americas
New York, NY 10020

McGraw-Hill Data Communications BOOK SERIES

McGraw-Hill, Inc.
1221 Avenue of the Americas
New York, NY 10020

- **Basic Guide to Data Communications, Edition 2**
- **Cases in Network Design**
- **Connectivity and Standards, Volume 3**
- **Data Communications: A Comprehensive Approach, Edition II**
- **Data Communications: Beyond the Basics**
- **Data Network Design Strategies, Volume 4**
- **Inside X.25: A Manager's Guide**
- **Integrating Voice and Data, Volume 3**
- **Linking Microcomputers**
- **The Local Area Network Handbook, Volume 3**
- **Network Management and Maintenance, Volume 4**
- **Networking Software**
- **Telecommunications and Data Communications Factbook**

Copyright © 1990 by McGraw-Hill, Inc. All rights reserved. Printed in the United States of America. Except as permitted under the United States Copyright Act of 1976, no part of this publication may be reproduced or distributed in any form or by any means, or stored in a data base or retrieval system, without the prior written permission of the publisher.

Library in Congress Cataloging-in-Publication Data

Basic guide to data communications / edited by Ray Sarch. — 2nd ed.
    p. cm. — (Data communications book series)
  ISBN 0-07-607026-3 : $34.95
  1. Data transmission systems. 2. Computer networks. I. Sarch,
Ray. II. Series: McGraw-Hill data communications book series.
TK5105.B364 1990
384.3—dc20
                                                  90-3255
                                                      CIP

Table of Contents

vii **Preface**

1 **SECTION 1**
NETWORKING AND INTERNETWORKING
2 Long-haul and local area nets — how do they differ? How are they similar? *William T. Brewer* (October 1986)
8 Understanding multiple LANs: The why and how of linking up, *George T. Koshy* (May 1986)
13 The choices in designing a fiber-optic network, *Marc A. Wernli* (June 1986)
18 The formula for network immortality, *Peter M. Haverlock* (August 1988)
25 The digital cross-connect: Cornerstone of future networks? *Bart W. Stuck* (August 1987)
33 Knocking on users' doors: Signaling System 7, *Walter Roehr* (February 1989)
41 Mastering SS7 takes a special vocabulary, *Daniel R. Seligman* (February 1989)
44 Get ready for T3 networking, *Stephen Fleming* (September 1989)

53 **SECTION 2**
LOCAL NETWORKING
54 A typology of local area networks, *Peter Gregory* (August 1986)
62 Save that LAN! Preventing network crashes, *Paulina Borsook* (April 1989)
70 FDDI: Getting to know the inside of the ring, *John F. McCool* (March 1988)

77 **SECTION 3**
NETWORK MANAGEMENT
78 Designing network control centers for greater productivity, *Kerry Kosak* (April 1988)
85 Troubleshooting network problems: By the numbers, *Gilbert Held* (May 1989)
90 What you don't know about T1 jitter can give you the jitters, *Kevin B. Flynn* (May 1987)
101 T1 outage ahead: A backup strategy could save your job, *Scott L. Ledgerwood* (July 1989)
106 DDS's latest wrinkle: User diagnostics in a separate channel, *Hugh Goldberg* (December 1988)

115 **SECTION 4**
SWITCHING AND SOFTWARE
116 New signs of life for packet switching, *Edwin E. Mier* (December 1989)
127 Surveying the software that manages telecommunications, *Nathan J. Muller* (March 1987)

135 **SECTION 5**
PERIPHERALS
136 What are the differences between printers? Here's a guide. *Don Dempsey* (February 1986)
143 Is there a place for optical disks in data networks? *Gilbert Held* (February 1986)

147 **SECTION 6**
APPLICATIONS
148 Making your network make money, *James Randall* (June 1989)
156 Audiotex: The telephone as data-access equipment, *Paul F. Finnigan* (November 1986)

163 **SECTION 7**
HOW TO . . .
164 Data wiring, or learning to live with spaghetti, *Brian Laughlin* (June 1987)
168 How to make and use null modem cables, *William Sheridan* (November 1987)
172 Making the most of the versatile breakout box, *Gilbert Held* (March 1988)
177 How to find phone-line faults and what to do about them, *Jack Douglass* (September 1988)
190 Protecting networks from power transients, *Kevin R. Sharp* (September 1987)
198 Cases in direct microcomputer connections: Nuts and bolts, *Arielle Emmett and David Gabel* (July 1986)
203 Modem connections: Practical, quick check, *Arielle Emmett and David Gabel* (August 1986)
205 ADPCM offers practical method for doubling T1 capacity, *Nathan J. Muller* (February 1987)

209 **SECTION 8**
STANDARDS
210 A user's guide to the CCITT's V-series modem recommendations, *Uyless Black* (June 1989)
217 Understanding T1 basics: Primer offers picture of networking future, *Daniel R. Ruffalo* (March 1987)
222 The hidden treasures of ESF, *Frank Bradley* (September 1986)
228 A tale of two standards — the T1 ESF (r)evolution, *Michael Lefkowitz* (October 1989)
233 Getting a handle on FDDI, *Kenneth J. Thurber* (June 1989)
236 Digital signaling: Which techniques are best — and why it matters to you, *William Stallings* (November 1988)

243 **SECTION 9**
QUESTIONS AND ANSWERS
244 Can users really absorb data at today's rates? Tomorrow's? *Hal B. Becker* (July 1986)
253 Consultants: For better or worse, business is booming, *John T. Mulqueen* (November 1988)
264 Leasing becomes a user's paradise (November 1988)
268 Minimize risk: Pick the right product — plus the right vendor, *Nathan J. Muller* (July 1988)
275 What makes a building intelligent? *Thomas B. Cross* (March 1986)
286 Is a private T1 network the right *business* decision? *Timothy G. Zerbiec and Rosemary M. Cochran* (July 1988)
299 Using testing to pick the right multiplexer, *John R. Curran* (July 1989)
304 Is ISDN an obsolete data network? *Gilbert Held* (November 1989)
309 Making sense of today's image communications alternatives, *Donald J. Ryan* (April 1987)

315 **SECTION 10**
GLOSSARY
316 Data Communications Glossary (March 1988)

Preface

When McGraw-Hill little more than a decade ago first published a collection of articles from Data Communications Magazine under the title "Basics of Data Communications," founding editor Harry Karp noted that "the field is still in its infancy". It has grown fast. With a small name change, *an update* in 1985 build upon the original work with all new articles. The idea was to acquaint readers not only with the fundamentals but also with the state of the art of Networking. The idea hasn't changed with this edition, but the content is entirely new, consisting of articles that have appeared in just the past four years.

That updating should help readers anticipate the trend that will drive data communications over the coming decade. Readers should bear in mind that the industry is still far from mature. As in any dynamic market, cost and vendor data are constantly changing, so for up-to-date vendor and product information readers should consult an authoritative source such as the current issue of the Data Communications *Basic* Guide.

Section 1
Networking and Internetworking

William T. Brewer, Air Training Command, Randolph Air Force Base, Tex.

Long-haul and local area nets—how do they differ? How are they similar?

This tutorial spells out the effect of different access techniques upon the throughput of each network type.

Many internetworking issues are not unique to local area networks (LANs), in spite of the emphasis in some popular technical literature. To place the real differences between LANs and long-haul networks into proper perspective, note that the architectural differences are in the lower layers. Specifically, the differences are in Layers 0, 1 (physical), and 2 (data link) of the OSI (Open Systems Interconnection) reference model, as shown in Figure 1. (The International Organization for Standardization, or ISO, does not define Layer 0 in the model. Still, many authors have conceptually extended the model to include transmission mechanisms by designating them as Layer 0.)

Key areas of distinction between network types in these lower layers are topology and access techniques. Once beyond the layers and sublayers that specify network topology and media access, both LANs and long-haul networks can and should be similar.

Let us first look at access techniques in general. The left side of Figure 1 shows that multiple levels of access may exist in a layered communications architecture. In general, the peer-to-peer operation of an access protocol allows a protocol layer to provide access service to a higher layer. For example, a subnetwork access protocol is the basis for the subnetwork access service provided by Layer 3 (Network) to Layer 4 (Transport). Likewise, a media access protocol typically operates in a sublayer within the data-link layer to give the data-link access to the transmission medium. Figure 1 shows a typical sublayering of Layer 2 into logical link control and media access control.

Generally, access techniques fall into three categories: centralized, distributed, and decentralized (see "Access techniques"). These classifications are idealized for a conceptual discussion. Real-world protocols are often hybrids, somewhere on a continuum between the two extremes of total centralization and total decentralization.

Furthermore, their position on this continuum may constantly change as network conditions vary. For example, some protocols operate on a decentralized basis under light traffic loads and move toward a more distributed nature as traffic loads increase. For more information on access protocols that adapt to traffic loads, see the following DATA COMMUNICATIONS articles: "A comparison of two 'guaranteed' local network access methods," February 1984, p. 143, and "Multiple access method embraces popular local net schemes," November 1983, p. 237.

Coordinate to transmit

Half-duplex transmission, which is sometimes used in long-haul networks, requires some type of media-access control. Since transmission on half-duplex links is limited to one direction at a time, transmitting and receiving stations must coordinate the line turnaround before the receiving station can access the link. Until this is accomplished, the receiving station is denied access to the medium.

To illustrate the distinction between media access and data-link access: Media access involves access to physical channels; data-link access involves access to logical channels. In some cases, a station could have access to the network's media yet be denied access to the data link's logical channel—and therefore could not transmit.

To further illustrate this point, consider the distinction between hard and soft turnarounds on a data link. When soft turnarounds are used, a station is unable to transmit until it gets permission from the other end of the data link, even though it may have complete access (permission to transmit) to the associated transmission medium. A hard turnaround is coordinated between Layers 2 and 0 across Layer 1 (Fig. 1); a soft turnaround is coordinated between Layer 2 entities.

Hard turnarounds are used for media-access control on half-duplex, point-to-point links, as previously discussed.

1. Architectural comparison. *Local area networks and long-haul networks differ in their lower layers. Shown is a typical sublayering of Layer 2 (data link) into logical link con-* *trol and media-access control. A media-access protocol typically operates in a sublayer within Layer 2 to give the data link access to the medium.*

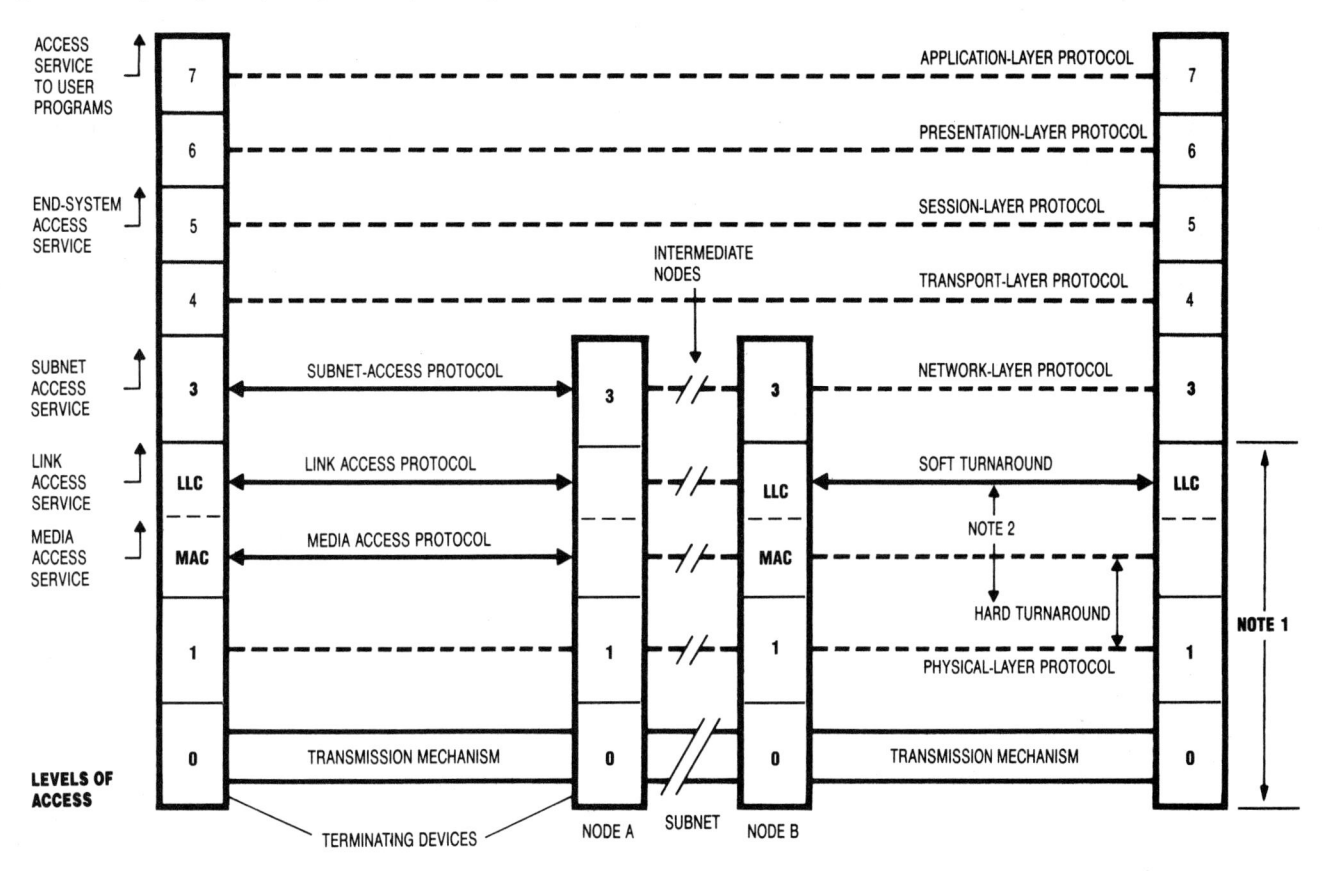

NOTE 1: AREA OF DISTINCTION BETWEEN LOCAL AREA NETWORKS AND LONG-HAUL NETWORKS.
NOTE 2: A SOFT TURNAROUND IS COORDINATED BETWEEN LAYER-2 ENTITIES; A HARD TURNAROUND IS COORDINATED BETWEEN LAYER 2 AND LAYER 0 ACROSS LAYER 1.

LLC = LOGICAL LINK CONTROL
MAC = MEDIA ACCESS CONTROL

On the other hand, soft turnarounds may be used on full-duplex, point-to-point links to provide data-link access. In effect, soft turnarounds may be used to provide half-duplex data-link operation even though the underlying transmission medium may be full-duplex. Reasons for using soft turnarounds on a full-duplex link may be traced to buffering, protocol, or processing limitations in the stations attached to the link.

People analogy

A good illustration of half-duplex operation is human interaction. People are essentially half-duplex; that is, they can talk, and they can listen, but they can't talk and listen at the same time. Hence they are half-duplex. On the other hand, the air people use for talking is a full-duplex medium. Because of the limitations of the human mind, people enforce half-duplex operation over this full-duplex medium. Computers often enforce a half-duplex protocol over a full-duplex medium for analogous reasons.

As we've seen, media access is not a problem that developed with the emergence of LANs. Data communi-

cators have been implementing media access by turning the line around on half-duplex data links for a long time. But media access in the form of line turnaround between two stations on a half-duplex link is relatively simple. By comparison, a LAN—as is the case in a complex network—may be shared by hundreds of devices arranged in a variety of topologies, with line turnaround required for many directions.

Figure 2a shows a broadcast topology typical of many LANs. Any of the three types of media-access techniques identified in Table 1 (centralized, distributed, and decentralized) could be applied to this topology.

Satellite-based networks provide a good example of broadcast topologies that use either decentralized or distributed media-access techniques. A distributed technique frequently used is time-division multiple access (TDMA)—even though the timing is centralized—and a decentralized technique is the contention technique previously discussed. This TDMA, in a sense, can be characterized as token passing. However, there is no token, but master status is still passed around the medium based on

Access techniques

Consider the operation of a typical school classroom. The air (the medium) is shared by members of the class in much the same way that communicating computers share a network. In both situations, the type of access technique used will determine the timing, duration, volume, and frequency of communications between students or between computers. Moreover, the amount of access control given to each participant, student, or computer is the key to classifying the access technique used as centralized, distributed, or decentralized. (See figure for the generic definitions of these terms.)

Centralized example. Using the classroom analogy, all access control is in the hands of the teacher—students talk only when permitted by the teacher.

Distributed example. A distributed access technique eliminates the teacher's function as permanent master. Instead, control of the medium is distributed equally among class members by allowing each student to temporarily act as a master for a fixed interval of time.

Decentralized example. Here all students try to act as the teacher at the same time. Obviously, this would result in conflict if every student wanted to contribute to a discussion at once. But this technique could be most efficient in situations where student contributions to the discussion were lengthy but infrequent.

The analogy in a computer network environment:

A centralized technique. Polling allows a single master station to control access to a network that is shared with a number of other (slave) stations.

A distributed technique. Token passing in a ring topology illustrates distributed access in computer networks. This technique makes all stations equal, each being a temporary master with temporary access to the transmission medium whenever it has the token. In a token-bus configuration, the token is explicitly addressed from station to station, based upon station addresses stored at each station. The sequence for passing the token on a bus creates a logical ring for distributing access to network stations.

A decentralized technique. Here, each station contends with all other stations on an equal basis for access to the transmission medium. If two or more stations try to gain control of the medium at the same time, a conflict occurs—resulting in no coherent transmission. The conflict is resolved according to precise rules (algorithms). Obviously heavily loaded networks could not use this access technique, but, with light loads, the result is high throughput and fast response.

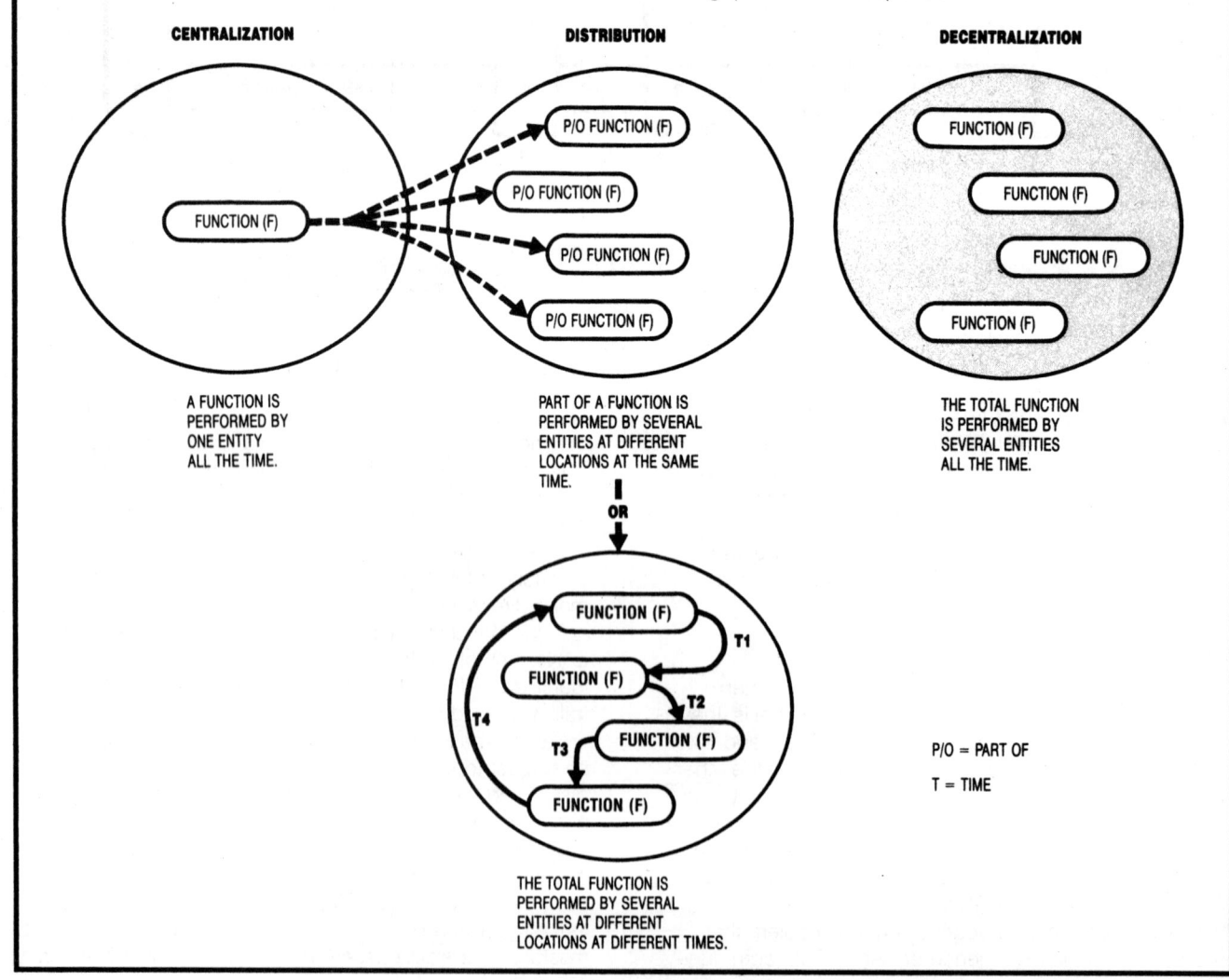

CENTRALIZATION

FUNCTION (F)

A FUNCTION IS PERFORMED BY ONE ENTITY ALL THE TIME.

DISTRIBUTION

P/O FUNCTION (F)
P/O FUNCTION (F)
P/O FUNCTION (F)
P/O FUNCTION (F)

PART OF A FUNCTION IS PERFORMED BY SEVERAL ENTITIES AT DIFFERENT LOCATIONS AT THE SAME TIME.

OR

FUNCTION (F) — T1
FUNCTION (F) — T2
FUNCTION (F) — T3
FUNCTION (F) — T4

THE TOTAL FUNCTION IS PERFORMED BY SEVERAL ENTITIES AT DIFFERENT LOCATIONS AT DIFFERENT TIMES.

DECENTRALIZATION

FUNCTION (F)
FUNCTION (F)
FUNCTION (F)
FUNCTION (F)

THE TOTAL FUNCTION IS PERFORMED BY SEVERAL ENTITIES ALL THE TIME.

P/O = PART OF
T = TIME

2. Similarities and differences. Shown are broadcast (A) and sequential (B) topologies typical of many LANs. A multisegment, long-haul network is shown in C. The architecture depicted in D is generally the same for all three. How routing is conducted from one station to another across multiple links is shown in E.

(A) MULTISEGMENT LAN

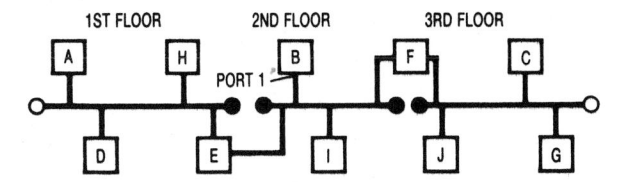

(B) MULTIRING LAN

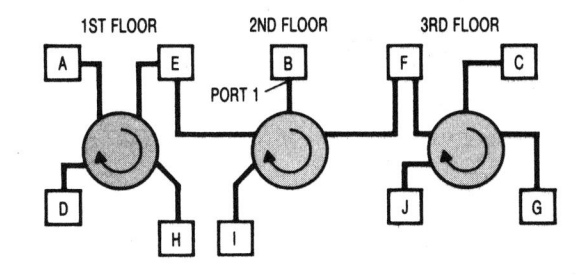

(C) MULTISEGMENT LONG-HAUL NETWORK

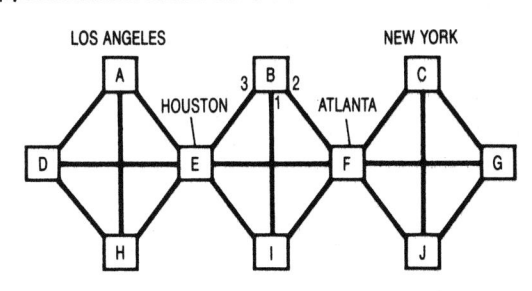

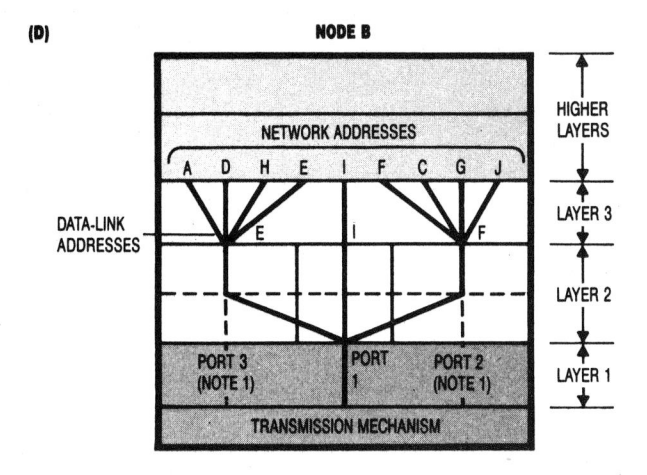

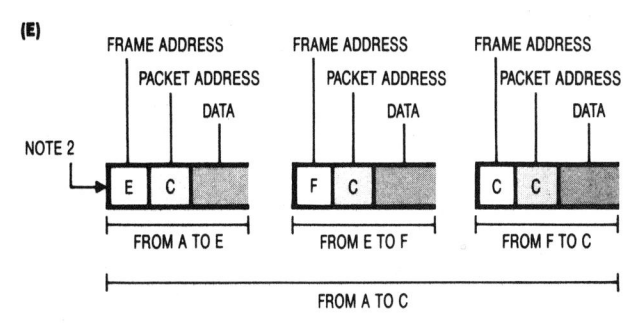

(D)

(E)

NOTE 1: IN THE LANs, ALL OF NODE B's DATA LINKS ARE MAPPED TO A SINGLE PHYSICAL PORT. IN THE LONG-HAUL NETWORK, EACH DATA LINK HAS A DEDICATED PORT.

NOTE 2: IN A LONG-HAUL NETWORK, FRAME ADDRESSES ARE NOT ALWAYS REQUIRED.

LAN = LOCAL AREA NETWORK

Table 1: Media access

	CENTRALIZED ACCESS	DISTRIBUTED ACCESS	DECENTRALIZED ACCESS
TOPOLOGIES	BROADCAST SEQUENTIAL POINT-TO-POINT	BROADCAST SEQUENTIAL POINT-TO-POINT	BROADCAST SEQUENTIAL POINT-TO-POINT
TECHNIQUE	POLLING/SELECTION	TOKEN PASSING	CONTENTION
STATION STATUS	PERMANENT MASTER/SLAVES	TEMPORARY MASTERS/SLAVES	ALL EQUAL
BEHAVIOR	DETERMINISTIC	DETERMINISTIC	PROBABILISTIC
APPLICATION	REAL-TIME HEAVY TRAFFIC (NOTE 1)	REAL-TIME HEAVY TRAFFIC (NOTE 1)	NON-REAL-TIME LIGHT TRAFFIC (NOTE 2)

NOTE 1: PROTOCOL OVERHEAD IS THE MAJOR FACTOR IN DETERMINING EFFECTIVE THROUGHPUT; THROUGHPUTS ABOVE 90 PERCENT ARE POSSIBLE.

NOTE 2: BOTH PROTOCOL OVERHEAD AND WASTED BANDWIDTH AFFECT ACTUAL THROUGHPUT; THROUGHPUTS CAN BE AS LOW AS 20 PERCENT.

possession of a particular time slot. In essence, a station's time slot is an implied token giving it access to the medium.

Satellite networks require special consideration in making comparisons between LANs and long-haul networks: They are long-haul as far as distance is concerned, yet they exhibit a broadcast topology and use access techniques characteristic of LANs. Another similarity to LANs is that they can be modeled as multistation links. So for the sake of our discussion, LANs and satellite networks are in the same class.

Same techniques

Figure 2b shows a sequential topology typical of many LANs. Once again, any of the access techniques described in Table 1 could also be applied to this topology.

The different access techniques affect the traffic load capacity and the responsiveness of the associated data link in either a deterministic or probabilistic way. In general, centralized or distributed access results in a network that behaves in a deterministic fashion, while decentralized access causes a probabilistic behavior.

In a deterministic design, the output can be determined from the input(s) with a high level of confidence. But in a probabilistic design, the output is not assured but probable, based on one or more random functions. If a deterministic-access technique is used, the carried traffic load and worst-case response time can be determined from the offered traffic load. On the other hand, if a probabilistic-access technique is used, only the probability of achieving a given response time and traffic-load capability can be calculated. Because centralized- and distributed-access techniques behave deterministically, they are better suited for real-time data flow, whereas the probabilistic nature of decentralized-access techniques limits them to non-real-time applications.

The access techniques described in Table 1 behave either deterministically or probabilistically, regardless of the topology. Polling/selection and token passing behave deterministically on both broadcast and sequential topologies because, in both topologies, the worst-case polling/selection and token-passing time intervals are known. This is not true for the contention-access techniques used on buses or rings, because access to the medium is a random function highly influenced by the traffic load on the link. These behavioral characteristics indicate that polled buses/rings and token buses/rings are suitable for real-time traffic; contention buses/rings are not. As is now apparent, the different types of media-access techniques are similar in many ways, regardless of the topology employed. Another point of similarity concerns the techniques used to give stations priority access to the transmission medium. For polled access on both broadcast and sequential topologies, a slave station can be given a higher access priority by having its address appear more than once in the master's polling list.

Token-based access requires slightly different techniques for priority access onto broadcast topologies than onto sequential topologies. On a token bus, the addresses of high-priority stations will appear more than once in the token-passing sequence. On token rings, high-priority stations can be created by causing lower-priority stations to defer their use of the token, either temporarily or for a fixed percentage of the time they have access to it.

Priority access on both contention rings and contention buses uses a similar concept. In both cases, priority access is achieved by a station increasing its persistency —via a programmed algorithm—in its attempts to access the medium. A more persistent station will attempt access more frequently than a less persistent station, thereby achieving a higher probability of gaining access to the medium.

The pluses and minuses
Traffic-load characteristics have a heavy influence on the selection of a particular media-access technique. Generally, deterministic protocols are better suited for heavy traffic loads than contention-based probabilistic protocols: They allocate the available transmission bandwidth more efficiently. But when traffic loads are light, deterministic protocols provide individual stations with slower response and less throughput in comparison with probabilistic protocols. The slower response results from stations having to wait their turn even though no other station may have anything to transmit; the smaller throughput results from limitations on the amount of data a station may send before it has to relinquish access to the medium.

Probabilistic protocols (contention-based access) have opposite traffic-handling characteristics. They behave poorly under heavy traffic loads because transmission bandwidth is wasted by stations contending for the medium. But under light traffic loads they provide stations with quicker response and higher throughput than deterministic protocols. Quicker response is possible because stations may immediately access the medium whenever it is idle; higher throughput results from the ability to quickly access the medium over and over again without the delay inherent in a token-passing or polling scheme. Indeed, under optimum load conditions some vendors claim the ability to provide a throughput of over 90 percent. However, under worst-case load conditions a contention protocol could limit throughput to less than 20 percent.

Data-link access
Media access is the lowest level of access in a network architecture. The protocols of data-link access—the next higher level—can be classified according to the same categories as those used for media-access protocols. (Table 2 shows three examples.)

Data links are, by nature, point-to-point. Therefore, access to them is not tied to any particular topology. Multipoint links are actually individual point-to-point data links that are "multiplexed" over the same physical channel. This multiplexing is accomplished by Layer 2 and is a lower-level analogy to the multiplexing that occurs in Layers 3 and 4. For example, Layer 4 can multiplex messages from more than one session over a single network connection. Layer 3, on the other hand, multiplexes packets associated with multiple network connections over a single data link. Layer 2 extends the concept to the multiplexing of frames associated with multiple data links over a single physical channel.

In Layer 0, transmission equipment can multiplex bits from multiple channels onto the same physical circuit. Layer 2 accomplishes its level of multiplexing by mapping multiple data-link addresses onto a single physical (Layer 1) address. Although the data links share the same physical channel, they behave as if they are established over dedicated channels. (Even when a station is in the broadcast mode, it would transmit to a single address that all stations are designed to recognize.)

IBM's binary synchronous communications (BSC) is used as an example of a centralized data-link access technique in Table 2. The concept behind the BSC polling/selection access technique in the data-link layer is the same as that described for the polling techniques previously described for media access. Yet their operational characteristics differ because they are implemented in different layers. BSC provides a software poll/select to control access to the data link, while hardware polling controls access to a transmission medium.

Analysis of data flow can give insight into the nature of polling/selection in the data-link layer. Protocols, such as BSC, create an unbalanced data link—that is, data flow across the link is not symmetrical (with respect to the slave stations). Polling/selection creates an unbalanced data flow

Table 2: Data-link access

	CENTRALIZED ACCESS	DISTRIBUTED ACCESS	DECENTRALIZED ACCESS
TECHNIQUE	POLLING/SELECTION	ADCCP (ABM MODE)	CONTENTION
STATION STATUS	PERMANENT MASTER/SLAVES	TEMPORARY MASTERS/SLAVES	ALL EQUAL
APPLICATION	UNBALANCED DATA FLOW	BALANCED DATA FLOW	BALANCED DATA FLOW

ADCCP = ADVANCED DATA COMMUNICATIONS CONTROL PROCEDURE
ABM = ASYNCHRONOUS BALANCED MODE

because all traffic flows to the master station in response to a poll and all traffic flows away from the master during the selection process. There is no direct data flow between slave stations.

Naturally, polling/selection can be efficient when traffic flow is primarily to and from a master station. But this type of access control is inefficient for traffic flow from one slave station to another.

Many masters
This operational mode does not hold for the distributed-access technique (Table 2). The Asynchronous Balanced Mode (ABM) of the Advanced Data Communications Control Procedure—better known as ADCCP—is an example of a distributed-access technique. This access technique allows any station to act as a master. Once again, the concept is similar to the distributed concept previously discussed with respect to media-access control, but the effect is different. Using distributed data-link access allows any station to set up a data link with any other station—a balanced data link. In other words, any station on the link can send directly to any other station on the link without going through an intermediate station.

Logical Link Control, Type 1, described in the IEEE 802 LAN standard, is an example of a decentralized data-link access technique (Table 2). Under the Type 1 protocol, data is transferred across a data link without going through a data-link establishment procedure. The fact that data-link access control doesn't exist to enforce an arbitrary data flow on the link permits a balanced data flow between stations.

Certain differences
Now that we've looked at topology and access techniques in some detail, let us put it all together. From an architectural standpoint, a single-segment (unbridged) LAN is a single multistation link, whereas a long-haul network is a concatenation of multiple links.

An accurate comparison of LANs and long-haul networks—as equivalents—must make use of a multisegment LAN. Figures 2a and 2b show two different types of multisegment LANs. Figure 2e shows how routing occurs from one station to another across multiple segments. Note the interplay of the data-link (frame) addresses with the network (packet) addresses. The data-link address is used to transfer frames from station to station on the same segment while the packet address is used to transfer packets between the bridges interconnecting the LAN segments. (A bridge between LAN segments operates similar to a node in a long-haul network. That is, the bridge routes packets from a data link associated with one physical channel to a data link associated with a different physical channel.)

Figure 2c shows a multisegment, long-haul network. Figure 2e again shows how routing occurs from one station to another across multiple links. As with the multisegment LANs, network addresses are used to route packets from node to node through the network, and data-link addresses are used to identify the logical channels assigned to each physical link. (Some data-link protocols do not provide a data-link address field because they are intended for use on point-to-point links that have only a single logical channel. For more information see DATA COMMUNICATIONS, October 1985, p. 124—part of "Inside SS No. 7: A detailed look at ISDN's signaling system plan".) By analyzing Figure 2, one can see that the Layer 3s in the LANs are doing exactly the same thing that Layer 3 is doing in the multisegment long-haul network. In the long-haul network, Layer 3 routes packets from an incoming point-to-point data link to an outgoing point-to-point data link. Similarly in the LANs, Layer 3 routes packets from an incoming multistation link to an outgoing multistation link. The only difference is the type of physical link—point-to-point versus multistation. These two types of networks differ in the nature of Layer 2 and below—Layer 3 and above are the same. We should also note that it is Layer 2 and below of the network architecture that distinguish one LAN from another LAN.

A significant point in this discussion is that Layer 3 is not aware of whether it is relaying packets across a LAN or a long-haul network. Layer 3 can operate this way because the lower layers "hide" the nature of the actual topology and access techniques from Layer 3.

In a LAN, Layer-2 addresses are used to create multiple logical channels across a shared network link. In long-haul networks, a single logical channel usually exists across each network segment. In both cases, Layer 3 is looking at logical channels, not physical channels. This means that Layer 3 cannot distinguish if it is operating in a LAN with multistation links or in a long-haul network with point-to-point links. The foregoing is true whether Layer 3 provides only intranetwork routing or both inter- and intranetwork routing. For a description of how Layer-3 functions are sublayered, see "The status and direction of Open Systems Interconnection," DATA COMMUNICATIONS, February 1985, p. 177.

The architecture depicted in Figure 2d is the same for all three of the network types shown, with two exceptions: 1) The LANs have a media-access sublayer because multiple stations are sharing a half-duplex network. 2) The data-link modules in the LANs share a common physical port, whereas the long-haul networks have a dedicated physical port for each data-link module. ■

William Brewer has 14 years experience in communications. Besides Air Force training, instruction, and requirements analysis, he has taught graduate-level courses in computer communications at the University of Southern Mississippi. He holds a master's degree in teleprocessing science and a bachelor's degree in industrial and vocational education.

George T. Koshy, Booz, Allen & Hamilton Inc., Lexington, Mass.

Understanding multiple LANs: The why and how of linking up

A consultant argues for the proliferation of multiple LANs in an organization that is bridged at the Data Link Layer.

In the late seventies and early eighties, computer users and vendors realized that they required networks to tie their diverse equipment together and to make their data processing more efficient. Controversy was fervent among vendors regarding the most appropriate single medium as well as the most appropriate single technique to access the medium. Today, such discussions have subsided because vendors and users alike have learned that neither one medium nor one access scheme will satisfy all needs at all times.

The emerging trend is toward the existence of multiple local area networks (LANs) within one organization—each one catering to the needs of a specific operation or a functional group. Multiple LANs within an organization need to be interconnected so that all users can communicate with all others if necessary. The devices that perform the interconnection are called bridges, providing high throughput and low delay so that users do not experience any significant performance degradation when communicating with other users attached to the conglomerate of LANs.

Why have multiple LANs?

This article consists of two parts. In the first part, the need for the existence of multiple LANs is described in detail. The second part deals with one issue of the architectural layer at which the interconnection should take place.

Local area networking products available today do not conform to a single standard. They exist on a variety of media, such as twisted pair, coaxial cable, and optical fiber; use two signaling schemes (baseband and broadband); and work with a variety of media access techniques, such as carrier-sense multiple access with collision detection (CSMA/CD), token passing, time-division multiplexing, and so on. There is wide support among all segments of the computer industry for the Institute of Electrical and Electronics Engineers (IEEE) 802 standards, and it is expected that within the next few years most LAN products will conform to one of these standards.

Currently, IEEE 802 standards support the following schemes:
- CSMA/CD on baseband cable.
- CSMA/CD on broadband cable.
- Token-passing bus on broadband cable.
- Token-passing bus on baseband cable.
- Token-passing ring on baseband cable.

Although they do not offer a single scheme, the IEEE 802 standards have reduced the number of options for new products.

A number of LANs may coexist in a single organization for several reasons:
- Number of stations.
- Security.
- Area of coverage.
- Media access schemes.
- Organizational growth.
- Maintenance.

The following is a detailed description of these reasons.

Number of stations. In any media access scheme the performance deteriorates with an increase in the number of stations. In CSMA/CD, the greater the number of stations, the greater the probability of collisions that reduce the effective throughput. In a token-passing scheme, the effect of the number of stations on the throughput and delay is more straightforward. The token has to pass through more stations. This reduces the time available for transmission of data and increases the time a station needs to wait in order to receive the token. In a token-passing ring network, adding more stations increases the perimeter of the ring that will reduce the throughput and increase the delay.

Security. The establishment of multiple LANs may improve the security of communications. It is desirable to keep different types of traffic that have different security needs on physically separate media. At the same time, the different types of users with different levels of security need to communicate through controlled and monitored mechanisms. Multiple LANs, rather than a single LAN, are necessary under such circumstances. For example, a LAN used by personnel or for in-house financial projections should be separate from one used for customer service or on the factory floor.

Area of coverage. In many situations, one LAN is not capable of covering all areas of a user organization, due to inherent limitations of certain media access schemes, performance, and geographical locations. Certain media access schemes put a limit on the maximum distance of the LAN. The most obvious example is CSMA/CD, which imposes a limit on the maximum distance for a given minimum frame size and transmission speed. This restriction is necessary for the effective detection of collisions. Increasing the minimum packet size increases the maximum distance, but this affects the effective throughput because frames will have to be stuffed with nondata characters. Reducing transmission speed also increases the distance, but this reduces the throughput and the number of stations that may be attached to the LAN. So a CSMA/CD scheme operates on the basis of a set of fixed values for these parameters.

For example, IEEE 802.3 specifies the speed, 10 Mbit/s; the minimum frame size, 512 bits; and the maximum distance, 1.5 kilometers (km), or 0.9 miles. In this LAN, the maximum distance between the coaxial cable and the stations, such as computers or terminal concentrators, is only 50 meters (64 feet).

Broadband LANs also do not cover all areas of large organizations. Even though CATV broadband cable can cover areas of 10s of kilometers, these LANs have restrictions, covering a maximum distance up to only a few kilometers. For example, a standard IEEE 802.3 broadband CSMA/CD LAN covers an area within a radius of 1.4 km (0.87 miles) from the headend.

Media access schemes. The nature of media access schemes makes it necessary in many cases for multiple LANs with different media access schemes to be set up. Each of the common access schemes has its individual merits and demerits that make it suitable for certain environments and unsuitable for others. For example, CSMA/CD performs well under light loading but cannot provide deterministic delays. The token-passing scheme on a bus topology provides deterministic delays but introduces relatively larger delays at low levels of loading. Token-passing rings also provide deterministic delays but are more vulnerable to failures in cables and stations. They have an advantage in that they can use optical fiber and run up to a few hundred bit/s.

The access scheme chosen for a LAN will depend on these characteristics, and an organization within one local area may have LANs of many different types. A manufacturer might use the General Motors-sponsored Manufacturing Automation Protocol (MAP) for its factory-floor communications, employing a token-passing bus LAN based on a broadband cable. Devices such as programmable contollers and robot controllers, which are directly involved in manufacturing operations, are attached to the broadband cable. The mainframe computers and peripherals at the same company might be tied together on a 10-Mbit/s token-passing ring, and the office computers and peripherals may be on a CSMA/CD bus. In this case, most communications would be confined within one type of LAN, but occasionally the office computers might need to talk to the mainframe or get information from the computers on the factory floor.

Traffic partitioning. Traffic originated at different sources must be partitioned into a number of groups, each with certain dominant characteristics. In most LANs, two major services are terminal-to-host communications and host-to-host communications. Terminal-to-host communications are characterized by small frame sizes and relatively fewer numbers of these frames. Host-to-host communications typically involve large frames and continuous generation of these frames. These two types of traffic should be put on different LANs having different characteristics. For example, terminal-to-host communications may be put on a channel operating at less than 1 Mbit/s, and host-to-host communications may be on a channel operating at 5 to 10 Mbit/s.

There are also administrative reasons for traffic partitioning. Divisions or groups within a large organization may require independence from each other. For example, a LAN for accounting and personnel departments should be separate from a second LAN used for the engineering department. Traffic can be monitored in different departments and users charged for their connect time for billing purposes. With multiple LANs, each department can grow and change its functions without affecting other sections of the company and without being affected by other sections of the company.

Organizational growth. Organizational growth could be the single most important reason for the existence of multiple LANs within an organization. If a department only has a small number of computers and peripherals, and this arrangement does not change significantly, then there is little incentive to create a LAN. If, however, the departmental computing resources are expected to change and grow, there is evey reason to have a LAN: With a LAN, the department's equipment will not have to be reconfigured every time there is a change in hardware or software. In cases like these, the motivation for establishing a LAN becomes a business rather than technological decision. This reason could be useful in convincing nontechnically oriented managers of the value of LANs.

Once a LAN is in place, the changing nature of most businesses results in the procurement of many different types of computers and peripherals for many different reasons. In most large organizations, a stable environment as far as computer networking is concerned is almost nonexistent. There will always be some part of an organization that is putting new computers into service or trying out a new piece of software or hardware. In such an environment it is advisable to divide the network into smaller sections that are independently managed, making it possible to run pilot tests without endangering the company's everyday operations.

Maintenance. Equipment that is modular in structure is easier to maintain. The same is true with networks. Even today's typical small networks of a few mainframes or minicomputers coupled with 10s of terminals are not easy to manage; networks are expected to grow into thousands of computers and terminals in the next few years, and it will be extremely difficult to manage such large networks as single entities. The solution is to divide the network into manageable sizes. Consider as an example an office complex wired with a baseband LAN using bus topology and the CSMA/CD access scheme. When the LAN does not function due to a faulty transceiver or controller on the station, it affects the entire user community. It is then difficult to locate the fault. If, on the other hand, the LAN consists of a number of separate segments, the improper operation due to a faulty component would be confined to that segment only. Such an arrangement also makes it easier to isolate the faulty component.

Mechanisms for interconnection

Having said that most large organizations will probably have multiple LANs within a limited geographical area, let us look at the possible means of providing the required interconnection between different LANs, whether local or remote. The interconnection between distant LANs will be more common than the interconnection between local LANs. The requirements and available means are different in these two situations; consequently, the solutions are also different.

LANs that are separated by long distances (perhaps up to thousands of miles) are typically interconnected using point-to-point lines operating at a few kilobits per second. These lines, which are leased from common carriers, are characterized by high cost and high incidence of bit errors (1 in 10^5).

Another common way to interconnect LANs as well as individual stations is via a Public Packet-Switching Network (PPSN). The PPSNs employ protocols that are different from the LANs, and their effective rate of data transmission is in the range of 10s of kilobits per second.

Private branch exchanges are usually used for long-distance connections and cannot usually handle enough throughput for efficient local communications. For this

1. OSI and 802. *Two IEEE sublayers correspond to one OSI Data Link Layer. The MAC sublayer handles addressing and identification of station networks.*

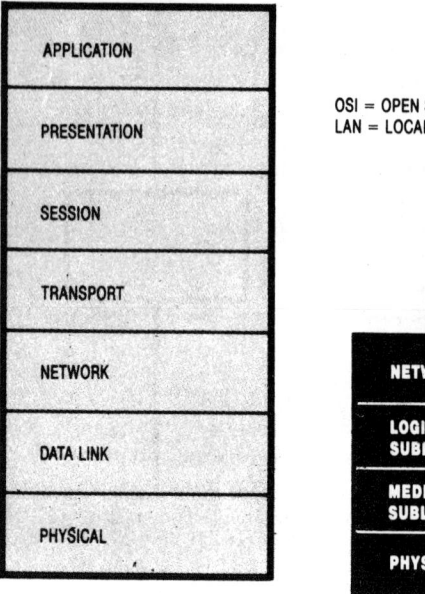

OSI = OPEN SYSTEMS INTERCONNECTION
LAN = LOCAL AREA NETWORK

reason, such considerations are not relevant to this discussion.

A long-haul network may be required to provide the interconnection of hundreds of host computers and 10s of LANs. In order to guarantee delivery in the event of link outages, there may be alternate paths in the topology. The links may use different speeds and transmission technologies. These factors make the routing of information among the stations and LANs attached to a long-haul network involve complex algorithms.

Local LANs may be interconnected using the same algorithms as those for long-haul interconnection. The Department of Defense's TCP/IP (Transport Control Protocol/Internet Protocol) is a good example. But many significant features of LANs make such complex algorithms unnecessary for interconnection when the LANs are close to each other. If the number of LANs is small and they are geographically close (within a few miles), they need not use expensive, low-speed lines leased from common carriers. Small numbers and geographical proximity can contribute to relatively fewer instances of lost connectivity that is due to hardware failures.

In such cases, interconnecting paths can be of a simple topology and would, therefore, not require an optimal path. Interconnecting devices that are all located within a limited geographical area can be easily managed.

Because the interconnection of local LANs is different from that in long-haul networks, the question arises: At which architectural layer does the interconnection take place?

2. Two LANs and a bridge. *A bridge makes decisions about switching frames between local area networks based on the address of a station. It provides the interconnection between LANs. Bridges can use different sorts of algorithms to determine the best method of network interconnection.*

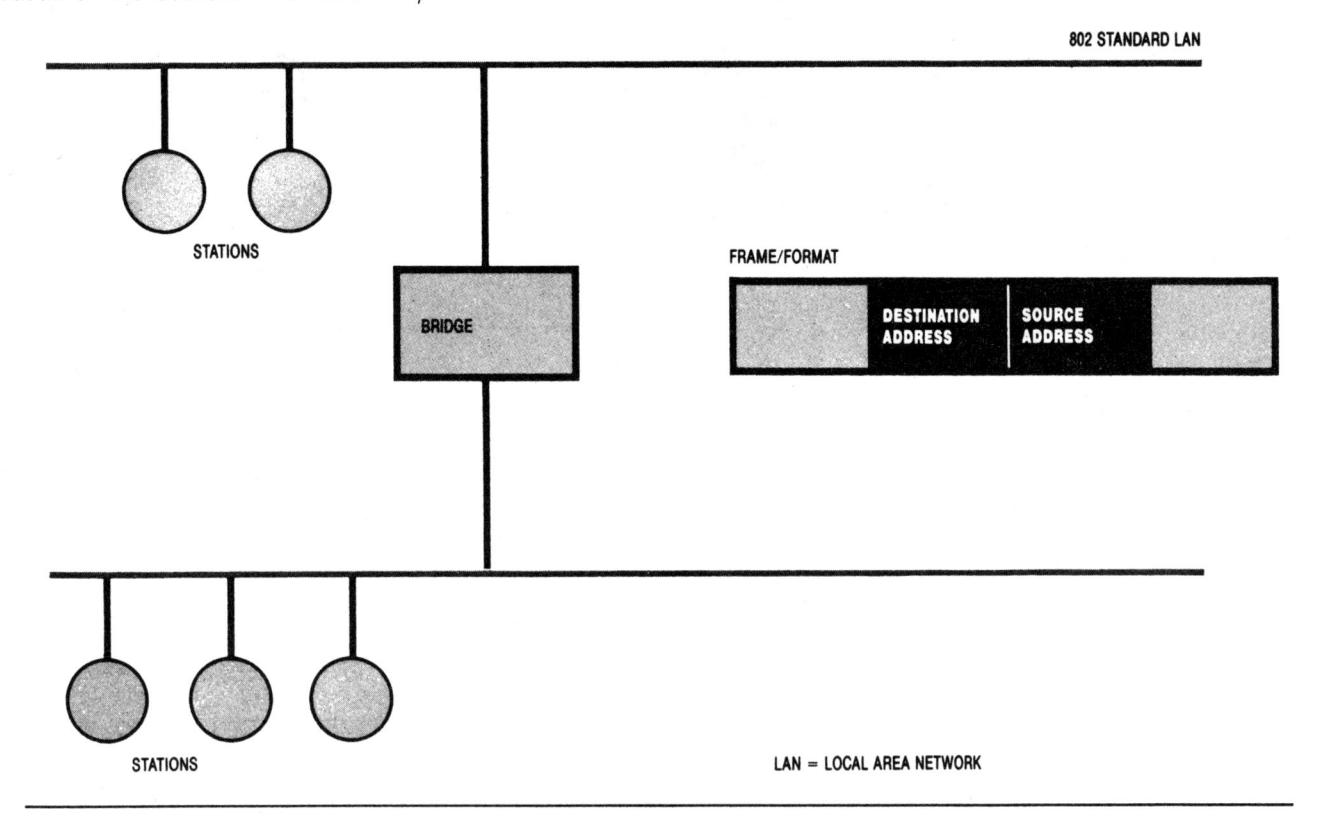

Decisions at the Data Link Layer

Figure 1 shows the OSI reference model and IEEE 802 model for LANs. In the IEEE model, the Data Link Layer consists of a logical link control (LLC) sublayer and a media access control (MAC) sublayer. The MAC sublayer involves addresses for stations to be identified in a network. Figure 2 shows two LANs connected through an interconnection device called a bridge. The bridge can make a decision about switching frames between the LANs on the basis of the address of a station. A number of simple algorithms may be used for making this decision. From a practical standpoint, the fact that interconnection between local LANs takes place at the MAC sublayer means that higher throughput will be achieved due to the relative simplicity in decision-making algorithms that are used at the MAC sublayer compared with other layers.

Bridges as defined above are possible between similar LANs. Even though IEEE 802 does not have a single standard, the similarities between the various standards are such that bridging between them is possible.

Figure 3 shows a configuration for a campus. It consists of four separate LANs—two baseband CSMA/CD networks, two broadband token-passing bus networks on one CATV cable, and one token-passing ring network. One 10-Mbit/s CSMA/CD baseband network connects the office machines, and the other 10-Mbit/s CSMA/CD baseband network runs the computer-aided design (CAD) room. A 20-Mbit/s token-passing ring creates the network for the mainframe computers and peripherals in the computer room. One 5-Mbit/s token-passing bus network ties together all data-gathering equipment requiring deterministic delays.

The LAN that is made up of a 10-Mbit/s broadband token-passing bus acts as a backbone interconnecting the other four LANs. Each bridge provides the interconnection between the backbone and one other LAN: thus Bridge 1 connects the backbone and one baseband LAN; Bridge 2 connects the backbone and the other baseband LAN; Bridge 3 connects the backbone and the token-passing ring; and, finally, Bridge 4 connects the backbone and the 5-Mbit/s token-passing bus LAN.

Algorithms for bridges

Among the many possible algorithms for decision making in bridges, two are significant for the present discussion. These two in particular have been proposed to the IEEE 802 committees. One, proposed by Digital Equipment Corp. (DEC), uses a nonsource routing scheme. Alternatively, IBM has proposed a source-routing scheme. Other proposals have been variations on these two methods.

11

3. Campus LANs. *How four different local area networks are configured on a typical campus using four bridges. Two baseband CSMA/CD (carrier-sense multiple access with collision detection) LANs are connected to two broadband token-passing LANs on one CATV cable and to one token-passing ring network.*

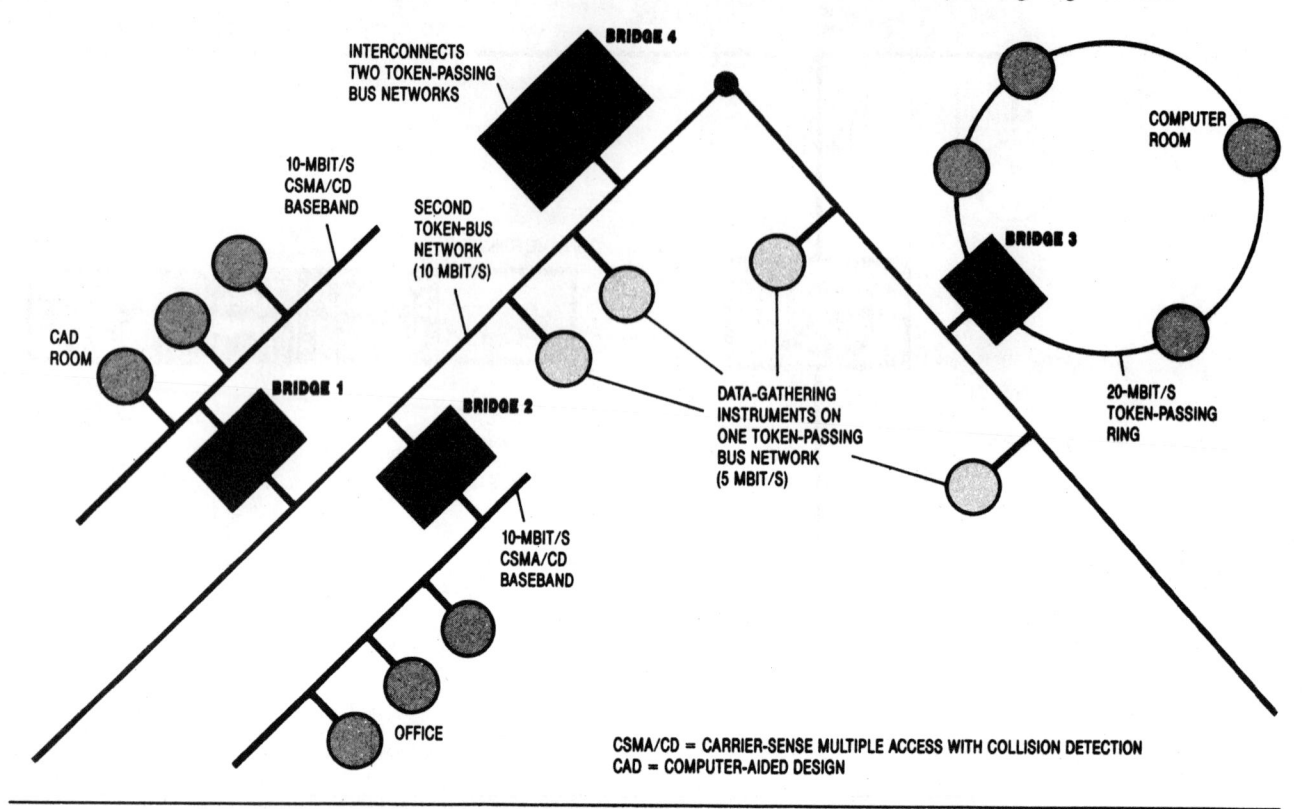

- BRIDGE 4 — INTERCONNECTS TWO TOKEN-PASSING BUS NETWORKS
- 10-MBIT/S CSMA/CD BASEBAND
- SECOND TOKEN-BUS NETWORK (10 MBIT/S)
- CAD ROOM
- BRIDGE 1
- BRIDGE 2
- 10-MBIT/S CSMA/CD BASEBAND
- OFFICE
- DATA-GATHERING INSTRUMENTS ON ONE TOKEN-PASSING BUS NETWORK (5 MBIT/S)
- COMPUTER ROOM
- BRIDGE 3
- 20-MBIT/S TOKEN-PASSING RING

CSMA/CD = CARRIER-SENSE MULTIPLE ACCESS WITH COLLISION DETECTION
CAD = COMPUTER-AIDED DESIGN

The DEC learn-and-decide scheme is shown in Figure 2. Here, the bridge connecting the two LANs maintains a database of the addresses of stations on each side. This database is empty to begin with and watches all frames that go by on the two LANs, learning the relative locations of the stations. This information is put into the database. When a new frame is picked up by the bridge, it searches the database for the destination address contained in the frame. The forwarding of the frame to the other side is based on the results of this search.

This simple algorithm requires no extra effort by end stations to switch frames through bridges, so that operation of the bridges is transparent. With this method, bridges do need to search the database for every frame before the next frame arrives. This DEC-proposed algorithm raises challenging design issues because the database entries are addresses that are up to 48 bits long.

The IBM algorithm works when the source station originating the frame sends the routing information within the frame itself. This enables the bridge to make the switching decision. For example, the frame might contain an ordered list of the addresses of the LAN segments through which the frame has to travel before it reaches its destination. This algorithm makes it easy for the bridge to make its switching decisions but requires the involvement of the end station. This means that bridge operations are not transparent to end stations.

The terms bridge and gateways are both used to refer to devices that perform the interconnection in networks. They should be treated as two separate types of devices. Both perform the general function of interconnection, but they do so at different levels in the architecture. Bridges, as proposed in this article, interconnect LANs using simple algorithms at the Data Link Layer. Gateways interconnect LANs and hosts in a long-haul network of arbitrary topology and use complex algorithms belonging to the Network Layer.

How is the distinction between gateways and bridges relevant to the user? The algorithmic simplicity of bridges enables them to have better performance characteristics, such as throughput and delay, compared with gateways. Gateways typically have throughput in the 56-kbit/s range, while it is not too difficult to accomplish throughput in the vicinity of 5 to 7 Mbit/s with bridges. Gateways need only be used when LANs are separated geographically or are not of the IEEE 802 type. In order to achieve maximum performance when a number of LANs are interconnected locally, bridges are necessary. ■

George Koshy has a B. S. in electronics and communications engineering from Kerala University, Trivandrum, India, and an M. S. from Massachusetts Institute of Technology. He has worked for more than 11 years on network hardware, software, protocols, and architecture. Prior to joining Booz, Allen, he worked for Digital Equipment Corp.

Marc A. Wernli, Northwestern Bell Telephone Co., Omaha, Neb.

The choices in designing a fiber-optic network

When do you use an LED as a light source? When a laser? And what about multimode versus single-mode fiber? Here are one expert's answers.

The many fiber-optic networks that have recently been installed use different combinations of light sources and fiber-cable types. A lot of questions have been raised concerning the advantages and disadvantages of these various combinations. This article attempts to answer some of these questions and to identify some of the applications for each combination.

Two types of light sources are used for fiber-optic networks. The most common, found in the first fiber networks, is the light-emitting diode (LED). The other that has gained popularity, enabling both the bandwidth and distance of fiber-optic networks to increase, is the laser.

Both the laser and LED are semiconductor devices that emit a beam of light when a voltage is applied. The two devices display different optical characteristics and have different sensitivities. Most of the devices are made from gallium arsenide (GaAs). They are also "doped" with other materials, such as indium, aluminum, and phosphide.

Figure 1a shows the optical power output of a typical LED as the modulating current through the device is increased. Note that the LED has almost a linear characteristic, emitting light pulses (the digital data) proportional to the current as it is changed from near zero to about 220 milliamperes (ma). A further current increase would, typically, result in nonlinearity or LED failure.

Compare the LED plot to that of a typical laser (Fig. 1b), which also shows the optical power output as the current through the device is increased. The laser has almost a switching characteristic—because of the plot's steepness—as the current is increased above the threshold level at "a," here about 28 ma. Lasers normally have a fixed "bias" current, just above the threshold level, that causes the device to emit a low light level. The additional modulating current resulting in a change from "a" to "b" results in the laser's light output changing from the threshold to a high level—that is, a light pulse. A laser is normally able to operate at bit rates higher than an LED's because a comparatively small change in current (from "a" to "b") causes a larger increase—almost two orders of magnitude greater—in optical output power than an LED's range.

The output power of an LED is spread over a wide range of wavelengths, resulting in the device having a spectral width of approximately 100 nanometers (100 10^{-9} meters—abbreviated nm). The laser has a much more narrow spectral width, in the range of 4 nm. (Figure 2 displays a comparison of the two spectral widths.) Since different wavelengths propagate at different speeds in a fiber cable, a device with a narrow spectral width will have less pulse dispersion than a device with a wide spectral width. This characteristic results in a laser able to operate at higher bit rates than an LED.

Below visibility

Fiber-optic light sources normally operate at the 850-, 1,300-, or 1,500-nm wavelength, which is in the infrared portion of the frequency spectrum. This is below (lower frequency) the visible-light portion, which is 400 to 700 nm. Most fiber-optic networks transmit digitally, with the network "bandwidth" indicated by the maximum data rate; most video transmissions are analog, with an increasing trend to digital.

The usable power of a laser or LED is the power that can be coupled into the fiber "pigtail" (connecting strand) from the light-source module. A fiber has a limited acceptance angle, and any light from an LED or a laser that is outside this angle will not be coupled into the fiber. Figure 3 shows the acceptance angle of a fiber—typically 30 degrees—and the output patterns of both an LED and a laser—typically 90 and 30 degrees, respectively. The acceptance angle and output patterns are cone shaped and can be made more compatible by having a lens on the end of the fiber. The coupling losses for a laser range from approximately 3 to 6 decibels (dB); for an LED, from 10 to 30 dB, depending on the type of fiber with which the LED is being coupled.

There are pronounced differences in the characteristics of LEDs and lasers. These differences turn into advantages and disadvantages for each device, some of which are noted below.

The advantages of an LED are:
- Low cost—approximately $150; a laser costs about $1,500, but the price is dropping each year.
- Long life—20 to 100 years; a laser lasts about five to 20 years.
- Less sensitivity to environmental changes—a temperature increase of 30 degrees Celsius (54 degrees Fahrenheit) decreases an LED's lifetime by a factor of 2; the same temperature increase decreases a laser's lifetime by a factor of 10.

The disadvantages of an LED are:
- Low output power—approximately -l0 to -l5 dB; a laser's output power is about 0 dB.
- Narrow bandwidth—normally less than 135 Mbit/s; a laser's bandwidth is greater than 1 Gbit/s.
- Ability to couple only to multimode fiber; a laser couples to either multimode or single-mode fiber (see below for a discussion of the fiber types).
- Wide beam of light; a laser produces a narrow beam of light.
- Wide spectral width—typically 100 nm; a laser's is much narrower—typically 4 nm.

It should now be apparent that each light-source device has its own suitable areas of application. If the wrong device is used in a particular application, the result will be either unacceptable performance or excessive cost.

Suitable sites
The LED light source can be used in fiber applications where the distance between network end points is no more than about 12 km (about 7.5 miles) and the data rate needed is less than l35 Mbit/s. (Repeaters—called regenerators—are generally used when longer distances are required; see below.) Multiple-fiber cable is used, with individual fibers spliced to new ones for additional distance where practicable. The maximum allowable distance between end points will vary, since it is dependent on the type of fiber used and the number of splices that are expected to be made. The LED's major application areas have been in campus environments and local area networks (LANs).

The laser should be used in applications where the end-to-end network distance is longer than 12 km—up to about 45 to 110 km (about 30 to 70 miles), after which regeneration is required—or the data rate required is greater than 135 Mbit/s. The laser is used in metropolitan area networks or in networks that have end points in different towns.

1. Optical power. Note in A that the light-emitting diode has almost a linear characteristic, emitting light pulses proportional to the changing modulating current. This contrasts with the laser's response in B, which displays almost a switching characteristic as the current is increased above the threshold level.

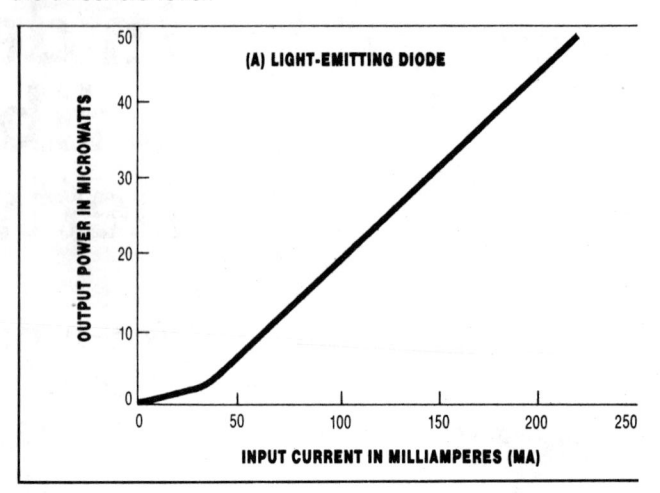

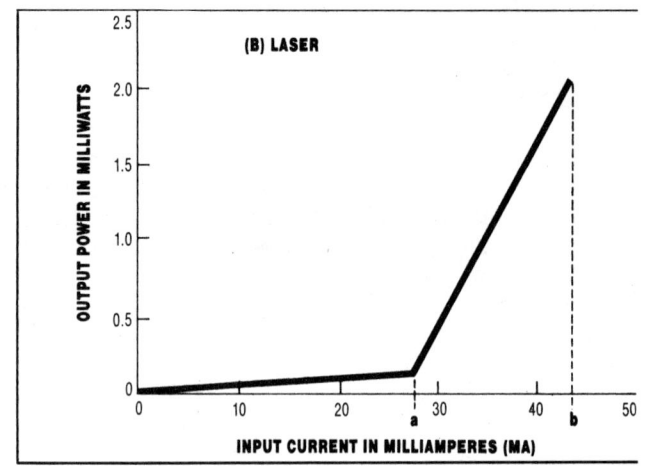

At present, the success of coupling LEDs to single-mode fiber has been limited. A slotted-aperture device, called the edge light emitting diode (in contrast to the older "surface" LED), is being tested for this coupling. The application has a high coupling loss (approximately 15 db), but can be used on single-mode fiber networks that extend less than 7 km (about 4.4 miles). While the conic emitted-light pattern cross section of the surface LED is circular, that of an edge LED is elliptical.

Cheaper, too
The perceived trend is to develop lasers that have longer lifetimes and are not sensitive to environmental changes. As these lasers are produced in quantity, their cost should drop to the $200-to-$500 price range. An additional capability of these lasers is a data rate beyond 10 Gbit/s. There is also an effort under way to develop LEDs that have a narrower light beam and will not have high coupling losses with single-mode fiber. The first practical versions of such products will probably reach the market

by early 1987.

Fiber cable is divided into two major categories based on the number of modes (paths) that light propagates along its glass core. The fiber cable that had the greatest usage prior to 1983 contained multimode fibers. This cable has an outer diameter of 125 microns and the core that the light travels in is 50 microns in diameter. (A micron is one millionth of an inch.) The core of this cable allows several modes of the light frequency to exist concurrently.

Most of the cable that is being used today still has a 125-micron outer diameter, but the core diameter is only 7 to 9 microns. This small core only allows one light path or mode to exist; therefore, the cable is called single mode. Note that multimode cable is easier to splice because of the larger diameter core.

Multimode fiber undergoes a light-power loss in the range of 2 dB/km and a data rate limited to approximately 135 Mbit/s. The loss associated with this type of fiber is a function of both distance and bandwidth: the distance-bandwidth multiple. Therefore, the greater the distance between network end points, the narrower the bandwidth (the more limited the data rate). The bandwidths of multimode fiber are in the range of 400 to 1,000 MHz-km—which accommodates a range of 45 to 135 Mbit/s—at an 850-nm spectral width, and 400 to 1,500 MHz-km (accommodating a proportionately higher data rate) at a 1,300-nm. spectral width. The losses in the fiber are due primarily to cable impurities absorbing light. (Incidentally, plastic-core optical-fiber cable has recently become available, but it generally has a reduced-distance capability compared to the more-dominant glass types. This performance inferiorty is due primarily to its greater incidence of impurities.)

Single-mode fiber has a loss in the range of 0.5 dB/km and a data rate limitation in the gigabits-per-second range. The data rate limitation is normally due to pulse dispersion, which is a function of distance. This dispersion is caused by the different wavelengths of light propagating at different speeds in the fiber, causing the pulses to broaden.

Presently, there is a greater demand for single-mode than multimode cable. (One exception: Some LAN applications use multimode 62.5-micron-core fiber cable. Multimode fiber normally has a 50-micron core.) This is because most fiber networks being installed today cover long distances (greater than 10 km) and carry high data rates (above 90 Mbit/s) that require single-mode cable.

Of course, multimode fiber should only be used where its distance and bandwidth limitations do not cause a problem. This would be in distribution networks in buildings, campus environments, and LANs.

Faster and farther
Single-mode fiber is best applied where there is a present or future need for data rates higher than 135 Mbit/s or a transmission distance greater than 10 km between end points within the network. Single-mode fiber applications would include metropolitan area networks and full-motion video transmission, with network end points in different towns.

Most of the research and development effort is directed toward single-mode fiber to reduce both pulse dispersion and loss. This includes better splicing materials and equipment. The two main methods of joining fiber cable are fusion splicing and fiber-optic connectors. Fusion splicing is accomplished by aligning the two fiber ends through a microscope and fusing the fibers together with an electric arc. This generally results in a splice with less than 0.1 dB of loss.

Optimizing the junction
Fiber connectors use various methods of aligning fibers, along with a refraction-index-matching gel between the ends of the fibers, to reduce losses due to an optical mismatch (refraction differences). Fiber connectors have losses in the range of 0.1 to 0.5 dB. Research and development on multimode fiber will probably be limited, because future improvements in light sources and wider bandwidth requirements will limit its uses—except in LAN applications.

The cost of fiber-optic cable has gone through a dramatic reduction—an order of magnitude—in the past few years and there is only a small difference (less than 10 percent) in price between single-mode and multimode fiber. The cost could continue to fall in the future depending on how long the present production volume continues. A more likely development is that future fiber will support much higher transmission rates for approximately the same price as today's fiber. (For information about fiber optics standards activities, see "Brewing standards conflict blurs fiber optics' future," DATA COMMUNICATIONS, February, p. 55.)

Not a static technology
Fiber-optic networks provide significant advantages over other types of data communications networks. To fully obtain these advantages, however, requires extensive planning and design to fit an organization's unique requirements.

In the past few years, fiber-optic networks have gone through many changes in maximum data rate, distance, and cost. During this same period, the design, installation, and maintenance of these networks have also gone through changes, to the point where many organizations are now offering services in the networks' design and installation.

Most fiber networks that were installed before 1983 had a maximum data rate of 45 to 90 Mbit/s and were limited to a metropolitan area. Some of the networks required regeneration every few miles. These networks used multimode-fiber cable and both LED and laser light sources. Some of the locations had alternative facilities utilizing a different technology in case of a fiber network failure. Many of these fiber networks had marginal economic advantages over other technologies; fiber was used where it was extremely expensive to accommodate certain data's additional bandwidth requirements with a different technology.

It is anticipated that the networks being installed today will have a service-failure rate of less than one every five years due to equipment, *if* a redundant

2. Spectral width. *The laser has a much narrower spectral width—therefore less dispersion—than the light-emitting diode: about 4 nanometers versus about 100.*

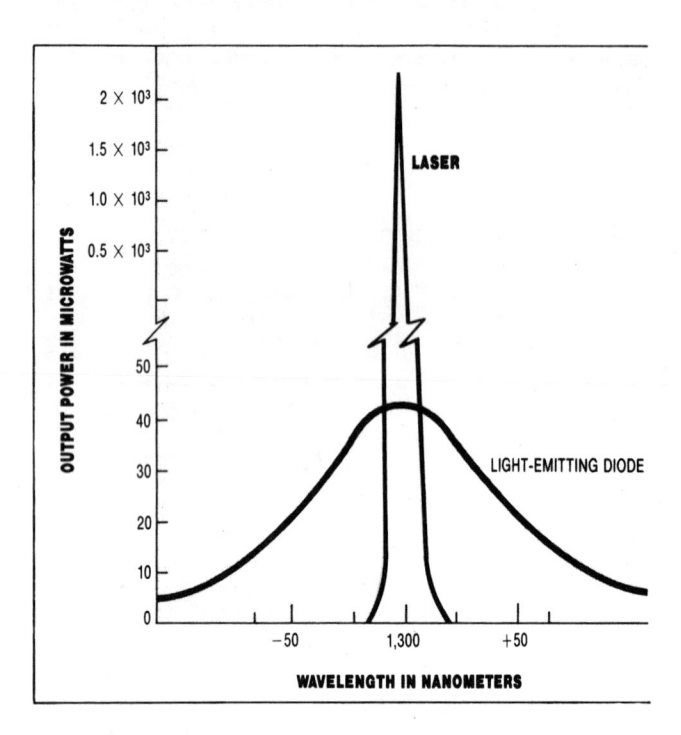

[Graph: Output Power in Microwatts vs. Wavelength in Nanometers, showing narrow LASER peak and broader LIGHT-EMITTING DIODE curve centered at 1,300 nm]

("protection") channel is provided. At present, the records of many networks show service failures occurring from every six months to a year due to fiber-cable cuts and human error.

In the past several years there have been many fiber-optic networks installed, and there are many more that are in the planning process. If all announced fiber networks are built, the result will be a transmission capacity that could not have been imagined a few years ago. A majority of the networks currently being installed are utilizing single-mode fiber cable with laser light sources.

The capacity of these networks is in multiples of 45 Mbit/s and ranges up to 1.2 to 1.7 Gbit/s. The distances range from a few kilometers to networks that cover several states. These networks have excellent economic advantages over other technologies (operating costs are lower because of less-costly maintenance), provide the primary facilities, and have no—or limited—alternative facilities for backup.

The future of many fiber networks exists in higher data rates (1 Gbit/s or more) and longer distances—greater than 50 km (about 30 miles)—without requiring regeneration. These areas are where much of the research and development is being directed today. The resulting networks will probably use improved types of single-mode fiber cable and laser light sources and be capable of carrying huge quantities of video and data.

Needs more attention
Future local fiber networks must also be able to economically distribute data signals from the large-capacity networks to various buildings, LANs, and individual locations. This area has not had nearly as much effort directed toward it as the high-capacity portions have. The smaller fiber networks and the portions of these networks that will distribute the signals from the large-capacity ones have more options for types of fiber and light sources, because of the reduced bandwidth and distance requirements.

The first decisions that have to be made about a small fiber network are the type of fiber to be used and the bandwidth required. The next step is to choose a light source based on the type of fiber chosen, the bandwidth, and the size of the network. Besides the network's initial bandwidth, future bandwidth requirements will have to be determined before any design can be completed. It may be difficult to estimate future bandwidth requirements. But the effort *must* be made because the findings can have a significant effect on the network design.

Economic decisions
Once the initial and future bandwidth requirements are quantified, the number of fibers to be used in the various sections of the network will have to be determined. It may actually be more economical to employ a larger number of fibers with lower individual bandwidths than to place the total bandwidth requirement on fewer fibers with higher individual bandwidths. The choice will depend on the distance between network termination points and how much of the total bandwidth requirement is for the future. A major decision factor will be based on the costs of high-speed (above 45 Mbit/s) versus T1 multiplexing equipment, with the latter having more fibers in the cable. The incremental cost of additional fibers in a cable is not as high as that of high-speed multiplexing equipment on a short (less than 12 km or about 7.5 miles) fiber network. An example of this is a network where new fiber-optic cable is being placed and the data rate (bandwidth) requirements are in multiples ranging from 1.5 to 45 Mbit/s. If the network is shorter than 5 to 10 km (3.1 to 6.2 miles), it is probably cheaper to increase the size of the cable and use individual multiplexers in the 1.5- to 45-Mbit/s range.

After the bandwidth and distance requirements of the individual fibers are identified, the types of fiber and light source can be determined. If multimode fiber is used, the light source can be either an LED or a laser, depending on the network length. An LED can be used if the network is small—no longer than the aforementioned 12 km; otherwise a laser may be required. If single-mode fiber is used, the light source will probably have to be a laser, for now.

Who does what
There are many organizations that sell fiber-optic services, which range from bandwidth on their existing networks to completely installed new networks. There are other options, one of which is leasing fibers, with the customer providing the light source and multiplexing equipment for the leased portion of the cable. A data-transmitting organization should go through a thorough analysis to determine what options are available, and

3. Outputs and angles. *Any light from a light-emitting diode or a laser that is outside a fiber's limited acceptance angle will not be coupled into the fiber.*

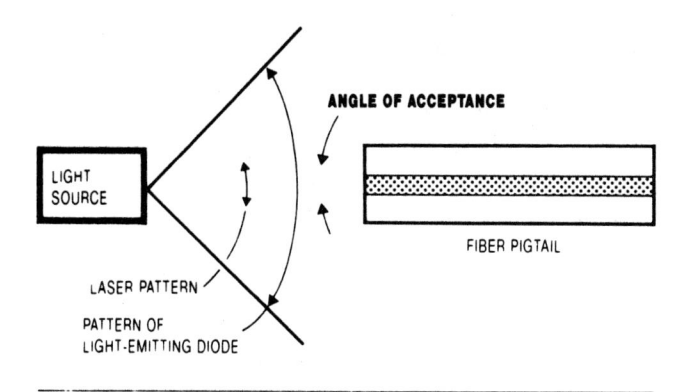

which of those are most suitable.

As is usually true of any network, the decision to build and maintain a fiber-optic network involves the commitment of capital dollars and the issues of how the network will be maintained and who will do the maintaining. A too conservative or an overly optimistic forecast of bandwidth requirements could cause a waste of capital dollars or a later expensive replacement or reinforcement of the network. If the decision is made to lease the fibers and own the multiplexing equipment, additional problems may be encountered. These include: trying to locate and clear troubles via several organizations involved with different portions of the network.

The decision to lease bandwidth conserves capital dollars and places the burden of maintenance and the provisioning of future bandwidth on someone else. With this burden placement comes the possible problems of bandwidth pricing and the reliability of the leasing organization to be responsive to maintenance requirements. The price of bandwidth can vary from a few hundred dollars up to several thousand dollars per megabit per second per month, depending on various factors. Some of these factors include shared versus unshared facilities, standard versus nonstandard bandwidths, transmission distances, and how quickly the initial investment is recovered. A data communications manager must have confidence in the abilities of any organization from which bandwidth is to be leased. ■

Marc Wernli is a staff manager in the engineering planning department at Northwestern Bell. He holds a B. S. and an M. S. in electrical engineering from the South Dakota School of Mines and Technology in Rapid City. He is also a member of the National Society of Professional Engineers.

Peter M. Haverlock, IBM Corp., Thornwood, N.Y.

The formula for network immortality

Availability is the sine qua non of networking, but at what cost? Increasing network reliability and serviceability is a better, and more affordable, path to high availability.

Availability, performance, and cost are three of the most important attributes of a well-run network, according to user surveys. In many businesses, availability is often *the* most important system requirement. Indeed, the cost associated with maintaining high availability is deemed unimportant if availability itself is threatened. But communications professionals can strike a balance between availability and cost without sacrificing performance—provided they understand the relationship between each of the attributes.

Too often, availability and reliability are used interchangeably. Reliability is an element of availability, as is serviceability. Network availability, in its broadest sense, is that characteristic of a communications link that provides connectivity to a user. Availability can be expressed as a value between one and zero, with one corresponding to 100 percent availability and zero to no availability. Availability is composed of two factors: reliability, which is expressed as the mean time between failures (MTBF), and serviceability, which is expressed as the mean time to repair (MTTR).

$$\text{AVAILABILITY} = \frac{\text{MTBF}}{\text{MTBF} + \text{MTTR}}$$

RELIABILITY—MEAN TIME BETWEEN FAILURES (MTBF)
SERVICEABILITY—MEAN TIME TO REPAIR (MTTR)

Availability is presented as the total operative and inoperative days and hours, which are noted as availability and unavailability in the table. The numbers cited in the table assume 24-hour-per-day operation over one year of 365 days.

In some organizations, availability is calculated on the basis of the hours that a network is actually in operation. In such cases, outages that take place outside operational hours are not included in the reported availability figures. Calculating availability in this fashion increases overall availability numbers, but it may not present a totally accurate picture.

Equation 1 shows that availability can be increased by either increasing reliability, expressed as the mean time between failures, or decreasing the time for serviceability, expressed as the mean time to repair. By lengthening the MTBF, the network will become more available if the MTTR is not increased. It also follows that if the MTBF is not affected and the MTTR is reduced, the availability of the network will be increased. Many networks make use of both techniques to achieve increased availability; redundancy is built into the network by deploying parallel trunks and alternate routes as well as automating failure-recovery systems.

Network communications links are frequently composed of complex serial components. Serial components usually add functions or reduce the cost of the network link, but they can also decrease availability. For example, a line multiplexer allows the concentration of multiple lines into one line; however, if the multiplexer fails, all the attached lines may become unavailable. Building parallelism into network designs is often the best way to offset any decrease in availability produced by serial component failures.

The use of automated service restoration also increases availability by decreasing the service time required to establish an alternate connection after a component or link failure. For example, a short power failure at a remote location may require the network operator at the host location to go through a set of procedures to reactivate the modem and the remote control units. The procedure can be accomplished through an automatic programmed interface that invokes the commands required to bring the remote location on line; the human operator is notified only if the procedure is not successful.

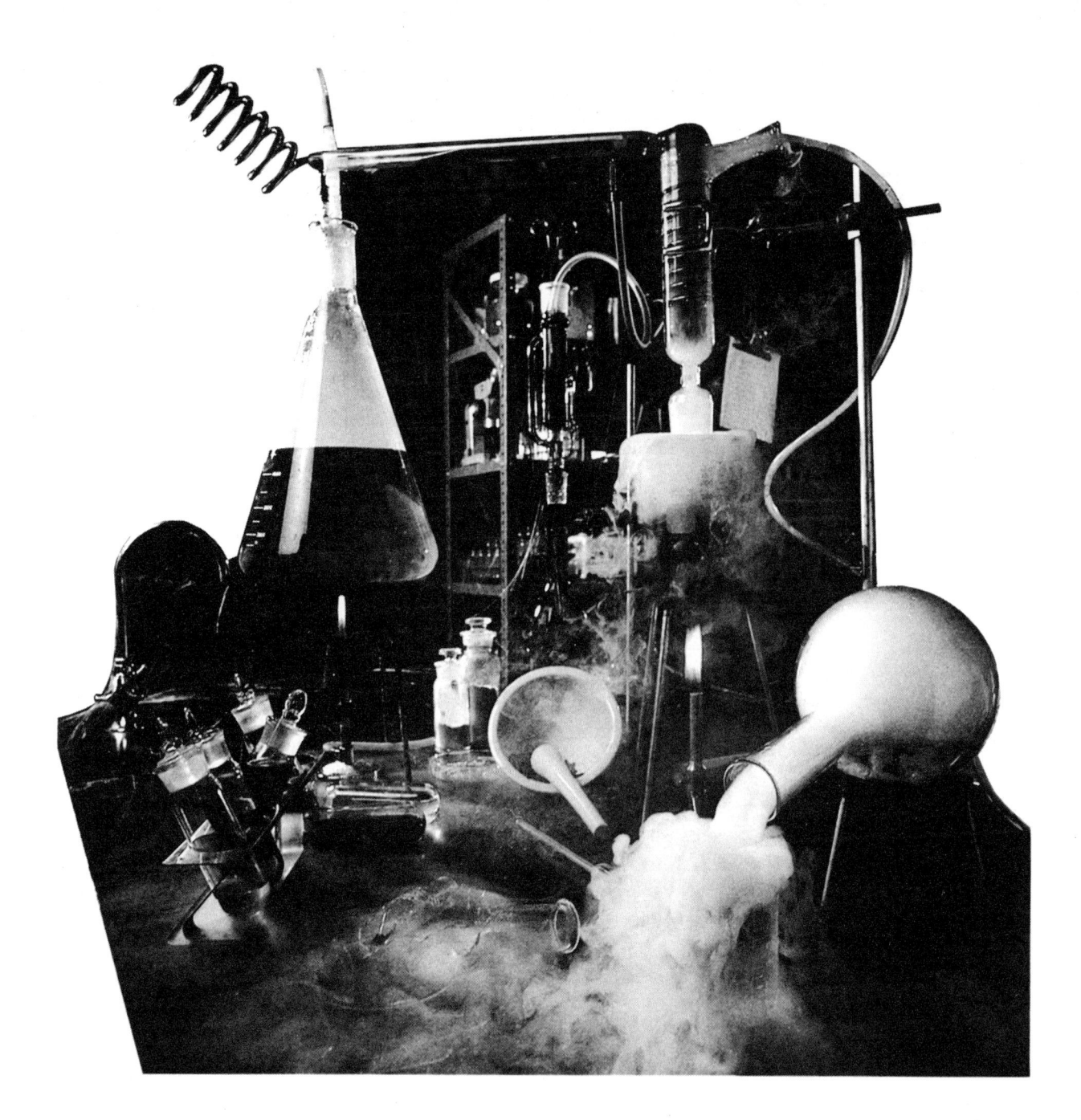

As a network grows, more serial components are added. Adding serial components only decreases availability since failure of a lone component can cause total system failure. System availability is the product of the individual availabilities shown in Equation 2.

$$\text{AVAILABILITY OF A AND B} = \left(\text{AVAILABILITY OF COMPONENT A}\right) \times \left(\text{AVAILABILITY OF COMPONENT B}\right)$$

In a network that is organized in parallel fashion, all components must fail to cause total system failure. System availability and failure (system unavailability) are complements of each other, as shown in Equation 3.

$$\text{AVAILABILITY} = 1 - (\text{UNAVAILABILITY})$$

The availability of a system with two parallel components is shown in Equation 4. According to the equation, the probability of system availability is 1 minus the product of the individual failure probabilities.

$$\text{AVAILABILITY OF A AND B} = 1 - \left(\text{UNAVAILABILITY OF COMPONENT A}\right) \times \left(\text{UNAVAILABILITY OF COMPONENT B}\right)$$

Figure 1 presents some examples of serial and parallel component availability. Components linked in serial fashion in the upper portion of the figure compare unfavorably to availability of components linked in parallel.

The figure uses Equations 2 and 4 to show that highly available systems can be created from unreliable components used in parallel. Failures are reduced because system failure will require the simultaneous failure of both parallel components (redundancy). This is highlighted in the parallel example with 0.8 availability, which produces a system availability of 0.96. Referencing Table 1, an availability of 0.8 has an unavailability of 73 days. Using the

Network availability by the numbers

AVAILABILITY	NON-OPERATING TIME DAYS AND HOURS		OPERATING TIME DAYS AND HOURS	
.64	131	10	233	14
.80	73	0	292	0
.95	18	6	346	18
.96	14	15	350	9
.97	10	23	354	1
.98	7	8	357	16
.9801	7	7	357	17
.99	3	16	361	8
.995	1	20	363	4
.997	1	3	363	21
.999	0	9	364	15
.9999	0	1	364	23
1.000	0	0	365	0

simple parallel design shown in Figure 1 decreases this outage to 14 days and 15 hours, with an availability increased to 0.96. The other example in Figure 1 shows the use of highly available components, 0.99 availability, in a parallel design producing an availability of 0.9999. If parallel components replace the serial components, the system availability will be the product of the improved parallel components, that is, 0.96 x 0.96 or 0.9999 x 0.9999. Thus, by using highly available components and parallel design, a very high degree of availability can be achieved.

Topology and performance
A well-designed network topology can increase network availability. The topology of a network is the routing of its physical or logical links. A logical circuit can be viewed as the ruler distance between two points. The physical circuit is the actual connecting path between the two points. The same network can have different logical and physical topologies. The topology of a network can affect network availability, performance, and cost because the pricing of a circuit is not always related to the actual physical routing.

Users can employ their knowledge of physical-line routing to improve network availability through redundancy, by using components with higher availability, and by decreasing the time required for network-problem determination.

Communications services can be divided into two major types: private or leased lines and the public network of switched lines.

The private line is a dedicated communications link between two or more locations; it offers volume-insensitive pricing for voice and data traffic in the United States. When first developed, Wide Area Telephone Service (WATS) was priced at a flat rate; however, within a few years, its pricing became traffic-sensitive. Because of the flat-rate pricing of private lines, other options are compared against their fixed monthly cost.

Figure 2 shows the monthly cost of a private line compared with direct dialing and two other discount offerings. Common carriers provide different types of bulk-discount offerings; for simplicity, they are referred to here as Discount A and Discount B. The slopes and Y-axis intercept may change for different types of communications services and varying physical or logical topologies since there is never a guarantee that one offering will be priced lower under all conditions.

Heavy communications traffic between two company locations will invariably lead to the selection of private-line configurations because of the fixed line costs. The chart only presents the tariff link cost of a connection: The private network's hardware and other support costs would need to be added to get a complete picture. This could affect the position and slope of the lines in the chart but not the general picture.

The basic routing of a private interstate circuit is shown in Figure 3 by the solid lines. The dial-access lines are shown as dashed lines between customer location A and the Local Exchange Carrier (LEC) central office in Local Access and Transport Area (LATA) 1. The routing of the circuit passes through the facilities of three carriers: the LEC at location A, the Interexchange Carrier (IXC) connecting the two central offices' exchanges near location A and B, and the LEC at location B. The circuit can be leased from the IXC, which in turn leases both ends from the LEC, or through separate arrangements for each service.

The LATA, which is sometimes described as a calling zone, is the geographic area that is serviced by the local common carrier. The LEC provides services between points within one LATA. An IXC provides services between LATAs as well as lines that carry interstate traffic.

The lines are available in either analog or digital formats.

1. Robust designs. By changing the configuration from a serial to parallel design, poorly performing serial components (top) operate more reliably (bottom).

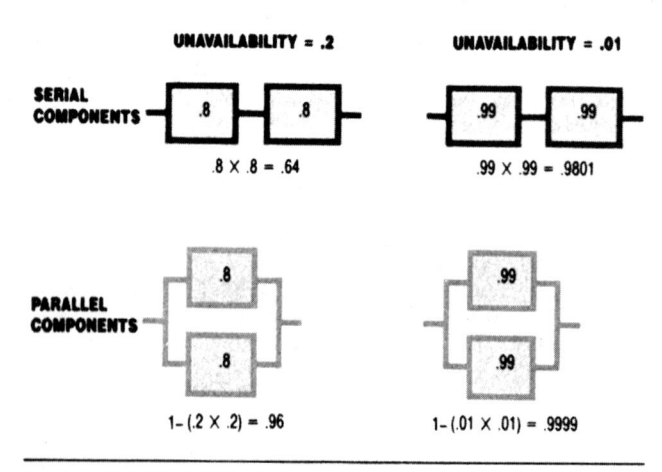

2. Private versus public. *Physical-line routing can be used to improve network availability. When heavy traffic is expected, private lines with fixed costs are best.*

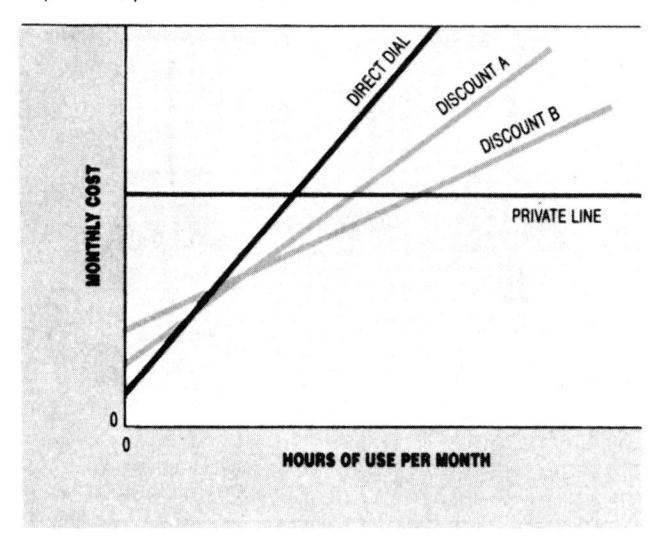

The termination interface at the customer's premises determines the format. An analog line may be transmitted in digital format over part of its path, but a digital line is digital over its entire length.

The digital line tends to be more accurate because it uses repeaters to precisely replicate the transmitted signal. Analog, on the other hand, is subject to greater errors because the analog wave form may be amplified or attenuated slightly out of phase or frequency as it travels across a link. Distortions also occur because the transmission properties of the line differ over a range of frequencies.

The goal of AT&T Dataphone digital service (DDS) digital lines is 99.9 percent availability. Such high availability is achieved through common carrier network redundancy and unique maintenance—despite the fact that DDS sometimes uses T1 circuits for transport. T1 circuits are designed for lower availability goals than DDS circuits.

T1's availability goal is 99.7 percent or greater. Nevertheless, a single failure can knock out the multiple communications links being multiplexed over the 1.544 Mbit/s line. AT&T's Technical Reference 62411 of October 1985 states T1's quality goals for error-free seconds of operation are 99.6 percent for less than 250 miles, 96.0 percent for 250 to 1,000 miles, and 95 percent for over 1,000 miles.

The public switched network, also known as direct dial, connects users to their destinations via a dialing sequence that is composed of an area code, exchange, and subscriber number. The public switched network may offer a different interoffice line each time a call is placed. Users, therefore, can never be certain of the quality of their connection.

For dial-in users, the direct-dial connection offers the convenience of dependable connectivity with reasonable availability. The actual degree of availability is dependent on line quality and modem technology. The public switched network can be used to back up private line speeds varying from 1.2 kbit/s to as high as 19.2 kbit/s for dial calls that are routed over high-quality circuits. The use of higher speed may require two calls; one sending, the other receiving.

When components are connected serially, they can adversely affect availability. Availability can be increased by configuring the components in parallel. In fact, unreliable components configured in parallel can produce a reliable system. Parallel components, configured for redundancy, provide the basis for high network availability. Network managers can use one of several options offered by common carriers to increase the availability of a network path. Those options include:

■ *Diversity.* Diversity is used to prevent two or more circuits from being routed through the same distribution cables and central offices. This option is not always available because of topology constraints, distribution cable routing, central office functions, and central office trunk routing. Sometimes diversity is implied because of the routing of different services (analog and digital) by the common carrier. The diversity option has a fixed monthly charge and an installation charge.

■ *Avoidance.* The user can specify that a line not be routed through a specific geographic area, such as new construction zones or areas subject to flooding. Again, because of topology constraints, this is not always practical.

■ *Multiple-carrier circuit routing.* This technique generally provides diverse routing for the interexchange portion of the circuit. The local channel portion of a point-to-point circuit is routed through the LEC's central office without diversification and then to the IXC central office. At the ICX, multiple-carrier routing is provided. However, the service is not always available because all locations are not serviced by multiple communications carriers. It is important to remember that some ICX carriers resell their services, so

3. Point-to-point? *The routing of a private interstate circuit can be circuitous: from dial-access lines to the LEC, then to the IXC and, finally, back to an LEC.*

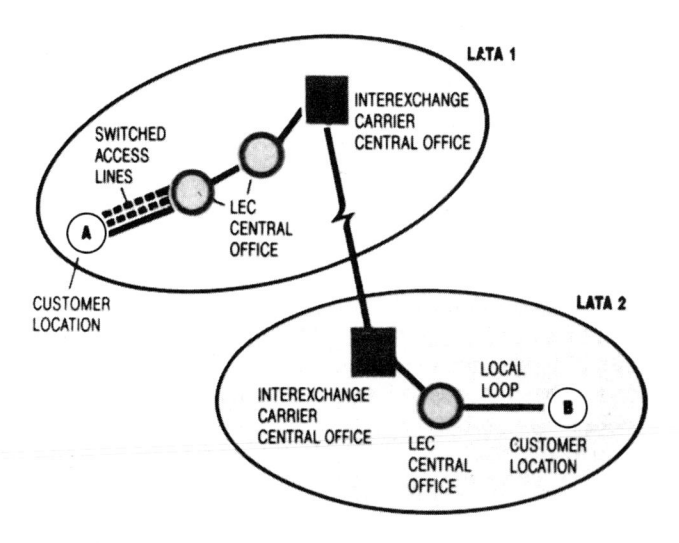

LATA = LOCAL ACCESS AND TRANSPORT AREA
LEC = LOCAL EXCHANGE CARRIER

verify that the multiple-carrier option is not a repackaged form of single-carrier routing.

■ *Parallel circuits*. This option is almost always available. To control costs users can mix high-speed 56-kbit/s circuits with slower, less-expensive, 9.6-kbit/s circuits. However, if diversity is not specified, the telephone company may route the circuits through the same cables and distribution frames from the customer's premises to the LEC. T1 circuits cannot ensure true parallelism because their multiple circuits use the same media and the same physical topology. Without route diversification, parallel circuits cannot offer protection against a cable-seeking backhoe.

■ *Switched network backup*. While not strictly an option, if a private line fails, public switched access lines can be used to provide low-speed transmission between two points. With a properly configured modem, a user can make the public switched network a backup for a failed private circuit.

A modem's performance depends on many factors, including the modem's technology, physical topology of the network, and the distance between nodes. Throughput and performance may suffer in a switched line environment, however, since switched lines tend to produce more errors than private lines. Just as with private lines, there is no guarantee that the switched circuits will be route-diversified. Also, multiple call attempts may be required in order to acquire a high-quality circuit, since all interoffice trunks are not created equal.

■ *Digital circuits*. Digital circuits provide better availability and fewer line errors than most analog lines. Digital data circuits have a design goal of 99.9 percent availability with 99.5 percent error-free seconds of operation. This specification is for end-to-end service.

A study of 6,500 point-to-point private analog line customers reported .56 failure incidents per month for each analog line. It is estimated that about 75 percent of the failures on an analog line are caused by the analog termination equipment. The cost for digital service for the ICX portion is about equal to that of analog service. The digital portion of the local circuit usually costs more than a comparable analog circuit.

■ *Line conditioning*. Higher modem operating speeds may require the control of amplitude, envelope delay distortion, harmonic distortion, and noise. This is accomplished by the installation of line conditioning or by building the electronics into the modem to provide similar line quality controls.

Common carriers provide two types of line conditioning. Type C is designed to minimize the effects of amplitude and envelope delay distortion; Type D conditioning controls the amount of harmonic distortion and also controls noise to tighter limits than Type C conditioning. There are various levels of Type C and D conditioning. Not all levels of conditioning are provided at each LEC central office. Many modems have automatic equalization; this provides some of the functions of line conditioning.

■ *Bridging options of multipoint lines*. Bridging connects two or more private lines at a telephone central office to provide a multipoint circuit. In a voice network, it is the basis for a conference call.

4. Better bridge. *A multipoint interstate private line is usually bridged at the Interexchange Carrier's central office, but using the Local Exchange Carrier's central office costs less.*

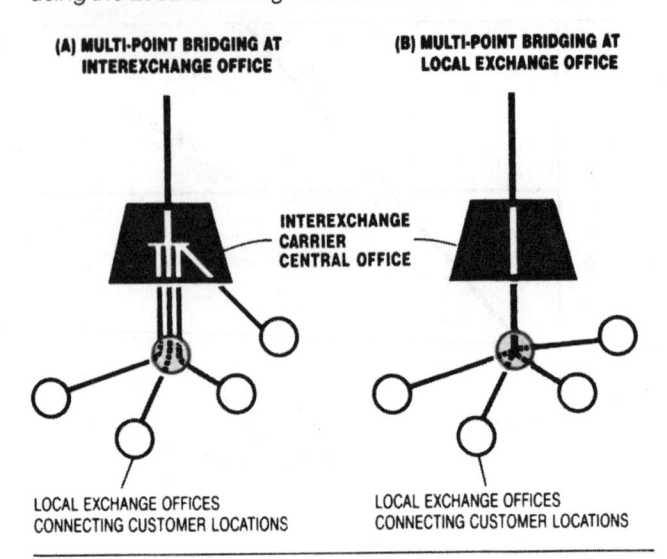

(A) MULTI-POINT BRIDGING AT INTEREXCHANGE OFFICE

(B) MULTI-POINT BRIDGING AT LOCAL EXCHANGE OFFICE

INTEREXCHANGE CARRIER CENTRAL OFFICE

LOCAL EXCHANGE OFFICES CONNECTING CUSTOMER LOCATIONS

LOCAL EXCHANGE OFFICES CONNECTING CUSTOMER LOCATIONS

A multipoint interstate private line that has multiple locations in the same LATA will usually be configured as a mini-star network with the interconnect points being bridged at the IXC's central office (Fig. 4A). However, it can also be configured using one of the LEC's central offices as the bridging hub configuration (Fig. 4B). This option usually produces a lower tariff link cost.

The question of which option provides greater availability cannot be answered from Figure 4 if more stations are to be added to the circuit. Assume that the circuit is complete except for a leg to a network processor. If the ICX is used as the contact point—the contact point is the carrier that will be called at the first sign of line trouble—then the MTTR should be shorter in the configuration shown in Figure 4A. If the LEC is the contact point, the configuration shown in Figure 4B should have a shorter MTTR. The point is that the repair time for the circuit may be lengthened when one carrier has to call the other carrier to do problem determination.

The assumptions made about repairs are based on failures caused by one of the end points on the star topology. The repair procedure would isolate the failed point and make the other points on the circuit operational. The failed component then would be repaired and the circuit reconfigured to its original topology. Again, an understanding of the topology and repair procedures used by the designated carrier can help in the availability design of the circuit. The carrier must also be able to isolate the trouble leg. The network processor leg is the most important; if that link fails, other stations on the circuit may not be available.

Adding it up

Communications cost is the aggregate of the amortized cost for capital equipment and communications services or tariff costs. The proportion of total communications costs also varies with the type of service and whether voice or data is being transmitted.

In voice networks, approximately 75 percent of the cost is allocated to tariff charges. After all, standard telephone instruments have little bearing on the total system communications cost.

Generally, data networks have a reversed relationship, with approximately 25 percent being spent on link tariff charges and the rest being spent on front-end processors, communications controllers, modems, or channel service units, remote control units, multiplexers, host and remote communications software, remote terminal hardware, hardware and software maintenance, and, of course, help-desk support for the remote network. Data networks also use such hardware as concentrators, multiplexers, modem technologies, and multipoint line bridging to lower network costs.

The percentage of communications costs allocated to links should start to shift as voice and data networks are integrated. In a digitally integrated network, the differentiation of voice and data line charges will blur. The Integrated Services Digital Network (ISDN) will also blur voice and data networks by combining voice and data connections over one physical line. The availability optimization processes for voice and data networks have similar goals.

Even though a line may be point-to-point, there are many private-line tariffs. Before AT&T's divestiture in 1984, there were about 200 special tariffs for pricing local circuits. Today there are more than 800 special private line tariffs (see "Making the most of post-divestiture tariffs for data network design," DATA COMMUNICATIONS, January 1987, p. 135).

The private-line pricing structure has been evolving since divestiture. With the escalation of installation charges and multiple tariff changes each year, a network manager will think twice before making network changes to take advantage of tariff pricing abnormalities, since they can change again within a few months.

Interaction: Availability, performance, and cost
Network optimization can be viewed as the process of balancing the design factors against one another to reach a network configuration that gives the best combination within the constraints specified. The interaction of the three major network requirements of availability, performance (response time), and cost is shown in Figure 5. The charts show the interactions of the three major design factors when one of the factors is held constant against the others.

Each variable, when held constant, affects all the others. The curve itself is a nonlinear, quasi-step function. Cost will produce a discrete step on a curve, but performance and availability may produce nonlinear steps. This is shown in greater detail in the close-up view in Figure 5C.

Changes in components, hosts, modem speeds, and line topology produce changes on the X and Y axis. If the speed of one network line is increased to 56 kbit/s from 9.6 kbit/s the user will notice the difference. But the change may have a minor effect on the total system performance for a network composed of many lines. The net effect of minor changes may almost appear to produce a continuous curve.

In Figure 5A, the same cost will produce greater avail-

5. Balancing act. *Network optimization is the process of balancing availability, performance (response time), and cost against one another.*

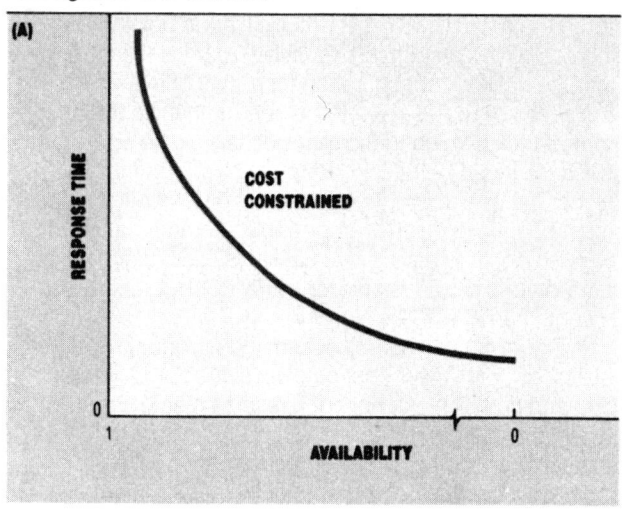

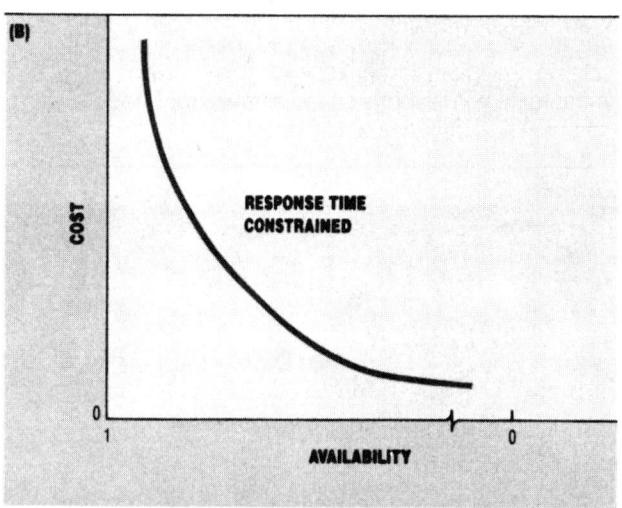

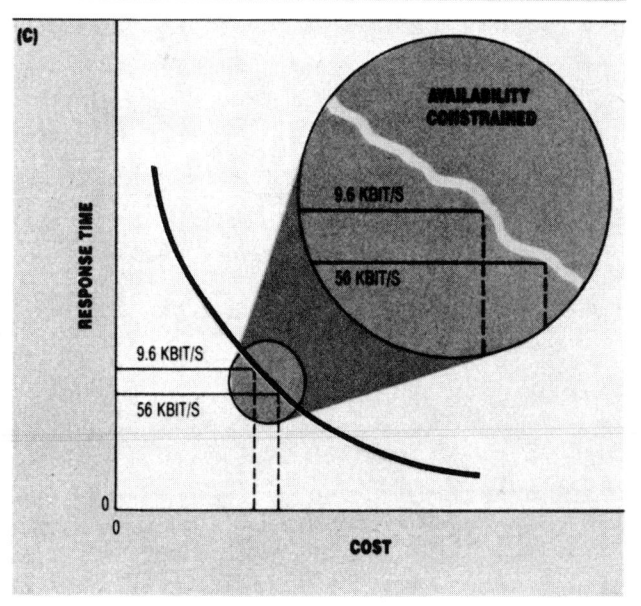

(A) RESPONSE TIME vs AVAILABILITY — COST CONSTRAINED

(B) COST vs AVAILABILITY — RESPONSE TIME CONSTRAINED

(C) RESPONSE TIME vs COST — AVAILABILITY CONSTRAINED (9.6 KBIT/S, 56 KBIT/S)

ability with lower performance or lower availability with greater performance. The figure applies to a large backbone system with alternate routes. The failure of one route can force the data to travel over multiple node hops, thus increasing the response-time delay. There is a cost built into the network configuration for a level of availability since the alternate routes have to be sized to handle the newly routed traffic. Voice traffic may not have to be sized because it can be off-loaded to the public switch. The higher the availability, the greater the data capacity that must be held in reserve for possible alternate routing. This will also apply to having two 9.6-kbit/s lines operating in parallel. This provides greater availability but less performance than one 19.2-kbit/s line.

In Figure 5B, the same performance produces greater availability with lower cost or lower availability with decreased cost. An example of a response-time constraint is when an analog line modem is replaced with a modem of the same speed but a newer technology. Cost has increased because of the cost of the new modem; availability should be improved because of the new technology. Response time has stayed the same, since there was no change in modem speed. There may be a slight improvement in response if fewer messages need to be retransmitted because of line errors.

In Figure 5C, the same availability produces greater performance with increased cost or lower performance with decreased cost. If a digital 9.6-kbit/s line is increased to 56 kbit/s, the system cost will increase as a result of the higher tariff, but response time will be decreased (improved performance). We are assuming that the availability of the two digital services is about identical. This is shown in the close-up view of the "availability constrained" chart, Figure 5C. In this example, the new 56-kbit/s line should provide extra capacity to provide greater throughput and improve response times. This assumes a similar workload before and after the installation.

Network availability can be improved through several means: redundancy, alternate routing, using higher-availability digital lines, and minimizing the length of any outage by automating network operations. Network managers will always strive to maximize availability and performance within cost constraints, but in the long term any increase in availability or performance generally requires a corresponding increase in cost. ∎

Peter M. Haverlock is a senior instructor at the IBM Telecommunication Education Center in Thornwood, N.Y. He received his B.S.E.E. from the University of Illinois and has served as an adjunct instructor at the U.S. Department of Agriculture Graduate School, Washington, D.C.

Bart W. Stuck, Probe Research Inc., Morristown, N. J.

The digital cross-connect: Cornerstone of future networks?

The device may well revolutionize digital networking. It can use T1 and T3, and is attracting IBM.

T1 is ubiquitous, with tens of millions of miles of transmission links throughout the continental United States. This has led to an explosion in demand for digital cross-connect systems (DCSs) for interconnecting different derived bit streams, such as 64 kbit/s. (The more popular term, DACS, which stands for Digital Access and Cross-connect System, is an AT&T product name.)

Since 1983, major corporations and private networks have become big users of T1 links, which are now standard service offerings of AT&T and other interexchange carriers (IECs), as well as local exchange carriers (LECs). (See the following DATA COMMUNICATIONS articles: "The anatomy and application of the T1 multiplexer," March 1984, p. 183; "T1 mux market heats up at high and low ends. Mergers ahead?" June 1986, p. 87; and "Private T1 networks call for powerful switches," June 1986, p. 127).

The demand for "high-capacity" point-to-point communications has led to the emergence of over 30 T1 multiplexer vendors as of 1986.

The DCS bit streams include DS-0 (data speed zero, or 64 kbit/s) and DS-1 (1.536 Mbit/s). One DS-1 equals 24 DS-0s (1.536 Mbit/s = 24 × 64 kbit/s). DS-1 is carried within a T1 link; an additional 8 kbit/s is reserved for framing and control, resulting in T1 operating at 1.544 Mbit/s.

Broadly speaking, carrier networks and private networks have evolved in a similar fashion. First-generation T1 products were designed to handle mainly point-to-point applications: Early T1 multiplexers for common carriers supported point-to-point T1/DS-1 digital transmission, as well as analog-to-digital (and digital-to-analog) conversion. The equivalents for private networks were the first-generation T1 multiplexers.

Second-generation T1 products enabled the interconnection, or networking, of multiple sites: For common carriers and major private corporations, DCSs multiplex and demultiplex digital bit streams containing both voice and data.

Compared with first-generation offerings, the second-generation products tend to have significantly greater software capabilities for installing, operating, and troubleshooting networks of devices. Third-generation products—only now emerging into the marketplace—will probably encompass higher levels of functionality than simply physical layer connectivity. These products incorporate functions such as protocol conversion (which might be an OSI presentation layer service) and message handling (generally regarded as an application layer function), as well as additional network management and testing features that cut across all levels.

Exactly what is a digital cross-connect system? Structurally, a DCS is a nonblocking time-division digital switch interconnecting synchronous bit streams. Typically, DCS connections are maintained for days, weeks, months, or years. In many respects, a DCS is a solid-state version of a wiring patch panel. The connections are typically between different bit streams with identical data rates: Dataphone Digital Service (DDS) rates of 2.4, 4.8, 9.6, and 56 kbit/s—which are then multiplexed onto a T1 link—or the aforementioned 64 kbit/s (DS-0) or 1.536 Mbit/s (DS-1).

Both switched and dedicated
Unlike a voice or data PBX or a telephone-carrier switch (which has extensive software for call setup, take down, and supervision), a DCS tends to have more rudimentary software. On the one hand, many telephone-carrier switches may not support permanent circuits—that is, circuits that must be kept connected for years. They were designed mainly to handle large volumes of telephone calls lasting typically five to 10 minutes.

On the other hand, it is quite common for a DCS to

control transmission links that may contain both switched-service traffic (such as voice) and private-line or dedicated services. Matrix switches that connect modems to host computers are comparable to DCSs. The big difference is that a DCS can handle voice as well as data.

The DCS was developed by vendors of transmission equipment—not of switching equipment—to simplify network administration and testing. Administration includes managing the configuration of every port on every printed-circuit line card; changing and rearranging the DCS configuration (programmed by filling in blanks on a terminal screen from a menu of items) in response to changes in user needs; and network load balancing, in response to time-of-day changes in tariffs; and to reconfigure the network in case of link failure.

Testing the status of each transmission facility and line card on a link-by-link, node-by-node basis is essential for proper network management. A T1 multiplexer capable of switching to a backup link in case of primary-link failure is the simplest example of a first-generation DCS.

A second-generation DCS allows physical connectivity between any two locations in a network. Once a user specifies the two communicating nodes and the required transmission capacity, the DCS-controlled network attempts to effectively establish a connection, according to user-defined cost criteria such as tariffs and deadlines. (By deadlines are meant the preset times at which a circuit switchover or a tariff-rate change occurs.)

The DCS is a critical component in both private and public networks that include central office transmission and switching equipment, customer premises voice and data communications equipment, and computers. The DCS allows:
- Control of digital communications links that transfer information-bit streams, such as voice, data, and image;
- Control of one or more virtual networks built on top of a single physical network, all managed by a special control network—special in that it uses, for example, X.25 or CCITT Signaling System 7 protocols; and
- Timely network administration, testing, and disaster recovery.

The strategic issue is simple: Should DCSs play a major role in these areas, or should alternative devices control the network? Alternatives include PBXs, which typically reside on a user's premises as part of a private network, and public-carrier switches.

The issue is further complicated by changes in technology, corporate organizations, and regulations. These changes include:
- Carriers starting to offer DS-3 (28 DS-1s), which carry bit streams of 28 × 24, or 672, DS-0 (64 kbit/s), or an aggregate of 43.008 Mbit/s over T3 (44.736 Mbit/s) facilities (framing and control needs make up the difference);
- The proliferation of fiber optic long-haul networks with numerous new tariffing options;
- Viable bypass networking alternatives such as satellite,

1. The anatomy of a DCS. *Synchronous DS-1 links are connected to input/output handlers, which in turn are interconnected by a processor-controlled time slot interchanger. To maintain a nonblocking architecture, the number of input links is equal to the number of output links. DCSs are available with up to 640 input/output links.*

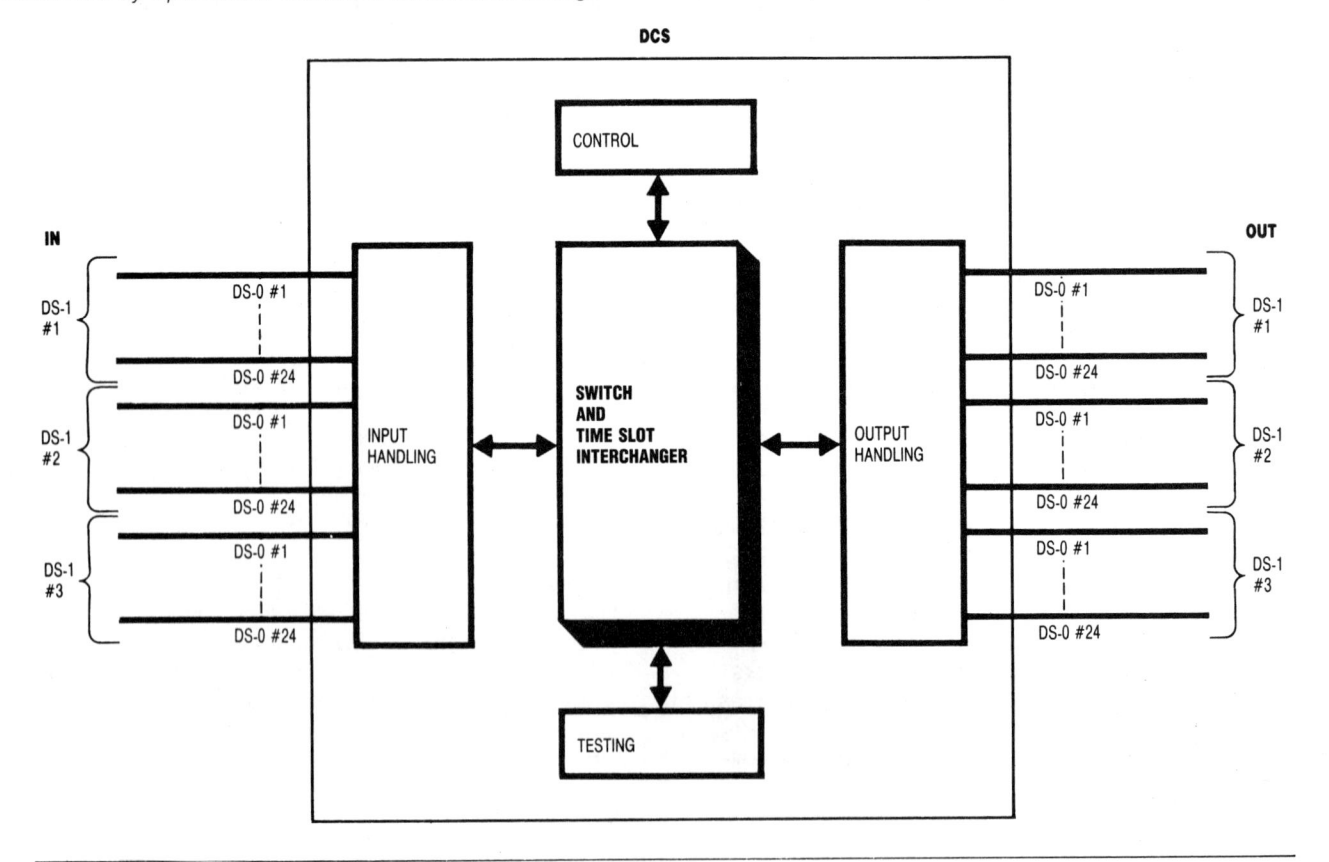

2. Concentration and segregation. *The DCS concentrates intermixed services. Segregation, the inverse of concentration, simplifies cabling requirements.*

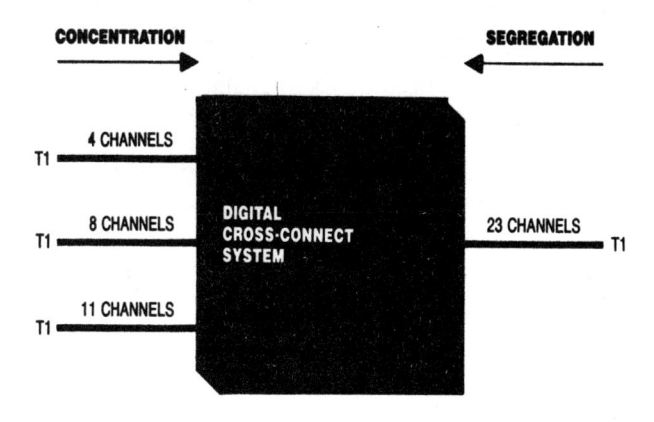

CONCENTRATION → ← SEGREGATION

T1 — 4 CHANNELS
T1 — 8 CHANNELS → DIGITAL CROSS-CONNECT SYSTEM → 23 CHANNELS — T1
T1 — 11 CHANNELS

CHANNEL = ACTIVE DS-0

---

digital microwave, and digital UHF (ultrahigh frequency) radio;
- The creation by many *Fortune* 500 firms of corporate information technology groups charged with voice/data computer communications services;
- The wave of mergers and acquisitions that requires rapid integration of voice and data communications services from two distinct corporate organizations; and
- The AT&T divestiture and resulting user and carrier loss of end-to-end network control.

All these changes further stimulate the need for a sound information technology business strategy.

Comes the evolution

DCSs are evolving toward two types of products. One, a high-performance cross-connect, is rich in software functionality, testing capabilities, and options. The other, a low-cost entry-level device, is a highly versatile voice/data multiplexer that is capable of analog/digital conversion and data rates from 75 bit/s up to at least 64 kbit/s.

These DCS products would typically be used to build two-level hierarchical networks. Numerous low-end devices would multiplex and switch voice/data bit streams onto a backbone network controlled by many fewer high-end devices.

Figure 1 is a block diagram of a DCS. Synchronous links are connected to input/output handlers, which in turn are interconnected by a special type of random access memory called a time slot interchanger. The time slot interchanger is controlled by a processor. Meanwhile, the processor provides access to links and circuit cards by internal or external test equipment.

To illustrate how the DCS works, assume all input/output links are DS-1 bit streams. That is, every 125 microseconds or 8,000 times a second, 24 envelopes of eight bits each enter and leave on each DS-1 link, providing 24 bit streams of 64 kbit/s (DS-0) for each link. To maintain a nonblocking architecture, the number of input links is equal to the number of output links. DCSs are available with DS-1 input/output links varying from two to as many as 640.

Suppose that DS-0 number 7 of incoming DS-1 number 3 is to be connected to DS-0 number 15 of outgoing DS-1 number 5. Bits associated with the input bit stream are read into the switch's random access memory and read out to the output bit stream. The switching is controlled by a table program that determines how bits are read in and out of memory; the table is managed by the processor. Control signals determine how to add to, delete from, and modify the table, according to a wide variety of events (such as a failure or time of day).

The current generation of digital cross-connects typically handle DS-0/DS-1 bit streams. The technology is moving in the direction of having identical digital hardware—but different software configurations (sets of programs)—for handling data rates from 1.2 kbit/s on up to the DS-0 or 64 kbit/s rate. VLSI (very large-scale integration) gate array (logic circuit) technology is making highly cost effective the interconnection of much higher bit rates: The first application interconnects DS-1 and DS-3—that is, cross-connecting 1.536 Mbit/s bit streams that are embedded within DS-3s (43.008 Mbit/s).

Furthermore, software technology is making possible the construction of networks of cross-connect nodes using distributed control to ease network modifications such as installations, changes, and disaster recovery. This software technology draws on algorithms developed by San Jose, Calif.,-based Tymnet for packet-switching networks. These algorithms are currently used by the Defense Data Network within its Transport Control Protocol/Internet Protocol (TCP/IP) suite, and by IBM for its Low Entry Networking (LEN) local area network (LAN) product offerings. Several vendors of second-generation DCS products—such as Network Equipment Technologies (NET), DCA/Cohesive, Spectrum Digital, and Stratacom—offer this type of networking software.

Concentration and segregation

For regulated carriers and major corporations that have both switched and nonswitched voice services, DCSs concentrate or consolidate special services—such as Dataphone Digital Service and Accunet T1.5—and switched services that might be intermixed among a

---

3. Good grooming. *Shown are two incoming T1 lines, each having a mix of traffic. The DCS grooms the bit streams to match the outgoing T1 lines' requirements.*

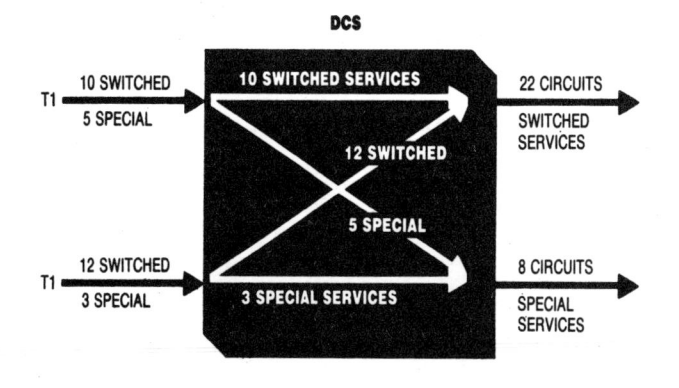

DCS

T1 — 10 SWITCHED / 5 SPECIAL → 10 SWITCHED SERVICES → 22 CIRCUITS SWITCHED SERVICES
                              12 SWITCHED
                              5 SPECIAL
T1 — 12 SWITCHED / 3 SPECIAL → 3 SPECIAL SERVICES → 8 CIRCUITS SPECIAL SERVICES

SPECIAL CIRCUIT = 1 UNSWITCHED DS-0
SWITCHED CIRCUIT = 1 DS-0

number of incoming links onto dedicated outgoing links. Concentration or consolidation increases the utilization, or "fill," of circuits and equipment. Segregation, the inverse of concentration, simplifies cabling requirements (Fig. 2).

A function closely related to segregation and consolidation is grooming. Grooming combines like types of traffic, and, in turn, allows direct routing to different destinations. In the example shown in Figure 3, two T1s are cross-connected, with each incoming DS-1 having a mix of switched and special (dedicated) services. The DCS grooms the bit streams to meet the outgoing DS-1's requirement of handling only one type of service.

A DCS can be used to drop and insert DS-0s, as shown in Figure 4. Typically, a number of DS-0s originate at one location and are dropped or terminated at an intermediate location. Meanwhile, additional DS-0s are inserted at the intermediate node and terminate at the far location.

In many data networking applications, analog data channels are connected in a multidrop arrangement. Part of the multidrop configuration is, inherently, a bridge, which literally bridges (interconnects) two or more circuits. Some analog bridges make it difficult to add, move, or delete circuits: Because cables must physically be moved, there exists the potential for disturbing all the other circuits on the bridge. Also, bridges make difficult the implementation of a broadcasting capability because of the drawbacks of a multidrop arrangement. Broadcasting is desired for quickly downloading software for file transfers and network-disaster-recovery applications.

A DCS addresses all these issues. The impact of adding, moving, or deleting circuits is potentially limited to just those affected circuits. There is a reduced chance that changes will have an impact on other circuits: Changes can be done by software, with no physical cable movement, and a broadcasting capability is a side benefit of the DCS design.

DCSs can be configured (programmed by selections from menus) to support subrate—less than DS-0 (64 kbit/s)—data cross-connections. Users can get more cost-effective service based on digital rather than analog technology, mainly because of the savings associated with multiplexing. Also gained are better diagnostics and trouble isolation capabilities. Meanwhile, carriers enjoy more efficient line and equipment utilization because of greater user demand.

Selected suppliers

DCS vendors come in two categories: those who address the needs of interexchange and local exchange carriers, and those who address the needs of major corporations and private-network users. The intent here is to cover a select number of DCS vendors. (Additional information is available from the individual vendors or the author.) The table is a brief product-comparison matrix summarizing the data from some of the leading vendors. Note that, with the exception of NET, the cost per channel today is about $1,000. NET's higher price is based on supplying greater built-in networking capabilities.

AT&T introduced the first digital cross-connect, the DACS (Digital Access and Cross-connect System), and

Selected vendor-product matrix

	ROCKWELL WESCOM 370 DCS	AT&T TECHNOLOGY DACS	DSC DEXCS1	NORTHERN TELECOM DNX100	TELLABS 532 TCS	NET IDNX
CROSS CONNECT:						
DS-1 TO DS-1	NO	YES	YES	YES	YES	NO
DS-0 TO DS-0	YES	YES	YES	YES	YES	YES
SUBRATE DS-0	NO	YES	YES	NO	NO	YES
MULTIPLE DS-0s	NO	YES	YES	YES	YES	YES
FEATURES:						
MULTIPOINT BRIDGING	YES	YES	NO	YES	YES	YES
ANALOG INTERFACE	YES	NO	NO	NO	YES	NO
VOICE CONFERENCING	NO	YES	NO	NO	YES	NO
AUTO SWITCH	NO	YES	YES	NO	YES	YES
CUSTOMER CONTROL	NO	YES	YES	NO	NO	YES
CONFIGURATION RANGE (DS-1s)	32-128	32-128	28-336	<249	32-256	2-16
PRICE RANGE ($K)	32-128	<128	34-160	NA	32-256	40-650

4. Drop and insert. *Originating DS-0s are terminated at an intermediate site. Additional DS-0s are inserted at the intermediate node and terminate at the far location.*

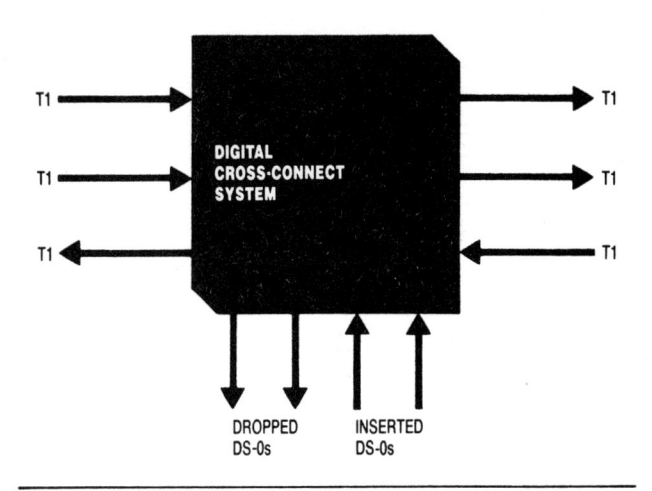

currently has the lion's share of the installed U. S. base. As of the close of 1986, AT&T was estimated to have shipped 2,000 of its DACS units.

The current product line supports 128 DS-1 channels, and the major user is AT&T. The product offering has a rich, wide-ranging set of features, including multipoint bridging and subrate data multiplexing. The local exchange carriers have held off ordering AT&T DCSs, in part because of cost effectiveness for initial service (the common equipment for future expansion must be part of the purchase), and in part because the initial product was in fact too small for some major urban installations. A DS-3/DS-1 cross-connect, and a DACS II capable of cross-connecting 640 DS-1s, are all in the works, as is a strong push for ISDN (Integrated Services Digital Network) support.

Northern Telecom Inc. (NTI), of Ottawa, Canada, is matching AT&T in both breadth and depth of DCS product line. Local exchange carriers (LECs) have said repeatedly they want at least one alternative supplier to AT&T (because of the dilemma of AT&T as an equipment vendor, as a major customer for private lines, and as a potential competitor), and NTI intends to fill that role. NTI markets a Tellabs DCS (532 TCS) as a low-end product, with the same DCS marketed by AT&T—as customer premises equipment—to businesses. NTI has devoted its own resources to the high end of the DCS product line, its DNX100.

Tellabs (Lisle, Ill.) began shipping its DCS 532 TCS in early 1985. It gained market presence by using the NTI sales and support organization to handle its product line via an OEM (original equipment manufacturer) agreement. Tellabs intends to grow its product line upward in capacity, and to reduce its cost to compete on price with other suppliers. Subrate data multiplexing may be introduced this year.

Rockwell Wescom (Downers Grove, Ill.) has successfully penetrated the independent telephone company market with both transmission and switching gear. Its internal semiconductor capability provides the potential to make Wescom a low-cost supplier of DCSs. Rockwell Collins (Richardson, Tex.) is examining the DCS market, and may well enter the DS-3/DS-1 as well as high-capacity (above about 300 channels) DS-1/DS-0 markets in the next two years.

DSC (Plano, Tex.) has been successful in selling to interexchange carriers (IECs) such as MCI and U S Sprint, and LECs such as Bell Atlantic. Its DCS line draws on its experience with these customers, and understanding and meeting their needs. Digital multipoint bridging and subrate data multiplexing are features that may soon appear in the DSC product line.

Venture capital has funded at least two DS-3/DS-1 cross-connect startups: Licom (Herndon, Va.) and Telinq (Richardson, Tex.). Each vendor is entering the market with products that would be used for DS-3/DS-1 cross-connects. A potential application, based on optical-fiber/digital-radio cross-connects, is in network disaster recovery.

Fresh territory
The offering of tariffed T1 service by carriers, as well as the potential for bypassing carriers using T1 facilities, has opened the customer premises market to DCSs:
■ Timeplex (Woodcliff Lake, N. J.) is currently the leading vendor in the T1 multiplexer market, claiming over 3,000 installed units. The bulk of the applications are point-to-point, with a standby or redundant T1 unit ready to be switched in automatically in the event of a primary T1-link failure. This is the lowest level of DCS functionality (one active link and one backup). Timeplex is currently evolving its product line to offer full DCS DS-1/DS-0 functionality and greater networking capabilities, as well as reducing costs across its product line to compete against numerous startup firms.
■ NET (Redwood City, Calif.) recognized the need for transparent, physical layer connectivity together with the capability to multiplex voice and data over a T1 backbone network. A key feature of its IDNX product line is its distributed control: Nodes are added to a network, then automatically configure themselves by interrogating each of the attached links. These actions build up the node's routing table, along with routing tables from each adjacent node. The process allows the entire network configuration and routing requirements to be automatically downloaded to a node with no human intervention, thus reducing operating costs.

Several hundred NET nodes are installed at a variety of major corporations. This vendor has the largest installed base of high-performance, second-generation DCSs. An interesting aside is that the control protocol used to interconnect NET nodes is based on CCITT's Signaling System No. 7 (see "Inside SS No. 7: A detailed look at ISDN's signaling system plan," DATA COMMUNICATIONS, October 1985, p. 120). The use of SS No. 7 may ease compatibility with carrier networks, thus more readily enabling a customer to use enhanced offerings such as "800" service and telemarketing. NET is actively soliciting business from carriers, as well as from major corporations.
■ DCA/Cohesive Network (Los Gatos, Calif.) offers a product, the CN-1, roughly comparable in functionality to NET's. There are a multitude of differences between the NET and DCA/Cohesive Network product lines (examples: the handling of voice, control-signaling protocols, and network initialization, routing, and fault-detection algorithms).

Over 100 nodes are installed at major corporations.
- Infotron (Cherry Hill, N. J.) offers a DCS, the NX4600, whose functionality is comparable to Tellabs's product. The NX4600 evolved from Infotron's existing statistical multiplexer product line and draws on the company's network-management computer experience. In addition, Infotron had a business relationship with the former Network Switching Systems (NSS)—which was terminated by NSS's recent absorption by Cambridge, Mass.,-based BBN Communications—which (now under the BBN name) is developing a product line comparable in functionality to NET's and DCA/Cohesive Network's. Finally, Infotron is examining opportunities in the DS-3/DS-1 DCS market. Infotron is actively soliciting business in the carrier marketplace as well as within major corporations and businesses.

Those that have recently joined NET's and DCA/Cohesive Network's market include: Spectrum Digital (Herndon, Va.), with a joint marketing agreement with Largo, Fla.,-based Paradyne (Spectrum Digital recently announced an acquisition offer by Micom, Simi Valley, Calif., which will not apparently affect the agreement with Paradyne.); Stratacom (Campbell, Calif.), with a joint marketing agreement with Mansfield, Mass.,-based Codex; and the aforementioned BBN Communications. And AT&T plans to distribute Tellabs's DCS product line as the carrier's Dataphone II Acculink multiplexer. This list is illustrative of some of the players in this new and emerging business; conspicuously absent, at this writing, is Digital Equipment Corp. (DEC).

Futures
Where is DCS going? A number of new synchronous transmission standards are emerging that will be deployed throughout public and private networks over the next decade in response to market needs and technology changes. One example is Syntran, which allows migration from current copper transmission networks to new fiber optic networks. Interface specifications are emerging for Syntran DS-3/DS-1 digital cross-connects, encompassing multiplexing of those data rates, as well as of switching DS-1s. A key advantage of Syntran-compatible products over many other offerings is that both DS-1/DS-3 multiplexing as well as DS-1 drop-and-insert can be offered. This often results in the use of one rack of equipment, instead of requiring two or more.

Sonet (synchronous optical networking) is a fast-emerging interface standard (though several years behind Syntran) for cross-connecting not just DS-3s but higher-capacity digital bit streams as well (typically multiple DS-1s). Sonet is intended for fiber; Syntran concentrates on microwave and copper. As ISDN evolves to support graphics and imaging applications, Sonet will take its place in the ISDN panoply of standards. Bell Communications Research (Livingston, N. J.) publishes technical interface specifications for Syntran and Sonet. These specifications are being discussed by the CCITT.

Other emerging fiber optic-based standards, such as the Accredited Standards Committee's (ASC's) Fiber Distributed Data Interface (FDDI), may well find their places in the DCS market, interconnecting local and wide area networks. The proliferation of optical fiber through both the interexchange and local exchange carrier transmission plants suggests that a significant portion of digital cross-connects will be purchased to interface to these facilities. The reasons for doing so are the same as for DS-1/DS-0 cross-connects: switching, testing, administration, and enhanced services.

Growing capabilities
DCS functionality is evolving in five areas: hardware, protocol conversion, message handling, network management, and testing.

The hardware is moving toward:
- higher speeds,
- physical connectivity to different transmission facilities such as Syntran and Sonet,
- VLSI supporting digital signal processors as well as time slot interchangers,
- innovative switching design based on "fast-packet-switching" types of distributed-control packet-switching networks, and
- specialized test equipment that may be an integral part of line cards or may be switched to access a particular line or card on demand.

5. The multinetwork. Illustrated is the key internetworking role DCSs play, whether the individual networks are public (evolving toward ISDN) or private.

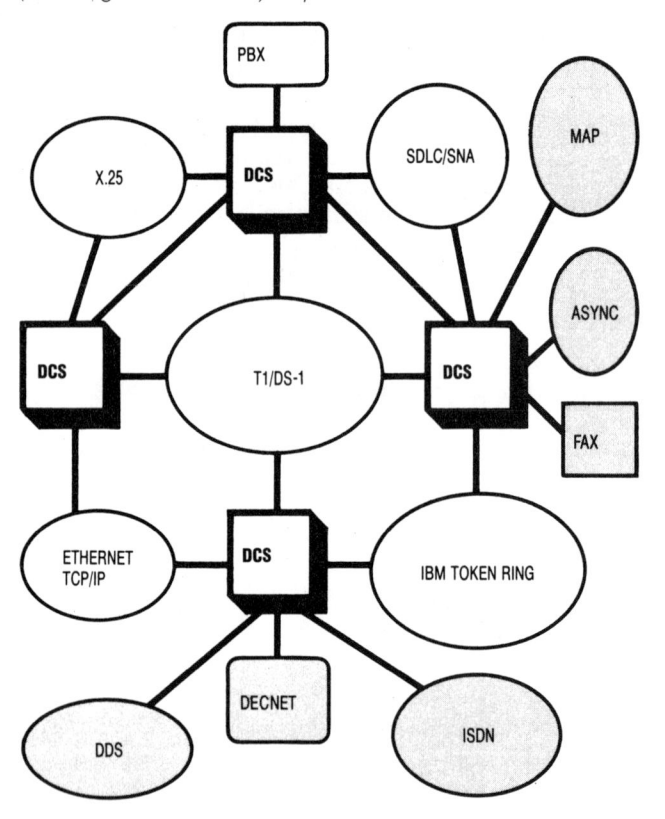

DCS = DIGITAL CROSS-CONNECT SYSTEM
FAX = FACSIMILE
DDS = DATAPHONE DIGITAL SERVICE
ISDN = INTEGRATED SERVICES DIGITAL NETWORK
MAP = MANUFACTURING AUTOMATION PROTOCOL
SDLC = SYNCHRONOUS DATA LINK CONTROL
SNA = SYSTEMS NETWORK ARCHITECTURE
TCP/IP = TRANSMISSION CONTROL PROTOCOL/INTERNET PROTOCOL

IBM's digital cross-connect strategy

Ellen M. Hancock, president of IBM's Communications Products Division, delivered an address to an IBM-users group in St. Louis on November 11, 1986. The subject was, "IBM directions in telecommunications." In particular, she said, "The mandate for connectivity is growing... not only within users' own corporate networks... but also among their networks... and those of other enterprises... this makes for new demands on IBM and other vendors... to offer higher bandwidth capacities." Among the areas she singled out for IBM product direction was "bandwidth management... to run an integrated voice and data network more efficiently," which is precisely what a digital cross connect system (DCS) does.

Similar statements were made on April 29, 1987, by Terry Lautenbach, IBM vice president and group executive, Information Systems and Communications Group, at an IBM-sponsored consultant liaison conference in Phoenix, Ariz. (Lautenbach is also a member of the IBM Corporate Management Board.) IBM had apparently decided to enter the DCS market; the only question remaining was when.

On June 16, 1987, IBM announced that it had nonexclusive worldwide marketing, installation, and service rights for the current and future releases of the Intelligent Digital Network Exchange (IDNX), a transmission resource manager (DCS-like) product line from Network Equipment Technologies Inc. (NET) of Redwood City, Calif. In addition, IBM decided to fund development work at NET that many believe could lead to the incorporation of unique IBM functionality into the IDNX. This may even mean extensive support for Systems Application Architecture (SAA).

SAA, the hot new buzzword of 1987, is an "architecture" being developed by IBM that will specify a set of interfaces for application programs, users, communications and networking, and network management. Initial versions of the new architecture are expected to be published in the latter part of this year. Target hardware for products using these new interfaces include IBM mainframes (S/370), midrange computers (including both S/36 and S/38), and PCs. It is likely that significant numbers of products in the commercial market that are compatible with SAA are still five years away. (Some refer to SAA as IBM's version of the Strategic Defense Initiative, or "Star Wars.")

In the interim, IBM will be hard at work on SAA. This implies developing products that conform to Systems Network Architecture (SNA) protocols for offerings such as: SNA Distribution Services; Netview for a common network-management interface based on existing IBM products such as Network Problem Determination Application and Network Logical Data Manager; Distributed Data Management-compatible products for data description, organization, and access; and Enhanced Connectivity Facilities-compatible products for protocol conversions and transformations.

IBM is rumored to be developing a DCS internally. If it is, Big Blue can draw on expertise within IBM/Rolm in Santa Clara, Calif., as well as established telecommunications groups within IBM such as those at Raleigh, N. C., Boca Raton, Fla., or La Gaude, France.

Many of the functions provided by a digital cross-connect system fall within the realm of the Integrated Services Digital Network. Therefore, vendors of PBXs and data communications equipment, as well as carrier vendors of transmission and switching equipment, can be expected to enter this market. Those entering will include the regional Bell operating companies (RBOCs)—provided Judge Greene frees them from manufacturing restrictions, in keeping with the Justice Department's recent recommendations.

IBM may choose to work with one or more of the regional Bell operating companies to meet market needs. The long-term intent of IBM may be to develop a product line of communications processors based on its existing front-end processors, cluster controllers, and modems—plus DCS technology.

The 1985 filing with the FCC by IBM on Computer Inquiry III, along with associated documentation and IBM presentations at industry forums over the past year, all suggest that IBM views DCS functionality as a key ingredient in meeting major mainframe-user data communications needs. The NET IDNX product line handles voice and data (physical) connectivity, transmission-capacity management, and can lead to protocol conversion services; it meshes perfectly with IBM's apparent business strategy.

The availability of industry-standard buses—such as Multibus (Intel), VMEBus (Motorola, Signetics, et al.), and PC bus (IBM)—has spawned numerous board-level vendors. Some of these vendors are developing test equipment that meets these bus-interface industry standards and that can be readily added to a DCS.

Protocol conversion capabilities are becoming increasingly rich. (Unfortunately with every year there are more, not less, protocols to convert among.) Whether this function should reside in a DCS or elsewhere remains moot. Typical protocol suites encompass IBM interfaces such as Synchronous Data Link Control (SDLC), Binary Synchronous Communications (BSC), and higher-level Systems Network Architecture (SNA) protocols; asynchronous interfaces and associated protocols from vendors such as DEC and Hewlett-Packard; network, transport, and session level protocols such as SNA, DECNet, or TCP/IP (Transmission Control Protocol/Internet Protocol); file-format conversion (such as from IBM fixed-length record-oriented formats to IBM PC variable-length byte-stream formats); and document-format conversion (from Wang to IBM to DEC).

Message handling requires a disk plus its controller for storage of messages for later delivery, as well as a file program running under an operating system with a file-transfer protocol. Current trends are to support this type of operating system under a real-time communications operating system (no file program, under 100-microsecond program-to-program switching, support for hundreds or thousands of simultaneously active programs). Message-handling formats are illustrated by IBM's Document Interchange Architecture (DIA) and CCITT/ISO X.400 Message Handling Service (MHS).

Network management is evolving to administer networks of hundreds of thousands of devices—such as computers, data communications products, and transmission links—from multiple vendors. Embryonic potential de facto interface standards such as IBM's Netview are starting to appear. Functions such as billing (for chargeback to users), access authorization (for security and control), test programs and diagnostics, and network planning and traffic engineering (for determining the usage of links and DCS subsystems) are all evolving under the rubric of network management.

DCSs are, in short, evolving toward communications processors. They are becoming modular platforms capable of supporting multiplexing, switching, testing, protocol conversion, message handling, network management, and networking of a wide variety of digital interfaces.

Big Blue and the DCS

IBM is committed to transmission-capacity management, as part of its overall strategic marketing direction, to meet its major corporate customers' needs. And a DCS is a product class that meshes with that thrust. IBM has the capability of developing its own DCS product line, presumably with the price/performance skewed toward its communications products and services. IBM would also use its internal knowledge of how SNA will evolve with time, or would draw on carrier offerings for providing this functionality (see "IBM's cross-connect strategy").

For common carrier services based on ISDN, digital cross-connects impact on them in three ways: 1. DCSs are used for private-line offerings of ISDN basic- [(2 64 16) kbit/s] and primary-rate [(23 64 64) kbit/s] services; 2. DCSs can be interfaced to supervisory data communications networks such as Signaling System No. 7; 3. DCSs interface telephone company computer-based operations-support entities such as the Trunk Integrated Record Keeping System (TIRKS), and LEC operations-support networks supporting X.25-type protocols.

Digital cross-connect systems play a key role in networking. Whether the network is a carrier-managed public network that is evolving toward ISDN or a corporate private network that is based on SNA, the DCS is an integral part of the scheme (Fig. 5). ∎

Bart Stuck, senior vice president at Probe Research, has S.B.E.E., S.M.E.E., and Sc.D. degrees from M.I.T. He was with Bell Laboratories for 12 years, working on a variety of computer communications devices and applications. He has written many technical papers on computer communications, and one book, "A Computer and Communication Network Performance Analysis Primer," Prentice Hall, 1985. He is chairman of IEEE Computer Society Project 802 Local Area Network Traffic Handling Characteristics Technical Advisory Group.

This article is based on material abstracted from a report, "DACS Digital Cross-Connect Systems: The Strategies and Markets to 1992," available from Probe Research, P. O. Box 590, Morristown, N. J. 07960 (201-285-1500).

Walter Roehr, Telecommunication Networks Consulting, Reston, Va.

Knocking on users' doors: Signaling System 7

The new standard for signaling between telephone central offices is spreading quickly—and promises a host of new user applications.

What will soon become the highest-volume data network in the world? It is not one of the value-added common carriers like Telenet or Tymnet. And neither is it a government or a military network. Here's a hint: The telephone industry is in the midst of deploying it. The answer is Signaling System Number 7 (SS7), a new, worldwide, packet-switched network specifically designed to handle telephone signaling needs.

In addition to providing the call setup and disconnection traditionally associated with telephone signaling, SS7 will foster a variety of new applications. Credit calls, 800 service, virtual private networks, and a host of other innovative services will be controlled by SS7.

SS7 did not spring from the collective intelligence of one telephone company's marketing department. It is the natural culmination of the evolution of computer-controlled digital switching. The earliest telephone switch signaling techniques emulated the pulses generated by a rotary dial. These pulses were carried on the same wires that carried the user's voice.

Tone signaling came later. It was introduced when multiplexing and carrier techniques made it impossible to signal by interrupting the battery current. Despite the fact that a variety of improved schemes were developed over the years, the tones continued to be carried in the user's speaking channel. It remained a channel-associated signaling scheme.

Moving the signals from a number of user channels onto a single common channel represents a big technical advance. Faster call handling, interdiction of fraudulent "blue-box" tones, and simpler administration are just a few of the many advantages of the common channel arrangement. Such advances could come about only in a computer-controlled switching architecture. In a sense, the common channel becomes a special-purpose data link between two computers that just *happens* to be controlling a telephone circuit.

The first common channel-signaling system to be standardized was Signaling System Number 6 (SS6), which was formulated under the auspices of the International Telegraph and Telephone Consultative Committee (CCITT). Number 6 operates on analog telephone systems using 2,400- or 4,800-bit/s modems. Despite initial worldwide enthusiasm, only North America widely deployed Number 6. In North America, SS6 is known as common channel interswitch signaling (CCIS). The rest of the world impatiently waited for a signaling system tailored for the emerging pulse-code modulation digital facilities: Signaling System Number 7.

The geographically uneven deployment of SS6 set the scene for a dichotomy in the development of SS7. North America has traditionally taken a relatively independent stance vis-a-vis telephone standards. In part, this can be attributed to the size of its network. The North American network represents approximately 40 percent of the world's telephones, and its huge size created special demands. For example, the North American network could not afford to wait for the rest of the world to decide whether common channel signaling was a good idea—it had to proceed with SS6. By deploying SS6 in North America, the pressure to implement SS7 was eased. However, non-North American administrations are not so fortunate. Verbal presentations at the International Switching Symposium (ISS '87) described SS7 introductions that were being accelerated because the existing tone-signaling systems were within months of being seriously overloaded.

The combination of traditional North American independence and different development priorities resulted in two major standards forums developing SS7 recommendations. The CCITT is developing an international version that

1. Out of band. *Both the interoffice signaling arrangement of SS7 and the ISDN access scheme use out-of-band signaling, but each protocol is unique.*

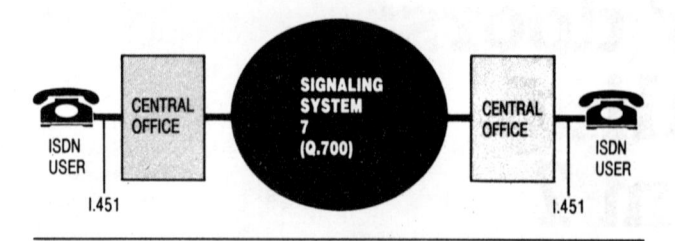

has room to accommodate national versions. In North America, the Exchange Carriers Standards Association T1S1.3 working group is developing its own version. Since ECSA is a recognized American National Standards Institute body, once the T1S1 work is completed, its products become ANSI standards.

In North America the acronym SS7 is used to refer to Signaling System Number 7, generally, and the North American version in particular. If it is necessary to note that the CCITT version is being considered, the acronym SS#7 is used. There are differences between SS7 and SS#7 that, while minor, do prevent direct interoperation.

SS7 is optimized for operation in conjunction with digital telephone systems. While a variety of analog and lower-speed digital transmission paths can be used, SS7 is designed with a 64-kbit/s channel in mind. The 64-kbit/s data links are used to establish a packet-switched network that is optimized for high-capacity, low-delay communications (see "Inside SS No. 7," DATA COMMUNICATIONS, October 1985, p. 120).

SS7 is used only in the backbone network between telephone company switches. One of the primary impetuses for its deployment in North America is the Integrated Services Digital Network; SS7 will support ISDN's enhanced services. However, SS7 is not the protocol users will employ on ISDN access links. An ISDN connection requires the cooperation of two entirely different common channel-signaling systems. Figure 1 shows this arrangement. The users communicate their desires using the ISDN access-signaling protocols, described in the CCITT recommendation I.451.[1] The backbone switches relay these user desires to other switches using the SS7 formats described in the Q.700 series of protocols.

It is interesting to compare these two protocols since, in many ways, they have very similar tasks. The access-signaling protocols in ISDN have a limited task—they only handle user access to the local switch. The signaling protocols do not support independent networks. Rather, they are merely a control mechanism for the affected circuits; they are performing a "network layer" routing function for those circuits. Thus, the I.451 protocol contains all of the required functions in Layer 3. Layers 1 and 2 are stock ISDN: The same Layer 1 is used for all ISDN applications, and the LAPD (Link Access Procedure-D) Layer 2 is used for all packet accesses.

SS7 is conceived as a separate signaling network. It has a seven-layer structure available. Currently, SS7 uses null layers 4, 5, and 6 for circuit-related signaling, but the full seven layers are available, and used, for functions other than circuit-related signaling.

If a PBX is involved in the connection, the user signals to the PBX using the I.451 protocol, and the PBX also uses the I.451 protocols on its public switched network trunks (Fig. 2). It is not necessary for the PBX to make the transformations that allow interworking of I.451 and Q.700—that is a task left to the telephone company switch. The only place that it currently seems likely that SS7 will appear on customer premises equipment is on tandem networks (Fig. 3).

Upper-level protocols

SS7 has a layered protocol structure similar to all modern data communications protocols, though the layers are called levels. The bottom three levels of SS7, which are collectively referred to as the message transfer part (MTP), provide a packet-switched network comparable to an X.25 network. The major differences between X.25 and the MTP are that the MTP provides only a connectionless service and it has a limited (14- or 24-bit) addressing capability. The addressing capability is sufficient for addressing switches themselves, but not for processes or users at the switch.

An SS7 packet switch, which is called a signaling transfer point (STP), is capable of routing the messages using the short addresses. STPs are used to avoid the need for signaling channels on all trunks. A pair of channels replaces the array of signaling channels that would otherwise be required (Fig. 4).

For call-control signaling, the characteristics of the MTP are ideal. The MTP minimizes the processing and transmission overhead and thereby reduces delay. But SS7 gets used for more than just call control. It has many additional uses, including a global address capability and connection-oriented service.

To provide these additional services, the signaling connection control part (SCCP) has been developed. Classic call-related signaling does not use the SCCP. Though the connection-oriented services are still being developed, SSCP global addressing capability is in place and functioning.

In North America, the ISDN user part (ISUP) will provide classic call-handling functions.[2] While ISUP provides functions in addition to the standard call setup and disconnect, it performs call handling extraordinarily well. Interexchange carriers (IXCs) that have deployed ISUP report decreases in call setup time of 3 to 7 seconds. Shaving seconds from a call is valuable if you are paying for switch ports, trunks, and local exchange carrier (LEC) connect time—not to mention enhanced user satisfaction.

But faster call setup is not the only thing ISUP offers. There are additional controls and features of ISDN to support, including: end-to-end signaling, 3.1-kHz speech, 7-kHz speech, 3.1-kHz audio, handling of multimode terminals, changing modes in mid-call, and user-to-user signaling.

The transaction capabilities application part (TCAP) was originally conceived to support two North American database functions: credit card calling and 800 numbers. The

2. PBX talk. *With the exception of tandem switches, SS7 is not being implemented on the customer's premises. If a PBX is involved in the connection, it is not necessary for the PBX to make the transformations that allow interworking of I.451 and Q.700 protocols—that is a task left to the telephone company switch.*

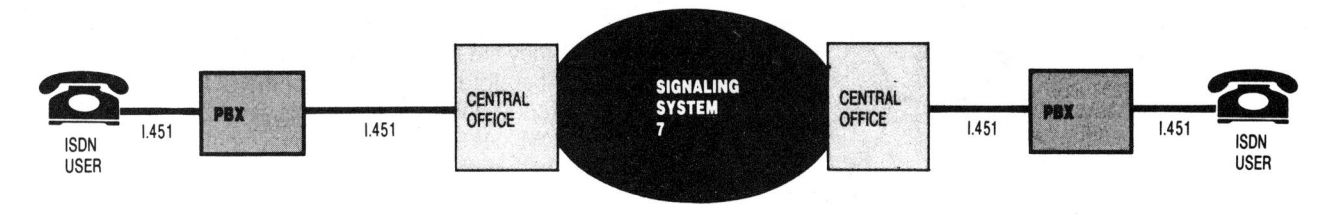

credit card calling database contains the association of telephone numbers and valid four-digit security codes. The contents of this database have been expanded to contain profiles of all lines and billable numbers and dubbed the line information database (LIDB). The 800-number database contains the association of an alias 800 number and the real 10-digit public network number, as well as the billing and interexchange carrier instructions for the number.

The TCAP capabilities address unique North American needs. Calling cards and 800 numbers are not yet widely used outside North America, and TCAP was a product of the North American T1 standards committee. The original TCAP, which is now referred to as Issue 1, was based on the X.409/410 protocols. It was balloted and accepted within the SS7 subcommittee, used as the basis of telephone company procurement specifications, and submitted as a U. S. contribution to the CCITT SS#7 working party.

The working party liked the concept but disliked the U. S. interpretation of X.409/410. CCITT proceeded to rework Issue 1 TCAP for inclusion in the 1988 edition of the CCITT recommendations. Various members of the U. S. delegation then attempted to have the CCITT version adopted as Issue 2 of the ANSI TCAP. This effort bore no fruit.

Currently, the only TCAP with any official status is Issue 1. Work on Issue 2 TCAP has started under an agreement that accepts the following: Issue 1 as the baseline; keeping backward compatibility with Issue 1; and movement toward CCITT TCAP as a worthwhile goal. This agreement ended an extended period during which no progress was made on TCAP because of a bitter disagreement regarding the status of Issue 1 TCAP.

While it is generally accepted that CCITT TCAP (Q.795) is a more elegant protocol, there does not appear to be any function Issue 1 cannot accomplish. There are claims that under some unusual circumstances—such as a loss or delay of a message—Issue 1 can enter a situation that requires a time-out for recovery. However, Issue 1 TCAP has been successfully tested in the field.

It should be noted that TCAP is not used during the actual establishment of a call. There had been some movement toward using TCAP during call forwarding, but that function is now once again firmly positioned within the ISUP. TCAP can be used to establish forwarding arrangements or to determine the suitability of a particular forwarding command, but the actual forwarding is accomplished using ISUP.

The inherent flexibility of the TCAP remote operations syntax readily allows more responsive and complex implementations of the classic database functions. A single 800 number could result in routing to different regional offices, based on the call origin. The 800 service can be easily enhanced with services of the "play announcement, collect digits" type, wherein the caller is queried by a recorded announcement for further information. A caller might hear, "If you are trying to reach Sales press 1, for Service press 2, for all other functions press 3."

Similar automated attendant services are currently available on some high-function PBXs and call-distribution switches, but this version could be embedded in the public network and result in routing the call, via the public network, to different lines and even different cities. While other kludges could be used for providing these features, TCAP provides a simple, straightforward implementation.

Database access for 800 numbers and calling cards provided the initial inspiration for TCAP, but there are myriad new functions, not directly involved in a call step-up, for which TCAP is the ideal vehicle. Some examples are:

■ *Camp-on.* A calling party, upon being informed that the called party is busy, can initiate a message indicating that the call should be set up whenever the called party becomes available. All that is kept in the queue is a record of the calling party's number.

■ *Call-forwarding management.* Both the updating of a subscriber's current forwarding address and the transfer of that information to a calling switch can be accomplished via TCAP messages.

■ *Call gapping.* This is the flow control of remote facilities (overload prevention). The request for call gapping, as well as the interval, is transmitted back to call sources by a TCAP message.

■ *Virtual private network management.* Instructions to remote switches that cause the rearrangement of the trunking in virtual private networks can be carried in TCAP message exchanges.

Operations, maintenance, administration

The operations, maintenance, and administration part (OMAP) of SS7 was designed for the care and feeding of the signaling network only, but recent developments have led to its being the leading candidate for the complete management of all aspects of the backbone circuit-switched network. OMAP defines the functional requirements that a management capability should provide,

3. A user SS7? *At the present time the only place that it seems likely that SS7 will appear on customer premises equipment is on tandem networks.*

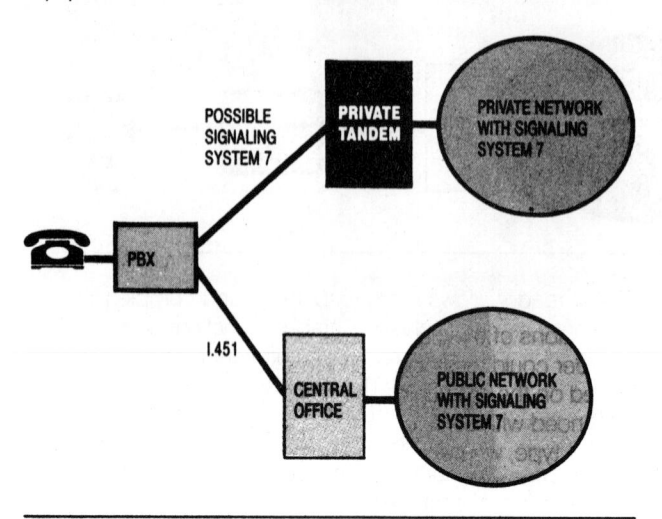

including the transmission of alarms, operational and performance statistics, program dumps, updates of tables and programs, etc. It also provides the means for formatting this information for transmission.

There are several arrangements for the management and control of SS7 networks and for applying SS7 to network management. Most basic management capabilities are built into the individual levels of the various protocols. Thus, Level 2 protocols include a running estimate of the average error rate to monitor link quality while upper levels have extensive reasonableness and format checks.

Any level that detects a problem informs the management entity: the operating system of the local network processor. The original SS7 deployment plans did not include native SS7 management—thinking was dominated by the existing environment in which a manufacturer's proprietary switch-management arrangements were in charge of the switch. First under AT&T patronage and more recently under Bell Communications Research (Bellcore), there have been moves to establish nonproprietary operations system standards using the BX.25 protocols to provide a generic management capability. The initiative led to SEAS, the signaling engineering and administration system. Manufacturers are required to provide a BX.25-based interface to their internal management entity. The regional Bell operating companies are currently going forward with plans to deploy SEAS central processors to manage their SS7 networks.

OMAP depends upon TCAP for the transmission of its messages. The remote operations capability of TCAP is just what OMAP needs for managing distributed processes—there is no need for OMAP to repeat that effort. The history of the parallel development of TCAP and OMAP is interesting. OMAP predates TCAP. There was early appreciation of the need for a network management capability. The initial OMAP efforts centered on functional requirements: What should be measured and what should be controlled. The design of a protocol to accomplish such functions came later. TCAP started as the database query protocol. Once the designers of OMAP started to consider the details of the protocol they needed, it was apparent that it already existed—it was TCAP!

The functions needed for managing the SS7 network are generic—they are needed for the management of any network. Therefore, recent drafts of the CCITT Study Group XI report on Operation Administration and Maintenance (COM XI-R 93-E) on Telecommunications Management Network protocols suggest that OMAP be used for the management of the backbone circuit-switched network. ISDN access networks would be managed using the D-channel protocols. Currently, the D-channel (I.450) protocols do not contain plans for detailed management functions. It is likely that the functionality built into OMAP (and TCAP) will be grafted onto these access protocols.

T1.11X, which specifies the measurements and controls to be implemented, has already gone out for letter ballot, and the July 1988 T1S1 meetings in San Diego incorporated suggested changes. During the July meeting the OMAP bearer protocol (T1.11Y) was approved by the TCAP subcommittee. There was some doubt, in that OMAP has chosen to more closely align itself with the CCITT recommendations than the ANSI/ECSA TCAP. The compromise that won approval for OMAP was the acceptance of the designation "Private TCAP" for OMAP messages. Since OMAP will be reusing some of the same identifiers for different purposes, this designation will allow discrimina-

4. Redundant redundant. *A signal transfer point (STP) handles message routing. A pair of channels replaces the array of signaling channels that would otherwise be required.*

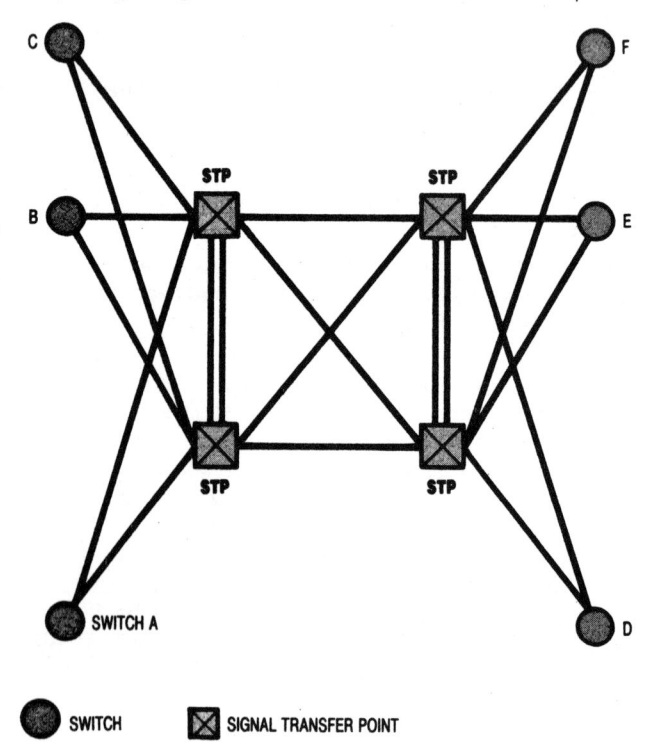

tion, on other than an addressed process basis, between OMAP and existing TCAP applications. Rapid formal approval of T1.11Y looks highly likely. Everyone appears to be pushing hard to keep OMAP rolling—there is a sense of urgency and cooperation.

Non-signaling applications

One of the ways a telephone company can have more control of its services and the switches it buys from vendors is to use simple switches and smart databases. This arrangement is shown in Figure 5. A service switching point (SSP) is any switch equipped with SS7 and TCAP. The database is contained in the service control point (SCP). The essence of the intelligent network is the use of these components to provide for unplanned services.

Just as the local switch need not have any knowledge of the real location of an 800 number or how to handle it, the local switch need not implement a feature the telephone company wishes to introduce. In both cases the switch can refer to a centralized database for instructions. Since the database and the instructions it contains are under the direct control of the telephone company, there is the hope that modifications can be introduced more quickly, uniformly across all switch models, and at a lower cost. The means for accessing the database is SS7 and TCAP—just as in the 800 function.

During 1987, the intelligent network was big news—every telephone company seemed to be rushing to deploy it. Lately, the ardor appears to have cooled. This cooling may be caused by the attention the telephone companies have had to devote to Open Network Architecture. ONA is a judicially mandated initiative that will result in the telephone companies separately tariffing the various components of their services. However, it is still likely that some form of intelligent network will appear.

One of the opportunities that ONA may provide is regulatory approval for providing additional services. With ONA, the telco monopoly advantage is eliminated because all value-added service providers are given access to the service components at the same price the company has to pay to use these services. SS7 plays a key role in several of these new services.

The significant fact about the SS7 network, from a non-signaling viewpoint, is that it has been designed from the ground up as a transaction network; it handles short messages without the overhead of setting up connections. One place this capability could clearly be advantageous is in general credit card validation checks. TCAP was designed to provide this function for calling cards being used to charge telephone calls, but clearly a more generic service is possible. Already telephone companies are establishing generic validation databases so calls can be charged to general-purpose credit cards as well as calling cards. The telcos could sell just transport service to the various credit validation centers, or they could be providing access to their own databases, if regulatory approval were gained.

While it is true that SS7 was designed for backbone signaling on the public network, recent developments

5. Future present. *Reconfigurable components are the essence of the intelligent network. SSPs are equipped with SS7, and databases are housed at SCPs.*

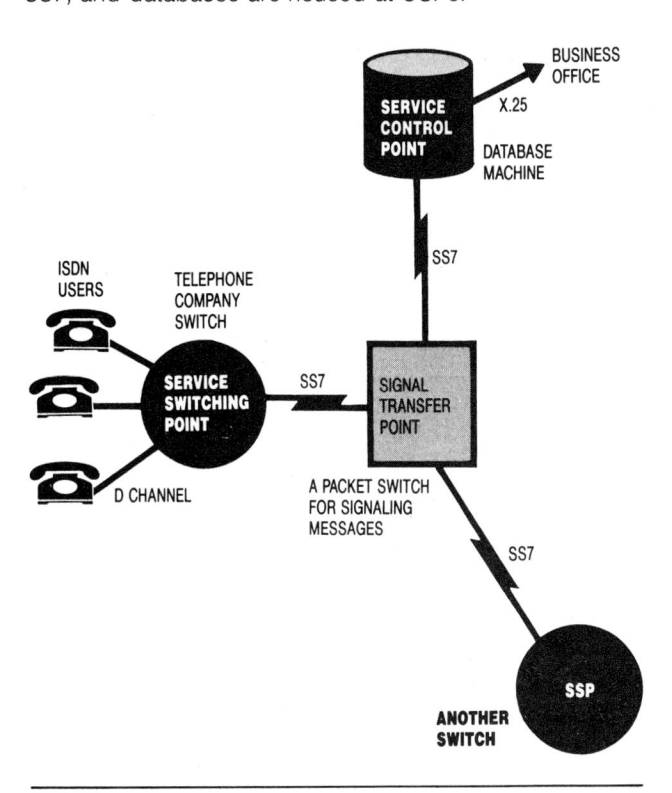

clearly indicate a wider role for SS7 within and between various private and public networks.

The simplest of these extended uses would be in private networks. Large private tandem networks have requirements that parallel those of the public network. Furthermore, private networks do not have the regulatory and operational constraints that can limit the utilization of the signaling network. In a private network, concerns such as capital investment, billing and charge-back, cross-subsidization, and security can be satisfied by executive fiat rather than a regulatory process.

Using a high-performance common channel-signaling system within a private network allows feature transparency across all of the switching nodes in the network. Management capabilities are also enhanced. TCAP and OMAP applications can be readily supported, and a private network could establish its own version of the intelligent network. Several vendors have already announced versions of SS7 for private tandem networks.

NEC offers SS7 as the standard tandem signaling technique on its line of NEAC 2400 PBXs. AT&T has not yet offered SS7 on its System 25, 75, or 85 PBX line but does provide SS7 on 5ESS switches offered to large organizations. The 5ESS is normally a central office switch, but it is offered as a PBX for very large private networks. As a central office switch it must have SS7; the capability is kept when the 5ESS is offered as a private switch. Northern Telecom has announced its Meridian Super-

Node, a private network version of its DMS family of telco switches. Thus, the SuperNode is approximately the equivalent of AT&T's 5ESS private network offering. One of the features Northern is touting on its SuperNode is the capability of providing Feature Group D access. Feature Group D is used by IXCs to provide access to their networks by the general public via the LEC. A private network using this arrangement would effectively be establishing itself as an additional IXC. A similar access by the private network to IXCs, with the SuperNode acting as the LEC, is possible. In both of these arrangements, SS7 would be used to provide signaling.

Not all PBX vendors agree with this arrangement: Both Siemens and IBM, which took over the Rolm product line, have declared that extension of the ISDN access signaling protocol is sufficient for tandem private networks. While this statement is patently true, since tandem networks are currently operated using in-band tone signaling, it is not clear that a signaling system designed for access should be forced to play a role for which it was not designed. It appears that by the time all the extensions are added, the complexity will be greater, the functionality will be less, and the extensions are likely to be nonstandard and proprietary. The larger, more sophisticated PBX customers apparently are aware of this, and there are numerous rumors of all PBX vendors starting to take SS7 more seriously.

SS7 rollout

Signaling System 7 has emerged from the standards committees and test beds and is currently operationally deployed in a number of public and private networks. However, this deployment, like any major software deployment, is not without its setbacks.

There are still occasional reports of bugs and temporary removal from service. Frequently, these bugs do not involve SS7 itself but rather the interaction of other switch software modules, such as trunk testing procedures or the generation of customer information tones with the SS7 modules. These setbacks may delay but will not prevent the ultimate deployment of SS7.

As might be expected, there are significant differences in the various telephone companies' approaches to SS7, but a clustering of similar attitudes falls out according to the LEC-IXC dichotomy. The LECs are most interested in additional services, database, and intelligent network applications of SS7. The IXCs, with the possible exception of AT&T, tend to be most interested in faster call completion.

This leads to very different priorities for establishing internetwork SS7 connections. The IXCs are impatient for the still faster call setups that internetwork connection would allow. The LECs focus on the vulnerability of the large databases that will be accessed and the need for security via a gateway screening function at the interconnection points. AT&T's schedule for releasing the interconnect software for the 2A STP is September 1989. For now, the IXCs have to be satisfied with IXC-to-IXC interconnections.

The IXCs—AT&T, MCI, and U S Sprint, as well as many of the small fiber-based companies—see faster call completion as the main SS7 boon. They are looking for two

A sampling of smaller interexchange carriers who have deployed SS7

INTEREXCHANGE CARRIER	SWITCHES W/SS7	REPORTED SETUP SAVINGS (SECS)	INTERCONNECTS NOW	INTERCONNECTS PLANNED	NOTES
ACC	5 DEX	4.5	1	3	1
LITEL TELECOMMUNICATIONS CORP.	3 DMS	3 TO 7			
MIDAMERICAN COMMUNICATIONS CORP.	12 DEX	6		1	
TELECONNECT CO.	6 DEX				2

DEX = DIGITAL SWITCH CORP.
DMS = NORTHERN TELECOM
1 = 800 NUMBER BASE COMING
2 = EACH DEX INCORPORATES A 'MINI-SCP' TO SUPPORT 800 SERVICE. NOT CURRENTLY PLANNING TO DEPLOY SIGNAL TRANSFER POINTS BUT DO SEE AN EVENTUAL NEED.

benefits from faster call setup: greater customer satisfaction and reduced access-time charges by the LECs.

AT&T had CCIS, the North American version of Signaling System Number 6, so it does not feel a great pressure for rapid deployment of SS7. SS7 is perceived as a way of doing things a little bit better, faster, or cheaper. Probably most important, it is a way of supporting ISDN. Deployment of SS7 is slated to follow the availability of the ISDN primary-rate interface at AT&T 4E ESS tandem switches. The schedule calls for 18 switches in 1988 and 68 in 1989. The total count of 4E tandems is 110, but not all need transition in order to allow universal access to SS7 and ISDN. The result is that AT&T will continue with a mix of common channel signaling based on SS6 and SS7 at least through the mid-1990s. Meanwhile, AT&T is experimenting with SS7 to the customer's premises.

MCI had some initial delays and made several false starts on SS7, but it is currently deploying SS7, and the company claims it will complete deployment by the end of 1988.

U S Sprint has been one of the most aggressive deployers of SS7. Sprint has established three pairs of STPs and two SCPs. This complex started supporting operational traffic in 1987. Sprint had problems bringing up SS7 on its DMS 250 switches, but these problems appear to be clearing up. Satisfying improvements in the call setup time within the Sprint network have been obtained. There are a number of smaller IXCs that have deployed SS7, a sampling of which is presented in the table.

If a LEC wishes to provide value-added services such as 800 service or credit card validation, common channel signaling is a necessity. In the pre-divestiture days of the U. S. telephone industry, common channel signaling was used for toll traffic. Toll traffic became largely the province of AT&T after divestiture. Most of the regional Bell operating companies (RBOCs) prefer building a new SS7 infrastructure to rebuilding a CCIS 6 environment. But the various

RBOCs have different opinions about how aggressive the rollout should be.

The two RBOCs with the most aggressive deployments of SS7 are Bell Atlantic and BellSouth. Bell Atlantic has major deployments in New Jersey and substantial deployment in Pennsylvania, Virginia, and West Virginia. BellSouth has STPs in Atlanta, Ga., and Birmingham, Ala., and plans early support of citywide Centrex services. Nynex is at the other extreme; it has yet to commit to any implementation plan and still talks about the number of services that could be provided via CCIS 6. Most of the SS7 action occurs among the major LECs, but there are some smaller independents that are starting to consider implementation and the possibility of shared signaling networks and databases.

BellSouth is proud to be the LEC leader in the deployment of SS7. It is now moving to deploy in all its major metropolitan areas. By the end of 1988 it plans to complete all equal-access tandems. BellSouth has a policy of converting an entire city rather than selectively by switches—a policy it developed during the early days of equal-access conversion.

Bell Atlantic is using AT&T STPs and will be implementing the database access functions, including a LIDB and the 800 number functions, when regulations permit. But the impressive commitment is that of Bell Atlantic, which is aggressively moving ahead with plans to implement SS7 on the local access switches in order to support customized local area signaling services (Class) in northern New Jersey, in the Washington, D. C., metropolitan area, and in a few locations in Pennsylvania. Class is used to identify the calling number to the receiving party.

Southwestern Bell has moved forward on SS7 in order to implement the 800-number database, which was scheduled to go on line during the last half of this year. However, the Federal Communications Commission has put that on hold. LIDB, the next milestone, is planned for 1989. The Southwestern Bell SS7 network currently consists of two pairs of STP/SCPs; the STPs were supplied by AT&T.

U S West is deploying three pairs of Ericsson STPs. It had originally planned to bring up the 800 database as the first use of SS7; with that on FCC hold, the next milestone is LIDB, scheduled for early 1989. Initial tests of the Ericsson STPs were good.

Ameritech is just starting to get serious about SS7. It recently closed the bidding on an STP buy, but things are expected to move along quickly now. Nynex has not yet progressed to committing to deploy SS7.

GTE will start deploying within its local exchange companies by November. It is using 2A STPs from AT&T. The first to go in will be in California. The first service planned is Class on its GTE 5 switches. Eventually, it plans to have a total of four regional STPs (two pairs)—one pair in California and the second in New England and the Midwest.

Vendors

In addition to AT&T and Northern Telecom, the two main vendors of central office equipment, Digital Switch Corp. (DSC) has carved a niche for itself as an SS7 hardware vendor. Initially, DSC specialized in STPs, but it has progressed to combine the SSP's tandem call-switching capability and the SCP's database capability in its MegaHub product. DSC also produces a small SS7 concentrator that is targeted at enhanced service providers. It generally is marketed with several low-speed, 9.6-kbit/s ports and one high-speed port. With 20 low-speed links, this device would sell in the $150,000 to $200,000 range. By way of comparison, a typical rule of thumb for an STP is $20,000 per 56/64-kbit/s port.

The performance of DSC's large STPs is impressive; it is currently rated at up to 80,000 message packets per second. A typical large X.25 packet switch handles 1,000 packets per second. There are two factors that account for the speed difference between SS7 and X.25 packet switches. The first is market pull—there is a clearly perceived need for these high levels of performance. The second is the lower processing load of the connectionless service used for SS7.

Test gear is also crucial to the successful rollout of SS7. Checkout before live-traffic activation, monitoring during operation, and rapid debug in case of failure, are of critical importance to network owners. However, there is significant disagreement about how best to provide this capability.

One means of supporting that need is the built-in capabilities described above under OMAP. In addition, there is agreement that some standalone test capability probably is needed. Bellcore has built a tester that it uses for checkout for its RBOC owners. Similarly, Bell Canada has built one to test equipment entering the Canadian network.

Several test equipment vendors have manufactured standalone equipment, but there is disagreement about how this equipment should be deployed. When compared with X.25, there is universal agreement that SS7 needs much less external testing: the specification is better; there is built-in monitoring capability; and significant redundancy and automatic switch-over are provided. This would argue that the main use of test boxes would be during implementation and troubleshooting.

On the other hand, the task is probably more critical than most X.25 applications. Furthermore, when SS7 is fully deployed, there will be more services and service providers intimately interconnected. X.25 does not have the same level of involvement in the applications. This would argue for wider deployment of test equipment. The initial SS7 installations have been something of test beds, so they have been heavily provided with patch, test, and monitor capability. As field experience accumulates, it is likely that there will be simpler installations. One of the determinants of the need for external test capabilities is the data link interface used. Loopbacks must be externally provided if the older V.35 interface is employed; the built-in loopback capability of the DS0A interface reduces the need for external hardware.

Protocol Technology Inc. (PTI) is currently recognized as the leading SS7 test instrumentation vendor. In July 1988, PTI announced it was planning to be acquired by Tekelec Inc., one of the other leading SS7 test equipment vendors. PTI's boxes have simulation as well as monitor capability and tend to be complex and expensive but very capable.

Tekelec has two SS7 testers available: its older 707 single-function machine and the Chameleon 32, which has dual 64-kbit/s ports. It has implemented MTP, SCCP, TCAP, ISUP, and TUP. The company's machines also have a simulation mode that is programmed with C language commands.

Atlantic Research has an SS7 module for its Interview-750 machine; it tests only the lower layers (MTP) of SS7. Currently, the company does not offer a simulation capability.

CXR Telecom offers a similar low-end test capability in its 845 and 841 digital monitors. The two devices are similar, differing only in the means used to store captured data. CXR Telecom markets its 84Xs as economical devices with limited capability; they cost approximately $8,500. The line does not offer a simulation mode and has not yet implemented protocols above MTP.

Northern Telecom produces an external test device for internal use; it is not offered for general sale. But it is an option on a switch purchase. Northern sees a limited market for the device. Hewlett-Packard, Scotland, has shown a tester built for the European market that implements TUP and MTP. It did not test SCCP, ISUP, TCAP, or OMAP.

In conclusion, SS7 provides the control base upon which a more innovative, responsive, global telecommunications complex can be built. This high-speed, high-volume, low-delay, packet-switched network is already at work in numerous locations and soon will be quite ubiquitous. But, like the adolescent it is, SS7 is still growing, expanding, and evolving. ■

Walter Roehr is an independent consultant who specializes in communications and computer technology. He has authored numerous articles and reference texts and follows Signaling System 7 developments closely.

Footnotes

[1] The content of I.451 also appears in the Q series of signaling recommendations as Q.931. The dual designation of this protocol reflects its dual parentage—part of ISDN (and therefore included in the I series) but developed by signaling experts in CCITT Study Group 11 (and therefore given a Q-series number).

[2] Outside North America there has been extensive deployment of the SS#7 telephone user part (TUP). This is an earlier, call-handling protocol with limited capability. ISUP provides all of the functions of TUP and a great deal more. There are no plans to deploy TUP in North America. Both TUP and the call-handling portions of ISUP interface directly with the message transfer part, without the intermediacy of the SCCP. TUP+ is being used in Europe to provide limited ISDN service.

Daniel R. Seligman, Codex Corp., Mansfield, Mass.

Mastering SS7 takes a special vocabulary

Forget the computer jargon, SS7 has its own terminology. Concepts familiar in a computer communications environment are often disguised in the SS7 lexicon.

For someone with a computer background, one of the most confusing aspects of Signaling System 7 (SS7) is its terminology. And concepts that are familiar to someone with a computer communications background are often disguised in the SS7 lexicon by unfamiliar names. Here's a handy translation.

In SS7, a network node is referred to as a *signaling point*. There are three types of signaling points. A *service control point* (SCP) supports applications that provide services such as 800 number service. A *service switching point* (SSP) is the point of origin of a request for services. And a *signaling transfer point* (STP) is, for all intents and purposes, a packet switch, capable of accepting a packet on an incoming channel and transmitting it on the appropriate outgoing channel.

The SS7 term most closely associated with a communications line is a *signaling link*. Strictly speaking, *signaling data link* refers to the physical properties of the communications line, while signaling link is reserved for a communications line capable of reliable message exchange between two adjacent signaling points. In general, multiple signaling links connect the same two signaling points for performance and reliability purposes. These multiple signaling links are referred to as a *link set* and correspond roughly to an SNA transmission group.

Similarly, a sequence of signaling points between the origin and destination of a message is referred to as a *signaling route,* and the collection of all routes between the origin and destination, a *signaling route set*.

Protocol Levels

SS7 consists of four layers, or levels, somewhat analogous to the Open Systems Interconnection (OSI) model layers as shown in the table. However, the terminology and the functions of the levels are not strictly in accord with the OSI model. Moreover, the venerable architectural rules that underpin the OSI model are often broken.

Signaling data link functions (Level 1) are concerned with providing a bidirectional communications path between two adjacent signaling points. This level corresponds directly to the OSI physical layer.

Signaling link functions (Level 2) support reliable delivery of messages between two adjacent signaling points and correspond rather closely to the OSI data link layer. Indeed, the signaling link protocol is quite similar to high-level data link control or synchronous data link control protocols. The signaling link functions are often called, collectively, the *link control function*.

Signaling network functions (Level 3) enable data messages and control information concerning outages and congestion to be exchanged between nonadjacent signaling points, corresponding more or less to the OSI network layer. Level 3 is also called the *common transfer function*.

The *signaling connection control part* (Level 4) supports several categories of connectionless and connection-oriented service as well as the addressing of individual applications on a signaling point. Such features are commonly associated with the OSI transport and higher layers.

The lowest three layers of SS7 are collectively called the *message transfer part* (MTP), a carryover from a time when these layers were thought to be sufficient to deliver user data between two remote signaling points. The MTP provides a datagram service between two signaling points.

The signaling connection control part (SCCP) was developed only as it became apparent that SS7 would have to support more than signaling and needed more explicit addressing and more sophisticated services between remote signaling points. The MTP and the SCCP are collectively referred to as the *network services part*.

The choice of SCCP as a name is unfortunate, since

SCCP is invariably confused with SSCP, even though the SNA System Services Control Point bears very little resemblance in function to the SS7 concept.

While SS7 does show the OSI influence, SS7 is characterized by a less than strict adherence to OSI principles. The signaling data link and signaling link functions correspond directly to the OSI physical link and data link layers. But the one-to-one correspondence ends at the link layer.

The signaling network functions are divided into two major categories: *signaling message handling* and the *signaling network management*. The signaling message handling is concerned with routing messages to their appropriate destinations—either to local applications or remote signaling points. It is consistent with the network layer functions of the OSI model. However, the signaling network management manifests some differences, both in terminology and in function, from what experience with computer communications would suggest.

In computer communications, network management is usually a feature that enables a user or an application program to monitor, control, and troubleshoot a network. But in SS7 parlance, the term signaling network management is used to describe how a signaling network functions. It refers to the signaling network's ability to: divert traffic from one signaling link to an alternative *(signaling traffic management)*; manage the state of an individual signaling link *(signaling link management)*; and exchange control messages to permit the network to adapt to outages and congestion *(signaling route management)*.

Signaling link management is concerned with such link-oriented activities as activation, deactivation, and restoration of signaling links. In a conventional computer context, these features are more likely to be associated with the data link layer than the network layer.

The SCCP is analogous to the upper half of OSI's network layer, while the signaling network functions comprise the lower half. SCCP is intended to support basic and sequenced connectionless services and three classes of connection-oriented services: basic, flow control, and error recovery with flow control. All grades of service are built upon the datagram service provided by the signaling network level. In one sense, such services seem more characteristic of OSI transport than the network layer.

Another unique feature of SS7 concerns its treatment of the fields in the message headers associated with the communications protocols at the various layers. If SS7 were handling communications in a computer communications context, its use of the fields would be suspect because fields are shared among different protocol levels. This violates the rigid separation characteristic of most computer communications protocols.

Figure 1 shows an example of an SS7 data packet or *message signal unit*. The fields corresponding to the various protocol levels are indicated.

The *service information octet* (SIO) identifies the type of message, its priority level (for congestion control), whether the SS7 network is domestic or international, and a limited address for the MTP user concerned with the message. The very presence of the field is necessary for the signaling link functions to distinguish the message signal unit from other types of signal units; the congestion and message type information is used by the signaling network functions; and the address is needed by SCCP or any other user of the MTP. Thus, a single field is used by three layers.

Routing is handled by the *routing label*. The routing label is made up of the destination address, or the *destination point code*, the source address, called the *originating point code*, and the *signaling link selection* field. The signaling link selection field is a bit configuration that permits load sharing among redundant signaling links. Both the SCCP and signal-

1. Message signal unit. *Certain fields in an SS7 packet are shared among different levels. This adds efficiency but makes it impossible to replace one protocol with another.*

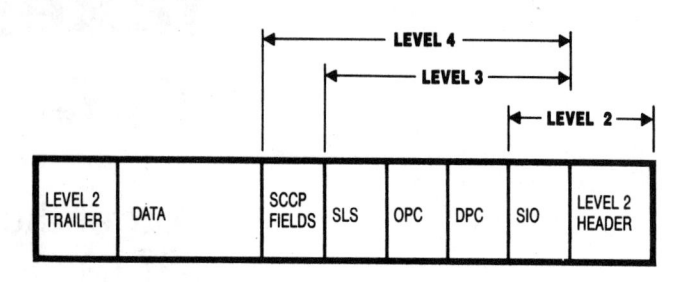

LEVEL 2 TRAILER	DATA	SCCP FIELDS	SLS	OPC	DPC	SIO	LEVEL 2 HEADER

DPC = DESTINATION POINT CODE
OPC = ORIGINATING POINT CODE
SCCP = SIGNALING CONNECTION CONTROL PART
SIO = SERVICE INFORMATION OCTET
SLS = SIGNALING LINK SELECTION

SS7 architecture and the Open Systems Interconnection model

ORIGINAL SIGNALING SYSTEM 7 LEVELS	OPEN SYSTEMS INTERCONNECTION LAYERS	REVISED SIGNALING SYSTEM 7 LEVELS
USER AND APPLICATION SERVICE PARTS	APPLICATION	USER AND APPLICATION SERVICE PARTS
	PRESENTATION	
	SESSION	
	TRANSPORT	SIGNALING CONNECTION CONTROL PART
SIGNALING CONNECTION CONTROL PART	NETWORK	SIGNALING NETWORK
SIGNALING NETWORK		
SIGNALING LINK	DATA LINK	SIGNALING LINK
SIGNALING DATA LINK	PHYSICAL	SIGNALING DATA LINK

ing network functions utilize the routing label. This is an example of three fields used by two different layers.

Common access to a single field makes it impossible to replace one level with a corresponding level without perturbing other levels. For example, DEC's replacement of its wide area network data link protocol with a protocol more suitable for an Ethernet would be impossible in SS7 without affecting other layers. The rigid structure of SS7 reflects its origins as a self-contained signaling architecture, which was developed prior to general acceptance of OSI layering and OSI principles.

Reliability issues

SS7 is characterized by a pronounced emphasis on reliability. In a computer communications environment, inaccessibility of services or inordinately long response times are occasionally acceptable. In a telephone service environment, on the other hand, major losses in revenue can result from even a few minutes of downtime. As a result, SS7 has highly developed reliability features.

Signaling links between adjacent nodes are generally deployed in groups of as many as eight. SCPs are laid out as mated pairs; identical service nodes are used in different geographic locations. STPs are also deployed in pairs. Numerous alternative routes typically connect SCPs with remote SSPs. The signaling network functions are designed to handle these redundancies. In addition, an elaborate exchange of SCCP messages between an SCP and its mate is required before an application can be taken out of service.

SS7 adapts to degradations and failures by propagating messages designating intermediate signaling points as *transfer-allowed, transfer-prohibited,* or *transfer-restricted* with respect to a given destination. The allowed and prohibited states indicate whether the signaling point is capable of routing traffic to the destination or whether an alternative route must be sought. This type of behavior is rather typical of computer communications environments. The restricted state, however, represents a refinement of this concept and indicates that the signaling point in question is still capable of routing traffic to the destination but the route is in some fashion degraded and that an alternative route should be used if possible. A restricted or prohibited signaling point is tested periodically for changes by an inquiry and response procedure called a *signaling-route-set test*.

SS7 supports a relatively advanced scheme for adaptation to congestion situations, as depicted in Figure 2. Each message is assigned a priority level. Congestion status is determined by the number of occupied transmit buffers associated with an outgoing signaling link. Three congestion statuses are defined for each signaling link, each characterized by three thresholds: *congestion onset, congestion abatement,* and *congestion discard*. Congestion abatement and congestion discard thresholds for a given congestion status are set respectively below and above the corresponding congestion onset threshold.

At congestion onset, warning messages are sent to appropriate signaling points. If the congestion situation does not improve, the number of occupied transmit buffers increases. When the congestion discard threshold is crossed, messages with priorities less than the congestion status are discarded. If the congestion situation improves, the number of occupied transmit buffers decreases, the congestion abatement threshold is crossed, and the congestion status is dropped to the next lower level. The congestion status of a congested signaling route set is periodically tested via an inquiry and response procedure similar to the signaling-route-set test called a *signaling-route-set-congestion test*.

---

2. Signaling link congestion. SS7 supports a sophisticated scheme for congestion management. For each signaling link, three congestion statuses are defined.

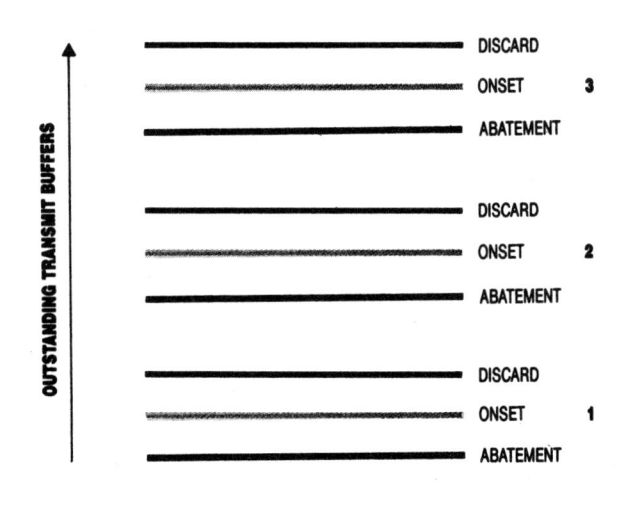

This scheme is far more complex than congestion control procedures in the more common network architectures. Contrast this scheme with, say, DECnet Phase IV where preference is given to messages routed through a node over messages originating at the node. In DECnet Phase IV, outgoing messages are simply discarded when predetermined buffer thresholds are reached. No messages are sent to neighboring nodes to indicate a congested situation.

SS7 remains uncomfortably poised between its telecommunications antecedents and its computer communications future. To the users in the computer world who will inherit it, SS7 presents the challenge of a different worldview and an emphasis on different capabilities than the more conventional computer network architectures. The first step toward mastering it is to understand SS7 terminology. ■

Daniel R. Seligman is a consulting engineer at Codex Corp. Until recently, he was a senior consultant at Technology Concepts Inc., Sudbury, Mass. He has authored several papers on computer network analysis and design and lectured on various data communications topics. Seligman received his Ph.D. in physics from Yale University in 1976.

Stephen Fleming, Licom Inc., Herndon, Va.

Get ready for T3 networking

DS-3 will be as commonplace as today's T1 because of coming availability and cost-effectiveness. Here's what to expect and how to implement the new technology.

Many corporate managers are administering T1 networks that are growing at a rate that puts crabgrass to shame, and new users are clamoring for more and more bandwidth. Increasingly, data communications managers are eyeing T3 equipment as a solution to the problems raised by this expansion. Carriers and vendors, aware of the growing interest, are offering equipment and services at the T3 rate (44.736 Mbit/s—commonly called 45 Mbit/s).

As an indication of increasing T3 acceptability, a recent study by Ken Bosomworth of International Resource Development showed the T3 equipment market climbing from $20 million in 1988 to a predicted $330 million in 1994. Similarly, he says, the T3 services market should go from $20 million in 1988 to $900 million in 1994.

To better understand many of the issues related to T1 and T3 networking, one should be familiar with North American regulations (see "The digital hierarchy"). They dictate how digitally multiplexed signals may be transmitted over the public network in the U.S. and Canada. Different hierarchies of signals are used abroad, making direct interchange of voice or data signals with North American networks impossible.

Before it can be justified, a T3 backbone must prove itself economically. In late 1988, AT&T amended its Tariff No. 9 to significantly improve the economics of T3 circuits. The previous tariff involved a complicated scheme of mileage bands. There is now a fixed charge of $6,000 per month and a simple mileage charge based on airline miles between cities. The charge varies from $180 per month for one-year contracts to $150 per month for three years to $130 per month for five years. Carriers other than AT&T offer similar arrangements, often for even lower prices.

A comparison of these charges versus standard T1 charges is shown in the figure. (The T1 calculations assume typical AT&T monthly rates of $2,600 fixed and $14.85 per mile with a 15 percent volume discount; the T3 calculations assume a three-year rate.) As can be seen, a T3 circuit can be cost-justified by as few as four T1s on links of less than 50 miles. (Recall that a T3 represents the equivalent of 28 T1 circuits.) At the other extreme, 10 T1 circuits will always cost more than a T3, regardless of distance. With non-AT&T carriers, the principle remains unchanged, although the break-even points may vary.

Flexibility and control

Implementing a T3 corporate backbone provides users with a measure of flexibility and control over the network. At the low-speed end, circuits may be either 56 kbit/s or 64 kbit/s. These may be used for voice or data services. Clear-channel circuits at 64 kbit/s may also be used for the bearer (B) channels of ISDN.

Intermediate circuits are often referred to as fractional T1 or FT1. These consist of some subset of a full T1 in multiple-DS-0 bundles. For example, one-half of a T1 (768 kbit/s) or even one-quarter of a T1 (384 kbit/s) may be adequate for many videoconferencing applications, without dedicating an entire T1 circuit. Many carriers have begun offering fractional T1 service to capture users who have outgrown 56-kbit/s services but who cannot yet justify a full T1. With the proper switching functions, these may be consolidated within a T3 networking multiplexer.

Full T1 circuits may be switched between sites on demand. The bit rates of these circuits may be 1.544 Mbit/s (the standard T1, including the framing bit), 1.536 Mbit/s (a T1 payload, without the 193rd framing bit), or 1.344 Mbit/s (24 channels of 56 kbit/s each).

The capability to switch this variety of circuits allows the user to put up and take down circuits of differing rates on the T3 backbone as requirements change, without having to work through an external network provider. This can take the form of reducing lead time for a circuit order, time-of-

T3 Networking

The digital hierarchy

Digital transmission techniques were introduced in the former Bell System in the early 1960s for efficient transport of voice signals. At that time, data formed an increasingly smaller percentage of network traffic. Therefore, the basic digital transmission structure is centered around human voice communication.

A plot of amplitude versus time for a speech sample would show significant high-frequency components. Luckily, a successful conversation (involving both understandable speech and a recognizable speaker) requires less than 4 kHz of audio bandwidth. After being processed by a low-pass filter, a speech sample loses its high-frequency components and is ready to be digitized.

The maximum analog frequency to be reproduced is 4 kHz. Therefore, according to the Nyquist theorem (the rate at which data can be transmitted without incurring intersymbol interference cannot be more than twice the bandwidth in Hertz), an 8-kbit/s sampling rate was adopted. By sampling the voice signal every 125 microseconds, its essential information is extracted in analog format and readied for digital encoding (see Fig. A). This pulse-amplitude modulated (PAM) signal contains all the information in the original signal up to approximately 4 kHz. (Because of operational considerations, the actual cutoff in digital telephony is lower than 4 kHz, but the principle remains the same.)

■ **Pulse-code modulation.** The modulation scheme chosen for early digital transmission standards is the easiest to implement: pulse-code modulation. The PAM signal is quantized (see Fig. B) by mapping into discrete amplitude levels, each with a unique binary code. (The example in the figure uses four-bit coding.) Naturally, additional discrete mappings reduce the quantization error and improve the fidelity of the coded signal. The example shows four-bit coding, for a total of 2^4—or 16—possible coding levels. Actual devices were designed to implement eight-bit coding, providing 2^8—256—quantization levels. This is sufficient for satisfactory reproduction of the human voice.

Note that by creating eight-bit codes 8,000 times per second (8 kbit/s), the bit rate of a digitized voice signal is eight multiplied by 8,000, or 64,000 bits per second. This is the basic 64-kbit/s channel that is the foundation of much of the digital network. Such a digital channel is often referred to as a DS-0 (digital signal, level 0).

■ **Time-division multiplexing.** The original deployment of digital transmission was driven by a desire to conserve copper pairs outside telephone offices. Each analog voice signal in the existing telephone network consumed a physical pair of copper wires from a subscriber location to a telephone central office. Once the basic building block was digital, it became feasible to multiplex the digital signals together into a higher-order digital signal. The interleaving method used, time-division multiplexing, led to defining the next level of the digital hierarchy as being equivalent to 24 DS-0 signals. This level is referred to as DS-1 or T1.

The multiplexing function to create a DS-1 signal was originally handled by a network element known as a digital channel bank or D-bank. Now, of course, numerous devices offer T1 interfaces.

■ **T1 format.** DS-1 is formed by byte-interleaving 24 DS-0 channels. The per-frame aggregate capacity, deduced from 24 channels of eight bits each, is 192 bits. Repeating the frame 8,000 times per second would result in an aggregate bit rate of $192 \times 8,000 = 1,536,000$ bits/second, or 1.536 Mbit/s.

This, however, is not the DS-1 rate, since a 193rd bit is added to each frame for timing and alignment purposes. This 193rd bit is called the framing bit and brings the aggregate bit rate to the T1 rate of 1.544 Mbit/s.

The framing bit is used to repeat a specific pattern throughout a "superframe" consisting of 12 frames. This pattern is used by receiving terminal equipment to identify and align the incoming bit pattern. The most common framing pattern used defines a D4 framing structure (named after the AT&T D4 channel bank). A newer standard, called extended superframe format (ESF), uses a 24-frame pattern (see "The hidden treasures of ESF," DATA COMMUNICATIONS, September 1986). The extended size of the superframe allows for the transmission of a six-bit cyclical redundancy check and for a 4-kbit/s embedded operations channel.

Note: Each voice circuit in a T1 appears to consist of a 64-kbit/s channel. In actuality, telephone switching re-

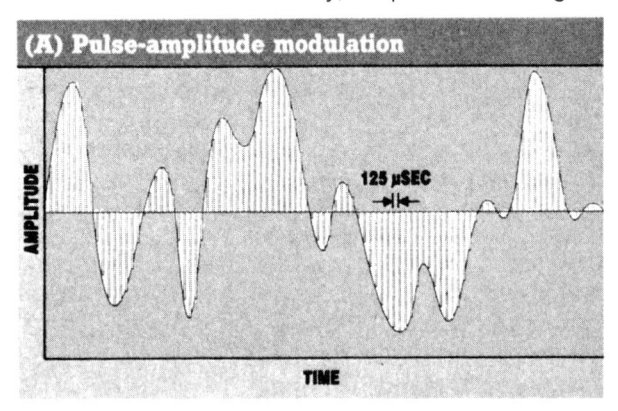

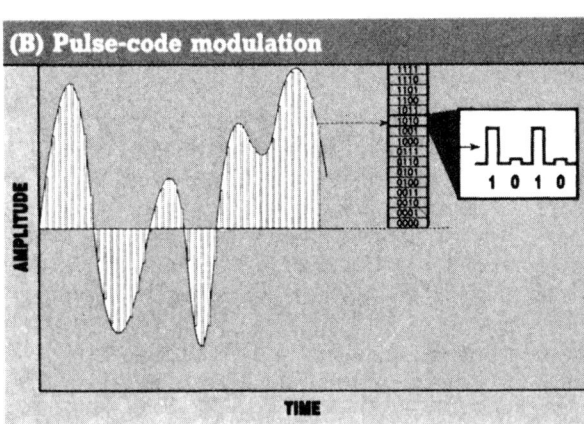

(A) Pulse-amplitude modulation

(B) Pulse-code modulation

T3 Networking

quired a fraction of this bandwidth to handle call-processing functions. In North America, this was handled through robbed-bit signaling: Every sixth frame, the least significant bit is removed from each eight-bit sample and used for signaling. This results in imperceptible degradation for voice traffic. Data traffic, however, can only rely on the untouched seven bits. Instead of a 64-kbit/s clear channel, therefore, DS-0 data circuits have an effective bit rate of only seven bits multiplied by 8,000 per second, or 56 kbit/s.

■ **T3 format.** At a rate of 1.544 Mbit/s, the T1 rate was sufficient for many needs, but not for all. On dense, high-volume routes, higher bit rates were required. The first step in this direction was made with the DS-2 rate, consisting of four DS-1s. (An intermediate rate, DS-1C [3.152 Mbit/s] is sometimes used, but is of no concern to this discussion.) The individual bits from each tributary are bit-interleaved.

DS-2 would appear to have a bit rate four times that of a DS-1, or 6.176 Mbit/s. In actuality, another layer of framing is added at the DS-2 rate. This framing ensures correct byte alignment as before, but also allows for variances in clock rates among tributary DS-1s (asynchronous operation). Special stuffing bits are included, as required, to ensure identical bit rates before bit interleaving. "Fast" signals receive less stuffing; "slow" signals receive more stuffing; adjustments are made continually to achieve a common reference level. These stuffing bits are removed at the far end of the transmission span. A total of 17 framing and stuffing bits are added to each DS-2 frame, leading to an aggregate DS-2 bit rate of 6.312 Mbit/s (8,000 × 17 added to 6.176 Mbit/s).

At this speed, the DS-2 signal can still be carried over copper pair, but the limitations inherent in copper transmission become more restrictive. Specially shielded cable is required to reduce crosstalk and susceptibility to electromagnetic interference. This cable requirement limited the acceptance of DS-2 installations, and it has never reached the wide deployment seen by DS-1 equipment.

By the end of the 1970s, however, a way around the limitations of copper pair was on the horizon. Transmission technologies based on the nearly limitless bandwidth of optical fiber were emerging from the laboratory, and a new layer of the digital hierarchy seemed appropriate. Based on technology available at the time, an asynchronous DS-3 rate was defined as the combination of seven DS-2 signals (equivalent to 28 DS-1s or 672 DS-0s). Framing and stuffing bits, as well as rudimentary error checking and internal communications, were added to the DS-2 tributaries to generate an aggregate bit rate of 44.736 Mbit/s.

Notice that the information content, or payload, of a DS-3 is equal to 672 64 kbit/s = 43.008 Mbit/s. The additional 1.728 Mbit/s of overhead represents the sum of the DS-1 framing bit, the DS-2 framing and stuffing bits, and the variety of DS-3 overhead bits. In terms of network efficiency, the DS-3 format devotes 96 percent of the transmission bandwidth to payload, with approximately 4 percent overhead.

Although the DS-3 was designed to be created from multiple DS-2 signals, there was an obvious inefficiency in using two separate devices for the DS-1-to-DS-2 and DS-2-to-DS-3 multiplexing functions. (The generic names of these devices are M12 and M23, pronounced em-one-two and em-two-three.) A new type of device was created, dubbed the M13 (one-three), which accepted DS-1 inputs and produced DS-3 output (and the reverse).

Note that the DS-3 (or T3) is often referred to as consisting of 28 DS-1s. This is correct, but it is more accurate to describe it as consisting of seven DS-2s. The DS-2 rate has not been eliminated, but simply shifted to an internal rate within the M13. None of the limitations of the DS-1 and DS-2 frame formats are removed by asynchronous DS-3 devices.

■ **North American digital hierarchy.** Coincidentally, as fiber optic technology exploded out of the laboratory, a far-reaching shift took place in the U.S. network. The divestiture of AT&T meant that no single entity would be capable of setting universal standards for the North American network. The technological advances did not slow, however, and higher and higher bit rates became economically feasible. After an abortive attempt at a DS-4 (274.176-Mbit/s) standard, major manufacturers basically went their individual ways with optical fiber equipment operating at a variety of bit rates. Overhead channels, multiplexing schemes, and the number and type of tributary were all decided on a per-manufacturer basis. Optical links between equipment from different vendors became impossible. DS-3, however, was retained as a common denominator and became the standard interconnect for all high-speed fiber gear designed for use in the public network.

Since all high-speed links were asynchronous, bit-stuffing penalties continued to mount. Multiple levels of bit-stuffing (DS-1 to DS-2, DS-2 to DS-3, DS-3 to proprietary) continued to require additional bandwidth for synchronization control. At the same time, the high bandwidth of optical fiber encouraged manufacturers to implement additional overhead functions. Payload efficiency dropped dramatically, but this was acceptable, given the vast capacity of these new transport elements. Hub offices began terminating dozens or, in some cases, hundreds of DS-3 signals.

By the late 1980s, the North American digital hierarchy looked like what is shown in the table.

North American digital hierarchy

LEVEL	BIT RATE	DS-3	DS-2	DS-1	DS-0	EFFI-CIENCY
DS-0	64 KBIT/S	—	—	—	1	100%
DS-1	1.544 MBIT/S	—	—	1	24	99%
DS-2	6.312 MBIT/S	—	1	4	96	97%
DS-3	44.736 MBIT/S	1	7	28	672	96%
3 x DS-3	≈ 139 MBIT/S	3	21	84	2,016	93%
12 x DS-3	≈ 565 MBIT/S	12	84	332	8,064	91%
24 x DS-3	≈ 1.2 GBIT/S	24	176	664	16,128	86%

T3 Networking

day circuit changes, or quick response to a temporary overload condition in some part of the network.

Realistically, T3 networks are not for everyone. Who can justify the investment required to operate a 45-Mbit/s circuit? One group that can is *Fortune* 500 corporations that have already installed nationwide T1 backbones. Smaller organizations with unusually high communications requirements (typically, service companies) also have T1 networks in place today. In any network where multiple T1 circuits have been placed or planned between locations, it may be appropriate to consider T3 service.

Another segment consists of organizations with rights-of-way, such as public utilities, railroads, pipelines, and state and local governments. One of the most cost-effective ways to implement a T3 network is to own the optical fibers required for transmission. Right-of-way organizations have an advantage, since they do not have to go through the negotiations necessary to lay a cable across private property and public thoroughfares. Although the up-front costs of a fiber installation can be significant, they are often offset by eliminating the recurring monthly charges associated with leased T1 or T3 circuits.

T3 technology issues

Once the decision to go to T3 has been made, a number of questions about technology need to be answered.

One of the choices to be made early in the process is whether to lease or purchase T3 circuits. The options involved in each choice are summarized in Table 1.

The first solution is the traditional way of managing communications: leasing the circuit from a service provider. This provider may be the local telephone company, an interexchange carrier (IXC), an urban-bypass organization, or a friendly right-of-way company. In each case, the service provider takes care of bringing a T3 pipe to the customer premises and keeping it working. The fees for such a service are often justifiable if the user organization is not set up for network monitoring, troubleshooting, and repair.

Alternatively, the T3 circuit may be leased only between carrier points-of-presence. Since T1 circuits to the premises are readily available, this combination avoids the problem of providing a dedicated fiber pair to the premises to complete a broadband connection: the "last-mile" problem. This option can be attractive when terminating an entire T3 at a private user's location is not feasible, either because of prohibitive placement cost or traffic patterns.

The alternative to leasing is to own the T3 transmission equipment outright. This implies that the user must have access to one of two facilities: an optical fiber cable or a digital microwave transmission path.

Optical fiber has a much higher transmission capacity than digital microwave. By installing a private cable, a user establishes ownership of transmission resources and, for a one-time cost, avoids the recurring expenses associated with a leasing arrangement. However, it is often impossible to install cable without owning a right-of-way. Placing private fiber cable is normally only practical for short-haul networks within a campus or urban area.

In addition, locating and repairing cable breaks (caused by construction, accident, or malice) can be time-consuming. To get around such difficulties, some users have resorted to leasing "dark fiber" from a telephone company, bypass operation, or IXC. Dark fiber means that the monthly charge pays only for dedicated access to the optical fiber and for cable maintenance; the user is responsible for providing optical multiplexing equipment, network monitoring, and terminal maintenance. This can be especially practical in an urban setting where a private right-of-way would be prohibitively expensive.

Because of the right-of-way and maintenance problems inherent in optical fiber cable, users have turned to digital microwave radio as a T3 transmission medium. Operating basically over line-of-sight paths, these networks provide reliable error-free transmission of a T3 signal across an urban area. Newer units can even be mounted indoors, transmitting through a window, so that tower installation and maintenance is eliminated.

Digital microwave radio has three problems. First, the electromagnetic spectrum is strictly licensed by the Federal Communications Commission. Overcrowding of the airwaves has closed off certain portions of the spectrum in densely populated urban areas. Second, strict spectrum allocations imply that digital microwave cannot be readily upgraded in bandwidth. While a 45-Mbit/s optical fiber can be readily converted to 565 Mbit/s, a 45-Mbit/s digital microwave setup is probably destined to remain at 45 Mbit/s.

Finally, digital microwave devices are inherently limited to line-of-sight distances—sometimes even shorter,

T1 and T3. *Using standard AT&T rates, a tariff comparison shows that leased T3 lines carrying the equivalent of 28 T1s are more economical than multiple T1 lines. For distances of less than 50 miles, only four T1s are required to break even.*

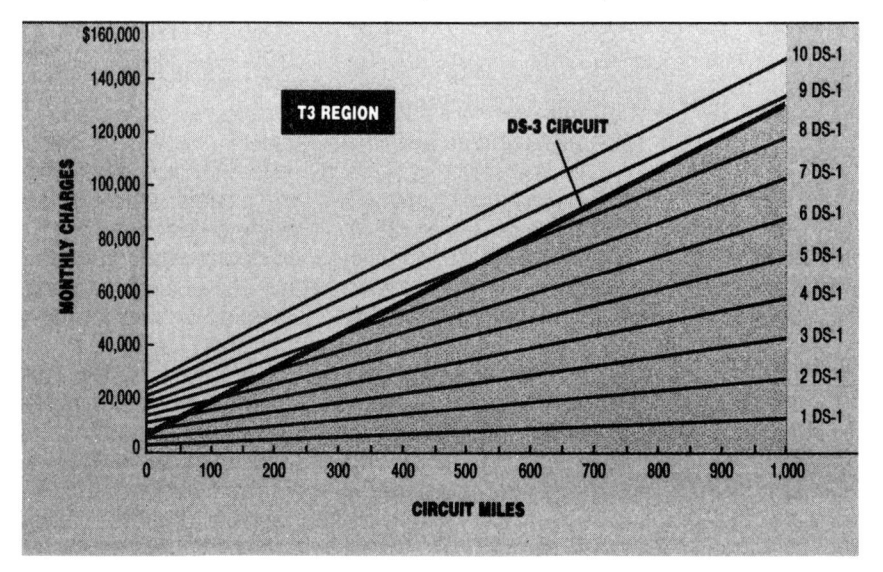

T3 Networking

owing to weather conditions or other hindrances. This is manageable in urban-distance settings, but can cause problems for interstate or national networks.

Many private networks mix optical fiber and digital microwave. The fiber can be used in high-density areas, with microwave hops to lower-density remote locations. Alternatively, the main network can be placed entirely on fiber, with T3 microwave used for emergency restoration in the event of a cable cut. Dual-media transmission is especially attractive to service-critical networks such as banks, airlines, and other on-line transaction-processing companies.

After choosing between leased and owned facilities, the data communications manager must decide what equipment to use to terminate these facilities. With leasing, the terms of the lease may dictate use of a particular vendor's equipment. When using private fiber cable or microwave, the terminal choices are entirely the responsibility of the data communications manager.

Table 1: Facility choices

	LEASED T3 CIRCUITS	OWNED OPTICAL FIBER	OWNED DIGITAL MICROWAVE
ADVANTAGES	SIMPLICITY MINIMUM STAFFING REQUIREMENTS PERFECT FOR LONG-HAUL T3 NETWORKING	ONE-TIME COST 'UNLIMITED' CAPACITY VARIED EQUIPMENT OPTIONS EASY UPGRADES COMPATIBILITY WITH NEW SERVICES PERFECT FOR CAMPUS ENVIRONMENT	ONE-TIME COST RAPID SET-UP PORTABILITY NO RIGHT-OF-WAY ISSUES PERFECT FOR METROPOLITAN AREA NETWORK
DISADVANTAGES	RECURRING MONTHLY COST LIMITED NETWORK CONTROL LIMITED FLEXIBILITY	REQUIRES RIGHT-OF-WAY VULNERABLE TO CABLE CUTS REQUIRES ON-CALL MAINTENANCE	WEATHER DEGRADATION FCC LICENSING RESTRICTIONS LIMITED BANDWIDTH

Equipment choices

All private optical networks share the advantages of near-limitless upgradability. The data rate of modern single-mode fiber reaches many tens of Gbit/s. Whether the fiber cable is owned or leased, users have abundant options when shopping for optical fiber terminals. The 1980s boom in optical installations for the public network has led to dozens of available products from numerous vendors; capacities currently range from a single T3 (45-Mbit/s) to 36 T3 circuits (1.7-Gbit/s). Future installations are expected to operate at even higher speeds. Although these Gbit/s devices are only of interest to telephone operating companies and IXCs, they will certainly be available to private-network users when the need arises.

Once transmission issues have been solved, the user must decide what T3 multiplexing equipment is required for the application. There are three major choices:
- Asynchronous M13s.
- DS-3 cross-connects.
- T3 add/drop multiplexers.

The traditional method of obtaining T3 circuits is via an M13 multiplexer. This device collects up to 28 T1 signals and uses two steps of time-division multiplexing to produce a T3. There are tens of thousands of M13s in service in the public network today; 10 years of manufacturing experience and economies of scale have brought them down to surprisingly low prices ($4,000 to $10,000). The rate and format of the M13 signal are defined in Bellcore document TR-TSY-000009.

These devices have been optimized for bundling T1 circuits for point-to-point transmission in the BOC and IXC markets. They are the T3 equivalent of the "dumb" channel bank—adequate for basic transport, but often inadequate for complex corporate networks. They are usually appropriate only in point-to-point networks that do not require much in the way of flexibility or performance monitoring.

A modification of the T3 standard, known as C-bit parity, was published by AT&T in document PUB 54014, which describes the Accunet T45 service offering. While not adding any flexibility or control to the M13 standard, C-bit parity does provide rudimentary far-end performance monitoring over T3 lines. This standard has not gained the widespread deployment of the traditional M13s.

At the other extreme is the new entry of 3/1 and 3/1/0 digital cross-connect systems (DCS). These are sometimes referred to as DACS (Digital Access and Cross-connect System) products, after the AT&T product line of the same name—or as wideband cross-connects. The types differ in that the 3/1 DCS demultiplexes DS-3 signals to the DS-1 rate, while 3/1/0 machines demultiplex through the DS-1 rate to DS-0, or 64-kbit/s, rate. DCS 3/1 or 3/1/0 devices incorporate an internal switching matrix, providing circuit-switched flexibility and significant network management features. The DCS excels in "hub-and-spoke" networks where T1 circuits from a variety of T3 sources must be interconnected. These products tend to be optimized for dozens or hundreds of T3 ports; although their features may appeal to corporate-network users, their capacity (and price tags) can be overwhelming.

A third multiplexing alternative exists in the form of the T3 add/drop multiplexer (ADM). As the name implies, these units allow the individual T1 circuits to be added and dropped at a particular site. When deployed along a T3 route, these devices can provide the T1 switching functions of large 3/1 cross-connects for a single T3 circuit. Some vendors also provide DS-0-level switching for some or all of the 64-kbit/s circuits within a T3. This provides the user with electronic control of the T3 bandwidth, network surveillance, capital-cost reductions at intermediate sites in a T3 route, and compatibility with the huge installed base of T3-based fiber and radio networks.

Synchronous ADMs can be especially valuable in overcoming the limitations of a T3 microwave network. By

T3 Networking

providing efficient bandwidth allocation, a synchronous T3 ADM can maximize the utilization of a single T3 pipe. With digital microwave, the difference between a single highly filled T3 and two poorly utilized T3s can determine whether a network is economically or technically feasible.

It is worth noting here that a fourth class of multiplexing equipment will be entering the market within the next few years. These devices, based on the Sonet hierarchy (see "Sonet calms choppy waters"), promise to offer a level of flexibility and performance well beyond the traditional M13. Because of their synchronous nature, Sonet networks will provide many of the benefits of the DS-3 cross-connects and T3 add/drop multiplexers for multi-DS-3-rate fiber. Since Sonet networks are incompatible with the installed base of fiber transmission, however, DCS machines or T3 ADMs will still be required to connect Sonet networks with the existing North American network.

T3 ADMs may be directly integrated into intelligent T1 multiplexer networks, acting as a higher-level circuit switch for a broad mixture of T1 tributaries. The same can be said for asynchronous M13 networks.

Although the DS-1 and DS-3 external interfaces are identical, the internal architectures are quite different. The asynchronous M13 bit-interleaves and bit-stuffs DS-1 signals to the DS-2 rate, repeating the process from DS-2 to DS-3. The T3 ADM, on the other hand, synchronously aligns each incoming DS-1, allowing identification of each DS-0 circuit. Therefore, the T3 ADM first demultiplexes the DS-1 tributaries into the component DS-0 signals. After passing through a time slot interchanger (TSI), the signals plus overhead channels are remultiplexed in a single stage from DS-0 to DS-3.

A DS-3 interface may be provided on one or both sides of the TSI. When equipped on a single side, the device acts as a DS-1-to-DS-3 multiplexer, with internal DCS. When equipped on both sides, the device can add and drop individual DS-0 or DS-1 signals to a DS-3 path. Unlike asynchronous designs, there is no limitation on how many DS-0 or DS-1 signals may be added or dropped.

By implementing the DS-0 internal switching matrix, the ADM provides far greater flexibility in circuit arrangement than the hard-wired multiplexing of an M13. The ADM can also switch proprietary or unframed T1 signals at the full 1.544-Mbit/s rate (rather than the 1.536-Mbit/s or 1.344-Mbit/s rates common to other devices). This is accomplished by arbitrarily splitting the signal into 24 bytes of eight bits each, carrying the 193rd bit separately in the T3 overhead, and reuniting the elements in the correct sequence at the receiving terminal. Unframed T1 video signals or non-D4-compatible T1 signals can be carried transparently within such a device.

In addition, the synchronous T3 transmission format (ANSI standard T1.103-87)—also known as Syntran—used in a DS-0 ADM integrates performance monitoring and an embedded control channel into the T3 bit stream. A nine-bit cyclical redundancy check (CRC9) is performed at the DS-3 rate for remote performance monitoring. Also, a 64-kbit/s embedded operations channel permits communications both between individual nodes and between the network and network management devices. For T3 users, the synchronous T3 format provides the same benefits that the extended superframe format (ESF) provides for T1 users.

Compatibility issues

Most data communications managers have learned the importance of compatibility with the public network the hard way. Proprietary interfaces, unless in a pure single-vendor network, often turn out to be more troublesome than useful. When choosing T3 network equipment, there are new network compatibility issues involved.

First, the equipment must be compatible with the existing T3 standards. Luckily, the T3 world consists of well-defined interfaces, so compatibility is not usually a problem here.

One area of concern with T3 is facility compatibility. A number of AT&T and Bellcore publications specify the interface required for a DS-3 signal to be carried over T3 equipment. These specifications make up the Digital Signal Cross-connect, Level 3 (DSX3) standard. The standard includes specifications for line coding, signal pulse shape,

---

Sonet calms choppy waters

No description of high-speed networking would be complete without a discussion of Sonet. This new standard, an acronym for Synchronous Optical Network, is supported by dozens of vendors and public network providers in North America, Europe, and Japan. It operates at multiples of T3 bandwidth. Initially, products will be offered at the following bit rates (OC stands for optical carrier): OC-1, 51.84 Mbit/s; OC-3, 155.52 Mbit/s; OC-12, 622.08 Mbit/s; OC-48, 2.49 Gbit/s.

Sonet brings order to the current chaos of high-speed fiber optics, where each vendor has established independent proprietary bit rates and protocols. In the United States, the first phase of the Sonet standard has been published as ANSI T1.105-1988 and T1.106-1988.

As a synchronous standard, Sonet is well-suited for switching tributary signals within a higher-bandwidth pipe. Initially, switching will be limited to T1 and DS-0 signals, but other service offerings will be defined as time goes on. One future example: a publicly switched Ethernet interface that would allow you to dial a 10-Mbit/s channel cross-country or around the world. Sonet networks operating at OC-3 and higher rates will also be used as the basis for interconnection of broadband services such as Distributed Queue Dual Bus metropolitan area networks and high-definition television.

Sonet is fully backward-compatible with the ANSI synchronous T3 format; it is partially backward-compatible with older asynchronous T3 equipment such as M13s. It does not affect users of digital microwave radio, since there is little need for a synchronous standard higher than T3 for these applications. It will be deployed by the BOCs in the early 1990s. Depending on its success in that arena, other network providers and corporate-network users will follow suit.

T3 Networking

clock rates, frame format, and other parameters of interest to equipment vendors. Any device meeting this DSX3 specification can transport over any T3 equipment, whether optical or microwave, from any vendor.

A second area of concern is terminal compatibility. Once the signal has been successfully transported, issues of terminal compatibility arise. Two major camps of terminal standards exist and have been formalized by Bellcore: the synchronous T3 and the asynchronous T3. These two signals are not directly end-to-end compatible, but must be translated by a third device.

The synchronous standard, being newer, is more fully documented and does not allow much vendor freedom in implementing the specifications. This ensures that any device built to this standard will work successfully with any other, regardless of vendor.

The asynchronous standard is older and has been interpreted differently by vendors. Many of them have added proprietary extensions to provide value-added features or to make up for deficiencies in the format (such as the C-bit parity variation, noted earlier). Their unique implementations of the asynchronous T3 interface can cause compatibility problems ranging from disabling minor features to major network inconsistencies. These solutions dictate that a user employ a single-vendor network.

Since installing T3 equipment in a private network almost always implies connection with new or existing T1 equipment, the issue of T1 compatibility must also be addressed. As with DS-3, AT&T and Bellcore have published details of the T1 interface, collectively referred to as the DSX1 specification. Again, the standards have left room for vendor interpretation, leading to possible inconsistencies.

The most common T1 interface consists of a 1.544-Mbit/s signal channelized according to D4 format. This allows network equipment to identify and switch individual DS-0 (64-kbit/s) signals. This standard was established by AT&T and is nearly universal within the public network. It is normally referred to as D4-channelized or DACS-compatible. The payload data rate of a channelized T1 is 1.536 Mbit/s.

The lockstep limitations of the D4 format led some T1 equipment vendors to ignore the 64-kbit/s boundaries and use a proprietary organization of data within the DS-1 frame. An unchannelized signal requires access to the entire 1.544-Mbit/s T1 format. This allowed more flexibility in transporting varied rates of voice and data, but created incompatibility with the DACS networks installed throughout the public network. Many vendors now offer both options: channelized for public compatibility and unchannelized for maximum bandwidth efficiency. Installations using both types of signals must ensure that their T3 equipment can transport both efficiently.

Yet a third variation exists with unframed T1 signals. These normally represent the output of certain T1 video codecs or encryption equipment. Unlike the unchannelized signals, these do not even meet the DSX1 framing standard, but only the clock rate and associated requirements. Again, in a network that must transport unframed T1 signals, it is important to verify that the T3 equipment will be compatible.

Future compatibility

Finally, it is important to note that the DS-3 formats do not represent the final step in network evolution. As higher bit-rate standards evolve, T3 equipment purchased today must be integratable into new networks that will be installed throughout the 1990s.

The user making the leap to T3 will find that all the network management capabilities of T1 products are still available. Indeed, by offering single-point monitoring of all T1 circuits in a network, the addition of intelligent T3 devices can actually make the network operator's life simpler, not more complicated.

Early in the T3 equipment decision-making process, a communications manager will realize that most T3 equipment is optimized for traditional BOC and IXC applications. This can be adequate in some circumstances, but these devices do not lend themselves to the sophisticated management and control requirements of private networks.

A new generation of T3 devices is appearing on the market from a number of sources—from traditional telephone company transmission-equipment suppliers to T1

Table 2: Performance monitoring parameters

PARAMETER	ASYNCHRONOUS T3	SYNCHRONOUS T3
DS1		
BIT ERROR RATE		✓
BIPOLAR VIOLATIONS	✓	✓
SLIPS		✓
CRC6 VIOLATIONS	ESF ONLY	ESF ONLY
AIS DETECT		✓
FRAME LOSSES		✓
ERRORED SECONDS		✓
SEVERE ERRORED SECONDS		✓
DS3		
BIT ERROR RATE	PARITY-BASED	CRC-BASED
PARITY ERRORS	✓	✓
BIPOLAR VIOLATIONS	✓	✓
CRC9 VIOLATIONS		✓
AIS DETECT	✓	✓
FRAME LOSSES	✓	✓
ERRORED SECONDS	✓	✓
SEVERE ERRORED SECONDS	✓	✓

AIS = ALARM INDICATION SIGNAL
CRC6 = 6-BIT CYCLIC REDUNDANCY CHECK

T3 Networking

multiplexer manufacturers to small start-up companies. All, however, have a common goal: to create intelligent T3 devices for the emerging private marketplace. These devices are a distinct departure from the "dumb" ones used in huge quantities by telephone companies and IXCs.

Communications managers will also have to analyze the T1 circuits currently used in their networks. For seamless operation, the T3 equipment should support all types of T1 circuits likely to be used. Managing different types of T1s on different types of T3 equipment ensures confusion.

Networks with an emphasis on data will tend to use unchannelized T1s in order to pack the maximum number of data circuits into the available bandwidth. This is especially common in networks where one vendor supplies all the T1 multiplexing equipment. These circuits will also be used for T1 video codecs, where channelization is meaningless.

Voice networks will tend to use D4-channelized circuits. Thesecircuits are generated by standard channel banks; they are alsoavailable on most modern T1 multiplexers. Naturally, D4-channelized T1s can also be used for transport of data at any number of bit rates, depending on the capabilities of the T1 equipment.

A possible complication arises with the availability of adaptive differential pulse-code modulation (ADPCM) equipment in private-network multiplexers. ADPCM transmits high-quality voice at 32 kbit/s, 21.3 kbit/s, or even 16 kbit/s, instead of 64 kbit/s. DS-0 switching implies that pairs, triads, or quads of ADPCM signals will be switched as units, which slightly reduces the efficiency of the switching matrix. The problem may be alleviated with the realization that T3 bandwidths bring an end to many of the original arguments for ADPCM. With 28 T1 circuits available, maximum utilization of a single T1 may not be an issue.

Finally, many vendors are considering the use of ESF circuits for enhanced fault isolation and troubleshooting. Although it may not be economical to convert all existing circuits to ESF, it is important to allow new circuits to take advantage of this improved range of functions.

Network surveillance consists of alarm reporting and performance monitoring to continually verify the health of the network. Alarms can consist of equipment failures, carrier failures, or entire node failures. Performance monitoring provides diagnostic information for individual circuits, either before or after a failure. Statistics can be reported for both T1 and T3 levels, as shown in Table 2. Effective use of performance thresholds can encourage preemptive equipment maintenance and minimize network downtime.

Surveillance in the public network is typically handled by multimillion-dollar surveillance centers operating on dedicated mainframes. In the private-network world, a dedicated microcomputer or technical workstation is often a more realistic alternative. The user's workstation is only half the issue. Comprehensive network surveillance requires both intelligent network management devices and intelligent network elements capable of measuring performance statistics such as slips, frame errors, CRC errors, and bipolar violations (see "How to detect frame slips in voice-band PCM channels," DATA COMMUNICATIONS, October 1988). Therefore, even sophisticated network surveillance can obtain and display only elementary alarm information from less sophisticated T3 devices such as M13s.

Many network management products really provide only network surveillance. Reaching into the network to rearrange circuits, either in response to a service request or to a service problem, often requires a technician moving cables on a patch panel.

Newer T3 devices solve these problems by giving the operator direct control over DS-0 and DS-1 connections within the network, resulting in such benefits as time-of-day switching of T1 or T3 or the reserving of bandwidth for an anticipated videoconference. Again, this requires comparable levels of sophistication both for the T3 network elements and for the centralized management software.

Survival

Network disaster recovery is critical at the T3 rate—not many networks can survive the simultaneous loss of 672 circuits. Disasters take many forms. Fiber optic cable cuts are not uncommon; with modern high-bit-rate fiber, a single cable cut can affect a quarter of a million circuits. Both long-haul and local-access circuits are at risk. Central office fires, such as the one at Hinsdale in Chicago, are rare but devastating. Even operator errors, such as disconnecting the wrong cable at the wrong time, can constitute a network disaster.

The first line of defense is battery backup and internal redundancy; T3 equipment built to BOC standards typically has multiple layers of protection switching built in, so that no single module failure can cause loss of service. The BOCs typically specify protection-switching times of 60 milliseconds or better to restore full service over backup modules.

The next defense is network redundancy: By routing redundant T3 circuits over separate physical links, users can protect against even catastrophic carrier-node failures. With excess bandwidth available on unaffected routes, manual or automatic disaster plans may be implemented to restore some or all circuits affected by the disaster. This can take several minutes—longer than the 60 milliseconds specified for equipment protection, but still greatly superior to the hours or days required for manual restoration.

The best defense is autonomous network recovery. For example, survivable T3 ring architectures provide rapid restoration of all circuits in a fraction of a second, without the lag time required to consult central human or computerized network management mechanisms. Such arrangements are now being implemented in the public network. Private users, with their sensitivity to even brief periods of downtime, will almost certainly follow suit. ■

Stephen Fleming has a BS summa cum laude in physics from Georgia Institute of Technology (Atlanta). He has worked at Bell Laboratories, where he specialized in optical fibers, and at Northern Telecom, where he specialized in multiplexers and cross-connects. He wrote this article when he was Licom's director of marketing for T3 and Sonet products. He has since returned to Northern Telecom.

Section 2
Local Networking

Peter Gregory, Applitek Corp., Wakefield, Mass.

A typology of local area networks

Confused by the array of LANs, some users fall back on switching. Pity. Only LANs may be able to support mixed-media services and high-powered workstations.

Local area network (LAN) technology is as suitable as data switches for solving data communications problems, if not more so. It will begin to serve the needs of voice traffic as well with the advent of voice digitization. As digital technology becomes pervasive in the third major application area—video—LANs will probably provide the common base that enables all three to be combined. As suggested in Figure 1a, voice and data applications today have limited overlap. Only some of the present data traffic is carried on LANs. The rest is handled through direct lines and through switches meant for voice. Current video applications include analog teleconferencing and digital facsimile.

In the future, technology will force the merging of voice and data, and their integration will provide a rich growth medium for the use of video (Fig. 1b). The addition of a videocamera to the workstation offers the opportunity for facsimile and digital teleconferencing from the desktop. Such video services can be integrated with voice and data through digital transmission and LANs.

Digital voice and video will emerge as applications for LANs over the next three to five years—within the lifetime of networks being planned today. Unfortunately, the ability of LAN technology to provide these capabilities may be restrained by standardization efforts that only address some areas of LAN potential. A network designed for 50 asynchronous terminals and two minicomputers will not support the coming range of wideband services.

The LAN's edge over the switch

Even so, and despite the widespread use of existing voice channels for simple data connections, LANs are coming into their own. They will eventually supersede analog and switching technologies in handling voice and video for the following reasons:
■ *Greater functionality.* Intelligence in the network interface units (NIUs) of many LANs can provide such services as conversion from asynchronous to synchronous protocols.
■ *Higher-speed interfaces.* These are made possible by local processors in the interface units.
■ *Greater network throughput.* Switches were not designed to handle high-speed data calls; most LANs were.
■ *Distributed control and management.* If a central switch fails, due to an internal problem or local power failure, a large number of users are stranded. The failure of NIUs, however, with only a few users each, confines the impact of the service interruption.
■ *Low installation costs for new applications.* This results from the ability to use cabling that has already been installed for a different purpose (a broadband network installed for videoconferencing, security, or data can also provide a backbone network).
■ *Lower reconnection costs for installed terminals.* To move a terminal, it is necessary only to reconnect to a local access point on the network (such as a departmental Ethernet) rather than having to wire each workstation back to a central switch.

When comparisons are made between digital switch and LAN technologies, cost is frequently mentioned as a distinguishing characteristic. However, this issue is often oversimplified by focusing on the cost of connecting to the switching device without including wiring and rewiring expenses. To make the role of these factors clear, figures from a variety of vendors and sources were combined into a graph showing a schematic relationship between network costs and the location of intelligence within the network (Fig. 2). The scale was removed for generality.

The location of network intelligence provides a basis for comparison. For example, a network with central intelligence might be based on a private branch exchange (PBX) or data switch; a distributed PBX could function at the building level; or a large, centralized LAN controller

1. Growth and integration. *Currently just one of users' data-carrying options (a), local area networks will boom as they bring digitized voice and video together (b).*

(A) CURRENT ENVIRONMENT

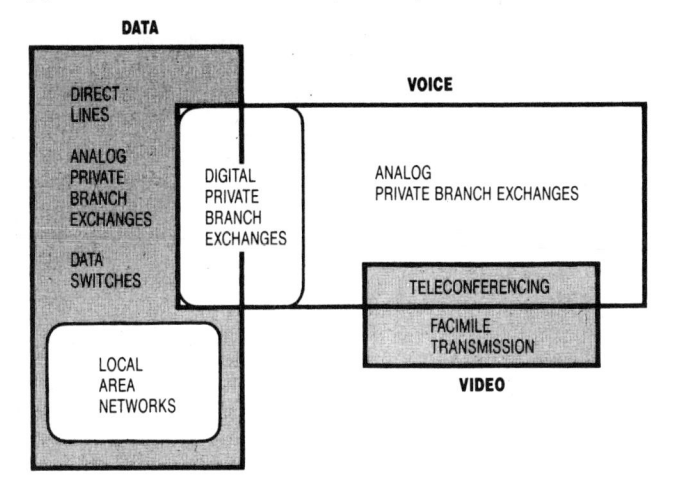

(B) FUTURE ENVIRONMENT

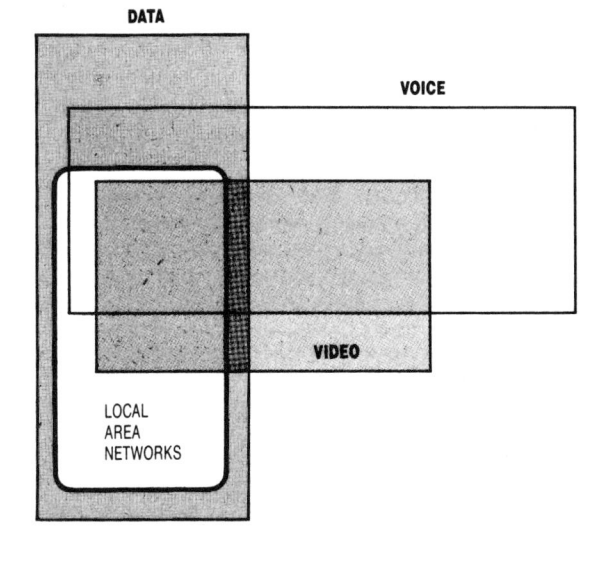

integrated services. To separate and classify some of the terms and concepts used in local area networking, a typology of LANs was devised. This schema can also help users understand trends emerging in the technology and anticipate industry developments.

Unfortunately for users, the universe of LANs is often discussed as though there were only one solution for all problems, which of course is not true. Much of the confusion arises because the distinctions among types of networks is unclear. To clarify the distinctions, the taxonomy has been based on the view that corporate networks consist of three levels:

- *Terminal or user-level networks.* Usually, LANs of microcomputers or networks of terminals attached to the same computer are homogeneous (that is, of the same terminal or processor type), exist to serve the work area or department, and serve related purposes (such as manufacturing or word processing).
- *Intrafacility networks.* These serve a single geographic location, which may include multiple floors of a building or multiple buildings on a campus. They are heterogeneous, joining various types of terminal networks and applications.
- *Corporatewide networks.* These connect the intrafacility networks found at multiple locations.

It is clearly desirable for applications to be capable of operating across all three levels with the maximum degree of connectivity. That is, each user's access to the corporatewide network should be limited by management decisions rather than by the technology of the network.

The technological boundaries between the layers should cause minimal operational interference. To this end, each level should be more sophisticated than the level beneath it to support the diversity of the lower level. It should also be faster, to carry the traffic of multiple terminal subnetworks without adding delay.

Figure 3 depicts the relationship of the layers. The axis labeled "function" represents the complex, high-level software interfaces in the network, while the "performance"

2. Distribution and dollars. *Networks built around a central unit cost less for device hookup and shared equipment but much more for cabling and recabling.*

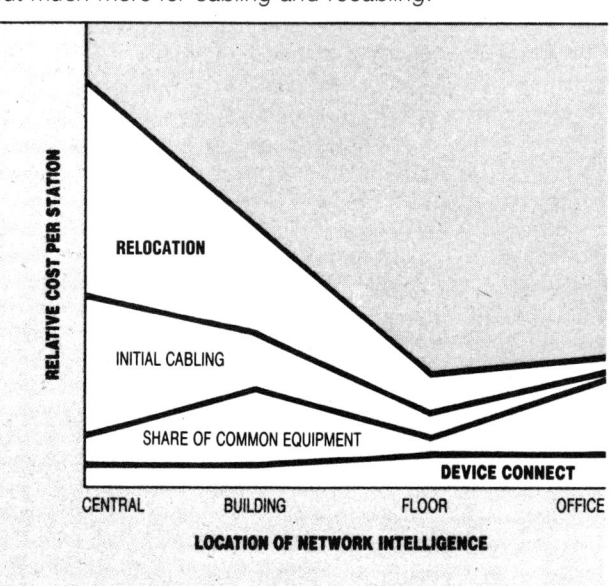

could provide networking for an entire floor, while individual offices could be served by small one- or two-port LANs.

It can be seen that lifetime relocation costs (that is, the cost of recabling in order to move a workstation) can more than offset the lower connection cost offered by a central switch. In a switch, the connection-cost saving comes, not from the lower cost of connecting a line to a circuit board, which is similar wherever the connection is made, but from the lower amortized cost of the common equipment (such as shared modems, packaging, frame or chassis, and power supply).

Sifting diverse alternatives

Of course, it is difficult to compare LAN and switch technologies as if they were monolithic categories. Like switches, LANs vary widely in cost and in their ability to adapt to technological trends, such as the evolution toward

3. The more, the broader. *Increasing the area that a network must serve demands more of the network. At each level, different criteria are used for selecting a network.*

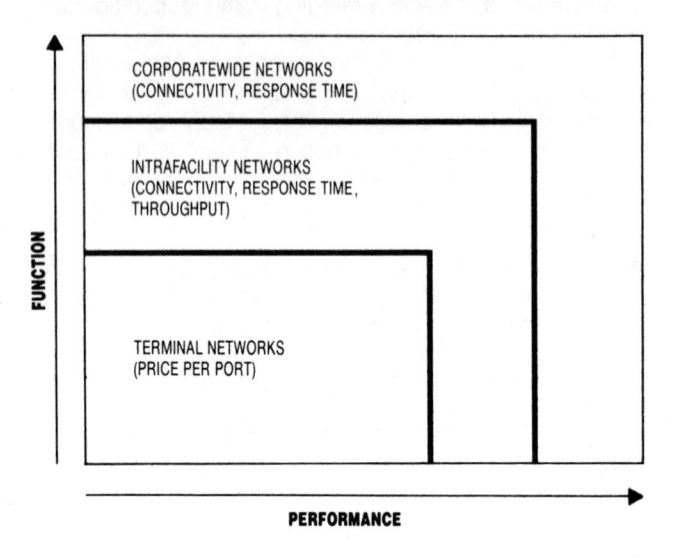

```
FUNCTION ↑
┌─────────────────────────────────────────┐
│ CORPORATEWIDE NETWORKS                  │
│ (CONNECTIVITY, RESPONSE TIME)           │
│  ┌──────────────────────────────────┐   │
│  │ INTRAFACILITY NETWORKS           │   │
│  │ (CONNECTIVITY, RESPONSE TIME,    │   │
│  │  THROUGHPUT)                     │   │
│  │   ┌───────────────────────┐      │   │
│  │   │ TERMINAL NETWORKS     │      │   │
│  │   │ (PRICE PER PORT)      │      │   │
│  │   │                       │      │   │
│  │   └───────────────────────┘      │   │
│  └──────────────────────────────────┘   │
└─────────────────────────────────────────┘
                          PERFORMANCE →
```

axis represents higher-speed connections and greater throughput.

The figure suggests that the primary focus in intrafacility networks is on connectivity and performance factors (response time and throughput). Throughput may be less significant at the corporate level because of the localization of traffic. Terminal networks are often judged on price per port. While important, this should not be the sole consideration. A high degree of manageability, operability, reliability, and performance of a terminal network may increase the price per port. However, these factors may be of greater importance in terms of user productivity. The lifetime cost of a network replete with such features may be less than that of a simpler network, which may need to be upgraded much sooner (see "Pricing LANs").

Support for terminal networks

Various communications devices and media can be located on the three-tiered model (Fig. 4). The inner box shows types of terminal networks. Typical media for the physical layer of terminal networks are baseband and broadband. Baseband is suitable for departmental networks, while broadband is useful for longer terminal networks or where the medium already exists.

Above the media in the figure are data link layer protocols: CSMA/CX represents CSMA, which does not listen for collisions; CSMA/CD, which detects them; and CSMA/CA, which avoids them. Users should be aware that, despite the hype about "industry standards," these networks are not interchangeable. That is, signals from one type of transceiver would travel to another type but not be responded to correctly. The situation is significantly worse in broadband, where the difficulty of interconnecting broadband modem technologies increases the problem of achieving physical-level compatibility. However, this problem is being addressed in the 802.4 efforts and may also be addressed by an 802.3 broadband standard.

Network types

Terminal networks are where LAN technology began and, as Figure 4 suggests, the 802.3, 802.4, and 802.5 standards have been developed around their needs. Token protocols are emerging as the preferred solution for terminal networks in which a heavier workload calls for higher performance. Token-bus networks may be baseband, but since they are found mostly in manufacturing environments,

---

Pricing LANs

In looking at the connect cost for various local area networks (LANs), it is interesting to consider the significance of, say, a $200 difference in the capital cost of network connections. Such a difference could be due to increased storage or processing hardware in the network interface units (NIUs), which might provide:
- Higher throughput and, thus, faster response times.
- Performance to accommodate high-level protocols.
- Ability to support higher-speed devices.
- Ability to adapt different user devices (such as asynchronous or synchronous terminals) through program control, obviating the need to replace the NIU.

A $200 capital difference in connect cost might seem less significant when compared with the productivity gain that might be experienced by a $40,000-per-year user who employs a $1 million network to access computers that may cost millions of dollars each. Amortized over four years, the extra expenditure can be equated to a productivity gain of 12 seconds per day for the user. Higher-performance networks can maintain response time while growing in size and complexity and serving the workstations brought on to replace simple terminals. A time savings may also come from the network's ability to recover from a power failure in seconds, rather than minutes. When some networks fail, only the device containing the network management program knows the configurations of each NIU. It must restart each one from scratch. Serial down-line loading of the configuration data can, on a medium-sized network, add 40 minutes to the time it takes to recover from a single power outage during the year. If the configuration data were stored in memory at each NIU, this time could be saved.

These and other factors translate into useful life for the network. While the lifetime cost is usually applied to the evaluation of computer projects, it is seldom applied to the evaluation of networks, even though their effective lives are often significantly longer than those of most computers installed today. This is because computers are replaced relatively quickly due to their rapidly declining price/performance ratio. An installed network will have to be in place longer, so its ability to adapt is crucial.

A lower initial connect cost per port due to cheaper network interfaces may hurt users in the long run. Such interfaces often lack the processing performance or memory to support higher-level protocols. This shortcoming limits the network's future growth potential.

4. Overall direction. In time, local area networking technology will evolve from simple baseband support of asynchronous terminals toward the integrated, multimedia use of intelligent workstations. While each of the network entities will continue to have a place, all are certain to develop along the two dimensions shown.

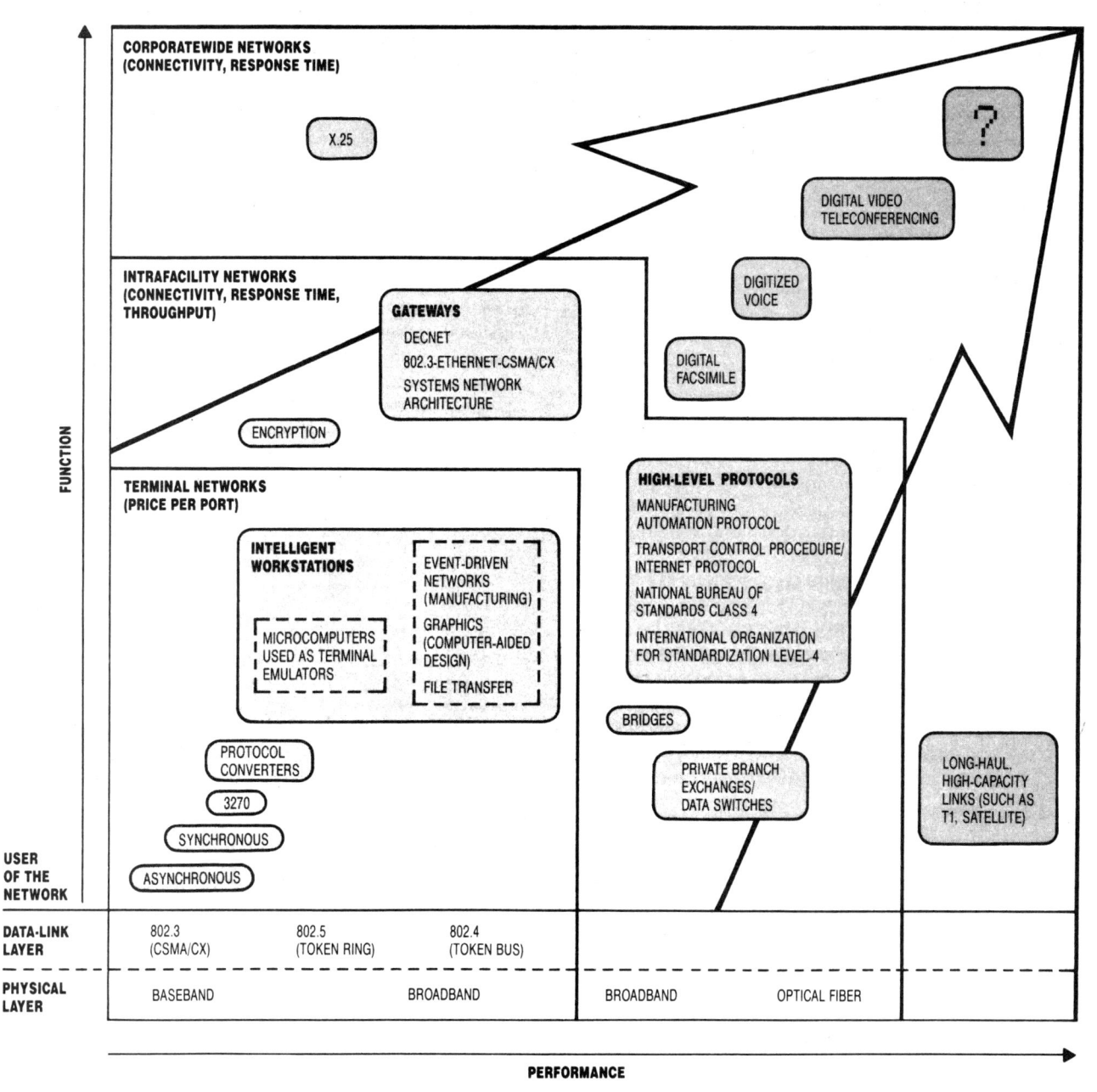

CSMA/CX = CARRIER-SENSE MULTIPLE ACCESS WITH COLLISION DETECTION OR AVOIDANCE

they ordinarily use broadband, which is more resistant to electrical interference. Token-ring networks may run over twisted pairs.

As shown in Figure 4, networks that support one type of terminal device or another vary in their function and performance.

■ Asynchronous terminals are the most common class of terminal installed today. However, networks of these devices have the lowest functionality and performance of any type of terminal network. For this reason, the devices are increasingly being replaced by intelligent terminals and workstations, which are rapidly declining in cost.

■ Synchronous terminals may use bit- or byte-oriented protocols. Such terminals are most often found in the proprietary networks offered by various computer makers. Each synchronous protocol was developed to enhance communications among a vendor's computers and terminals. However, the variety of terminal types means that terminals are not interchangeable.

■ 3270 networks rate higher along both dimensions (performance and function) than those consisting of other types of terminals. The large-screen 3270 terminals are quite complex in terms of the number of function keys they have and operations they can perform. Also, while asynchronous devices are limited to speeds of 19.2 kbit/s or less and synchronous terminals can communicate at up to 56 kbit/s, the 3270 specification includes an unusual 2-Mbit/s bus protocol between the terminal and the controller.

- Protocol converters are shown as having a higher level of functionality because they enable, for example, ASCII devices to appear as terminals that use the synchronous data link control (SDLC) protocol. Sophisticated LANs incorporate protocol conversion at the network interface. Such functionality also demands higher performance so that response time to the user does not suffer.
- Intelligent workstations offer the highest functionality and performance of any terminal environment. The spread of microcomputers in corporations is rapidly becoming the major network design factor. The upgrading of asynchronous terminals to computer-based workstations both changes the nature of the communications (from bursty interaction to synchronous block transfers) and substantially increases traffic volumes. Many networks that could handle low-speed devices may produce erratic response times or even blocking when intelligent workstations or higher-speed computers are added.

In the upper right corner of the figure's terminal-network box are the most demanding terminal environments today: event-driven networks requiring guaranteed response times (characterized by manufacturing applications), high-volume graphics (such as computer-aided design), and file transfers. All three represent the microcomputer as a terminal operating in high-performance mode.

There appears to be a strong correlation between the power of the workstation and the amount of data generated onto the network. This presents a great challenge to network designers and managers, since the workstation is in its infancy. Some forecasters say that workstations operating at speeds of 10 mips (million instructions per second), this being slightly faster than an IBM 3081 processor, will be available sometime between 1988 and 1990. While it is not yet clear how these will be used and what kind of traffic they will generate, there is a strong possibility that their extra power will be used for image processing. Thus, microcomputers will be the pivotal factor in moving video and voice onto LANs, as is suggested by Figure 1.

The intrafacility network

The era of combined video cameras and workstations has been ushered in by the Datapoint Minx, Widcom's 56-kbit/s desktop teleconferencing devices, and others. In the future, multimedia workstations will serve the full range of user needs for local computing, remote database access, and voice and video transmission. Admittedly, the price of a coder/decoder (codec) to translate video signals into 56-kbit/s data is unacceptably high today for individual offices. However, the digitization of video signals is under active development. The technology that supports a 10-mips workstation is going to substantially reduce the cost of codec processing in the next five years. Such advancement and the high payoff from reduced travel time and increased efficiency will make for rapid acceptance of desktop video as the technology emerges.

Intrafacility networks have many similarities to metropolitan area networks, since a campus may extend for several miles. As shown at the base of the middle box in Figure 4, broadband and optical fibers are the most suitable media for the physical layer because of their ability to operate over longer distances. Baseband is not appropriate for intrafacility communications today because the technology is limited to shorter distances. For example, the 802.3 standard will perform collision detection only if the network is less than 2,500 meters long.

Broadband offers greater flexibility than lightwave gear because of the general availability of cable and the associated headends, amplifiers, and other equipment used in broadband community antenna television (CATV) plant. Broadband can also support long networks and multiple subchannels. A state-of-the-art modem broadcasts 10 Mbit/s in a single 6-MHz channel and can be tuned under software control to operate at any point of the spectrum between 20 and 375 MHz. A dual-cable network can support 60 channels (600 Mbit/s of data bandwidth).

Thus, broadband modems can select a frequency band from anywhere in the CATV range while other applications use the rest of the spectrum. This flexibility is an important attribute in intrafacility applications. The frequency of the data channel can be moved to accommodate new uses of the shared cable, which can grow to 100 or even 600 Mbit/s in bandwidth.

Optical fiber is emerging as an alternative medium for intrafacility applications. However, the use of passive fiber equipment, which attenuates the signal each time the fiber is split in order to attach a network interface device or start a new branch, limits the distances over which lightwave networks can be used. An additional disadvantage is the propagation of phase jitter through a passive fiber network. The newer active fiber-optic taps regenerate the optical signal, enabling jitter to be reduced and providing a stable signal throughout the entire network. These taps permit a bus architecture to be constructed in fiber over long distances.

As experience is gained in lightwave installation and maintenance, this technology may make optical fiber viable for networks several miles in length at costs comparable to broadband. Also, parallel lightwave networks can be connected by bridges, forming the equivalent of multiple-channel broadband networks.

Intrafacility networks must effectively process the traffic generated by multiple terminal subnetworks, which may present the intrafacility network with both short and long packets of asynchronous and synchronous data. LAN technology faces its greatest challenge in intrafacility networks, which must handle a wide variety of traffic patterns as well as high volumes while maintaining consistent response times and high throughput. Interestingly, while much of the standards activity has been generated at the data link level for various types of terminal subnetworks, no corresponding activity has focused on the intrafacility network, clearly the most vexing environment for the network designer.

Both connectivity and performance are vital in intrafacility networks. Performance cannot be provided by simply increasing the signaling speed of the network. This is because the access protocol is more significant than the

Network protocols and user-data throughput

Local area networks (LANs) transmit data in packets. Certain bits added to the user's data enable correct transmission. The size of the packet containing the user data will depend on the application as well as the speed and nature of the device initiating the transaction. For example, computer-to-computer transfers are fast enough to be able to use long data blocks; providing good response time to interactive users, however, may mean sending a packet as soon as a user types in a character or two (in "echoplex," or host-echo protocols). Packet size also depends on the protocol that encapsulates the user data and provides addresses, check fields, and other needed information.

For example, according to the IEEE 802.3 standard, the Ethernet protocol would enclose 10 characters (80 bits) of user data in a packet almost 10 times that length for transmission on the network. A 64-bit preamble is used to wake up the modem, followed by a 48-bit destination address, a 48-bit source address, a 16-bit type field, a 32-bit cyclic redundancy check, and finally the 80-bit user-data field. Then comes a 288-bit pad field (the standard requires a minimum user-data field of 368 bits or enough padding to make up the difference) and a 96-bit guard. The guard, which lasts for 96 bit-times (the time it would take to transmit one bit on the network) at 10 Mbit/s, ensures a 9.6-microsecond interval between packets in order to avoid packet overrun.

The example shows that only 80 out of a total of 672, or 11.9 percent, of the bit-times associated with the packet actually represent user data (akin to shipping a pack of cigarettes in a container truck). This figure may seem odd, but not alarming, until other considerations that diminish the usable portion of channel capacity are taken into account. In carrier-sense multiple access with collision detection (CSMA/CD), many sources recommend that the maximum planning level for network traffic should be 25 percent of the signaling speed of the channel. Seventy-five percent should be set aside for peaks in traffic and for the fact that, at heavier loadings, increased collisions between packets on the network may begin to be seen by users as erratic response times or even blocking.

As a user network grows in the number of connected devices and speed, it may become necessary to operate multiple channels with bridges between them, especially for the intrafacility backbone. A packet transmitted to a device on an adjacent channel will appear on both subchannels, creating some duplication in traffic. Even though a single-channel network may be practicable at the outset, a performance plan for the network must anticipate the addition of channels to accommodate future growth. Although traffic will be localized to the best of the network manager's ability, in a multichannel network with limited transmission speed an allowance of 30 percent for interchannel traffic seems reasonable, leaving 70 percent (of the available 25 percent) for legitimate network business.

Network and session management and high-level protocols all add traffic to the channel. If 20 percent of the remaining capacity is allowed for these, only 80 percent of 70 percent of 25 percent, or 14 percent, of the network's signaling speed is available for user-data packets. Since only 11.9 percent of the data presented to the network in the 10-character example is user data, approximately 11.9 percent of 14 percent, or 1.67 percent, of the signaling speed of the network is actually devoted to carrying user data when the channel is filled to its planned capacity. In a 5-Mbit/s network, this means that the channel would be full with only 83 kbit/s of user data and may begin to exhibit fluctuating response times at higher loading.

These numbers apply, of course, to the 10-character example. As the standard requires a fixed-minimum packet size, the same packet will be transmitted even if the data is less than 10 characters. If the network carries interactive sessions, there may be many one- and two-character packets, bringing down the average number of useful characters per packet. This average greatly affects throughput. For instance, if user data accounted for only one character rather than 10 per packet, a mere 0.167 percent of the network speed would be available because each packet would carry just one-tenth of the usable information. In the real world, networks carry a variety of packet sizes. Intercomputer traffic usually generates packet sizes in the hundreds of bytes, with a corresponding increase in efficiency. Still, many one- or two-character packets are generated during interactive input and output.

The example shows the effect of one particular link-layer protocol on throughput. Other factors, such as the transmission of mixed-length packets or synchronous and asynchronous traffic on the same network, also place demands on the access protocol. The effects on performance of digitized voice and extreme network length have not yet been fully explored. These will require further innovation in the access method in order to utilize LAN technology effectively. Subnetworks running under standard 802.3, 802.4, or 802.5 protocols will serve departmental needs, but the intrafacility backbone will have to be considerably more versatile.

To compare the maximum channel throughput available with different access protocols, allowing for variations in the packet size and length of the network, a model has been developed and programmed in APL. Its purpose is to examine the performance that can be expected in intrafacility applications. The model uses a number of algorithms that calculate the amount of overhead due to the packet format, the effect of network length on packet length, and the time intervals between packets or transmissions. It does not take into account, however, the effects of software, modem performance, phase jitter, token loss, or the packet loss that occurs during a period of unusually heavy contention. Calculations were made for various access protocols at different speeds (see table).

The examples are all based on a three-mile analog broadband network, with the exception of the token ring, which is assumed to be digital lightwave. Networks of this length were chosen to demonstrate that ordinary terminal-network protocols may lose efficiency when they are used at facility-wide distances.

One network type that may be unfamiliar to readers is the optimized token bus. In a LAN of this type, network interfaces are able to determine their own distance from the headend. The protocol incorporates a packet-length field that lets listening nodes waiting to transmit determine when the preceding packet will end. The nodes can then time their transmissions so that packets are nose-to-tail along the network. Such protocols seem well-suited to longer networks.

The token ring example also deserves comment. The topology in the example is a single large ring, which is assumed to connect 3,000 workstations to 100 wiring centers, 30 each, at an average of 100 feet from the wiring center. In this and the token bus examples, 10 percent of the workstations are assumed to be transmitting at any one time. Increasing the percentage of nodes transmitting to 30 percent has little effect on the performance of the ring, although reducing its size increases its efficiency a great deal.

The token ring figures illustrate how a ring structure creates an extremely long network because a double path goes to each station from its local wiring center. In the example, the ring length amounts to 214 kilometers. The time taken for the token to pass an average half circuit to the next transmitting device is 0.5 milliseconds, the equivalent of 50,000 data bits at 100 Mbit/s. This illustrates the reduced efficiency of the network in handling data due to gaps in transmission at an increased signaling speed. Hoisting the signaling speed to 100 Mbit/s cannot alone compensate for how the access method processes short packets at great distances. (An entirely different picture emerges when networks are used to transfer long blocks over short distances. In that case, most access methods seem efficient.)

Comparing protocol efficiencies

ACCESS PROTOCOL	TRANSMISSION SPEED (MBIT/S)	USER PACKET SIZE (BYTES)			
		1	10	100	500
CSMA	5	0.02	0.17	1.12	1.63
CSMA/CD	5	0.03	0.29	2.16	3.96
	10	0.03	0.30	3.02	6.85
TOKEN BUS	5	0.01	0.08	0.69	2.22
	10	0.01	0.10	0.92	3.37
TOKEN RING	10	0.01	0.13	1.30	6.52
	100	0.01	0.14	1.37	6.83
OPTIMIZED TOKEN BUS	10	0.10	0.99	6.78	9.13

transmission speed in handling the variety of packets that will be encountered (see "Network protocols and user-data throughput"). High-speed networks are most efficient when they are kept full because any gap between transmissions translates into a proportionately greater loss of channel capacity as the speed increases. Also, the gaps between transmissions become longer because faster packets take less time to enter onto the network.

For this reason, multiple channels at 10 Mbit/s can provide greater efficiency than a single 50- or 100-Mbit/s channel. In addition, increasing the signaling speed of the devices attached to the network increases their cost. This makes for an expensive way to serve the low-cost asynchronous terminals still required on many networks.

What's at the middle level
In an intrafacility environment, multiple terminal subnetworks will be interconnected. This can be accomplished by several mechanisms:

■ PBXs or data switches may provide access to long-distance communications from the local environment.
■ Bridges connect similar networks. Broadband bridges are an economical way of combining the widely used baseband Ethernets into a unified network. Such bridges provide filtering to keep the data of a given network from unintentionally traveling to another. A protocol-transparent bridge can process packets without having to know the protocol that created them. Like PBXs, bridges are relatively fast but simple.
■ High-level protocols are very important for linking terminal networks. These have been defined for the manufacturing industry through the Manufacturing Automation Protocol (MAP), for the Department of Defense through the Transmission Control Protocol/Internet Protocol (TCP/IP), and for general applications through the efforts of the National Bureau of Standards (NBS) and International Organization for Standardization (ISO). Levels 3 and 4 of ISO's OSI (Open Systems Interconnection), the network and transport layers, respectively, are particularly important. Such protocols promise a great measure of functionality for intrafacility networks.

Many computer vendors, including Digital Equipment Corp. (DEC), IBM, and Hewlett-Packard, are now developing MAP/ISO Level 4 interfaces. These vendors are moving in a fortunate direction, since the new Level 4 interfaces will permit users to connect any devices needed to get a particular job done across any network that provides support for Level 3, regardless of the network's data link protocol. Users should plan to take advantage of the flexibility offered by common network- and transport-layer protocols, rather than wait for vendors to standardize "down to the wire" by solving the technically demanding problem of interconnecting their units at all levels.

For example, a user can select computer A because of its laser printer to operate with computer B because of its higher processing power. As long as both machines use common intermediate-level software, the connection can be made. The question of whether they both use the same signaling method on the network and have compatible modems for broadband communications is much less important. Such compatibility will take much longer for the industry to develop and certify. In the meantime, users are free to choose whichever of the wide variety of local transport networks on the market best suits their needs.

Like workstations, LAN technology is just beginning. Its evolution will provide more flexible and powerful solutions for device interconnection. The door should not be closed on these potential solutions in the desire to accelerate standardization between levels 1 and 3 of OSI.

- Gateways, which may interconnect Ethernet, Systems Network Architecture (SNA), Decnet, and others, are sophisticated but relatively slow.
- Encryption can be performed at the intrafacility level and will increasingly be required. If the terminal networks perform the encryption, their various schemes must be coordinated or translated by the intrafacility network. Encryption methods range from the simple to the complex. If such security is normally on an as-called-for basis, it does not require particulary high performance. (Making encryption, like protocol conversion, part of the routine communications process puts more pressure on the network to perform.)

Consistent and complete network management is a major requirement at the intrafacility level. Network managers, responsible for seeing that the individual terminal subnetworks have developed and been protected in a way acceptable to users, may have implemented special network-management processors that monitor the networks and the devices attached to them. Since the intrafacility network joins multiple terminal subnetworks, the management capabilities at that level must be as global as possible so performance information can be gathered for the network as a whole. They must be consistent with the methods used at the lower level and also be adequate to the task of managing the backbone network.

Spanning the organization

Communications between locations involves the use of private or public long-haul networks. X.25 and T1 (1.544-Mbit/s) capabilities are important features of corporatewide networks (see the outer box of Figure 4). While X.25 is also a significant method of connecting terminals to hosts and hosts to hosts at different levels, X.25 was shown only at the highest level to simplify the model.

Equipment and techniques for handling X.25 and T1, as well as the extensive network-management capabilities that go with automatic routing and recovery, have been extensively pioneered by the manufacturers of digital data switches. In 1986, T1-speed interfaces began to emerge on LANs. Extensive investments are being made in tools that can manage traffic across multiple independent LANs interconnected with T1 bridges. These bridges can perform traffic filtering and routing.

X.25 is the most complex entity at this level, in terms of software interfaces. The long-haul links are the fastest. Digital facsimile, in contrast, is a standalone, relatively simple, low-speed means of linking any two users in a corporation. It relies on paper delivery for the "last mile" but warrants inclusion because it is a digital imaging technology. A more complex wideband application will be deployed in terms of digitized voice. Finally, digital videoconferencing will make the greatest demand of any existing application on corporatewide networks and their tributaries. What networking frontier will follow full-motion color interactivity between any two users and provide an even greater challenge is as yet unknown.

The superimposed arrow in Figure 4 suggests the time dimension. All communications networks, including LANs, must be capable of supporting growth in traffic volume, performance, and functionality. They will be driven by increasing demands as connected workstations and host computers become more powerful, as specialized subnetworks become integrated into a single network through high-level protocols, and as integrated-media applications emerge. The arrow also reflects the history of the LAN, from its roots in baseband asynchronous support within a limited work area to a foundational technology for the full range of corporate communications.

Against this perspective, it is clear why baseband LAN vendors feel they must develop a capability in broadband to meet intrafacility requirements. Such capability calls for much more than the addition of a broadband modem to a baseband CSMA/CD product. Achieving efficient transmission in a long-distance network requires the integrated design of protocol, digital, and analog components.

While the technology necessary to interconnect networks that are several miles in length is more complex than that suitable for campus or terminal networks, the backbone must also offer greater flexibility and higher capacity. Broadband networks that offer speeds lower than the 10 Mbit/s currently available on baseband hardly provide a growth base for the evolution of facility-wide networks.

Value in the local area network must be seen in terms of useful life, that is, its ability to absorb additional terminals of increasing complexity while continuing to offer consistent response times, high reliability, rapid recovery from failure (either internal or external), and sufficient processing power. User productivity is the objective. The network should enable users to work in a way that makes them most productive without requiring them to adapt their working habits to the network's capabilities (or shortcomings).

The three network levels represent a single communications service that today is based on a heterogeneous mixture of technologies. For example, traffic from a digital data switch on a campus at one side of the backbone network may go through analog public circuit-switched lines and then to a LAN at another campus. The adjoined digital and analog technologies underlying this connection introduce boundaries between the different layers, where the necessary translating devices reduce performance. The advent of digital technology into voice and low-cost video communications will bring tremendous pressure to reduce the impact of technological boundaries and to provide access among multiple locations on a network that harmonizes work-area, campus-wide, and long-distance communications. ■

Peter Gregory is vice president of marketing and sales operations at Applitek Corp., Wakefield, Mass. Prior to joining Applitek, Gregory was vice president of planning at Cray Research in Minneapolis. Before that, Gregory was director of systems marketing for IBM Europe during his 18 years with IBM. Gregory is a consultant to the Los Alamos National Laboratory and a director of Scientific Computer Systems of Wilsonville, Ore.

Paulina Borsook, DATA COMMUNICATIONS

Save that LAN! Preventing network crashes

Practical wisdom and first aid for LANs from industry experts, seasoned consultants, customer-support technologists, and savvy network managers. Hot tips and musts to avoid.

It's unglamorous, but it's true: Most of what usually goes wrong with a local area network can be prevented by good planning, careful installation, and attention to cabling. These factors are the cause of 90 percent of the problems that occur most frequently, according to network managers, consultants, and customer-support technicians. For the remaining 10 percent, however, it's a finger-pointing toss-up between hardware, applications software, and operating system revisions.

Judith Estrin, Bridge Communications' cofounder and executive vice president of Network Computing Devices, a Mountain View, Calif.-based start-up, says that since "networking has become pervasive" and standards have begun to proliferate, everybody now buys—and installs and uses—local area networks as if they were simple point-to-point operations.

But local area networking is still complex, and finding and diagnosing problems is still largely beyond the capability of most nontechnical network users. It needs to be "taken seriously," according to Estrin. Dirk Martin, product manager of customer-support marketing for 3Com Corp. (Santa Clara, Calif.), agrees that vendors push the "plug-and-play concept." All too often, though, Martin cautions, "it will plug, but not play."

Because LANs have not yet become commodities, network managers will need to maintain close and ongoing relationships with their LAN vendors' technical-support organizations. These organizations should have proficient, in-house familiarity with the third-party products they sell, adequate debugging tools such as the Network General Corp. (Mountain View, Calif.) Sniffer, and experience with a wide range of installations. Networks are more than boxes with cards, a protocol or two, and some software.

So, what kind of animal husbandry do network managers need to learn and apply to their LANs? What are the tricks they can use to ensure LAN domestic tranquility?

Estrin divides LAN troubleshooting problems into five general categories, providing at least a logical starting point for isolating difficulties. Those categories are:
- Cabling and media
- Topology and design
- Internetworking
- Protocols
- Network management

Cabling
Brad Walker of LTV Aircraft Products Group (Dallas, Tex.) and LAN manager extraordinaire says that one of the most common causes of network problems is installation done on the cheap. Users who go with low-bid contractors who don't understand the mechanical and electronic issues will end up with far more costly problems once the network is up and running.

Here's one bit of advice: To find cabling flaws, have technicians do the boring, mundane work of testing cable and connectors. That's how Curtis Washington, senior systems support engineer at TRW Information Networks (Torrance, Calif.), was able to determine why the Cleveland Clinic Foundation's broadband LAN was failing its doctors.

The foundation's M.D. educational television channel kept disappearing. During the once-a-year cable certification, the inadequate signal level was traced to an overheated wiring closet.

Walker says one of his most commonly encountered network problems occurs every couple of months. "Some goofball decides, unannounced, to move his workstation," he says. And by unplugging that station's connector from the LAN, electrical continuity in the cable is broken.

3Com's senior support engineer Mark Zaller notes that one user's mystifying network glitch turned out to be the result of grounding both sides of his Ethernet.

Figures vary, but most practiced network troubleshooters believe that anywhere from 70 to 90 percent of network problems can be attributed to cabling mishaps—the electronics may just not be as robust as it should be for a normal work environment. Thomas Reid, Communications Network Manager at Ohio University (Athens, Ohio), may have the last word of caution on cabling: "Don't let anyone do unauthorized installations on your network."

Topology and network design
In spite of the temptation to perform acts of network derring-do, it's imperative to stay within LAN specifications. Pushing LAN topologies to the breaking point is more prevalent, it seems, with Ethernet than with Token Ring, not only because Token Ring Multistation Access Units (MAUs) demand a more structured approach, but also because the token topology has not been around as long as Ethernet. People tend to follow the prescribed Token Ring recipes because they haven't yet learned to do otherwise (see "Hot tips for Ethernet" and "Hot tips for token ring").

Imaginative topologies and LAN network designs that exceed specifications can typically result in loops, dual paths, and untraceable problems. There's another reason for keeping to specs: When vendors are called in to fix network problems, they may refuse to service the network unless it is shown to conform to specifications.

Even so, LTV's Walker notes that ingenuity in network modification often is the result of necessity, and "sophisticated users probably deserve respect for the integrity of what they have done."

Segmentation tops virtually everyone's recommendation list as helpful for achieving a sound LAN design, for reasons of both troubleshooting and security. LAN consultant Mike Hurwicz of MTI Group (Nashville, Tenn.) advises that networks should be subdivided into segments as small as practicable, following the networking good-housekeeping rules of defining segments by workgroup, keeping local traffic local, making sure no one has to log on over a bridge, and minimizing bridges. Users should not routinely need to go over more than one bridge.

Routers' superior intelligence will also keep local problems local, constructing "a firewall" against broadcast storms and other disasters, as Marshall Rose, Director of Software Engineering at the Wollongong Group (Palo Alto, Calif.), puts it. Even when these broadcast messages don't cause network avalanches, they can still gum up the works. Cisco Systems (Menlo Park, Calif.) software engineer James Forster refers to broadcast messages as "Trojan Pigs," which can subtly eat up from 2 to 10 percent of network's bandwidth, as well as CPU utilization. This is still another good reason, he says, to go with routers instead of bridges.

Finally, bridges that are intelligent enough to act on the differences between source and destination addresses can still be stupid enough to not realize when they have been programmed incorrectly. And when they are, they can generate a pattern of network misbehavior that makes no sense at all, says consultant Bill Hancock, vice president of engineering for Essential Resources Inc. (New York, N. Y.).

When bridges have to be used, it's advisable to place them in LANs to create a series of triangles, so that when one path fails, another is available. Curtis Washington articulated the general consensus of networking experts

---

Hot tips for Ethernet

Slidelocks. Ethernet slidelock attachment hardware is notorious for coming loose or looking securely fastened when it is not. Consider replacing it with screwdown lugs similar to RS-232-C. Many Ethernet problems can be traced to loose AUI connections. Characteristic of loose transceiver connections in particular are collisions occurring 50 to 100 bytes into a packet.

Infant mortality rate. Stress-test minihubs and transceivers one small segment at a time before installing them on an Ethernet. If these are going to fail, they are likely to do so right away—push them repeatedly at the beginning of a network installation to prevent marginal network operation later on.

Metal filings. Fragments from drilling into transceiver shields to install taps can cause shorts between shields and inner cores, causing time-out errors. Use magnets or fine soldering tools to remove particles.

CRC errors. Among the easiest Ethernet problems to resolve, they are usually the result of of an individual Ethernet controller failing. They may also be caused by error-prone remote links—use bridges to isolate these lines from the network at large.

Jabbering. Usually caused by a failing transceiver. The high error rates often cause individual nodes to drop from the network map. It may be difficult to track the jabbering point of origin. Client complaints of time-outs and nodes with high error rates or time-outs are likely clues when there are many devices on the network that are not continuously active.

Alignment errors. Common on extended fiber optic Ethernets. Tuning the fiber path reduces attenuation, minimizing alignment errors.

Racks. Install repeaters in racks at their central site so that all back panels are facing in the same direction. Using the visual cues of the devices' light displays, it's easy to spot atypical patterns of collisions and segmentations and discern unusually heavy traffic.

Physical spec. With Ethernet, it is easy to accidentally exceed the standard physical specifications, causing many collisions or slower response times on stations at the remote end of the LAN. Collision fragments, particularly longer fragments, are a symptom.

Cabling hints. Be very careful not to move vampire taps around once they are made; don't try to make vampire taps without the right tools. PVC- and Teflon-coated cabling use different size connectors. Choose twisted pair or fiber over Cheapernet.

that stars are preferable to buses and should be installed wherever possible.

For troubleshooting purposes, Forster believes that it is necessary to build trapdoors, essentially alternative paths to get to the outskirts of a network, so that users don't blind their networks to their remote portions. This is important when networks are becoming overloaded or problems seem to be concentrating in a particular segment of the network. A good network design isolates breakdowns and makes it possible to work around trouble spots. Users have to be able to shut down misfiring network components without bringing down the entire network.

Theories of network design can take up an entire five-foot bookshelf on their own, but Karen Summerly, an independent network site planner from Oakland, Calif., points out that at the very least, network planners need to consider whether they need to design networks for maximum growth and flexibility, or maximum cost savings, or maximum workplace aesthetics (that is, where cabling is pleasantly out of sight but devilish to reach and reconfigure). Building architecture, projected company expansion, and corporate culture may all need to be factored in.

When making plans for their LANs' future, network managers of course also need to consider migration paths and resist the temptation to buy that which is new on the assumption that it is necessary. Yes, a LAN based on FDDI (the Fiber Distributed Data Interface) is faster, for example. But managers need to give careful thought to where to put that improved velocity (and added expense) and whether their applications really require it at all.

Internetworking

As most network managers know, it's the boundaries between different protocols and different vendors' products that cause the biggest heartaches.

Independent consultant Pete Maclean of San Francisco

Hot tips for token ring

Mixed media. Because token ring networks can run over different kinds of cable, there is the temptation to mix and match. Don't. The resulting mismatched twisted pairs may create puzzling intermittent problems. One user, for example, encountered one set of errors on one portion of his token ring cable and another when transmission was sent through a media filter. It appeared that his network interface card was out of spec.

As it turned out, however, the user had ordinary telephone wiring on the media-filter segment, and the malfunction occurred because the wrong pairs were twisted together.

Different token ring vendors' products vary on the number of ports allowed per Media Access Unit (MAU), on whether or not baluns are used, and on the kinds of cable that can be used on trunks and backbones. Token ring is not a technology to start running in-house interoperability experiments with, those with experience say.

Token errors, damaged frames. Most likely these are the result of bad cables or loose connectors. If stations start receiving bad packets from their neighbors, it is not likely to be noise, as would be encountered over long-distance lines. Unless the microcomputer cards are overheating, the LAN shouldn't be causing error reports.

Crazy MAUs. Make sure your network is designed to take misfiring MAUs off-line automatically.

Bit-slots. Token ring network adapter cards can fit into either 8-bit or 16-bit microcomputer slots. Simple enough to get right, but this is a parameter that's often overlooked.

Jumpers. Token ring cards for both workstations and servers offer a welter of choices for DMA (Direct Memory Access), I/O (Input/Output), and interrupts. As ports, users, and software changes, these options need to be tracked and adjusted, along with the types and lengths of cable runs.

Clicks. When a device on a token ring is turned on, there should be an audible click as it inserts itself into the ring. This click signifies that the device and the MAU to which it connects are talking to each other. If the click is not heard, the problem is with the device, not the network. Check that the right software driver is inserted into the unit's configuration file.

Broken cable. A "transmission fail" message means there is a cable break; if the user was not in mid-processing, there should be no damage to either the network or the application. Even if the break occurred in the middle of working, there still may be no damage—provided reconnections are made quickly and the number of retries is below a specified number.

Stack overflow. This would be an error message signifying that memory addressing is wrong on the token ring card. Memory addressing may have to be changed.

Competition. Token ring cards often compete with enhanced memory and enhanced graphics adapter cards, so that all three functions land on top of each other in the 640-kbyte-to-1-Mbyte memory locations reserved for ROM Bios functions.

These functions may have to be remapped in this memory chunk; or alternatively, certain pieces of hardware and software may have to be disconnected from the network. A particular monitor may not work; a version of Lotus 1-2-3 that checks expanded memory may not work either.

TSR. Terminate and stay-resident programs may similarly befuddle the function of token rings. These fancy drivers, on-screen clocks, easy exits to DOS, background checks on the presence or absence of electronic mail, and other utilities are the first thing to get rid of when mysterious errors crop up. These TSR battles are common and most likely will get worse and not better as users add new tools to their workstations. OS/2 may resolve some of these problems.

says that this is an area where managers shouldn't scrimp on tools: "Network monitors and analyzers should not be considered luxuries," he says. While it may be possible to run a single-vendor, single-protocol network without these devices, it is probably impossible to run a large heterogeneous network without them—and without the trained in-house staff to use them. By nature, third-party maintenance agreements do not carry the onus of ultimate responsibility and, therefore, do not address the complexities or offer the accountability needed in large mixed networks.

While the expensive personnel and equipment may be difficult to sell to upper management, Walker says that cutting corners here is "stupid; the cost of a network being down is incalculable." He likens the cost for ongoing training of support staff and capital expenditure for network analyzers to outlays for the hammers, screwdrivers, and

Hot tips for TCP/IP

Bottlenecks. When Transmission Control Protocol/Internet Protocol (TCP/IP) networks working over high-speed LANs such as Ethernet are linked over a lower-speed remote connection (such as a 9.6-kbit/s or a 56-kbit/s line), the associated gateways will start to buffer madly and eventually run out of memory.

When consistently busy, the gateways will begin to drop packets, and sending machines will endlessly be resending transmissions, wondering why they are not getting proper acknowledgments. A horrific bottleneck ensues.

In 1988, a retransmission algorithm called "slowstart" was developed to address this problem; it adaptively throttles back sending hosts when round-trip packet retransmission time begins to degrade.

Sendmail. This is an electronic-mail manager that presents problems when interacting with diverse electronic-mail protocols. Considered by some to be designed more for the computer science theorist than the network administrator, it may create difficulties when mapping TCP/IP mail from the well-understood world of the Internet onto UUCP or other networks.

Extraordinarily complex in the way it handles reformatting issues, the utility may even make it difficult to determine if it's configured correctly for all the E-mail formats the host node may encounter. The difficulty lies in the mechanics of the actual configuration rather than the design of the utility itself.

IP addressing. This is a common problem when users either give two devices the same IP address or the wrong IP address. Typically, a machine with a wrong IP address won't answer an Address Resolution Protocol (ARP) packet, which is sent out to inquire about addresses. When two machines have identical addresses, difficulty arises in sorting out the identical ARP counterclaims of the legitimate machine and the imposter. Checking the Ethernet addresses of the machines may give a clue as to which claim is false and which is true. Simple misconfiguration is usually the culprit.

Confusion between hosts and routers. In TCP/IP, hosts handle applications and generally talk to only one router. Routers may occasionally get confused and send data to a host, thinking the latter is a gateway. The host should send an Internet Control Message Protocol message back to the router, telling it that it is confused and to redirect gateway traffic elsewhere.

The IP design philosophy calls for bad packets to be thrown away, rather than propagated. However, a misleading packet sent to a host (by a router thinking it is a gateway) may end up being sent back to the router, where it then ping-pongs between the host and the router up to 15 times. This eats up bandwidth and prevents the router from doing its business.

Diskless workstations. Use of a LAN as a replacement for the backplane of a computer is proliferating, but users underestimate the amount of disk activity involved in everyday operations. Paging and swapping memory for large applications used by diskless workstations takes up a large amount of network bandwidth.

If file transfers or virtual-terminal functions undertaken by standard workstations are also going on, there is a very high probability that paging and swapping will be disrupted and overall network performance will degrade. Conventional wisdom dictates that a second network may need to be set up entirely for the diskless workstations, with each workstation having its own network connection to the server.

Domain name problems. TCP/IP's "hierarchical domain" naming scheme suffers from the usual problems of distributed replicated databases. Data consistency is a concern, as is what to do when part of the database cannot be addressed.

If users get their entries into this branching structure correct on the first try, there should be no problem. But entries that are almost correct can be very difficult to track down and fix; users can type in a wrong name that looks right and end up literally searching the globe for the right corresponding address. Reconfiguring existing software to fit domain names can be very tricky. This will only get worse when the OSI directory function, which is even more complicated, comes into being.

Broadcast storms. More common in earlier versions of 4.2 BSD Unix than now, these floodings of a network with endlessly replicated who's-on-the-network broadcast packets can bring a LAN or WAN to its knees. One workstation not correctly programmed to ignore these background broadcast packets can send out additional packets, which in turn triggers similar responses on other workstations so configured, with a catastrophic multiplier effect.

pliers necessary for routine building maintenance. Upper management needs to be trained to regard network maintenance expenditures as still one more fixed cost of doing business.

Protocols

The biggest problem here may be that the network manager who knew which protocols were running where and what their quirks and idiosyncracies were left years ago, without having designated a clear succession of experience or responsibility.

When new versions of protocols arrive, the carefully obtained collective network experience of several years may be lost. The new versions of the software may be installed on the LAN with default, as opposed to customized, parameter settings and options. And the peculiar needs of that network will have to be learned all over again.

For example, protocols set to operate with LAN-to-WAN (wide area network) remote Unix applications and requiring character-at-a-time remote echoing may not be able to tolerate the half-second delay of satellite links; a network manager familiar with the problem can reset time-outs to compensate for the lag (see "Hot tips for TCP/IP"). Further, no one may still be around who is familiar with the predicament.

Protocols need to support both interactive transactions and file tranfers. Unfortunately, one tends to exist at the expense of the other, and interactive communications often get short shrift in most protocol implementations, which may not have the mechanisms to ensure the primacy of interactive sessions over file transfers.

Spending the time to get to know your protocols may be rewarding in terms of improved network performance. For example, DECnets configured out of the box for use over long-distance networks may operate in packets of 576 bytes; for LANs, they could be reconfigured to operate with 1,500-byte packets, improving network efficiency (see "Hot tips for DECnet").

Protocols such as NetWare can be programmed for single or multi-user reading and writing, so that programs can either be read in slow small-number-of-byte chunks, or in faster large-number-of-byte chunks (see "Hot tips for NetWare" and "Hot tips for NFS").

Hot tips for DECnet

Slipping between protocols. Diskless VAXes use one protocol, Maintenance and Operations Protocol (MOP), to access their operating system and then switch over to another, Systems Communications Services (SCS), to downline-load the rest of what they need. If there are problems in starting up VAX operations, it can be very difficult to determine where they have occurred between the two protocols. Terminal servers similarly shift from MOP to another protocol, Local Area Transport (LAT).

Proprietary. Many parts of what is considered DECnet, such as SCS and LAT, are proprietary to Digital Equipment Corp. (DEC), and the specifications have not been published. Users may have to effectively reverse-engineer these protocols.

Terminal servers. Terminal servers expect packets in the correct order from MOP. If, for some reason, packets do not arrive in the right order, the terminal server may not have gained enough operative intelligence from MOP. It will then time-out and restart.

On congested networks, the terminal servers may endlessly start, quit, and restart, without ever knowing what information to ask for to complete their intialization. In large DECnet installations this can create problems if there is a massive network failure, such as a power outage. Some terminal servers may never get back on line without being assisted in rebooting. This can be compounded if bridges are involved.

Complexity. Aside from MOP, LAT, and SCS, plain-vanilla DECnet also uses Digital Data Communications Message Protocol. DEC itself has 14 different operating systems. The average VAX runs and uses about eight protocols but can run up to 20.

Xerox Network Systems (XNS), TCP/IP, NetWare, and X.25 are only some of the available options, and each can fail in unique ways not reflected in DEC documentation. There is the rumor, for example, that DECnet and XNS cannot coexist on the same medium.

Error reporting logjams. The same network failure can cause several different parts of the network to generate error reports. And there may be enough of a multiplier effect so that after the problem is fixed, the events may still be queued in the error logger.

Peer-to-peer. DECnet operates peer-to-peer, with no centralized authority tracking network connections. Machines simply either accept or reject connections to and from each other. However, when things go wrong, no one machine knows who is connected to whom; there is no DEC equivalent to IBM's NetView. Polling won't necessarily solve the problem because many DECnet users may be intermittently on line.

Line communications lost. This and "network partner exits" are the two most common DECnet error messages. These messages tend to crop up no matter what the problem. While they typically refer to hardware problems, they can also occur with software. For example, one user got the "line" error message when a buffer was too large for a PDP-11 to handle downloading from a VAX.

Failsafe. DECnets tend to be reliable and easy to install. Because of this, users may not have gone through the hand-holding and coaxing common to other networks and may thus have gained relatively little information on how to handle problems when they occur. When problems do arise, one manual may refer to error messages available only in another manual.

Older versions of Ethernet can accidentally enable trailers, which may suit some operating systems fine, but offend others. Furthermore, understanding how the protocols operate may make it clear that the number of network retransmissions is a sign of a software glitch, not an indication that it is time to go out and buy more stations. There always remains a temptation to think that the purchase of more and faster equipment will solve all LAN problems.

Remember, too, that just because implementations work separately it does not mean that they work together. Even CCITT standards have gray areas of interpretation. If all else fails, try switching vendors or versions. And don't forget applications-level protocols: The way a word processing program may store a backup text file to disk may have just as many consequences to LAN management as the status of a Netbios driver.

Network management

According to Louis Delzompo, Sun Microsystems Inc. (Mountain View, Calif.) product line manager for native networking, network gurus are often more concerned with problem management than change management, but change management may present more everyday problems to the network administrator.

Network management experts and harware-software combinations are often more concerned with fine-tuning peformance than, for example, making it possible for users to know when a network printer has run out of paper—a representative lower-level concern with little technical dazzle but of real interest to users. Network devices that are self-sensing will begin to come into use, but these may also introduce more sets of options for LAN managers to worry about. However, these may eat up server capacity and network bandwidth in the process.

Every network manager has to develop an individualized network management database (see "The dream database"). Counters that monitor events in real time are valuable, but they also use up precious network server memory and performance time. A problem log converted into a database file as a table of complaints may save time and make clear patterns of network disruptions. Doing so will aid in the preventive maintenance that can catch serious problems before they start to spread and cause real damage. Everyday familiarity with network performance can help network managers develop their intuition for how their networks should look—and to know when something is going awry.

A more interesting aspect of network management arises when networks break down. Often when networks fail, the attendant fancy network management utilities fail as well, leaving the administrator with the problem of trying to determine whether the network should be restored first or the network monitoring functions.

Simple network diagnostic tools should be available when complicated network management fails. For exam-

---

Hot tips for NetWare

Dirty cache buffers. If all cache buffers are dirty—that is, holding information not yet written to disk—then the server may run out of space to do its work and have to write to disk before it can process requests from applications. This is a slow and inefficient way of doing business.

If 50 percent or more of the cache buffers are dirty, users may either add memory, reduce the number of users, or remove applications. Alternatively, decreasing the number of buffers will free up memory if, at peak, they constitute 20 percent or less of the total available.

FAT. The File Allocation Table (FAT) maintains the size and location of files. Fatal FAT errors mean that the disk is bad. While NetWare can continue to operate after a fashion, this error message means the server could not read or write to either copy of FAT.

The server can function carelessly because FATs are cached, but once the server goes down, it won't come back up again. The trick here is to run a file-by-file backup. Backing up the disk as a whole will only cause a replication of the bad FAT.

Thrashing. When the server gets too many requests for available buffers, thrashing—or swapping buffers back and forth—will take place, thus degrading response time. Any thrashing is cause for concern. An upgrade may be the only solution.

Re-executed requests. If workstations are making repeated requests to the file server, the server may be having hardware problems (such as a bad board) or it may simply be overloaded.

Disk requests. As a rule of thumb, 80 percent or more of disk requests should be serviced from cache. Anything less is a sign that the server is overloaded.

Hot fix table size. This measure of faulty disk performance should be tracked weekly. If hot fixes to incorrect disk writes are increasing rapidly, throw the disk away.

Volumes. Check to see if the number of files during peak use of this disk partition is close to its maximum. If so, increase the maximum number of files. As the volume reaches maximum, it may crash. Also, check on the number of allowable and open files; if the average and peak number of files is way below what is allowable, adjust the maximum downward.

Packets. Discarded packets shouldn't appear if a network is designed correctly. If a server's power plug has been kicked out, users may still be sending messages to it, thus creating discarded packets. Discarded packets can come from destinations designated "unknown" or more than 16 bridges away. Lost outgoing and incoming packets are another sign of an overtaxed server.

Read and write errors. If this happens, reformat the disk. Then replace it if these errors continue. There shouldn't be any physical disk errors.

ple, using a binary search technique can help. Here, if point A cannot talk to point B but there are lots of cables and transceivers in between, it may be useful to see if it is possible to talk to a device set midpoint. Troubleshooters can either move farther away from the the midpoint incrementally, if communications up to that point are O.K., or move back toward the initiating point until a sound connection is achieved.

Network security needs to raise its ugly head, for the argument can be made that any network can be destroyed by the least privileged user. Multipathing and backdoors, which improve networking reliability and ease network troubleshooting, can also jeopardize network security. The recent publicity of viruses and hackers may bring network security issues to the attention of those who had never considered them a problem before, causing concern where it may not be necessary.

Network managers have to be thinking about the trade-offs between flexibility and security. Aside from FDDI, networking technology will probably not be making any huge leaps over the next few years. In turn, security, not management, may become the hot networking issue.

Rules of thumb

In addition, there are some hard-won networking bits of advice that may be able to save network managers some of the irritation that is their destiny. As Mike Hurwicz puts it: "Network managers are always either trying to prevent things from going wrong or having to deal with things that have gone wrong." Here a few pointers that may save LAN managers some grief:

Cherchez le toaster oven. Weird, intermittent problems occurring at regular intervals are often the result of cables and network devices placed too near machines setting up interference. 3Com's Dirk Martin reports that elevators, with their large magnets' and electric motors' heavy morning and afternoon rush-hour loads, brought down an entire network.

Bill Hancock says that a maddening error on an Ethernet was caused by a transceiver connection that was set too near a fan: Its oscillations jiggled the slidelock connector, playing havoc with the LAN.

Cables draped over fluorescent lights or too close to microwave ovens have also been implicated—lunch hour in this case was a clue to one network glitch. Mysterious once-a-week network interruptions have been caused by cables placed too near heavy-duty arc welders, which are used only on a weekly basis, or in the pathway of forklifts that only perform certain warehouse tasks one afternoon a week.

Even more primitive are the similar kinds of physical errors caused by sloppy installations. Telebit Corp.'s (Mountain View, Calif.) director of field technical support, Richard Vaughan, knows of one installation where strange disk errors cropped up twice a day, the result of an automated mail cart smashing into a disk server as it

Hot tips for NFS

NFS server not responding. This message probably means the server has timed out. It is a symptom of an overly congested network or possibly an indication that a time-out default is set too low.

Use the operating system's "Traffic" utility to check for congestion. If the load is within the network average of about 30 to 40 percent, then increase the length of the time-out. This will, however, have a negative effect on overall network performance.

I/O performance. If a server continues not to respond, use the server's "Perf Meter" tool to check on I/O performance. If the number of I/Os is near the theoretical maximum of 30 per second per controller, it's overloaded. Move files and applications off the server.

RPC Info. Run this utility from any machine on a network. It can check on the types of Remote Procedure Call (RPC) information available on any other machine on a network. It can determine whether NFS is active on that machine, which is another useful bit of information if a server is generating error messages.

Segmenting. There should be no more than 80 nodes per LAN segment. As the number of nodes on a segment nears 80, begin planning another segment.

Diskless workstations. To cut down on paging and swapping bottlenecks, figure on a maximum of 10 to 15 diskless workstations on the fastest NFS servers, and about seven to eight on entry-level servers.

Hardmount, softmount. While hardmounting—the freezing of an application when interrupted—is useful for critical applications, it is not necessary in most instances. Consider resetting the initial hardmount and foreground default settings of NFS devices to suit the applications. Switching the setting to background will allow other applications to be used while a failing application is frozen in hardmount. Softmounting all applications gives users maximum network flexibility. Use softmount where possible.

Net stat. Run this utility daily. It checks the cumulative operation of device interfaces. The number of collisions or packets lost shouldn't be above 20 percent. If the number is higher, a controller is getting bad. Replace it as soon as possible.

Consider this preventive maintenance. While it can only be invoked at one machine for that machine, it can specify what hardware and software is being served, how many bad calls have been made, and how many transmit or receive errors have occurred.

Top eight. Look at the top eight sending and receiving machines. If any unit is in the 30 to 40 percent range, the chances are that it is having problems, or that its associated transceiver is jabbering.

Flow control. NFS's datagram protocol does not now support adaptive retransmission algorithms, so users wanting to connect NFS-based networks over slower-speed gateways may run into bottleneck problems. A slowstart algorithm may bring some relief.

made its mail drops. The disk had been placed in the device's track, the result of a lack of space.

A case of four token ring stations disappearing to their server was solved by looking to a MAU placed on the floor. The unit had only been moved a few inches, but doing so had jiggled every cable—hence all relays shut down from the noise. Resetting the relays made the server rediscover the existence of the missing stations.

One of the more bizarre anecdotes of this sort, from Curtis Washington, involves the 40,000-node Air Force Logistics Command complex of LANs. Transfers between three far-flung DECnet subnets took far too long for no detectable reason—particularly after VAX communications start-up and shutdown problems had been solved and broadband amplifiers running higher than spec had been tuned down.

The problem, and the solution, finally surfaced when a storm, kicking off 100-mile-per-hour winds knocked out the computer room, necessitating a restart of the entire network. Some minute network component had clearly been crying out to be physically reset—and on a network that large, attempting to track it down would have been impractical.

Blame it on the new kid. As Cisco Systems' Forster puts it, the network subarea most recently changed is the area most likely to be the cause of problems. Vaughan stated it more strongly: Assume every change is catastrophic. The chances are that when one change is made (such as upgrading software), it will be decided that this is also the time for every other small and not-so-small change that has been in the offing to be made, compounding the problems of error detection and correction.

A corollary of this law is what Harry Saal, president of LAN test-equipment manufacturer Network General, calls "too good network performance." After a new card or network gizmo is installed, it may process packets far more efficiently than its predecessor (for example, forwarding packets at a much higher rate much closer together). And this could overwhelm small or nonexistent buffers of the other, installed devices, which then could start missing packets, having to retransmit, and generally creating a classic bottleneck.

The best solution, unfortunately, is to upgrade the entire network, which brings users back to the original axiom: when things go wrong, look at what's newly installed first.

Human, all too human. Mistyping has been the source of more than one network mishap. An incorrect phone number prevented middle-of-the-night network backups from taking place; the irate recipient of the erroneous nightly phone call was ready to call in the FBI to track down the intiator of what seemed to be a prank call. Misentered line speeds or costs have resulted in LAN traffic destined to go from San Francisco to Los Angeles making a detour by way of Japan.

Other rules to live by. Harry Saal is an optimist, noting

The dream database

What should go into a network management database is a subject of much research. The Internet's Management Information Base project, for example, goes into elaborate bit-and-byte detail. Here, however, is a general list of suggestions.

No network management database can possibly contain all of the following data or entries. But, as Mike Hurwicz of MTI Group (Nashville, Tenn.) says, every detail helps, down to knowing what kind of keyboards are attached to the workstations. As with any database, however, the repository for network management information is only as useful as the timeliness and the accuracy of its entries.

Location information. A physical map showing node and server locations is useful. Possible database entries include room numbers, desk locations, floor and building numbers, wiring closet, hub, and tap locations, device serial numbers, user names, network administrator names and phone numbers, node names, resource or logical names, IP addresses (if applicable), and Ethernet addresses (if applicable).

Who's connected to what. What servers are attached to the workstations? Which versions of which operating systems and what files are stored in each server? Which of these are kept locally in each workstation? Track network-licensed software and individually licensed software. What peripherals are attached to each device, and what cards and options are installed within each device? Record types of cables, length of cable runs, numbers of repeaters, servers, and users.

Performance information. Log packets received and transmitted, error rates (particularly on the network's heaviest users), instances where packets are too long or too short, CRC and alignment errors, numbers of collisions, statistical measures of network traffic highs, lows, and averages over time.

Where applicable, record classes of connections, electronic-mail traffic (balanced against file transfers), number of messages sent out, average age of messages waiting in queues, any retransmissions above predefined numbers, and listings of invalid addresses. Record the status of routing algorithms, listings of links that come down and go back up frequently, and the numbers of errors per gateway.

Security information. Who should have access to what? And for how long? Privilege levels.

---

that "all problems are solvable. It's their recognition that's the problem." Brad Walker, ever the realist, says that "Everyone has a list of problems that they can't solve. Forty percent will be solved by the next release of the software or hardware. Fifty percent will be solved by users tinkering with their own networks, or from solutions figured out by other users with similar networks. And 10 percent will always be with us." ∎

John F. McCool, Advanced Micro Devices, Sunnyvale, Calif.

FDDI: Getting to know the inside of the ring

This route map and phrase book on Fiber Distributed Data Interface suggests that unequaled fault tolerance, coupled with high data rates, is within easy reach for LANs.

Local area networks (LANs) are turning up in increasing numbers in the office and on the factory floor. Despite various protocol schemes, network designers are eagerly awaiting the next LAN generation. Applications in parallel processing, industrial control, internetworking, and real-time voice and video demand data rates that far exceed the standard protocols in use today. The Fiber Distributed Data Interface (FDDI) provides a solution for the designer eager for increased network bandwidth. This article uncovers the operation of FDDI's protocol by examining ring use, control of data transmission, and the procedures used to recover from ring errors.

FDDI is the protocol employed for a 100-Mbit/s token-passing physical ring using a fiber optic medium. The emerging FDDI standard is a result of the work of the American National Standards Institute X3T9.5 committee. The FDDI Media Access Control (MAC) executes a timed-token protocol. The timed-token approach allows the FDDI to offer synchronous and asynchronous service. The synchronous service provides guaranteed bandwidth and response time that suit the requirements of voice, video, and industrial-control data communications. The dynamic bandwidth sharing of the asynchronous service can be used for bursty traffic. Network access is deterministic in that the maximum time it takes for a token to circulate the ring is guaranteed. That is, network nodes always know how long it will be before they see the next token.

The three main application areas of the FDDI are back-end, backbone, and front-end. Back-end networks are used to connect mainframes and minicomputers along with associated high-speed peripheral controllers. Physical distance, typically, is not a major concern in back-end applications, since all the devices on the network often reside in the same room. These networks require high data rates to match the speeds of the devices they serve. Located at the nerve center of a computer facility, back-end networks must guarantee high reliability.

The backbone network finds its home in the campus environment. In an office setting, the backbone network connects many lower-speed LANs via gateways. Backbone networks must have sufficient speed to handle the aggregate loading from the lower-speed networks. With the guaranteed response time of FDDI's timed-token protocol and the inherent safety of the fiber media, FDDI is equally suited to be backbone network on the factory floor.

High-powered workstations coming to the desktop will place greater demands on existing office LANs. These front-end networks provide a communication channel between computers and shared resources within an area. The FDDI will not only reduce bottlenecks as front-end networks grow, it will also introduce new services. Specifically, FDDI's synchronous bandwidth scheme opens the door to real-time voice and video operation across the network.

For these diverse applications, FDDI's support of high data rates, its redundant dual ring that offers fault tolerance if the primary ring fails, and its ability to span large distances are appealing features.

Network topology

FDDI can accommodate up to 500 stations with a total fiber-path length of up to 100 kilometers. The standard defines two station types:
- Class A stations have two physical links to the ring.
- Class B stations have one physical connection and are used in conjunction with a wiring concentrator. These stations sit only on the primary ring, trading redundancy for the lower cost of a single media connection.

Figure 1 illustrates an FDDI network composed of Class A and Class B stations. The wiring concentrator is actually a special case of the Class A station. It has two connections

1. Network topology. *Class-B stations are connected only to the primary ring and do not have the fault-tolerance advantage available with the redundant ring.*

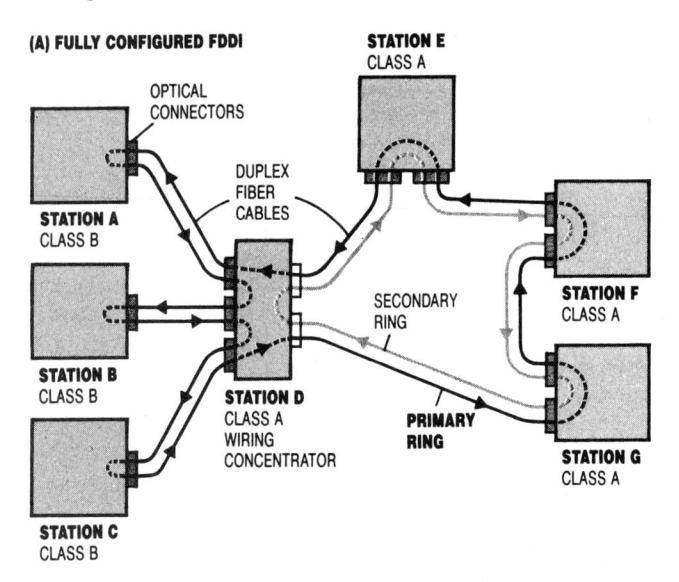

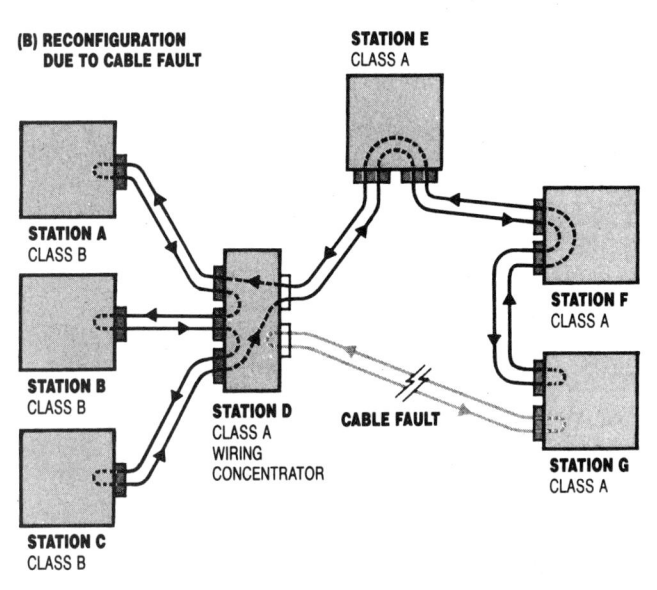

(A) FULLY CONFIGURED FDDI

(B) RECONFIGURATION DUE TO CABLE FAULT

FDDI = FIBER DISTRIBUTED DATA INTERFACE

to the main ring, with single connections to the Class B attachments. Figure 1A shows a fully configured ring with no broken cables. The arrows indicate the direction of data flow on the counter-operating rings. The Class B stations are connected only to the primary ring via the concentrator. All stations are attached to the ring with a duplex fiber cable. The cable houses both fibers in a single jacket and the two fibers can be terminated with a single duplex connector. Class A-to-Class A can connect to concentrator-to-Class B with the same hardware.

Figure 1B shows the same FDDI network suffering from a cable fault between Station D and Station G. The FDDI compensates by channeling the data back through the secondary ring. (Whether to allow any traffic on the secondary ring during normal operation is currently being debated in committee.) When the faulty link is detected by the neighboring Stations G and D, it is isolated.

Built for speed

FDDI is similar to the IEEE 802.5 token-passing ring. In fact, many of the initial FDDI concepts evolved from the 802.5 standard. There are, however, a number of key differences that make FDDI better suited to high-speed operation.

One important area that sets the FDDI apart from other low-speed LAN protocols is its data-encoding method. The 802.5 physical-layer protocol uses a differential Manchester scheme. In this scheme, each data bit transferred to the network requires a transition in the middle of the bit cell (the time it takes to transmit one bit of information). If the bit is a zero, an additional transition is made at the beginning of the bit cell.

The FDDI uses a group-encoding scheme referred to as 4B/5B. The group-encoding technique maps four bits of data to be transmitted into a five-bit code output to the network. The five-bit codes are selected to ensure a maximum of three bit times between level transitions, which is required to guarantee sufficient clock information at the receiver. With the 4B/5B scheme, 100 megabits of data translates to 125 Mbit/s on the network. Using the differential Manchester scheme would require a 200-Mbit/s rate. The lower data rate translates to lower-speed light-emitting diode transmitters, positive-intrinsic-negative diodes, and digital front-end logic, resulting in lower costs.

The Media Access Controller protocol is similarly tuned for high-speed operation. The MAC scheme is designed to allow for nibble-wide (four-bit) or byte-wide (eight-bit) manipulation. In other words, the MAC can function by processing and altering the incoming data stream as a series of bytes as opposed to bits. Bit-level manipulation would require processing hardware equal to the 100-Mbit/s network data rate. Nibble-wide or byte-wide processing reduces the required processing speed accordingly.

Not only are the FDDI protocols streamlined for high-speed operation, but the MAC algorithm itself is also modified to take full advantage of the available bandwidth. Another area where the 802.5 and FDDI rings diverge relates to issuing tokens after data transmission. In the 802.5 ring, a station must wait for the first packet it transmitted to circulate the ring and return to its receiver before it can issue a token. FDDI allows a station to issue a token immediately following the last packet it sends. This scheme does not require a station to hold the token, tying up available bandwidth for a period of time.

Strong as the weakest link

The easiest way to examine the workings of the FDDI is to follow the development of an FDDI ring from its start-up. Figure 2A shows a three-node network upon initialization. The internal interconnections between the physical layer components (PHY) and the MACs are detailed. In this example, all three stations are Class A. The direction of data flow in the network is signified by the arrows.

During start-up, the ring is broken down into a series of minirings. A miniring is made up of two PHYs and at least one MAC. Link integrity is guaranteed at the PHY level through a physical-connection management protocol. The physical-connection manager exchanges a series of FDDI control characters called line states to execute a handshake. Each PHY has its own line manager so that both minirings connecting to the station function independently.

Once the handshake is complete, the physical-connection manager signals the active condition to station-connection management, which represents the next layer of protocol that is responsible for the internal connections within the node. After both line managers determine that their respective links are functional, the station-connection protocol switches the node into the through mode.

Figure 2B shows Station B in the through mode. Since station-connection management operates asynchronously between stations, not everyone will reach the through mode at the same time. This effectively expands the ring; more and more minirings are joined by stations entering the through mode until the ring reaches the final configuration shown in Figure 2C.

Physical-connection management and station-connection management continue to operate even after the final configuration is achieved. The physical-connection manager can detect a broken or damaged link with its neighboring PHY and lower the signal, indicating that the link is available for use. This allows the station managers in the neighboring nodes to respond by channeling the data flow back onto the secondary ring. In this manner, a faulty link is isolated from the FDDI.

Up and running

After a ring is established, two things must occur. First, a token must be issued. A reliable mechanism must ensure that only one station can transmit at a time, so one and only one station receives the opportunity to issue this token. Second, it is useful to establish an upper bound on the time it takes for a token to circulate around the ring. This upper bound should be determined by the station whose application requires the fastest token-rotation time.

The MAC claim process determines which node will be responsible for issuing the token as well as the average- and worst-case token-rotation times. The claim process begins when one or more MACs detect the need for ring initialization and enter the claim state. In the claim state, an FDDI MAC continually transmits a packet called a claim frame. This frame begins with a start delimiter followed by a single-byte frame-control (FC) field. The FC field for claim frames uniquely identifies these packets. The destination-address and source-address fields in the claim frame are both set equal to the address of the originator. The first four bytes of the information field contain the station's bid for the target token-rotation time (TTRT).

FDDI MAC receivers continually process incoming claim frames. When a claim frame is received, the incoming bid is compared with the station's requested TTRT. Claim frames received with bid-field values greater than the requested

2. Growth of an FDDI ring. In (A), the ring data paths form three separate rings. Link b-c is operable through the connection-management handshake.

(A) RING AT START-UP

(B) STATION B IN THROUGH MODE

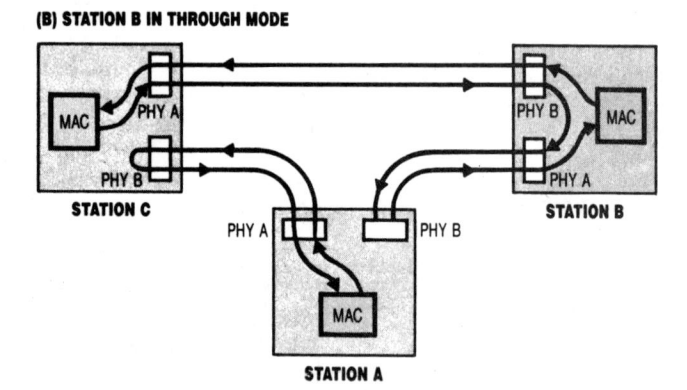

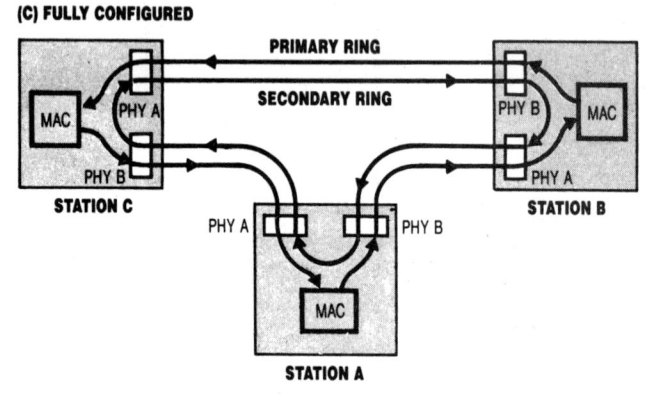

(C) FULLY CONFIGURED

MAC = MEDIA ACCESS CONTROL
PHY = PHYSICAL LAYERS

value, referred to as higher claims, represent requests for a TTRT faster than the time bid by the receiving station. Likewise, lower claims signify requests for a slower TTRT.

The claim process is designed so that the station requiring the fastest TTRT will win the bidding. Should two or more stations happen to request identical time values, the bidding is resolved by comparing the length and magnitude of the address fields. The MAC defers to requests for a faster TTRT. MAC stops transmitting its own claim frames when the first higher claim is received. Subsequent higher claims are repeated. Conversely, MAC begins or continues to transmit its claim frames when a lower claim is received.

Every MAC receiver remembers the bid value of the last higher claim. When the claim process is complete, this value represents the negotiated TTRT. Eventually, every station on the ring will defer to the station requesting the fastest TTRT. This station realizes that it has won the bidding process when it receives its own claim frame. The claim winner then initializes the ring by issuing a token.

Dividing the pie

The claim process determines how often a token will be received by a station on the FDDI ring. This does not guarantee that the station will be able to capture the token and transmit data. In order to provide that guarantee, the FDDI supports synchronous and asynchronous transmission service. Asynchronous data can only be transmitted when the token arrives at a station earlier than expected. Synchronous data can be sent whenever the token arrives.

In order to maintain the TTRT negotiated in the claim process, the amount of data each station can transmit under the synchronous service must be limited. The sum of the maximum allowable synchronous transmission times by all stations is bound by the negotiated TTRT.

When a station receives the first token after the claim process, the negotiated TTRT is remembered. The FDDI protocol is designed so that the negotiated TTRT translates into the average token-rotation time seen by a given station. The protocol also guarantees that the worst-case delay the token will experience while circulating the ring will never exceed twice the negotiated TTRT.

FDDI provides this guarantee by ensuring that the sum of the times required for synchronous transmission from all stations (the synchronous-bandwidth pool) plus the sum of the times required for asynchronous transmission from all stations (the asynchronous-bandwidth pool) is no greater than the TTRT. But instead of fixing the limit on asynchronous transmission, the FDDI timed-token protocol has the ability to dynamically transfer any unused bandwidth from the synchronous pool to the asynchronous pool.

The percentage and allotment of synchronous bandwidth are determined by the bandwidth-allocation process. At the conclusion of this process, each station requesting synchronous bandwidth will be assigned a time value. This value represents the maximum time the station can transmit using the synchronous service on a given token rotation. The sum of these values around the ring yields the value of the synchronous-bandwidth pool. Hence, the available time remaining for asynchronous transmission is determined by the outcome of bandwidth allocation.

Ring scheduling

To limit the average token-rotation time, each station controls the amount of data it forwards to the ring. For synchronous transmission, the amount forwarded is limited by the number assigned by the bandwidth-allocation algorithm. For asynchronous transmission, the amount of data forwarded is variable. The amount of time available for asynchronous transmission is a function of the unallocated and unused bandwidth on the ring.

To control access to the network, FDDI uses the TTRT negotiated in the claim process in conjunction with two internal timers, called the token-rotation timer (TRT) and the token-holding timer (THT). As the name implies, the TRT measures the time between the receipt of tokens. It is said to expire when it reaches a value that exceeds the target token-rotation time. If this occurs, a late counter (LC) is incremented, and the TRT will begin to count from the time of expiration until receipt of the next token. The second timer, the THT, measures the time that the station holds the token while sending asynchronous packets.

The rules for data transmission on FDDI depend upon the type of data to be sent. For transmission of synchronous data, the rules are straightforward. The amount of synchronous data that can be transmitted on a given token opportunity is limited by the bandwidth-allocation process. Bandwidth allocation ensures that if every station transmits its maximum allotment of synchronous data, the negotiated TTRT will not be exceeded.

The transmission of asynchronous data is slightly more complicated, since the maximum time allotted for transmission is not constant. Instead, a station can transmit asynchronous data until the unused bandwidth on the ring is exhausted. The two timers are used to determine the amount of unused bandwidth on a given token rotation.

Basically, asynchronous transmission can occur on any token rotation that is faster than the TTRT. The difference between the TTRT and the actual token-rotation time is a measure not only of unused asynchronous bandwidth, but also of any unused synchronous bandwidth for that particular token rotation. This difference dictates the amount of time available for asynchronous data transmission.

The mechanics of controlling the asynchronous transmission lie in the operation of the timers within each FDDI station. When a token arrives, the TRT is set equal to the TTRT. The TRT immediately begins to count down; it expires if a zero value is reached. If this occurs, it is reloaded with the target time and the LC is set. If a token arrives and the LC is zero (indicating early token arrival), the value remaining on the TRT is loaded into the THT. Again, the TRT is reloaded with the target-rotation time. The THT will count down only during asynchronous data transmission. When the THT expires (reaches zero), the station must wait for the next early token arrival to send asynchronous data.

Figure 3 illustrates an example of this operation by displaying the values of the TRT, THT, and LC for a particular station on an FDDI ring. In this example, the negotiated target rotation time is 100 milliseconds (ms). This station's synchronous bandwidth allotment is limited, in this example, to 30 ms. Significant events are indicated along the timer line with letters.

Event (a) marks the arrival of a token. The token is not captured because there is no data to transmit. The TRT is set to the 100-ms target value. At event (b), the token arrives back at the originating station 40 ms earlier than the target time. The 40-ms time is remembered by loading the

73

3. Fairness doctrine. *The FDDI protocol promotes fair and deterministic access to network resources for all stations. This is done using a timer that measures the time between token arrivals, a timer that controls how long a token can be held for transmission, and a counter that indicates the number of times the token arrives later than expected.*

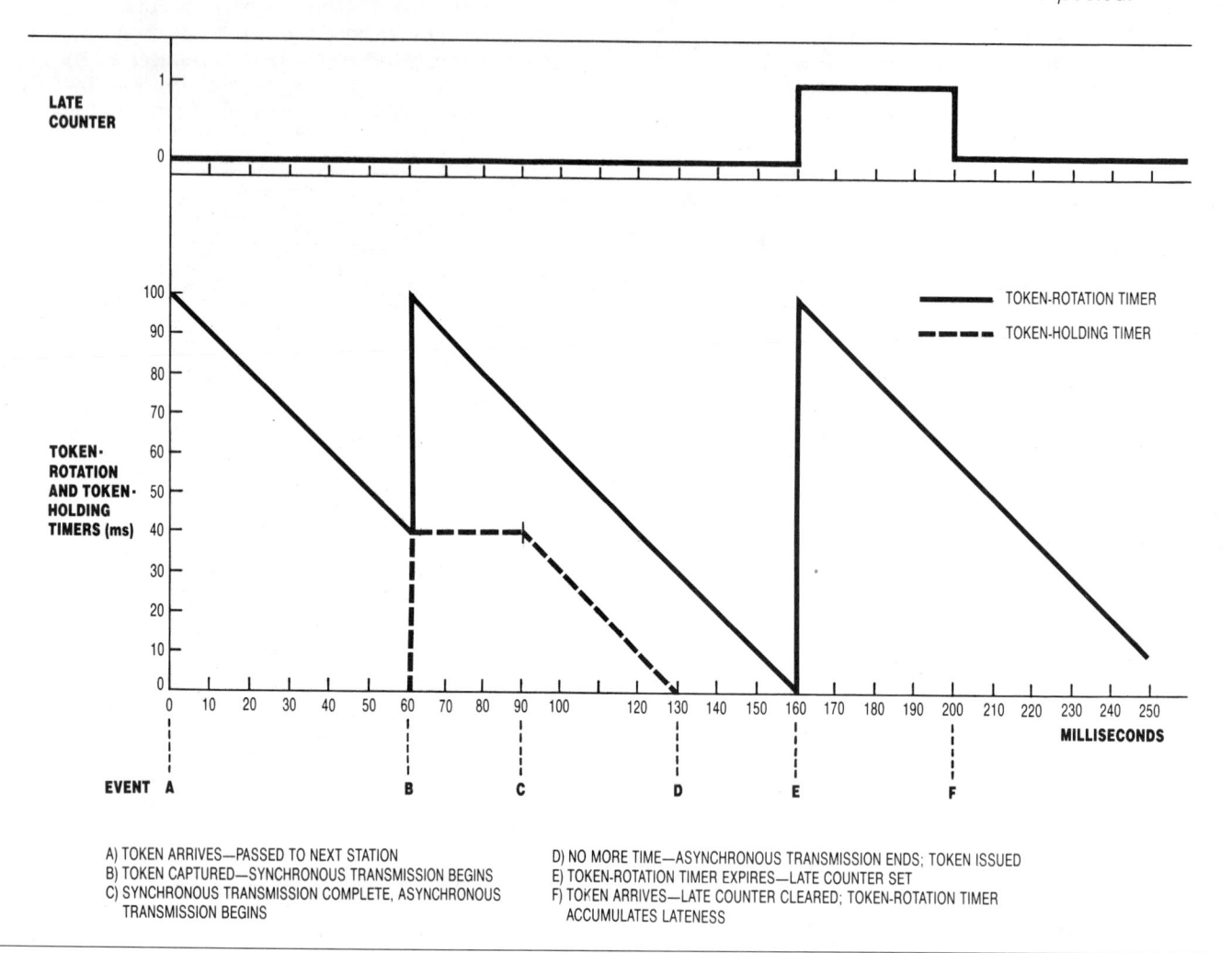

— TOKEN-ROTATION TIMER
--- TOKEN-HOLDING TIMER

A) TOKEN ARRIVES—PASSED TO NEXT STATION
B) TOKEN CAPTURED—SYNCHRONOUS TRANSMISSION BEGINS
C) SYNCHRONOUS TRANSMISSION COMPLETE, ASYNCHRONOUS TRANSMISSION BEGINS
D) NO MORE TIME—ASYNCHRONOUS TRANSMISSION ENDS; TOKEN ISSUED
E) TOKEN-ROTATION TIMER EXPIRES—LATE COUNTER SET
F) TOKEN ARRIVES—LATE COUNTER CLEARED; TOKEN-ROTATION TIMER ACCUMULATES LATENESS

TRT remainder into the THT. The TRT is set and begins counting. The station begins to send its 30-ms allotment of synchronous data.

The fact that the TRT is reloaded at (b) is significant. In this way, FDDI stations count their own data transmission against the next token-rotation time. This allows for fair access to the available asynchronous bandwidth.

The station sends its entire synchronous-bandwidth allotment from (b) to (c). At (c), asynchronous transmission begins and the THT begins counting. Event (d) marks the expiration of the THT. No more asynchronous transmission can occur. Since the station has already used its allotted synchronous bandwidth, a token must be issued.

Event (e) marks the expiration of the TRT. The LC is incremented and the timer is reloaded, because the timer expired before the token arrived. Finally, at (f), the token arrives and the LC is cleared. The TRT is not reloaded, however. This allows the FDDI station to accumulate the lateness (the measure of how much later than the expected TTRT the token arrived; by not resetting the timer, a record is kept of how tardy the token's arrival was from the previous rotation time). This accumulation of lateness is required to guarantee the upper bound of twice the negotiated target time.

The timed-token protocol is further refined in FDDI to include the concept of priority. Asynchronous frames can be categorized into eight priority levels. Each priority has an associated time value. This time is compared against the time remaining on the THT. If the priority time is less than the time remaining on the THT, frames with that priority assignment can be transmitted. Those frames will continue to be transmitted until the value of the timer falls below the threshold.

Access restricted

In applications where large bursts of traffic are applied to the ring from high-speed storage devices, it may be desirable to set up a dialogue using the ring's unallocated bandwidth. FDDI provides a means for multiple stations on an FDDI ring to use the entire available asynchronous bandwidth. The restricted token is the mechanism for exclusive use of the asynchronous bandwidth pool.

Restricted tokens are distinguished by different frame-control fields. The winner of the claim process always initializes the ring by issuing the unrestricted token. Like the unrestricted token, the restricted token can always be captured for the purpose of transmitting synchronous data. Asynchronous transmission requests, however, capture the restricted token only when enabled by the management protocol outside of MAC.

Restricted-access control follows a simple rule. A station wishing to initiate a restricted dialogue can do so only by capturing an unrestricted token. This prevents multiple restricted dialogues on the same ring. The initiator informs the participants that restricted dialogue has begun and issues the restricted token. After receiving the information from the initiator, participants can enable their MAC for asynchronous transmission on restricted tokens. Finally, one of the stations involved in the dialogue will act as the terminator; the restricted token is captured, the final dialogue message is sent, and the unrestricted token is issued.

What can go wrong?
Realizing that we don't live in a perfect digital world, FDDI's designers gave it the means for detecting and isolating persistent ring errors. The most obvious problem happens when somebody pulls the plug. Should the power go off, an FDDI node equipped with optical-bypass relays will channel light from the primary optical inputs to the primary optical outputs and similarly on the secondary ring. The FDDI standard is designed to operate with up to three consecutive stations optically bypassed.

Another obvious fault occurs when the optical fiber between two stations is removed or broken. The physical connection between FDDI stations is actually a pair of fibers. This fiber pair represents one link of the primary ring and one link of the counter-rotating secondary ring. When a link of either type is broken, the problem can be detected by the physical-connection managers in the stations on both sides of the break and by the MACs monitoring the dialogue on that ring.

At the MAC level, cable faults are manifested as periods of silence. The MAC could react in response to the following possible events depending upon its state at the time of the break:

- First, the MAC could detect that the token is missing. This is determined by the fact that the token has already been late once (LC = 1) and the TRT expired.
- Had the MAC just seen the token prior to the break, it might have reacted to the fact that it had not seen a valid transmission in an abnormally long time. MAC maintains a valid-transmission timer that measures the time between properly formed frames. The error is recognized when the valid-transmission timer crosses a threshold value.

If either error is recognized, the MAC will try to recover by initiating the claim process.

If the cable fault is not corrected, the claim will fail. The MACs will realize that the time spent in claim recovery has been excessive. This sends the ring into the beacon process. In the beacon state, the MAC continually transmits a specially formed frame with a unique frame-control field called a beacon frame. The MAC continues to send these frames until it receives a beacon from farther up in the link. If another station beacon is received, the MAC repeats subsequent frames. Eventually, the only station left beaconing on the ring will be that station located downstream from the cable fault.

Even as the MACs attempt recovery of the broken ring, the physical-connection and station-connection managers at both sides of the break are at work correcting the problem. The physical-connection manager downstream from the break fails to detect line activity. In response, the downstream connection manager informs its station-connection manager and forces control symbols in the other direction. This informs the upstream neighbor of the problem and causes it to indicate an inactive connection. Had both fibers been detached, the physical-connection managers in the two stations would reach an independent conclusion that the link was not functional.

With the physical-connection managers indicating a faulty link, the data paths in the stations on both sides of the break are altered to use the secondary ring. As the ring is repaired, the beacon frames being transmitted will start to return to the originator. The MAC receiving its own beacon frames will realize the ring has been healed. This MAC will stop beaconing and begin the claim process to re-initialize the ring.

Besides overt problems such as loss of power and interconnection, subtle problems can occur. Marginal links can result from faulty components, improper connection mating, or violation of the station-distance limits. A marginal link may work well enough to go undetected by the physical-connection manager while still degrading network performance. In FDDI, packets are protected by a 32-bit cyclic redundancy check (CRC) value transmitted in the packet's frame-check-sequence field. On reception, the validity of packets is determined by checking the CRC.

Packets are also transmitted with an error-indicator field following the end delimiter that can be altered as the data flows around the ring. All packets are transmitted with the error indicator as an R, or reset, symbol. When a station detects a CRC error, it alters the error indicator at the end of the packet to an S, or set, symbol. If the indicator was received as an R, the station knows it was the first to recognize the error and increments an error counter. Subsequent stations will see an S-error indicator and will not increment their error counters. In addition to the error counter, each station maintains a count of valid frames received. Thus, stations with abnormally high ratios of error count to frame count point to a marginal upstream link.

FDDI standards offer a rich set of features designed to meet the requirements of many network applications. Network use can be tailored to suit a variety of needs. ∎

John F. McCool is a section manager with Advanced Micro Devices, specializing in high-end networking products. He earned his B. S. E. E. from Drexel University in Philadelphia in 1982.

Section 3
Network Management

Kerry Kosak, Desience Corp., Malibu, Calif.

Designing network control centers for greater productivity

A little ergonomics in network control center design goes a long way toward improving output and boosting NCC staff morale

Despite the fact that networks play a key part in corporate activity, little attention is being paid to the nerve center of this function: the network control center. The corporate approach to control center design today runs the gamut from models of efficiency to routinely backlogged, poorly utilized resources. Although a properly designed environment is not the final answer to maximizing human and hardware productivity, recent studies have confirmed that it can go a long way toward improving a less-than-ideal situation.

Part of the problem is that private networks are still novel at many companies, so the concept of a specialized place dedicated to network operations tends to get short shrift. Another factor is that there are few historical studies of optimal command center design.

At the heart of the problem, though, is the intensity of the human/machine interface. The problem is not without precedent. Consider recent technological history: The same problem has already been faced in the scientific and financial communities, both of which provide an excellent starting point for deciding how to build a better data/voice network control center.

Perhaps one of the most vivid images of the last two

1. Form and function. Functional requirements should dictate network control center design. Financial trading requires quick and constant access to two primary sets of equipment: on-line monitors and a telephone. Since traders often work in groups, a systematic means of clustering is needed. And the trading floor aesthetics are also important.

decades is the rows of NASA controllers monitoring individual data terminals during a spacecraft launch. With at least one monitor per person and numerous monitors per spacecraft function, there was need for a well-organized environment that allowed both individual monitor attention and attention to the project's full progression. This was accomplished by arranging low banks of monitors, one per analyst, facing wall displays providing an overview of the entire project.

If the ergonomics of control center design seems to be overstatement of the obvious, consider the following specific design parameters:
- What is the optimum height of the monitor so that it can be the primary focus but still be looked over if needed?
- How deep should the counter in front of it be?
- How close can the monitors be to one another?
- How close can the people be?
- What accommodations should there be for telephones, lighting, and wire management?
- How do you provide for equipment service and changes?

All of these issues contribute to formulating preliminary mechanical-design needs, but equally important is an understanding of each job function and specific needs associated with carrying out that function. To illustrate the importance of function, consider a well-designed trading module used by financial institutions.

The job of trading requires quick and constant access to two primary sets of equipment, the on-line monitors and the telephone. Further, because traders often work in groups, a systematic means of clustering people in either an open floor plan or in rows is a prerequisite, and equipment changes are constant.

Therefore, a well-designed trading module requires flexibility for differing floor plans, modularity to handle diverse and changing equipment, a high level of equipment density, and adequate space for documentation and personal storage (Fig. 1).

To add a little more sophistication to the design equation, factor in the trend toward using the trading floor as a showplace in many financial institutions. Suddenly, aesthetics become relatively important and hidden-wire management, as well as data, telephone-line, and power access must all be juggled without jeopardizing crucial mechanical and ergonomic design elements.

Organization

Designers of specialized environments, such as those seen in financial institutions, have amassed a body of experience that other on-line applications can use. When the lessons learned on the trading floor are combined with the ergonomic work done by many companies and institutions, a substantial pool of data is available that can be applied to the specific needs of the network control environment.

The first thing that is obvious when entering a network

2. Pain in the neck? Viewing tiers of monitors can often lead to fatigue and neck strain, but when the screens are angled 10 degrees from the vertical, they become easy to see from either a sitting or a standing position.

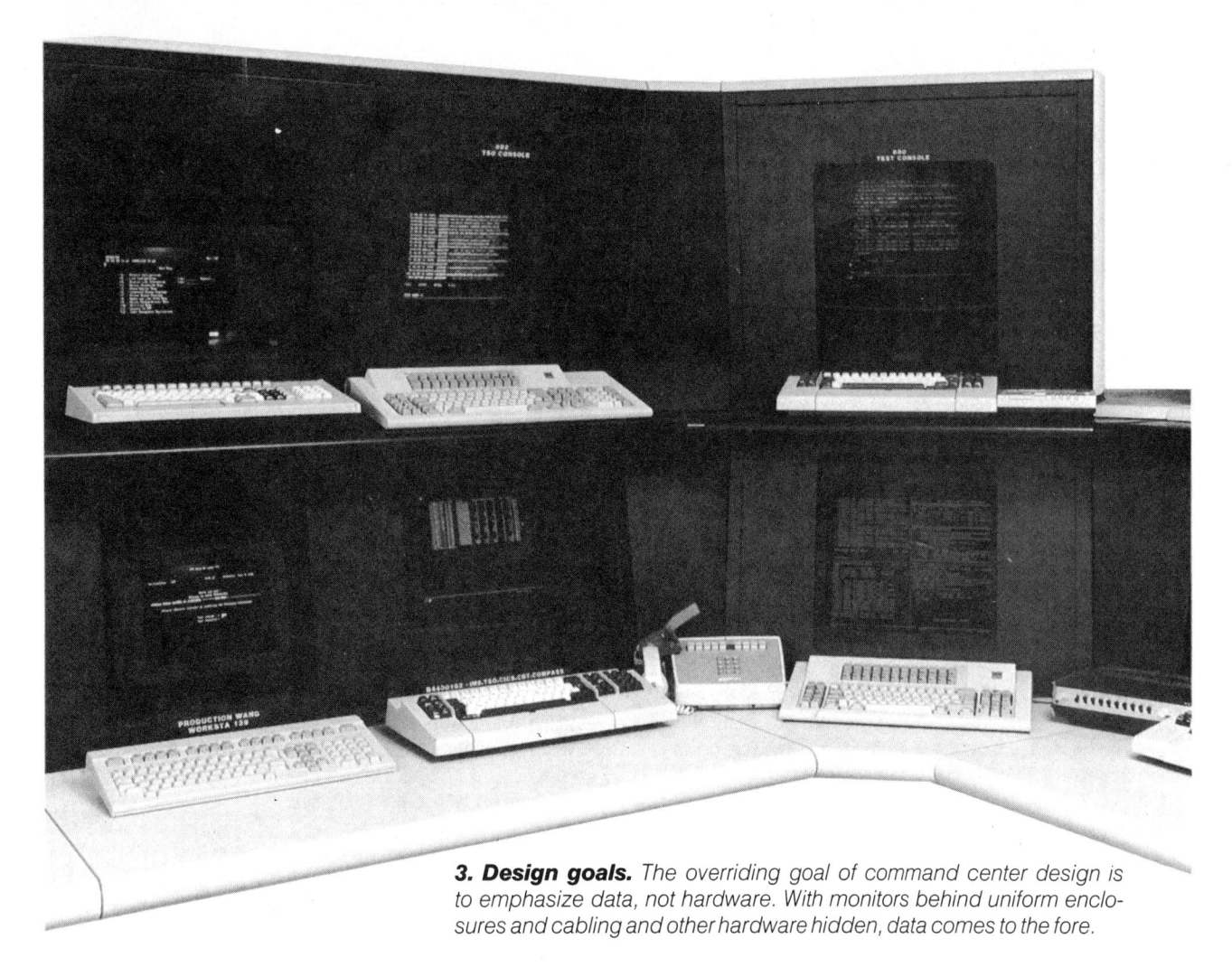

3. Design goals. *The overriding goal of command center design is to emphasize data, not hardware. With monitors behind uniform enclosures and cabling and other hardware hidden, data comes to the fore.*

control center is the ratio of monitors to personnel. In the financial environment, there are generally three or four monitors per person in a defined workstation. In the network control center, it is more common to find several people interacting with common monitors.

This arrangement is further complicated by the fact that different staff operations often share the same space. For example, it is not uncommon to see systems analysts, technicians, and a help desk all in the control area, all sharing the same hardware to one degree or another. Therefore, organization, ease of presentation, and access to a high density of monitors become critical concerns—problems that can be easily complicated when space is restricted or at a premium.

The design solution is vertical stacking. However, since a person may view a stacked monitor from either a sitting or a standing position, optimizing the dimensions and layout of the stacks is critical. Setting the design dimensions compatible with people from five feet to six feet, two inches tall will cover approximately 95 percent of the population. Beginning with a standard desktop height of 29 inches supporting the first tier, the second monitor tier will top out at just about six feet. This height precludes realistic options for a third tier, since it would be almost impossible to access and difficult to see from a sitting position.

Designing the monitor location in the second tier for viewing from a seated position creates other problems. First, because every monitor generally requires that a keyboard be placed in front of it, there should always be a shelf with enough depth to handle the largest keyboard in use (approximately 12 inches deep). Therefore, the viewer will always be looking up and over the shelf. A straight vertical presentation of the second tier monitor can be easily viewed by someone in a standing position but is difficult to see when sitting.

The optimum relationship between an upper and a lower screen is to have both fall within a 20-degree cone of vision of the seated analyst. This requires that each monitor screen be angled approximately 10 degrees from the vertical, which facilitates seeing both screens from either position (Fig. 2).

At the network control site for one of the largest insurance companies in the United States, these design techniques permitted the consolidation of three staff groups into a control area 40 percent smaller than the area previously reserved for the systems analysts. With the addition of two more groups to the same work area, management reported that the ability to quickly pull together people from diverse disciplines for any given problem resulted in a higher level of efficiency and improved customer service.

Accentuating the functional

Beyond organizational and staffing aspects, the functional and mechanical needs of the control center hardware must be addressed. The mechanical layout must provide easy access to monitoring equipment in both tiers, and such things as data lines, power, and air-conditioning access are all essential aspects of the well-designed network operations center. The design of the screen-support stack should be adaptable enough to handle a diverse range of monitor sizes and types and be structurally solid enough to avoid any chance of tipping over when loaded with monitors. These are primary concerns in any design that is freestanding in an open control room space.

Lighting and glare reduction

The most overlooked aspect of control room design is lighting. Generally speaking, most control rooms have too much light and the wrong type. At the center of the problem is screen glare. The reflective nature of the monitor-screen surface in a highly lit environment can become a major distraction to an operator at a terminal. Part of the problem can be alleviated by using a nonreflective surface to cover the monitor, although high levels of light can still wash out the data.

Another aspect of the lighting problem is that despite the fact that it is easier to read a screen in a low-light environment, analysts have reading, writing, and keying tasks to perform on an ongoing basis. The optimum solution for these seemingly conflicting needs is not as complicated as one might imagine. The key is simply to provide controlled light only where needed. This can be accomplished by providing adequate task illumination on the horizontal work surface, supplemented with adjustable indirect ambient lighting kept at minimal levels.

The best solution appears to be built-in direct lighting from a position overhanging the work surface. By using louvered grilles, light can actually be channeled to spill on the horizontal plane of the desktop in front of a monitor. This will provide adequate task lighting for operators without creating a wash or reflection on the monitor screen, while allowing ambient lighting to be reduced significantly.

What happens when area lighting is poorly planned? The experience of a large East Coast securities company sheds some light on this type of problem. The company's new command center was designed to be situated in the room with the mainframe and the support hardware. It was placed on a platform six inches above the computer floor. The additional height, combined with a generally high level of fluorescent lighting, immediately caused glare problems, even though nonreflective screens were in place.

Although the network-operations personnel were looking forward to an integrated control environment, the lighting conditions caused problems. Most of the personnel were frustrated, a few openly complained that they could not work there. The lighting problem added more stress to the settling in and bringing network operations on-line.

The lighting problem was eventually corrected by reducing the overhead light directly above the control environment. But it did require electricians to reopen ceiling access for a period of days, thereby delaying the start-up of a fully functioning installation.

In the grand scheme of things, glare may seem an oversight, but only because it was easily correctable. One only had to hear the complaints of the analysts to understand how critical the proper design of lighting is to the entire command center.

The lighting issue underscores the single overriding goal in control center design: Emphasize the data, not the hardware. In fact, in the perfect environment, all data is contrast-enhanced and well presented; all hardware is practically invisible and almost totally silent (Fig. 3).

A well-designed network control room eliminates all visual distractions. Irregular monitor shapes, cabling, and other hardware are obscured by enclosing the monitors in a dark, nonreflective cabinet. However, enclosing monitors requires forethought to provide functional solutions that facilitate accessibility, ventilation, and wire management.

Another major distraction is noise. Noise is important when deciding on the proximity of the command center to printers and other distractions associated with network hardware. Many companies have used glass enclosures contiguous to the actual hardware area to set off the command center. This helps organize space as well as cut down the noise level in the command environment.

To analysts with so many critical responsibilities, providing an area secure from hardware noise is a definite advantage. In this environment, enclosures can reduce the low-frequency hum of the monitors. There is also a variety of enclosure setups that can reduce printer noise by as much as 90 percent.

Advance planning: the critical criteria

How can networking professionals plan for the future in operations center design? In most instances, the impetus for designing a new command environment is the projected growth of the network. At the command center, growth is compounded by other concerns, such as the phasing in and out of computer hardware and telecommunications equipment. All of these factors have an obvious impact on proper design.

One way to get a handle on these issues is to examine an individual company and follow its planning and design decisions. For security reasons, the company will be called the ABC Corp. It is a holding company for firms in a variety of related industries.

Several years ago, following a change in management, ABC began an aggressive program of acquisition. Some companies remained self-contained subsidiaries, while others were folded into the parent company for economic reasons.

Under this regime, the company's revenues have increased more than fivefold, while management information systems (MIS) capabilities have increased proportionately. At the beginning of the acquisition process, the MIS function was performed in a single large room, but it soon became a series of installations spread throughout a midwestern city. Before MIS consolidation began, three mainframes were located in different parts of the city.

One of the first steps for integrating MIS functions was to build an advanced network consisting of both fiber optic and leased lines. The experience gained from this venture gave MIS operations personnel the confidence to assume responsibility for monitoring and maintaining telecommunications throughout the company.

Three years ago, ABC management realized that it was approaching critical mass and began the planning process

4. Workin' on the railroad. *As the network control center becomes equivalent to the nerve cneter of an entire company, it becomes the paradigm of corporate culture and capabilities. The layout of Burlington Northern's network operations center made monitoring and control operations easier, while the improved asthetics made the command center a company showplace.*

for a centralized command environment that could match projected company growth into the next decade. Three overriding concerns directed their efforts:
- Accommodating all present and future mainframe needs.
- Consolidating the monitoring setups for telecommunications and MIS environmental and support services.
- Planning a three-phase expansion to facilitate growth.

ABC's new data center, only recently completed, is an impressive example of the importance of advance planning. The command center is the geographic center of an installation that takes up the entire floor of a medium-size office building. As such, the command center serves as a functional hub for all the diverse operations it monitors and maintains. The semicircular, double-tiered monitor banks built of modular enclosures, the back wall containing all security, power, and environmental monitoring equipment, and the nearby lounge area for the analysts are all the result of comprehensive planning.

Within the security area, taking up roughly half the floor, are all printing, mainframe, disk-drive, telecommunications, and power resources. The other side of the floor houses offices for the management and support staff. In each of the areas, color schemes, furniture, wall treatment, and lighting have been coordinated for continuity as well as for the needs of specific working environments.

Despite the striking visual impact, an equal amount of precise planning lies behind the walls to accommodate expansion. First, power, cooling, and environmental monitoring and control have all been overbuilt, allowing the raised floor area to be expanded by more than 20 percent with easy access to needed services. Non-weight-bearing modular walls have been used extensively to allow expansion and reconfiguration of the existing center. All of these elements are geared for anticipated MIS growth, which is expected to double again by the end of the decade.

ABC hired a consulting contractor to both plan and execute the work. According to the network-operations manager, this decision was made early in the discussion phase, since ABC realized the importance of support services and that control center design was one area where it lacked the proper expertise.

ABC knew its specific operational needs, but it relied upon the consultants to provide recommendations about power and environmental monitoring—including water detection, main and backup air-conditioning, and Halon fire suppression—as well as security.

A majority of the support-function monitors has been integrated into the back wall of the center. This was done to make the command center a completely functional nerve center in the event of an emergency, an operational consideration often overlooked in the design phase of new centers. Such features as multizoned fire suppression, two-tiered security, and redundant cooling are added dimensions to traditional plans that can become important for both expansion and emergency contingencies.

Human elements

Hardware is not the only important issue, however. As the example of area lighting demonstrated, the needs of the personnel must also be given high priority. Once the explicit design criteria have been met, attention should be paid to the specific needs of the individuals.

The personnel staffing the center should have adequate storage for personal effects and basic supplies. Additionally, storage space for hardware and software documentation should be both plentiful and accessible.

Where monitor banks are stacked two tiers high on a desktop base, adequate work space should be accounted for in the design. However, desktops that are part of the monitor tiers should be set back deeply enough to accommodate either two keyboards (front and back) or a single keyboard and standard binders of documentation. This allows the analyst to use the documentation and keyboard simultaneously on the work surface without requiring cumbersome under-counter pull-out trays or using the analyst's lap as an extension of the work surface. This need is apparent when a software analyst works for several hours without adequate surface area.

Consideration should also be given to where the analysts can spend their time when not specifically working in the control environment. In highly secure areas, one might follow the example of ABC, which built an analyst lounge right off the main secure corridor between the disk-drive operations area and the command center.

Operators' performance can also be enhanced by providing safety features such as structural stability, fireproof construction, abatement of potential radiation, and rounded edges on all exposed surfaces.

The corporate image

As the network control center becomes equivalent to the nerve center of a company, it becomes the showplace of corporate capabilities. So, beyond space, mechanical, and ergonomic needs, aesthetics is playing an increasing role in the location and design of the command center. There is no question that an aesthetic environment can become an integral part of a company's identity, but like all other aspects of the optimum design, it must be factored into the design equation without detracting from other needs, as in the Burlington, N.H., network control center of Burlington Northern Railroad (Fig. 4).

Finally, under all circumstances, the command center must be designed to be redesigned. It must be able not only to account for an ever-changing array of monitoring and technical setups but also be adaptable to changing space configurations and provide hardware and service access. Telecommunications, power, and ventilation also must be considered, as should cable management.

For example, at one IBM manufacturing plant, after just 18 months, the increasing responsibilities of network operations forced a 40 percent expansion of the network control center. By using a modular design that allowed for easy expansion and reconfiguration, the expansion could be made cost-effective and carried out in a fraction of the time required for an entire custom-built design.

In the final analysis, command center design is not simply a function of space allocation and furniture. An enormous amount of advance planning is required for centralized control centers, especially in departments that have significant growth projections. To be effective, questions of morale, hardware, peripherals, and even the building's architecture have to be considered. Eliminating any single aspect can substantially decrease the center's effectiveness and longevity. ∎

Kerry Kosak, President of Desience Corp. in Malibu, Calif., received a Bachelor of Architecture degree from the University of Oregon in 1969. He also completed graduate courses at the Harvard School of Design.

Gilbert Held, contributing editor, DATA COMMUNICATIONS

Troubleshooting network problems: By the numbers

The 'seven testing commandments' are not really cast in stone, but knowing how to use them should help to rapidly solve data communications problems.

The complexity of many data communications networks has prompted more than a few network managers to count as much on prayer for the identification and resolution of problems as on technicians. While it is always good to have divine providence on your side, it is also important to have a good plan of attack—a set sequence of diagnostic procedures that will help you speedily isolate and correct the causes of communications problems.

With a methodical set of procedures to follow and questions to ask, you can narrow the scope of your investigation. These procedures will, in turn, enable you to focus your efforts upon determining the most probable causes of the problems. In certain situations, using the procedures will help to resolve problems before they actually materialize.

The recommended procedures represent a practical method for isolating the cause (or causes) of existing or potential communications problems.

1. Define the problem

Although this may appear to be an obvious first step, users often just report that they cannot communicate. In such instances, patience by control center personnel is truly a virtue: It is invaluable in working with persons who have little communications experience.

To help define a user's communications problem, follow the guidelines of newpaper reporter questions. That is, the control center specialist should determine what happened, when it occurred, and to whom and to what it occurred. (The whom refers to the user; the what: equipment, circuit, and/or dial network used.) Then this information can be used in conjunction with the background and experience of the control center personnel. This procedure results in either a rapid recognition of the cause of the problem or a basis for further problem determination efforts.

As an example of the ability to recognize a problem quickly, assume that a user calling with trouble stated that data keyed at a terminal did not appear on the terminal's screen. If data entered in the form of a computer sign-on message had been received at the terminal, both continuity and connectivity would have been proven. Therefore, the most probable cause of the problem would be an improper duplex setting in hardware or software. To better understand the cause of this problem—which accounts for about 5 percent of all trouble calls—let us review terminal and computer transmission modes of operation.

What is displayed on the terminal's screen depends on the terminal and computer transmission modes of operation. The user may have one, two, or no characters displayed for each character keyed in (Fig. 1).

If a terminal is in half-duplex mode, it echoes each transmitted character to its screen (Figs. 1A and 1C). If in full-duplex mode, it simply transmits each character without echoing it to the screen (Figs. 1B and 1D). At the computer site, the response to the terminal's transmitted character depends on the computer's transmission mode of operation. If the computer operates half-duplex (Figs. 1B and 1C), it simply accepts each received character. On the other hand, if the computer operates full duplex (Figs. 1A and 1D), it both accepts and echoes each received character back to the sending device. Therefore, for the Figure 1A case, the keyed character appears twice; for Figure 1B, no character display occurs; and for Figures 1C and 1D, a character is displayed once for each key depression.

Since it is relatively difficult to change the computer's transmission mode, in most cases an incorrect-character display problem is resolved by changing the terminal mode of operation. This is usually accomplished by changing a switch setting on the terminal, or, if one is using a PC, changing a setup parameter in the software via the keyboard.

Unfortunately, most communications problems are not as simple to isolate and correct as an improper character display. When a problem is not immediately recognizable, a quest for additional information is usually in order.

2. Determine the symptoms

In a complex communications environment, an examination of a problem's symptoms may provide the required information for its isolation and resolution. Determining the symptoms normally begins with determining if the problem is occurring on a random or defined basis—then attempting to correlate the symptoms to hardware, software, or the communications facility. Normally, randomly occurring problems are more likely to be associated with the communications facility than with data-dependent hardware or software. Conversely, a problem that occurs on a defined basis, such as losing communications whenever block X is transmitted, is more likely due to either hardware or software.

One example of a randomly occurring problem is a cluster of terminals that, at random intervals, terminates a user's computer session while redisplaying the sign-on logo of the installation.

Prior to installing 19.2-kbit/s modems, the circuit supporting two remotely located control units and their associated terminals used 14.4-kbit/s modems without any reported significant problems. Once those modems were replaced by the 19.2-kbit/s devices, all remote terminals would randomly "lose" their session in progress and redisplay the organization's sign-on logo. The randomness was once a day, twice a day, or sometimes not at all during a day. Needless to say, when this problem materialized, the organization's technical control center was flooded with complaining calls: A total of 64 workstations were supported by two control units fed by one line.

Using the line-quality monitoring capability incorporated in the 19.2-kbit/s modems, technicians in the control center examined the analog-line parameters. They determined that each time a log-on screen was redisplayed on the remote-site terminals, the 15-minute window in which the modem counted impulse hits always showed at least one—sometimes several—hits during the hit-recording period. Based on Bell System leased-line publications, up to 15 hits within a 15-minute period is considered acceptable. What required further investigation was the reaction of the 19.2-kbit/s modem to a severe hit. (A severe hit is one that lasts more than a few milliseconds and causes the modem to retrain [re-equalize].)

The vendor's manual stated that the modem would retrain under certain situations. The retraining resulted in a delay of approximately 1.5 seconds until the communications controller could reestablish communications with the control unit. Next to be examined were the ACF/NCP (Advanced Communications Function/Network Control Program) macro instructions for defining the type of line between the communications controller and the control unit. It was determined that the macro that controlled time-out and reinitialization was set to one second, which was the vendor's default recommendation.

While the one-second setting was acceptable for the previously used modems, its duration was too short to work correctly with the higher-speed modems. The resolution of this problem, by changing the macro to two seconds, was a simple task: reprogramming the NCP.

3. Use equipment indicators

One of the most valuable resources of communications equipment is the set of indicators included with most devices. Many times, an indicator's status is sufficient to determine the cause of a communications problem. And the status may often be determined simply by a glance at the indicator (is it illuminated?).

For an example of the potential use of equipment indicators, consider the front panel display of a US Robotics 2,400 bit/s standalone modem, one of many popular modems used for communications over the switched telephone network.

If a user complains that transmission is "very slow," a lack of illumination of the High Speed (HS) indicator will most likely provide the clue to the cause of the reported problem. In this situation, a lack of illumination indicates that the modem is not operating in its high-speed mode. The cause of this problem could range from a prior PC user

---

1. Quantity dependency. *From zero to two characters are displayed for each keyed-in character, based on the terminal and computer transmission modes of operation.*

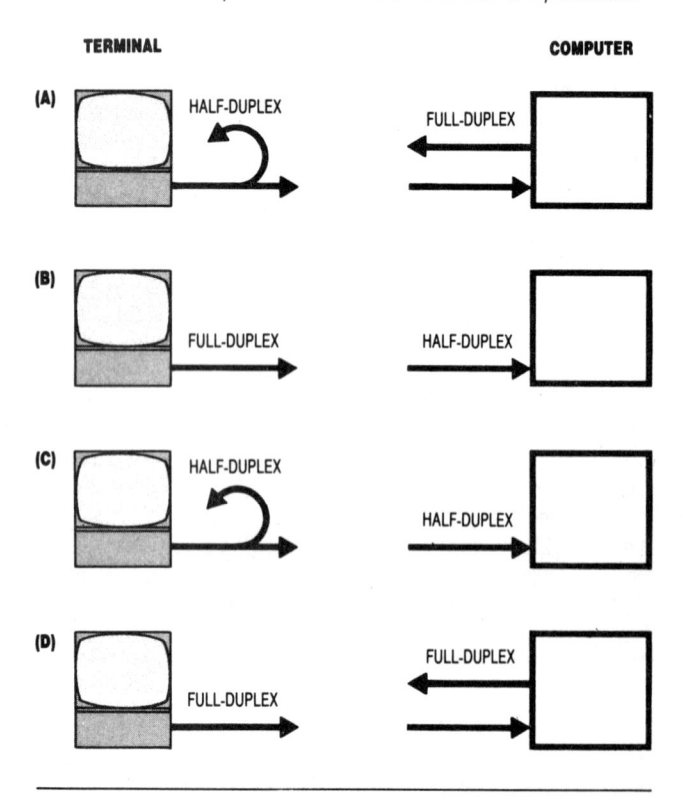

TERMINAL		COMPUTER
(A) HALF-DUPLEX	← →	FULL-DUPLEX
(B) FULL-DUPLEX	→	HALF-DUPLEX
(C) HALF-DUPLEX	→	HALF-DUPLEX
(D) FULL-DUPLEX	← →	FULL-DUPLEX

2. Protocol plots. *With Ring-Up, DTR is activated after an RI signal is received. With Hot DTR, it stays activated, except for a short period at the end of a call.*

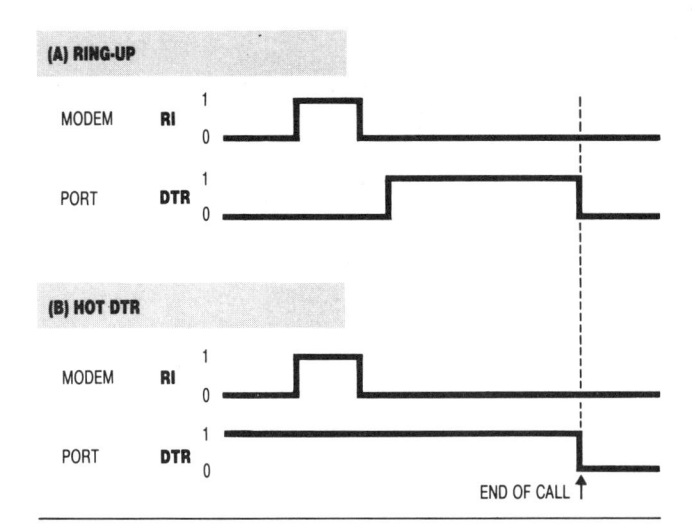

who reset the communications software data rate, to the user dialing an incorrect rotary group. In the latter situation, the organization might have one rotary group connected to 1,200-bit/s modems and a second rotary group connected to V.22*bis* 2,400-bit/s modems. Thus, dialing the 1,200 bit/s rotary group would result in the user's V.22*bis* modem operating at 1,200 bit/s.

If the Auto Answer (AA) indicator is illuminated, the modem has been placed into its answer mode of operation. While this is an appropriate setting to receive calls, it precludes the next user from originating calls until the modem is placed back into its original mode of operation. When this occurs, the AA indicator lamp will be extinguished, permitting the user to originate calls.

Another common problem reported by users involves the question, "Is the computer up?" This usually occurs when a user previously connected to the computer obtains no response to a keyboard actuation. Here, the status of the Carrier Detect (CD) indicator normally defines the cause of the problem, since a lack of illumination means that the connection was lost.

The Off-Hook (OH) indicator denotes whether or not the modem has control of the line. Although most modems are manufactured with a jack into which the plug of a telephone can be connected, it is fairly common for office personnel to temporarily disconnect a modem from a telephone company outlet to plug a telephone directly into that business line. Unfortunately, it is also common for office personnel to forget to reconnect the modem to the line after they finish using the telephone. Then, when the modem user powers up the terminal or PC and tries to use the modem, the attempt will obviously be unsuccessful. For this type of problem, the failure of the OH indicator to illuminate serves as a guide to the cause of the problem.

The Receive Data (RD) indicator on the US Robotics modem is designed to flash in tandem with the modem's receiving and demodulating data from the line. Thus, this indicator flashing in the absence of data being displayed on the attached terminal could indicate a failure in the terminal's receive logic or a possible break in the cable that affects the connector's pin 3. For the latter case, note that the modem passes received data on pin 3 to the attached data terminal equipment (DTE).

Similar to the RD indicator, the Send Data (SD) lamp flashes in tandem with the modem receiving outgoing data on pin 2. With the user keying in data, determine the status of the SD indicator. Control center personnel can then determine if data is reaching the modem from the attached DTE.

The Terminal Ready (TR) indicator is illuminated when the modem receives a DATA TERMINAL READY (DTR) signal from the attached DTE. If this indicator is not lit, the DTE could either be defective or, more probable, not powered up.

The last two indicators on the modem front panel, Modem Ready (MR) and Analog Loopback (AL), can also be used to determine the cause of frequent problems. If MR is not lit, the modem is either not powered up or the lamp is defective. A lack of power is the probable cause, since LEDs almost always outlast their communications devices.

If the AL indicator is illuminated, the modem is in its analog loopback self-test mode of operation, precluding it from transmitting data. Thus, unless the self-test mode is desired, the user would key in a command to take the modem out of analog loopback.

While the preceding discussion focused on one particular modem, readers should recognize that most communications devices provide similar indicators. Thus, recognizing what the illumination—or lack of illumination—of a particular indicator means can be of valuable assistance in isolating communications problems.

4 Know the types of connections

To receive a proper response to data transmitted over the switched network, the auto-answer modem must be configured to work with the modem-control protocol of the host computer. Two popular modem-control protocols used by host computers are Ring-Up and Hot DTR.

In the Ring-Up protocol, the computer does not generate a DTR signal until the modem activates a ring indicator (RI) signal to indicate an incoming call. The DTE then activates the computer's DTR signal to answer the call and keeps it activated until the end of the call (Fig. 2A).

In the Hot DTR protocol, the DTE activates the DTR signal in advance of the RI signal. However, the DTE does not answer the incoming call until it detects the RI signal (Fig. 2B). The DTR signal then remains activated until the end of the call, when it is deactivated for a period of time long enough to terminate the call.

If the computer port operates in the Hot DTR mode, the modem's DTR control option should be set to DTR on, which tells the modem that DTR is initially activated. If the computer port operates as Ring-Up, the modem's DTR option should be set to DTR off.

Most computer ports operate in a Ring-Up mode, result-

3. Ring-Start adaption. *A conventional null modem cable can be made compatible with Ring-Start operation by strapping pin 6 to pin 22 at the Ring-Start port end.*

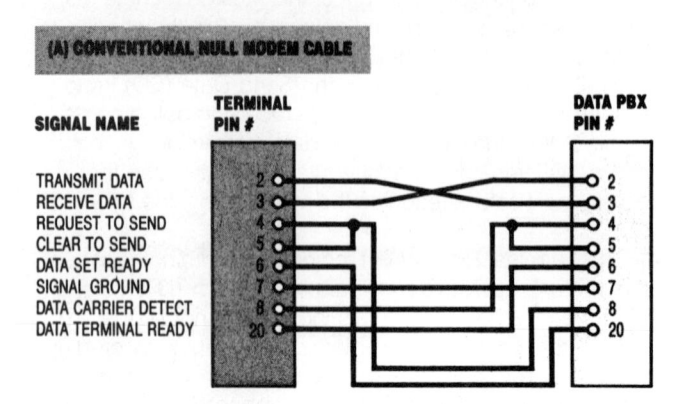

(A) CONVENTIONAL NULL MODEM CABLE

SIGNAL NAME	TERMINAL PIN #	DATA PBX PIN #
TRANSMIT DATA	2	2
RECEIVE DATA	3	3
REQUEST TO SEND	4	4
CLEAR TO SEND	5	5
DATA SET READY	6	6
SIGNAL GROUND	7	7
DATA CARRIER DETECT	8	8
DATA TERMINAL READY	20	20

(B) RING-START NULL MODEM CABLE

SIGNAL NAME	TERMINAL PIN #	DATA PBX PIN #
TRANSMIT DATA	2	2
RECEIVE DATA	3	3
REQUEST TO SEND	4	4
CLEAR TO SEND	5	5
DATA SET READY	6	6
SIGNAL GROUND	7	7
DATA CARRIER DETECT	8	8
DATA TERMINAL READY	20	20
RING INDICATOR		22

ing in most modem factory settings for the DTR signal being normally off. But, if you connect a modem whose DTR setting is off to a Hot DTR port, incoming calls will not be answered: The modem will be set to respond to a DTR transition, while DTR is always normally activated.

5. Understand interface requirements

One of the keys to making incompatible devices compatible is to understand interface requirements. For example, consider a terminal that is to be directly cabled to a port selector or data PBX that operates in the Ring-Start mode. Here, Ring-Start is a communications requirement for a voltage on pin 22 of the communications device's connector. Pin 22 is reserved for the RI conductor to initiate operation.

If you fabricate a conventional null modem cable to connect the terminal to the data PBX port, RI will never become activated (see "How to make and use null modem cables," DATA COMMUNICATIONS, November 1987, p. 165). This becomes obvious from an examination of the null modem cable in Figure 3A. Here you will note that the terminal never uses pin 22: This conductor is not included in a conventional null modem cable.

To obtain an RI signal at the data PBX, an existing conductor should be strapped to pin 22 at the data PBX port's cable end. The normal procedure in this case is to strap pin 6, the DTR signal's pin, to pin 22. In this way, when the DTR signal goes "high" at the terminal (pin 20), it will generate an RI signal on pin 22 at the data PBX cable end (Fig. 3B).

Although the Ring-Start null modem cable will work in most situations, a word of caution is in order. Some devices can be set to respond to the RI signal going high for either a short time or being on for the duration of a session. Other devices may only be able to respond to a short-duration RI signal. Note that the cable illustrated in Figure 3 activates an RI signal as long as DTR is high; it cannot be used with a device that requires a short-duration RI signal.

6. Use built-in diagnostics

Most modern communications devices contain a series of built-in diagnostics that can be used to isolate problems. Such diagnostics range from a self-test to different types of loopback tests.

A self-test is designed to test the internal circuitry of a communications device for faults. When this test is initiated, the device normally generates a test pattern that is routed through its circuitry to a pattern comparator. The comparator compares the received test pattern to what should be received if the device were functioning properly. If the received test pattern does not match the pattern stored in the comparator, an error indicator will light up. Other devices have more sophisticated self-testing capabilities that indicate a failure by board—or even by board module—to facilitate the replacement of a defective component.

Concerning loopbacks, let us again use modems to illustrate the versatility of this set of internal diagnostic tools. By using a progression of loopback tests in sequence, the cause of a transmission problem can be isolated.

The local digital loopback verifies the operation of the attached DTE and the continuity of the cable between the DTE and the modem. Activating local digital loopback makes the local modem "break" its connections to the line and connect the modem's transmitter and receiver leads to each other. This connection causes data to be echoed back to the DTE without modulation or demodulation occurring. When this test is initiated, you can use the terminal's keyboard to generate a data pattern and observe the results on your screen.

The local analog loopback tests the digital and analog circuits of the modem to determine if they are operational. Activating local analog loopback makes the local modem break its connections to the transmission line and connect its line-side (analog) transmitter and receiver leads to each other. This test provides an indication of the modem's operational ability. Plug a bit error rate tester (BERT) into the modem's connector, and inject random bit patterns into the modem. If the BERT shows no errors when the modem is in analog loopback, you can safely eliminate the local modem as the cause of a communications problem.

Remote analog loopback permits both the local modem and communications facility to be tested. When this loopback is initiated, the remote modem's analog-side transmit-

4. Balancing the load. *Based upon an analysis of events provided by the statistics port of a data PBX, port class sizes are adjusted to better reflect actual network usage.*

(A) ORIGINAL CONFIGURATION

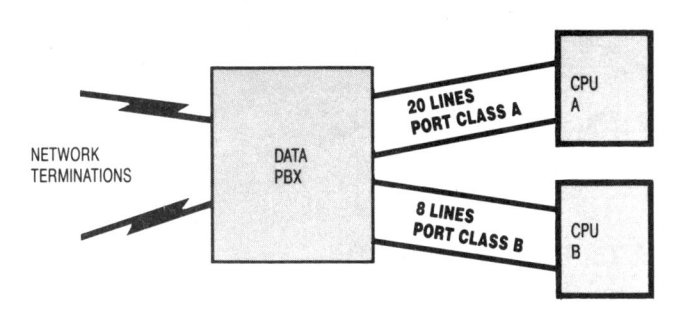

(B) ADJUSTED CONFIGURATION

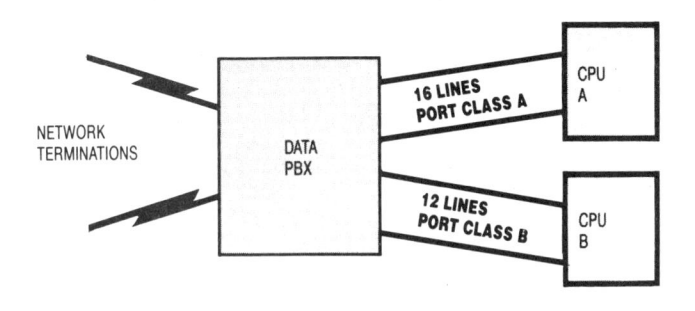

ter and receiver leads are disconnected from their modem's internal circuitry and connected to each other. This permits the operation of the local modem and the transmission line to be checked.

The fourth loopback, via the remote digital loop, permits a full end-to-end test of both modems and the communications facility. When this test is initiated, the remote modem's connections with the remote DTE are broken and the digital-side transmitter and receiver leads are connected to each other. Data received by the remote modem is demodulated and remodulated, permitting the operation of the remote modem to be checked.

By initiating the four loopbacks in sequence, you can verify the operational status of the local DTE and the cable between it and the local modem, the local modem, the communications facility, and the remote modem. About the only equipment whose status cannot be checked from a local site are the distant DTE and the cable between it and the remote modem. However, personnel at the remote site could initiate a local digital loopback on their modem to complete end-to-end testing.

7 Examine event reports

Many communications devices—including multiplexers, concentrators, and data PBXs—have a statistics port. As activity occurs, a data record defining the events that transpired is routed to this port.

Normally, a dumb ASCII terminal is connected to the statistics port, thus providing a mechanism for control center personnel to observe a description of the device's network activity as it occurs. Since a dumb ASCII terminal has no storage capability of its own, once the data scrolls off the screen, it is lost (unless, of course, a printer is employed).

If the dumb terminal is replaced by a PC operating a communications program, you can both display events as they occur and record the data to disk. Then, you could use the resulting database to obtain information that may not be readily observable by viewing individual events as they occur.

As an example of the use of the statistics port, consider a data PBX that generates an event record each time a user requesting access to a port class (group) is placed into a queue. Assume that the data PBX also generates a record when the user exits the queue and is cross-connected to a port in the desired port class. It becomes possible to determine queuing problems prior to users reporting them, reducing user dissatisfaction with network resources.

By the use of a database program or the development and use of customized software, you could generate reports by time of day. These reports would denote the number of users in a queue and the average time duration they spend there. By analyzing such reports, you could rebalance the number of ports routed, as a port class, to different CPU resources that are also connected to the data PBX.

Figure 4 illustrates one possible adjustment in a network configuration based on the analysis of statistics generated by a data PBX. In Figure 4A, 20 ports were assigned as port class A and routed to CPU A, while eight ports were assigned as port class B and routed to CPU B.

Suppose an analysis of a report generated from recorded statistical port data indicates that access requests to port class B are being excessively queued while no requests for access to port class A are being queued. As a result of this analysis, four lines from port class A might be removed and added to port class B (Fig. 4B). This adjustment to port class sizes better reflects actual network usage requests, eliminating or reducing the previously observed queuing in port class B. If the timing of the adjustment is right, user complaints would be averted.

As previously mentioned, the seven commandments for communications testing and troubleshooting are not cast in stone. However, remembering what they mean and how they can be used will enable readers to more rapidly isolate and alleviate communications problems. ∎

Gilbert Held, director of Macon, Ga.-based 4-Degree Consulting, is an internationally recognized author and lecturer on data communications subjects. Besides twice receiving the Interface Karp Award, he has been recognized by the American Association of Publishers for technical excellence in developing microcomputer software. He is also editor of the Auerbach Journal of Data and Computer Communications.

Kevin B. Flynn, Telecommunications Techniques Corp., Gaithersburg, Md.

What you don't know about T1 jitter can give you the jitters

There are as many different causes of error-inducing T1 jitter as there are conflicting 'standards' for measuring it.

There exists today a myriad of different performance specifications for T1 timing jitter—the ever-so-slight variations in time of the transmitted digital signal. Data communicators are naturally asking: "Why is there no agreement on what constitutes an unacceptable degree of jitter? Which specification applies to my network? And how do I measure jitter, anyway?"

Jitter should not be ignored—its effects can be disastrous in a T1 network. In this era of deregulation, with equipment and carrier service being provided by many different vendors, the measurement of timing jitter must be well understood and its parameters well defined.

As an example, consider an actual jitter amplitude-versus-frequency plot measured on a T1 circuit running from New York to California (Fig. 1). The link consists of a mix of metallic wire pairs, microwave radio, optical fiber, and multiplexers and demultiplexers. Is this amount of jitter low? Excessive? Is it within specifications? What specifications?

What is timing jitter?

The T1 signal is made up of pulses representing logical ones that alternate in polarity. A logical zero is represented by the absence of a pulse (no signal). Timing jitter is the deviation in time between when the pulse transitions actually occur when they ideally should—and when the digital decoding gear expects them to occur.

This jitter is, in effect, unintentional phase modulation, which has both an amplitude and a frequency component. The jitter's amplitude is the magnitude of the phase deviation; its frequency is a measure of how rapidly the phase is changing. The measurement gauge for the amplitude is called the unit interval, which is the time period (648 nanoseconds) that it takes one bit to pass a fixed point at the T1 transmission rate (1.544 Mbit/s).

Figure 2a shows a "snapshot" of a fixed data pattern being transmitted by a T1 signal that has sinusoidal jitter modulation. At this particular instant in time, phase shifts can be seen in the second and third pulses. (Note that a pulse width equals one-half a bit period.) Figure 2b is a composite view of the same T1 signal as viewed on an oscilloscope. The blurred edges indicate the amplitude, or range, of the jitter modulation. Figure 2c shows a plot of the jitter function (t), which is the expression used to represent phase deviation over time. This plot reveals the jitter amplitude of 0.33 UIpp (unit intervals, peak to peak), and the jitter frequency of 1,000 Hz.

Jitter that has a frequency of less than 10 Hz is referred to as wander, which, because of the very low frequency and long wavelength, requires different specifications and different methods for measurement. Wander is not covered further in this article.

When one hears of jitter of up to 10 or 12 UI, the question may be asked: How can an amplitude possibly exceed 1 UI, or 360 degrees? The answer is that the phase excursion accumulates bit by bit—literally—and does not all occur over one bit period. In general, if the phase shift from one pulse to the next exceeds 0.25 UI, or 25 percent variation of a bit period, bit errors can occur. This is explained more later.

In the real world, jitter is not sinusoidal, nor does it occur at a single frequency. It is usually a complex waveform that is a composite of many frequencies at many amplitudes. One type is called systematic jitter, which is a byproduct of the clock-signal-recovery and data-regeneration functions of T1 line repeaters. Systematic jitter is directly related to the data content of the T1 signal, and it can accumulate as the signal goes through multiple repeaters.

Another jitter type is called waiting-time jitter, which results when a T1 signal is demultiplexed out of higher-rate carriers, such as DS-2 (6.312 Mbit/s) or DS-3 (44.736 Mbit/s). To synchronize a T1 signal being extracted from a

1. Sample spectrum. *This is an actual plot of the jitter amplitude versus frequency on a T1 link between New York and California. The circuit consists of a mix of metallic wire pairs, microwave radio, optical fiber, and multiplexers and demultiplexers. Is this amount of jitter low? Excessive? Is it within specifications? What specifications?*

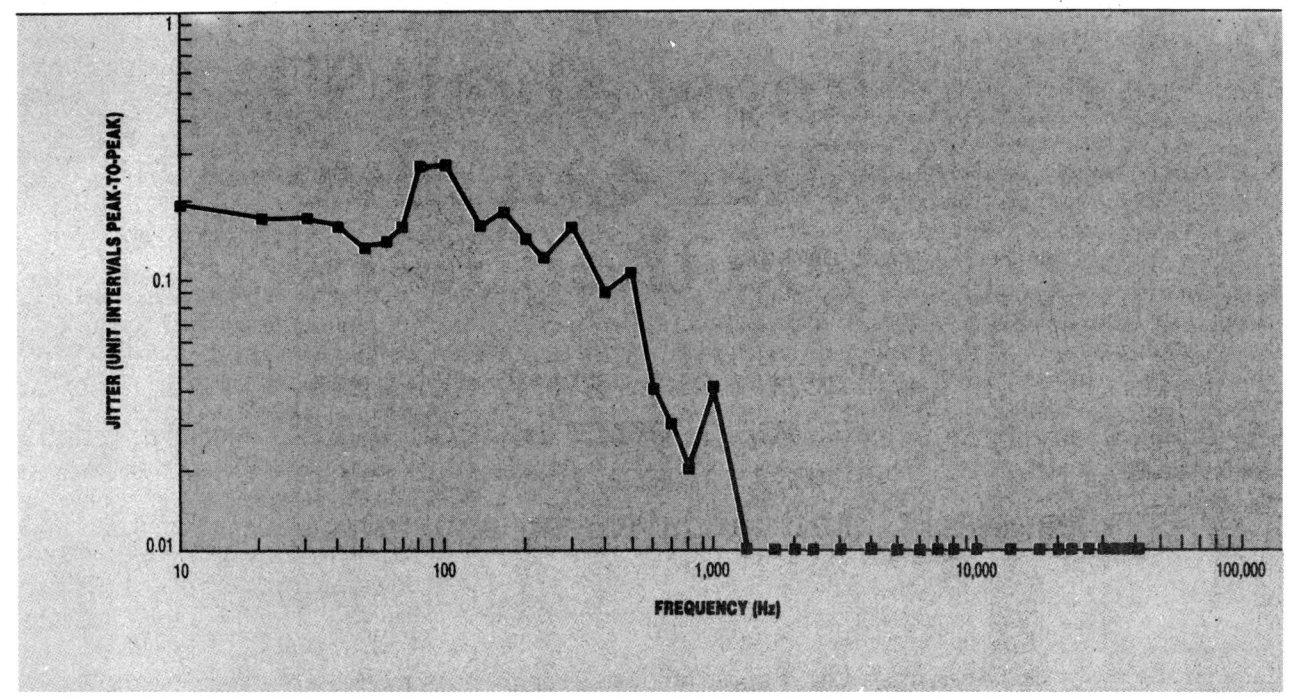

DS-3 carrier, for instance, the demultiplexer must delete certain overhead "stuffing" bits that are added as part of the multiplexing process. This creates gaps in the bit stream that are smoothed out by buffering.

The demultiplexer, however, waits to recognize a stuffing bit before deleting it. And this waiting time allows the development of large phase shifts, which cannot be fully filtered out.

Jitter has also been traced to faulty repeaters, especially when operating under high-temperature or high-humidity conditions. Other sources of jitter include crosstalk, power-supply electrical noise, faulty components, oscillator phase noise, and environmental noise.

Impairments

Perhaps the foremost problem caused by T1 jitter is an increase in error rate. Bit errors occur when the receiving circuit incorrectly samples the incoming pulses. A T1 receiver must recover a clock signal from the incoming data in order to sample subsequent pulses and regenerate the digital bit stream. The recovered clock signal defines the instants in time at which decisions are made as to whether or not a real data pulse, denoting a binary 1, is present.

Figure 3 illustrates a received T1 signal and the clock signal recovered from it. At each rising edge of the clock (Fig. 3d), the receiver "looks at" the voltage level of the input (Fig. 3b), and, if the voltage exceeds a certain threshold, the receiver detects a logical one. If the voltage is lower than the threshold, a logical zero is detected. To ensure the highest probability of making the right decision, the rising clock edge should be in the middle of each pulse. This is called mid-bit sampling.

A clock recovery circuit tracks the input frequency changes and tries to maintain the mid-bit phase relationship. However, it cannot instantaneously adjust for phase shifts from one pulse to the next; therefore, any pulse that is shifted in phase by more than 50 percent of its width (0.25 UI) will be sampled incorrectly. The example in Figure

2. Not-so-pretty picture. *Note the phase shifts in the second and third pulses (A), composite view (B) and phase deviation versus time (C) reveal the jitter amplitude.*

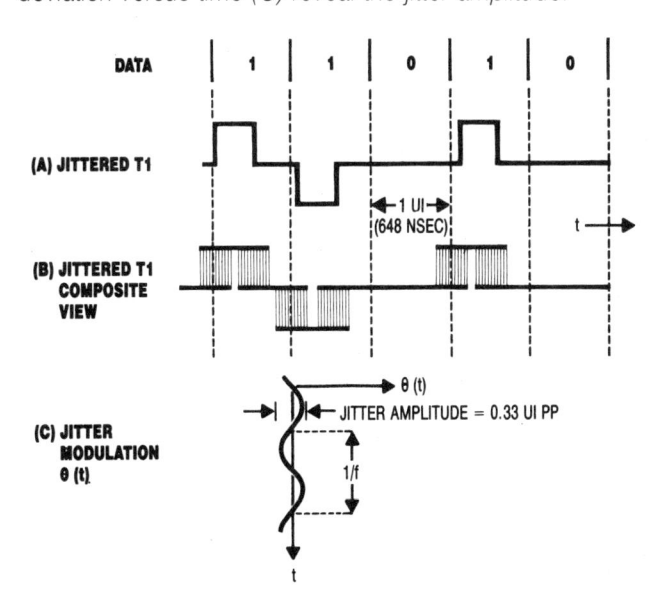

f = JITTER FREQUENCY = 1,000 Hz
NSEC = NANOSECONDS
UI PP = UNIT INTERVALS PEAK-TO-PEAK

3e shows that two bit errors were caused by the inability of the recovered clock to adjust instantaneously to the phase shift of the third pulse.

Figure 3 also illustrates the importance of a high ones density (greater than 12.5 percent) in the transmitted bit stream. Each pulse helps realign the clock for mid-bit sampling. When a long string of zeros occurs, no alignment information is received and the clock drifts toward its natural or free-running frequency. The combined effects of clock drift and jitter raise the probability that the next pulse that comes along will be incorrectly sampled.

The pulse sampling process is akin to a sharpshooter in a shooting gallery. This person, analogous to the recovered clock, can easily hit the ducks (T1 pulses) as they move by, as long as there is no variation in their movements. The shooter is able to track slow variations (jitter) in the movement of the ducks and continue to hit them. But as the speed variations increase in size or frequency, the shooter cannot adjust quickly enough and starts missing ducks. This corresponds to the bit errors that occur when the clock samples incorrectly.

Jitter specifics

It is the pulse-to-pulse phase deviation that causes the clock to miss the incoming bits. This deviation is a result of both the amplitude and the frequency of the jitter. A mathematical demonstration of this relationship follows.

First, consider the expression for sinusoidal phase modulation:

$\theta(t) = A \sin wt$,

where A = jitter amplitude (peak) in radians, and w = jitter frequency in radians/sec. The slope of this function, which is the rate of change of the phase, determines how much the pulses will vary from their ideal position over a given time interval.

An expression for the slope can be found by differentiating $\theta(t)$ with respect to time, which gives:

$d\theta/dt = wA \cos wt$, in radians/second.

By integrating the slope over a time period T equal to the maximum time between pulses (15 zero periods × 648 nanoseconds per period), an expression for the maximum phase shift between pulses is obtained:

maximum phase deviation = $2A \sin wT/2$, in radians.

For most cases, the period of the jitter frequency will be much larger than T, and the small-angle approximation, $\sin x \cong x$, can be used to reduce the expression to:

maximum phase deviation $\cong AwT$, for $1/w \gg T$.

This expression clearly shows that the pulse-to-pulse deviation caused by jitter is a function of both the amplitude and the frequency of the jitter. It is this important principle that has become the basis for most of the jitter specifications today. A more useful form of the expression can be obtained by converting to UIpp and Hertz:

maximum phase deviation $\cong 0.03$ Kf, in UI, where
K = jitter amplitude in UIpp, and f = jitter frequency in kHz.

With values of 1 UIpp and 8.4 kHz, a maximum phase shift of 0.25 UI results, which is 50 percent of a pulse width. A recovered clock signal that "expects to see" the pulse at the midpoint could, therefore, miss it entirely (Fig. 3). The same result would occur with jitter of 10 UIpp at 840 Hz.

Because the slope of the modulating jitter function

3. Clock and data. *The receiver samples the input's voltage level (B) at each clock pulse (D). Two bit errors (E) were caused by the inability of the recovered clock to adjust.*

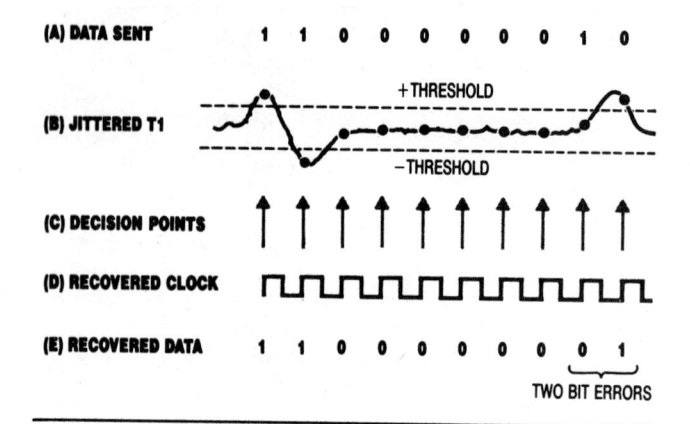

determines how severe the jitter is, a high-amplitude, low-frequency jitter is just as damaging as a low-amplitude, high-frequency one. This is shown graphically in Figure 4, where two sinusoidal jitter functions of different amplitudes and frequencies produce the same maximum slope. The two different jitter signals would have the same effect on error performance.

Overflow

Another problem caused by jitter is buffer overflow. Multiplexers that combine many asynchronous T1s use a buffer to clock data in at the T1 rate and clock it out at a higher rate, such as DS-3. These buffers can overflow, or be depleted, if the frequency of the input T1 fluctuates too widely—a condition directly related to the phase jitter. These uncontrolled "slips" can cause data loss and framing-synchronization loss.

Digital access and cross-connect switches (DACS) typically employ input buffers to allow for timing variations. A whole frame of data can be held in these buffers and, in the event of an overflow, may be deleted. This is called a controlled slip, where frame synchronization is maintained but at the expense of lost data.

Still another problem created by T1 jitter is the degradation of digitally encoded analog waveforms, such as audio, video, or voice-band data. When these signals are transmitted on a jittered T1, and then reconstructed back to their analog forms, a phase modulation is placed on the waveform. This occurs because the clock that controls the digital-to-analog conversion is derived from the recovered clock, which has jitter similar to that on the received T1.

Inconsistent standards

Jitter specifications have been promulgated by organizations including AT&T, Bellcore, and the CCITT to cover four areas: jitter tolerance at an input, output jitter, jitter transfer from input to output, and overall network jitter limits. These specifications have evolved as T1 carriers have proliferated and as more knowledge about T1 operational characteristics has been acquired. Because of this informal process, there is now a lack of consistency among these specifications, and confusion is a common result.

An example of this inconsistency is the terminology used

4. Same degradation. *The maximum slope of the modulating jitter determines the jitter's severity. Here, different amplitudes and frequencies are equally damaging.*

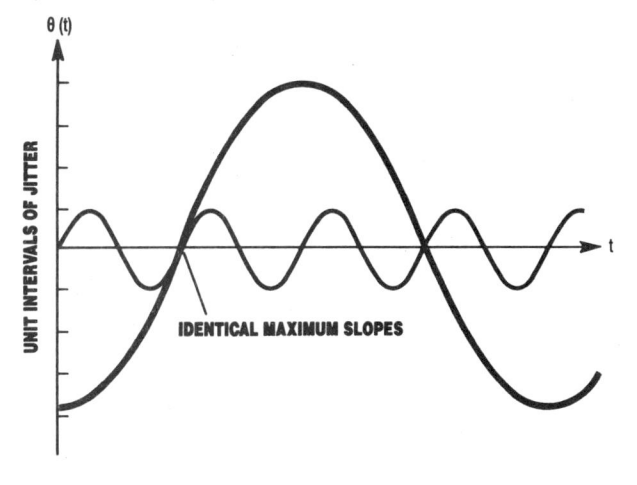

to express jitter amplitude. Units of measure include degrees, radians, nanoseconds, percent, bits, time slots, and unit intervals. More recently, the unit interval has become the accepted standard unit of measure for jitter amplitude. Specifications that express jitter in other ways should be converted to unit intervals to simplify testing and comparison with other specifications. (One UI is equivalent to each of the following: 360°, 2π radians, 648 nanoseconds, 100 percent, one bit, and one time slot.)

Jitter tolerance, or jitter accommodation, defines the amount of jitter that can be tolerated at an input before errors start to occur. Because of the amplitude-frequency relationship mentioned earlier, jitter tolerance is usually specified with a mask, which is an amplitude-versus-frequency curve that indicates the maximum jitter that must be tolerated at a device's input.

A collection of some of the most widely used masks is shown in Figure 5 and listed in Table 1. (Each mask is coded to match a specification group defined in the table.) The table also lists the reference document number and title, as well as any conditions required when testing.

5. Masks. *These are some of the most widely used masks. Notice the large disparity between them. At a frequency of 200 Hz, for example, asynchronous multiplexers must tolerate up to 5 UIpp, as specified by AT&T. However, the CCITT specification for a second-order multiplexer requires a tolerance of only 2 UIpp.*

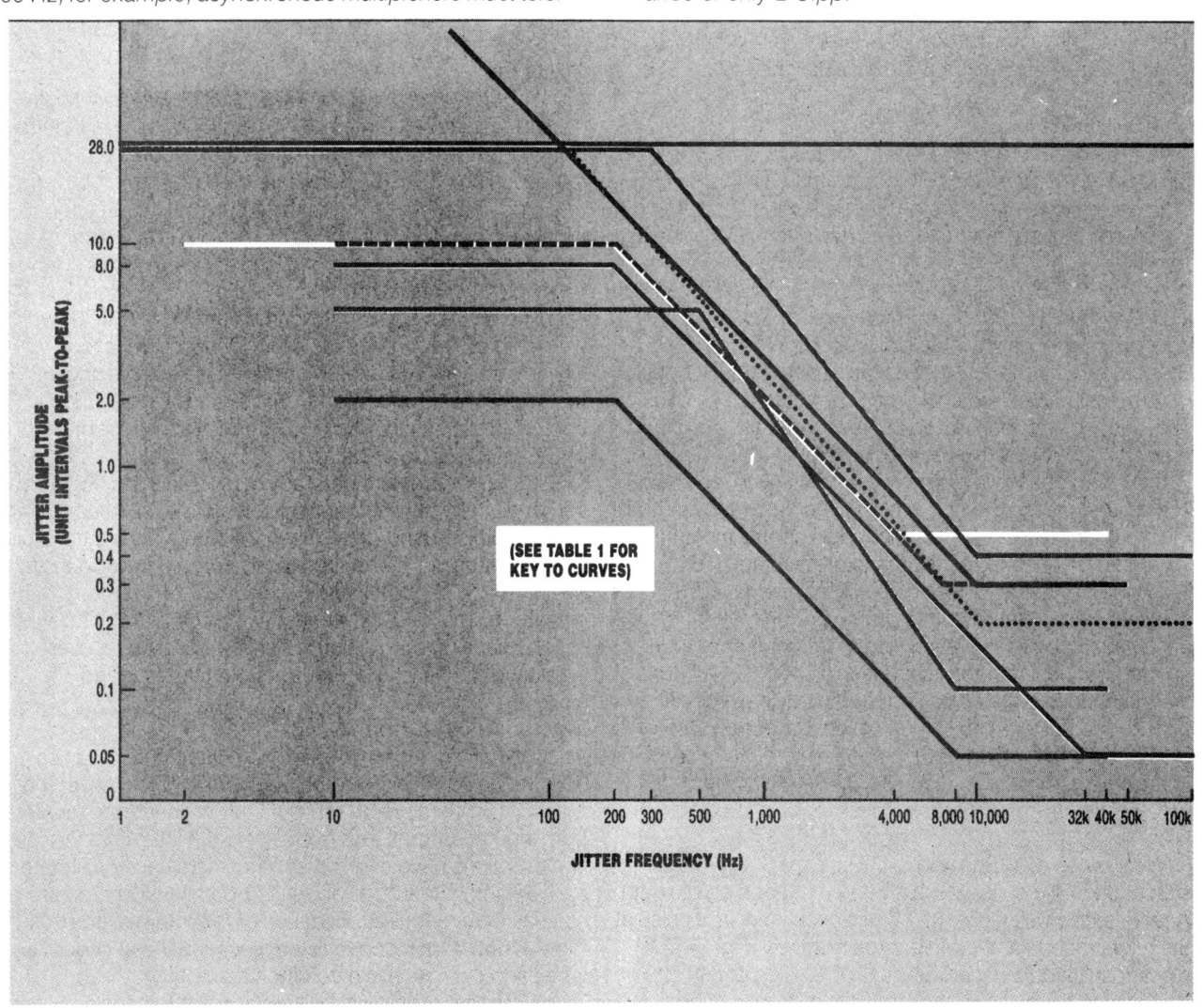

Table 1: Jitter tolerance specifications

DOCUMENT	TITLE	CONDITIONS (PATTERN, MODULATION, INPUT LEVEL)	JITTER TOLERANCE LIMITS	
AT&T PUB 43802 (7/82)	DIGITAL MULTIPLEXES REQUIREMENTS AND OBJECTIVES	QRSS, SINE	5 UI PP	10 Hz TO 500 Hz
AT&T PUB 62411 (9/83)	HIGH CAPACITY DIGITAL SERVICE CHANNEL INTERFACE SPECIFICATION	QRSS, SINE, +7.5 TO −35.5 dB	−28.2 dB/DEC	500 Hz TO 8 kHz
AT&T PUB 41457 (5/85)	SKYNET DIGITAL SERVICE (PRELIMINARY)	QRSS, SINE, +7.5 TO −35.5 dB	0.1 UI PP	8 kHz TO 40 kHz
BELLCORE TR-TSY-000009 5/86	ASYNCHRONOUS DIGITAL MULTIPLEXES REQUIREMENTS AND OBJECTIVES	SINE		
BELLCORE TA-365-23232-84-01 (4/84)	GENERIC REQUIREMENTS AND OBJECTIVES FOR 96 CHANNEL INTEROFFICE DIGITAL PAIRED CABLE SYSTEMS (PRELIMINARY)	SINE		
BELLCORE TA-TSY-000038 (7/85)	SINGLE MODE INTEROFFICE DIGITAL FIBER OPTIC SYSTEMS	SINE		
AT&T PUB 43801 (11/82)	DIGITAL CHANNEL BANK REQUIREMENTS AND OBJECTIVES		−20 dB/DEC	<10 Hz TO 10 kHz
AT&T PUB 60110 (12/83)	DIGITAL SYNCHRONIZATION NETWORK PLAN		0.3 UI PP	10 kHz TO 50 kHz
BELLCORE TR-TSY-000303 (9/86)	INTEGRATED DIGITAL LOOP CARRIER SYSTEM GENERIC REQUIREMENTS			
BELLCORE TA365-23221-84-01 (4/84)	DIGITAL CROSS CONNECT SYSTEM (PRELIMINARY)			
BELLCORE TA-TSY-000241 (11/85)	ELECTRONIC DIGITAL SIGNAL CROSS CONNECT FRAME REQUIREMENTS AND OBJECTIVES (PRELIMINARY)			
AT&T PUB 41451 (1/83)	HIGH CAPACITY TERRESTRIAL DIGITAL SERVICE		8 UI PP	10 Hz TO 200 Hz
			−20 dB/DEC	200 Hz TO 32 kHz
			0.05 UI PP	> 32 kHz
AT&T CB 143 (1/83)	DIGITAL ACCESS AND CROSS CONNECT SYSTEM TECHNICAL REFERENCE AND COMPATIBILITY SPECIFICATION		28.5 UI PP	
AT&T CB 123 (8/81)	DIGROUP TERMINAL AND DIGITAL INTERFACE FRAME TECHNICAL REFERENCE AND COMPATIBILITY SPECIFICATION			
CCITT REC. G.743 (RED)	SECOND ORDER DIGITAL MULTIPLEX EQUIPMENT OPERATING AT 6.312 MBIT/S	215-1, SINE	2.0 UI PP	10 Hz TO 200 Hz
CCITT REC. Q.502 (RED)	DIGITAL TRANSIT EXCHANGE INTERFACE		−20 dB/DEC	200 Hz TO 8 kHz
CCITT REC. Q.512 (RED)	COMBINED DIGITAL LOCAL/TRANSIT EXCHANGE INTERFACE		0.05 UI PP	8 kHz TO 40 kHz
CCITT REC. G.824 (RED)	THE CONTROL OF JITTER AND WANDER IN DIGITAL NETWORKS BASED ON 1.544 MBIT/S HIERARCHY			
AT&T CB 127 (10/79)	M1C MULTIPLEX COMPATIBILITY SPECIFICATION	FOR t = TIME THAT PHASE SLOPE > 2,000 Hz	T(SLOPE-2,000) ≤ 2.5	
AT&T CB 128 (10/79)	M12 MULTIPLEX COMPATIBILITY SPECIFICATION	FOR t = TIME THAT PHASE SLOPE > 1,550 Hz	T(SLOPE-1,550) ≤ 5	
AT&T CB 129 (10/79)	M13 MULTIPLEX COMPATIBILITY SPECIFICATION	FOR t = TIME THAT PHASE SLOPE) > 1,550 Hz	T(SLOPE-1,550) ≤ 5	
AT&T PUB. 62411 (10/85)	ACCUNET T1.5 SERVICE DESCRIPTION AND INTERFACE SPECIFICATIONS	QRSS, SINE, DSX-1 (FOR DTE)	28 UI PP	<10 Hz TO 125 Hz
			−22.3 dB/DEC	125 Hz TO 10 kHz
			0.2 UI PP	10 kHz TO 100 kHz
		QRSS, SINE, DSX-1 (FOR SYNCHRONIZER)	28 UI PP	<10 Hz TO 300 Hz
			−24.2 dB/DEC	300 Hz TO 10 kHz
			0.4 UI PP	10 kHz TO 100 kHz
CCITT REC. O.171 (10/84)	SPECIFICATION FOR INSTRUMENTATION TO MEASURE TIMING JITTER ON DIGITAL EQUIPMENT	JITTER GENERATION TEST INSTRUMENT	10 UI PP	2 Hz TO 200 Hz
			−20 dB/DEC	200 Hz TO 4 kHz
			0.5 UI PP	4 kHz TO 40 kHz
		JITTER MEASUREMENT TEST INSTRUMENT, 215-1	10 UI PP	10 Hz TO 200 Hz
			−20 dB/DEC	200 Hz TO 7 kHz
			0.3 UI PP	7 kHz TO 40 kHz

UI PP = UNIT INTERVALS PEAK-TO-PEAK

Notice the wide disparity between the masks. At a frequency of 200 Hz, asynchronous multiplexers must tolerate up to 5 UIpp, as specified by AT&T. However, the CCITT specification for a second-order multiplexer (one that extracts T1 from DS-2) requires a tolerance of only 2 UIpp. A channel bank must be able to handle I5.4 UIpp, while a CSU (channel service unit) that interfaces to AT&T's Accunet T1.5 service must accommodate 28 UIpp.

Notice that the jitter tolerance mask for a DACS, per AT&T CB143 (CB stands for Compatibility Bulletin) is flat over the required frequency range: The only criterion used in creating the specification was to ensure that the input buffer does not overflow or "underflow"; the effects of input sampling errors were not included. The same holds true for AT&T's three multiplexer specifications, CB 127, 128, and 129, which give both the input buffer sizes of the multiplexers and a formula for the maximum time during which the jitter function can exceed a certain slope.

Making measurements

Testing for jitter tolerance requires that the error rate be monitored while input jitter is varied. This is accomplished with a BERT (bit error rate tester) and a jitter generator. The latter either "jitters" the T1 output of the BERT or supplies a jittered clock to the BERT.

A typical test configuration is shown in Figure 6a, with a jitter generator as an integral part of the BERT. (In the figure, DSX-1 refers to the DS-1—or T1—signal at the cross-connect, which is the patch panel.) A specification for a jitter generator is given in CCITT Recommendation O.171. It gives recommended frequency and amplitude ranges that are included in Table 1. However, it should be noted that there are some AT&T tolerance masks that exceed the specified CCITT ranges.

Four important parameters that must be defined for testing are data pattern, jitter modulation, pulse shape, and the "threshold of intolerance." It is absolutely essential that these parameters are controlled and recorded; otherwise, results can vary widely.

The type of data pattern that is used is important because of the effects of systematic jitter. Generally, a QRSS (quasirandom signal source—a Bell term) is used, which is a $(2^{20}-1)$-bit pseudorandom pattern, with strings of 15 or more zeros suppressed. It has been demonstrated that such a pattern adequately simulates random data in a repeatered T1 line.

For some equipment, however, a pseudorandom pattern cannot be used for the T1 data. For example, channel banks and T1 demultiplexers require a properly structured signal that can be demultiplexed down to 56-kbit/s channels. A T1 signal with pseudorandom data cannot be used because the bit error rate cannot be monitored. Instead, a pseudorandom pattern is applied to one of a multiplexer's low-speed ports. The T1 output is jittered and applied to the T1-demultiplexer input (the test point).

One way to test T1 multiplexers using this procedure (Fig. 6b): The BERT transmits a pseudorandom pattern on one of the tributary channels at 56 kbit/s, while the jitter generator operates in "through" mode, simply jittering the T1 that passes through it. Ideally, the other channels should contain live data so that the composite T1 looks as random as possible at the demultiplexer input.

6. Testing. *A typical test configuration (A) has a jitter generator as an integral part of the tester. For a multiplexer, a different configuration (B) is used.*

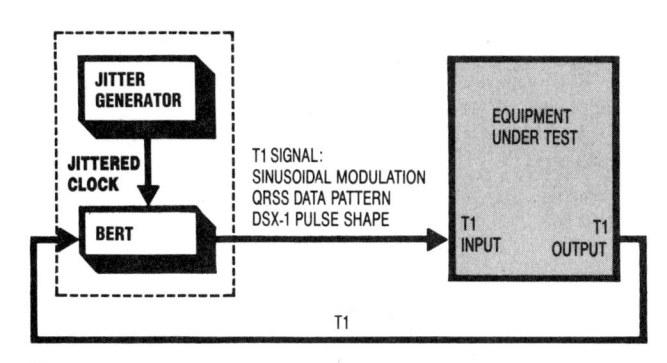

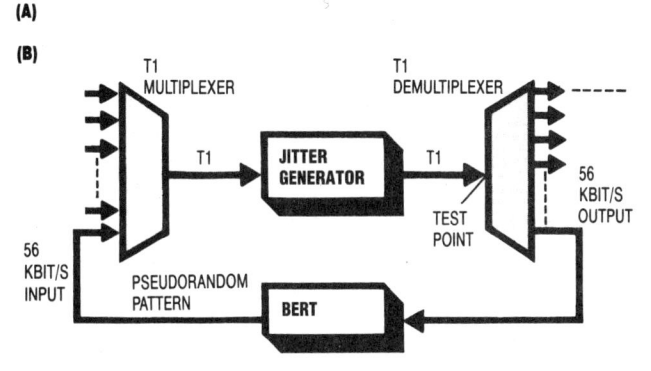

BERT = BIT ERROR RATE TESTER
QRSS = QUASIRANDOM SIGNAL SOURCE

Sinusoidal jitter modulation should be used when testing for specification compliance. Other modulating waveforms, such as square and triangle-shaped waves, contain harmonic frequencies that can exceed mask limits even when the fundamental frequency does not. And this could falsely indicate that specifications are not being met. However, other waveforms can be used for "stressing" the equipment or more closely simulating real jitter. For example, a ramp- or sawtooth-shaped modulation can simulate the type of jitter produced by an M13 multiplexer (AT&T terminology, pronounced "em one three," meaning a multiplexer that combines T1 signals into a DS-3 signal).

Pulse shape and cable length

Specifying the T1 pulse shape at the equipment input is important because the definition of jitter is given in terms of the location in time of the pulse transitions. Any lengthening of these transition times (due to the distortion of the square-wave pulse shape) will cause an ambiguity in defining the amount of jitter present. The longer the cabling, the more pulse distortion and spreading will occur at the input.

If there is insufficient signal equalization performed by the receiver, a lower equipment tolerance for jitter will result. Generally, the digital cross-connect DSX-1 signal should be used for testing, which is at a level of 0 dBdsx (0 decibels relative to the DSX point) and provides a pulse with fairly steep edges—a rise time of less than 135 nanoseconds. Note, however, that some specifications require that the jitter tolerance apply with up to 35.5 decibels of signal loss, which corresponds to the signal loss over 22-gauge cable at up to 6,000 feet.

Jitter-tolerance testing should be performed by applying jitter at a fixed frequency, and then increasing the jitter amplitude until the threshold of intolerance is reached. This threshold should be defined to ensure consistent and repeatable results, yet most specifications fail to give an adequate definition. For example, one specification states that terminal equipment must "operate satisfactorily" with jitter up to the limits given in a mask. This qualitative criterion is ambiguous because satisfactory operation for one user may be unacceptable to another.

A better definition is given in AT&T PUB 62411 (dated October 1985), which defines the threshold as the point at which an onset of errors (1 to 5) occurs in a 60-second interval. Measurements should be made at numerous frequencies until enough data is gathered to enable a comparison to the appropriate jitter-tolerance mask. If the results show that the mask limits were exceeded at every frequency tested, then the tested equipment has adequate jitter tolerance.

Timing sources

Output jitter, or generated jitter, is defined as the amount of jitter at a T1 output when there is no jitter at the input. The input in this case refers to the signal from which the transmit timing is derived (the "synchronizer" input), which may not necessarily be the data input. For instance, as applied to a channel bank in loop-timed mode (where the channel bank output T1 derives timing from the T1 input of the channel bank's demultiplexer side, rather than from an oscillator), the input would be the received T1 signal. If the channel bank is acting as the source of timing for the network, then the input source is the channel bank's own internal oscillator.

A collection of commonly used output jitter specifications is shown in Table 2. Note that most of the specifications give one jitter amplitude limit that applies over all jitter frequencies. Testing for compliance with these specifications requires that a wideband jitter measurement be performed on the output.

Most jitter test sets available today provide a maximum range of 10 Hz to 40 kHz. Additional band-limiting is required to test the AT&T Accunet specification (PUB 62411), which splits one usable band into two: 10 Hz to 8 kHz, and 8 kHz to 40 kHz. CCITT Recommendation 0.171 specifies a frequency range for jitter measurement equipment, which has been included in Table 1 and Figure 5.

The ratio of the output jitter to the input jitter is a device's jitter transfer. The input is again defined as the T1 source from which the transmit timing is derived. A jitter transfer characteristic indicates the amount of allowable jitter amplification and the required jitter attenuation from input to output. It is usually given in the form of a gain-versus-frequency mask.

This mask specification is necessary because a certain amount of jitter reduction in the recovered clock is desirable to reduce accumulated jitter. However, as explained earlier, the recovered clock must track the incoming jitter in order to correctly sample the received data. These two conflicting requirements are addressed through the use of jitter transfer masks, which permit a slight amount of jitter amplification at lower frequencies but require attenuation of the jitter at higher frequencies. This characteristic is much like a low-pass filter, which attenuates noise but allows the desired signal through. Some common jitter-transfer specifications are shown in Table 3.

Determining equipment's jitter-transfer characteristics requires both a jitter generator and a jitter-measurement device. Typically, a QRSS pattern is used, with sinusoidal jitter applied at amplitudes that are one half of those specified in the jitter tolerance mask. The measurement is simplified if a sweeping (automatically stepping through a series of frequencies) jitter generator and a synchronized jitter spectrum analyzer are used.

Simplifying the interface

A fourth type of specification is the network jitter limit, which defines the maximum permissible jitter at a particular interface point in a network. The purpose of one such specification—CCITT G.824—is to enable the satisfactory interconnection of digital network components to form national/international digital paths or connections.

Network limits are also specified by common carriers for points where customers interface to their networks. This greatly simplifies interfacing to a network, or designing intercarrier connections, because knowledge of specific equipment within the network is then unnecessary. The single network-jitter limit ensures that the jitter tolerances of all equipment in the network are adequate.

Determining the correct jitter specification to use depends largely on the application. For equipment manufacturers, the choice is clear because most jitter specifications were written for specific types of equipment. Channel banks, cross-connects, multiplexers, repeaters, remote terminals, and switches all have unique jitter specifications. However, careful attention must be paid to the version of the specification and whether it has been superseded by a more recent specification.

For users who lease a T1 facility, a required specification is one that defines the maximum jitter going into and coming out of the network at the network interface. (AT&T PUB 62411 is an example of one such specification.) The user must ensure that the CSU (channel service unit) that interfaces to the network can tolerate the maximum received network jitter. The jitter at the CSU output must also be less than the maximum allowed into the network.

Budgeting jitter

Therefore, network implementers must use jitter specifications for both equipment and networks. When designing a network, a jitter budget can be formulated by referring to the jitter-tolerance specifications for each device. The maximum allowable jitter at each input can then be roughly estimated by using output jitter and jitter-transfer specifications. To aid in estimating the amount of jitter accumulation that occurs for random T1 data over a repeatered circuit span, the amount of accumulated jitter varies almost linearly with the number of repeaters.

If error rates are excessive, but the network output's jitter level does not justify such a high bit error rate, measurements should be made at equipment inputs to determine if any jitter tolerance limits are being exceeded. This

Table 2: Output jitter specifications

DOCUMENT	TITLE	CONDITIONS	OUTPUT JITTER LIMIT
BELLCORE TR-TSY-000009 (5/86)	ASYNCHRONOUS DIGITAL MULTIPLEXES REQUIREMENTS AND OBJECTIVES		LESS THAN 0.3 UI RMS AND LESS THAN 1.0 UI PP
BELLCORE TA-365-23232-84-01 (4/84)	GENERIC REQUIREMENTS AND OBJECTIVES FOR 96 CHANNEL INTEROFFICE DIGITAL PAIRED CABLE SYSTEMS (PRELIMINARY)		
BELLCORE TA-TSY-000038 (7/85)	SINGLE MODE INTEROFFICE DIGITAL FIBER OPTIC SYSTEMS		
AT&T PUB 43802 (7/82)	DIGITAL MULTIPLEXES REQUIREMENTS AND OBJECTIVES		LESS THAN 0.3 UI RMS
AT&T CB 127 (10/79)	M1C MULTIPLEX COMPATIBILITY SPECIFICATION		
AT&T CB 128 (10/79)	M12 MULTIPLEX COMPATIBILITY SPECIFICATION		
AT&T CB 129 (10/79)	M13 MULTIPLEX COMPATIBILITY SPECIFICATION		
BELLCORE TR-TSY-000303 (9/86)	INTEGRATED DIGITAL LOOP CARRIER SYSTEM GENERIC REQUIREMENTS		LESS THAN 0.2 MICROSECOND RMS (0.44 UI PP)
AT&T PUB 62411 (10/85)	ACCUNET T1.5 SERVICE DESCRIPTION AND INTERFACE SPECIFICATIONS	QRSS OR LIVE TRAFFIC	LESS THAN 0.5 UI PP NO BANDLIMITING 0.01 UI PP 10 Hz TO 8 kHz 0.25 UI PP 8 kHz TO 40 kHz 0.25 UI PP 10 Hz TO 40 kHz
AT&T CB 113	LOW POWER LINE REPEATER COMPATIBILITY SPECIFICATION	ALTERNATING 8 BIT REPEATING PATTERNS	LESS THAN 25 DEGREES PP (.07 UI PP)
AT&T PUB 62411 (9/83)	HIGH CAPACITY DIGITAL SERVICE CHANNEL INTERFACE SPECIFICATION	ALTERNATING 8 BIT REPEATING PATTERNS	LESS THAN 0.07 ±.015 UI PP
AT&T PUB 41457 (5/85)	SKYNET DIGITAL SERVICE (PRELIMINARY)	ALTERNATING 8 BIT REPEATING PATTERNS	
CCITT REC.G.743 (RED)	SECOND ORDER DIGITAL MULTIPLEX EQUIPMENT OPERATING AT 6.312 MBIT/S		LESS THAN 0.33 UI PP
CCITT REC G.824 (RED)	CONTROL OF JITTER AND WANDER IN DIGITAL NETWORKS BASED ON 1.544 MBIT/S HIERARCHY		LESS THAN 2.0 UI PP 10 kHz TO 40 kHz LESS THAN .05 UI PP 8 kHz TO 40 kHz

QRSS = QUASIRANDOM SIGNAL SOURCE   UI PP = UNIT INTERVALS PEAK-TO-PEAK
RMS = ROOT MEAN SQUARE

requires that a spectrum analysis be performed on the demodulated jitter so that the amplitude-versus-frequency relationship can be examined.

A wideband measurement is not adequate, because a single reading cannot verify if a mask is being exceeded. For example, a measurement of 3 UIpp may be within the mask at one frequency, but may exceed the mask at another frequency. Fortunately, the newest generation of jitter test instruments includes sweeping spectrum analyzers that measure jitter in numerous frequency bands and indicate the relationship to the mask.

Note that a frequency-sweep analysis allows only one frequency band to be examined at a time, and a simultaneous measurement of the jitter spectrum cannot be made. Accurate results *can* be obtained by making numerous sweeps and accumulating the results in each band. By comparing the measured spectrum with the jitter tolerance mask, areas can be identified where the mask is exceeded or where there is very little margin. To aid in quickly analyzing a jitter spectrum, a new metric called percent of mask can be used (see "Un'masking' jitter").

Plotting the measured jitter spectrum at key network nodes when service is initiated provides a "fingerprint" of the jitter performance. If problems later arise, new plots can be made to compare to that fingerprint, which will show any degradation and may even give clues to the source of the problem. Abnormalities, such as peaks in the spectrum plot, can be caused by crosstalk, power-line hum, or demultiplexers' waiting-time jitter.

Crystal-balling

Recognizing the need for consistent standards for network jitter and its measurement, the ECSA (Exchange Carriers Standards Association) has established a working subgroup to study jitter. It is part of the T1X1.3 working group of the technical subcommittee on carrier-to-carrier interfaces. T1X1.3 consists of experts who represent many of the major U. S. common carriers and equipment manufacturers. Its goal is to document a framework and philosophy for the control of T1 jitter and wander.

The completed document will provide:
- Recommended network jitter and wander specifications at hierarchical digital interfaces;
- A framework for the specification of individual digital devices;
- Characterization guidelines for network and equipment jitter performance; and
- Standard measurement methodologies.

The finished work will serve as a foundation for the revision of CCITT Recommendation G.824, "The Control of Jitter and Wander Within Digital Networks Based on the 1.544-Mbit/s Hierarchy," which is currently incomplete.

Table 3: Jitter transfer specifications

DOCUMENT	TITLE	CONDITIONS	JITTER TRANSFER LIMITS	
AT&T PUB 43802 (7/82)	DIGITAL MULTIPLEXES REQUIREMENTS AND OBJECTIVES	OUTPUT IS DS-1 FROM DEMULTIPLEXER	≤ 0.1 dB GAIN < −40 dB/DEC < −20 dB/DEC	0 TO 350 Hz 350 TO 2,500 Hz 2.5 TO 15 kHz
BELLCORE TA-365-23232-84-01 (4/84) BELLCORE TR-TSY-000009 (5/86) BELLCORE TA-TSY-000038 (7/85) CCITT G.743 (RED)	GENERIC REQUIREMENTS AND OBJECTIVES FOR 96 CHANNEL INTEROFFICE DIGITAL PAIRED CABLE SYSTEMS (PRELIMINARY) ASYNCHRONOUS DIGITAL MULTIPLEXES REQUIREMENTS AND OBJECTIVES SINGLE MODE INTEROFFICE DIGITAL FIBER OPTIC SYSTEMS SECOND ORDER DIGITAL MULTIPLEX EQUIPMENT OPERATING AT 6.312 MBIT/S	FOR M12 DEMULTIPLEXER	≤ 0.5 dB GAIN < −40 dB/DEC < −20 dB/DEC	10 Hz TO 350 Hz 350 Hz TO 2.5 kHz 2.5 kHz TO 15 kHz
AT&T PUB 62411 (9/83) AT&T PUB 41457 (5/85)	HIGH CAPACITY DIGITAL SERVICE CHANNEL INTERFACE SPECIFICATION SKYNET DIGITAL SERVICE (PRELIMINARY)	QRSS QRSS	< 0.5 UI PP −20 dB/DEC −13.6 UI PP	10 Hz TO 8 kHz 8 kHz TO 40 kHz AT 40 kHz
AT&T PUB 62411 (10/85)	ACCUNET T1.5 SERVICE DESCRIPTION AND INTERFACE SPECIFICATIONS (PRELIMINARY)	TRANSFER FUNCTION MUST FALL BETWEEN MASKS	LESS THAN: GREATER THAN:	−20 dB/DEC 20 Hz to 1 kHz −40 dB/DEC 1 kHz TO 5 kHz −20 dB/DEC 1 Hz TO 30 Hz −40 dB/DEC 30 Hz TO 150 Hz
BELLCORE TA-365-23221-84-01 (4/84)	DIGITAL CROSS CONNECT SYSTEM (PRELIMINARY)		≤ 0.2 dB GAIN −20 dB/DEC	0 TO 0.1 Hz > 0.1 Hz

DEC = DECADE
QRSS = QUASIRANDOM SIGNAL SOURCE
UI PP = UNIT INTERVALS PEAK-TO-PEAK

The T1X1.3 study is progressing rapidly, and it should resolve many of the problems existing with the present assortment of jitter specifications. The proposed network jitter specifications will allow for the interconnection of different national and international digital networks and should ensure that all equipment jitter-tolerance requirements are satisfied.

The equipment specification will provide thorough definitions of jitter tolerance, jitter generation, and jitter transfer. It will also propose such standard test parameters as data pattern, pulse shape, and modulation type.

The characterization guidelines will include mathematical models of jitter accumulation and generation for networks having repeaters and multiplexers. This will provide network designers with a valuable aid for budgeting and predicting jitter performance. Finally, the measurement methodologies will present standard testing configurations and procedures that will enable the performance of repeatable tests with usable results.

It is the goal of AT&T, other common carriers, and the Bell operating companies to evolve to the point where their networks are totally synchronous. A step toward this is the development of the synchronous DS-3 format, which will not use bit-stuffing techniques for multiplexing and therefore will not create waiting-time jitter.

Also, there is a trend to design equipment to be more tolerant of jitter, and even to "dejitterize" T1 signals passing through. These steps are not enough, however, to totally eliminate jitter in T1 networks. It will be many years—even decades—before all older equipment is replaced. Even then, the jitter created by data pattern, environmental effects, and crosstalk will still be around. ∎

Kevin Flynn is an engineering manager and project leader at Telecommunications Techniques, responsible for new product development. He holds a B. S. E. E. from the University of Utah.

Further reading

C. J. Byrne, B. J. Karafin, and D. B. Robinson Jr., "Systematic Jitter in a Chain of Digital Regenerators," *Bell System Technical Journal,* Vol. 42, November 1963.

D. L. Duttweiler, "Waiting Time Jitter," *Bell System Technical Journal,* Vol. 51, 1972.

C. E. Huffman, J. K. Blake, *Asynchronous Multiplex Jitter,* Rockwell International/Collins Transmission Sys. Division, Technical Bulletin 523-0605721-00283J.

Transmission Systems for Communications, Bell Telephone Laboratories, fifth revision, 1982, chapters 29 and 30.

M. Amemiya, M. Aiki, T. Ito, "Jitter Accumulation for Periodic Pattern Signals," *IEEE Transactions on Communications,* Vol. Com-34, No. 5, May 1986.

Strategy for the Control of Jitter and Wander within Digital

Un'masking' jitter

Jitter spectrum analyzers have become indispensable tools for determining compliance with specifications and for troubleshooting problems caused by jitter. A new measurement has been introduced recently to aid in analyzing measured jitter spectrums. Called percent of mask, it is the ratio of measured jitter at a specific frequency to the value specified as the maximum jitter that must be tolerated—called the jitter tolerance mask—at that frequency. The result is expressed as a percent.

For example, if a spectrum analyzer measures a 100-Hz jitter component of 5 Ulpp, and the mask value of jitter tolerance at that frequency is 10 Ulpp, then the percent-of-mask reading would be 50 percent.

Therefore, the percent-of-mask method gives the user:
- A quantitative measure of how severe the jitter is in each frequency band.
- The amount of headroom (margin) there is under the mask.
- A quick go/no-go indication of compliance with the specification.

A value of greater than 100 percent means that the jitter tolerance mask has been exceeded.

The percent-of-mask method is under study by IEEE P1007 standards group that is responsible for developing standards for pulse-code-modulation test instrumentation. A recommendation is expected in favor of this nonproprietary "template" method as a technique for describing jitter performance.

The figure shows the front of a test instrument that incorporates a jitter spectrum analyzer, with the percent-of-mask result displayed. The rating of 54.0 percent tells the user that, across the frequency spectrum, the worst-case frequency band had jitter that was 54 percent of the mask value. This verifies that the jitter does not exceed the tolerance mask given in AT&T PUB 62411. It also shows that there is still quite a bit of headroom (100 percent minus 54 percent) left under the mask.

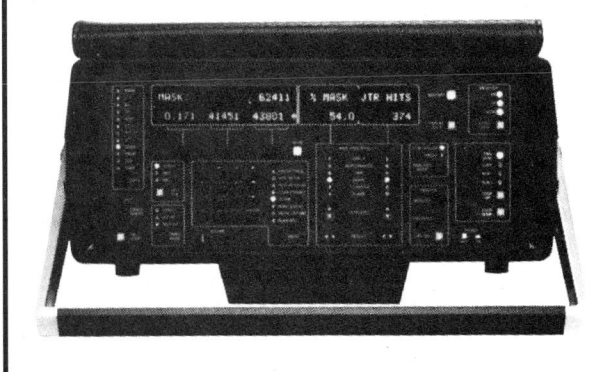

Networks based on the 1.544-Mb/s Hierarchy, ECSA T1X1.3 subgroup proposal T1X1.3/86-008.
Synchronous DS-3 Format Interface Specification, Bell Communications Research, TR-TSY-000021, Issue I, June 1984.

100

Scott L. Ledgerwood, Case/Datatel, Cherry Hill, N.J.

T1 outage ahead: A backup strategy could save your job

Lose a high-speed link and become the center of some very negative attention. With T1 backup, they might not even know.

A network built with T1 circuits is a double-edged sword. When operating normally, it is cost-effective, can transmit high volumes of voice and data traffic at 1.544 Mbit/s, and can even handle full-motion video signals. This is the "good edge" of the sword's blade.

The T1 sword's other edge—the "bloody" one—comes into play when a T1 channel is damaged or its information flow is otherwise interrupted. All of T1's pluses are quickly forgotten as users and network operators scramble to recover the circuits and restore communications. Network horror stories exist where companies have been out of service (and, in many ways, out of business) for several hours—even days.

A network outage is sometimes so critical, in fact, it can reflect badly on the network manager—the reason why major outages are referred to as "career influencing." Consequently, network managers have compelling reasons to be concerned about minimizing the potential damage of an interruption in T1 service. This "job insurance" starts with network backup and restoration procedures that must be thoroughly defined and ready to take effect when (not if) a major link fails.

Among the various backup alternatives for T1 circuits is route diversity, in which dedicated analog and digital circuits are configured as redundant links, ready at all times to accept the interrupted data traffic. Other backup alternatives include switched digital services, such as AT&T's Accunet Reserved T1.5 and Switched 56, and packet-switched services.

In general, network backup techniques for T1 channels include three primary elements: hardware, software, and circuit facilities. Hardware includes products like T1 multiplexers, digital cross-connect systems (DCS), and "smart" multiplexers (also called nodal processors) that have alternative-routing capabilities. Software within each device provides alternative network-routing schemes, network-test and -diagnostic capabilities, and network-outage reporting. The third element, circuit facilities, covers the actual transmission path for backup links, and is the area users have the least control over.

Not all T1 users have identical needs for backup. Companies using T1 links for applications that are not time-critical (administration, sales activity reporting, and certain types of billing) can live with occasional unscheduled downtime, and may not need T1 backup at all.

A second class of users relies on T1 connections for mission-critical communications that cannot be interrupted, even for very short periods of time. Examples of this level of need include: airline reservation systems, international financial networks, publishing systems, and so on. For these users, loss of T1 can mean major loss of productivity and revenues; hence, substantial costs for the redundant links of the routing-diversity approach are justifiable.

T1 dependence and diversification
Although there are many T1 users in the first two application categories, most users fall into a gray area between the highest and lowest levels of T1 dependence. This third group will suffer greatly without its T1, but perhaps cannot cost-justify an entire secondary T1 path to be used only in the event of a primary link failure. In the area of data communications, these users can often get by with slower service during a T1 outage, and consequently are excellent candidates for backup via Switched 56 and similar digital services. Another backup option for this level of T1 dependence is AT&T Accunet Reserved T1.5 service, as explained below.

Regardless of the level of dependence of your organization, the reality is this: The majority of T1 users, by far, have no backup capability.

Route diversity normally is used when a T1 network has

1. Route diversity. *In this three-site network, traffic among the sites can be balanced so that if any link is lost, the remaining links can sustain normal communications.*

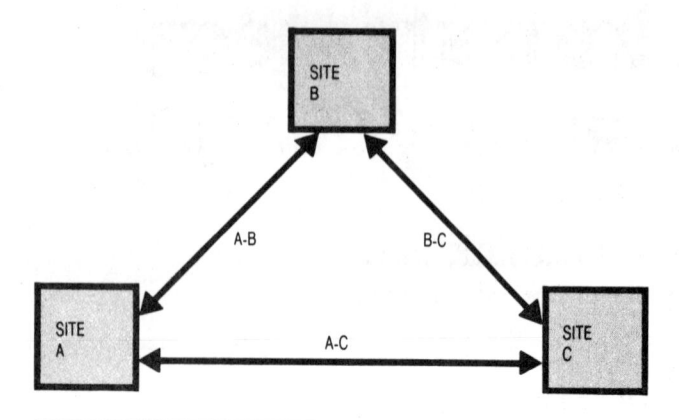

three or more sites. However, it can also be used in a simple point-to-point network.

In its most basic application, the point-to-point technique requires providing two paths—a primary and an alternative—between sites. Each path can use a different type of service, or the same type of service routed differently to reduce the potential of a common failure affecting both paths. If the primary T1 path fails, traffic is automatically switched to the backup link.

A crosstown, point-to-point scenario could employ a short-haul digital-microwave link, backing up a T1 line leased from a local telephone company. It is equally feasible to use microwave as the primary link, backing it up with the leased T1 line. The cost to back up the T1 line in this situation is relatively inexpensive: A typical two-point digital microwave channel, including radios, towers, antennas, and electronics, costs (one time) about $25,000. Compare this to about $650 per month for a dedicated 56-kbit/s channel, or $250 to $1,500 per month for a regional T1 channel.

With route diversity on a three-site network (see Fig. 1), data and voice traffic among sites A, B, and C can be balanced so that if any link (A–B, A–C, or B–C) is lost, the remaining links provide sufficient bandwidth to sustain normal communications while repairs are made.

Most modern T1 nodal processors provide alternative-routing features. One of these is "table-based" routing, in which the network manager programs the nodal processor with network end points and traffic-routing instructions. A sophisticated alternative to this is dynamic routing, sometimes called "algorithm-based routing," where software in the nodal processor dynamically computes alternative routing, using criteria initially set up by the network manager. In the latter case, no complex routing tables are needed.

Another nodal-processor feature, called priority bumping, routes traffic considered higher in priority or in bandwidth usage while slowing down or shedding lower-priority traffic. When network sites are located within the same city or Local Access and Transport Area, circuit costs for a route-diversity solution are generally considered affordable. As mentioned previously, a two-point T1 circuit within a city, New York for example, averages about $1,500 per month.

If the sites to be backed up are hundreds or thousands of miles apart, however, route-diversity backup is considerably more expensive: Monthly T1 costs jump rapidly to tens of thousands of dollars. Even with the likelihood of continuing T1 rate reductions, route diversity for multiple sites located more than a few hundred miles apart may still be too expensive for many users.

Using switched T1

One backup alternative to redundant T1 circuits is AT&T's Accunet Reserved T1.5 (switched) service. It is provided through a DCS located in specially designated AT&T central offices. Local access to this service is through T1 circuits from the customer's premises to the AT&T network serving central office, also called a point of presence (POP). Costs for Accunet Reserved T1.5 are based on three rate elements: usage charges, call setup charges, and local channel charges.

Accunet Reserved T1.5 service was originally targeted for video teleconferencing networks. To boost usage, AT&T has been promoting the service as a backup alternative to dedicated T1 service. One particular application is for high-speed file transfer between a user's computer center and a "hot-site" backup computer facility. In practice, when a primary T1 channel fails, traffic is switched to a backup T1 access line and AT&T is notified to activate Accunet Reserved T1.5 service.

An important limitation to note is that the normal response time to establish Accunet Reserved T1.5 service is 30 minutes or more. This delay results from the time required by the carrier to set up T1 service through DCS equipment.

Voice vs. data

A key consideration when establishing an overall T1 backup plan is how to handle voice communications. Most voice circuits derived from T1 channels are used for PBX-to-PBX traffic (typically using channel banks or related devices).

Here is the easiest and quickest backup solution: If a T1 line fails, the PBX's least-cost-routing feature can be modified, usually within 15 minutes if the user has been trained to access and modify this feature. (It could take as long as three to four hours if the PBX vendor has to be summoned to make the programming changes.) With the modification, outgoing calls are completed using existing local and long-distance facilities. Typical of these facilities are AT&T Megacom and MCI Prism, both of which are distance-sensitive long-distance services (in contrast to traditional banded WATS-like services).

In this scenario, users can still complete outgoing calls as usual. However, the cost for usage in the interim period (while the T1 circuit is being restored) will be higher than with T1.

If this approach to backing up voice traffic is acceptable, then backing up a T1 line really means backing up the data traffic embedded in that T1 line. Since most private T1 networks have a voice/data traffic ratio of 80:20 or greater, techniques used to back up the data channels in a T1 network can be very different from backup for voice.

Applications running at speeds slower than 56 kbit/s can be restored quickly via Switched 56 service. Typically, the user dials a prestored 10-digit number (700-XXX-YYYY) from the console of the nodal processor to effect the restoration; the resulting reconnect time is under a minute in ideal circumstances.

Applications running at speeds greater than 56 kbit/s, such as videoconferencing and CAD/CAM are often bandwidth-sensitive and normally must be reassigned alternative T1 facilities, such as Accunet Reserved T1.5 service.

Dial-up backup
Switched 56-kbit/s digital communications service is a dial-up usage-sensitive digital service that is accessed via dedicated lines that connect the customer with a common carrier's central office (see "The how and where of switched 56-kbit/s service," DATA COMMUNICATIONS, August 1986). AT&T currently offers interstate Accunet Switched 56 service in over 80 cities. Other major common carriers, such as MCI and US Sprint, offer their own versions of the service.

AT&T's Accunet Switched 56 network uses T1 channels to connect designated AT&T Accunet Switched 56 central offices to 4ESS switches. These switches have been specially modified to support the Accunet Switched 56 network, which is completely terrestrial and is available principally in the U.S.

Similar to Accunet Reserved T1.5 service, Accunet Switched 56 service requires a dedicated local channel from the customer's premises to the Switched 56 central office. Either a 56-kbit/s or T1 channel can be used. Single digital channels (such as AT&T Dataphone Digital Service lines) are used by customers with moderate access requirements (less than three 56-kbit/s lines), while T1 access is used by customers who need multiple access points or who wish to consolidate access for various telecommunications services.

Important note: Digital access lines must be present at both the originating and terminating ends of a connection, and a Switched 56 call can be made only to cities served by the service.

If Switched 56 service is used for T1 backup, connections can generally be made in a matter of seconds to reestablish data communications in case of a T1 link failure. When advanced nodal processors are in place, devices using T1 at the time of an outage may be switched over to alternative paths, without losing their sessions. Voice traffic is usually routed to the switched telephone network using the same T1 access as the data.

One of the advantages of choosing Switched 56 for T1 backup is that it can be used for other applications. Some are: overload relief (a process in which excess traffic on T1 channels is routed over 56-kbit/s service); videoconferencing; digital facsimile; and polled access to sites not on the T1 network.

The savings
Table 1 compares the costs, between two sites, of three backup alternatives: Accunet Reserved T1.5, Accunet Switched 56, and route diversity (a full-time backup line). The potential savings in monthly access-line and usage charges are shown for Accunet Reserved T1.5 or Accunet Switched 56 T1-channel backup by substituting either service for route diversity.

In this comparison, the two sites are assumed to be 350 miles apart—the approximate distance between San Francisco and Los Angeles. Service is terminated in one port at each end of the connection. The customer offices at each end are assumed to be 10 miles from their AT&T POPs. Another assumption is that, of the 24 possible DS0 (56-kbit/s) channels on the T1 line, six contain data traffic; these are backed up by Switched 56 service. Voice traffic will be routed by the PBX over standard voice facilities.

The standby costs include those for local T1 access lines, for a duplicate San Francisco Los Angeles T1 channel (needed for route diversity), and the monthly access (or minimum) charges needed for Accunet Reserved T1.5 or Switched 56 service.

As the distance between the two sites to be backed up

Table 1: Cost comparison, intrastate/interLATA application

	ROUTE DIVERSITY	ACCUNET RESERVED T1.5	ACCUNET SWITCHED 56
FIXED MONTHLY ACCESS LINE CHARGES			
LOCAL T1 ACCESS 2 CIRCUITS @ $250	$500	$500	$500
SF-LA T1 LINE	6,000	–	–
MONTHLY USAGE CHARGES			
CONNECTION CHARGE RESERVED T1.5	–	700.80	–
MINIMUM USAGE 12 TOTAL CIRCUITS @ $75 EACH	–	–	900
TOTAL STANDBY COST (ASSUMES NO OUTAGES)	6,500	1,200	1,400
SAVINGS OVER ROUTE DIVERSITY	–	5,299.20	5,100

NOTE: IN THIS EXAMPLE, USING 56-KBIT/S ACCESS LINES IN PLACE OF T1 LINES DOES NOT INCREASE SAVINGS, PARTICULARLY BECAUSE MULTIPLE CIRCUITS ARE BEING BACKED UP. 56-KBIT/S INTRASTATE INTERLATA ACCESS LINES COST $316 PER MONTH IN CALIFORNIA. SIX CIRCUITS AT EACH END OF THE CONNECTION RAISES THE ACCESS LINE FIGURE FROM $500 TO $3,000.

Table 2: Cost comparison, interstate/interLATA application

	ROUTE DIVERSITY	ACCUNET RESERVED T1.5	ACCUNET SWITCHED 56
FIXED MONTHLY ACCESS LINE CHARGES			
LOCAL T1 ACCESS			
1 CIRCUIT—LOS ANGELES	$250	$250	$250
1 CIRCUIT—NEW YORK	1,524	1,524	1,524
LA-NY T1 LINE	31,800	—	—
MONTHLY USAGE CHARGES			
CONNECTION CHARGE RESERVED T1.5	—	700.80	—
MINIMUM USAGE 12 TOTAL CIRCUITS @ $75 EACH	—	—	900
TOTAL STANDBY COST (ASSUMES NO OUTAGES)	33,574	2,474.80	2,674
SAVINGS OVER ROUTE DIVERSITY	—	31,099.20	30,900

increases, the savings achieved by using switched backup rather than route diversity are even more dramatic. In Table 2's example—a T1 link connecting Los Angeles with New York City—the line-charge savings are more than $30,000 per month.

Both Accunet Reserved T1.5 and Switched 56 are attractive T1-backup options. Accunet Reserved T1.5 allows both voice and high-speed (Mbit/s) data traffic to be readily backed up. The most important factor favoring Switched 56 backup is its quick recovery time, measured in seconds, as opposed to the approximate half hour needed when establishing an Accunet Reserved T1.5 connection. Of course, employing the Switched 56 data rate may result in reduced throughput during the T1-backup period.

If a T1 channel fails, applications already in progress on the Switched 56 service are preempted, either immediately ("hard bumping") or upon session completion ("soft bumping"). How the preemption occurs is determined by the new application's priority; the multiplexer is preprogrammed to prioritize channels based on user requirements. High-end nodal processors can be programmed with many different levels of application priority, determining what sessions will be hard-bumped, soft-bumped, or maintained.

The customer premises equipment needed to implement switched backup of T1 includes, at a minimum: a T1 multiplexer with two full-duplex T1 links, a channel-adapter card to store dialing codes, and a dedicated access line that connects the customer's premises to the carrier's POP. It is assumed that the T1 multiplexer supplier includes switched-service support in the equipment design, as well as the following attributes:

■ Switchable T1 ports with logic that recognizes when the primary T1 link has failed.

■ Data-channel cards that "instruct" the Accunet central office switch to access the backup 56-kbit/s circuits. This access includes the capability to dial backup Switched 56 circuits and to automatically answer incoming Switched 56 calls (additional detail below).

■ Storage of phone numbers for backup connections. (Switched 56 service is accessed via 700-prefix numbers.)

Several major T1 multiplexer suppliers currently provide or plan to support these features.

Figure 2 shows a T1 multiplexer configured to back up a dedicated T1 line with Switched 56 service. The multiplexer has two operational T1 links. If the primary T1 link fails, multiplexers at both sites sense this failure and switch to the backup T1 link, which is connected to the local interexchange carrier POP.

At the same time, each data-channel card at the main site's multiplexer is directed by the multiplexer software to dial the preprogrammed Switched 56 telephone number designated for its equivalent channel in the distant multiplexer. Up to 24 DS0 channels provided by a T1 line could be backed up in this fashion. In most applications, backup facilities will be needed for as many as five or six high-priority data channels.

Backup for the hub/star

Figure 3 depicts how a hub/star network using T1 circuits can be configured to provide Switched 56 backup. As in the previous example, backup T1 lines to the closest AT&T central office are provided in each city in the network. Note: Further savings can be realized in some applications where only a single T1 line at the hub—as backup for the three

2. Point-to-point backup. *The multiplexer backs up the primary T1 line with Switched 56 service. The T1 line links the multiplexer to the local Class 4 switch.*

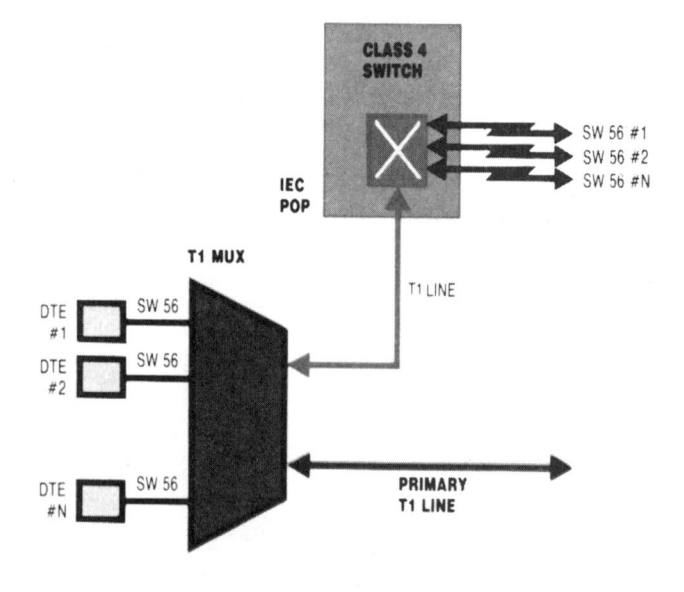

DTE = DATA TERMINAL EQUIPMENT
IEC = INTEREXCHANGE CARRIER
POP = POINT OF PRESENCE
SW = SWITCHED
SW 56 = 56-KBIT/S SWITCHED CIRCUIT

3. Hub/star backup. *The network uses T1 circuits to provide Switched 56 backup. The backup T1 lines connect the multiplexers to the closest IXC POP in each city.*

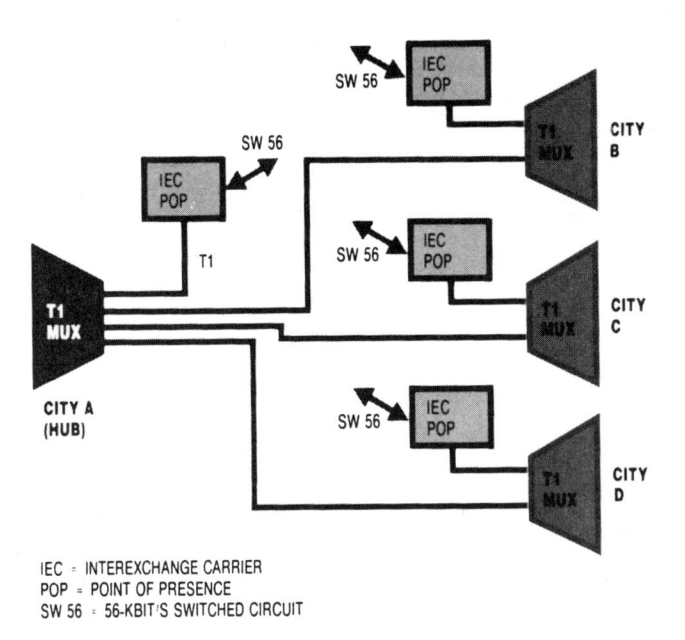

IEC = INTEREXCHANGE CARRIER
POP = POINT OF PRESENCE
SW 56 = 56-KBIT/S SWITCHED CIRCUIT

remote sites—is able to support all DS0s.

Many corporate and government-agency networks take the form of a hub/star naturally, with communications lines emanating from the headquarters site to regions or branches. The need to have backup provisioning is driving these networks into ring or mesh configurations, strictly to provide route-diversity backup of T1 lines. In some applications, such as voice communications (in which the PBX routes calls over alternative voice-grade circuits) or digital facsimile (which can absorb some delays without overall service degradation), this route-diversity-backup strategy is not necessary, and the switched-backup approach will more than suffice.

The significant cost savings possible by avoiding redundant T1 lines has already been illustrated. The bottom line is that if the natural topology of your network is a hub/star, continue that strategy, and use route-diversity backup where necessary. But, where practical, back up the T1 lines with switched services. ■

Scott Ledgerwood is director of product planning for Case/Datatel. He has been with the company since 1985 and is responsible for identifying and selecting new product opportunities, and coordinating them with the company's engineering and sales departments. He holds a BS in industrial engineering from Oregon State University.

Hugh Goldberg, General DataComm Inc., Middlebury, Conn.

DDS's latest wrinkle: User diagnostics in a separate channel

Digital service with a handy side channel is now a reality. But how does one use it? And will it herald a new era for DDS?

Over the past decade, Dataphone Digital Service (DDS)—AT&T's trademarked offering, whose generic term is digital data system—has established itself as one of the premier private-line data offerings. But DDS has not been without flaws. Even with its lack—until recently—of a user-diagnostic channel, the outcome of its long competition with standard analog leased lines for data transmission has been a see-saw race with no clear winner. The secondary-channel capability could make a difference.

The vagaries of both local and nationwide tariffs have made DDS more attractive some years, only to be brushed aside in favor of analog in others. Stories of less-than-perfect digital service abound, causing some users to abandon digital for analog leased lines. But it is too late to alter the future course of data transmission. Simply stated, telephone companies and their customers favor digital transport: The tariff contains guaranteed performance criteria and bit-error rates generally lower than with analog transmission.

Analog facilities used for data transmission have had one key advantage over conventional DDS: the ability to transmit diagnostic data between host and tributary locations without affecting production-data flow. With these secondary diagnostic channels, remote terminals are monitored and controlled from a master location. Tests are performed, statistics logged, and problems anticipated before the communications network has been completely disabled.

The predominant method for adding diagnostics over analog facilities has been frequency-division multiplexing (FDM). A secondary (diagnostic) channel occupying a very narrow band—generally less than 200 Hz—above or below the primary channel carries data from a diagnostic controller to various remote modems. The primary, or production-data, channel is bounded by 600 and 2,400 Hz; the entire bandwidth is 300 to 3,400 Hz.

By adequately filtering each frequency band, neither the primary nor secondary channel is affected by the other's data flow. Since an analog leased line passes signals in a 3,100-Hz band transparently (that is, in any format), both primary and secondary channels act independently.

Digital transmission, on the other hand, is not transparent. The signal that is generated by the user's data service unit (DSU) is limited to passing binary information, and only at the channel's fixed data rate. This signal is completely reconstructed (regenerated) at the first central office (CO) and at every major point along the network, until it reaches its final destination.

Ineffective robbery

There has been no suitable way to pass diagnostic information along with the digital production data. Even robbing data bandwidth from the primary channel—as in time-division multiplexing (TDM)—is not completely effective, because it does not allow primary and secondary data to flow independently.

For DDS diagnostic equipment that uses TDM techniques, remote tributary stations in a multipoint DDS application cannot accommodate polling of the primary channel at times different from its secondary channel. Also, such an approach does not permit tests to be run on suspect remote equipment at arbitrary times, since there is only one path through conventional DDS's digital hubbing equipment (the multipoint junction unit or MJU).

To reach its full potential, digital transmission needed a diagnostic means similar to analog that supports both primary- and secondary-channel data simultaneously and independently. Toward this end, a secondary channel capability was developed by Bell Laboratories for both

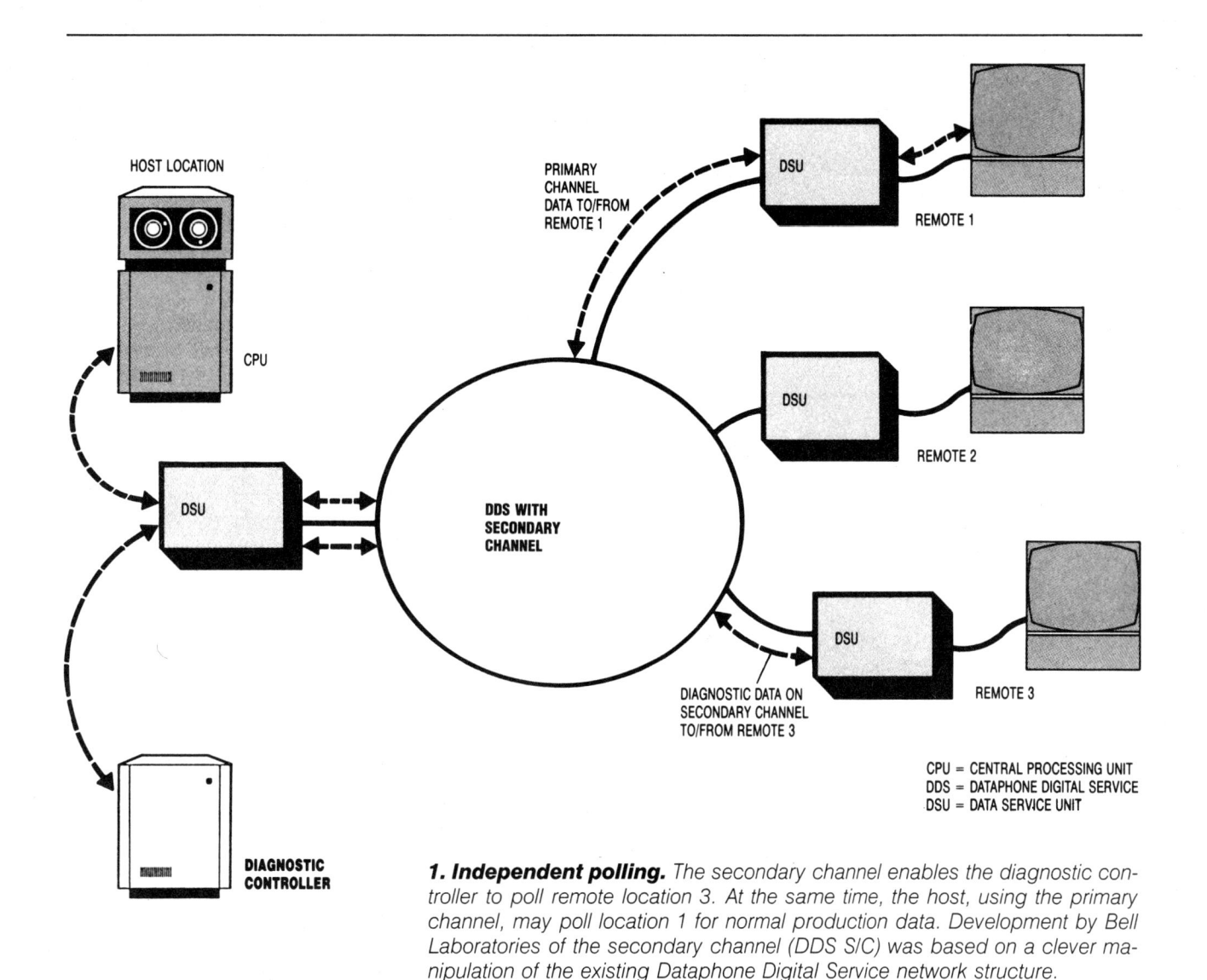

1. Independent polling. *The secondary channel enables the diagnostic controller to poll remote location 3. At the same time, the host, using the primary channel, may poll location 1 for normal production data. Development by Bell Laboratories of the secondary channel (DDS S/C) was based on a clever manipulation of the existing Dataphone Digital Service network structure.*

subrate (2.4-, 4.8-, 9.6-kbit/s) and 56-kbit/s DDS. Known as "DDS with Secondary Channel" (DDS S/C), this development was based upon a clever manipulation of the existing network structure. With DDS S/C, both primary and secondary channels may be polled separately (Fig. 1), from the same or different remote DSUs, since diagnostic data may be passed independently of the primary channel's production data.

Many networks require master diagnostic consoles that control the data communications equipment at all remote locations, whether attended or unattended. Clearly, this implies a diagnostic overlay to the existing production data network.

DDS S/C accommodates the overlay requirement by providing the transport means needed to pass diagnostic information between host and remote tributary stations without disrupting activity on the primary data channel. Information concerning the remote's "health" or the activity of the attached terminal equipment can be passed to the master console. This allows analog-like network control, permitting the network manager to anticipate problems, log network statistics, print management reports, and take appropriate action for disaster recovery.

Other possible applications exist for DDS S/C's channel. These include piggybacking low-speed (generally 1.2-kbit/s or less) applications like alarm monitoring, surveillance, and environmental control onto a high-speed (up to 56-kbit/s) data application. The secondary channel may also be used to carry encryption algorithms to ensure the privacy of sensitive information during transmission. The object is to save overall line charges by using one digital private line instead of two.

Why diagnose?
DDS has proved to be highly reliable. It is the only private-line data service with performance guarantees for error-free seconds (99.5 percent) and network uptime (99.95 percent) built into the tariffs. (In comparison, AT&T's Pub.

62411 specifies T1 "design objectives" of 95 percent error-free seconds and downtime of less than 26 hours per year for a long-haul circuit.) Yet if DDS is so reliable, then why are network diagnostics—requiring DDS S/C—necessary?

Outlined below are five general categories of network diagnostics and control that are supported by a secondary channel. Only one category, network testing, may be considered a function of DDS's performance record:

1. Host control over remote optioning. The diagnostic controller can send commands over the secondary channel to option or re-option remote DSUs under the control of the host diagnostic console. This optioning may be performed independently of the production data. As long as the DSU option selections are programmable (soft), commands sent over the secondary channel can completely re-strap the remote device without any hands-on technical personnel.

2. Surveillance—remote DSU/terminal interface. Each remote DSU can report the status of its terminal equipment interface to the diagnostic controller. This can be done over regular polled intervals or on a demand basis. The DSU-to-terminal interfaces may be categorized as: Control, such as *Request to Send* (RTS) and *Data Terminal Ready;* Clock, transmitter and receiver timing; and Data, both transmitted and received.

3. Remote alarming. Certain conditions can be reported to the host as alarms. Although similar to interface surveillance, alarm decisions are made by the remote DSUs and communicated over the secondary channel to alert the diagnostic controller. The alarm criteria may be based on abnormal conditions internal to the DSU, or on external conditions, such as the condition of a terminal interface lead. In this manner, the failure of an internal component or the loss of a *Data Terminal Ready* interface signal could be relayed to the host as an alarm.

4. Performance testing of the network and equipment. This category includes an evaluation of overall signal quality. Testing can be performed over either the primary or secondary channel. In preventive-maintenance testing, the secondary channel may be the vehicle for both loopback and end-to-end testing.

DDS S/C testing may be called predictive—similar to the way the extended superframe can predict the performance of a T1 data channel (see "The Hidden Treasures of ESF," DATA COMMUNICATIONS, September 1986, p. 204). While it need not interfere with production data on the primary channel, the testing is statistically representative of the performance of both channels. Secondary channel data is transmitted via the network C bit (discussed later in the derivation of the secondary channel), which always accompanies the primary channel data bits. The very same impairments that degrade secondary-channel performance do so to the primary channel, and in the same way.

Maintenance testing cannot be done in this manner with conventional analog diagnostic modems, which derive their diagnostic channels using FDM techniques. Since there is not linkage between the primary and secondary channels with analog facilities, testing on the secondary channel cannot be correlated with the signal-quality performance on the primary channel.

Primary-channel, end-to-end, or loopback testing completely disrupts production-data flow and is therefore only performed at initial service installation or when data has stopped flowing.

5. Reference information stored within each remote. Remote-equipment serial numbers and hardware- or software-revision levels, resident within each remote DSU's firmware (stored memory), can be transmitted back to the host controller on demand. In this way, the network manager can perform a complete inventory of the field equipment from the host diagnostic console without dispatching any personnel. User-defined information, such as DDS-circuit and multipoint-drop identification numbers, may be programmed by the network manager to establish a map of all the digital terminations.

Justification

Take, for example, a nationwide brokerage service that has chosen DDS because it needs reliable, error-free data communications. This firm may choose a DDS S/C network over conventional DDS to better facilitate an integrated disaster recovery plan.

With the primary DDS channel carrying brokerage-transaction information, the secondary channel provides a means of transport between the host location's diagnostic data controller and all of the remotes. Since the primary and secondary channels are independent, they may be polled separately.

Under normal conditions, the secondary channel carries status information from the tributary stations back to the master. Noninterfering "surveillance" tests may be run on a continuing basis between the DSUs and the transaction terminals. In this way, the diagnostic controller can monitor the remote office locations, logging usage statistics and looking for potential problems—such as intermittent power and streaming—before they impact primary-channel data flow. (Streaming is a condition in which a terminal holds its RTS continuously on after its transmission back to the host has been completed.) Since diagnostic intelligence is built into the DSUs, the need for technical personnel at the remote sites is greatly reduced.

If a problem is suspected, the diagnostic controller interacts with the remotes over the secondary channel to pinpoint the problem, without affecting production data. The network operator can perform both end-to-end and loopback testing on the secondary channel, to further isolate the problem. Testing on the primary data channel is performed only as a last resort, since it will take the entire circuit down.

If a network failure does occur, the firm's disaster recovery plan provides for immediate, though temporary, service restoral while the defective element is being isolated and repaired. Using the diagnostic controller, the firm's dial-up circuits would be used in place of failed subrate or 56-kbit/s circuits. Data continues to flow over the backup link (such as AT&T's Accunet Switched 56 service), while trouble-shooting and repair procedures continue on the faulty link until the problem is resolved.

For many critical data applications, anticipation of error

conditions that could become catastrophic problems, combined with the ability to take remedial action that readily restores service, cost-justifies a diagnostic network using DDS S/C with dial backup. The degree of a company's reliance on the flow of production data from its remote locations will be the deciding factor in determining whether the added cost of the equipment and service is justified. In the case of our hypothetical brokerage firm, the loss incurred from eight hours of downtime during a peak traffic period may well have been greater than the added equipment costs for DDS S/C.

The carrier's perspective

DDS S/C is a powerful adjunct to nationwide DDS because it is potentially most useful for medium-size to large networks—having more than 25 DDS terminations—with widely dispersed locations. While nationwide DDS S/C may be the most desirable application, it is also the most difficult to deploy in today's post-divestiture environment.

A nationwide DDS network requires the coordinated involvement of major interexchange carriers (such as AT&T, MCI, and U S Sprint) and various local telephone companies. Since the local telephone companies own the DDS hubs (test sites), they must provide much of the new, upgraded equipment required to implement DDS S/C. For nationwide DDS S/C to be effective, the service must be made available in all major geographic markets. This means that the interexchange carriers must have the appropriate interLATA (Local Access and Tariff Area) tariffs and the local telephone companies must have the access tariffs in place.

While the primary market is nationwide DDS S/C, the secondary market, which addresses locally provided DDS S/C, has already been deployed by several regional Bell operating companies.

Until recently, the RBOCs have not pushed for DDS S/C. The reasoning: Most of the network equipment that would require replacement—such as MJUs and OCUs (office channel units)—is found at the DDS test sites and is therefore owned by the RBOCs. Even though the expense to upgrade the facilities would be borne by the local telephone companies as access providers to nationwide DDS, the major portion of the revenues from increased DDS usage would go to the interexchange carriers.

Also, ISDN (Integrated Services Digital Network) continues to create confusion about its potential impact on DDS. The RBOC network planners must resolve concerns that traveling down the road of DDS S/C will not lead them to implement an outdated technology.

Most of these concerns, however, have been overshadowed by an increased awareness that the RBOCs must compete with each other—as well as with the interexchange carriers—for investor interest and for customer attention. DDS S/C represents a tangible migration toward future digital transport schemes, such as ISDN. Also, the regional Bell operating companies no longer view DDS S/C service as limited to only nationwide. New intraLATA digital services will benefit from the advantages of DDS S/C to make an even more effective offering.

Finally, users have been pressuring both the local and interexchange telephone companies for a digital service that can readily support network diagnostics.

2. The backhaul problem. *With conventional point-to-point DDS service, a subscriber with two locations separated by one mile might have to pay for a 100-mile charge.*

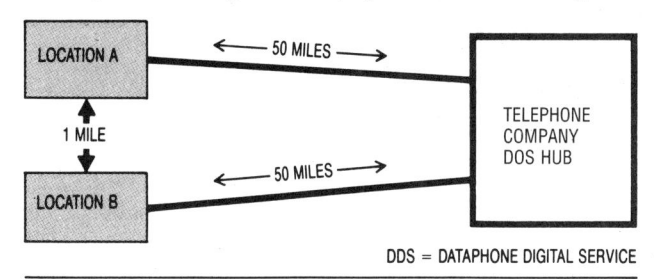

DDS = DATAPHONE DIGITAL SERVICE

The physical means by which DDS is deployed can add substantially to the expense of the service. Conventional DDS is a hubbed service. That is, all remote user terminations must be connected by way of one of the approximately 110 DDS test sites throughout the country. If, for example, locations A and B of a point-to-point link (Fig. 2) are spaced one mile from each other but 50 miles from the nearest test site, the effective mileage charge will be 100 miles, since each channel must be "backhauled" to the test site 50 miles away. While hubbing facilitates complete digital-network testing, the added backhaul mileage can make DDS very expensive compared with analog transmission.

Lower cost

Generic digital services, also known as hubless DDS, is offered by the various local telephone companies. It provides a lower-cost, intraLATA digital service by minimizing and, in some cases, almost totally eliminating the backhaul mileage. While the generic services may differ in form, the apparent end result to the user is very much the same as conventional DDS. The three common methods used to effect generic service are:

■ Completely eliminating the connection to a test site through the interconnection of subscriber terminations at the nearby CO (Fig. 3A). Telephone company dial-up diagnostics and control may be performed from a remote test site. The subscriber's data passes through a minimally equipped Class 5 central office just to get from location A to location B. Only in the case that both user locations are directly served by the same DDS test site would the backhaul distance be the same for conventional DDS as for the hubless solution.

■ Placing local digital nodes closer to the subscriber, such as in a Class 5 CO, also can reduce the service-mileage charges (Fig. 3B). These nodes are simpler and less expensive than normal hub facilities, yet perform similar network test functions. Control—such as initiating a test—is still performed from the test center.

■ Aggregating remote digital terminations and multiplexing them over T1 fiber facilities to the test site (Fig. 3C), with

3. Hubless DDS. *Three common methods to minimize backhaul mileage costs: (A) Interconnect subscriber terminations; use dial-up for testing from the test center. (B) Place "mininodes" close to the subscriber; control is still from the test center. (C) Aggregate remote terminations; multiplex them via T1 to the test center.*

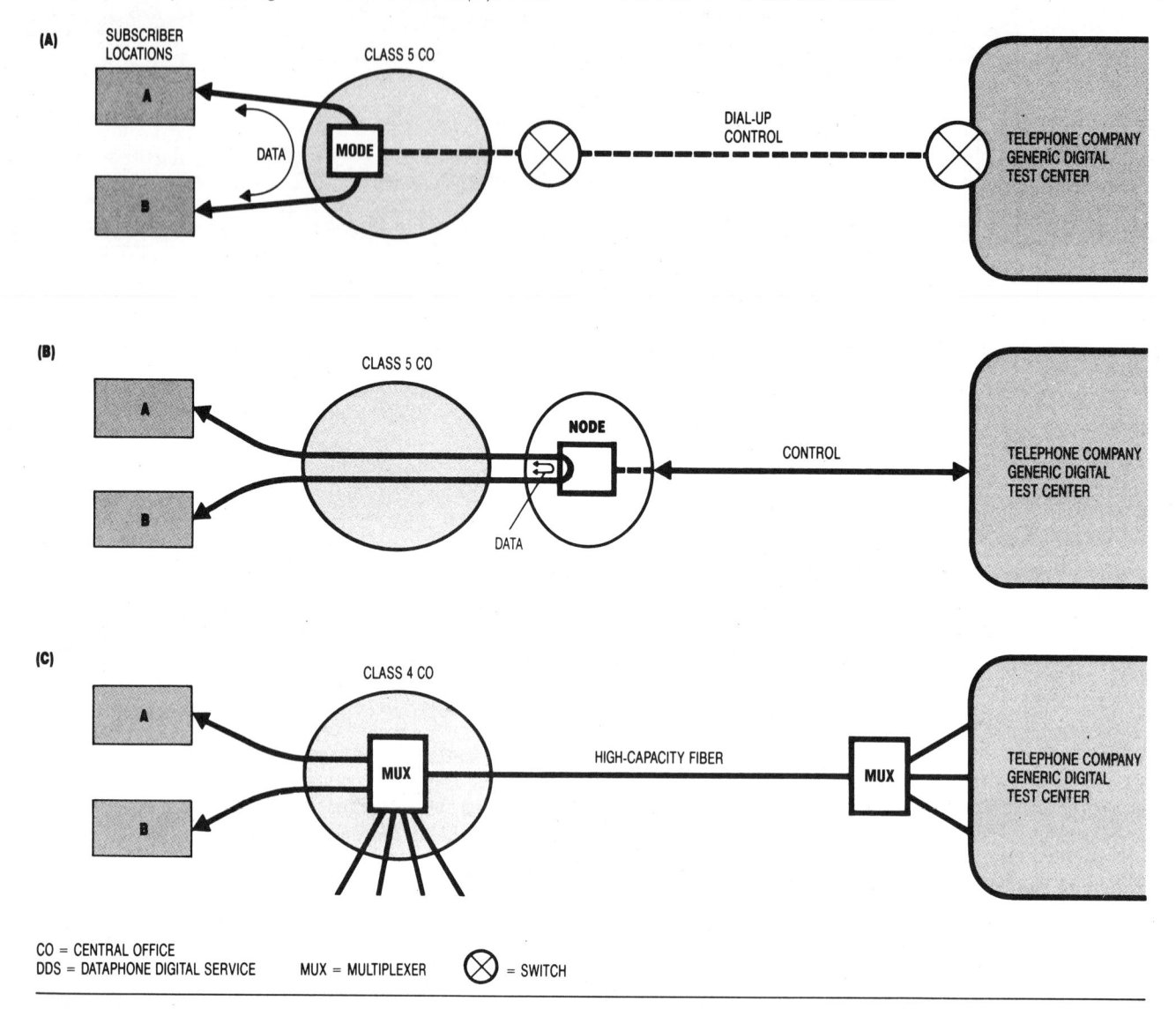

CO = CENTRAL OFFICE
DDS = DATAPHONE DIGITAL SERVICE
MUX = MULTIPLEXER
⊗ = SWITCH

the remote multiplexer located at the CO. While this method does not eliminate the necessity of backhauling, it lowers the cost by sharing the high-capacity transport cost to the test site among many DDS terminations.

The cost advantages of generic intraLATA digital service, coupled with the diagnostic potential of the secondary channel, makes generic DDS S/C an attractive offering at an overall lower cost to the user than conventional DDS without secondary channel. And if hubless techniques can be used for access to conventional (nationwide) DDS, the overall service ends up costing less.

For the user in a position to implement DDS S/C entirely within one LATA (intraLATA), the following advantages over nationwide DDS S/C deployment become apparent:
- Only one telephone company need be involved in providing the entire service. This eliminates the requirement for other telephone companies to file companion secondary-channel tariffs.
- For intrastate usage, only one state public utility commission is involved, simplifying the tariff procedure.
- No interexchange carrier is required.

IntraLATA DDS S/C represents a standalone offering—that is, no interconnection with nationwide DDS is required. In a sense, generic digital service may be viewed as a bypass opportunity for the RBOCs, since it eliminates all other service providers. In the future, generic digital services may well interface nationwide DDS to provide more-affordable digital service.

Since DDS S/C is an adaptation of the existing network, many of the conventional DDS elements must be replaced for DDS S/C operation. Figure 4 details the equipment between the user's data terminal and the elements of a

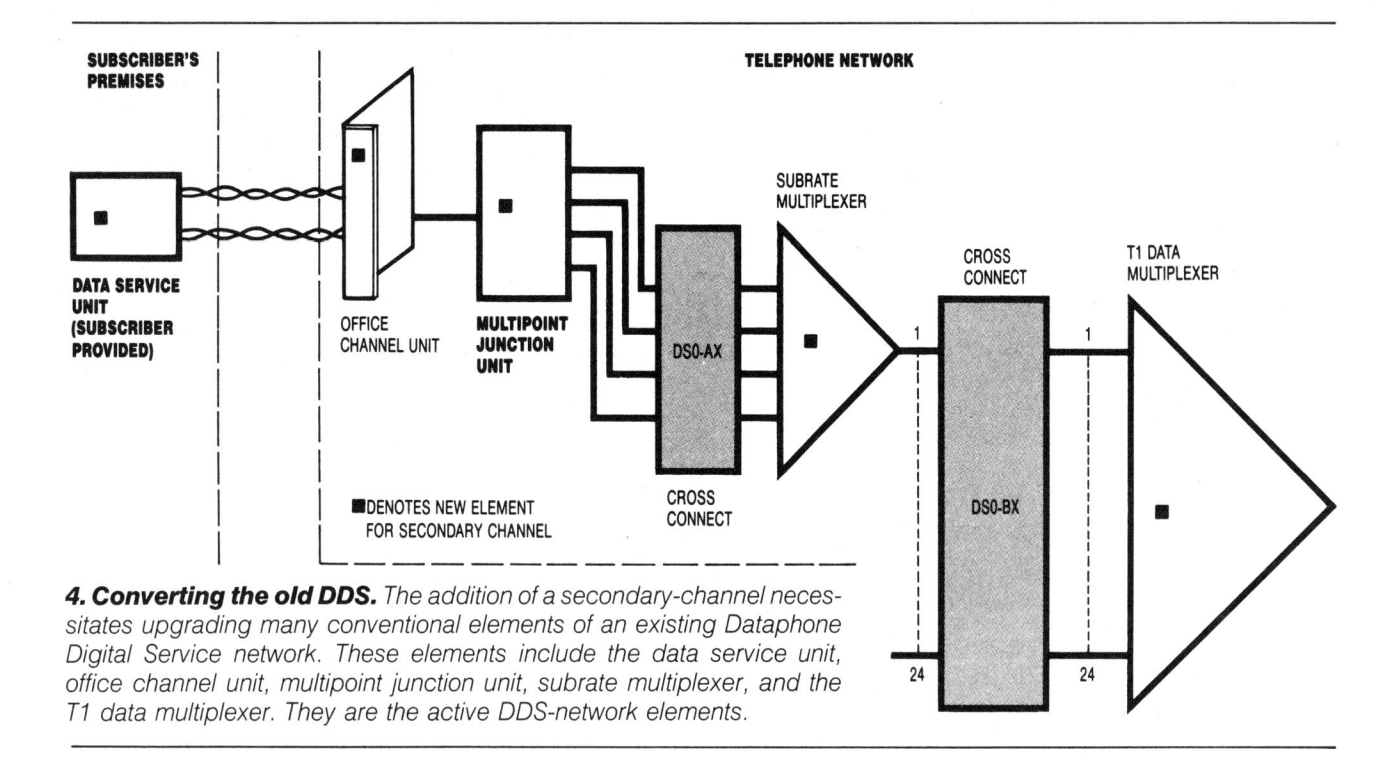

4. Converting the old DDS. *The addition of a secondary-channel necessitates upgrading many conventional elements of an existing Dataphone Digital Service network. These elements include the data service unit, office channel unit, multipoint junction unit, subrate multiplexer, and the T1 data multiplexer. They are the active DDS-network elements.*

conventional DDS network.

Briefly, digital data originates at the subscriber's data terminal equipment attached to a DSU. This data, in binary form, is converted by the DSU into an "alternate mark inversion" (AMI) format (detailed later). The AMI signal travels across the subscriber's access loop, enters the local CO, and provides the input to the telephone company's OCU. The OCU regenerates the signal and translates it to 64 kbit/s.

For multipoint, polled applications, an MJU permits one host location to serve multiple tributaries. For more efficient use of the network, the subrate OCU data drives a subrate data multiplexer (SDM)—via a cross-connect (DS-0A X)—where the OCU data is aggregated with other subrate channels to form one 64-kbit/s (full DS-0) stream. 56-kbit/s data, converted by the OCU to a full DS-0 rate, requires no additional processing.

Combinations of aggregated subrate and 56-kbit/s data (converted to 64 kbit/s) provide the 24-channel input to a T1 data multiplexer, forming the 1.544-Mbit/s output data stream. Each active element (shown with an asterisk in Figure 4) requires modification to operate within a DDS S/C network.

Secondary-channel capability is being quietly added to the DDS network, without regard to the RBOCs' concerns. AT&T, as the largest supplier of DDS-network equipment, has already developed DDS elements that accommodate either conventional DDS or DDS S/C as a field-selectable option. Virtually all new circuit packs (AT&T's term for plug-in, printed-circuit boards) shipped since mid-1986 have this capability. With the projected growth of DDS, the installed base of older, nonselectable equipment will comprise an ever-decreasing percentage of the digital network.

But how did this come about? How can an independent secondary channel be derived from a network that had already been designed, is deployed, and cannot be changed in structure? That was the challenge to AT&T's network equipment design engineers during the mid-1970s.

Deriving the secondary channel

The answer focused on one bit, reserved by the network to ensure a minimum number of timing-pulse transitions in the subscriber's data stream and used to pass network status information during idle periods. This bit, called the network control or C bit, was the key that unlocked the secondary channel for DDS.

In DDS, the C bit (Fig. 5) is transmitted as a digital one when the user's terminal requests access to the channel (RTS is on). In 56-kbit/s applications (Fig. 5A), the C bit occupies one position of the 8-bit DS-0 "word" (octet), leaving the seven remaining bits for the user's data. (In this application, the seven user-data bits are transmitted at 56 kbit/s. The 56-kbit/s—or seven-bit—structure is part of a DS-0 [64-kbit/s] eight-bit octet.) For the subrate speeds of 2.4, 4.8, and 9.6 kbit/s (Fig. 5B), the DS-0 octet is formed as a combination of six data bits, the C bit, and one multiplexer framing bit.

Because a long string of zeros does not provide pulse transitions, the T1 repeaters used throughout the network may lose timing synchronization. With the C bit continuously set to a one, the user may transmit an unrestricted stream of data, including continuous zeros, since every eighth bit is guaranteed to be a one. The secondary channel for DDS is derived from this C bit. By giving the user's DSU access to this bit once every third octet, a virtual data path is established for the secondary channel.

5. The key to S/C. *The C bit had been reserved by the network to indicate the subscriber's channel activity and to ensure a minimum number of timing-pulse transitions.*

(A) 56-KBIT/S STRUCTURE, DS0 OCTET

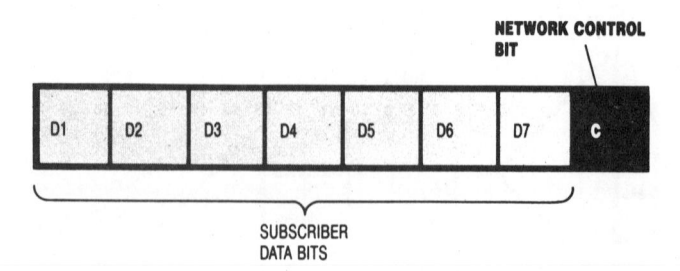

| D1 | D2 | D3 | D4 | D5 | D6 | D7 | C |

SUBSCRIBER DATA BITS (D1–D7); C = NETWORK CONTROL BIT

(B) SUBRATE STRUCTURE, DS0 OCTET

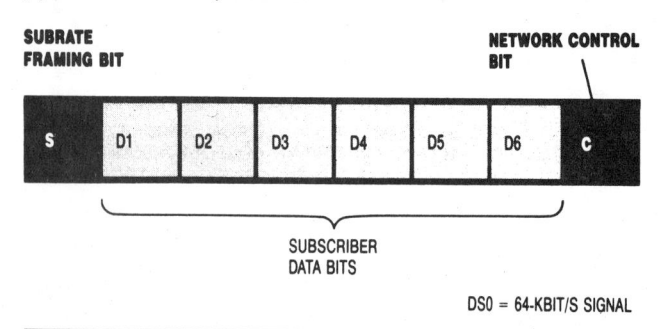

| S | D1 | D2 | D3 | D4 | D5 | D6 | C |

S = SUBRATE FRAMING BIT; SUBSCRIBER DATA BITS (D1–D6); C = NETWORK CONTROL BIT

DS0 = 64-KBIT/S SIGNAL

Data transmission at the subrates differs from that of 56-kbit/s service. Since subrate data streams are frequently multiplexed into one DS-0 slot, one bit position must be reserved for subrate-multiplexer framing. This leaves six bits for the subscriber's data.

The computation of the secondary-channel data rate for 56-kbit/s DDS is performed by multiplying the full DS-0 rate of 64 kbit/s by 1/8 (which represents the C bit's portion of the DS-0 stream) and by 1/3 (since the user's equipment has access to the C bit once every third octet). This results in a secondary-channel data rate of 2,666 2/3 bit/s [$64 \times 1/8 \times 1/3$].

Dividing the 2,666 2/3 bit/s rate by the number of corresponding 9.6, 4.8, or 2.4 kbit/s subrate multiplexer channels—alternatively, the number of times the same subrate channel's data is repeated in a DS-0 channel when no subrate data multiplexing is performed—gives the secondary channel data rate for the subrate speeds. Thus, each of five 9.6-kbit/s channels that fill a DS-0 would have a secondary-channel rate of 533 1/3 bit/s; each of ten 4.8-kbit/s channels, 266 2/3 bit/s; each of twenty 2.4-kbit/s channels, 133 1/3 bit/s.

The secondary channels are derived from, and therefore synchronized to, the DDS network. In their raw form as synchronous speeds from 2,666 2/3 to 133 1/3 bit/s, they are not particularly useful. Data used at these rates is generally for asynchronous transmission, even with the various diagnostic devices. Therefore, the secondary channel is most useful if the DSU performs a format and speed conversion to the nearest-lower standard ASCII asynchronous data rate: 2,666 2/3 to 2,400 bit/s; 533 1/3 to 300 bit/s; 266 2/3 to 150 bit/s; 133 1/3 to 75 bit/s.

With conventional DDS, serial binary data is converted by the DSU to an unframed AMI format before being sent across the access loop to the serving CO's OCU. For conventional DDS, both the DSU and OCU communicate over the access loop at the same rate as the subscriber's data terminal equipment. Thus no "overspeed" (discussed below) is required.

Loop signals

For conventional DDS, two control signals are passed from the subscriber's DSU to the network:
- *Control mode idle,* transmitted when the terminal's RTS signal is turned off.
- *Excessive zeros,* transmitted when the terminal is sending six or seven consecutive spaces, for subrate or 56-kbit/s service, respectively.

Each of these control signals is passed by using bipolar violations: two successive pulses of the same polarity that violate the alternate-mark-inversion encoding rule.

Since DDS S/C must always keep track of the subscriber's secondary-channel use of the C bit, the data that flows across the subscriber loop must be framed, thereby requiring overspeed transmission: For subrate DDS S/C, each six user data bits must be accompanied by two extra bits (one frame bit and one C bit), resulting in a requirement for the data to be transmitted at 4/3 (8 6) times the normal, primary-channel data rate. That is, for a primary-channel rate of 9.6 kbit/s, the loop-transmission rate would be 12.8 kbit/s; for 4.8 kbit/s, 6.4 kbit/s; and for 2.4 kbit/s, 3.2 kbit/s. For 56-kbit/s DDS S/C, a framing bit and a C bit must be added to the seven data bits, resulting in a 9/7 overspeed, or 72 kbit/s.

At the telephone company's CO, the frame bit for the subrate subscriber loop's data is replaced by the appropriate SDM framing bit. The frame bit for 56-kbit/s data is completely eliminated by the OCU. The added C bit with both the user's secondary-channel data and control information is carried through the network.

Technical issues remain

Pulse-code modulation (PCM), a T1-based transmission, was deployed more than 25 years ago. It still serves as the basis for communications between wire centers for the telephone network that we use today. While it has withstood the test of time, two fundamental design decisions have made movement to an all-digital network for both voice and data more difficult.

The first of these was the lack of a nationwide synchronization plan for T1 transmission. This shortcoming had to be resolved, in part (the T1 circuits needed for DDS), before DDS could be deployed. Nationwide DDS requires network synchronization from one (centralized) master timing source. Much of the remaining T1 network capacity—not needed for DDS—remains unsynchronized. Had PCM/T1 transport been deployed, with all transmissions synchronized to one master timing source, total nationwide digital implementation would be a much simpler task today.

ISDN requires the network to become completely synchronized and will force this issue.

The second problem concerns the inability of the original PCM/T1 to transport long strings of zeros (such as more than 15 in succession). In a voice environment, preventing excessive zeros by eliminating one of the 256 possible encoded states (namely, eight consecutive zeros) is not a problem — its omission would not be noticed. But for data transmission, an all-zeros octet must be handled the same way as any other; it cannot be selectively omitted.

At the time of T1's inception, AMI was selected as the encoding scheme to be used for wireline transmission. AMI provides a straightforward transformation from digital ones and zeros to alternating pulses and no pulses, respectively. Since zeros are encoded as no pulses, a long string of zeros would appear as a "no-signal" state. Yet any attempt to convert a long string of zeros seemed an unnecessary burden to a voice network, since the all-zeros octet could simply be eliminated from the analog-to-digital conversion process, as mentioned earlier.

As it has turned out, the weakest links in T1 data transmission are the repeaters, found at specific intervals along a wireline. These devices must have pulses to recover timing synchronization from the signal they receive, so that they can completely regenerate a degraded T1 input signal into new, full-level output. The excessive-zeros problem plagued the initial DDS design and continues to haunt the telephone network in transporting all new data services that use T1 transmission in their structure.

All of the restrictions placed upon DDS S/C originate from the inability to send continuous zeros through the repeaters. Any DDS S/C data condition that results in an octet of all zeros is considered illegal. Both subrate and 56-kbit/s DDS S/C have potential conditions that will result in a string of eight zeros.

'One' assurance

Figure 6 defines the subrate channels with the associated subrate framing patterns. Channels 1 through 5 are used for 9.6 kbit/s, 1 through 10 for 4.8 kbit/s, and 1 through 20 for 2.4 kbit/s. With six bits used for data, one bit for subrate framing, and the remaining bit for the C bit, conventional DDS ensures that at least one of the eight bits (octet) is always a one — namely the C bit. But with the C bit controlled by the user's DSU once every third DS-0 octet, the opportunity exists to create eight consecutive zeros: six data zeros, one subrate framing bit as a zero, and the C bit transmitting a secondary-channel bit as a zero.

In the near term, the only way around this problem is to restrict subrate usage to a 40 percent DDS S/C-loading factor (Fig. 6 tabulates which channels are usable for DDS S/C). Therefore, only subrate channels with frame-pattern ones assigned become candidates for DDS S/C subrate data. This does place an administrative burden on the local telephone companies, which may have a cost impact on secondary-channel DDS service.

As to the 56-kbit/s DDS S/C usage, this service may not transmit a network control (C) bit as a zero if the associated seven user-data bits are also zeros. The network control (C) bit would be zero, for example, to indicate that the primary channel's RTS signal is turned off (control-mode-idle state).

The problems at 56 kbit/s cannot be solved administratively, as with subrate DDS S/C, because no equivalent to a subrate frame bit is available that can be forced to a one. This poses two difficulties: First, it precludes a multipoint DDS S/C service at 56 kbit/s. Second, it constrains the combination of primary-channel and secondary-channel data and thereby makes the channels interdependent, as opposed to truly independent.

Since the combination of primary- and secondary-channel data must never be all zeros, encoding algorithms have been developed to prevent this condition. AT&T's technical reference for DDS S/C states that, for 56-kbit/s transmission, an all-zeros, primary-channel data state must be accompanied by a one (or a forced one) in the secondary channel. While this does preserve the integrity of the primary channel's data, it can result in errors in the secondary-channel data stream. Even worse, a state of continuous zeros in the primary channel completely disables the secondary channel, because it must then send all ones to comply with the technical reference.

Until the various technical issues are resolved, the use of digital facilities will be restricted. Specifically, subrate DDS S/C service will be limited by the telephone com-

6. Framed channels. *Shown are the 20 subrate channels with their framing patterns. Conventional DDS ensures that at least an octet's C bit is always a one.*

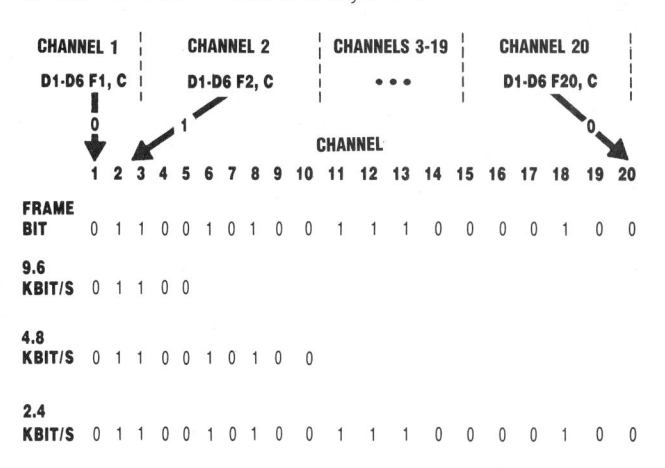

DATA RATE	USABLE DDS S/C CHANNEL NUMBERS	UNUSABLE DDS S/C CHANNEL NUMBERS
9.6 KBIT/S	2,3	1,4,5
4.8 KBIT/S	2,3,6,8	1,4,5,7,9,10
2.4 KBIT/S	2,3,6,8,11,12,13,18	1,4,5,7,9,10,14,15,16,17,19,20

C = NETWORK CONTROL BIT
DDS S/C = DATAPHONE DIGITAL SERVICE WITH SECONDARY CHANNEL
DX = USER DATA BIT
FX = NETWORK SUBRATE FRAME BIT WITH CHANNEL

panies to a 40 percent utilization when subrate data multiplexing is required. While the split of conventional DDS versus DDS S/C can be established at the CO—where the former can use the remaining 60 percent—what if a major telephone company customer decides to change over to DDS S/C? What if all the telephone company's major customers decide to migrate to DDS S/C over a very short period of time? As designed today, this problem can only be solved by adding capacity.

As for 56-kbit/s DDS S/C, the problem precludes multipoint service. What remains is a point-to-point service that may require certain code restrictions on the user's primary- and/or secondary-channel data.

The B8ZS solution

The most promising solution to problems with subrate and 56-kbit/s DDS S/C (as well as with T1 data transport) lies with an encoding technique that permits unrestricted, clear-channel T1 transmission. (Clear-channel means that the full bandwidth is available to the user.) This technique is known as binary 8 zero substitution (B8ZS). With B8ZS, a string of eight zeros (no pulses for eight-bit intervals) is replaced with a word, framed with two successive pulses of the same polarity that intentionally violate the alternate-mark-inversion encoding rule (a bipolar violation). This method is similar to that used in DDS to send long strings of zeros across the subscriber access loop.

What are the prospects for DDS S/C? Although hesitant at first, the local telephone companies are now convinced of DDS S/C's importance. AT&T, the major U. S. interexchange carrier, is fully committed to this service. As analog private-line tariffs continue to rise, DDS will become increasingly attractive to the user community. And the secondary channel will help fuel this growing popularity.

DDS S/C is just the beginning of a whole new breed of enhancements to digital data transport. Services such as switched digital service (see "The how and where of switched 56-kbit/s service," DATA COMMUNICATIONS, August 1986, p. 19) and a new 19.2-kbit/s subrate offering are made possible by replacing older, conventional network elements with innovative technology. ■

Hugh Goldberg is the product-line marketing manager for all digital transmission products at General DataComm. Earlier at the company, he held various engineering management and project engineering positions. As a committee member of the Electronic Industries Association and the Exchange Carriers Standards Association, he contributed to various industry standards. He holds an M. S. E. degree in electrical engineering from the University of Pennsylvania in Philadelphia.

Section 4
Switching and Software

Edwin E. Mier, editor at large, DATA COMMUNICATIONS

New signs of life for packet switching

X.25 packet switching has always had its place. But now that includes linking LANs and hauling SNA data. And with OSI gaining momentum, packet backbones are a way to cover all bases.

What do corporate giants Westinghouse, American Airlines, Manufacturers Hanover Trust, and United Parcel Service have in common? Each of these firms, and many others, have recently decided that their next-generation data networks would be based on X.25 packet-switching backbones.

"The packet backbone is more reliable, more versatile [than existing, proprietary network architectures]," says Bill Jewell, managing director of communications engineering for American Airlines (Fort Worth, Tex.), "so it fits many standards." (By versatile, Jewell means that the new network can handle more multivendor equipment and a greater variety of traffic.) American announced in March that it had contracted with Northern Telecom for a new multimillion-dollar, multiyear packet-switching backbone network. This network replaces a predominantly IBM-based, leased-line network. Initially, the network will be used primarily for internal traffic; later, it will be used for American's SABRE reservation service.

Another recent convert to the packet backbone is the Online Computer Library Center in Dublin, Ohio. OCLC announced in mid-November that it will spend $63 million over the next five years to install and operate a new backbone packet-switching data network. OCLC's major applications are internal traffic and access from various customer devices. The existing network is a mixed bag: asynchronous dial-up customer devices, with internal traffic handled by 3270 and other methods.

Why the dramatic upsurge in new packet networks? According to OCLC and others, there are a host of reasons that involve both current and future network requirements.

"We want to maximize our connectivity, we want to be less vendor-dependent, and we want to accommodate very different kinds of technology at our network end points," says Fred Lauber, OCLC's manager of telecommunications systems engineering and project manager for the new packet-switching backbone.

(The OCLC network is being installed, and packet equipment supplied, by Telenet.)

Packet switching? The old Defense Department data-transport technology developed in the 1960s? Sure, it's served Arpanet well, but isn't it mainly for wide-area TCP/IP networks? For those Unix- and VAX-based academic networks?

Not any more. While the latest and greatest developments in T1 networking (and its downsized derivatives, fractional T1 and switched 56-kbit/s service) have dominated the trade press lately, the packet-switching industry has hardly been idle.

A spate of recent trends and developments, including cheaper and more powerful packet-switching hardware and new software for marrying LANs and SNA traffic with X.25 nets, have significantly bolstered packet switching's capabilities, applicability, and esteem in the eyes of users and vendors.

Indeed, it is the rosy prospects for packet-switching's future that underlie the technology's renewed appeal. And this has caught many industry analysts by surprise. Just a few years ago, analysts were writing off packet switching as a mature and stagnant technology that faced only declining market prospects.

In a major 1987 network-technology overview, the Boston-based Yankee Group had forecast that over a five-year period (1987 to 1992), the number of private global packet networks (those traversing at least one national border) was expected to grow from perhaps 150 to 600. But a few months ago, the Yankee Group revised that forecast, noting that the number was growing much faster than expected.

According to Jack Freeman, senior analyst for data communications at Yankee Group, "it now seems there

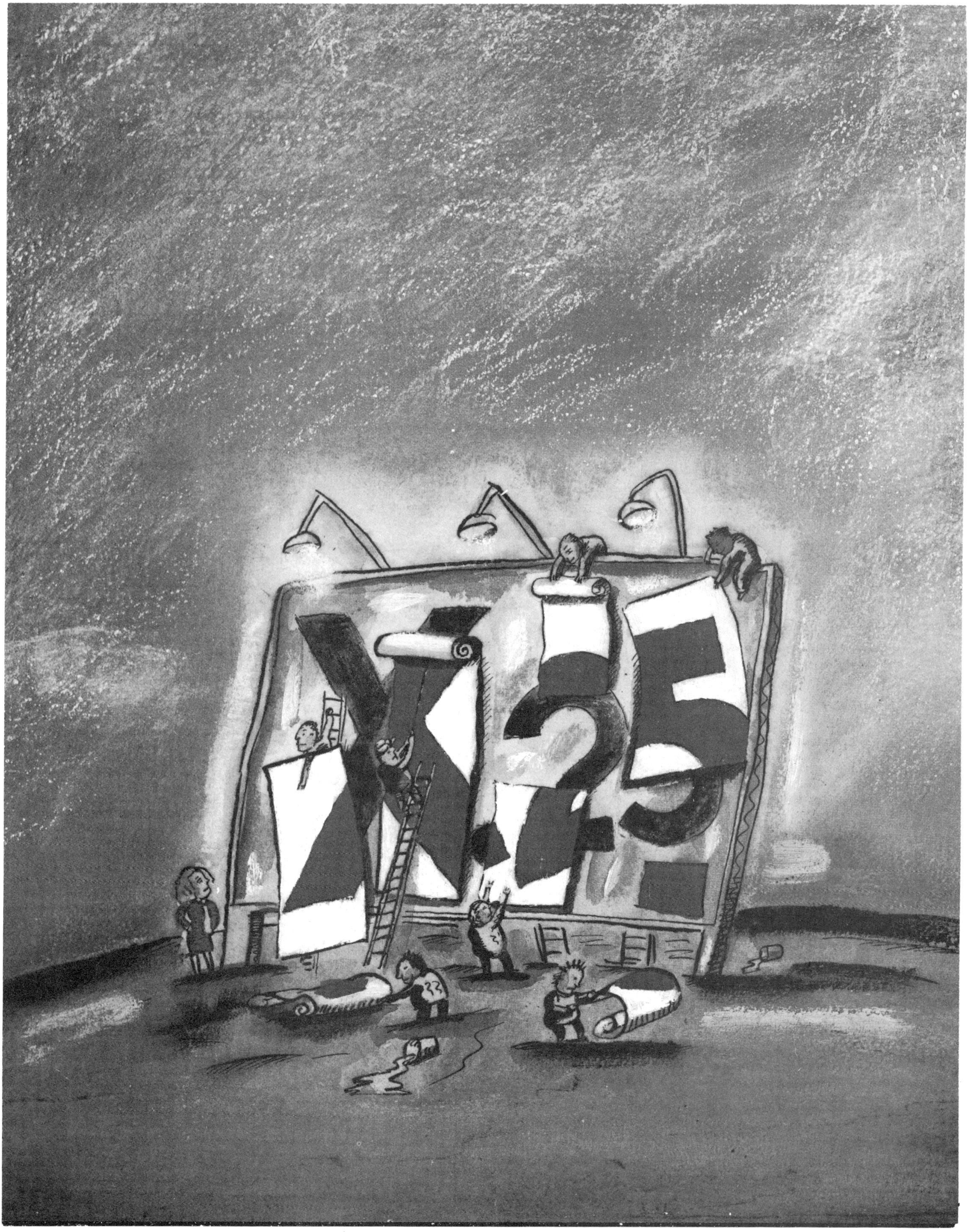
X.25

Packet Switching

could easily be over 1,000 such global packet backbones by 1992." He adds that there are currently "from 200 to 250" such networks, "and it's growing very fast."

What's new
Among packet switching's technical developments:
- *Adaptability for SNA.* Though X.25 and SNA have for years been regarded as diametrically opposed networking technologies, IBM terminal-to-host and computer-to-computer traffic can now be carried along with other traffic types over a packet network as quickly—and some say even more efficiently—than over dedicated SNA leased lines.
- *LAN to WAN.* As a technology for linking LANs to WANs, and to remote LANs, X.25 packet gateways and transport backbones are becoming as popular as point-to-point bridges (and are being deployed in ever greater numbers, by some market estimates). Packet-network gateways typically interact with LAN stations using the Netbios (and soon, Named Pipes) software interface and the Server Message Block (SMB) client-server protocol.

Other router-class gateway devices operate on the LAN as TCP/IP nodes and communicate through a wide-area packet network with other TCP/IP nodes. And new LAN-to-packet-network gateways are promising support for other popular LAN protocol stacks and client-server protocols (such as the XNS adaptations of older 3Com LANs, as well as those of Novell and Banyan).

What's more, new public data network services designed expressly for LAN-to-remote-LAN connectivity (such as one from Reston, Va. based Telenet, due out next month) will debut next year.
- *More packets, lower prices.* During the 1980s, packet-network price-performance ratios improved by an order of magnitude. According to Northern Telecom, a leading supplier of high-capacity, general-purpose backbone packet networks, the capital cost per 100 packets per second (pps) of private-packet-network throughput has dropped from more than $100,000 in 1979 to about $16,000 today (Fig. 1).

And within the last few years, packet-network call-processing rates (the number of virtual-circuit call setups and tear-downs that can be handled per unit of time) have soared. Where a packet network might have processed 50 calls per second two years ago, it might now handle more like 500 calls per second, according to Carlton Rice, Northern Telecom's manager of network engineering. What has mainly brought about this increase in call-processing speed is faster processors and streamlined call setup procedures.
- *X.25 ubiquity.* Every major computer vendor—including IBM—now offers an integral X.25 packet-network interface. These typically consist of a high-speed (typically 64-kbit/s) synchronous line interface, along with software customized for maximum packet input/output directly into the data format of the vendor's computer. Integrated interfaces eliminate the PAD protocol conversion that had been a chokepoint of sorts at the host-connection end of the packet network.

And since 1976, when X.25 was first standardized, it has

1. Plummeting packet prices. *During the 1980s, the cost per 100 pps throughput has dramatically dropped, from more than $100,000 in 1979 to about $16,000 today.*

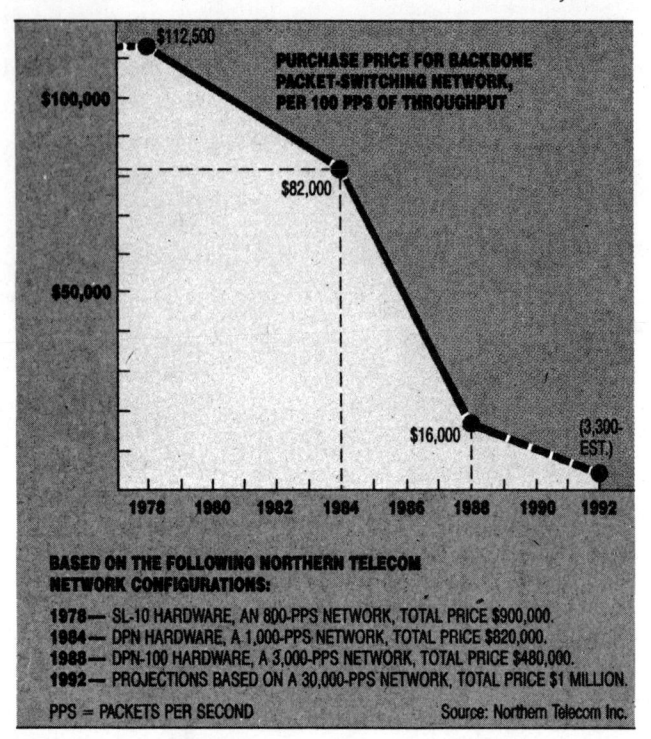

PURCHASE PRICE FOR BACKBONE PACKET-SWITCHING NETWORK, PER 100 PPS OF THROUGHPUT

- 1978: $112,500
- 1984: $82,000
- 1988: $16,000
- 1992: $3,300 (EST.)

BASED ON THE FOLLOWING NORTHERN TELECOM NETWORK CONFIGURATIONS:
- 1978— SL-10 HARDWARE, AN 800-PPS NETWORK, TOTAL PRICE $900,000.
- 1984— DPN HARDWARE, A 1,000-PPS NETWORK, TOTAL PRICE $820,000.
- 1988— DPN-100 HARDWARE, A 3,000-PPS NETWORK, TOTAL PRICE $480,000.
- 1992— PROJECTIONS BASED ON A 30,000-PPS NETWORK, TOTAL PRICE $1 MILLION.

PPS = PACKETS PER SECOND   Source: Northern Telecom Inc.

been revised, enhanced, and refined in subsequent 1980, 1984, and 1988 versions. Users and vendors report few problems anymore in mating X.25-based packet equipment from different vendors.
- *Voice and (packet) data?* Where X.25-based packet transport has long been a mainstay in many of the world's developed countries, except the U.S. (largely because of the relative affordability and availability of leased lines, including digital data service and T1), the efficiencies and other benefits of packet switching, including the prospects for implementing mixed-media traffic over the same packet backbone, are winning over many new converts—even in the U.S.

New high-capacity packet switches (30,000+ pps) can now handily fill T1-capacity trunks. And all indications are that real-time, toll-quality voice will routinely ride along with data on packet backbones within two to four years (see "Less processing, higher throughput"). Telenet and others offer this capability today in specially engineered private packet networks. (Telenet inserts software-based fast-packet switches that it OEMs from Campbell, Calif.-based StrataCom between its packet switches.)

The catalyst for mixed-media (voice, data, video, graphics) backbone packet switching will be frame-relay and fast-packet specifications that are now being defined in the standards community. (Frame relay is a streamlined mode of packet switching based on the CCITT's Link Access Procedure-D, which minimizes packet-layer processing. Fast-packet switching is an embryonic packet-transport technology featuring small, fixed-length packets—called cells—and fast, silicon-based logic execution.)

Packet Switching

■ *And then there's OSI.* With the U.S. Government's OSI procurement doctrine (GOSIP) effective in August 1990, X.25 packet-switching support will be required for all new systems and networks involving wide-area data communications that are bid to the government after that time. Since the U.S. Government is the largest purchaser of computer and data communications equipment and services in the world, this will accelerate the widespread deployment of OSI standards-based computer networking, for which X.25 is currently the only wide-area protocol set encompassing Layers 2 and 3 (the data link and network layers, respectively).

Vendors who are now busily implementing OSI's higher-layer protocols, as Retix Communications is, say that the software mechanisms defined for tying in OSI's higher layers, enabling access to and egress from X.25-based packet networks, are straightforward and efficient.

Big Blue packets

Most agree that a fundamental incompatibility between X.25 packet switching and IBM terminal-to-host networking had long stifled the widespread deployment of packet backbones, especially in the U.S. and especially in the IBM-dominated general-business sector. But this is not the case anymore. Indeed, as IBM proceeds to migrate SNA away from the terminal-to-host, hierarchical structure and toward computer-to-computer, peer-to-peer networking, some argue convincingly that packet-switched backbones can handle SNA network traffic even better than IBM's own leased-line-based designs.

Driven by customer demand, first in Europe and more recently in the U.S., IBM has made several key product introductions (some would say concessions) that enable IBM SNA data to be efficiently transported via packet-switching networks. As a result, the IBM-X.25 incompatibility that existed five years ago has largely disappeared.

Five years ago, many IBM networks were still running character-oriented Bisync (Binary Synchronous Communications, or BSC), which does not relate well to the bit-oriented nature of X.25 and its HDLC (high-level data link control). In fact, the public packet carriers developed a special protocol called Display System Protocol (DSP), which significantly improves the flow of Bisync traffic over a packet network. (DSP has become a de facto industry standard and is also now supported by many private packet network equipment makers.)

Even with DSP, however, transporting Bisync traffic via packet network is less than an optimal, or elegant, solution—especially when compared to the IBM polled, cluster-controller-to-front-end, leased-line approach.

This fundamental incompatibility began to dissolve with the spread of synchronous data link control (SDLC) in IBM networks. Yet, while the bit-oriented SDLC could be much more efficiently handled by X.25 packets, there remained the IBM-network requirement for host polling of remote SDLC devices. Passing polls added considerable, unnecessary data packets to an intermediate X.25 transport network, until packet-network designers discovered they didn't have to carry this polling traffic at all: They could identify and intercept the polls at the host end, issue their own at the terminal end, and not have to devote network bandwidth to transporting them.

But the real marriage of IBM's SNA and X.25 packet switching came about just a few years ago with IBM's general introduction in North America of an IBM front-end processor software package called NPSI (Network Packet Switching Interface). IBM had already furnished NPSI to its European customers for a few years, but demands for it in the U.S. became too loud for IBM to ignore.

NPSI lets IBM SNA traffic take on the look and feel of X.25 packets, using an X.25-oriented, IBM-developed frame format called QLLC (qualified logical link control). These frames can then be zipped through packet networks virtually intact. With NPSI in the front-end (along with the 37X5's basic operating software, the Network Control Program), polls are not even issued anymore—they are intercepted by NPSI.

Packets versus leased lines

Using the DSP protocol for transporting older Bisync terminal traffic via a packet network involves considerable protocol conversion. In general, the more processing required to adapt non-X.25 traffic to a packet network, the lower the throughput, the higher the response time, and so on. (A comparison of different terminal types and their adaptability to packet transport is shown in the table.)

The fastest way to get SNA data through a packet network is by encapsulation. In encapsulation, the IBM frames (typically 3270 or 5250 terminal data streams) are kept intact and bundled up within X.25 packets. On leaving the packet network, the X.25 wrapping is stripped off. Encapsulation is usually employed in packet networks for passing IBM QLLC data to a 37X5 front-end processor running NPSI.

In other environments, the packet network needs to do

> **Bisync traffic via packet net is less than an optimal solution.**

more than merely encapsulate the IBM frames. At a minimum, the recognition and interception of polls at the host end is required (along with issuance of polls at the remote, terminal end).

Packet-switching equipment vendors vary in the degree of processing that their gear applies to IBM SNA data as it enters, transits, and then leaves the packet network. Telenet's approach, for example, is to convert SNA data into its own internal frame and packet format. This is done, says Alan Taffel, Telenet's vice president of strategic marketing, so that IBM terminal traffic can be switched to non-IBM processors via the packet network, with possibly substantial protocol-conversion processing.

In other cases, SNA traffic is carried more transparently.

Packet Switching

Less processing, higher throughput

If the remarkable increase in packet-processing rates and throughput can be attributed to any single network-design trend, it is that more and faster processors are being used and that they are performing less software-intensive processing.

According to John McQuillan, president of McQuillan Consulting (Cambridge, Mass.) and a noted expert in network-equipment design and performance, protocol processing (such as is done in the asynchronous-to-X.25 processing of a PAD) is a heavy additional burden on a single-processor packet switch.

McQuillan says that a single-processor packet switch can process from five to 10 times more packets by not also having to perform protocol processing. When multiple protocol conversions are being handled by the same processor, the drain on throughput is magnified even more.

Indeed, based on the performance data available from suppliers of single-processor packet equipment (such as low-end, standalone packet switches and PC plug-in boards for LAN-to-packet-network gateways), packet throughput in the range of 300 to 500 packets per second (pps) can be achieved, given the 16- and 32-bit microprocessors that are typically employed today.

Users should keep in mind that as they add protocol processing to a packet processor, the packet throughput will drop. And depending on the complexity of this additional software-intensive protocol handling, this drop could be significant. A single-processor packet node, theoretically capable of pushing out 500 pps, could be constrained to perhaps only 50 pps by the addition of a lot of protocol processing.

Multiprocessor designs, especially in sizable nodal packet switches (such as those from BBN, Telenet, Northern Telecom) can obviate this throughput degradation, their designers claim. In fact, the architecture of today's large packet switch—consisting of multiple line controller cards, protocol-processing cards, and packet-switching controller cards, all connected via a multi-megabit/s bus—is functionally not unlike today's LAN configurations.

Indeed, some experts see the protocol-processing function that used to be integral to packet switches being performed much more efficiently on a LAN.

"PAD functions are now being done more cost effectively by LANs," says McQuillan. He maintains that the traditional appeal of packet switching—"to multiplex a lot of low-speed terminals to high-speed devices"—is "no longer important." Instead, he says that the promise and prospects of packet backbones for efficient, general-purpose, wide-area transport is the new draw and that anything other than raw packet transport and switching is being pulled out of the packet network to achieve greater throughput performance.

Frame relay promises to streamline packet switching even more—and enable at least a doubling of raw-packet throughput from the same amount of processing power. Frame relay gets its name from the frame designation of data units at Layer 2 (data link layer) of the OSI model. In essence, typical Layer 3 (network layer) functions, where most X.25-based packet processing is now performed, are relieved from the frame-relay packet network (see figure and table).

The long-term design trend, most designers agree, is for many software- and memory-intensive functions—such as correct packet sequencing and error correction—to be moved into the devices that are connected by the frame-relay packet network. Frame-relay operation, largely defined in the CCITT's specifications for Link Access Procedure-D (Q.921), still provides for the detection of errors, for example, but bad packets are summarily dropped. It is up to the source and destination devices to correct such errors, usually through retransmission.

Because X.25-based packet networks are centered on the CCITT's X.25 Recommendation, which is only a standardized convention for access to a packet network, packet-equipment and switch suppliers have always used their own proprietary protocols and architectures within their packet networks for internodal traffic transport and management.

Because of this, most believe that frame-relay switches will be able to be conveniently inserted into existing packet networks and that an X.25-to-frame-relay interface will enable the efficient marriage of the two.

Frame relay will still use much the same packet-processing hardware base as today's packet-switching equipment, most agree. This means that a packet node based on, for example, an 80286 chip, could be reworked to become a frame-relay switch instead of an X.25 switch. But where a node might pump out 100 X.25 packets per second, it would be able to do perhaps 200 to 500 frame-relay packets per second.

Existing hardware designs will be inappropriate, however, for the generation of packet switches that come after frame relay (mid- to late 1990s). Prototypes of packet switches based on asynchronous transfer mode (ATM), or so-called fast-packet operation (also called cell relay by Bellcore), have already been demonstrated. These perform almost no software-based processing and instead perform packet-manipulation functions based on silicon-embedded logic, which is much faster.

ATM fast-packet switches will serve as the basis for the switched multimegabit/s data services that are being preannounced by local and long-distance carriers and data-transport service suppliers. These will appear initially for metropolitan-area transport, mainly as a network facility for linking multimegabit/s LANs.

Unlike X.25 and frame-relay packet switching, where packet size is variable, fast-packet switching uses standard 48-byte cells (as distinguished from Layer 2 frames and Layer 3 packets), plus a 5-byte header. Current designs and prototypes are heralding throughputs of millions of packets per second, which leads some to doubt whether private backbone-type packet networks will ever

Packet Switching

have the throughput requirements to justify such high-horsepower switches (with correspondingly high price tags) through the next decade.

Fast packet will unquestionably be capable of mixed-media transport—real-time voice, data, graphics, video. It is still unclear whether frame relay, by comparison, will offer the capability even for packetized, real-time voice transport. New 32-bit processors (80386, 68020) might enable it, the experts say, but they also agree that frame relay, while a significant enhancement over X.25 packet switching, is not designed to support real-time voice traffic.

—E.E.M.

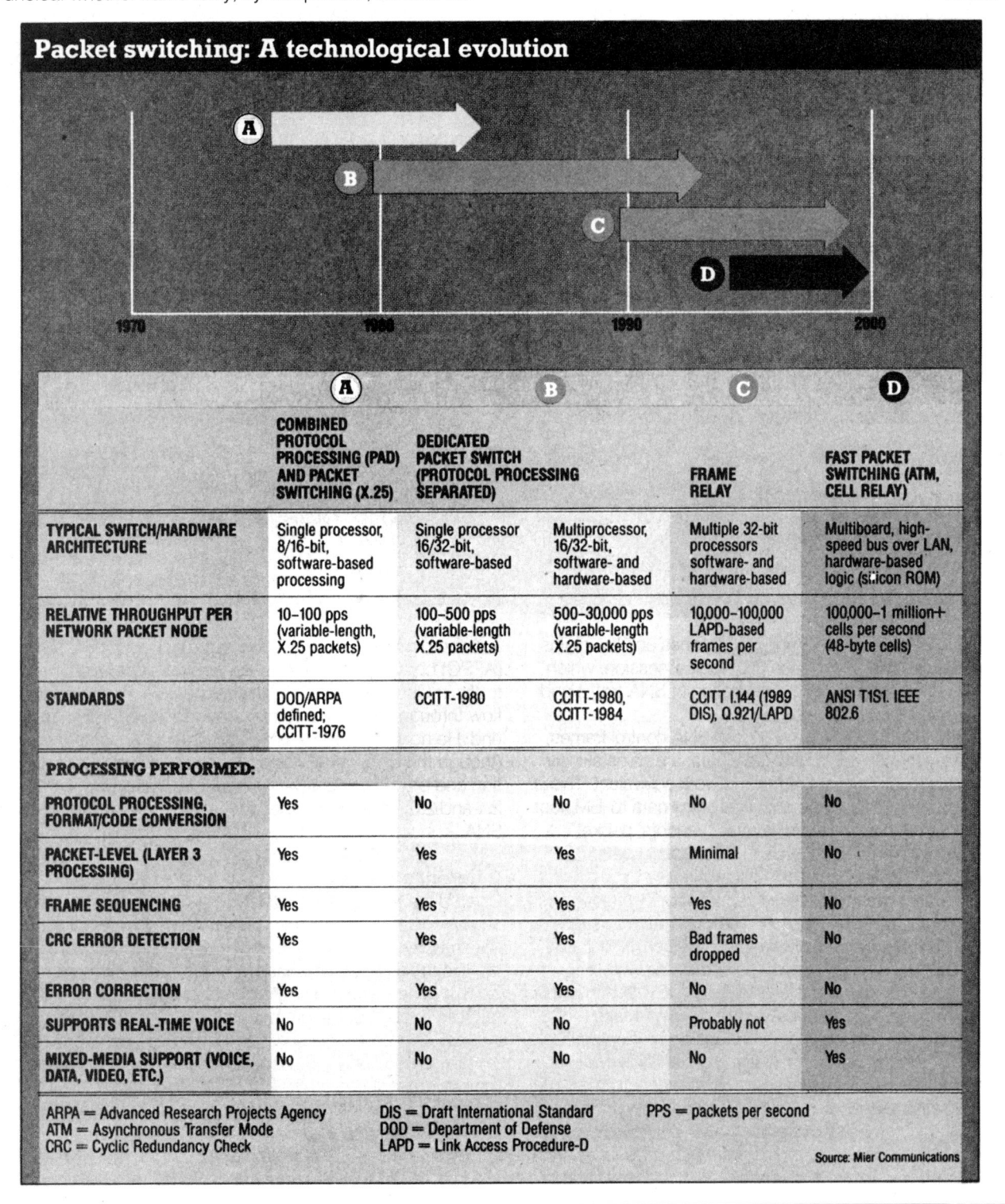

Packet switching: A technological evolution

	A COMBINED PROTOCOL PROCESSING (PAD) AND PACKET SWITCHING (X.25)	**B** DEDICATED PACKET SWITCH (PROTOCOL PROCESSING SEPARATED)		**C** FRAME RELAY	**D** FAST PACKET SWITCHING (ATM, CELL RELAY)
TYPICAL SWITCH/HARDWARE ARCHITECTURE	Single processor, 8/16-bit, software-based processing	Single processor 16/32-bit, software-based	Multiprocessor, 16/32-bit, software- and hardware-based	Multiple 32-bit processors software- and hardware-based	Multiboard, high-speed bus over LAN, hardware-based logic (silicon ROM)
RELATIVE THROUGHPUT PER NETWORK PACKET NODE	10–100 pps (variable-length, X.25 packets)	100–500 pps (variable-length X.25 packets)	500–30,000 pps (variable-length X.25 packets)	10,000–100,000 LAPD-based frames per second	100,000–1 million+ cells per second (48-byte cells)
STANDARDS	DOD/ARPA defined; CCITT-1976	CCITT-1980	CCITT-1980, CCITT-1984	CCITT I.144 (1989 DIS), Q.921/LAPD	ANSI T1S1, IEEE 802.6
PROCESSING PERFORMED:					
PROTOCOL PROCESSING, FORMAT/CODE CONVERSION	Yes	No	No	No	No
PACKET-LEVEL (LAYER 3 PROCESSING)	Yes	Yes	Yes	Minimal	No
FRAME SEQUENCING	Yes	Yes	Yes	Yes	No
CRC ERROR DETECTION	Yes	Yes	Yes	Bad frames dropped	No
ERROR CORRECTION	Yes	Yes	Yes	No	No
SUPPORTS REAL-TIME VOICE	No	No	No	Probably not	Yes
MIXED-MEDIA SUPPORT (VOICE, DATA, VIDEO, ETC.)	No	No	No	No	Yes

ARPA = Advanced Research Projects Agency
ATM = Asynchronous Transfer Mode
CRC = Cyclic Redundancy Check
DIS = Draft International Standard
DOD = Department of Defense
LAPD = Link Access Procedure-D
PPS = packets per second

Source: Mier Communications

Packet Switching

Good and bad fits for packet-backbone transport

TERMINAL COMMUNICATIONS	EXAMPLE	SUITABILITY FOR PACKET TRANSPORT	COMMENT
CHARACTER-MODE, FULL-SCREEN, WITH ECHO-BACK	VT100	POOR	ECHO-BACK GENERATES UNNECESSARY PACKET TRAFFIC CHARACTER-MODE TRANSMITS SINGLE CHARACTER AT A TIME, MAY REQUIRE A FULL PACKET FOR EACH CHARACTER
TTY-MODE	ANY TTY EMULATION	FAIR	TRANSMITS ONE LINE OF DATA AT A TIME, WHICH PERMITS BETTER PACKET UTILIZATION THAN CHARACTER-MODE
BISYNC CLUSTER CONTROLLER, POINT-TO-POINT	IBM 3274 BSC	FAIR	BLOCK-MODE, GOOD FOR FILLING PACKETS, BUT CHARACTER-ORIENTED FRAME STRUCTURE REQUIRES CONVERSION TO BIT-ORIENTED X.25/HDLC STRUCTURE
BISYNC TERMINALS, MULTIPOINT	IBM 327X BSC	GOOD	POLLING IN MULTIPOINT CONFIGURATION CAN BE ELIMINATED; BEST IF PACKET NETWORK SUPPORTS DSP PROTOCOL FOR BSC DEVICES
SNA/SDLC CLUSTER CONTROLLER	IBM 3174 SNA/SDLC	GOOD	SNA/SDLC BIT-ORIENTED STRUCTURE MEANS FAST PACKET FORMATION; POLLS CAN BE INTERCEPTED/SIMULATED; A LONG PACKET SIZE USUALLY BEST
APPC/LU6.2 DEVICE	PC, PS/2, SYSTEM/36	EXCELLENT	ESPECIALLY EFFICIENT OVER PACKET NETWORK WITH NPSI FRONT-END PROCESSOR AND USING QLLC FRAME STRUCTURE

APPC = ADVANCED PROGRAM-TO-PROGRAM COMMUNICATIONS
BSC, BISYNC = BINARY SYNCHRONOUS COMMUNICATIONS
DSP = DISPLAY SYSTEM PROTOCOL
HDLC = HIGH-LEVEL DATA LINK CONTROL
LU = LOGICAL UNIT
NPSI = NETWORK PACKET-SWITCHING INTERFACE
QLLC = QUALIFIED LOGICAL LINK CONTROL
SDLC = SYNCHRONOUS DATA LINK CONTROL
TTY = TELETYPEWRITER

Source: Mier Communications

Northern Telecom, for example, establishes and maintains an X.25 virtual circuit for each SNA logical session, which provides a clear one-to-one association of SNA traffic and packet-network resource allocation.

In some vendors' packet products, SNA control frames, which may or may not contain user data, are painstakingly converted to their closest packet-network equivalent. This is helpful in tying in management and control data to IBM host-based network management. In other vendors' packet products, all SNA frames—whether control or user data—are passed via encapsulation. This maximizes throughput and response time but makes the packet network effectively transparent to the SNA network. The price paid is usually in a separate network management arrangement, which is required for the packet network, in addition to whatever management arrangement is used for the IBM SNA network.

"Network management is a problem," says Maks Wulkan, executive vice president of Eicon Technology (Montreal). Eicon's products, deployed generally for LAN gateway access to remote IBM processors via packet networks, offer several session-layer interfaces for packet-network transport. For SNA traffic, these include 3270/LU2, 5250/LU7, and APPC/LU6.2. Another handles basic ASCII/VT100 asynchronous communications. And recently, Eicon added a software option for handling IBM's QLLC.

According to Wulkan, Eicon's approach for LU6.2 (APPC) communications is to encapsulate this type of traffic in QLLC packets, which provides the most efficient flow through the packet network and to the IBM NPSI front-end. He notes that by passing SNA traffic transparently (though the Eicon products do take care of poll interception and physical unit device emulation, notably PU Types 2.1 and 2.0), "the packet network knows nothing about SNA."

Different strokes

Using a packet backbone solely to replace a greater number of leased lines in an all-IBM network probably doesn't pay in most instances. A packet network would likely reap savings for the user's organization over an extensive network of point-to-point leased lines in monthly facilities costs, but the payback for the cost of the packet-network components—such as the processors—could take an exceedingly long time. Even if the monthly leased-line bill was reduced from $20,000 to $10,000, the $10,000 saving might have to be spent for packet equipment, amortized over, say, four years.

However, in a network with many multipoint lines, which are handling mainly IBM terminal-to-host communications, a packet backbone network can have considerably more

Packet Switching

appeal. There are several reasons for this:
- In multipoint configurations, IBM host polling of terminals can become an unwieldy portion of the overall traffic. Where polling on a point-to-point circuit usually accounts for only a minuscule portion of the overall line traffic, this can grow in a multipoint environment to a point where individual user response times suffer unacceptable degradation. The elimination of polling through a packet-switching network can ameliorate this.
- Multipoint circuit pricing has become exceedingly complex, with the result in many cases being sharply higher overall monthly costs owing to new per-circuit connection charges levied by the local telephone companies. Packet-network topologies invariably use many fewer leased-line circuits to accommodate many more devices. And if engineered properly, a packet network can usually handle high-peak data-traffic spurts, and even sustain considerable network growth, without having to add transmission facilities (though data-rate upgrades on select links may be needed from time to time).
- A packet-switching twist called fast select enables very short transactions (like credit card authorizations, automated teller machine personal identification number verifications, and similar point-of-sale-type transactions) to be transmitted extremely efficiently. Already supported in Northern Telecom's packet switches, for example, fast select allows a single, short call setup packet to carry a brief data message to the destination and the destination to acknowledge receipt and respond in a single, equally brief call tear-down packet.

For these reasons, packet backbones may be justified as a transport replacement for multipoint environments, even where there is only IBM terminal-to-host traffic. Usually, however, the decision to go with a packet backbone hinges on additional factors, such as the ability to readily switch user's connections.

The right stuff

Many large-network users have a mix of terminals, PCs, minicomputers, and hosts. And one reason packet backbones are in growing demand today is that they readily enable users at any network-attached device to switch from one destination to another, even when different protocols are required, and over the same network link.

The heightened appeal for packet switching in this regard comes from the additional software support many packet-equipment suppliers now offer. Typically, support is now included for the following:
- PAD protocol conversion for asynchronous terminal traffic—usually to asynchronous hosts—may be supplemented with particular terminal-emulation software support (such as for VT100 or 220 terminals, Hewlett-Packard async devices, and Honeywell VIP terminals).
- IBM 3270 Bisync, usually combined with support for DSP or specific Bisync/3270 device emulation.
- IBM 3270 SDLC, emulation of an SNA 3270 cluster controller, or remote standalone 3270 display terminal.
- IBM 5250 SNA/SDLC, emulation of the terminal series used with IBM minicomputers.
- X.25, which will typically be based on the CCITT's 1984 or 1980 versions of the standard. Sometimes connection between one vendor's PAD supporting the 1980 version and another vendor's packet switch supporting the 1984 version can be a problem (especially during call establishment, since the switch offers services and features from the 1984 specification that the 1980 PAD doesn't recognize). To handle such cases, equipment can sometimes be set to run in 1984-suppressed mode, so that communications with 1980-based devices can be accommodated on a line-by-line basis.
- X.32, which defines X.25 features for support over a dial-up (or switched), synchronous connection. This involves user identification and setup negotiation features that typical, leased-line X.25 connections do not require.
- SNA/QLLC, special support for IBM NPSI and the IBM-defined QLLC packet format. A newer version of QLLC, called ELLC (for extended logical link control), has been issued by IBM and will no doubt be supported by packet-equipment suppliers that already handle QLLC. ELLC is the SNA-via-packet-network protocol that IBM is supporting for networking its midrange computers (System/36, System/38, AS/400) via packet networks. It reportedly provides better error-recovery capabilities than its QLLC predecessor, because ELLC keeps more error-recovery decision making at the data link level. By comparison, QLLC reportedly defers many error-recovery decisions to higher-level SNA protocols.
- X.75, for connections between packet networks (private to public, private to private, public to international).
- Any of several leading LAN client-server protocols, such as the SMB of Netbios-compatible LANs. These are supported mainly in the new genre of packet-switching LAN gateways.
- APPC/LU6.2 (IBM's Advanced Program-to-Program Communications/Logical Unit 6.2 protocol), which can be

Packet-equipment suppliers now offer greater software support.

implemented in several ways. One of the most common is where a LAN-to-X.25 gateway or PAD processes the IBM-defined verbs from other LAN workstations (usually PCs). In this way, the PCs don't have to run the full APPC protocol software themselves (requiring from 400+ Kbytes in an MS-DOS PC to more than 2 Mbytes in an OS/2). In this case (supported in such LAN/X.25 gateways as those from Eicon Technology), the PCs send only the APPC verb to the X.25 processor, which then initiates and performs the appropriate APPC protocol function.
- Support for higher-level protocol stacks, on top of X.25, such as TCP/IP. In such products, like those available from Frontier Technologies (Milwaukee, Wis.), the X.25 gateway with TCP/IP support effectively becomes a LAN router.

Packet Switching

- Any combination of the above protocols.

It is unlikely that many networks would need to implement all of these protocol conversions in the same backbone packet network. And it would probably be unwise to do so, since protocol processing is a processor- and memory-intensive operation. As the number of different protocols that need to be supported grows, throughput drops. In most networks, only a few are needed.

"Ninety-five percent of what most are looking for [in packet-network protocol support] is Bisync, 3270/SNA, asynchronous PAD, and X.25," says David Jeanes, manager of data network market analysis with Bell Northern Research (Ottawa). "You need more memory available for multiprotocol systems," he adds.

The LAN connection

The spate of relatively new equipment manufacturers who are specializing in LAN gateways to packet networks seem to reflect the newness of LANs in general. Manufacturers like Eicon and Frontier are recent entrants into the packet-switching marketplace.

But like the LAN industry in general, these specialized-gateway makers are growing rapidly (Eicon, for example, claims 25,000 of its gateways are already installed, and that its products are OEMed to some 40 to 50 resellers and system integrators).

It seems, too, that these LAN gateway specialists are particularly adept at developing efficient software for tying LANs to wide area networks. The traditional packet-switch and PAD manufacturers, by comparison, seem these days to be more focused on hardware development to improve throughput and call-processing performance in backbone packet networks.

Naturally, the LAN-gateway makers are obliged to ensure that their products work with the leading backbone packet-switch suppliers, as well as with the major public data networks of the world. Users should query these gateway suppliers on their connectivity and compatibility experiences with the specific backbone packet equipment they are either already using or considering.

Unfortunately, there are no de jure standards yet that specify how LAN traffic is to be mapped to packet-switching WANs or connections maintained through packet backbones to other, remote LANs. As a result, implementations vary greatly in how this is achieved, what particular features are supported, and in relative performance.

A better approach than IBM's?

To understand the diversity of approaches being taken, consider several of Eicon Technology's SNA/LAN-to-packet-network implementations.

Eicon's appearance to LAN nodes takes several different forms. Currently, communications to the gateway across the LAN uses Netbios; the LAN stations, in the role of clients, use a redirector function to access the gateway (supplied by Eicon, which takes about 10 Kbytes of the workstation's memory). The gateway handles packet call setup and communications through the packet network to the remote IBM host.

The redirector function initiates SMB sessions with the Eicon gateway, which assumes the role of a server. The SMB message informs the gateway to which host and application a virtual circuit through the packet network needs to be established. For 3270 or 5250 terminal communications, the LAN stations need to have software for the terminal emulation; the gateway assumes the identity of the appropriate cluster controller to the host.

The operation is different, however, in the case of APPC/LU6.2 communications (Fig. 3). Eicon supplies software that loads onto the PCs (or PS/2s) needing to establish APPC communications. As opposed to IBM's approach, which is to load APPC/PC on MS-DOS PCs (or the full APPC protocol module from the Communications Manager of OS/2 Extended Edition), the Eicon approach is for the LAN workstations to send only APPC service-request verbs. The Eicon gateway processes these verbs and initiates the appropriate APPC protocol actions and messages.

Eicon boasts of the efficiency of its approach. The memory requirements on the LAN workstations are much smaller than if they handled all APPC processing on their own, and the amount of trans-LAN traffic related to APPC communications is minimized, says Wulkan.

But even more important to operation over a packet network, the Eicon gateway-based approach involves a single physical unit appearance to the remote IBM host. This is key because the PU definition to the host front-end is the basis for host-issued polls (and not LU existence in SNA networks). And with a single PU in the gateway, polling from the SNA host is minimized. If polls need to be passed to LAN workstations (as when the stations handle all their own APPC processing, and each has both PU and LU entities defined to the host for it), then this additional traffic can unduly burden the packet transport network.

When the Eicon gateway handles cluster-controller processing and emulation across the packet network to a NPSI host, the response time that is achieved is as good as a direct leased-line connection through an IBM 3174 cluster controller.

In fact, according to Wulkan, independent user tests show that response times through an Eicon gateway are, in some cases, even better than through a 3174 cluster controller for clusters of from one to 10 terminals (PCs emulating 3270 terminals). The normalized data (supplied by Eicon) indicates a 4.0-second response time for a 10-node 3174 cluster, and 3.5 seconds for an Eicon LAN configuration supporting 10 terminal-emulation LAN workstations.

"The data shows our technique doesn't degrade performance," says Wulkan. The analysis is not an exact apples-to-apples comparison, however, since the Eicon approach was measured as a cluster-controller gateway on both Ethernet and token ring LANs, communicating using the QLLC encapsulation technique over a packet network to a remote NPSI host. The IBM 3174 can operate as a gateway on a token ring, or it can be configured to handle QLLC communications over a packet network to a NPSI host, but IBM documentation

Packet Switching

clearly points out that the 3174 cannot handle both attachments at the same time.

The spread of OSI presages a rapid proliferation of packet backbones. But the good news for users today is that existing packet networks should be readily adapted to handling high-level OSI communications (in addition to whatever protocols and connectivity are supported currently).

"X.400, for example, is a message-switching network that has been designed to overlay on top of a packet-switching network," says John B. Stephensen, senior vice president of technology at Retix, which has pioneered OSI protocol implementation in a variety of network and processor environments. "For wide-area OSI communications," he adds, "X.25 is the only thing that exists."

According to Stephensen, higher-level OSI protocols will access a packet network through a new OSI protocol standard called ISO-IP (its formal name in OSI circles is the Connectionless Network Protocol, or CLNP; the ISO-IP is used to distinguish it from the Internet Protocol of the TCP/IP protocol suite).

Technically, both X.25 and OSI higher-level addresses are variable in length. In practice, however, an X.25 address (the data terminal equipment address) is usually 14 digits. And the OSI address (called the IP-NSAP—network service access point—address) can be up to 24 bytes in all.

"For OSI, you need to follow any of the eight NSAP address formats," says Stephensen. These formats, for carrying and passing on existing address standards like

2. Two APPC methods. IBM's APPC approach (A): Load APPC/PC on MS-DOS PCs. With Eicon's approach (B), the LAN workstations send only APPC service-request verbs across the LAN. The PC gateway processes them and initiates the APPC protocol actions and messages. This involves a single physical unit appearance to the IBM host.

(A) IBM APPC

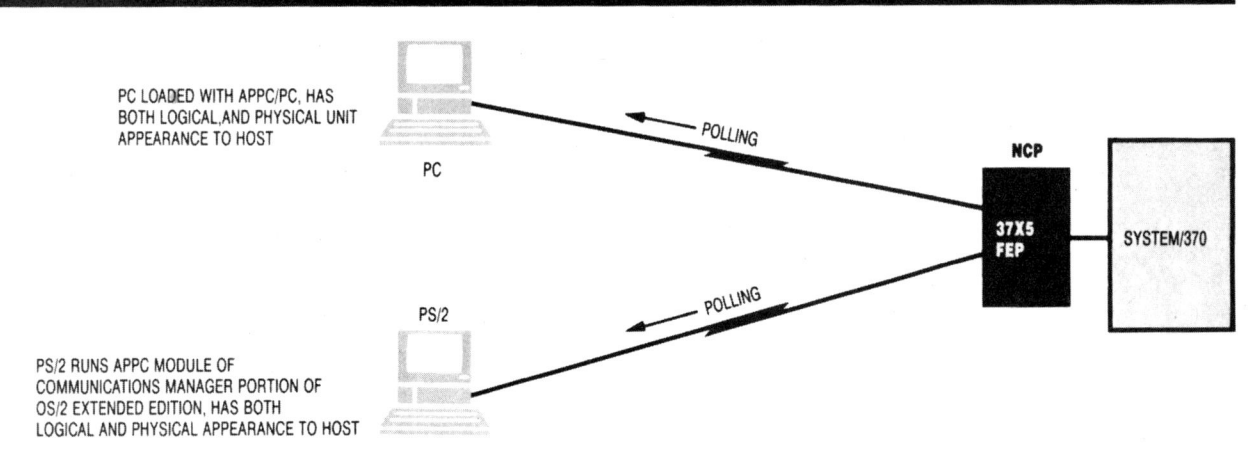

PC LOADED WITH APPC/PC, HAS BOTH LOGICAL AND PHYSICAL UNIT APPEARANCE TO HOST

PS/2 RUNS APPC MODULE OF COMMUNICATIONS MANAGER PORTION OF OS/2 EXTENDED EDITION, HAS BOTH LOGICAL AND PHYSICAL APPEARANCE TO HOST

(B) Eicon APPC

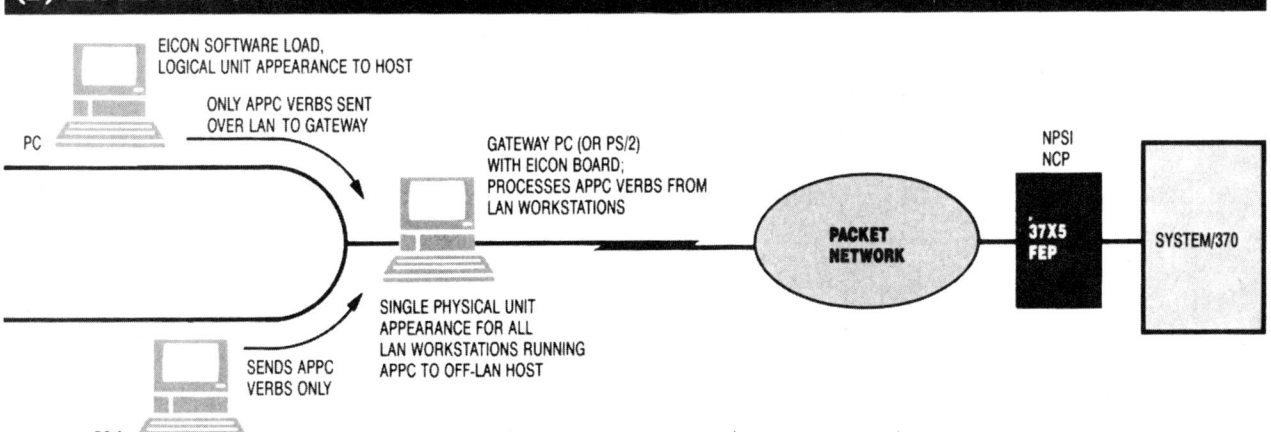

EICON SOFTWARE LOAD, LOGICAL UNIT APPEARANCE TO HOST

ONLY APPC VERBS SENT OVER LAN TO GATEWAY

GATEWAY PC (OR PS/2) WITH EICON BOARD; PROCESSES APPC VERBS FROM LAN WORKSTATIONS

SINGLE PHYSICAL UNIT APPEARANCE FOR ALL LAN WORKSTATIONS RUNNING APPC TO OFF-LAN HOST

SENDS APPC VERBS ONLY

APPC/PC = ADVANCED PROGRAM-TO-PROGRAM COMMUNICATIONS FOR THE PC
FEP = FRONT-END PROCESSOR
NCP = NETWORK CONTROL PROGRAM
NPSI = NETWORK PACKET-SWITCHING INTERFACE

Packet Switching

Telex numbers, telephone numbers, even ISDN addresses, are all clearly delineated in a separate OSI standard: ISO document 8348, Addendum 2.

Forward spin

The state of packet switching is clearly evolving in response to changing times. And while many of the recent developments—packet price-performance ratios, software links, LAN-to-packet gateways—have positioned packet switching to enjoy an unprecedented proliferation in the next decade, other advances are still needed before packet backbones are viewed as the best long-term selection for most users.

More attention needs to be paid to separating packet-network control from transport, for example. Sources, such as packet switch vendors, report that so-called separate-channel control for packet-network operation is being actively studied and explored, both as part of standards activities involving frame relay, for example, and also in private development labs as a technique holding great promise for unheard-of packet throughputs in future generations of packet switches. (In standard packet switching, control packets preempt user-data packets. Separate-channel control, as the term implies, keeps control packets on a channel separate from user-data channels.)

The separation of control and transport is also a key to packet-switching operation over ISDN, which most agree is a marriage that simply must work. Conventional packet switching, characterized by the LAPB link-control protocol, is constrained to operating within the ISDN D channel, which offers only limited bandwidth for data transport. (At this writing, dial-up X.25 over a B channel is not yet a reality.)

LAPD—devised for ISDN connections—is a substantial improvement over LAPB toward achieving separate-channel packet control and enabling full 64-kbit/s, DS-0 packet bandwidth on a dynamic demand basis.

There's little question that packet backbones deployed in the coming decade will be based on 64-kbit/s DS-0 and 1.544-Mbit/s T1 facilities. Most packet gear already supports full-line utilization at 64 kbit/s, and several can also now fully load T1 facilities. (Telenet, for one, uses T1 facilities as part of its packet network.) What's more, the competition in the U.S. for T1 and fractional T1 bandwidth facilities makes their use as trunks in packet backbones inevitable. ■

Edwin E. Mier, editor at large for DATA COMMUNICATIONS, *is also president of Mier Communications Inc., a communications and networking consultancy in Princeton Junction, N.J. Mier publishes the* CONNECTIONS *series of loose-leaf information services and computer-networking guides.*

Nathan J. Muller, Telecom Planning & Analysis, Huntsville, Ala.

Surveying the software that manages telecommunications

A consultant's crash course lays out mainframe, minicomputer, and microcomputer options that address communications costs.

Over the years, businesses have become adept at quantifying most aspects of their operations to eliminate waste, increase worker productivity, and control overhead. But when it comes to applying the same level of scrutiny to telecommunications, a substantial line item on most corporate budgets, there are still few, if any, controls. Until relatively recently all but the largest firms shrugged off the cost of telecommunications as merely a necessary business expense.

Recognizing that accurate and comprehensive information is necessary for the effective management of telecommunications is commendable. But to thoroughly evaluate available software packages, assess the reliability of potential vendors, and ensure trouble-free implementation requires both an appreciation of the various approaches to telecommunications management and an understanding of how various programs fit specific organizational needs.

The microcomputer solution

Microcomputers may be used to collect, poll, and process call records and provide reports on demand. Many other benefits of microcomputer-based telecommunications management deserve attention (Table 1).

Inexpensive floppy disks can be used to store call records conveniently for later reprocessing, historical inquiry, and traffic analysis. Floppy disks are much simpler to use than the magnetic tapes commonly used to store data for mainframe processing. Menu-driven microcomputer products provide the user with choices that quickly retrieve reports and perform database maintenance, allowing users with little or no experience to be instantly productive. Some microcomputer software programs include features that allow users to customize telecommunications reports.

The same hardware can be used for call accounting and for other telecommunications management jobs, such as database and telephone directory maintenance, polling, inventory control, service-order tracking, traffic analysis, and network optimization. In fact, sophisticated windowing programs and other background mode techniques now allow the microcomputer to record call data while the operator performs other tasks. For example, while calls are being recorded, the operator can use another window to access an electronic telephone directory, check the status of a service order, or run a spreadsheet on the telecommunications budget. Such multitasking capabilities provide telecommunications managers with additional justification for purchasing standalone gear and to preempt management concerns about dedicating a microcomputer to call-record collection. Finally, hardware support for microcomputers is widely available and, for the most part, reliable.

But the apparent convenience and user-friendliness of microcomputer-based telecommunications management often obscures its inherent limitations. Despite the impressive collection and storage capacities of some microcomputers—as much as one million call records a month—what really counts is the number of call records that can be processed at one time and how long it takes to format and run the final reports. A microcomputer that can collect up to 500,000 call records a month from 2,200 extensions, for example, may produce only summary reports, or retrieve and print call data one station at a time. This may not be adequate for running detailed and consolidated usage reports on a timely basis. Depending on the number and complexity of reports required, and the rating scheme used to cost each call, processing that many call records can consume as much as 120 man-hours per month, requiring the supervision of a full-time operator.

Many vendors unintentionally confuse prospective customers when they use the term "processing." To equate it with "call collection" alone is misleading. Processing actually refers to the systematic execution of operations on a call record to arrive at a desired result—that is, calls priced approximately and arranged in a meaningful report format. Call collection, then, is only the first step in a much more complicated process that leads to report generation. When vendors say that their microcomputer-based machines can "process" or "handle" 50,000 calls an hour, what they are really trying to say is that when their microcomputers function as call collectors, they can collect and store 50,000 raw call records.

Generally, microcomputers cannot rate calls according to appropriate tariffs for intra- and interstate or intra- and inter-LATA (Local Access and Transport Areas) calls. The same holds for calls to Canada, Mexico, Hawaii, Alaska, and international (011) locations. With their limited memory, storage, and computing capabilities, microcomputers must approximate rather than accurately rate calls using V&H (vertical and horizontal) tables. These tables provide, among other things, exchange coordinates that are used for calculating the distance of calls. But this method is only 90 percent to 95 percent as accurate as rating calls with actual tariffs, which may be close enough even for high-volume users.

Using the V&H costing method, Xtend Communications Corp. in New York, for example, can collect and price up to 30,000 calls per hour in real-time with a microcomputer; it can have some reports ready in only 30 seconds. (This kind of performance is more the exception than the rule.)

Microcomputers virtually require that users take full responsibility for quality control. It is often a full-time job to monitor equipment and keep it running smoothly. Although microcomputer software costs much less than that for mainframes, the limitations of most microcomputers should be carefully weighed against the promise of short-term savings.

Table 1: Summary of microcomputer processing

ADVANTAGES	DISADVANTAGES
MULTIFUNCTIONAL: COLLECTION POLLING REPORT PROCESSING DATABASE MAINTENANCE	LIMITED MEMORY AND PROCESSING POWER
MULTITASKING CAPABILITY	
REPORTS ON DEMAND	
INEXPENSIVE	LIMITED CALL-RATING ACCURACY
CONVENIENT USER FRIENDLY	REQUIRES USER TO BE RESPONSIBLE FOR TURNKEY OPERATION
	LIMITED REPORTING FLEXIBILITY
HARDWARE SUPPORT READILY AVAILABLE; ECONOMICAL FOR SINGLE-SITE TELECOMMUNICATIONS NETWORKS WITH LESS THAN 500 EXTENSIONS	

If user call-costing and -reporting needs are relatively simple, the microcomputer processing option may be the best choice. This alternative also gives the added benefits of convenience and multiple functions. As needs change, and insight and expertise in telecommunications management grows, software modules and memory capacity can be added at only an incremental cost. The microprocessing option is also an effective way for telecommunications managers to end their dependence on the MIS/DP (management information systems/data processing) shop and retain total control of their corporate mission. From top management's perspective, the microprocessing option should stop the finger-pointing between MIS/DP and telecommunications.

Alternatively, users can migrate to minicomputer or mainframe products, perhaps with the same vendor. When the time comes to make that decision, the user will have built up the knowledge base from which to make more informed choices.

Minicomputer processing

Minicomputers constitute another on-site processing option. For many years this method was used almost exclusively by the hotel and motel industry for on-demand billing. Vendors developed specialized hardware and software packages for this lucrative market niche. But as the market became saturated, many of these vendors enhanced their offerings for broader use. Today, approximately 150 vendors compete with about 500 software offerings in a market that will approach $225 million in revenue by the end of 1988.

Because today's microcomputers can provide nearly the same storage capacity and processing power as medium-range minicomputers, the market for minicomputer-based telecommunications management products is not expanding. Advances in microcomputers have come faster than advances in minicomputers and mainframes. However, many mainframe software vendors also offer their products for use on minicomputers.

For the most part, the following discussion of mainframe processing options also applies to minicomputer telecommunications management packages.

Mainframe solutions

Mainframe processing comes in two versions: service bureau and license agreement.

With a service bureau, the user provides the vendor with call detail records through magnetic tape or floppy disk, or through electronic transmission over telephone lines under a polling arrangement. The vendor uses its mainframe computer to process the data and to generate the reports requested by the customer. A reasonable turnaround time for this kind of report processing is one week.

Under a license arrangement, the user typically signs an agreement with the vendor. The document authorizes use of the software at one or more sites where the user's hardware is located. Such a license agreement is common practice among vendors because it allows them to exercise more control over the proprietary nature of their software than copyright laws usually afford with an outright purchase. Under a license agreement the user is obligated to maintain confidentiality and adhere to provisions in the

Table 2: Summary of minicomputer/mainframe processing (License Arrangement)

ADVANTAGES	DISADVANTAGES
VIRTUALLY UNLIMITED MEMORY AND PROCESSING POWER	MAGNETIC TAPE MAY PROVE CUMBERSOME AND TAX MAINFRAME RESOURCES
PRECISE CALL RATING	HIGHER UP-FRONT COSTS FOR SOFTWARE
INCREASED REPORTING FLEXIBILITY	REQUIRES KNOWLEDGEABLE DATA PROCESSING PERSONNEL; MINIMUM TURNOVER
TIMELY REPORT PROCESSING	REQUIRES USER TO TAKE CHARGE OF TURNKEY OPERATION
ECONOMICAL FOR MULTI-NODE USERS WITH MORE THAN 500 EXTENSIONS	

agreement governing the use and disclosure of the software product.

The licensed software package usually includes tariff tables required for accurate call rating and a database of V&H coordinates for assigning city and state locations to long-distance calls made over bulk-rated facilities. It also includes a database defining the characteristics of the user's telecommunications setup that will use this data to generate the desired reports.

Site license versus service bureau

Choosing between the license or service bureau may hinge on internal capabilities, specifically the amount of time and effort the MIS/DP shop wishes to expend in becoming experts at telecommunications management (tables 2 and 3). Installing new tariff tables, updating the database to reflect changes in the network, and verifying input data and report runs are all time-consuming chores that require expertise and staff continuity. Ultimately, it may be easier and more economical to use a reliable service bureau for such tasks. A good service bureau also provides assistance in interpreting the reports.

Businesses with a large number of extensions or account codes, coupled with constant equipment moves and changes, should ask if the vendor offers a front-end capability for entering and uploading this data to the mainframe. Menu-driven microcomputer data entry permits users to easily record, review, and edit the database—a more convenient and accurate process than filling out forms for keying by the vendor's data-entry staff.

Remember that with multinode networks that use private branch exchanges from different manufacturers, each PBX type formats call records differently. Trying to handle a variety of formats on an in-house mainframe may take up valuable processing time and cause program maintenance nightmares for the MIS/DP staff.

Distinct disadvantages arise when a telecommunications management application uses a data processing center that relies heavily on magnetic tape. Since magnetic tape is not pollable and since different PBX types use proprietary call record formats, the data stored on each magnetic tape must be preprocessed into a common format before mainframe report processing can take place. Depending on the number of PBX types the network has, this could turn into a cumbersome procedure that wastes mainframe resources and increases the chance for human error.

Magnetic tape drives are mechanical devices that require scheduled preventive maintenance. Calls are not recorded during maintenance downtime unless redundant magnetic tape hardware is operating—a very expensive proposition.

Furthermore, it is not always easy to spot a malfunctioning magnetic tape drive; a misaligned head, for example, can cause call-recording problems. Many times such a malfunction is not discovered until a technician stumbles on it during a preventive maintenance visit—or when the MIS/DP manager notifies the telecommunications administrator that a blank tape was sent to the data processing center. Even more basic, it is easy for inexperienced operators to mistakenly install a magnetic tape on the drive unit. This can result in lost call records, wasted computer time, and delayed report processing. Moreover, magnetic tape reels can be lost in transit, damaged from mishandling, or destroyed in an accident.

Magnetic tapes require careful administration and security for keeping track of spares, backups, tapes in transit, tapes awaiting processing, and blanks ready to be used. Not only does this burden the user with unnecessary overhead costs, but one foul-up can throw a tightly scheduled data processing operation into chaos. The

Table 3: Summary of minicomputer/mainframe processing (Service Bureau)

ADVANTAGES	DISADVANTAGES
VIRTUALLY UNLIMITED MEMORY AND PROCESSING POWER SUPPLIED BY VENDOR	DELIVERING DATA THROUGH MAGNETIC TAPE OR FLOPPY DISK IS RISKY
PRECISE CALL RATING	NOT ECONOMICAL FOR RAPIDLY GROWING COMPANIES WITH CONSTANT EQUIPMENT MOVES AND CHANGES
NO CAPITAL INVESTMENT; ONLY MONTHLY PAYMENTS FOR THE SERVICE	
INCREASED REPORTING FLEXIBILITY	LONG-TERM VIABILITY OF SERVICE HINGES ON CONTINUED SUCCESS OF VENDOR
REASONABLE TURNAROUND TIME FOR REPORTS	
ECONOMICAL FOR TELECOMMUNICATIONS NETWORKS WITH UP TO 1,000 EXTENSIONS AND LIMITED DP RESOURCES	
CUSTOMER SERVICE AVAILABLE ON CONTINUING BASIS	
QUALITY CONTROL IS ASSURED	

alternative—submitting finished reports late—may result in stale information that is of limited use to the telecommunications manager.

Pollable solid-state collection devices, black boxes that hang off PBXs and are responsible only for collecting call records, eliminate these problems. They are relatively inexpensive: from less than $3,000 for a store-and-forward device like Account-a-Call's Tadpoll to $6,000 for Sarasota, Fla.-based ComDev's intelligent STU-3B, which is available only through distributors. These devices install easily and quickly without PBX modifications or service interruptions. Because they can be polled, they also provide substantial cost savings in labor, magnetic tape shipping, and mainframe processing.

If reports are processed on an in-house mainframe and the network involved is composed of different PBX types, these store-and-forward devices do nothing to simplify the task of format translation. Although they operate unattended and store as many as 60,000 call records, they do not have the intelligence necessary to convert this data into a common call record format, a chore that will ultimately tax mainframe resources. However, for recording needs on a homogeneous network, these low-cost call data collectors perform this simple task reliably.

Alternatively, look for an intelligent Station Message Detail Recorder (SMDR) that will process call records from virtually any PBX into a common format. Although they cost more, these smart devices make data collection and report processing much easier, and they provide flexibility in choosing additional PBXs for network expansion. They can be purchased without regard for PBX type (see figure). An additional benefit is that a single device can accept data from multiple PBXs simultaneously. For example, ComDev's STU-3B collects data from up to six PBXs simultaneously, while Telco Research's TRU Recorder records data from up to 15 PBXs simultaneously. If saving money on gear is an objective, look for a service bureau that will poll inexpensive store-and-forward data collectors and assemble the diverse call record data in a common format for call costing and report processing.

In addition to eliminating the risk, labor intensiveness, and cost of magnetic tape delivery, the polling process can enhance data integrity by auditing the data from the point of origin to the point of delivery. Blocks of data are sequentially numbered at the point of origin and are "checkpointed" as they are teleprocessed to the destination polling equipment. In this cyclic redundancy check, the number of data blocks is verified by both the sending and receiving units. Sometimes the ACK/NAK (acknowledgment/negative acknowledgment) process is used to confirm the receipt of data. In the event that incomplete or damaged data arrives at the network poller, repolls are initiated automatically until all data blocks are accounted for and arrive at the destination error-free.

Polling provides a degree of flexibility to data collection in that the process may be initiated as demand warrants or according to a routine late-night schedule that takes advantage of lower transmission costs. And most pollers

Multinode teleprocessing. *SMDRs can collect data from diverse PBXs, formatting it for use by a service bureau or on-site data processing center. SMDR buyers need not consider the type of PBX sending data. Although up-front costs are greater than with store-and-forward devices, overall network management costs may be less.*

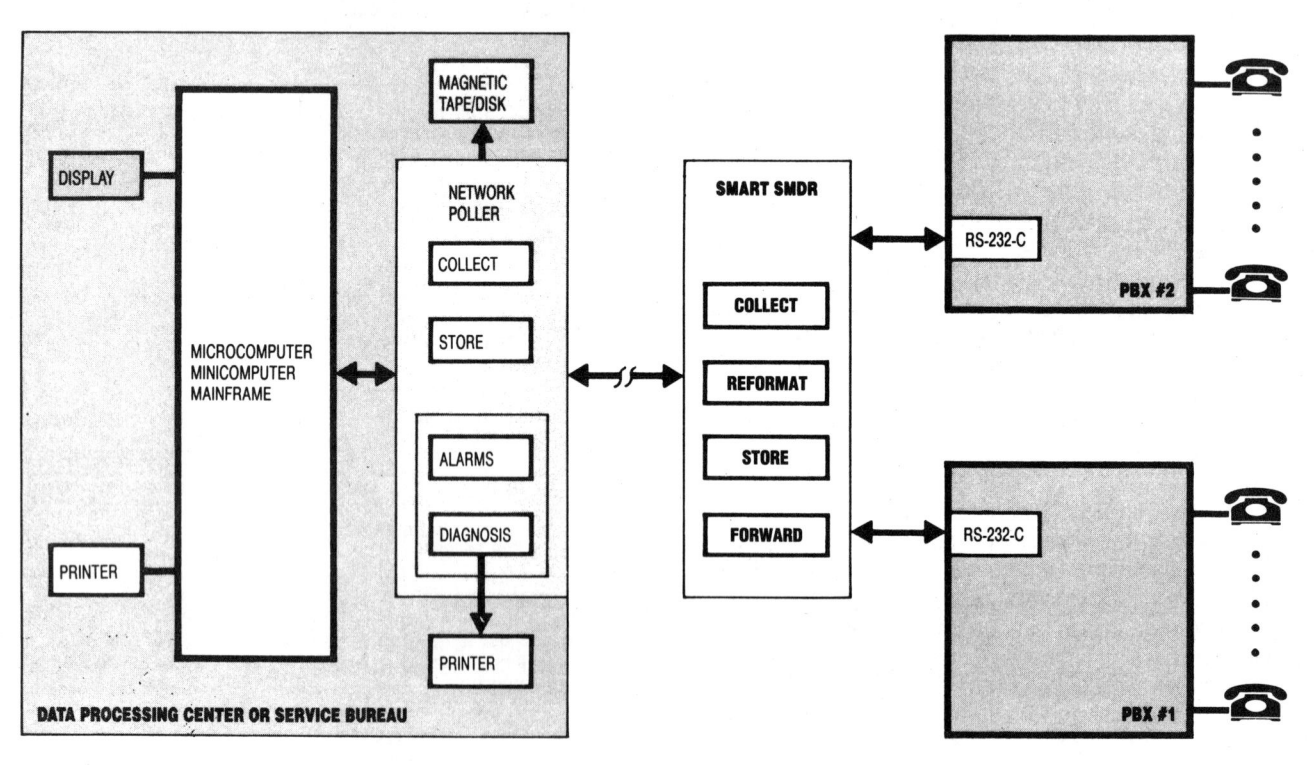

PBX = PRIVATE BRANCH EXCHANGE
SMDR = STATION MESSAGE DETAIL RECORDER

are designed for unattended operation. If users have high call volume and plan to use their microcomputers in a multitasking mode, polling must be done more frequently because there is less memory available for storage.

But even the selection of polling equipment requires careful evaluation:
- In the event of a power outage, will the poller turn off and stay off, or will it restart automatically and initiate a repoll when the power resumes?
- If there are different SMDR types on a multinode network, will the poller adjust automatically to the error-checking protocol of the SMDR device being polled?
- Does the poller have enough intelligence to switch lines automatically or to hang up and dial again when it encounters poor line quality?
- Does the poller allow remote activation for polling on demand?
- Does the poller furnish a complete report of its activities?
- Does it have the capability to perform remote diagnostics on PBXs as well as on the SMDR devices?

Answers to these questions are critical to the long-term reliability of data collection and, ultimately, to the viability of in-house report processing on multinode networks. When these questions are applied to most microcomputer-based pollers, there may be trade-offs between reliability and convenience and low cost. Unlike their minicomputer or mainframe equivalents, microcomputers may not have the intelligence necessary to automatically reinstate polling after a power outage.

The comprehensiveness of tariff tables used by the vendor ultimately has an impact on the accuracy of cost allocation. With the implementation of LATAs in 1984, there are now many different rate structures for inter- and intrastate calls, and others for inter- or intra-LATA calls. With 164 LATAs defining the service areas of the major telephone companies and another 25 for independent telephone companies, the task of rating calls is complex. Thus find out how the vendor developed and implemented its new rating package when the LATA schema went into effect after the divestiture of AT&T. Also find out if its customers experienced any problems related to the changeover.

Answers to these questions may determine the reliability of vendor service and indicate future responses to changes in the operating environment.

Other points to keep in mind include:
- The advantages of being able to rate calls differently from department to department.
- In addition to costing calls by tariff, costing may be user-defined as a flat cost-per-call, cost-per-minute, or cost-per-minute with differential rates for the first and each additional minute.
- Calls placed over bulk facilities may be costed at the equivalent DDD (direct distance dialing) rate, or calculated as a percentage of the total corporate telecommunications cost.
- Time-of-day costing allows the application of appropriate evening, weekend, and holiday discounts to DDD calls and calls made over alternative interchange facilities.

When used in conjunction with account codes, any of these costing schemes can be used for client billing. Some software vendors are adept at providing all of these rating options and will even work closely with users to determine their exact requirements.

A thorough assessment of organizational needs will also determine the importance of having a vendor who can accurately rate calls originating and terminating in the same state. Calls originated and terminated in California are rated differently from calls originated and terminated in New York. Consequently, if a company has multiple locations, extra tariff files have to be maintained to rate intrastate calls. Although this information is readily available from such reputable organizations as CCMI/McGraw-Hill, some vendors are not properly equipped for such an undertaking and will try to make a case that other, less accurate call rating schemes, such as flat costs per minute, may also work.

Network optimization

Post-divestiture competition has resulted in more frequent and more complex tariff changes, making it almost impossible for telecommunications managers to evaluate everything available to ensure an optimally configured network. If a voice network has 500 or more extensions and relies extensively on alternative carriers and bulk billed services, a network optimization study should be performed at least annually, or more frequently as changes in available services, equipment, and network configuration dictate.

Network optimization studies yield valuable information that can be used for the following purposes:
- Ensure maximum savings with alternative carriers by finding out how they serve specific calling patterns.
- Justify FX, Tie Line, or WATS services with accurate and comprehensive information useful in making decisions.
- Determine through "what-if" analysis the potential impact of proposed tariff changes on the long-distance bills.
- Validate network reconfiguration proposals for top management review and approval.
- Set the pace for corporate fiscal responsibility.
- Sharpen the company's competitive edge with an efficient telecommunications network.

Paradoxically, vendors and consulting firms specializing in network optimization exclusively are severely handicapped compared with those that offer call accounting on a license and service bureau basis. While on first inspection the network optimization companies appear to be less biased, the second group of vendors have the advantage of already maintaining tariffs and huge databases, endowed with the computing power necessary to provide comprehensive call accounting services. Generally, they are going to be more reliable and thorough when it comes to providing network optimization services.

In addition, call accounting firms can accommodate the data from a number of different PBX types. Generally, the turnaround time for a network optimization study will be shorter than with vendors that lack these capabilities because call-accounting firms already know the correct call record format used on each PBX and can read the data without encountering translation problems.

Even if network optimization is only a remote consideration, users may want to choose a call accounting vendor that has a reliable track record with such services. The charges for network optimization can be as much as 20 percent less because database setup has already been done to provide call accounting. A reasonable turnaround

Table 4: Communications management vendors

Vendor	Software	Freestanding	Vendor	Software	Freestanding
THE ABACUS GROUP BELMONT, MASS.		●	MICRO-TEL INC. NORCROSS, GA.	●	
ACCOUNT-A-CALL CORP. BURBANK, CALIF.	●	●	MOSCOM CORP. EAST ROCHESTER, N.Y.	●	●
ADAX INC. NORCROSS, GA.	●		OLENTANGY ASSOCIATES COLUMBUS, OHIO	●	
AMERICAN TELEMANAGEMENT SOFTWARE INC. CINCINNATI, OHIO	●		OPCOM SUNNYVALE, CALIF.		●
CDR OF WASHINGTON VIENNA, VA.	●	●	SOFT-COM (FORMERLY SURE COMMUNICATIONS) NEW YORK, N.Y.	●	
COMMERCIAL SOFTWARE INC. NEW YORK, N.Y.	●		STONEHOUSE & CO. DALLAS, TEX.	●	
COMMUNICATIONS DESIGN CORP. STAMFORD, CONN.	●		SUMMA FOUR INC. MANCHESTER, N.H.		●
COMMUNICATIONS GROUP INC. KING OF PRUSSIA, PA.	●		TECHTRAN INDUSTRIES INC. ROCHESTER, N.Y.		●
COMMUNICATIONS SCIENCES INC. ISELIN, N.Y.	●		TEKNO INDUSTRIES BENSENVILLE, ILL.		●
COMPUTERWARE INC. DALLAS, TEX.		●	TELACCOUNT INC. SAN RAFAEL, CALIF.	●	●
CONTROL KEY CORP. PEABODY, MASS.		●	TELCO RESEARCH CORP. (A SUBSIDIARY OF NYNEX) NASHVILLE, TENN.	●	●
CREATIVE MANAGEMENT SYSTEMS (A SUBSIDIARY OF CINCINNATI BELL INFORMATION SYSTEMS) McLEAN, VA.	●		TELCOM MIS INC. UPPER DARBY, PA.	●	
DMW SOFTWARE INC. ANN ARBOR, MICH.	●	●	TELECOM MANAGEMENT BATON ROUGE, LA.	●	
INFO GROUP FRAMINGHAM, MASS.	●	●	TELECOMMUNICATIONS SYSTEMS MANAGEMENT INC. HARVESTER, MICH.		●
INFORTEXT SYSTEMS INC. SCHAUMBURG, ILL.		●	TELEPHONE BUDGETING SYSTEMS NEW YORK, N.Y.	●	
MBG ASSOCIATES LTD. WESTBROOK, CONN.	●		XIOX CORP. SAN MATEO, CALIF.	●	●
MCS INC. PITTSBURGH, PA.	●		XTEND (A SUBSIDIARY OF THE COMPUTOLL GROUP) NEW YORK, N.Y.	●	●
MDR TELEMANAGEMENT LTD. MISSISSAUGA, ONT.	●				

MATERIAL ABRIDGED BY PERMISSION FROM DATAPRO RESEARCH CORP.
CHART DOES NOT DISTINGUISH BETWEEN USER AND SERVICE BUREAU SOFTWARE.

time for a service bureau network optimization study is four to six weeks, depending on the number of network nodes plus the nature and scope of transmission facilities to be considered.

But caution should be taken with network optimization vendors who promise a certain percentage of savings or base their fees on a percentage of savings. Usually such vendors will not allow much input about the type of long-distance and bulk-billed services to be included in the study. These vendors want to make such decisions themselves because they can then deliver the greatest amount of savings and thus higher fees for themselves.

Also, be on guard with a vendor who happens to be a subsidiary of a telephone company. Impartiality may take a backseat to achieving larger corporate objectives.

If total control over the network optimization process is desired, and the extra time and effort to become proficient in network planning is available, there are microcomputer-based traffic analysis and network optimization packages available. Such packages include tariff and availability information for all major long-distance carriers. Some packages include a database of services available on an exchange-by-exchange basis, especially useful for comparing calls to cities that may not be on different discount carriers, and so will cost more than on-network calls. Also included in these packages is a program for analyzing real-time calling patterns, which can be used to select the most appropriate long-distance services.

Although such packages are effective for optimizing a single location, performing optimization studies on each node of a large nationwide network can be cumbersome and time-consuming, requiring dedicated staff. In this case, the mainframe processing capabilities of a service bureau might be more efficient.

Vendor reliability
Be wary about using the service bureaus of PBX manufacturers or equipment vendors. Being hardware-oriented, their call-accounting capabilities are usually limited to their own brand of PBX, which could limit equipment choices when it comes time to expand the network. When software problems arise, hardware vendors can be very slow with problem resolution.

Find out if telecommunications management is a major or minor part of the vendor's business. If it is only a sideline, the pressing needs of call-accounting customers may not receive top-priority treatment.

Before committing to a vendor:
- Insist on reviewing product technical documentation for scope and clarity—and to verify the claims of salespeople. If the in-house MIS/DP shop has problems attracting and keeping qualified staff, the quality of technical documentation may prove to be critically important if the choice is made to license mainframe software.
- Consider the ability of the vendor to customize software to meet unique organizational requirements.
- When calling references, be sure to ask about the timeliness with which customization was completed, the cooperativeness of the vendor in ironing out bugs in the program, and whether the final product matched the buyer's expectations.
- If a reference who no longer uses the vendor's products appears, find out why the company changed vendors.
- If a vendor appears to be giving away too much to get business, be suspicious. Getting telecommunications management at a bargain price will do no good if the vendor goes out of business and leaves no ongoing support. The call-accounting industry is extremely volatile. Some of the best-known companies are only marginally profitable; others have gone under and resurfaced as new entities with scaled-down product offerings and severely limited levels of customer service.
- Don't accept standard contracts. All provisions of the contract are negotiable, including price and terms. As in any other business transaction, the seller sets the price and the buyer sets the terms. Just because a contract is typeset doesn't mean users can't spell out the terms in as much detail as they deem necessary.
- If custom software is part of the purchase, throw in a penalty clause for late delivery, or a "weasel" clause that delivers a full refund if the product doesn't perform as promised after a reasonable prove-in period.
- To guard against the loss of technical support, make sure that the purchase includes a program source code in the event that the vendor goes belly-up or discontinues the product. The source code should be deliverable automatically from an escrow account or from a third-party specializing in such services. Be advised that this provision in the contract requires the assistance of an attorney who is experienced in matters of software protection—it's too easy to overturn these provisions in court. Also, make certain that whenever the product is updated, the source code in escrow is also updated.

If vendors balk at any of these notions, hand them a list of their competitors who are eager to get the business (Table 4).

Look before you leap
Whether a microcomputer, minicomputer, or mainframe call-accounting package, it carries a commitment to a long-term relationship and a dependency on the vendor for tariff updates, software enhancements, customer service, and so on. Vendors must make the case that they will be around to provide support for many years to come. It is the user's responsibility to exercise due diligence with respect to vendor selection by obtaining customer references, as well as credit and financial information. An added measure of caution is called for when dealing with privately held firms. In this industry it is these companies that have been most prone to mismanagement—falling behind in product development and having serious problems with cash flow.

If the decision is made to rely on a consultant for advice, show that individual no mercy; be alert to potential under-the-table relationships with vendors. Some consultants are paid retainer fees by vendors, given as an incentive to bring in new business. Insist on a thorough justification for all decisions. ■

Nathan J. Muller is an independent communications consultant in Huntsville, Ala. He specializes in network planning, as well as hardware and software evaluation. Muller's 15 years of industry experience has included positions in engineering, operations, field service, sales, and marketing. He has a graduate degree in management from George Washington University.

Section 5
Peripherals

Don Dempsey, Xerox Corp., El Segundo, Calif.,
and Cindy K. Parkinson, Xerox Corp., Fremont, Calif.

What are the differences between printers? Here's a guide.

With a little study you can identify the major types, how they work, how they compare, and where they're best suited.

Confusion abounds not only in the terminology for the communications and computer industries, but also in references to their peripheral gear—particularly printers. For data communicators, printers are essential when network and other data must be recorded beyond the electronic or magnetic form. With technologies changing so rapidly, it is often hard to keep up with the jargon, let alone the definitions.

Just what is a dot matrix printer, and how does it differ from a daisywheel unit? What is thermal-transfer technology? How do laser printers work, and where do ink jets fit in? What are the advantages and disadvantages of each type? Which printing method is best-suited for which application? The answers are detailed below.

Greatest impact

Daisywheel printers have become the industry standard for letter-quality printing. Their fully formed characters are generated by the impact of a hammer on the tip of a wheel spoke that is implanted with a letter. This spoke strikes a ribbon leaving the designated letter on the paper. The result is a clear, crisp character that looks as though it had been typed on a typewriter.

Some of the newest daisywheels have a dual-hammer construction in which two characters, nine spokes apart, can be struck on the same print line. This construction, with the use of a double-row extended-character-set printwheel, makes all the characters available without a shifting or carriage motion, which can both slow the printing speed and cause wear on the printer mechanism.

The "print-on-fly" capability is another innovation of daisywheel printers that helps to increase their speed. This technique allows the machine to print characters without the carriage coming to a complete stop. It requires split-second timing of the carriage, printwheel, ribbon, and hammer motion. To achieve this timing, firmware-based algorithms calculate various motion and distance parameters—including present carriage velocity, distance to next character, printwheel rotation, and hammer "flight" times—by looking ahead to the following sequence of characters. Based on these results, the carriage velocity adjusts upward or downward between characters to optimize the printer speed.

Besides the print quality, a major advantage of the daisywheel printer is its high reliability. Most of these workhorses of the business world offer more than 4,000 hours MTBF (mean time between failures), with the printwheel life reaching as high as 10 million impressions. A wide variety of daisywheel printers are available, ranging in price from $500 to $3,000. The higher-priced units have such features as faster speeds, extended character sets, and graphics capabilities. The cost per copy (page) ranges from $0.04 to $0.07.

The newer high-speed daisywheels mentioned earlier, with speeds up to 80 cps (characters per second), are often fast enough to function in a shared-resources environment. One printer can handle the printing needs of up to 16 individual workstations in either a local area or remote network. High-speed daisywheel printers are priced at $2,000 to $3,000. As we shall see, dot matrix printers, while generally faster, offer less professional-quality printing; thermal-transfer and laser printers both have high speed and good print quality but are much higher priced (see table).

In addition, new daisywheels offer ECS (extended-character set) capability: Careful design of a 200-character printwheel enables a user to construct up to 400 characters by overlapping existing characters to

Printers at a glance

TYPE	FEATURES	COMMENTS
DAISYWHEELS	LETTER-QUALITY PRINTING 20-80 CPS WORD PROCESSING, PROFESSIONAL CORRESPONDENCE PRINTHEAD LIFE: 10 MILLION CHARACTERS 58-65 dBA $500-$3,000; $0.04-$0.07 PER COPY 4,000-6,000 HOUR MTBF	ECS CAPABILITY FOR SCIENTIFIC, TELETEX, FINANCIAL, APPLICATIONS. CANNOT DO EXTENSIVE GRAPHICS.
DOT MATRIX	NEAR LETTER-QUALITY AND DRAFT PRINTING 60-400 CPS SPREADSHEETS, NUMERICAL DATA GRAPHICS CAPABILITY PRINTHEAD LIFE: 500 MILLION CHARACTERS LESS THAN 58 dBA $200-$2,000; $0.05-$0.12 PER COPY 5,000-7,000 HOUR MTBF	COLOR RIBBONS ARE AVAILABLE. PRINT QUALITY NOT AS GOOD AS DAISYWHEEL.
THERMAL TRANSFER	PROFESSIONAL-QUALITY PRINTING 6 PAGES PER MINUTE DOCUMENT PROCESSING, INTEGRATES TEXT AND GRAPHICS, MULTIPLE WORKSTATIONS PRINTHEAD LIFE: 3.6 MILLION CHARACTERS LESS THAN 52 dBA $3,000-$10,000; $0.15-$0.25 PER COPY 2,500 HOUR MTBF	COLOR POSSIBLE. GOOD COMPROMISE BETWEEN DAISYWHEEL AND LASER.
COLOR INK JET	COLOR GRAPHICS, TRANSPARENCIES 20 CPS CAN MERGE TEXT AND GRAPHICS PRINTHEAD LIFE: 500,000 CHARACTERS LESS THAN 55 dBA $1,000-$10,000; $0.07-$0.20 PER COPY 2,000 HOUR MTBF	THREE-DIMENSIONAL GRAPHICS. CAN DO WHOLE LANDSCAPES. NOT DESIGNED FOR TEXT PROCESSING.
LASERS	LETTER-QUALITY PRINTING 8-120 PAGES/MINUTE HIGH-VOLUME DOCUMENT PRODUCTION CAN DO GRAPHICS, LOGOS, SIGNATURES GOOD FOR LOCAL AREA NETWORKS, DATA AND WORD PROCESSING, PUBLISHING, AND ENGINEERING APPLICATIONS 46-75 dBA $5,000-$450,000; $0.01-$0.03 PER COPY	EXTENSIVE CAPABILITIES. HIGHLY FLEXIBLE PRINTING CAPABILITIES TO SUIT BROAD RANGE OF APPLICATIONS.

CPS = CHARACTERS PER SECOND
dBA = AUDIBLE DECIBELS
ECS = EXTENDED CHARACTER SET
MTBF = MEAN TIME BETWEEN FAILURES

form new ones. For example, in the world of accounting and banking, an ECS wheel can be used for printing unusual symbols, including the designations for foreign currencies. Legal application printwheels are available as well as scientific, statistical, mathematical, teletext, and multilingual types. The latter provide over 16 European languages on a single ECS wheel. Simple business graphics are also possible, such as bar and line charts.

The major disadvantage of the daisywheel is its speed. By comparison, dot matrix printers operate at up to 400 cps; thermal transfers, up to six pages per minute or 300 cps (at an average 3,000 characters per page); and laser printers, as many as 120 pages per minute or 6,000 cps. Besides the limitation to simple graphics mentioned earlier, daisywheel printers use a noisy impact mechanism. Although some vendors have managed to reduce the noise to 57 dBA (audible decibels) from the standard 65 dBA, they are still noisier than nonimpact printers. (Zero dBA is the weakest sound a healthy human ear can detect.) To better understand these levels, note that the rustle of leaves in a forest is approximately 15 dBA; quiet voices in a library, 35 dBA; the average sound of a typewriter in a business office, 65 dBA; a heavy truck, 90 dBA; and a jet plane on take-off, 125 dBA.

Needled characters

Dot matrix printers are giving daisywheels a run for their money with an ever-improving quality of print. Matrix characters are formed by the impact of "needles" on a ribbon in a matrix pattern, most commonly 9 by 7. Matrix printheads range from seven to 24 vertical-plane needles.

A major advantage of dot matrix printers is high speed, ranging from 60 to 400 cps in draft-quality mode, which is below letter quality (Fig. 1a). Highly reliable as well, their MTBF ranges up to 7,000 hours. Printhead life on some models reaches 500 million characters. These printers are generally less expensive than those using daisywheels: Most sell for less than $1,000, with a $0.05 to $0.12 per-copy cost. Some of the slower (such as 60 cps) draft-quality printers are even priced at less than $500. They are also quieter than most daisywheels, at less than 58 dBA.

One distinct advantage of the dot matrix printer is its graphics capability. It offers line graphics (to produce block diagrams and tables), mosaic graphics, plus bit-image graphics—which allow each of the eight upper printhead pins to be individually selected by program for custom design of symbols and characters. Densities up to 240 dpi (dots per inch) are available in this mode, enabling the reproduction of complex images with fine technical detail. Color is also possible.

Dot matrix printers have traditionally been used for spreadsheets and other heavily numeric output requirements, mainly for communications that are internal to a company. With the relatively new double-pass capability, dot matrix printers produce near letter-quality characters (Fig. 1b). Therefore, these printers can now be used for business correspondence and other text applications. In double passing, the printhead goes over the same line a second time, with a slight shift in placement that fills in the gaps in each character, producing a more fully formed character. This reduces the speed of the printer to about 60 cps—usually fast enough for correspondence. Many print fonts are available for versatility in size and formation of characters, such as elongated, compressed, emphasized (double strike), superscript, subscript, bold (double strike, with the second offset from the first), and shadow printing. Unique characters not in firmware may be created via software commands.

The major disadvantage of the dot matrix printer still centers on print quality. Although the double pass produces a highly readable and quite acceptable print quality, it still does not measure up to the letter quality of a daisywheel, which is required for professional correspondence. For color applications, the dot matrix does not produce the variety or vibrance of an ink jet printer (see below).

Heat and pressure
Thermal transfer is one of the newer nonimpact printer technologies. A combination of heat, pressure, and capillary action causes dots to form characters on plain paper. An ink donor film—somewhat similar to a typewriter ribbon—contacts the heated printhead while electrical pulses selectively heat the printhead elements. A pressure roller places the paper against the ink donor film and the printhead. Where the print elements are heated, ink is transferred and fused to the paper (Fig. 2). A roll of donor film, 400 meters (about 1,250 feet) long, is estimated to last for at least 1,200 printed sheets of paper, or 3.6 million characters.

The advantages of thermal transfer printers include speed (the previously noted 300 cps), quiet (less than 52 dBA), and print quality that surpasses most dot matrix units and rivals some daisywheel and laser printers. Their print quality is due to a resolution of 200 by 200 dots per square inch with nonsmudge, nonfade characters. In addition, since images are created by a pattern of dots, similar to that of dot matrix printers, the creation of complex graphic images is also possible. Thus, both text and graphics can be integrated in the same document through software-controlled font changes. Unlike the first thermal units, plain paper can now be used with today's thermal transfer printers. These units offer a 2,500-hour MTBF.

Thermal printers are used primarily for business letters and reports. Other applications include word and document processing, with such features as automatic underscore, bolding (bold characters), margin justification, subscript, and superscript—similar to the capabilities of a daisywheel printer. In addition, they offer such features as the ability to draw line segments with simple control commands—a versatility that daisywheel units do not have. These printers are also applicable to a shared-resource environment, supporting a clustered group of workstations or attached to a local area network.

Some thermal transfer printers can also print in more than one color, using donor rolls with multiple color bands. After a full page is printed in one color—where applicable—the print medium is returned to the beginning of the page and the next color is printed. Other thermal transfer printers make use of various-color donor films for the printing of one-color documents.

One disadvantage of thermal transfer printers is their cost. At $3,000 to $10,000, and a $0.15 to $0.25 cost per copy, they are far more expensive than daisywheel units, although they do offer the noted advantages for the price. Some users say that the print quality looks more like a clean photocopy than a typed document. Moreover, there are some registration difficulties and waste of ink donor film (one color may be used up sooner than others) with color printers.

Like an oil can
Color ink jet printers produce imaginative graphs and images in clear, vibrant colors. They use either a continuous-stream, electrically charged method to direct the ink or a drop-on-demand electric vibrating method. The drop-on demand process is similar to the operation of an oil can: The bottom of the can represents the transducer; the spout is the nozzle; and the oil is the ink.

Four individually keyed, user-replaceable cartridges of colors—yellow, magenta (deep purplish red), cyan (greenish blue), and black—can be mixed to reproduce seven basic colors, including violet, green, and red. The machine's ability to mix colors, however, producing half tones and shades, makes a multitude of hues possible. Each cartridge, containing 2.5 cubic centimeters of ink, can produce 125,000 characters.

With color ink jet technology, simple bar graphs and

1. Twice looks better. *The speed of draft-quality (A) dot matrix printers ranges up to 400 cps. With the relatively new double-pass capability, these printers produce near letter-quality characters (B). This reduces the speed of the printer to about 60 cps—usually fast enough for correspondence.*

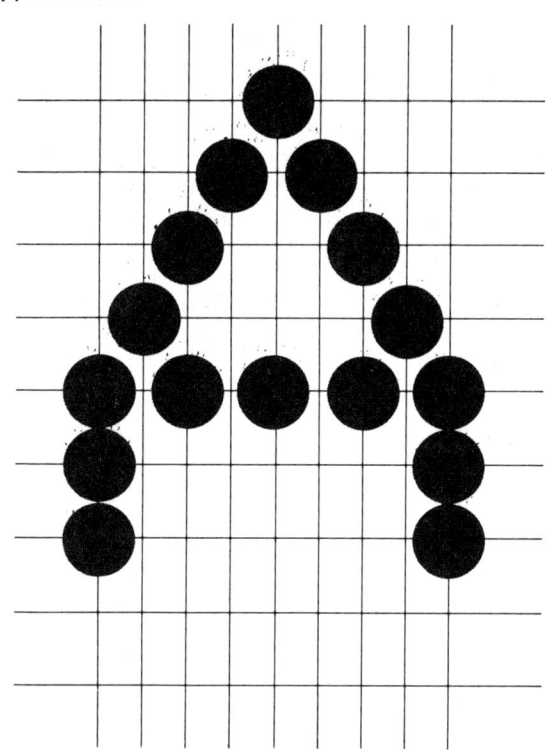

(A) DRAFT QUALITY

(B) LETTER QUALITY

pie charts are things of the past. Three-dimensional color presentations are now possible. In addition, software control can produce not only circles and curves but also bit-mapped landscapes and images with a resolution of 120 dpi.

The medium may be either plain paper, clay-coated paper, or transparencies. Clay-coated paper, which has special sizing (chemical treatment), creates balanced absorbency and promotes proper spreading of the ink. It also helps to retain the dye molecules to enhance both the shape of the characters and the color intensity.

These printers can merge text with color graphics, have a low noise level—less than 55 dBA—have an MTBF of about 2,000 hours, and are relatively economical. Cost per copy is $0.07 to $0.20, compared with $0.20 to $0.50 for pen plotters.

Applications for these printers include color graphics for group presentations; complicated CAD/CAM (computer-aided design/computer-aided manufacture) drawings, providing rapid visual discrimination; medical reports and graphics, where color can be a valuable aid in describing patient status; and product design, where ideas can be tried and changed relatively inexpensively before a final hand-drawn copy is produced.

The main disadvantage of the color ink jet printer is its speed: a fairly slow 20 cps (in text mode)—although improvement is expected in about a year. Although it can integrate text with graphics, this printer is not designed for, nor is it capable of, text processing. It tends to be sensitive to vibration and has occasional problems because of clogged nozzles.

The laser shows a great deal of promise in its application to printers. Electronic printers using lasers combine the technologies of digital computers, with their capacity for high-speed (microseconds) handling of information; lasers, with their high-resolution (300-by-300 "spots" per square inch) imaging qualities; and xerography, with its ability to produce letter-quality printed output on cut-sheet paper.

A laser printer creates an image of the entire page to be printed by "writing" on a cylindrical drum (similar to that of a photocopier) with a laser beam and transferring this image to paper. The laser beam is focused on a tiny spot that scans repeatedly along the length of the rotating drum, which is coated with a light-sensitive, electrostatic material. The scanning beam is turned off and on, creating a pattern on the drum that can be transferred to paper. The process is similar to that used in a copier (Fig. 3).

Text and graphics data is transmitted to the printer, with an entire page formatted before printing begins. In addition to the scanning and printing components, these printers require circuitry and software to encode the text and graphics before the image is "beamed" onto the drum.

Two types of lasers are common: the solid-state infrared semiconductor variety and the earlier visible-light gas type. The solid-state laser, currently popular in compact-disk players, is about half the size of the gas unit; otherwise, there is very little difference distinguishing the two.

Laser printers offer a wide range of speeds, from eight to 120 pages per minute (about 400 to 6,000 cps). By comparison, a high-speed daisywheel printer produces roughly one page per minute.

Laser printers are designed for data processing, word processing, publishing, and engineering applications. They can produce complex graphics, business forms, logos, and signatures. Both portrait (vertical) and landscape (horizontal) orientations are possible in the same job. Also, a wide range of readily selectable (by firmware) font styles and sizes is available for a flexible (nonuniform) page appearance. The available page-formatting commands include centering, tabbing, and bolding. Text, data, and graphics can all be integrated on one sheet. Many models support duplex processing—that is, sequentially printing on both sides of a page.

The key parameter a potential user of a laser printer should determine is the recommended average monthly page volume, or AMPV. The manufacturer designs its printer to handle a particular AMPV, which is known as the centerline. This is the median point on a bell curve for the expected number of machines in use. Therefore, some machines will run at higher volumes than the centerline, some lower. The engineers will design the machine, the types of parts to be used, and the given maintenance philosophy around this centerline performance.

2. Heat and pressure. *In thermal transfer, an ink donor film contacts the heated printhead while electrical pulses selectively heat the printhead elements.*

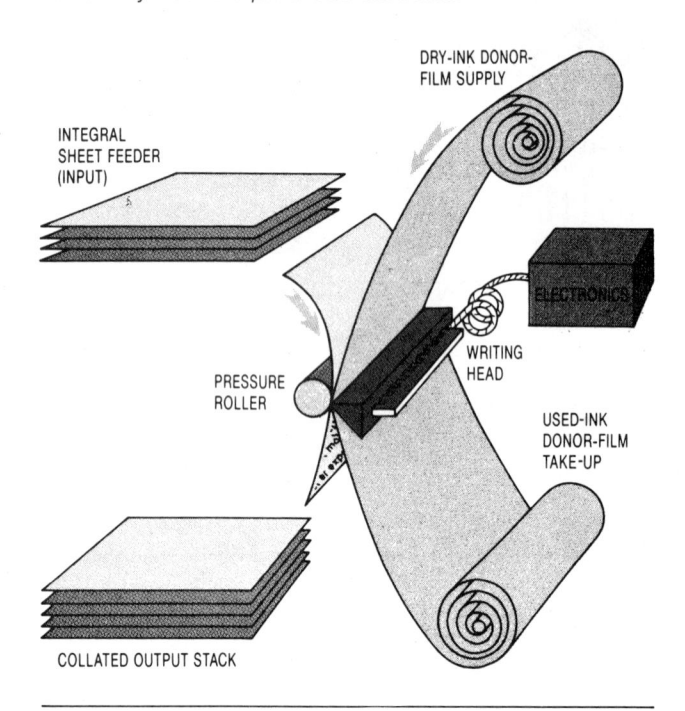

Production variations
At the low end, with an AMPV of 3,000, there are the desktop laser units that produce eight pages per minute. A shared-resource laser printer, at 10 to 30 pages per minute, has an AMPV of 5,000 to 70,000. At the high end, producing at least 50 pages per minute, is the laser machine with a 250,000 AMPV.

Reliability is a function of volume on a given laser machine—except for the laser source unit, which normally outlasts the other elements. For optimum reliability, it is important that the user buy the printer that is geared to the application. Otherwise, the reliability may mistakenly be perceived as poor. The manufacturer would expect a certain service-call frequency based on the AMPV. Typically, for a 10,000-AMPV laser printer, a service call could be expected for about every 20,000 pages produced. (The relationship is not linear.) If the printer is run consistently higher than its centerline, the service technician will be at the customer site more frequently. The reliability is not worse; the user has merely run more volume through the printer in a shorter time frame than would the average user.

Because laser printers use a nonimpact technology, their printing mechanisms tend to be much quieter than those of impact printers. But the noise due to the cooling fans and the paper-handling mechanisms could make these machines the noisiest types, depending on size. Generally speaking, the larger the printer, the noisier it is likely to be. A typical noise range in the operating mode (standby mode is quieter—close to zero dBA) is 46 to 75 dBA. Note that the printers at 75 dBA are designed to operate in a computer room environment, not the office.

For printers in general, cost per copy is a function of consumables (paper and ink, primarily) cost, service costs, and depreciation of the printer. Paper is the only item that remains constant for all machines: roughly $4.80 per 1,000 pages. A range for all other costs is $0.01 to $0.03 per page. (These costs are defined similarly for all the printer types mentioned in this article.)

Laser printers are used in a multitude of environments, including offices, distributed data processing locations, centralized data centers, and in-plant printing and publishing departments. In this last application category laser printers have a major advantage: They usually eliminate the need to preprint material, inventory and store it, and throw it out when it becomes obsolete. With a laser printer, it is often possible to print on demand.

Among their wide range of applications, laser printers are ideal for multiple workstations in a local area or remote network. Data to be printed can be transmitted from various locations, with the information ranging from short electronic-mail messages to whole volumes. Because of its advantages the laser printer varies widely in price—from $5,000 to $450,000.

Price versus performance is the key to determining

3. Production speed. *Laser printers combine a high imaging resolution of 300-by-300 "spots" per square inch with speeds of about 400 to 6,000 cps.*

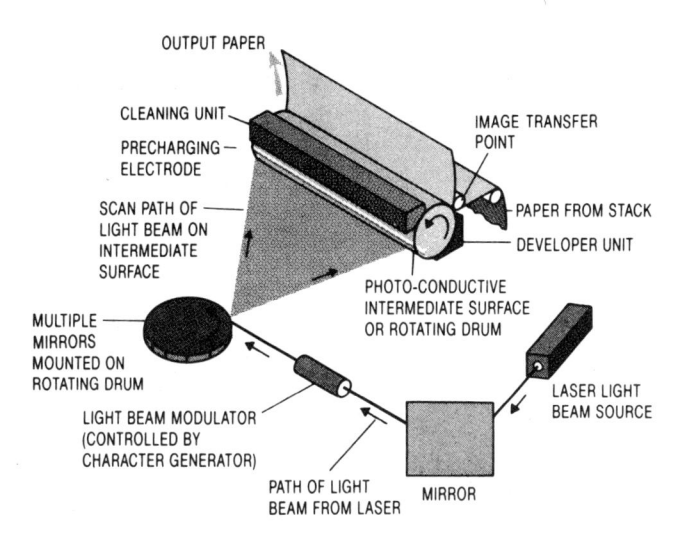

[Diagram labels: OUTPUT PAPER; CLEANING UNIT; PRECHARGING ELECTRODE; IMAGE TRANSFER POINT; SCAN PATH OF LIGHT BEAM ON INTERMEDIATE SURFACE; PAPER FROM STACK; DEVELOPER UNIT; PHOTO-CONDUCTIVE INTERMEDIATE SURFACE OR ROTATING DRUM; MULTIPLE MIRRORS MOUNTED ON ROTATING DRUM; LASER LIGHT BEAM SOURCE; LIGHT BEAM MODULATOR (CONTROLLED BY CHARACTER GENERATOR); PATH OF LIGHT BEAM FROM LASER; MIRROR]

the best use of a printer. Hobbyists and other microcomputer owners usually look for inexpensive printers. For under $1,000 they will find a slow daisywheel printer—under 20 cps—that would limit the possible applications. Dot matrix printers in this price range are faster—80 to 150 cps—but offer fewer features and have poorer print quality than do more expensive models (see above). For most nonbusiness applications, either printer type will be adequate.

In the medium-speed range (about 40 cps for daisywheel printers), unit prices run from $1,000 to $2,000. These machines are prevalent in many business applications. In the legal and educational fields, with high text-processing usage where letter quality is important, daisywheel printers are most appropriate. In the engineering environment, where graphics and numeric printouts are important, perhaps a faster (400-cps) dot matrix printer would be more useful.

In finance and accounting, where a substantial need for numeric output might require a fast, draft-quality dot matrix printer, there is a conflict: Financial statements and letters to clients need letter-quality printing. Here, a double-pass, correspondence-quality dot matrix printer appears to be appropriate.

To go one step further, business managers and educators may well be intrigued by the ink jet printer—especially by the impact that its color capability could make in their respective fields. As should now be apparent, the major application needs of users determine the best printer for them.

Near the top of the line, with speeds over 60 cps and prices above $2,000, are daisywheel printers with extended character sets. These printers can function with multiple users in a networked office environment. Thermal transfer printers, which can integrate text and complex graphics, also fall into this range. Less expensive than laser printers but faster than daisywheel units, they might be a good compromise for a business with high-volume production needs—such as law, medicine, and technical writing, which typically need about 3,500 pages per month. Laser printers are, of course, the Cadillacs of the industry, offering a wide range of applications for the smallest of offices to the largest of corporations.

Expectations and buying tips
The growth in the data communications and computer industries—which include the machine that is the vital source of hard copy, the printer—has been driven by improvements in both microprocessor and semiconductor-memory technologies. This trend should continue as microelectronics is increasingly used. This will bring increased reliability, easier maintenance, and reductions in spare elements, repairs, weight, and noise. Also on the way are improved sheet feeding, compatibility with an increasing number of different computers, and approaches that merge the functions of desktop professional computers with desktop printers.

With their reliability (4,000-to-6,000 hours MTBF), high-quality printing, and reasonable cost, daisywheel printers should always have a place in the printing world. It is estimated that they will have 25 percent of the market by 1987. Dot matrix printers, with their continually improving character quality, high speed, and graphics capability, are encroaching on the daisywheels. The dot matrix units' market share is projected to reach up to 60 percent by 1987. Although ink jet, thermal transfer, and laser printers do not have a large market share today—a combined 2 percent—their share is expected to grow throughout the next decade. They are exciting technologies that will continue to improve and become more affordable.

How should a prospective buyer decide which printer to acquire? Needs and applications should be considered first: How much speed and print quality are needed? Are there any special applications, such as those requiring scientific notations? It is also important to consider operator-related factors, such as ease of operation. Is unattended operation possible? If so, are alarms provided for paper jams and other problems?

Ease of operation is facilitated by "drop-in" printwheels and printheads as well as high-capacity (500,000-character life) snap-in ribbon cartridges. A line of accessories should be available, including a range of sheet feeders, bidirectional tractor feeders (for fanfold paper), and printwheels that offer a variety of character types. Supplies should be readily available, such as ribbons for daisywheel and dot matrix printers, donor ink rolls for thermal transfer printers, and ink cartridges for color ink jet printers.

Compatibility is an important factor. Does the printer have the proper interface for the intended computer? A variety of interfaces should be available, such as RS-232-C, IEEE 488, and Centronics parallel.

And, of course, reliability is of prime importance. For daisywheel and matrix printers, an MTBF of 4,000 hours is essential, while 2,000 hours should be the minimum for ink jets and thermal transfers. Dot matrix printers can be expected to run 5,000 to 7,000 hours. The mean time to repair should range from 15 to 30 minutes. In addition, some companies offer a spares-refurbishment program that provides up to a 40 percent cost savings over that of new parts—a very attractive feature.

Each type of printer has certain unique qualities and advantages that meet different application needs. Understanding what each printer has to offer helps simplify the decision-making process. Determining one's own needs, however, is the first step. ∎

Don Dempsey, with Xerox since 1968, is vice president of OEM marketing and sales—disciplines with which he had been concerned while at IBM for five years. Dempsey has a B. A. in mathematics/physics from St. Peter's College, Jersey City, and an M. A. in mathematics from the University of Detroit. Cindy Parkinson has been in marketing/communications at Xerox for two years. She has a B. A. in English from Stanford and is working toward an M. B. A. in marketing from San Francisco State University.

Gilbert Held, U. S. Office of Personnel Management, Macon, Ga.

Is there a place for optical disks in data networks?

This year's Karp Award winner examines the application and potential of this ultra-high-capacity storage technology in future data networks.

Optical disk technology is moving out of the laboratory and into a worldwide computer and communications marketplace. By providing storage capacities hundreds to thousands of times greater than conventional magnetic media, computer professionals already are eyeing this technology with more than a passing interest. But how about in the information networking biz? Regrettably, this new media's impact on data communications has not gotten the attention it deserves—at least not up until now.

In a typical communications-intensive application, such as database distribution, how does optical disk technology stack up against more traditional storage facilities used in communications? Do all optical disks have the same performance characteristics? Only through an understanding of the technology's metes and bounds can networkers hope to exploit this, or any other innovation, for improved efficiency, capacity or economy.

The storage capability of optical disk media can be difficult to comprehend when compared with conventional magnetic media such as Winchester drives or floppy disks. Imagine trying to hold fifteen hundred 5¼ inch diskettes in your hands; the storage capacity of all those floppies would be roughly equivalent to just one 3½ inch optical disk. Not only does the optical disk weigh just a fraction of an ounce, but it can be neatly tucked into a person's shirt pocket.

With a data storage capacity several orders of magnitude greater than conventional magnetic media, the per-stored-byte cost of optical disk is, as might be expected, just a fraction of the cost of magnetic media. Based upon storage cost and capacity alone, it appears optical storage will eventually capture a substantial portion of the market presently dominated by magnetic media products.

Magnetic disk technology is in competiton with three distinct types of optical storage media. And before the impact of optical storage on communications networks can be assessed, it is necessary to distinguish these different types of optical disks.

All optical disk technology shares some basic hardware elements. These include a laser source, a disk, and a positioning servomechanism. The servo moves the assembly that actually performs the recording, reading, and read/write functions on the optical disk. The disks themselves can be classified into three categories based on their recording ability: read-only, write-once, and erasable media.

Prerecorded data

The CD-ROM, or Compact Disk-Read Only Memory, was pioneered by several companies, including Sony Corporation and N. V. Phillips. As indicated by the name, prerecorded data on the disk can only be read. In a sense, a data-carrying CD-ROM disk is similar to an audio CD disk: it involves the mass replication of a prerecorded disk, which can be read by relatively inexpensive hardware. CD-ROM disk storage capacities currently range between 550 and 600 Mbytes depending upon the format structure used to write the data.

Although a few misplaced 1s and 0s on an audio CD disk might not be noticed by an audiophile, a comparable situation with a CD-ROM disk drive could result in serious problems. This is because a single incorrect bit could affect the meaning of a byte containing the bit. And this might even distort all the succeeding data stored on the disk. Imagine the problems that could result if the misread byte represented a decimal point in a large financial transaction.

To minimize the potential of recording and retrieval errors, CD-ROMS routinely employ a sophisticated error-correcting technique based upon a Reed-Solomon error-detection and correction code (where extra overhead bits are required to ensure data integrity). This code reduces the probability of an uncorrected bit error to approximately one in 10^{12}. By comparison, in data communications a typical bit error rate of one in 10^6 is usually considered acceptable for most applications.

The loading of a CD-ROM disk with data is a time-consuming process that can require three to five weeks to complete. First it is necessary to generate a magnetic tape according to a predefined format, which generally is established by the organization that has the facilities to create a "master" CD-ROM disk. Once the tape is submitted to the disk-processing organization, the data will either be transferred to a master disk in sequential order, or in-house software will be used to generate a comprehensive data index, which is then recorded onto the master optical disk along with the data.

It would require almost 24 hours to transmit 600 Mbytes via a 56-kbit/s DDS facility; 1 Gbyte would require 39 hours.

During the disk-creation process a laser beam is used to burn tiny indentations approximately one micron wide (about 50 times thinner than a human hair) onto the plastic-coated disk. The presence or absence of an indentation on the disk corresponds to a digital 1 or 0. The indentations—called ablations—are, then, the mechanism for encoding binary data onto the disk.

When the disk is inserted into a CD-ROM player a low-power laser in the optical assembly illuminates a track on the disk. Binary digits are read by deciphering the differences in reflectivity between the indented and non-indented spots on a track.

Only after the master CD-ROM has been created can the processing firm begin mass replication of the disks. As noted, this process is time-consuming, which clearly is a drawback. As noted, this process is time-consuming, and the delay time involved in the transmit-and-manufacture procedure render this technology unsuitable for dynamically changing data.

Another type of optical disk can be written to only once. Development of write-once read-many-times (WORM) optical disks actually predates current CD-ROM technology, though early WORM drives had a number of technical problems. Complex electronics were needed to decode data from the disks. And the media itself lasted no more than a few years. In the early 1980s, the 3M Company developed a preformatted WORM disk, which both extended the media shelf life and reduced the complexity of the electronics required to retrieve the data from a disk.

With the 3M preformatting process a series of blisters are formed on a track by a high-powered laser. When the preformatted media is placed in a WORM drive, a low-powered laser produces just enough heat to burst the prerecorded blisters. During a disk-read operation, a laser in the WORM drive illuminates the disk's surface. Since the burst blisters provide higher contrast than the surrounding area, they are easily recognized by simple electronics and can be interpreted as either a binary 1 or 0.

Unlike the CD-ROM industry, which has standardized its disk diameter and recording formats, the WORM drive industry is fragmented. Some WORM vendors are producing 12-inch drives; others are building 5¼-, 8-, and 14-inch drives. Although several vendors have discussed standardizing recording formats, proprietary recording techniques and formats are still the rule. For users, this means that data recorded on one WORM drive cannot be read by another.

Most popular WORM drives presently use 5¼- and 12-inch diameter disks. Their storage capacities range from 350 Mbytes for a single-sided 5¼-inch disk to more than 1000 Mbytes (1 Gbyte) for a single-sided version of the 12-inch disk.

Although prototype erasable optical disk drives have been working in laboratories around the world for more than five years, the first commercial drives are not expected to reach the consumer marketplace until late 1987 or early

Table 1: Application areas for optical disk technology

DATABASE DISTRIBUTION
SUPPLEMENT ON-LINE INFORMATION NETWORK SERVICES
IN-STORE CATALOG ACCESS

1988. The erasable optical disk technology that holds the greatest promise at the present time is based on technology called magneto-optic recording.

Magneto-optics uses the heat produced by a laser to influence the magnetic field of a data-carrying spot (or magnetic domain) on a magnetic disk. By heating a particular spot on a magnetic disk, it is possible to change the orientation of its magnetic field. Polarized light reflected from the spot will change its degree of rotation depending on the magnetic field's orientation. Electronics in the magneto-optic drive's head assembly then interprets the orientation of the reflected light as a 1 or 0 binary condition.

The first erasable disks reaching the commercial marketplace are expected to be 3½-inch diameter. Although their storage capability will initially be limited to between 40 and 100 Mbytes, many industry observers predict that by the early 1990s, 5¼-, 8-, and 12-inch diameter disks should be available—providing erasable storage capacities in the Gigabyte range.

Optical applications

Though erasable optical disks still have a way to go before they can be fully integrated into commercial networksized, CD-ROM and WORM disks presently offer data processing and data communications managers a new range of planning options. Table 1 lists three areas where the new optical disks could have a major effect on existing communications applications.

For example, several types of databases lend themselves to distribution via optical-disk media by virtue of the large CD-ROM and WORM drive storage capacities. Financial reports, internal manuals, and legal and medical abstract databases could be stored on optical disk. Or the technology could be used to supplant database updating that is now performed on-line; overnight mail delivery of an optical disk could be a viable alternative to data-communications applications now heavily dependent on telecommunications.

Another area where optical disks are expected to have a significant impact is on user access to on-line information networks. Currently over 50 commercial organizations offer access to a variety of databases at prices ranging from $2 to $200 per hour. During 1986, several firms began to condense portions of their databases onto CD-ROM masters. CD-ROMs are currently being marketed as either replacements or supplements to on-line database access service.

With the price of CD-ROM optical disk players expected to decline from about $1,000 at the beginning of this year to $250 or less by mid-1989, it is only a matter of time before the CD-ROM drive becomes as common a peripheral as a personal computer printer. Since the unit cost to master and produce a CD-ROM can fall to under $3.00 for quantities of 10,000 disks, it appears that the day of the CD-ROM database library may be fast approaching. This could eventually limit the utility of on-line information to the retrieval of data concerning current events. Last week's stock prices, articles printed in the last quarter, and other subjects too timely to publish and distribute via CD-ROM could still be accessed on-line.

A third area where optical disk technology could significantly affect existing practices is in-store catalog access. Currently many large retail organizations provide customer access to inquiry terminals located in their stores. These terminals—connected by communications links to the organization's data processing facility—provide on-line query capability as well as offering the means for placing orders.

Though WORM optical drives can only write information to a disk once, their tremendous storage capacity makes them ideal for storing and updating catalog information. By using pointers on the disk, updated information could be recorded on a WORM drive late in the search of the revised WORM database. Once the customer has spotted what he or she is after in the electronic catalog, the order can be placed directly through the database using the databases's dial-up facilities to complete the transaction.

Optical economics

To appreciate the economics associated with optical storage, compare it to the cost of distributing large database updates via a data communications network. Table 2 lists the time required to transmit 100 Mbytes of information at data rates ranging from low-speed 1.2-kbit/s asynchronous transmission to a high-speed 1.544-Mbit/s T1 data rate. It is important to note that the transmission times indicated in Table 2 do not reflect the overhead associated with a transmission protocol or the need to retransmit data when transmission errors occur. Thus, the transmission times listed in Table 2 are optimum; they presume that line conditions are perfect and thus require no transmission overhead.

Table 3 shows the time required to transmit the entire contents of two types of optical disks at different data rates. The capacities shown assume that optical recording is done on only a single side of each disk. For computational purposes, the capacity of the CD-ROM disk was assumed to be 600 Mbytes; the WORM disk was assumed to have a storage capacity of 1 Gbyte.

Table 3 shows that the distribution and updating of large databases via optical media is probably more practical and cost effective than attempting the same activity by any communications facility other than T1 lines. For example, it would require almost 24 hours to transmit 600 Mbytes via a 56-kbit/s Dataphone digital service (DDS) facility, while 1 Gbyte would require 39 hours to transmit. By comparison, most express-mail carriers, including the U. S. Postal Service and Federal Express, can deliver an overnight envelope containing an optical disk by 10:30 A.M. the next business day.

Table 2: Transmission time per 100 mbytes

DATA RATE	TRANSMISSION TIME
1.2 KBIT/S	185.2 HOURS
2.4 KBIT/S	92.6 HOURS
4.8 KBIT/S	46.3 HOURS
9.6 KBIT/S	23.2 HOURS
19.2 KBIT/S	11.6 HOURS
56.0 KBIT/S	3.9 HOURS
1.544 MBIT/S	8.6 MINUTES

Table 3: Time to transmit the contents of an optical disk

DATA RATE	COMPACT DISK READ-ONLY MEMORY (600 MBIT/S)	WRITE-ONCE READ-MANY (1 GBYTE)
1.2 KBIT/S	1,111.2 HOURS	1,852 HOURS
2.4 KBIT/S	555.6 HOURS	926 HOURS
4.8 KBIT/S	277.8 HOURS	463 HOURS
9.6 KBIT/S	139.2 HOURS	232 HOURS
19.2 KBIT/S	69.6 HOURS	116 HOURS
56.0 KBIT/S	23.4 HOURS	39 HOURS
1.544 MBIT/S	51.8 MINUTES	1.4 HOURS

Table 4: Write-once read-many database distribution cost

A. FIXED AND VARIABLE COST ELEMENTS

FIXED COST:	TWO WORM SYSTEMS @ $7,500 = $15,000
VARIABLE COST:	WORM DISK @ $75.00
	EXPRESS MAIL @ 10.35

B. THREE-YEAR LIFE CYCLE EXPECTED COST

MONTHLY DATABASE UPDATE FREQUENCY	THREE-YEAR LIFE CYCLE COST
1	$ 18,073
5	$ 30,363
10	$ 45,726
15	$ 51,089
20	$ 76,452
22	$ 82,598
30	$107,178

The time delay between sending data to be mastered and receiving the required CD-ROM disks precludes its use for timely database updates. Users can consider installing WORM optical disk drives at their central data processing location and at remote locations, which presently receive database updates via telecommunications facilities. The cost of each WORM drive is about $7,750, while a 1-Gbyte optical disk can be obtained in quantity for about $75. The costs associated with using two WORM drives and the U. S. Postal Service's Express Mail for the distribution of WORM disks are shown in Table 4.

The fixed and variable cost elements associated with WORM database distribution are listed in Part A of Table 4. In Part B, a three-year life cycle cost was computed based on varying frequencies of database updating occurring during a month. It should be noted that a monthly database update frequency of 22 corresponds to updating the database every working business day for a month for organizations operating on a Monday-through-Friday schedule.

Cost variations

As indicated in Part B of Table 4, the three-year life cycle cost of distributing a database on WORM media can vary widely. With a single monthly database update the three-year life cycle cost is slightly over $18,000. When update frequency increases to 22 times per month (or once per business day), the corresponding three-year life cycle cost exceeds $80,000. At a frequency of once per day during a 30-day month, the cost of distributing a database on WORM media will slightly exceed $107,000 over a three-year period.

As Table 3 shows, the time required to transmit the contents of an optical disk could make data transmission of databases obsolete in all cases except those where very high speed transmissions are used. Since T1 lines are rarely used exclusively for data transmission, a 56-kbit/s DDS facility was selected for cost comparison between the use of a transmission network and the distribution of the database via optical media. Table 5 shows the monthly and three-year cost of a 56-kbit/s DDS facility based on varying distances between two computer locations.

Comparing the data listed in Part B of Table 4 with the data presented in Table 5, it is apparent that the distribution of a large databases via optical media is an economically viable alternative to conventional high-speed data networking. For distances between computer centers exceeding about 1,000 miles, the distribution of a database on optical media can be significantly less than the cost of a transmission facility—regardless of the monthly database update frequency.

For 500-to-1,000-mile distances between computer centers, the cost of distributing a database on optical media, at a frequency of 20 times per month or less, will be less expensive than the cost via 56-kbit/s DDS transmission. Only when the distance between computer centers is substantially under 500 miles and the monthly database update frequency is high does the use of 56-kbit/s DDS become economically viable.

With a storage capacity several orders of magnitude beyond that available with conventional magnetic storage, optical disk technology is about to provide data processing and data communications managers with new alternatives to information distribution. In certain situations it may be possible to substitute optical disk storage for on-line access to central computers. In other situations, however, it may be more cost-effective not to use the new technology and instead use more traditional storage mediums coupled with lower speed and lower cost data communications facilities. Managers will have to do their homework if the true potential of optical storage is to be realized in communications networks. ■

Gilbert Held, chief of data communications for the U. S. Office of Personnel Management at Macon, Ga., is an internationally recognized author and lecturer. Recipient of an American Association of Publishers Award, he is the author of 12 books and over 60 technical articles.

Table 5: 56-kbit/s DDS service cost

MILEAGE	MONTHLY COST	THREE-YEAR COST
250	$1,413	$ 50,868
500	$2,125	$ 76,500
1,000	$2,925	$105,300
1,400	$3,725	$134,100
2,000	$4,525	$162,900

Section 6
Applications

James Randall, Independent Consultant, Jamesburg, N. J.

Making your network make money

Business-savvy communications managers can produce revenue for their company by turning a corporate overhead utility into a product-offering profit center.

In the next decade and into the next century, the technical data communications manager seeking personal success will be measured by more than hard-won technical competence. Bottom-line performance will be of growing importance and will determine advancement up the corporate ladder, as well as the bonuses and prestige earned en route.

It is communications professionals who devise methods for interconnecting all the dispersed computing power in the postdivestiture world. Unfortunately, data and telecommunications operations have grown so fast, often with a damn-the-torpedoes mandate, that apart from panicked intervention to keep the information flowing, there is precious little time to plan with care, manage with an eye on the bottom line, and operate the way Ma Bell taught us: recover all direct costs, plus a guaranteed return on investment (ROI).

This new corporate profit center can be called the Private Multi-Vendor Network/Computer Utility and Asset (PMVN/CU&A). And it can be exploited for maximum bottom-line contribution, career advancement, and growth within the corporate milieu.

Predivestiture

Remember the characteristics of predivestiture telecommunications services provided by "the phone company"? Immediate dial tone, the envy of the rest of the world; transparent support services from equipment installation to new product introductions; a monopoly on all parts of the telecommunications service utility from the handset on your desk to the private branch exchange at the receptionist's station in the lobby to Centrex and "long lines" services connecting to the rest of the world.

These are some of the qualities that made Ma Bell unequaled as a communications service provider. And a very effective quasi-political lobbying effort on behalf of all the Bell operating companies ensured that the fundamental revenue concept upon which Ma Bell built her success—recovery of all direct costs plus a guaranteed ROI—was the way tariffs were determined.

The telephone operating companies wielded considerable power before their state public utility commissions (PUCs). Consider, for example, the following anecdote.

About a dozen years ago, Robert Abrams, the current Attorney General of the State of New York, was Borough President of Bronx County, New York. He was seeking the Democratic nomination for the state office of Attorney General. Abrams was "running against the phone company" and the Public Service Commission (New York's PUC) as a consumer advocate. He made some radio commercials in which he asked: "In the last four years, do you know how many tariff increases the New York Telephone Company requested from your Public Service Commission?" After a pause, Abrams answered his own question: "91," he said. Then he asked: "Do you know how many were granted?" Then, after an even longer pause, Abrams responded: "91."

It is memorable after all these years because it stated simply how powerful the phone company was in getting its way before a public utility commission, whose job ostensibly was to protect the interest of the subscriber while simultaneously ensuring that New York Telephone received a fair return on its investment.

Postdivestiture

The character of the postdivestiture telecommunications and computer world is a very different one for the technical data communications professional. Management Information Systems (MIS), the data processing and data distributing corporate department, is being challenged for control of the larger portion of the overall MIS-PMVN/CU&A budget. The challengers are the communications activities, which are growing apace with distributed computer power—the direct result of the microcomputer revolution. These two contenders now rival MIS in laying claim to the larger share of growing budgets.

The immediate challenge for technical data communications managers is to seize the opportunities presented by the growth of distributed computing and the spread of network capabilities to gain control of the asset. How? By controlling the budget for that asset.

Divestiture has permitted many new players to enter the communications/computer business. This multivendor supermarket can be exploited by savvy technical data communications managers for lower product-acquisition costs, better performance and service support, and growing profits for their profit centers, provided any one vendor can be prevented from becoming too dominant.

Keeping qualified vendors at arm's length is essential to the independent crafting of your own performance specifications. Tables can be turned by exploiting the desirable features of informal proposals to identify the best products and services offering those features. This process will also enable you to discover the needs unique to your organization, which may require costly features only available on special order.

Then, with clear product or service requirements stipulated in the request for quote (RFQ) format, communications managers are in control because they have defined what they want to buy. With a number of proposals in hand from qualified suppliers, outright purchase, try-and-buy, beta-site testing, leasing, and other ways of obtaining equipment and services can be considered.

Defining requirements, determining which of your users would pay to connect to your network, and exploiting multivendor offerings for the best deal is a far cry from the overhead allocations of data and telecommunications costs, which is the most persistent and conspicuous hangover from the predivestiture days (see table). Data communications managers are faced with four major challenges: marketing the network, designing the network, setting performance standards, and building a team. This will determine the success of the PMVN/CU&A.

Marketing the network

To the technical professionals who manage today's networks, the idea of marketing the network may appear a violation of the inherent service mentality. But marketing the network is central to making the PMVN/CU&A produce revenue (see Fig. 1). This is the revenue that affects the bottom line and ultimately, when properly accounted for and managed, leads to profits for the PMVN/CU&A profit center, profits for the corporation as a whole, and bonuses and promotions for the leader of the PMVN/CU&A department and those who help produce the revenue. These profits may not be trivial either in the amount or the proof they provide of the value of the PMVN/CU&A.

Such an approach is almost universal in companies that develop products, and it is almost totally absent from

Comparison between innovative and traditional leadership

INNOVATIVE	TRADITIONAL
VISIONARY	SOMEONE ELSE'S VISION
DEFINES OBJECTIVES	REACT TO UNQUALIFIED DEMANDS
INITIATES TASK-ORIENTED PROBLEM-SOLVING	AD HOC, CHAOTIC ACTIVITY
SETS SPECIFIC STANDARDS FOR PERFORMANCE OF THE NETWORK AS WELL AS REVENUE PRODUCTION	OBSCURE, ELASTIC, OR NONEXISTENT STANDARDS
ESTABLISHES LINE OF AUTHORITY REWARD ARRANGEMENTS	STAFF/ADVISORY FUNCTION: HIERARCHICAL CONTROL, OFTEN PUNITIVE
BUILDS ROUNDTABLE, TEAMWORKING ATMOSPHERE IN WHICH INDEPENDENT SOLUTIONS ARE ENCOURAGED	JOB DESCRIPTION IS PRIMARY PREOCCUPATION OF CONTENDING GROUP MEMBERS
IMAGINATIVE, CREATIVE	RESPONSIVE, REFLEXIVE

organizations whose tradition is providing a service. What worked well for the phone company—recovery of costs plus a guaranteed ROI—must be updated and streamlined: There is no PUC to lobby for tariff increases to cover costs and ROI. The PMVN/CU&A that is managed like a high-tech product company has the best chance of producing the growing revenue (see Fig. 2).

The first and most important step toward producing that growing revenue is to determine what your users want and what they will pay for it. Hence, the marketing approach.

Marketing is the activity of determining what potential users want and are likely to pay for, then marshalling the resources to satisfy those needs at a profit.

Selling, by contrast, is the activity of developing leads, qualifying them as prospects, determining if they can both make a buy decision and meet the payments, and getting a favorable decision—closing.

The selling skills that will be needed by technical data communications managers in the 1990s, will be almost equally divided between getting plans, proposals, and budgets approved by upper management and persuading associates to actively innovate in the planning and implementation of the vision for PMVN/CU&A.

Selling the plan

Selling a marketing plan and a budget (which, combined, are the PMVN/CU&A business plan) is a far cry from product-flogging. The kind of selling required is the kind done every day to investment bankers by entrepreneurs seeking financing; to foundations that are importuned regularly to support one scholar's efforts over another's; or to senior management in high-tech companies by those seeking support of a new product.

Anyone who has an agenda and needs the approval and collaboration of those in more powerful and influential

1. Marketing cycle. Marketing a service that has always been available may seem unnecessary, so the transition from telecommunications provider to profit-and-loss department may be formidable. The flow chart, freely adapted from product development use, describes the steps that will meet demand and command user fees.

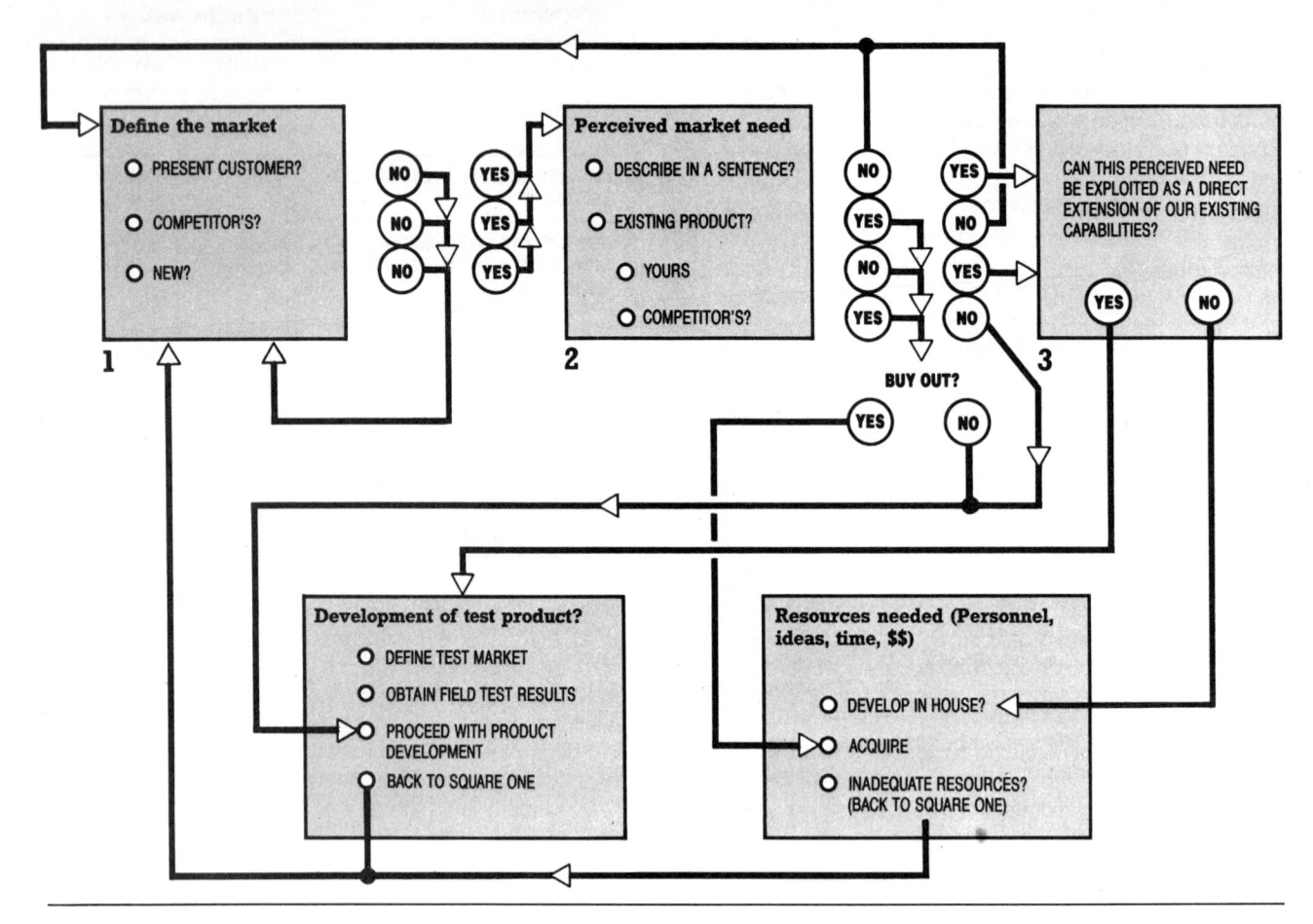

positions must know how to sell and how to sell with facts, plans, and quantified data—not hopes.

Managers also have to know how to sell their associates. Associates are not easily motivated, but they can be led. The essence of leadership is having formed an inner vision of what needs to be accomplished and then articulating that vision for all those involved with the PMVN/CU&A enterprise. In such a collegial, peer-to-peer endeavor, there are no bosses, only a collection of variously gifted associates, painstakingly selected to implement the shared vision.

Of course, teams are not built from scratch. Within existing telecommunications and distributed computing operations are established ways of doing things and people who are doing them. Any heavy-handed approach to force change implies dissatisfaction or disapproval with current staff and methods.

The conversion of department members to your way of thinking involves consulting with them, factoring in their ideas, fully disclosing your program, and continuously seeking their agreement as plans evolve. This constitutes selling your associates at the most diplomatic level. Commitment to seeking their counsel in order to make the PMVN/CU&A a success is the underlying principle. This way, rewards and challenges are shared.

This type of leadership was the way Dr. J. Robert Oppenheimer ran the Manhattan Project. He had his opponents within the project, but he always heard them out. An amazing level of loyalty emerged. It is also the way the famous Skunk Works of Silicon Valley and other high-tech venues are run.

Once all the managerial essentials are in place (see "The essential PMVN/CU&A"), attention can be turned to the design of the network, the group's bread and butter.

Designing the network
The essentials are in place. The data communications manager is the leader, reporting to upper management. The manager is responsible for the nuts and bolts of the PMVN/CU&A, as well as the growing revenue it produces. The manager is rewarded based on how well the PMVN/CU&A works and how much revenue it produces.

No doubt, an extensive and active telecommunications infrastructure is already in place, passing voice, data, and images in both directions and to all kinds of users throughout the organization. This existing network must be audited to discover its extent, where it goes, who's connected to it, and what kind of information is passed and with what quality.

This auditing function is time-consuming and fraught with ambiguity. Many pieces of terminal equipment will be orphans; no one will admit to owning them—so budget-center assignment is impractical. Depreciation allowances thus become nebulous. Cost or salvage as the determinant in assigning value to the asset becomes a guessing game. Never mind. The network in place *must* be rendered in block diagram form, with as much detail and accuracy as possible.

A standard for current valuation of equipment should be established, so that replacement cost, salvage cost, and title assignments can be determined. Time spent on determining an asset's worth should be measured against the asset's reasonable present value. For example, a laser printer priced at $5,000 a few years ago may now have a replacement cost that is a fraction of that.

The laboriously gathered information, the end product of systematic site surveys, will be the first data entries for a computer-based inventory control system, which will track all network and terminal equipment by manufacturer's name, model number, serial number, and to whom it is assigned (itself tracked by name, telephone extension, physical location, and profit center to which the device is charged) plus the purchase price and date of purchase. It is essential that this database be kept clean and up to date.

All requests for terminal moves, circuit additions, and cutovers, as well as the purchase of all data terminal equipment (DTE) and data circuit-terminating equipment (DCE) assets, should be entered into the inventory system *before* any new microcomputers, modems, or local area network servers are purchased.

A tall order? Indeed. Finding out just what's on a network and who has it is the most difficult part of designing the network. Some network managers may feel that this is beneath them. But consider that it was always Ma Bell's way of tracking products, which consisted of terminal equipment and network services. She knew who had what and what it was earning in revenue.

Once managers have a reasonably good idea of what makes up their networks and what's connected to them, the marketing plan dictates the next step: establishing schedules and priorities for implementing that plan.

All work to be done, whether it is as simple as moving a microcomputer from one location to another or as intricate and potentially disastrous as a major hot cutover, should be described in writing as a task (Fig. 3).

Once the task is described and the degree of difficulty or the level of commitment of in-house resources is estimated, a decision can be made regarding the use of in-house employees. Alternatively, bids can be solicited from qualified consultants.

The bottom-line mentality encourages the use of outside specialists. Only a cost-passthrough organization with no bottom-line concerns can have on staff every conceivable kind of specialist. In fact, service organizations, such as the predivestiture telephone companies, could afford to do just that since they operated on the recovery of all direct costs, plus a guaranteed ROI. Your products, PMVN/CU&A services, however, operate most effectively when all costs are accurately identified and built into user fees.

2. Engineering cycle. *While regarded as an arcane offshoot of science, replete with complex formulas, incomprehensible handbooks, and practitioners who are out of touch with reality, engineering is simply codified trial and error. The flow chart depicts how a design is refined until an optimum result is obtained.*

The engineering cycle in product development

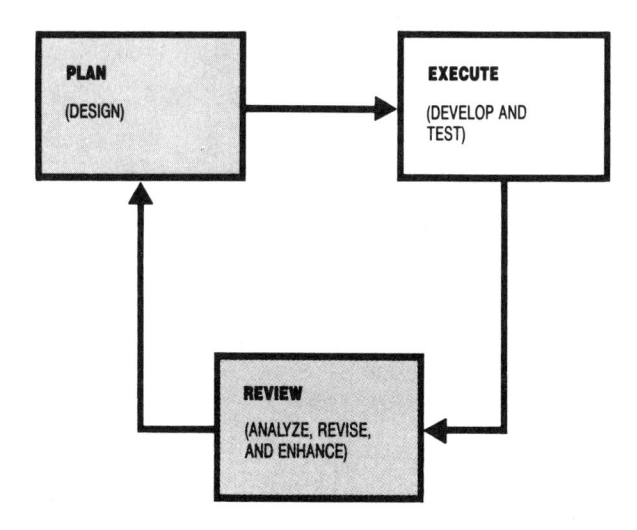

PLAN (DESIGN) → EXECUTE (DEVELOP AND TEST) → REVIEW (ANALYZE, REVISE, AND ENHANCE) → (back to PLAN)

The PMVN/CU&A as a revenue producer, developed using the engineering cycle

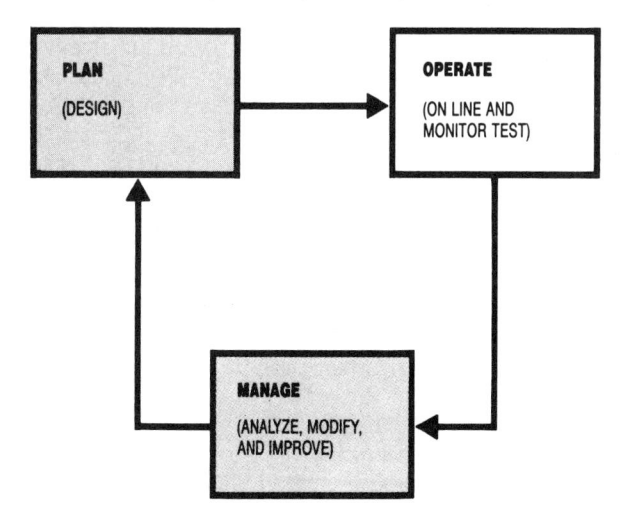

PLAN (DESIGN) → OPERATE (ON LINE AND MONITOR TEST) → MANAGE (ANALYZE, MODIFY, AND IMPROVE) → (back to PLAN)

PMVN/CU&A = PRIVATE MULTIVENDOR NETWORK/COMPUTER UTILITY AND ASSET

> **The essential PMVN/CU&A**
> **The management**
> ■ A data communications manager reporting to upper management.
> ■ A business plan blessed by upper management.
> ■ A team that is committed to implementing a shared vision.
> ■ A marketing group that has carefully solicited and recorded what the users want and what they will pay for.
> **The network**
> ■ A topographical schematic of the PMVN/CU&A, using industry-accepted symbols, showing all nodes, switches, multiplexers, and circuits, including data rate capacity and supplier.
> ■ An inventory of both data circuit-terminating equipment and data terminal equipment connection arrangements determining which is which, listing manufacturer, model and serial numbers, and physical location, plus who and what budget center is assigned to it.
> ■ Gateways to other networks and common carrier services.
> ■ LANs: location, type, and manufacturer.
> ■ Network control and monitoring functions. Location, types of information delivered, and remote network control capability.

Averaged costs, plus general and administrative costs, all have a negative impact on profit. Assigned costs for defined tasks can be marked up to carry your profit burden and contribute to positive bottom-line growth. Properly selected consultants can do jobs that you need to have done and add to the bottom line. The design of networks and the pre-installation modeling of networks, however, should be kept in-house. After all, who knows your business better than you do?

If anything goes wrong, data communications managers want to be able to identify the problem quickly, determining how it happened without having to deal with alibis and explanations. All network control and monitoring design and testing should also be kept in-house.

Any network design that is undertaken, either as an enhancement of existing capability or an expansion of the existing network topography or carrying capacity, should always be viewed as temporary. This is where the brains of the PMVN/CU&A team should be applied so that the improvements in a given technology can be factored in without too much rework and new users can be accommodated with a minimum of surprises.

A horror story
Broadband metropolitan two-way transmission appeared to network designers to be an added benefit when made available through the installation of CATV networks a decade ago. Had designers modeled part of the proposed network, however, its pitfalls would have become apparent.

LAN designers in New York City, for example, saw this broadband CATV backbone snaking its way through tunnels, subways, and sewers as a boon to the development of broadband LAN technology. It seemed much more promising than the limited data-carrying capacity of a 10-Mbit/s Ethernet.

Entertainment programming, however, is one-way, send-only distribution, whereas data transmission requires both transmit and receive over the same cable infrastructure. Thus was born the split-band division of the CATV radio frequency spectrum; one portion for transmission and another for reception.

Unfortunately, this scheme drastically reduced the number of subscribers that could get point-to-point or multidrop service because the useful, effective bandwidth had been reduced to accommodate both transmit and receive capabilities on a single CATV infrastructure.

Using the existing CATV scheme as a point of departure, the engineers at Wang Laboratories thought they had a better way: a two-cable network where one cable carried all outbound traffic (transmit) and a second, identical cable carrying all inbound traffic (receive).

The advantage to broadband LAN users was that they could use full CATV bandwidth on each leg. This benefit seemed so overwhelmingly favorable that the slight drawback of requiring a matched pair of circuit interface devices (CIDs) for every LAN access seemed a mere quibble. It was more than a quibble, however, and the additional cost and complexity of this approach remains a problem.

Making sure that CIDs track together and are installed together and in fact, like misshapen twins, go through life together for optimum performance, was a feat of technical wizardry that simply could not be delivered because of the inherent instabilities of commercially available CIDs at the time. Technical improvements in drift control have markedly improved CIDs from a variety of sources. But unfortunately, the stigma associated with unstable CIDs affected the acceptance of Wangnet (and, therefore, the size of the Wangnet user base). The limited installed base, in fact, is insufficient to justify retrofitting it with vastly improved CIDs.

Success story
Twisted-pair cable can be substituted for more expensive coaxial cable through the addition of a simple, passive, impedance-transforming device (which effectively connects a balanced circuit to an unbalanced circuit, hence the acronym, balun). IBM 3270-type terminals and terminal controllers, usually interconnected via coax, can now, over distances of several hundred feet, be interconnected using baluns with existing twisted-pair installed in the wall or floor. Multiple twisted pairs can be freshly installed, with designated pairs set aside for specific services such as voice, while other pairs are used as an effective low-cost, baseband LAN.

Savings can be significant, particularly if the existing twisted pair is disconnected or additional capacity is lying unused in the walls and floors of a site. However, maximum home-run distances—the total distance the cable must run,

3. Request form. *To earn revenue, you must know where terminal equipment is, who is using it, and the nature of the work being performed. A record such as this one will make it easier to quote prices and assign personnel to tasks.*

A TYPICAL PMVN/CU&A WORK ORDER REQUEST FORM

```
NAME_____ LOCATION_____ EXTENSION_____

BUDGET CENTER_____ EMPLOYEE NUMBER_____ NETWORK ACCESS NUMBER_____
BRIEF DESCRIPTION OF WORK TO BE PERFORMED:


DESIRED COMPLETION DATE_____  WILL YOUR PROFIT CENTER PAY PREMIUM RATES
                                FOR OVERTIME?  YES_____ NO_____
PRESENT USER EQUIPMENT CONNECTED TO THE PMVN/CU&A
          ITEM              MODEL #           SERIAL#
Terminal Equipment


Video Display Terminals


Personal Computers


Word Processors


Printers


Modems, Circuit Interface Devices


Budget Center Manager_____
Do you want a written quote?  Yes _____ No _____
For PMVN/CU&A Operating Group Only:
Site Survey required?  Yes _____ No _____
Inventory Control verifies equipment complement?  Yes _____ NO _____
Technician Assigned_____
```

turns and all, from the farthest point to, say, a terminal controller—must be tested in situ for the maximum data rate that can be transmitted before unacceptable waveform degradation takes place.

In this success story, the installing contractor, an outside consultant to a major bank, set up a test bench in unoccupied space at the site and proceeded to drive various twisted-pair/balun combinations at a variety of lengths, some in excess of the longest to be used in the application with a variable-rate data source. The consultant monitored the outputs for attenuation versus length, rise-time degradation, leading and trailing edge overshoot, and group delay for a standard pulse.

A clear narrative describing the tests was written by the outside consultant's project engineer. Simple block diagrams showing the test configurations were part of the test procedure. Oscilloscope pictures were taken and annotated with calibration data for amplitude and time. And all of this was done *before* any cable was pulled into the walls and floors.

Several valued results accrue to both the client and the contractor when such a sensible engineering approach is employed. There is a recorded baseline of data showing actual, live performance for actual cable and balun configurations. Testing is done off-line, before installation. As the actual installation proceeds, before-and-after comparisons can be made to benchmark the live network for future performance reference. The client and the contractor are then more comfortable with each other because they are confident of results, which are predictable.

Setting standards

The PMVN/CU&A should be viewed as a product that offers certain features to the range of users established by the marketing plan. This product should appeal to current users and be capable of being enhanced and expanded for future users and needs.

Largely because of the hangover from Ma Bell's regime, networks are viewed as vast, complex, and impenetrable conglomerations of technology incapable of being understood in the whole, save by the geniuses who designed them.

This is nonsense. If the product approach is used, then the PMVN/CU&A can be described in written form (using both specifications and block diagrams). It becomes a utility performing certain information-carrying functions and describes in detail what is required of a potential user's equipment to become attached to the PMVN/CU&A.

The written specifications should be widely dispersed, updated on a regular basis, and reduced to a computer model with graphics. The topography of the current network should include a well-labeled block diagram complete with place names, node locations, backbone and tail-circuit data-rate capacity, equipment names, and model numbers. An inventory summary should be published and could even be made available through a microcomputer-accessible electronic mailbox. A user directory should also be made widely available to all users and potential users in the same way.

When users and potential users know what's available to them, word of mouth takes over, and given the choice, instead of going their own way, most users will become rate payers.

Of course, good old word of mouth works both ways. Lousy service gets talked about, too. The leaders of the PMVN/CU&A are Ma Bell's progeny, so why not make every effort to emulate her most significant achievement: telecommunications services of unrivaled quality that also produce abundant and growing profits.

Multiple vendors of varying size are available to supply most PMVN/CU&A products. A well-crafted RFQ or request for proposal (RFP) solicits their interest in your project on your terms. The recent Pentagon scandals center around a single, powerful customer being manipulated by its contractors and unscrupulous consultants and being told by suppliers what it wanted.

One way to avoid being overly dominated by a single vendor is to be sure that all vendors get the same information on your firm and its organization by publishing information on key people, including their relationships to each other. Horror stories abound of the favored vendor dominating the customer, providing excessive support that supplants an independent in-house capability and eventually leads to sloppy procurement practices and lazy, dependent buyers.

Until there is an independent way of establishing specifications without the collaboration and collusion of suppliers and consultants, bribery and chicanery will continue. There is a lesson here for those who aspire to make the PMVN/CU&A pay. That lesson is: If you don't understand the existing and emerging technologies that can be applied to your PMVN/CU&A well enough to write your own specifications and RFQs and RFPs, go back to school or into another line of work.

Qualified consultants can be a boon to the leaders of the PMVN/CU&A. They have several qualities to recommend them. It is the temporary nature of the assignment and the consultant's own specialized skills that helps yield an independent judgment of hardware and software proposals.

The drawback to retaining consultants is that they can become family members, bringing some perceived indispensable skill to the enterprise. If the talents retained are so critical or in such constant demand, develop a job description, discuss it with PMVN/CU&A staff, and see if one of them won't take it on. If the consensus is that someone is really needed, go into the market and find one.

Finally, network monitoring and control in the PMVN/CU&A is similar to documentation where high-tech products are concerned: It is often the last thing considered. Documentation of a product from its inception is de rigueur

---

Words to live by

A few pearls of wisdom for technical data communications professionals who want to control their destiny and grow in their careers:

- He or she who fashions the budget controls the asset—and vice versa.
- He or she who helps increase revenue is entitled to a portion of the increase.
- Staff jobs seldom lead to the top.
- Line jobs are risky and exciting and lead to the top.
- Forget not your technical education, so that bits, bytes, baluns, and modems cease to have a meaning grounded in reality and become buzzwords to impress the uninitiated.
- Heed the advice of technicians, even unto the third helper, for theirs is a wisdom unknown to technocrats.
- Remember, networks improve and grow by cutting over live circuits.
- The self-made man or woman relieves the Almighty of an enormous responsibility. No one's accomplishments are solely his or her own.

---

in any well-run engineering and product-development operation. Like inventory control, network monitoring and control is a top-priority project and should begin right up there with the inventory site survey.

Revenue is the other half of the PMVN/CU&A performance standard. Revenue measures the productivity of an asset. In the case of the PMVN/CU&A, the criteria for measuring performance have traditionally been technical standards: data rates available, downtime, bit error rate, and so on.

If the PMVN/CU&A is to turn a profit, become market-driven, and provide growth opportunities for the professionals who run it, attention has to be paid to revenue and other bottom-line considerations, such as depreciation, book value, title, ROI, and cost/benefit analysis. As much time needs to be spent on these financial matters as on developing the network.

Remember the marketing plan, site survey, and inventory system? This is where they pay off. If managers know who has what equipment where, then they can begin to develop an internal tariff structure (that's right, just like Ma Bell). They can charge users "connect" charges—such as for connect time or for the total number of packets accepted and delivered—and equipment charges (if the asset belongs to PMVN/CU&A). In addition, communications managers can begin to factor into those charges some portion of the total cost for underwriting capital expenditures.

Managers can begin to write down the capital advanced or borrowed to build or enhance the PMVN/CU&A. This will be based on the marketing plan. The improvements should reflect user wants, and their capital budget will show where the income will come from to pay both long-term (capital) and current expenses.

When senior managers are presented with a plan crafted around technology plus a marketing plan and a predicted source of revenue, they will be hearing language they understand.

Just as the PMVN/CU&A should be monitored for performance from its inception, so should the revenue production side be subject to regular review. In any income-producing activity, managers should be looking for growth (both in absolute amounts and in increases over the previous accounting period), return on invested capital, break-even point, overhead underwriting, and delinquent accounts.

Sometimes, however, a write-off and write-down is appropriate. A major New York bank installed a broadband LAN that is now only being used to 12 percent of its capacity. The bank is in a Catch-22 situation. It cannot attract enough users because of the network's poor performance reputation, so the bank cannot demonstrate to upper management that it can bring in revenue to pay for the necessary improvements. The only alternative is to take full depreciation against the asset and, when it reaches zero, close it down.

Building a team
Bureaucracies are defined by structure, lines of authority, and superior/subordinate reporting arrangements. When growth is minuscule and the tasks repetitive and mundane, this structure can get the job done. Bureaucracies are resistant to change, innovation, or expansion of function, and this is why they ultimately require subsidies to keep them operating.

The communications team that is envisioned in this article will be entrepreneurial, performance-driven, and dollar- and promotion-rewarded (see "Words to live by"). Problems are seen as opportunities, a challenge wherein skills can be tested, something new learned, or both.

Several preconditions must exist to get the PMVN/CU&A functioning as needed. Autonomy must be granted by upper management with one person reporting to the chief executive officer or the chief financial officer. MIS and the PMVN/CU&A have to be combined on some equitable basis—for the division of function as well as rewards. Naming a chief information officer is a start, provided someone is qualified who also has a direct line to the CEO.

In the future, there will be a growing pool of technical professionals trained in both engineering and computer science who are eager to take a leadership role. The new MIS-PMVN/CU&A can and should be on a par with other profit/loss departments in status, visibility, and budget. ■

James Randall has a BSEE from Brooklyn Polytechnic Institute. He has worked in sales and engineering in the electronics industry for more than 30 years.

Paul F. Finnigan, Voicemail International, Cupertino, Calif., and James G. Meade, Words Co., Fairfield, Iowa

Audiotex: The telephone as data-access equipment

Videotex was to put data in easy reach. Voice mail uses ubiquitous telephones as terminals. Now their offspring promises the best of both.

Airlines, investment firms, physicians, retailers, and other users are beginning to discover the potential of audiotex. It brings the spirit of videotex to plain-vanilla voice mail by adding a new software component: the audiotex interface. This software allows a database host to pass data to a voice-mail computer, where it is interpreted and delivered over the telephone as a natural, spoken-voice message.

Audiotex users can store a virtually unlimited vocabulary in the voice-mail computer, a store-and-forward mechanism for digitized voice. Words, sentences, paragraphs, and longer messages are each stored and assigned a number. Through the audiotex interface, the voice-mail computer matches incoming ASCII data from the company database with these stored messages, combines them, and relays them to the caller.

For example, a caller telephones an airline's flight information number and is greeted by a recorded instruction (Fig. 1). Pressing the "1" key on a Touch-Tone telephone leads to information on the status of a flight, whereas "2" might lead to arrival and departure times, "3" to frequent flier mileage, "4" to seat availability, and so on.

After an exchange with the caller, the audiotex software on the voice-mail computer formulates a terminal-style inquiry for the host and receives a database response. It interprets the response, selects and combines words or phrases from a stored vocabulary of prerecorded voice snippets, and plays back the completed answer to the caller over the telephone.

Rationale and uses for audiotex

By itself, voice mail has found limited acceptance. Users tend to think of voice-mail computers as overgrown answering machines. Thus only a few hundred of the units have been sold. Merely replacing pink telephone message slips in the office is not perceived as sufficient justification for spending $20 or $30 per person per month.

Many users, however, are concluding that while such mundane office tasks may not have provided an economically feasible rationale for voice mail, audiotex applications do. Trans World Airlines, for example, now has several audiotex setups in place, including a scheduling application that serves several thousand crew members a day (see "TWA flight assigner").

In another application of audiotex, Pacific Southwest Airlines offers arrival and departure information and flight schedules by telephone. Passengers use Touch-Tone telephones to answer verbal prompts for their "from city" and "to city." Pacific Southwest's computer searches the database for the routes between those cities and delivers flights and times to the caller.

The financial industry is another prime candidate for audiotex, given the mass of constantly changing information on stocks, bonds, prices for gold and silver, and so on. Currently, people sit at computer display screens dispensing such information over the telephone. Audiotex provides an attractive alternative, as evidenced by the success of Dowphone (see "Dialing for dividends").

Audiotex is also being used to deliver medical updates. It is safe to say that all physicians rely on the *Physician's Desk Reference,* a standard loose-leaf reference volume published annually. In the past, updates would arrive in the mail every month or so, and doctors or their assistants would have to replace pages from their binders. Now physicians can keep current on such critical information as drug interactions by dialing an audiotex service, keying in the code number for the drug in question, and listening to the *Physician's Desk Reference* update.

Retailers can use audiotex to advertise goods and services via digitized voice. Audiotex acts as a voice bulletin board of items available for sale. The caller listens to descriptions of the items and orders by pressing Touch-

1. Interaction. *In audiotex, information goes from Touch-Tones to database inquiries and then from data responses to composites of stored digital speech.*

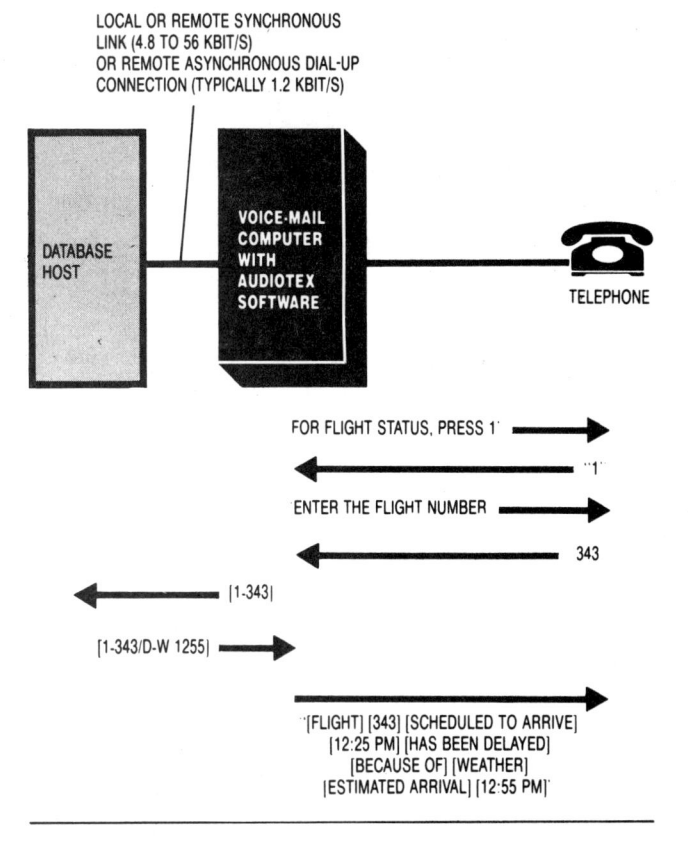

```
LOCAL OR REMOTE SYNCHRONOUS
LINK (4.8 TO 56 KBIT/S)
OR REMOTE ASYNCHRONOUS DIAL-UP
CONNECTION (TYPICALLY 1.2 KBIT/S)
```

[DATABASE HOST] — [VOICE-MAIL COMPUTER WITH AUDIOTEX SOFTWARE] — [TELEPHONE]

→ FOR FLIGHT STATUS, PRESS 1
← "1"
→ ENTER THE FLIGHT NUMBER
← 343
← [1-343]
→ [1-343/D-W 1255]
→ "[FLIGHT] [343] [SCHEDULED TO ARRIVE] [12:25 PM] [HAS BEEN DELAYED] [BECAUSE OF] [WEATHER] [ESTIMATED ARRIVAL] [12:55 PM]"

Tone keys to denote item number, quantity, and the caller's credit card number. If the credit card is not valid, the voice-mail computer refuses to fill the order. Otherwise, it asks for the caller's name and shipping address, which the caller announces. This information, stored in verbal form, is later entered manually by an operator. The rest of the information about the order has been entered directly into the computer by the caller via audiotex.

This type of arrangement is already proving itself. One Los Angeles entrepreneur, for instance, had 200 hours of caller time to his bulletin board in one recent month. An average of one minute per call meant that 12,000 transactions had been handled. As a voice mail-order house, the retailer does not even have to own a store. The audiotex machine takes the orders, and the retailer ships the goods via United Parcel Service.

The voice-mail processor

In developing audiotex applications, TWA and others have drawn on previous experience and accumulated new insights into what works and what does not. Informal tests of people using audiotex have shown, for example, that the most effective way to give instructions in an audiotex application is first to tell people they are going to have to make a choice, then list the choices, explain each choice one at a time, and, finally, ask for a decision—allowing the callers to interrupt and make a choice at any time.

Three is a good number of choices to give, and six is a maximum before people are unable to remember the

TWA flight assigner

Like all airlines, Trans World Airlines faced a two-hour telephone nightmare each day. Reserve flight attendants (crew members who are needed, on short notice, to handle a variety of situations caused by weather, holiday travel, and flight changes) call the airline daily between 7 P.M. and 9 P.M. to receive their flight assignments. In a successful effort to unclog its switchboard, TWA installed audiotex.

Traditionally, TWA reserves called an answering machine, which delivered a list of names of the people with flight assignments. Since up to 100 people might be calling at once, there were many busy signals. Those who did hear their names on the list called an 800 number to receive their assignments from a scheduler, who often had to put callers on hold. With this inefficient setup, the reserves made multiple telephone calls and wasted a great deal of time waiting.

With TWA's audiotex implementation, the crew member dials the 800 number of a voice-mail machine, which asks for an identification number and a password. The voice-mail computer then sends TWA's crew management computer (which is an IBM 9083) a digital command to list any assignments for the person with the given I.D. and password. The TWA computer responds in digital form.

Based on the information from the TWA computer, the voice-mail computer delivers a voice message from the stored vocabulary. The computer might simply say: "You are released until Monday at 7 P.M.," the next call-in period. However, if there is an assignment, the computer constructs a message such as: "You have been assigned to Flight... one hundred fifty ... August twenty... eleven hundred hours... local time.... To acknowledge your assignment, press 1. To speak to a scheduler, press 9."

If the caller presses "1," the voice-mail computer delivers a notice to the crew-scheduling computer saying that the person has received the message and accepted the trip. If the caller presses "9," the voice-mail computer switches the crew member directly to a live scheduler.

With the audiotex setup, assignments that the TWA scheduling department has entered on a computer display terminal are delivered automatically over the telephone. Callers listen to information intended specifically for them instead of to a list of names (which might not even include their own). They also make one call instead of two.

TWA expects the average connect time to be half that of a manually handled call because the length of each call is just the length of the assignment. There are no discussions about the assignment or, for that matter, about weather, politics, or sports. If reserves have no assignment, the message is three or four words. If they do have one, the message is still brief. By limiting the amount of time callers are on the phone and serving each caller more quickly, audiotex cuts down on the cost and aggravation of communications.

> **Dialing for dividends**
>
> Investors want news about events that affect the financial world as soon as they occur. They can get such news by listening to the radio, by watching television, or by calling Dowphone. An audiotex service from Dow Jones & Co., Dowphone already has 30,000 subscribers and is adding more at the rate of 1,000 a month. As they would for other information services, subscribers pay a yearly fee plus the bill for connect time.
>
> To get news and stock information directly from the Dow Jones database, subscribers call Dowphone, key in their identification numbers on Touch-Tone telephones, and listen. Dowphone reads the latest business and financial headlines automatically. To listen to stock quotes on a specific company, callers press the "6" key at the ready tone.
>
> When the computer voice asks for a company code, callers key in identification numbers from their printed directories. For example, 5009 brings information about AMF Inc., 4205 about Boeing Co., 5918 about Zenith Radio Corp., and so on.
>
> Subscribers can select stock quotes on more than 6,500 companies. They can also get frequently updated business news on 58 industries and market reports on precious metals and commodities. To select news, they press "7" at the ready tone and then identify their choices by directory number. In this case, for example, entering 9067 brings stock market news on bankruptcies, 9310 yields industry news on aerospace, and 9102 results in information on the U. S. dollar in foreign exchange markets.
>
> Dowphone subscribers can set up portfolios of their own stocks so that, when they give their I.D. number at sign-on, Dowphone automatically reads them information on the companies for which they hold stock. They can put up to 100 companies in their personal stock portfolio and an equal number in their news portfolio.

options well enough to make good decisions. People tend to remember the first and last choices that are presented to them but not the ones in the middle.

The software that makes audiotex possible runs on voice-mail processors. Such machines are composed of specialized cards or printed circuit boards (Fig. 2).

Telephone-line coupler cards connect outside telephone lines with the voice-mail computer. Regulated by the Federal Communications Commission, they present a balanced interface to the telephone lines, primarily by performing echo suppression.

The coupler cards connect with the line cards, which contain microprocessors and audio buffers (memory). The line cards recognize the Touch-Tones from the caller's telephone. For example, a "1" tone may mean send a message, an "8" may mean replay a message, and so on. The line cards also convert incoming analog voice into digitized information that can be stored.

The rate of sound digitization is typically from 16 to 32 kbit/s. At the higher speed, voice quality is equivalent to that of commercial telephone transmissions. The encoding method may be adaptive differential pulse code modulation or continuously variable slope delta modulation.

The line cards not only recognize Touch-Tones and digitize sound but also reverse the process to generate Touch-Tone signals and convert digital signals into analog voice. Segments of digitized sounds are stored in the memory buffers of the line cards. If a message exceeds the length of a single buffer, the next segment of it goes into a second buffer. Logic in the computer cards can then join the separate segments. By having two or more buffers for each line, it is possible to move the data of one buffer in or out while another buffer is in use, thus continuously recording or playing back messages.

The line cards connect over a bus with computer cards

2. Hardware. *The cards handle various voice-mail functions, such as electrical line handling, Touch-Tone detection and interpretation, and processing.*

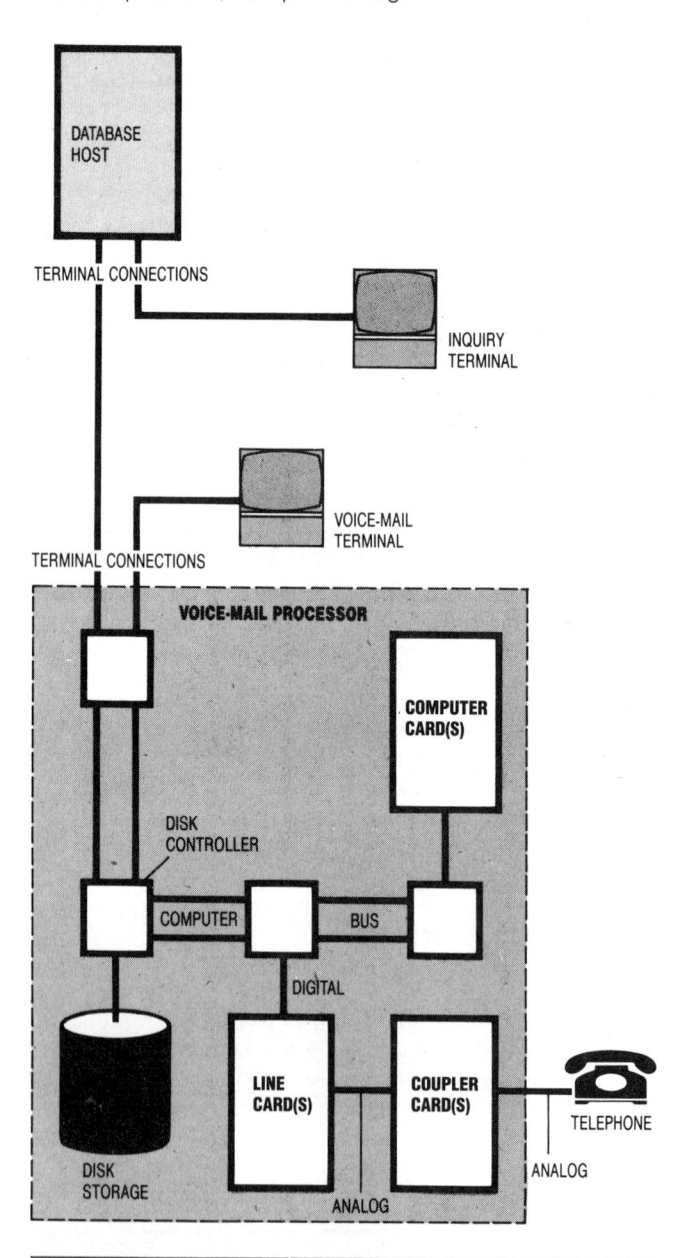

3. Software. *Code that links voice and data machines contains portions that act on behalf of the users and a portion that may multiplex calls on a single host port. The telephone user processes track the sessions of individual callers, while the host interface program routes and buffers traffic and allocates ports.*

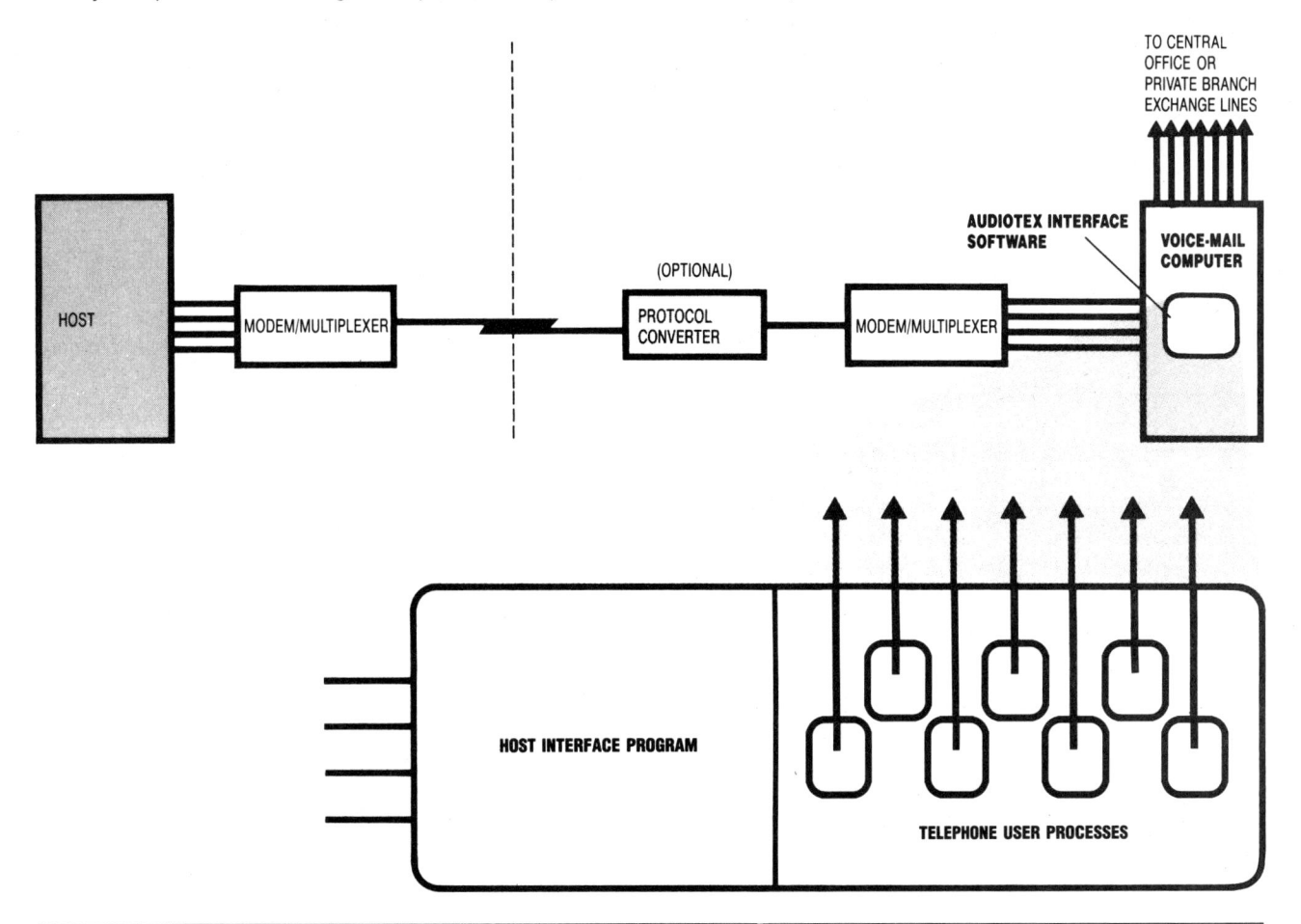

that contain logic for assigning addresses, storing and forwarding messages, and issuing or recognizing commands. Together, the computer cards constitute the central processing unit (CPU), which is as powerful as a minicomputer.

Key functions of audiotex

When a speaker begins recording a message, the CPU gives that message a number corresponding to a specific storage location on disk. To transfer a buffer of audio data to the disk, the CPU establishes a transfer path from the line card through the computer bus and the disk controller to the disk. Because the data moves directly from the line card to the disk, the CPU does not have to be involved in the transfer of data to the disk, which nets a significant saving in the load on the CPU.

Audiotex also uses the voice-mail processor's fixed-file capability. Logic in the CPU can piece together fixed files of stored information to form messages. Voice mail uses fixed files for prompts and instructions; it uses standard words to denote date and time. Fixed files are recorded in the same way as other messages. Because they are very short, fixed files are kept by the typical voice-mail processor in a separate file structure so that they can be accessed as readily as possible.

Just as the computer cards provide continuous speech by piecing together message segments, they also build prompts by linking individual words or phrases in the fixed file. Voice-mail configurations may contain more than one vocabulary, which allows the potential for prompting in several languages. A vocabulary may also contain specialized words and phrases, such as the messages in TWA's crew-scheduling application.

Software: The audiotex interface

If a particular audiotex installation is based on voice-mail hardware, it stores natural-voice message fragments in a vocabulary and uses data from the external host to construct phrases and sentences. Another form of audiotex uses a speech synthesizer such as Digital Equipment Corp.'s DECtalk. The synthesizer does not sound like a natural human voice but offers a compensation: It can speak any ASCII-coded text instead of being restricted to a prerecorded vocabulary.

The version based on voice-mail hardware requires that information in a database can be accessed by the audiotex interface software (Fig. 3). Such software runs under the voice-mail processor's operating system and consists of two parts. The host interface program (HIP) interacts with the host while the telephone user processes (TUPs) act on behalf of the callers.

Each TUP is responsible for answering the telephone, issuing prompts, receiving Touch-Tones, formatting caller data into host-inquiry syntax, and playing the appropriate portions of the vocabulary depending on the host's response.

In general, the HIP takes inquiries from the TUPs, passes them on to the host, receives responses from the host, and sends the responses back to the correct TUP. In addition to routing messages between the ports and the TUPs, the HIP buffers messages in memory allocated to it. That is, the HIP assembles the entire incoming message before handing it to the TUP for playback.

The HIP also determines when host ports are available and allocates them (as in Figure 2, where there are four ports into the host). When the caller submits an audiotex inquiry, the HIP forwards it to the host if a port is available. Otherwise, it holds the inquiry until a port is released at the conclusion of another caller's transaction. In this arrangement, the main duty of the HIP is to schedule the use of host ports.

However, rather than having the TUPs contend for exclusive host sessions over each of four ports, an alternative software design is to have one host session per telephone user. With the HIP operating in time-sharing mode, all such sessions can be in progress at once, multiplexed over a single physical connection.

In this case, when the HIP gets a request from a TUP to send something to the host, it puts appropriate envelope characters at the beginning and end of the inquiry to indicate which line is talking. On the return trip, it strips off the envelope and uses it to route the message to one of the TUPs. Of course, this requires software either in the host or in the protocol converter (if one is used) to handle the envelope protocol.

Possible relationships

Although many voice-mail processors are based on general-purpose computers and could, in principle, be programmed to maintain the database for the application, there is often an existing database on a host machine being accessed by inquiry terminals. Thus it is more efficient for the voice machine to gain access to the host's information than to maintain the information itself.

There are several possible relationships between the database and the audiotex software that will vary among different types of applications:

■ *Duplicate database.* If the audiotex computer does not directly change the database from which it derives information, it can bring the data to the voice-mail computer, where it will then be stored. The transfer of information may be via local area network or, if the computers are at a distance, over a packet-switching connection.

■ *Duplicate database with automatic capture.* If the data in the main database changes rapidly and there is a frequent requirement for information from the whole database, the most efficient design is, once again, to maintain a duplicate database within the audiotex computer but to feed updating information directly to the audiotex database whenever changes occur.

Some database programs can be set up to send a continuous stream of update notifications to display terminals. This may be either a complete set of transaction information or only those transactions that a certain display has been programmed to receive. If the software on the host has this capability, the audiotex machine can maintain a database that is updated automatically, without requiring an inquiry or a response.

■ *Duplicate database with timed capture.* If information from the whole database is frequently required but changes to that database are relatively infrequent, the best design may be to maintain a separate database on the voice-mail computer and update it automatically at a rate based on the anticipated rate of change to the main one.

■ *Selected data with timed capture.* If the type of inquiry is such that there are a large number of requests for the same restricted set of information and the information changes infrequently, the load on both computers can be reduced and response time improved if these particular bits of information are periodically retrieved and stored by the audiotex machine.

For example, a commodity-price computer receives frequent requests for the London price of gold. However, the price is fixed and can change only twice a day. Thus, the audiotex machine is programmed to request the price and change information automatically at set times. This information is then stored in the audiotex computer so that requests can be answered without recourse to the host.

■ *Direct inquiry.* Where the values on the main database change frequently but there are relatively few requests for items from that database, the best relationship between the audiotex computer and the host may be direct, or on-demand, inquiry. The audiotex computer may retrieve items directly from the database when audiotex access is requested. This alleviates the need to have a possibly costly duplicate of the database.

Where the audiotex application produces a direct change in the database, as in cases where receiving an order reduces available inventory, direct inquiry is the preferred approach. Inquiry is the normal mode employed by display terminals, so the probability is high that using audiotex would require little or no change to the host's database software.

Simulating a terminal

The link from the voice-mail computer to the host will typically be in standard text format, simulating an ASCII terminal. However, other terminal protocols can be accommodated, either with a modification of the audiotex software or with a separate protocol converter. One example is the Sabre 6-bit code used in airline audiotex applications, where the two machines are linked through off-the-shelf Sabre-to-ASCII protocol converters. Another example involves 3270 binary synchronous communications. Typical speeds between the two machines are 1.2 or 2.4 kbit/s for remote connections and 9.6 kbit/s for local links.

Some database inquiry languages permit a terminal to submit multiple inquiries without waiting for the responses. Where multiple inquiries are allowed, audiotex can use a single data link for callers on several telephone lines, as in the single-link software design mentioned above. (If multiple inquiries are not available, of course, inquiries must either be queued or sent via multiple paths.)

A data link can serve several telephone inquiries simultaneously if the style of transaction is complete, that is, if the inquiry contains sufficient information to retrieve response data without relying on values passed during a previous transaction. Similarly, for complete transactions, the response must contain sufficient identifying data to link it to the inquiry.

Some transactions are open-ended, however, as where separate inquiries are used to establish the identity of the caller, to find the availability of a part in inventory, and to initiate the shipping of the order. In complex applications where users submit a barrage of intricate queries, this type of arrangement may require a data link to the host machine for each simultaneous call. Although the host machine may be configured to handle a large number of terminal connections, the audiotex machine would be burdened with superfluous hardware. The remote data links would then drive up communications costs.

The alternative, as described previously, is to use a special protocol converter or host software facility to simulate a number of terminals. Each telephone inquiry is then assigned a virtual terminal identifier that remains valid until the end of the call. In this case, the terminal connection between the host and the audiotex machine is most likely a synchronous remote link at 4.8 to 56 kbit/s, but it may also be a lower-speed link over the public switched voice network.

Dial-out

In a relatively new application of audiotex, users do not have to dial in. The audiotex machine dials out. Voice-mail messages may be automatically delivered on the basis of instructions (date, time, attempts, and interval) received from another computer. Either the voice-mail processor or the database computer may originate the request for delivery.

Experience with audiotex applications has found that people do not always have time to listen if they are not sure the information they receive is important for them. And people forget to call in, particularly if they do not know whether any valuable information awaits them.

The dial-out capability enables the audiotex machine to call someone by telephone or, for time-critical information, by radio pager (beeper). For example, investment advisers at Risk Arbitrage Monitor Inc., a Wall Street firm, provide a service that dials out to notify clients of information they have requested.

A financial adviser may want to notify investors of a change in their investment positions on a certain company. To make all the calls to perhaps 200 clients might take hours of calling, informing, and playing telephone tag. And the investors contacted first might profit over those who receive the time-critical information later.

With dial-out audiotex, the information provider calls a voice-mail computer and records a recommendation (Fig. 4). The recorded message is stored in a particular location (a voice-mailbox) reserved for that particular dial-out application. By using different box numbers, the information provider can indicate the urgency of the message, the industry that the information pertains to (for example, telecommunications), and perhaps even the company discussed in the message. This voice-mailbox arrangement also provides security because, to access its contents, a caller must know the seven-digit box number in addition to the seven-digit password required for initial log-on.

The information provider also selects the number of a distribution list of subscribers who have signed up for news on this particular subject. The distribution-list number and box number are passed to the central computer of a network paging service, which identifies the local paging-service computer and pager number of each subscriber in the group. The central computer then notifies the paging service in each appropriate city.

The local paging service transmits an alert and the box number to the individual pagers, which beep and display the box number and perhaps the other information associated with the message (urgency, industry, or company). With this, the client knows to retrieve the time-critical

4. Alerting the masses. *Dial-out audiotex with a radio pager tie-in lets an investment adviser notify hundreds or thousands of clients with a single call.*

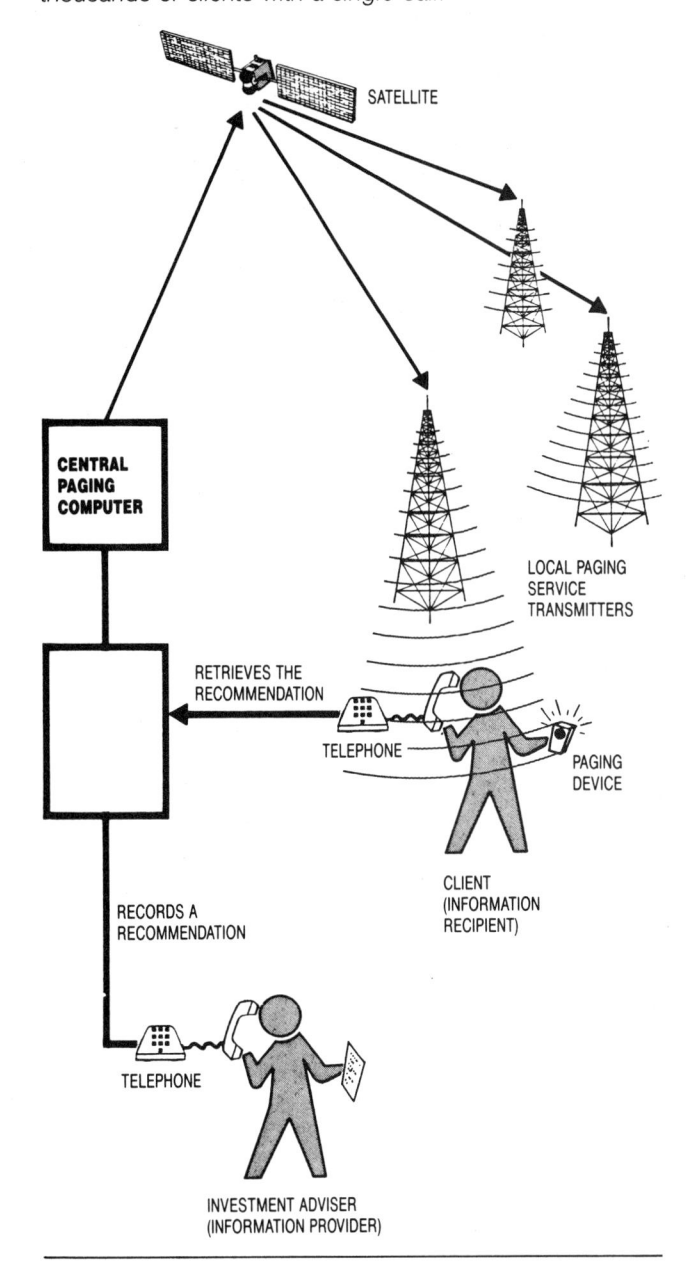

message.

Dial-out capability allows audiotex to simultaneously alert two hundred or even two thousand subscribers to a news broadcast. Subscribers then receive the message by calling the voice-mail computer, entering a subscriber password, and then entering the box number displayed on the pager.

The elapsed time for the broadcast is the time for the information provider to dial an 800 number, enter a password, select a box number and a group number, record and edit the message, and initiate the page alert. From the time the sender has completed and sent the message, beepers may go off within seconds in as many as 35 cities.

Coming attractions

Audiotex does not have to end with dispensing information. With the computer's "if this, then that" capability, business people can benefit from extensive computer resources directly over the telephone.

For example, currently a subscriber to voice mail can use the telephone keypad to send a deferred message. Answering the computer's questions, the subscriber goes through a series of simple steps to indicate delivery date, time, number of tries, and retry interval, and to specify delivery (for example: "Tomorrow beginning at 8:30 A.M., four attempts at delivery, one every fifteen minutes").

With the next generation of voice-mail software, users will be able to set up comparable if-then conditions for the computer. "If my stock is $200 a share, call me," the investor can instruct the audiotex service. "Page me as soon as it happens."

In a more advanced application, the investor could specify: "If the composite of my stocks goes up or down more than three points, call me." The investor would not even have to call in to find out what is going on. If any stock in the portfolio moves significantly in either direction, the audiotex computer would call, once an hour at several locations if necessary, or transmit a page alert to wherever the investor might be.

Paul F. Finnigan has 30 years experience in the design of computer and telecommunications hardware and software. Chairman and founder of Voicemail International of Cupertino, Calif., Finnigan conceived and designed Dowphone, the first commercial product utilizing audiotex. He also developed the crew-scheduling application for Trans World Airlines and an automated reservation service for Pacific Southwest Airlines.

James G. Meade, Ph. D., is an author and president of Writing Or Related Design Services (Words Co.), a Fairfield, Iowa, consulting company. Specializing in voice communications, he writes frequently for industry trade publications and prepares a monthly office automation column for users of Digital Equipment Corp. computers. Meade was formerly a senior writer for DEC.

Section 7
How To . . .

Brian Laughlin, Damac Products Inc., Santa Fe Springs, Calif.

Data wiring, or learning to live with spaghetti

A survey shows how networkers cope with the computer-generated tangle of twisted-pair and coaxial cable: Most just grimace and bear it.

Beneath the streamlined veneer of today's paperless office sprawls a proliferating mess of wire. The clutter accompanying computer power and data communications cabling is epidemic, to be sure. But it is also a problem that many users simply sweep under the rug. What's more, one recent survey indicates that this path of least resistance is not only the most popular but also, possibly, the most efficient.

A survey of 2,000 DATA COMMUNICATIONS readers, whose names were supplied to the survey group, reveals that over 80 percent of the respondents consider their workplace wiring to be a shambles (see "The question is wiring"). Even so, only 38 percent of survey participants said that they would consider enlisting a consultant for help.

Why not? Most of those surveyed (44 percent) cited cost as the main reason they weren't interested in trying to solve cable clutter; 38 percent said they were concerned it would cause equipment downtime. Other reasons cited for not disturbing the status quo included personnel downtime, space considerations, uncertainty about future plans, the "if it ain't broke, don't fix it" syndrome, company politics, and plans to relocate.

In the context of the survey, equipment downtime referred to that period between the unpatching and repatching of terminal devices that would be affected. Computer equipment and its power supply would likely not be shut down during this time. Personnel downtime was defined as users' temporary lack of access to their regular terminals.

Typical comments from respondents include, for example: "The spaghetti is a mess, but it takes too much time to clean it up." "Since this situation arises from lack of or poor planning, we handle it as the problem hits us." "Shall we call in a consultant or louse it up ourselves?" "Is there one easy way to control wiring confusion?"

In sum, the data processing manager, facilities manager, or communications manager faced with the tangle of computer-to-terminal wiring would just as soon ignore the disorder. Perhaps, the study indicates, this kind of thinking may be the most constructive.

In the past few years, computer terminals have become commonplace in virtually every department throughout companies of all sizes. Along with the obvious advantages of computer technology, however, has come a wiring nightmare for building managers. To address this, several manufacturers have designed an assortment of "data wiring systems." These encompass a host of different approaches to organizing the flow of data between computers and terminals. Such schemes have ranged from simple patch panels to elaborate and complicated data switches and local area networks (LANs).

But unless a company is buying a new computer, moving into a new facility, or rearranging an existing plant, there is little motivation to make major revisions in wire management. Simply cleaning up the clutter does not seem to warrant the cost of ripping out one set of wiring and replacing it with another. As long as users can get along with things the way they are, common sense says to leave well enough alone.

While sound planning could prevent cable disarray in most cases, usually very little attention is paid to it before it becomes a problem. Not until it is time to move into a building is the task of wiring given much thought. This lack of vision occurs despite the fact that the typical installed cost of data wiring is $200 to $300 per terminal. And while an average number of terminals might be in the 100 to 200 range, there could be as many as 1,000 or more.

Understandably, the many problems facing users can breed procrastination when it comes to wiring. As the number of terminals in a particular environment increases, such problems multiply. What's more, there is no single standard for connecting terminals to a computer within a

The question is wiring

The following are selected questions and responses from a survey of user plans and attitudes regarding data network wiring. Of the 2,000 data communications professionals queried about their data wiring, 163 (8.15 percent) responded by the cutoff date.

Not all the respondents answered all the questions, which accounts for fewer than 163 answers in questions 1 and 2. Other questions, such as number 5, allowed for multiple answers and therefore received more than 163 responses.

Question 1: Do you experience problems with data wiring disarray or clutter within your facility?
Answers: Yes, 81 percent. No, 19 percent.

Question 2: If data wiring clutter became a problem at your present site, would you consider turning to a wire management consultant for help?
Answers: Yes, 37.5 percent. No, 62.5 percent.

Question 3: What are the inhibiting factors solving a cable clutter problem within your facility? (I ore than one answer is applicable, please list i. order of importance.)
Answers: Cost: 44 percent. System Downtime: 38 percent. Other: 18 percent.

Question 4: Who else in your company becomes involved in computer-to-terminal wiring? (If more than one answer is applicable, please list in order of importance.)
Answers: Data Processing Manager: 27 percent. Facilities Manager: 23.5 percent. Facilities Engineer: 16 percent. Telecommunications Manager: 22 percent. Wire Management Consultant: 0.6 percent. Other: 11 percent.

Question 5: What products presently on the market do you feel offer the best solution to cable clutter? (If more than one answer, please list in order of importance.)
Answers: Point-to-Point Wiring: 8.5 percent. Coax Eliminator/Twisted-Pair Wiring: 19.5 percent. Multiplexing: 22.5 percent. Data Switches: 20 percent. Local Area Networking: 23 percent. Other: 6.5 percent.

Fifty-seven respondents said that they use in-house staff to solve data wiring clutter. About one-third of this number said they handled such problems themselves. One respondent was unaware that wiring consultants existed.

When respondents were asked who would be their first choice for help in resolving wiring problems, the positions most often named first were: Data Processing Manager: 23; Facilities Manager: 7; Facilities Engineer: 5; Telecommunications Manager: 12; and Wire Management Consultant: 1.

When asked their first choice of wiring option, respondents answered: Point-to-Point Wiring: 3; Coax Eliminator/Twisted-Pair Wiring: 16; Multiplexing: 12; Data Switches: 13; and Local Area Networking: 16.

1. Distribution center. At the heart of this wiring plan, computer ports and terminal ports home in on a single, central distribution center. Patching between computers and terminals can therefore be accomplished quickly, and connections can easily be changed in order to accomplish the addition or rerouting of terminals.

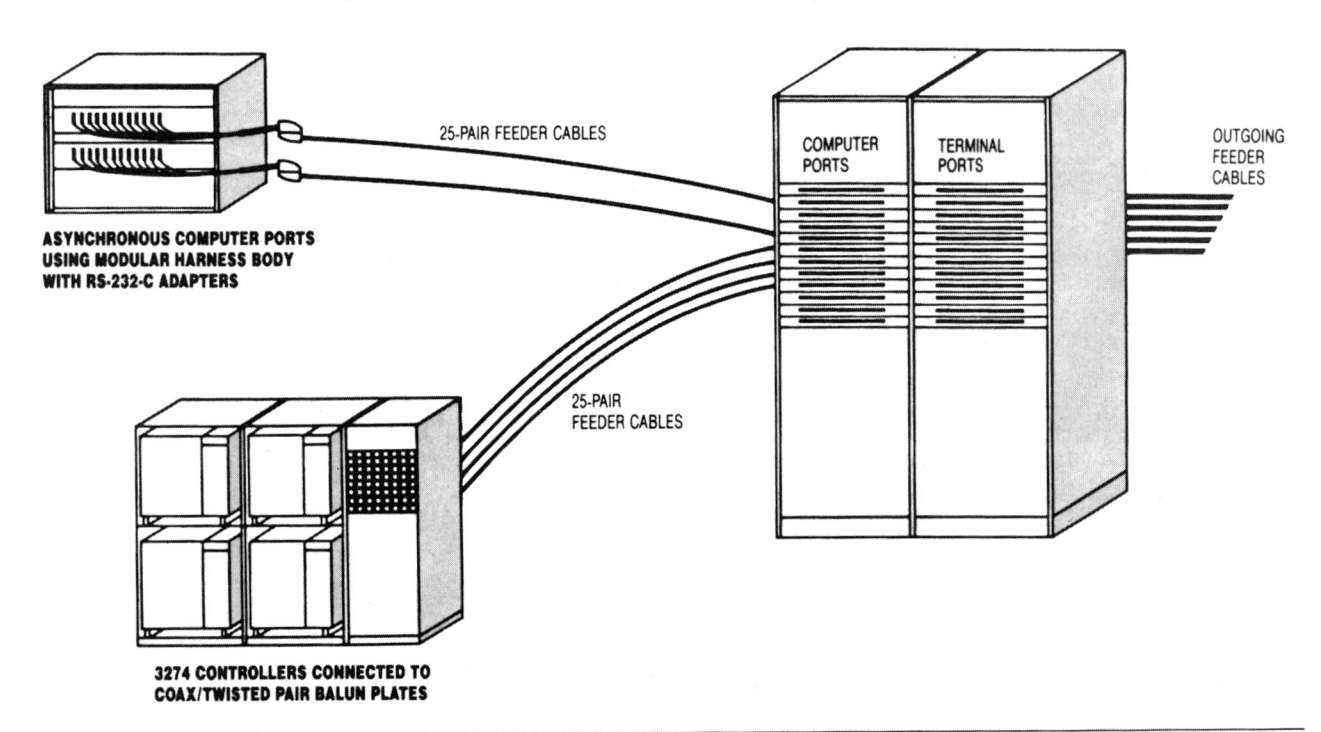

building. To a great extent, suppliers of data wiring schemes are driven by manufacturers of data communications hardware.

The IBM 3270 terminal family, for example, operates at signal speeds close to 2.4 Mbit/s. The company now has a LAN that runs at 4 Mbit/s, and it is predicting a network in the next few years that will operate at 16 Mbit/s. Most other local terminal connections and configurations support lower-speed transmission rates, the most common being 1.2, 9.6, and 19.2 kbit/s.

The wiring industry must accommodate vast differences in device signaling rates—and signal speed has a great deal to do with the type of wiring the user chooses. The wiring problem is compounded when a decision is made to substitute one brand of mainframe computer for another. Changing from an IBM computer to one from Digital Equipment Corp., for instance, requires complete rewiring because the two types of machines support very different transmission specifications.

Coaxial maze

Many user facilities contain miles of bulky, expensive coaxial cable because traditional IBM terminal networks mandated a point-to-point wiring scheme that could use only coaxial cable. For every terminal, a separate cable would be run from a computer through the floor, up the ceiling, down into the wall, and out into an office. And every time a terminal was added, the same process would be repeated. Before long, cabling would be strung throughout the building.

Recently, more attention has been given to using multipair wiring, where a single cable contains many discrete wire pairs, allowing it to accommodate many different terminals and speeds. With this cabling, an office can be wired once with passive components from the work site, back to a distribution center, and from there to the computer.

A multipair approach gives wiring managers much more flexibility in retaining existing wiring when computer equipment is changed. Also, it obviates running cable all the way back to the computer or disrupting the office workplace when more terminals are added. (Figure 1 shows typical changes that can be made at a distribution center.)

Much reluctance to cleaning up cable clutter stems from uncertainty. No one, it seems, is sure that existing wiring is going to be adequate five years hence. With continual change in data communications and computer technology, users have little confidence that what they plan now will accommodate their computer hardware and networking needs in the future.

Devoting the resources to designing an effective wire management program runs counter to most users' thinking. Nevertheless, it can, and should, be done. A wiring plan should be based on the computer hardware purchased today, not five years from now. And communications managers should buy wiring that can handle their present equipment, because they have no way of knowing what will be available in 1992.

Postponing the purchase of, say, a personal computer in hopes of buying a better model at lower cost may be a wise decision. Selecting a data wiring scheme, however, does not allow that luxury. The choice is this: To spend two to three times the amount on a cabling plan that, with luck, takes into account every parameter of possible change (but which still might not be workable in the future); or to spend much less on a cabling configuration that handles present requirements and offers reasonable prospects for growth. In short, plans need to be put into effect based on an assessment of hardware needs for the next year or two—five or 10 years from now.

Options

In setting up a wire management plan, there are plenty of alternatives. In addition to point-to-point wiring—which in general is bulky, hard to manage, expensive to run, and particularly difficult to rearrange—users today can choose from alternatives that include twisted-pair, multipair wiring, multiplexing, data switches, LANs, and fiber optics.

The "wireless" options of LANs and data switches can greatly increase communications flexibility, but they still need to be supported by some type of wiring. (Figure 2 shows a typical twisted-pair wire layout.)

Twisted-pair, multipair wiring provides fully discrete, point-to-point connections that don't require programming or hardware changes. It is lightweight, inexpensive, and flexible. The basic 25-pair trunk cable is only one-half inch in diameter and serves up to 25 terminals for about half the cost of coaxial cable. While twisted pair cannot support the distances that coaxial cable can, or provide the noise immunity of optical fiber, it still is a viable alternative for distances up to 1,000 feet.

Twisted-pair wiring can carry both synchronous and asynchronous signals and can, therefore, support hardware from many different manufacturers. In certain situations, however, twisted pair has limitations—such as when wide bandwidth, or broadband, video channels are required.

As the high-end capabilities of twisted pair are becoming better understood, and as more effective transmitters and receivers are being designed, the range of applications supported by twisted-pair cabling continues to expand. Its low cost and ease of connectivity make it the medium of choice today in many inside-building wiring plans.

The decision to add multiplexing or data switching as part of one's cabling plan adds from $100 to $400 per terminal. Both options offer increased flexibility, but this may not always be necessary. Many multiplexing products and data switches have operational restrictions and cannot, for example, handle both high- and low-speed signals.

A big advantage, however, to adding a multiplexing capability, compared with plain old twisted-pair wiring, is the significant increase in transmission distance that can be obtained. Multiplexers can be a particularly good choice if a group of terminals is located several thousand feet away from the computer.

Data switching provides instant reconfigurability, but at a relatively high cost. Many users do not require such a high degree of versatility. What's more, many users are discovering that LANs are not always compatible with different kinds of computers. For example, an IBM Token Ring may be ideal for linking certain IBM networks, but it generally cannot accommodate multivendor networks.

Optical fiber has the advantage of being able to support very high data rates while offering virtual immunity to noise.

2. Building wiring plan. *While the requirement to accommodate video channels can completely change a wiring configuration, shown here is a distribution scheme designed for distances up to 1,000 feet. Multipair cabling is able to work along with hardware from multiple vendors, and the range of applications continues to be flexible.*

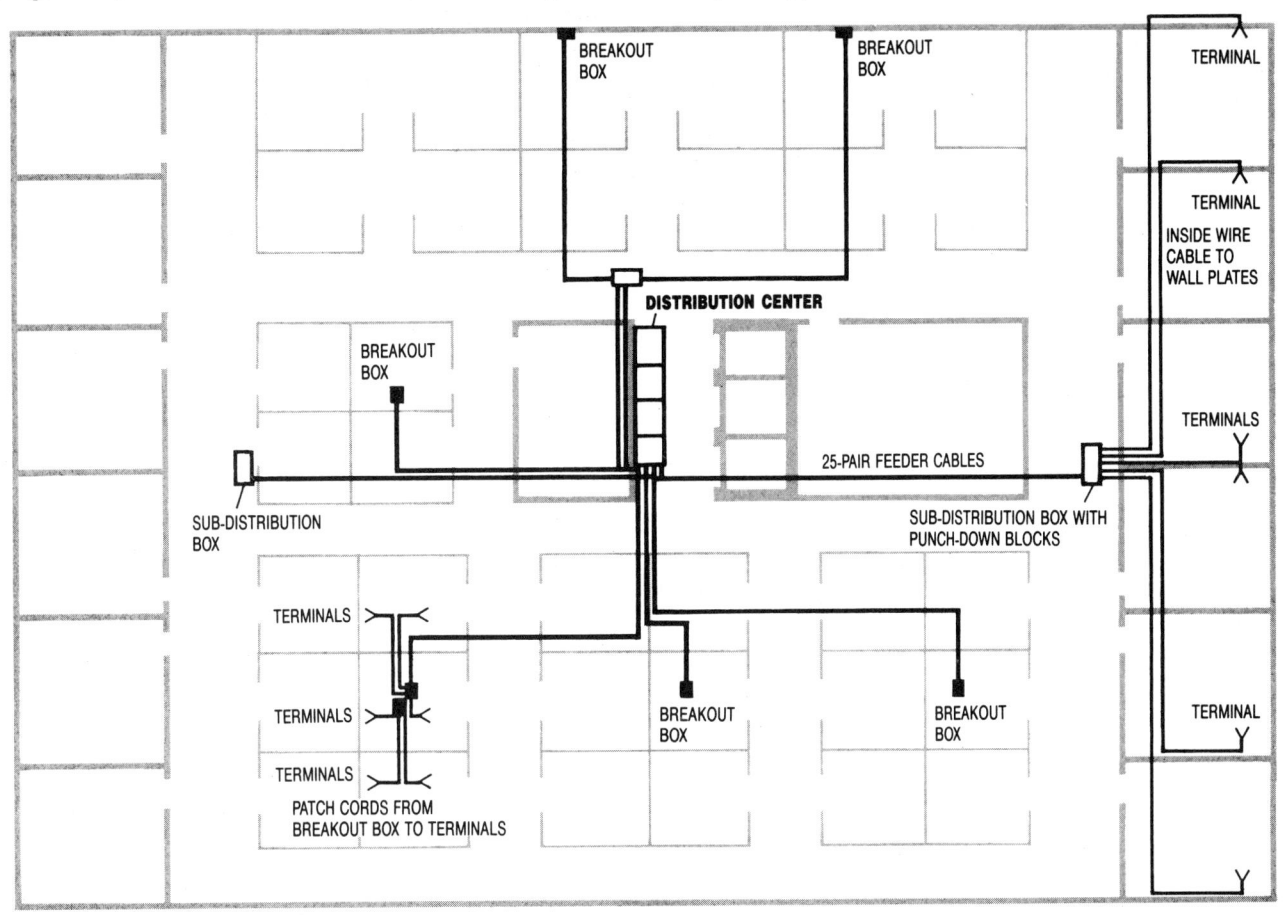

However, this medium demands greater skill for installing connectors and splices. It also requires more expensive interface devices, which are necessary to convert the signals from optical to electrical.

In specifying a wiring scheme, it is important to take into account such special requirements as video transmission. Video uses up a large amounts of bandwidth, which mandates very high-speed, expensive cabling. For video, a completely separate wiring subnetwork is recommended.

Many data processing and communications managers are unaware of the wide range of wiring options available today. (Some may not even realize that they have a cable clutter problem.) There is, however, a trend toward enlisting the aid of a consultant who specializes in this increasingly complex field. Similarly, more and more contractors who specialize in data wiring installation are assuming the role of consultant.

A few years ago, companies devoted exclusively to the provision and installation of data wiring were impossible to find. There are a few today, and their number is growing, but it still takes a little effort to locate them. One way is to ask the manufacturer of the computer hardware.

Network and data processing managers will generally devote considerable resources to studying their computer configurations. But many tend to overlook wiring until the consequences demand attention. Because the cost of wiring—which can be as high as $250,000—is still a relatively small amount compared with $5 million or more for mainframe computers, the wiring issue is neglected.

Another reason that wiring receives last-minute treatment is that computer manufacturers, more concerned with selling mainframes, have traditionally avoided this aspect of the installation. Vendors selling terminals or peripherals also rarely participate in this area. In short, data wiring has been the poor stepchild that has received very little attention from those who should be more concerned.

After acknowledging that they do, in fact, have a problem with data wiring clutter, managers must decide whether it is worth solving. A relocation of an office or a comprehensive reorganizing of an existing plant are two good opportunities to try to fix the problem. In many cases, simply replacing point-to-point coaxial wiring with a more flexible and less costly twisted-pair distribution network will result in a dramatic untangling of the web. ∎

Brian Laughlin has been vice president of Damac Products Inc. for three years. Prior to that he was a consultant for 10 years in the design and construction of office buildings. He earned a B. A. in business from Loyola University, Los Angeles, and an M. B. A. from the University of California, Irvine.

William Sheridan, Telecomputing Strategies Ltd., Rancocas, N. J.

How to make and use null modem cables

To link two computers or a computer to a terminal over a short distance requires nothing more than a cable — with some of its wires crossed. Here's how to build your own.

Modem cables are used to connect a terminal, printer, or computer (the data terminal equipment, or DTE) to a modem (the data circuit-terminating equipment, or DCE). Such cables typically conform to the Electronic Industries Association's (EIA) Recommended Standard RS-232. Since all 25 leads on the interface are connected end-to-end, the modem cables ensure success in linking DTE to DCE.

However, some applications call for the direct connection of two DTEs without intervening modems and data transmission facilities. For example, a user may wish to connect a terminal to a computer in the same room or building. Compensating for the absence of modems and transmission lines requires a special cable, terminated into RS-232-type connectors, that is variously called a "null modem cable," a "dummy modem," or a "modem eliminator." Null modem cables simulate interface signals, making the DTEs think the signals are coming from modems, when they are actually coming from themselves or from the attached DTE.

In many cases, users can purchase the needed cable from such suppliers as Black Box Corp. (Pittsburgh, Pa.), Micom Systems Inc. (Simi Valley, Calif.), or RAD Data Communications (Englewood, N. J.). In other cases, however, it may be more economical, expedient, or appropriate to devise one's own cables. To understand the construction of a null modem cable, it is helpful to know something about the RS-232 standard. (Unless otherwise noted, RS-232 refers, throughout this article, to the latest revision, RS-232-D.)

At first glance, the subject of electrical and physical interface hardware appears straightforward. However, it harbors many misconceptions that need clarification. One of the most common is that RS-232, the widely known interface standard, specifies a protocol for error-protected and flow-controlled communications. Actually, RS-232 is merely a set of rules, agreed to by members of the EIA, that govern the physical and electrical properties of connections between the DTE and the DCE.

Another common misconception is that RS-232 is a single, unchanging standard. In fact, RS-232-C, the old workhorse of data communications interfaces, is being replaced by RS-232-D, one of several more or less successful offspring of Revision C (see "Standards update").

Crossover
Essentially, a null modem cable takes the place of a circuit with modems on each end by transposing certain control leads. To understand why this is required, consider the Transmit Data signal on pin 2 of the RS-232 interface cable. If the cable is standard, all wires run straight through, and the terminal's Transmit Data lead is connected to the computer's Transmit Data lead (that is, pin 2 at one end is connected to pin 2 at the other). Obviously, the Transmit Data lead of the terminal should be connected to the Receive Data lead of the computer and vice versa.

When two DTEs are connected through modems, this transposition takes place in the modems. This is because the modems (or, in the less automated case, their users) assign one modem as the call originator and the other as the call recipient. Transmit and receive frequencies are specified for the originating modem and reversed for the receiving modem. Without modems, the transposition must be made in the interconnecting cable.

In addition to the crossing of Transmit Data and Receive Data, most setups other than very simple terminals require that some of the control leads be modified to make the interface work properly. Figure 1 shows a null modem configuration for connecting a common type of asynchronous terminal to a computer. In this example, at each DTE, two DTE-originated signals, Request To Send (pin 4) and DTE Ready (pin 20), are jumpered at the connector to their

Standards Update

Officially, RS-232-C was to be gradually replaced by three standards beginning in 1977: RS-449 (using 37-pin and 9-pin connectors) supplemented by the RS-422 and RS-423 electrical specifications. These standards were to provide higher data rates and additional functionality. However, RS-449 never succeeded in finding its niche. The Electronic Industries Association (EIA) issued RS-232-D (Revision D) in January 1987 and RS-530 in March 1987.

Both of these standards include a specification of the familiar D-shaped 25-pin interface connector. RS-232-C, on the other hand, merely made reference to the connector in an appendix, explicitly stating that the connector was not part of the standard.

RS-232-D provides new functions (see "RS-232-D signal summary") that support testing of both local and remote DCEs, while RS-530, which also provides the test functions, achieves higher data rates than RS-232 (greater than 20 kbit/s). It does this by specifying the use of balanced signals at the expense of several secondary signals and of the Ring Indicator signal provided in RS-232 (see "RS-530 signal summary"). To say that the signals are balanced means that each signal, such as Transmit Data or Receive Data, uses two wires with opposite polarities, which minimizes distortion. The elimination of Ring Indicator suggests that RS-530 is not intended for use in dial-up applications.

The foreword of the RS-530 standard states that it is intended to gradually replace RS-449. In the author's opinion, RS-449 never caught on because it specifies two different connectors, neither of which is the nearly universal 25-pin connector. Both RS-422 and RS-423, however, survive. They specify the electrical characteristics of the interface and are referenced by RS-530 as well as by other EIA standards.

In addition to the differences noted above, RS-232-D changed some signal names (for example, Data Terminal Ready, DTR, became DTE Ready and Data Set Ready, DSR, became DCE Ready). It also modified the use of Protective Ground to provide shielding, added signals to support modem testing, and generally brought the standard up to date and in line with the international standards. One can safely assume that EIA expects to continue the use of the already ubiquitous RS-232 into the foreseeable future.

The international standards that deal with comparable interfaces are CCITT V.24, CCITT V.28 and ISO International Standard IS2110, issued by the International Telegraph and Telephone Consultative Committee (CCITT) and the International Organization for Standardization (ISO). Generally, devices built to one standard are compatible with devices built to another. However, in accordance with Murphy's Law, slight but problematic differences can sometimes arise.

A word of caution: Null modems for use with RS-530 will certainly differ from those for RS-232. Users should refer to RS-422 and RS-423 as well as RS-485, a standard that provides guidance for connecting multiple drivers and receivers to the same pair of wires. This standard will be applicable in most null modem designs. —WS

Table 1: RS-232-D signal summary

PIN NO.	CIRCUIT	SIGNAL DESCRIPTION
1	–	SHIELD
2	BA	TRANSMITTED DATA
3	BB	RECEIVED DATA
4	CA	REQUEST TO SEND
5	CB	CLEAR TO SEND
6	CC	DCE READY
7	AB	SIGNAL GROUND
8	CF	RECEIVED LINE SIGNAL DETECTOR
9	–	RESERVED FOR TESTING
10	–	RESERVED FOR TESTING
11	–	UNASSIGNED
12	SCF/CI	SECONDARY RECEIVED LINE SIGNAL DETECTOR/DATA SIGNAL RATE SELECT (DCE SOURCE)
13	SCB	SECONDARY CLEAR TO SEND
14	SBA	SECONDARY TRANSMITTED DATA
15	DB	TRANSMITTER SIGNAL ELEMENT TIMING (DCE SOURCE)
16	SBB	SECONDARY RECEIVED DATA
17	DD	RECEIVER SIGNAL ELEMENT TIMING (DCE SOURCE)
18	LL	LOCAL LOOPBACK
19	SCA	SECONDARY REQUEST TO SEND
20	CD	DTE READY
21	RL/CG	REMOTE LOOPBACK/SIGNAL QUALITY DETECTOR
22	CE	RING INDICATOR
23	CH/CI	DATA SIGNAL RATE SELECT (DTE/DCE SOURCE)
24	DA	TRANSMIT SIGNAL ELEMENT TIMING (DTE SOURCE)
25	TM	TEST MODE

Table 2: RS-530 signal summary

PIN NO.	CIRCUIT	SIGNAL DESCRIPTION
1	–	SHIELD
2	BA	TRANSMITTED DATA
3	BB	RECEIVED DATA
4	CA	REQUEST TO SEND
5	CB	CLEAR TO SEND
6	CC	DCE READY
7	AB	SIGNAL GROUND
8	CF	RECEIVED LINE SIGNAL DETECTOR
9	DD	RECEIVER SIGNAL ELEMENT TIMING (DCE SOURCE)
10	CF	RECEIVED LINE SIGNAL DETECTOR
11	DA	TRANSMIT SIGNAL ELEMENT TIMING (DTE SOURCE)
12	DB	TRANSMIT SIGNAL ELEMENT TIMING (DCE SOURCE)
13	CB	CLEAR TO SEND
14	BA	TRANSMITTED DATA
15	DB	TRANSMITTER SIGNAL ELEMENT TIMING (DCE SOURCE)
16	BB	RECEIVED DATA
17	DD	RECEIVER SIGNAL ELEMENT TIMING (DCE SOURCE)
18	LL	LOCAL LOOPBACK
19	CA	REQUEST TO SEND
20	CD	DTE READY
21	RL	REMOTE LOOPBACK
22	CC	DCE READY
23	CD	DTE READY
24	DA	TRANSMIT SIGNAL ELEMENT TIMING (DTE SOURCE)
25	TM	TEST MODE

1. Asynchronous. One possible asynchronous null modem cable crosses the Data leads, passes the Shield and Ground leads through, and jumpers several other leads, an arrangement that allows the DTEs to present signals to themselves that they think are coming from the remote DTE and thus save on the number of wires used.

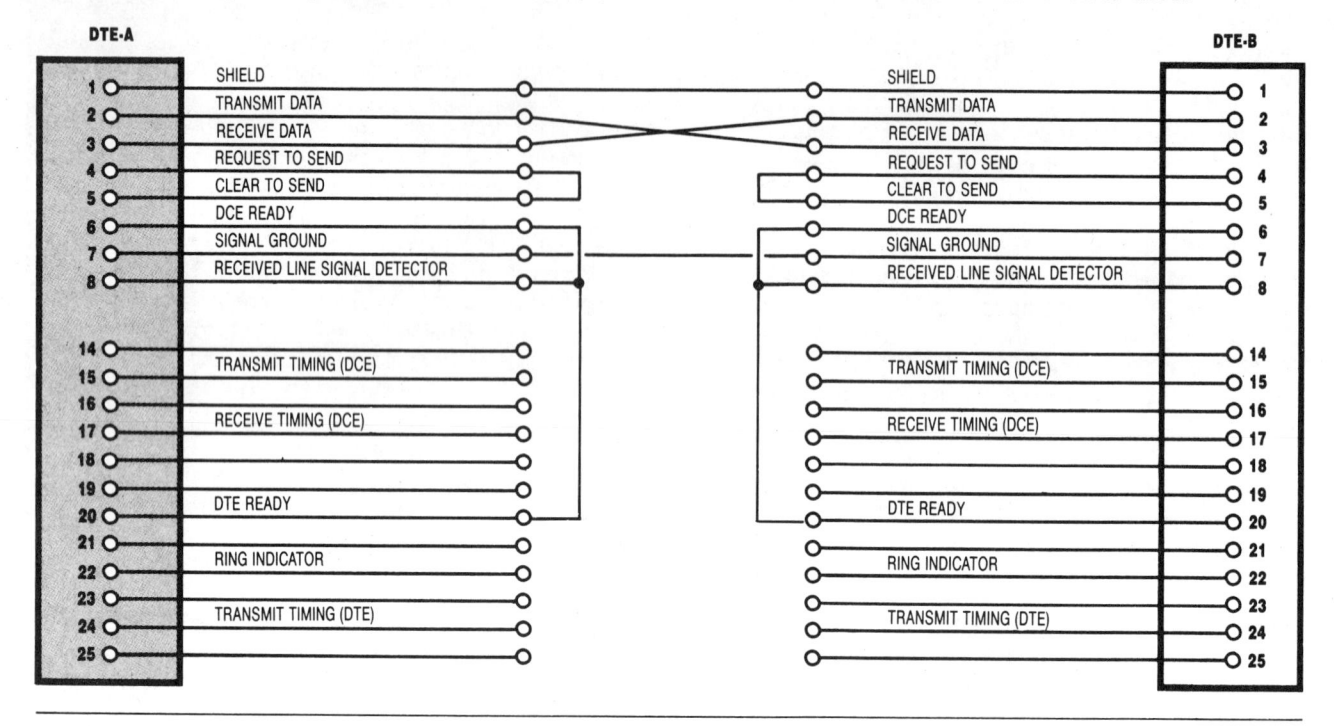

2. Synchronous. This case differs from asynchronous in that certain control leads must be run across the cable while timing leads are hooked to an external source. As before, the transmit and receive data leads are crossed, the shield and ground pass through, and the Clear and Request To Send leads are jumpered at the connector.

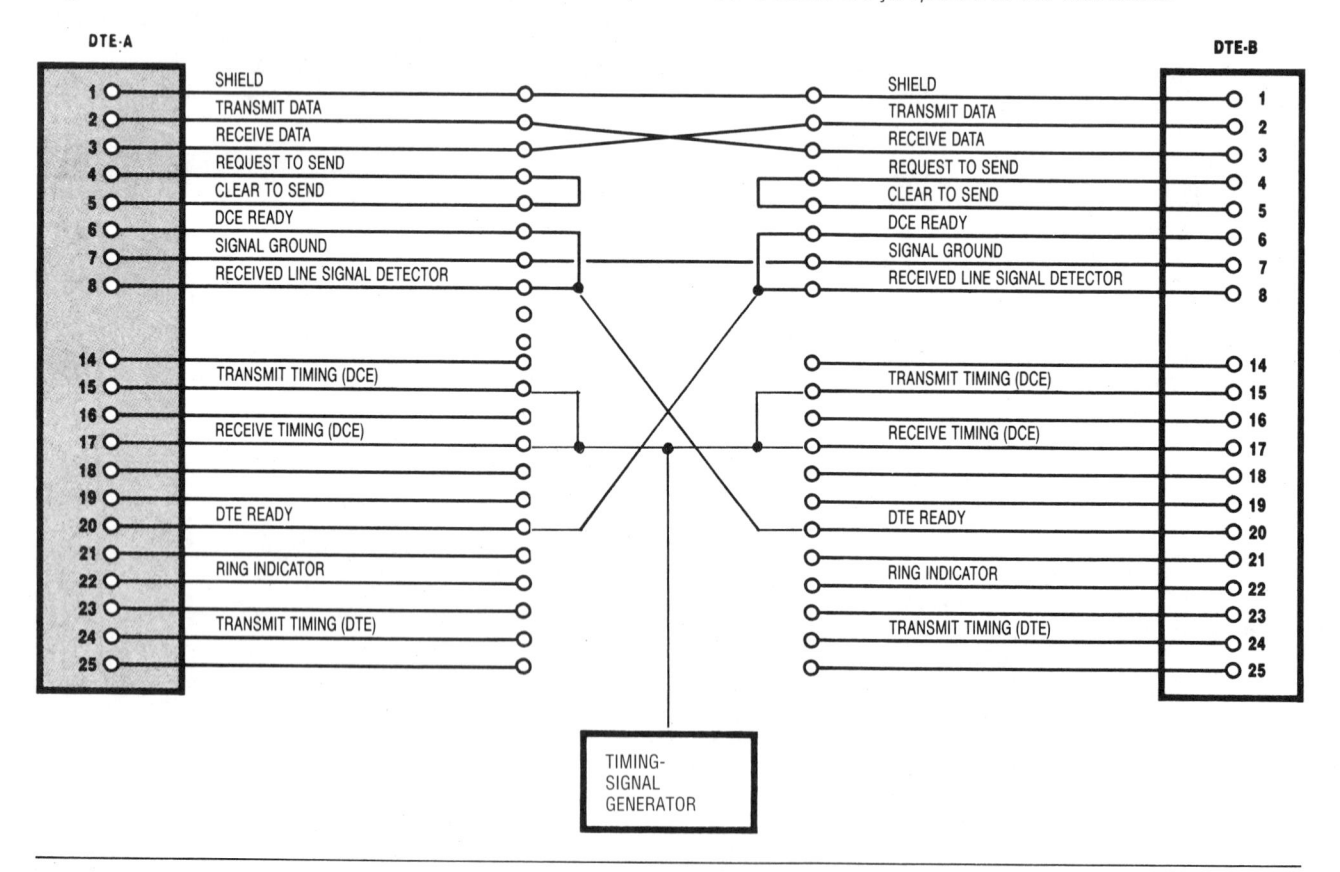

3. Tick, tock. *This figure shows the timing relationship between the clock signals and the data passing over a synchronous communications interface. The bits begin when the clocks go positive, as from 12 to 12 volts, and are sampled at their midpoint when the clock signal goes from positive to negative.*

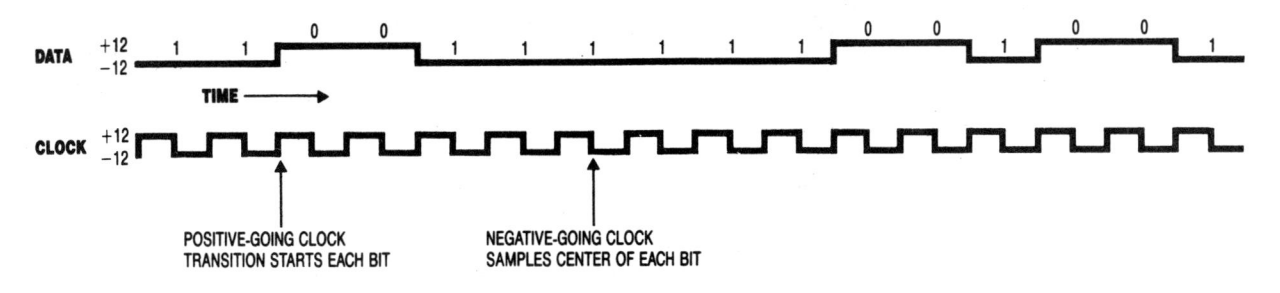

POSITIVE-GOING CLOCK TRANSITION STARTS EACH BIT

NEGATIVE-GOING CLOCK SAMPLES CENTER OF EACH BIT

counterpart modem-originated signals, Clear To Send (pin 5) and DCE Ready (pin 6).

Received Line Signal Detect (pin 8, formerly Carrier Detect) is also jumpered to DTE Ready at both ends because the DTE is usually informed when the modem is ready and an end-to-end connection is in place. When a DTE turns on Request To Send and DTE Ready, this arrangement makes that DTE think it is connected to a modem that is ready to send or receive data, even though the other DTE may not be connected.

Synchronous null modems
Synchronous terminals need clock signals for the timing of data transmission and reception, adding another degree of complexity to the interface. In a null modem connecting synchronous terminals, all clock signals must be supplied from an external timing-signal generator (Fig. 2). Most synchronous terminals require that an external source (usually a modem) supply clock signals on pins 15, Transmitter Signal Element Timing (DCE source), and 17, Receiver Signal Element Timing (DCE source). Pin 15 normally is driven by an oscillator in the modem, which tells the DTE when to transmit the next bit. Pin 17, which tells the DTE to look for a new data bit on the Receive Data line, is kept in harmony with the remote modem by being adjusted on the basis of the incoming signal. Unlike in the asynchronous null modem cable, DTE Ready is here transposed with DCE Ready and Receive Line Signal Detect and run across the cable. This is because synchronous DTEs must know that the DTE on the other end is up and running before attempting to exchange data.

Moreover, it is extremely important that the clock signal used as the Transmit Timing for DTE A also be used as the Receive Timing for DTE B and vice versa, otherwise numerous garbled transmissions can be expected. As shown in Figure 3, each bit is started when the clock signal changes from negative to positive. Since each bit lasts a full clock cycle, the clock transition from positive to negative can be used to sample the center of each bit in the data stream.

In cases where one or both DTEs supply transmit clock, an external source is not required, but the Transmit Clock signal (pin 24) of a DTE supplying clock must be connected to the Receive Clock (pin 17) of the other DTE. Such terminals are rarely encountered.

One of the most important signals on the interface is ground, especially for applications involving synchronous transmission. The result of careless ground connections can be numerous transmission errors or, in some cases, the inability to communicate at all. Two separate wires were specified by RS-232-C, Protective Ground (pin 1) and Signal Ground (pin 7). Protective Ground was replaced in RS-232-D by the Shield lead, which specifies that pin 1 be a common connection point for the shield of a shielded cable used to suppress electromagnetic interference (EMI). The standard recommends that pin 1 not be connected at the DCE but only at the DTE end, so that the shield does not form a circuit that might give off EMI.

The frame of both devices (the DTE and either the DCE or the other DTE) should have a solid grounding connection. Typically, a DTE or DCE gets alternating-current power through a three-wire connector, the third wire being the common Protective Ground. If a three-wire connector is not used, the user should investigate how best to get a proper ground. The Signal Ground is usually connected to Protective Ground internally (RS-232-D specifies connection through a 100-ohm resistor) and is also connected with the remote device's Signal Ground via the interface wire specified for that purpose.

Operation without modems has led to diverse interpretations of the RS-232 standard. Some asynchronous terminals (especially printers) use one of the control signals, either Request To Send, Clear To Send, or DTE Ready, for flow control. This allows the terminal to tell the other DTE, typically a computer, that it is or is not ready to receive data. It is not unusual to connect the DTE Ready and DCE Ready signals at one DTE while leaving them unconnected at the other DTE.

Some terminals require Received Line Signal Detect, while Ring Indicator, used for automatic answering of phone lines, is inappropriate for a null modem. To reduce cost, some DTEs are designed to use less than the full complement of RS-232 interface signal wires. In such cases, the DTE may require jumper wires or specific switch settings. ∎

William Sheridan entered the computer field in 1955 at the Eckert-Mauchly Computer Corporation (now Burroughs/Sperry Univac), where he worked while attending Pennsylvania State University. He received training in electronics in the U. S. Army during the Korean War, a B. A. in math from Penn State, and an M. S. E. E. from the University of Pennsylvania. Since then, he has worked as a logic design and software engineer and in various management positions. He is currently an independent consultant.

Gilbert Held, 4-Degree Consulting, Macon, Ga.

Making the most of the versatile breakout box

Handy and economical tools for troubleshooting all kinds of data communications problems, active and passive breakout boxes can prevent finger pointing when networks fail.

A portable, hand-held tester used primarily to examine the condition of the conductors at the physical-interface level, the simple breakout box, in the right hands, can be one of the most powerful tools available for testing and troubleshooting communications.

There are many types of breakout boxes, ranging from simple monitoring devices to units that permit the operator to readily change the state of leads, patching one conductor to another. Most breakout boxes are designed for use on RS-232-C interfaces, while some work with wideband V.35 interfaces or Centronics parallel printer interfaces. The discussion here focuses on devices designed for use on the ubiquitous RS-232-C interface, although general descriptions contained in this article, without reference to specific RS-232-C conductors, are also appropriate to breakout boxes designed for use on other types of physical interfaces.

The breakout box was originally designed to provide a visual indication of the state of the conductors at the physical interface. This examination can be between data terminal equipment (DTE) and data communications equipment (DCE), between two DTEs, or between two DCEs. The simplest type of breakout box is passive, providing a number of light-emitting diodes (LEDs), which are lit or not, depending on the voltage level on a particular conductor.

One end of a breakout box normally contains a "male" plug DB 25-P connector, while the opposite end of the breakout box contains a "female" socket DB 25-S connector. In the RS-232-C standard, DTEs and DCEs are supposed to have female DB 25-S connectors, while the cable connecting DTE to DCE has male DB 25-P connectors on each end.

In most situations, the breakout box can be easily inserted into either end of the cable connection between DTE and DCE (Fig. 1). The top portion of the figure shows the standard cabling of a DTE to a DCE; the bottom shows how the breakout box can be inserted between one of the devices and the cable. In actuality, the breakout box can be inserted between the DTE and a cable connector, between the DCE and a cable connector, or right between DTE and DCE. To allow insertion directly between devices, many breakout box manufacturers have incorporated two ribbon cables to tie the separate device connectors to each end of the test unit.

Some of the more expensive breakout boxes have dual-gender connectors attached to each end of the ribbon cable connected to the device. These ensure that the technician using the breakout box will always be able to insert it into a network segment, regardless of the type of cable end or device connectors encountered.

Passive breakouts
Basically, passive breakout boxes (Fig. 2) provide the user with the ability to monitor either all or a subset of the conductors at the physical interface. Some lower-cost units allow the user to monitor only pins 2, 3, 4, 5, 6, 8, and 20—the key data and control leads used with most asynchronous transmission applications. Others include two rows of interface-circuit probe points and an additional LED display labeled TEST, with a patch point wired to the TEST LED. This creates a spare LED.

A typical passive breakout box will monitor eight interface leads at one time; the TEST LED is used to provide the operator with the ability to monitor any other lead. This is an economical design, since LEDs normally cost more than probe points. Also, by reducing the number of LEDs, both the size and the complexity of the breakout box are reduced. Typical retail cost for such devices ranges between $75 and $100.

1. Using the box. *Breakout boxes can be installed between a DTE and a DCE, between two DCEs, or between a cable and either a DCE or DTE.*

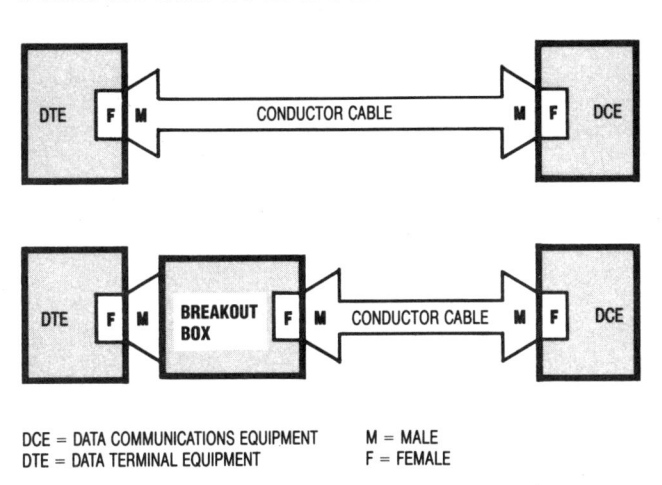

[Diagram: DTE—F M—CONDUCTOR CABLE—M F—DCE]

[Diagram: DTE—F M—BREAKOUT BOX—F M—CONDUCTOR CABLE—M F—DCE]

DCE = DATA COMMUNICATIONS EQUIPMENT M = MALE
DTE = DATA TERMINAL EQUIPMENT F = FEMALE

When a single row of unicolor LEDs are included in the breakout box, the device is considered a "single-state monitor," a definition that is derived from the RS-232-C standard for data and control signals. In the RS-232-C specification, a positive voltage at or greater than +3, and less than or equal to +15, is defined as a "logic 0" or "space." A negative voltage at or less than -3, but not less than -15, is defined as a "logic 1" or "mark." Here, voltages between the logic 0 and logic 1 delimiters are considered a transitory state.

When only one set of LEDs is used in a breakout box, the LEDs normally light up in response to a positive voltage, denoting a logic 0 or signal space. The absence of illumination on the LED can indicate either a negative voltage or a transitory voltage. Thus, only when the LED is illuminated can the breakout box user be assured of the state of the conductor's signal.

In comparison to single-state breakout boxes, the use of a second row of LEDs changes the device into a "tri-state" unit. This type of breakout box normally uses red and green rows of LEDs, with a pair of LEDs assigned to each conductor to be monitored. Generally, breakout boxes are designed to illuminate red LEDs when a positive voltage is present and green LEDs when a negative voltage level occurs. Thus, if neither LED is lit, the monitored conductor is in a transitory (no-voltage) condition.

As an alternative to the use of dual rows of green and red LEDs, some breakout boxes employ a single row of LEDs that can be illuminated in either color. While this type of device is functionally equivalent to a breakout box that uses two separate rows of LEDs, it does permit color-blind people to use the device.

Still other breakout boxes are constructed with dual pairs of red and green LEDs. One pair of LEDs is used on the DCE side of the interface; the second pair is used to represent leads on the DTE side of the interface.

Since a passive breakout box can only monitor the condition or state of interface conductors, its role is limited to the examination and verification of control signal conditions. As an example of a possible use of this device, consider a dial-in modem connected to a computer port.

Suppose users complained that the only response to dialing the switched telephone network number of the line connected to the modem was constant ringing—the classic "ring no answer" (RNA) communications problem. By inserting a passive breakout box between the modem and the computer port, the operator of the breakout box can usually determine the culprit initiating the RNA.

Port diagnosis
Prior to receiving a call, the computer port will normally have pin 20 (Data Terminal Ready, or DTR) "raised," or in the ON condition. If this condition is not observed, the chances are very high that the computer port is the RNA culprit. Potential solutions to the problem range from removing and reinserting the board on which the computer port is located (known as reseeding), replacing the board with a spare, or checking the computer's communications software.

The next step in this observation process is to determine if the modem has conductor 6 (Data Set Ready, or DSR) in the ON condition. If not, the modem will not pass the RI (Ring Indicator) signal to the computer port when an incoming call arrives, thus causing the RNA predicament.

The breakout box user may then arrange for an associate to dial the modem while the tester observes the control signals. The absence of pin 6 or pin 22 (RI) being ON means that the modem is probably causing the RNA condition. Possible solutions to this problem can range again from the reseeding of a board in the modem, refas-

2. Passive box. *With a mini patch cord, the status of any conductor can be displayed on the TEST LED. Here, the Ring Indicator (pin 21) lead status will be displayed.*

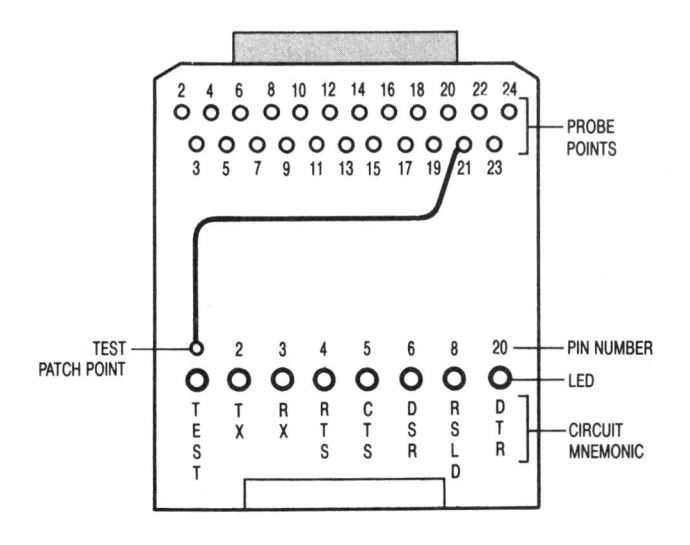

[Diagram of breakout box showing probe points numbered 2-24 (even) and 3-23 (odd), with TEST PATCH POINT connected to pin 21, and LEDs labeled TEST, TX, RX, RTS, CTS, DSR, RSLD, DTR for pins 2, 3, 4, 5, 6, 8, 20]

TX = TRANSMIT   DSR = DATA SET READY
RX = RECEIVE   RSLD = RECEIVE SIGNAL LINE DETECT
RTS = REQUEST TO SEND   DTR = DATA TERMINAL READY
CTS = CLEAR TO SEND   LED = LIGHT-EMITTING DIODE

173

tening connectors, or replacing either a modem board or the whole modem.

If both the DSR and RI signals are high (register a positive voltage), then the computer port is not correctly responding to the modem. This indicates that the computer port, and possibly also the communications software, need to be examined. In many instances, the deactivation of one or a group of lines by the computer console operator, through either a standard operating procedure or testing, may not have been followed by an appropriate command to place the line back into service. In such situations, a request to the computer operators to reactivate line "XXX" should cause the DTR signal to reappear and return the connection to normal.

Active breakouts
In comparison to a passive breakout box, an active breakout box contains patch and cross-connect probe points for both DTE and DCE sides of devices undergoing tests. In addition, an active breakout box contains a set of switches that can be used to break open the data and control lines of the physical interface. These devices are also commonly called breakout switches.

Some active breakout boxes are battery-powered, while other devices are powered from the line they are monitoring. At the high end of this product category, several breakout boxes include positive- and negative-voltage sources that can be used with jumpers or mini patch cords to simulate control signals. These normally sell for between $275 and $350.

In a typical high-end, active breakout box, the positive- and negative-voltage sources are included so an operator can simulate any of the RS-232-C conductor signals he or she may require. This control-signal simulation is accomplished by the operator first patching one end of a jumper wire (supplied with the breakout box) to the appropriate voltage source.

The operator can then connect the opposite end of the jumper wire to one of the 50 probe points on the device, each of which is associated with a simulated conductor signal on the DTE or DCE side of the breakout box.

As an example of the use of the voltage sources and probe points, consider an operator who wants to observe the reaction of a device to the presence of a RI signal but does not have a dial-network circuit available in which to place an actual test call. By connecting the active breakout box to the RS-232-C port on the device and then patching a jumper wire from the positive voltage source to the probe point associated with pin 22 (RI), the operator can simulate the occurrence of that signal. Then, by observing the other LEDs, the operator can note the response of the device to an RI signal.

Probe points
The two rows of 25 probe points on a typical active breakout box can be used for patching and simulating RS-232-C data and control signals at either side of the device. This all-inclusive patching capability permits the operator to use a jumper wire to connect any signal or data conductor on one side of the device to any other signal or data conductor on the same side or the opposite side of the device. To understand the value of using probe points, consider an operator that is working with a ring-start communications device, such as a port on a port selector.

If the operator desires to connect a terminal directly to the port selector, no RI signal will occur (since the connection bypasses the switched telephone network). In this situation, the technician would examine other control signals activated by the terminal and determine the effect of jumping one of the terminal control signals to the RI signal.

By using the probe points, the technician could, for example, first cable the active breakout box to a port on the port selector. One jumper wire could be used to patch a positive voltage to the DTR probe point, thus simulating that control signal without actually cabling the terminal to the port selector port. Next, the technician could jumper the DTR probe point to the RI probe point, in effect forcing the RI signal to become active whenever a DTR signal is present.

If the operator then notices the flashing of an LED on either pin 2 or pin 3, this would indicate that the port selector is activated by forcing the RI signal high. It would then begin to transmit a sign-on message to a nonexistant terminal simulated by the use of the active breakout box. The LED may flash either on pin 2 or pin 3 because the port on the port selector may be configured as either a DTE or a DCE. If it is configured as a DTE, data will be transmitted on pin 2, whereas if the port is configured as a DCE, data will be transmitted on pin 3.

Once the required jumpering is noted, the operator can use the information to fabricate an appropriate cable. For the previous example, pin 20 (DTR) would be jumpered to pin 22 (RI) in a cable to ensure that each time a directly connected terminal was turned on, the port selected would receive the required RI signal.

Connectors and switches
The dual-gender connectors that come with the cables attached to an active breakout box ensure that the device can be connected to any standard RS-232-C connector, without requiring the operator to search for an adapter. To understand the utility of dual-gender connectors, consider the RS-232-C cabling standard. In this standard, DTEs and DCEs are supposed to be built with female socket connectors, while cables connecting the devices are supposed to have male connectors on each end, allowing such cables to be fastened to both devices.

However, in reality, DTEs and DCEs may not conform to the connector standard, and the resulting cable used to connect the two devices (a DTE to a DTE or DCE) will likewise deviate from the standard. With the inclusion of dual-gender connectors, breakout box operators do not need cable adapters or "gender-mender" devices.

The 25 breakout switches on an active breakout box can be used to break open data and control lines when the left side of each switch is pushed down. When examining the operations of two devices, the breakout switches are useful for enabling and disabling data and control signals. By using these switches, a technician can easily examine the effect of changes in control signals of one device on another, without requiring that the devices be operating.

Consider the previous example where a terminal is directly connected to the port of a port selector. To find out if the port selector interprets a drop of the DTR signal as a disconnect request, the operator could simply flip the DTR breakout switch to drop that control signal. Then, by either examining the port selector console or the port interface on the port selector, the operator will be able to determine if the absence of DTR causes the port selector to disconnect the terminal.

On the port interface, a technician will first note some activity on either pin 2 or pin 3 (again, depending on whether the port is configured as a DTE or DCE). This is evident because the green LED associated with that pin will light up. This occurs because, according to the RS-232-C standard, a transmitter will always be at a negative voltage when not transmitting.

The pin-reversal switch enables the operator to easily reverse pins 2 and 3 in an RS-232-C test application, such as when connecting two DTEs or two DCEs together. Some breakout boxes, however, require an operator to use two jumper wires to patch the probe points of pin 2 to pin 3 and pin 3 to pin 2.

Active vs. passive

The patching and control-signal simulations of active breakout boxes enable them to be used in a variety of situations where a passive device may be of little or no use. Consider the versatility of the active breakout box in several typical communications scenarios.

■ Suppose a communications port on a microcomputer is directly cabled, through a conduit, to a port on a protocol converter located in a computer room. After the microcomputer loads its communications program and enters its terminal emulation mode, it turns out that data entered from the keyboard fails to be displayed on the microcomputer's monitor. Since there is a possibility that (1) the communications cable was crimped when snaked through the conduit, (2) the software was configured incorrectly, or (3) the protocol converter was not operating correctly, problem elimination should be used to isolate the impairment. By using an active breakout box, in this case as a loopback plug (taking a signal received and looping it back), the technician obtains a mechanism for physically checking the cable.

Figure 3 illustrates the use of an active breakout box as a loopback plug. By inserting the device between the cable and the protocol converter port, it can be used to check the continuity of conductors in the cable by using breakout switches with jumpers or mini patch cords.

In the example, Transmit Data (TD) is patched to Receive Data (RD), Request to Send (RTS) is patched to Clear to Send (CTS) and DTR is patched to both DSR and Data Carrier Detect (DCD). The switches on the breakout box for each of the circuits are placed in the open position, thereby disabling any signals emanating from the port on the protocol converter.

3. Loopback plug. *Looping back signals can be accomplished through an active breakout box. This allows testing of both transmitting devices and cables*

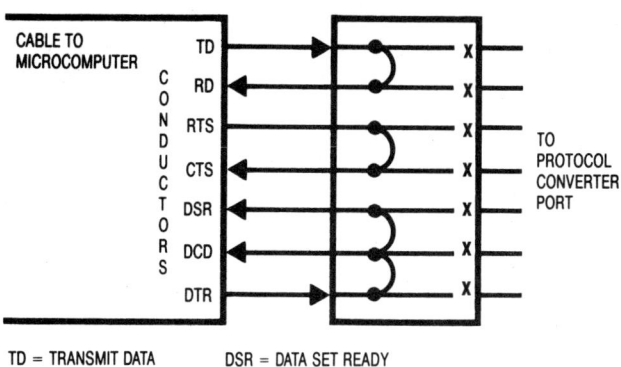

TD = TRANSMIT DATA
RD = RECEIVE DATA
RTS = REQUEST TO SEND
CTS = CLEAR TO SEND
DSR = DATA SET READY
DCD = DATA CARRIER DETECT
DTR = DATA TERMINAL READY
X = INDICATES A BREAKOUT SWITCH IN OPEN POSITION

Although the breakout box will only confirm whether or not the microcomputer is functioning as a terminal, the breakout box could also be connected directly to the computer's communications port. If characters are echoed back to the computer's display when the breakout box is connected to the computer's communications port, while no characters are echoed back when the device is inserted between the cable and the protocol converter port, then the technician can safely assume that the cable is defective.

■ With interface modification, an active breakout box probably finds its primary use. By using its patching capability, technical control center personnel can determine special cabling requirements that may be necessary to make devices with incompatible control signals compatible.

Consider the direct connection of a terminal device to a port selector that operates as a ring-start device. This means that the port selector must receive a signal on pin 22 (RI) in order to be placed in operation. Since a directly cabled terminal does not provide an RI signal, the technician could insert an active breakout box between the cable and the port selector port connector, then, through the use of jumpers or mini patch cords, attempt to derive the required signals prior to fabricating a cable. In this situation, one possible solution might be to jumper or patch DTR to RI. Then, when the terminal is turned on and DTR becomes high, it forces RI high, activating the port selector.

■ Another common data communications problem is determining whether an interface device operates as DTE or DCE. While the original RS-232-C standard was developed to govern the serial data interchange between DTE and DCE equipment, it is now quite common to have DTEs connected to DTEs and DCEs connected to DCEs. In such situations, technicians must first determine the "personality" of each device to be connected (whether DTE or DCE) and the conductor flow requirements, and then fabricate the appropriate cable to permit the incompatible devices to communicate.

4. Null modem. *By using the breakout box, users can easily determine what kind of conductor cabling will be required to make a null modem.*

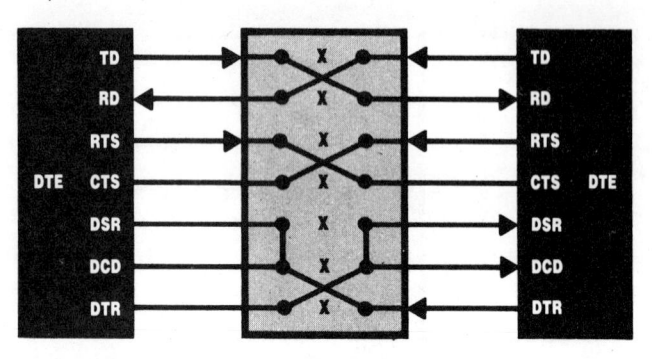

TD = TRANSMIT DATA
RD = RECEIVE DATA
RTS = REQUEST TO SEND
CTS = CLEAR TO SEND
DSR = DATA SET READY
DCD = DATA CARRIER DETECT
DTR = DATA TERMINAL READY
DTE = DATA TERMINAL EQUIPMENT
X = INDICATES A BREAKOUT SWITCH IN OPEN POSITION

In the example where a microcomputer is cabled to a protocol converter, another incompatibility problem can arise if the protocol converter port is configured as a DTE device. To verify this, the technician can connect a breakout box to the port of the protocol converter. Since the RS-232-C standard specifies that a transmitter will always be at a logic 1 (negative voltage) when not transmitting, the green LED associated with pin 3 on a three-state breakout box will light up if the protocol converter port is configured as a DCE. If the protocol converter port is configured as a DTE, then the green LED on pin 2 will be illuminated.

Since some protocol converters can be programmed through a configuration port, it might be possible to simply change the port to a DCE port in order to achieve compatibility with the microcomputer operating as a DTE. If this is not possible, then the technician must determine the appropriate control signals and data path connections required to develop a null modem cable to connect one DTE to another. This can be accomplished by either examining the manuals of the protocol converter and the microcomputer's asynchronous communications adapter to determine their control signal requirements or by using a breakout box to determine the required control signals.

The technician can connect the breakout box to the protocol converter port to observe its control signal outputs. This is accomplished by noting which red LEDs are lit. (At rest, they generate a positive voltage.) Next, the technician can verify the control signal inputs to the protocol converter port by first patching pins 2 to 3 and 3 to 2, which connects the transmit-data and receive-data conductors of the microcomputer to the appropriate transmit and receive conductors on the protocol converter port. This procedure is called for because it was previously determined that the protocol converter port is configured as a DTE and because conductors 2 and 3 must be reversed for two DTEs to operate.

Once pins 2 and 3 are reversed, the technician can apply a negative voltage (control-off) to each potential input and note the results. This is accomplished by placing one end of a mini patch cord into the negative voltage source on the breakout box and the opposite end of the patch cord to each potential input source.

If the protocol converter port stops operating when a negative voltage is applied on a conductor, a working control input has been located. The control inputs on the microcomputer's asynchronous communications adapter can be similarly determined to develop a DTE-to-DCE wiring chart. This can then be used by the technician to verify null modem conductor assignments. Figure 4 illustrates the use of an active breakout box, configured as a modem eliminator cable, to verify the conductor arrangement prior to fabricating the required cable.

Cable verification

Pin connections of a cable can also be examined by using an active breakout box. If cable has not been installed, each end of new cable can be connected to the breakout box, and the operator can apply either a positive or negative voltage to each of the conductor probe points on one side of the breakout box and examine the LEDs on the other side. Open conditions (broken connections) and continuity of conductors (where voltages flow evenly end-to-end) can then be noted.

To illustrate the use of an active breakout box to perform cable testing, assume one end of a mini patch cord is connected to a voltage-source probe point. If the operator patches the other end of the cord to pin 2 and the LED associated with pin 3 on the other side of the device lights up, this indicates that pins 2 and 3 are reversed. Similarly, if the operator patches the other end of the cord to pin 20 and pins 6 and 8 light up on the other side of the breakout box, this indicates that DTR is tied to DSR and DCD.

If a cable is already in place, it is usually too difficult to remove for testing. In such situations, an active breakout box can be placed at one end of the cable and a passive breakout box placed at the other end. A positive or negative voltage can be patched to each conductor probe, with results noted at the end of each cable.

As indicated, the breakout box is a very useful and practical piece of network diagnostic hardware. Because of its low cost and high usefulness in testing and troubleshooting, it is quite common for technicians to carry one around in the way that engineers used to wear slide rules. And since other types of communications test equipment— line monitors and protocol analyzers—are now being manufactured with built-in breakout boxes, this added functionality can be viewed as a testament to the versatility of the handy, standalone breakout box. ■

Gilbert Held, director of 4-Degree Consulting, is an internationally recognized author and lecturer on data communications subjects. Twice a recipient of the Interface Karp Award and a winner of the American Association of Publishers Award, Held is the author of 15 books and more than 60 technical articles. He also conducts seminars on data communications testing, troubleshooting, and capacity planning.

Jack Douglass, Universal Data Systems, Huntsville, Ala.

How to find phone-line faults and what to do about them

When reporting phone-line problems, it helps if you speak telephonese. Here's a guide to recognizing and pinpointing many common problems.

Phone line problems waste time and money. For data communications users, transmission anomalies appear as flawed data. If the data is asynchronous and there is no form of error correction—either within the modem or as a function of the user's software—the errors will appear directly on the user's screen and may readily be identified as such. With numerical data, where the correct character cannot be inferred from the errored result, the entire file will need to be retransmitted.

If error correction is used, it happens in several ways:
- If the data is asynchronous and an error-correcting protocol is used, the errors are automatically corrected when the modem detects the error and retransmits that portion of the file.
- If error correction is part of the communications software, the computer retransmits the errored portions of the file before the data reaches the modem.
- If the data is synchronous the communications protocol usually handles the error correction by automatically retransmitting the errored blocks of data.

In all three cases, data retransmissions result in greater connect time, increased long-distance charges, and increased computer charges if the user is connected to an information service. If data transmission is a large part of the user's operations, the cost of retransmissions due to bad connections can be hundreds of dollars per year.

Fortunately, transmission errors can usually be significantly reduced by getting the telephone company to correct the line problems. But resolving problems with the local telephone company can be difficult and frustrating. This is because many modem users have a limited knowledge of the types of impairments that affect a modem's performance, and the phone company only performs a limited test on the line when a complaint is called in. The phone company does not perform complete line impairment because many people mistakenly call the phone company with complaints when the problem is with the user's equipment and not with the phone line.

Since the divestiture, this problem has grown worse. In some cases, the local telephone companies lack the money or personnel to resolve the problem. Of course, problems with private leased lines are usually easier to resolve than those with the public switched telephone network (PSTN) lines because private lines have a controlled transmission path from customer premises to customer premises.

In general, there are nine different types of natural or man-made line impairments that affect the performance of the modem and cause it to have a higher error rate.

1. Noise. This impairment is inherent to the line design or induced by transient energy bursts. There are several types of noise: (1) Gaussian noise (Fig. 1A), also called white, thermal, or shot noise, is the background hiss that can be heard on a telephone line. It is the result of many independent current or voltage pulses such as the random motion of electrons. (2) Impulse noise hits (Fig. 1B) are high bursts of energy with durations from a few milliseconds to hundreds of milliseconds. It is caused by electrical storms, switching and signaling equipment, power sources, and other electrical systems. (3) Cross talk noise (Fig. 1C) is caused by the signal on one pair of wires interfering with an adjacent wire pair. (4) Ground-loop or common-mode noise (Fig. 1D) is caused by potential differences of external noise sources such as those that occur between two different grounds. (5) Quantizing noise (Fig. 1E) is a result of the difference between the signal presented to a coder/decoder (codec) and its equivalent quantized value. Codecs are used to convert analog signals to digital signals for transmission over high-speed digital data links.

Codecs are typically used on T1-carrier links. Currently,

most codecs operate at 64 kbit/s. Some lower-cost telephone services use 32-kbit/s adaptive delta pulse code modulation (ADPCM) codecs to allow twice as many telephone calls as the 64-kbit/s codecs through the same T1 carrier. However, 32-kbit/s codecs cause more quantizing noise. Therefore, modems over 2.4 kbit/s will have a higher error rate when operated through 32-kbit/s ADPCM codecs. (6) Signal reflections and standing waves (Fig. 1F) are noises caused by local impedance mismatching, which causes the signal to be reflected back to the originating device. The delay of these signal reflections is usually less than 1millisecond. (7) Echo (Fig. 1G) is noise caused by reflections of the transmitted signal at distant points in the network where the line impedances are dissimilar. Most of these reflections occur in the hybrids that convert the two wires of the local phone lines to the four wires that connect the telephone company central offices.

The delay of the echoes varies from 50 ms (milliseconds) to 100 ms on terrestrial circuits and up to 700 ms on satellite circuits. Older telephone circuits reduce the echoes with echo suppressors (electronic switches). However, newer terrestrial circuits and satellite circuits within the continental United States use echo cancellers (electronic circuits that cancel the echo by adding the inverse of the echo signal to the echo).

2. Attenuation. This impairment is the loss of signal level (Fig. 2) as it passes through the telephone line. Such loss of energy is normally measured in decibels (dB). The equations for dB are:

$$dB = 10 \log (\text{power out/power in})$$
$$dB = 20 \log (\text{voltage out/voltage in})$$

Further, there are several other related terms that the telephone company uses. One is dBm. As defined by the telephone company, dBm is a power-level measurement unit based on a 600-ohm impedance at 1,004 Hz referenced to one milliwatt. In other words, 0 dBm is 1 milliwatt (mW) of power at 1,004 Hz measured with a termination of 600 ohms. The equation for dBm is:

$$dBm = 10 \log (\text{power level/1mW})$$

Another common term is dBrn. With dBrns, signal levels are referenced to -90 dBm. In other words, -90 dBm is equal to 0 dBrn. This unit of power-level measurement permits the phone company to express the negative dBm signals in terms of positive numbers. The phone company usually measures signals with a C-Message filter in front of the meter. Such a filter has a frequency response similar to the hearing response of the human ear. This allows the phone company to relate the signal level to the psychological effect of the signal on a human being. The filter also reduces the strong 60-Hz component that is seen on many phone lines and reduces the measured noise level by about 1.8 dB. Signals that are measured with a C-Message filter are expressed in terms of dBrnc.

The term dBrnC0 is also used by the phone company to express signal levels. DBrnC0 is measured in terms of dBrns, with a C-message filter, and with respect to a reference "Zero Transmission Level Point" called the TLP0.

1. Noise. (A) gaussian: line hiss; (B) impulse: engery bursts; (C) cross talk: signal couplings on adjacent wires; (D) ground loop: currents between different ground potentials;

(A) GAUSSIAN OR WHITE NOISE

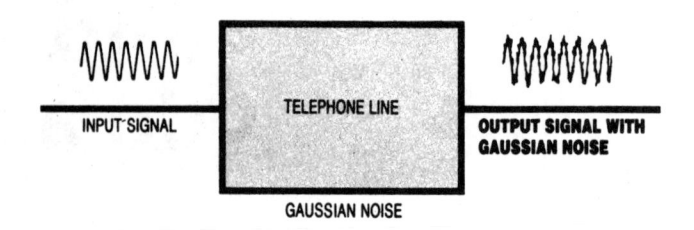

(B) IMPULSE NOISE

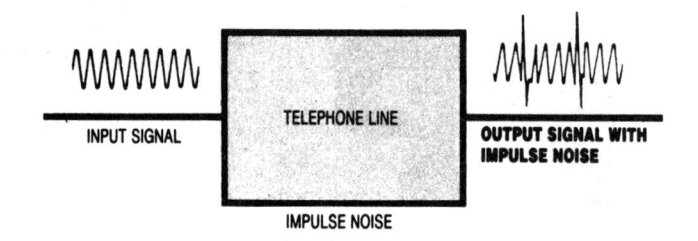

(C) CROSS TALK

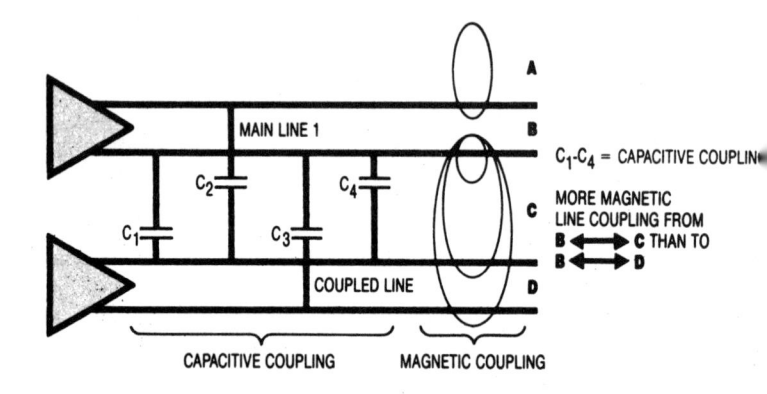

C_1-C_4 = CAPACITIVE COUPLING

MORE MAGNETIC LINE COUPLING FROM
B ↔ C THAN TO
B ↔ D

(D) GROUND LOOP

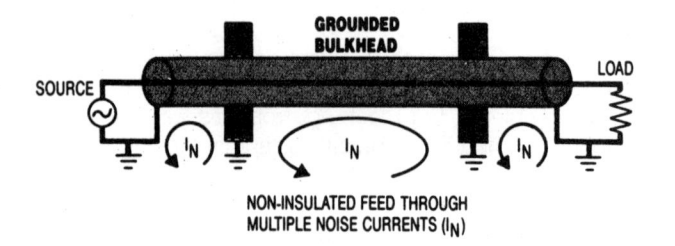

NON-INSULATED FEED THROUGH
MULTIPLE NOISE CURRENTS (I_N)

(E) quantizing: difference between codec output at either end of T1 carrier; (F) signal reflection: impedance mismatching; (G) echo: signal reflections.

(E) QUANTIZING NOISE

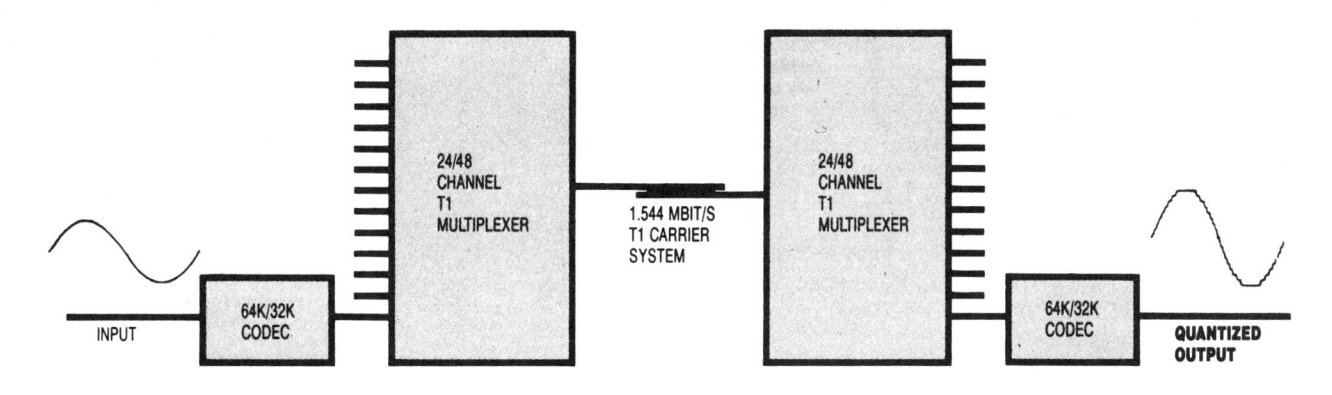

(F) SIGNAL REFLECTION AND STANDING WAVES

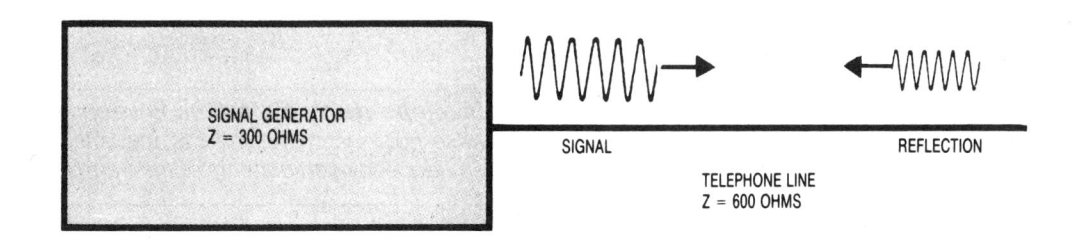

(G) ECHO

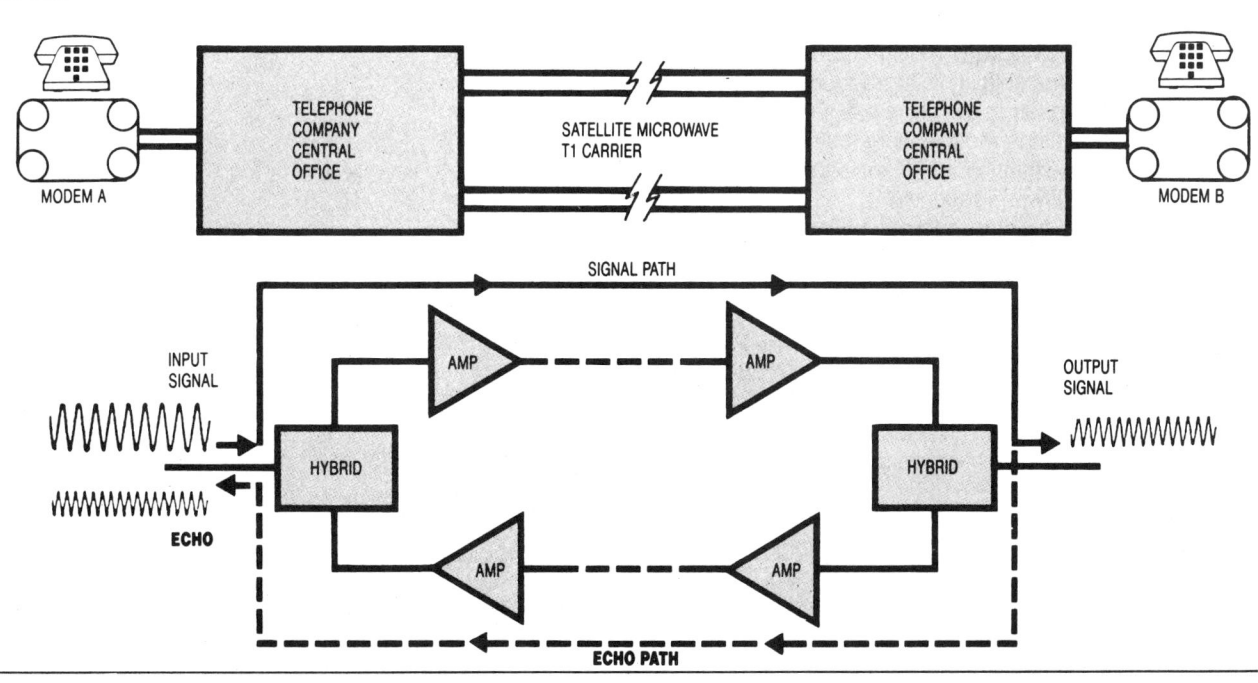

2. Attenuation. Attenuation is loss of signal energy as the signal passes through the telephone line. This is usually seen as a loss in the signal's amplitude.

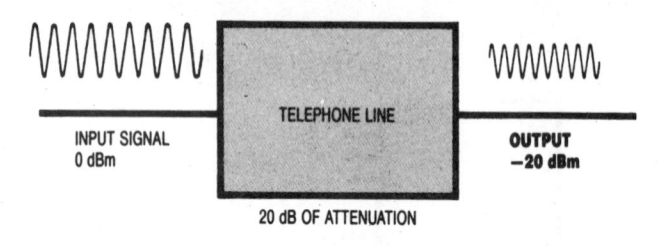

3. Attenuation distortion. Attenuation distortion is the loss of signal energy that affects the relative magnitudes of various frequency components of the transmitted signal.

The TLP0 at the customer premises is usually +3 dB. Therefore, to find dBrncs when dBrnC0s are specified, subtract the TPL0 (3 dB) from the dBrnC0 level (i.e., 71 dBrnC0 is 68 dBrnc).

3. Attenuation distortion. This is the signal-level loss that affects the relative magnitudes of various frequency components of the transmitted signal (Fig. 3). These losses are usually greater at the upper and lower edges of the passband. The causes of this distortion include capacitive and inductive reactances, filters in carrier systems, loaded cables (acting as low-pass filters), transformers, and series capacitors (acting as high-pass filters).

4. Envelope delay distortion. The fourth type of impairment is envelope or group delay distortion (Fig. 4). This is phase nonlinearity where the delay is greater at the edges of the passband. Envelope delay distortion (EDD) affects or upsets the time relationship between various frequency components in a transmitted signal. In other words, low- and high-frequency components of the signal take longer to pass through the network than do freuencies in the center of the passband (1,800 Hz). This delay is produced by inductive and capacitive reactance in the network.

5. Frequency translation. The fifth type of impairment (Fig. 5) consists of the shifting of all frequency components in the modulated signal. These shifts are generally due to oscillator drift or offset in the telephone carrier system. The shift may be positive (shift to a higher frequency) or negative (shift to a lower frequency).

6. Jitter. The sixth type of impairment (Fig. 6) is of two types: phase jitter and amplitude jitter. Phase jitter (Fig. 6A) results in a pure tone having an associated FM spectrum. In some cases this spectrum is random, and in other cases it takes the form of discrete a.c. power frequencies. Phase jitter is caused by coupling from power-line-associated equipment and ringing generators. Amplitude jitter (Fig. 6B) results in a pure tone having amplitude modulation. The causes of amplitude modulation are similar to the causes of phase jitter.

7. Intermodulation distortion. Intermodulation distortion (IMD) is sometimes called nonlinear distortion (Fig. 7). The difference between harmonic distortion and IMD is the method of measure. IMD is measured with four tones, and harmonic distortion is measured with two tones. This type of impairment is caused by nonlinearities such as clipping

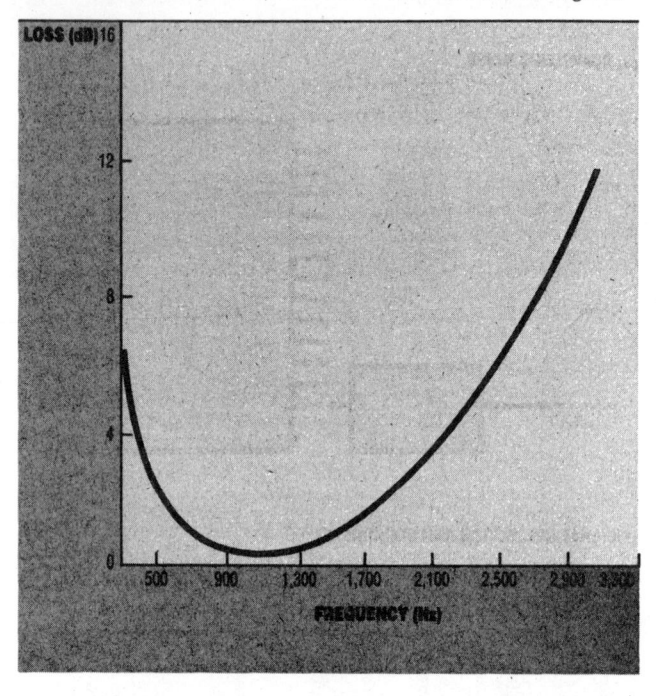

4. Envelope delay distortion. Envelope delay distortion is phase nonlinearity that affects the time relationship between frequency components of the transmitted signal.

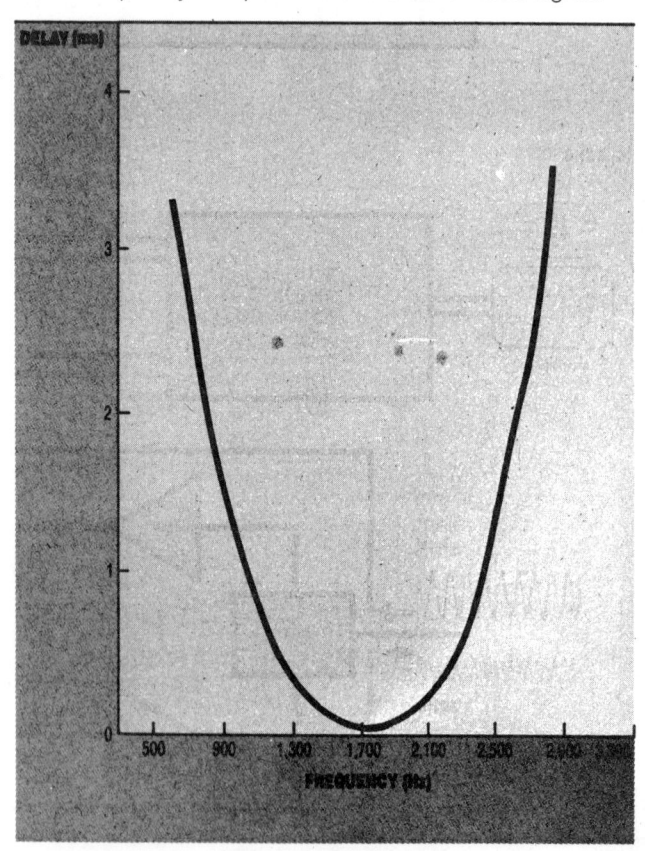

5. Frequency translation. Frequency translation is the shifting of all the components of a frequency to a higher or lower frequency.

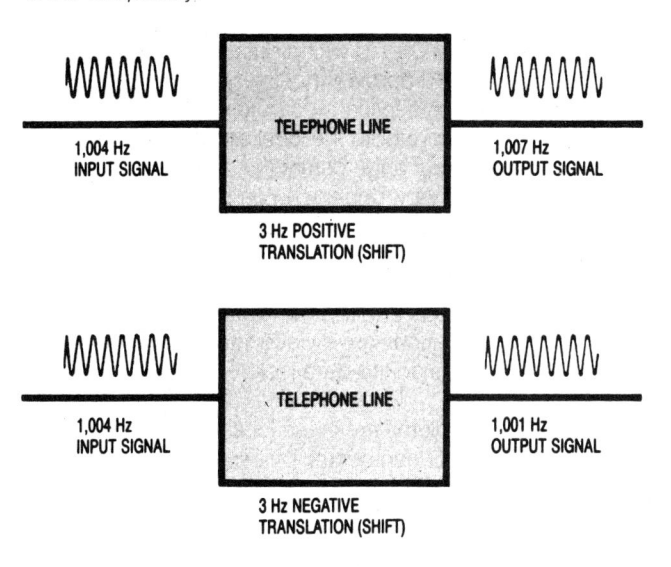

[Figure: 1,004 Hz input signal → Telephone Line → 1,007 Hz output signal. 3 Hz POSITIVE TRANSLATION (SHIFT)]

[Figure: 1,004 Hz input signal → Telephone Line → 1,001 Hz output signal. 3 Hz NEGATIVE TRANSLATION (SHIFT)]

6. Jitter. (A) phase jitter is the result of a pure tone having an associated FM spectrum; (B) amplitude jitter is the result of a pure tone having amplitude modulation.

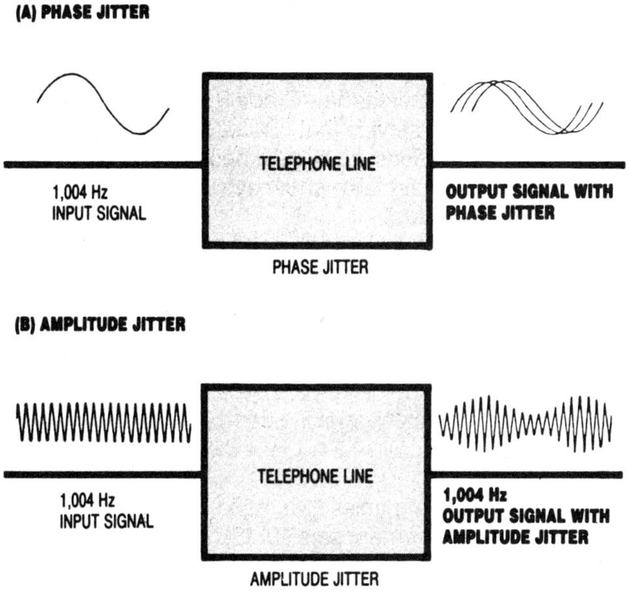

(A) PHASE JITTER

[Figure: 1,004 Hz input signal → Telephone Line → Output signal with phase jitter. PHASE JITTER]

(B) AMPLITUDE JITTER

[Figure: 1,004 Hz input signal → Telephone Line → 1,004 Hz output signal with amplitude jitter. AMPLITUDE JITTER]

or limiting the signal as it passes through the telephone system. It results in extraneous frequencies, which are multiples of the original frequencies. (For example, 500 Hz fundamental frequency has a second harmonic of 1,000 Hz and a third harmonic of 1,500 Hz.)

8. Single frequency interference. The eighth impairment is single (discrete) frequency interference (Fig. 8). This is the addition of one or more discrete frequencies to the signal as it passes through the line. For example, routing the telephone lines very close to a.c. power lines would result in a strong 60-Hz component and its harmonics being present with the signal.

9. Transient impairments. These impairments are not continuously on the line; they come and go. Dropouts (Fig. 9A) are transient impairments that result in sudden large reductions in signal level that last for more than several milliseconds, while gain hits (Fig. 9B) are sudden increases in signal level that last for several milliseconds. Phase hits (Fig. 9C) are another type of transient impairments that result in sudden changes in the phase of the signal. Phase hits are caused by switching to an out-of-phase carrier system or sudden substitution of a broadband facility having a different propagation delay time. Impulse noise is sometimes considered a transient impairment.

Impairment limits

There are basically two types of analog telephone lines used for data communications: private leased/dedicated lines and the PSTN lines. Private leased lines are permanently connected 24 hours a day; a call does not need to be placed to transfer data. Private lines may be point-to-point or multidropped. PSTN lines are dial-up lines that are only connected when a call is placed. They are only point-to-point circuits and cannot be multidropped.

The specifications for private leased lines are uniformly specified under Federal Communications Commission tariffs, while the specifications for the PSTN are not. The latter are specified by the local Bell operating companies (BOCs) and long-distance carriers. Until recently, the specifications for private leased/dedicated lines were spelled out in FCC tariff 260. This tariff called out the specifications for the 3002 unconditioned line—the basic private line service. In addition to this service, C and D conditioning were specified. The new specifications for private leased lines are specified under FCC tariffs 9, 10, and 11, and Bell Publication 43202. These documents specify a series of 10 different line types with the Type 5 line (Fig. 10A) most nearly matching the 3002 characteristics. Under the new tariffs, C conditioning (Fig. 10B) and D conditioning (Fig. 10C) are still available. With C conditioning, filters are added to the line to improve the EDD and attenuation distortion characteristics. C conditioning is available in four grades—C1, C2, C4, and C5. C5 conditioning provides the best characteristics. Curves comparing the various types are given in Figure 11.

Most modems don't require C conditioning because they contain internal equalizers that correct for the attenuation distortion and EDD. In many cases, the lines already meet the C limits without the user having to request it. D conditioning provides improved signal-to-noise ratio and harmonic distortion characteristics by engineering the routing of the line through specific types of carriers. D1 conditioning is for point-to-point lines. D5 conditioning is for multipoint lines. Modems operating at speeds of less than 12 kbit/s normally do not require D conditioning. As with C conditioning, in many cases the line already meets the D limits without the user requesting it. In most cases, the

7. Harmonics. *Intermodulation distortion (harmonic or nonlinear) results in extraneous frequencies that are multiples of the fundamental frequency.*

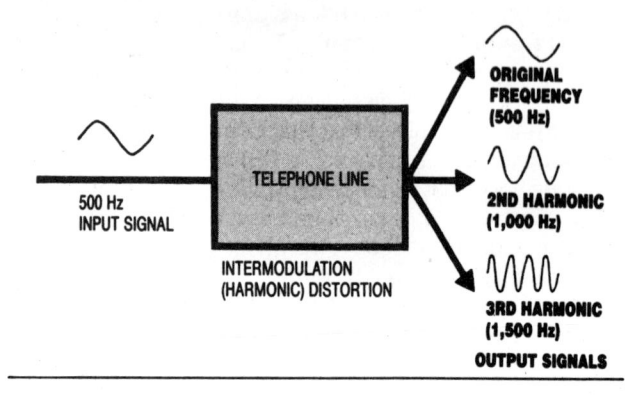

8. Interference. *Single frequency interference is the addition of one or more frequencies, such as a 60-Hz component, resulting from passing near an a.c. power line.*

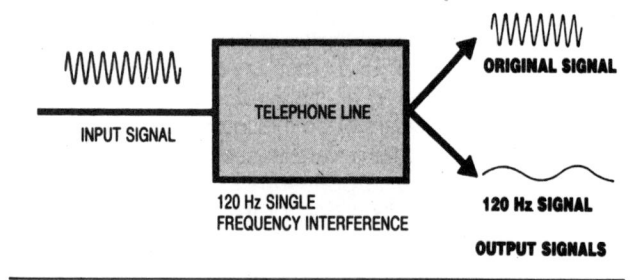

9. Gains and drops. *Some common transients are (A) sudden reductions in signal level; (B) sudden increases in signal level; (C) sudden changes in signal phase.*

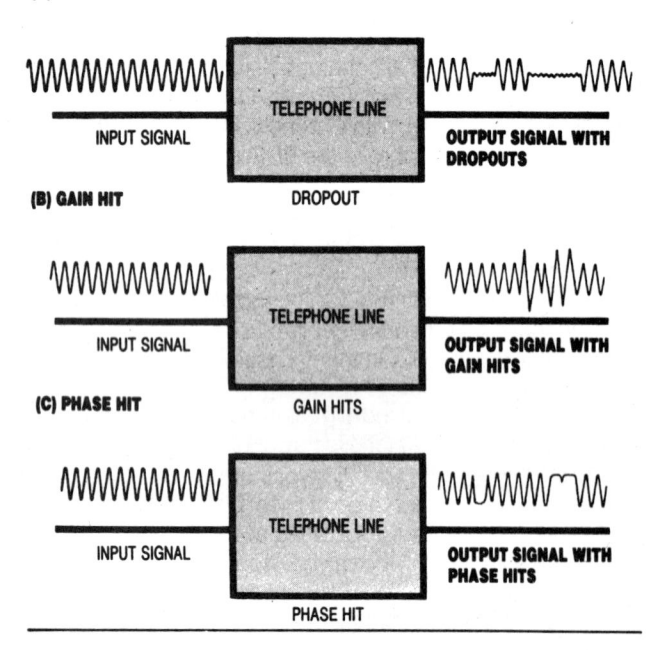

basic Type 5 service is sufficient, and conditioning need only be ordered if problems are experienced with the line.

Characteristics on the Public Switched Telephone Network (PSTN, the dial-up network used in the home or office) are only guaranteed with a data jack (RJ-45S and RJ-41S) and when "improved data service"—sometimes called "data access service"—is purchased. This service must be ordered from both the local exchange carrier (LEC) or the interexchange carrier (IC). The guaranteed characteristics will vary, depending on the LEC and IC being dealt with. It should be noted that these characteristics are not guaranteed on every call but are guaranteed only on seven out of 10 calls. The typical PSTN specifications that some LECs and ICs follow are provided in Figure 12. These specifications are divided into types: Local loop (Fig. 12A) and data-jack-to-data-jack (Fig. 12B) specifications.

Most PSTN problems are in the local loop rather than in the connection between central offices. Since divestiture, it is more difficult to get the telephone companies to support the data-jack-to-data-jack specifications because multiple carriers may be involved. With a permissive jack (for example, the ubiquitous RJ-11 jack) there are no guarantees on the characteristics: If you can talk on the line, it is within specification. In the future, it is expected that there will be various grades of service. For example, there could be three grades of service. Grade 1 is expected to be a permissive service with very minimal line characteristics that may contain low-speed ADPCM codecs. Grade 2 is expected to be a data service that will not contain any low-speed ADPCM codecs and will have about the same characteristics as exist today. Grade 3 is expected to be an enhanced data service that will not contain any low-speed ADPCM codecs; it will have better characteristics than are presently available and may support higher data rates (e.g., 19.2 kbit/s).

The EIA TR30.3 subcommittee and the Exchange Carriers Standard Association (ECSA) T1Q1.1 subcommittee are presently working on standardizing the line characteristics for the PSTN, but these standards are not expected to be completed for another one or two years. The line characteristics of data-grade service are expected to be very close to the characteristics given in Figures 12A and 12B.

Test equipment

There are many companies that manufacture transmission impairment measurement sets (TIMS): Hewlett-Packard, Hekimian Laboratories, Ameritec, Bradley, and LP Com.

Some TIMS equipment measures all the parameters that have been discussed, while others only measure some of them. The cost of TIMS equipment varies from about $500 to about $15,000, depending on features and capabilities. It is best to initially buy a good-quality TIMS that measures as many parameters as possible and has a speaker to allow aural monitoring of the line. One needs to be able to measure most of the parameters because the phone company will typically find the obvious problems, such as high-level noise, attenuation distortion, and line loss.

A good-quality TIMS is important to ensure accurate

measurement and to ensure credibility of the measurements when talking with the phone company. When a problem is reported to the telephone company, it will, in most cases, connect a TIMS and an aural monitor (speaker) to the line. If it is testing a private leased line, it will loop-back the network channel-terminating equipment (NCTE). If it is testing a PSTN line, it will send a technician to the customer's premises to do the testing.

TIMS parameters

A good-quality TIMS will usually measure seven sets of parameters: level and frequency, peak-to-average ratio (P/AR), noise, envelope delay distortion, intermodulation distortion, jitter, and transient impairments.

■ *Level and frequency.* This TIMS setting is used to measure the receive signal, which is used to calculate 1,004-Hz line loss. Line loss is calculated by taking the transmit signal level (i.e., 1,004-Hz signal at 0 dBm for a private line and -9 dBm for a PSTN line) minus the level received at the other end. Line losses on a private line are 16 dB ± 4 dB, and 30 dB maximum on PSTN lines. Gain slope and frequency translation (shift) are also measured with this setting. Gain slope is a three-point measurement of the attenuation distortion, which is measured at 404 Hz, 1,004 Hz, and 2,804 Hz. Slope is calculated by taking the difference between the signal level received at 1,004 Hz (reference) and the signal levels at 404 Hz and 2,804 Hz. Slope on a private line is between -2 dB (gain) and +10 dB (loss). On a PSTN line, slope is less than +14 dB (loss). Frequency translation is measured by subtracting the receive frequency from the transmit frequency (1,004 Hz). Maximum frequency translation is specified at ± 3 Hz on a private line and ± 5 Hz on a PSTN line. However, translation greater than 1 Hz is almost never seen.

■ *P/AR.* P/AR is the peak-to-average ratio of the transmission line. It allows measurement of the channel dispersion or the spreading, in time, of signal amplitude due to transmission imperfections. The P/AR test signal has a peak-to-average ratio and a spectral content that approximates a data signal. P/AR is a figure of merit for the channel, giving an indication of the general quality of the line. It is affected by many factors, but envelope delay distortion affects this parameter the most. P/AR is also affected by noise, bandwidth reduction, gain ripples, nonlinearities, such as compression and clipping (clipping of a waveform when an amplifier is driven beyond its capacity), and other impairments. P/AR is expressed as a number between 0 and 100, where 100 is the best quality line. Most lines have a P/AR between 85 and 100. Lines with a P/AR of 60 to 75 probably have a fair amount of envelope delay distortion or some other parameter that is out of specification.

■ *Noise.* Noise measurements are divided into three types: message circuit noise, noise with tone, and signal-to-noise ratio. Message circuit noise is the noise level measured with a quiet termination (i.e., line terminated but no transmit signal) at the transmitting end. Message circuit noise gives a good indication of the local loop noise but does not indicate the noise generated in the carrier system. Mes-

10. Within 'spec'? Specifications for private leased/dedicated lines are defined under Bell Publication 43202 and FCC tariffs 9, 10, and 11.

(A) TYPE 5 LINE (PREVIOUSLY 3002 LINE) SPECIFICATIONS

PARAMETER	IMMEDIATE ACTION LINE
1. LOSS DEVIATION (dB)	± 4.0
2. C-NOTCHED NOISE (dBrnC0)	51

3. ATTENUATION DISTORTION #(dB) BETWEEN:
    504 AND 2,504 Hz
    404 AND 2,804 Hz
    304 AND 3,004 HZ
	
	 -2.0 TO +8.0
	 -2.0 TO +10.0
	 -3.0 TO +12.0

4. SIGNAL-TO-C-NOTCHED NOISE RATIO (dB)	≥ 24
5. ENVELOPE DELAY DISTORTION (μs) BETWEEN 804 AND 2,604 Hz	1,750
6. IMPULSE NOISE THRESHOLD* (dBrnC0)	71

7. INTERMODULATION DISTORTION (dB)
    R2
    R3
	
	 ≥ 27
	 ≥ 32

8. PHASE JITTER (DEGREES PEAK-TO-PEAK)
    20-300 Hz
    4-300 Hz
	
	 ≤ 10°
	 ≤ 15°

9. FREQUENCY SHIFT (Hz)	± 3

\# = (+) MEANS MORE LOSS.
* = 15 COUNTS IN 15 MINUTES AT SPECIFIED THRESHOLD.

(B) CONDITIONING SPECIFICATIONS

	ATTENUATION DISTORTION RELATIVE TO 1,004 Hz		ENVELOPE DELAY DISTORTION	
	FREQUENCY RANGE (Hz)	VARIATION (dB)	FREQUENCY RANGE (Hz)	VARIATION (MICROSECONDS)
C1	1,004-2,404 304-2,704 304-3,004	-1.0 TO +3.0 -2.0 TO +6.0 -3.0 TO +12.0	1,004-2,404 804-2,604	1,000 1,750
C2	504-2,804 304-3,004	-1.0 TO +3.0 -2.0 TO +6.0	1,004-2,604 604-2,604 504-2,804	500 1,500 3,000
C4	504-3,004 304-3,204	-2.0 TO +3.0 -2.0 TO +6.0	1,004-2,604 804-2,804 604-3,004 504-3,004	300 500 1,500 3,000
C5	504-2,804 304-3,004	-0.5 TO +1.5 -1.0 TO +3.0	1,004-2,604 604-2,604 504-2,804	100 300 600

(C) CONDITIONING SPECIFICATIONS

SIGNAL-TO-C-NOTCHED NOISE RATIO	≥ 28 dB MINIMUM

INTERMODULATION DISTORTION (4-TONE)
    SIGNAL TO SECOND ORDER MODULATION PRODUCTS
    SIGNAL TO THIRD ORDER MODULATION PRODUCTS
	
	 ≥ 35 dB MINIMUM
	 ≥ 40 dB MINIMUM

11. Distorted. *Attenuation and envelope delay distortion curves are shown for a standard, 3002-type leased analog voice-grade line (A) and a C1-conditioned leased line (B). As is the case with analog leased lines, envelope delay is greater at the edges of the passband. The conditioned line has minimal delay distortion in the 900-to-1,700 Hz band.*

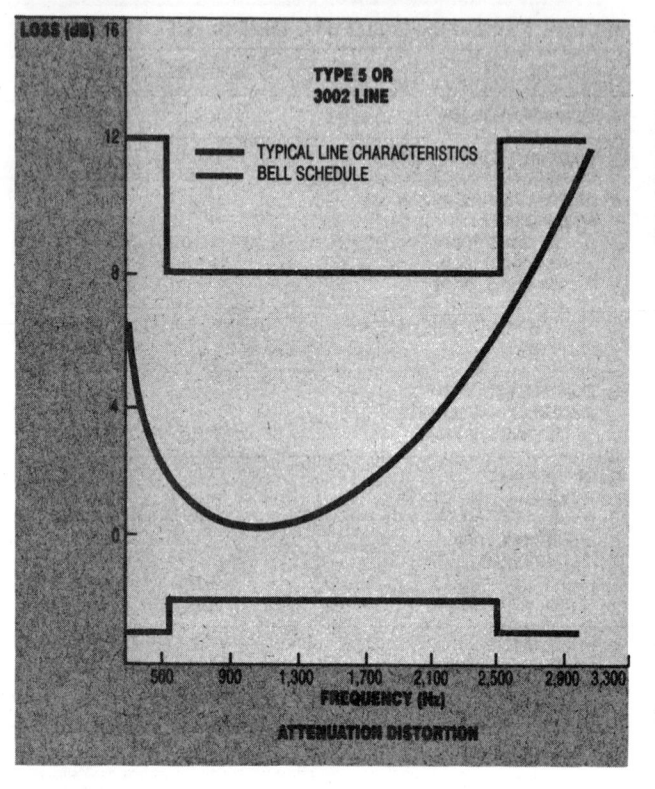

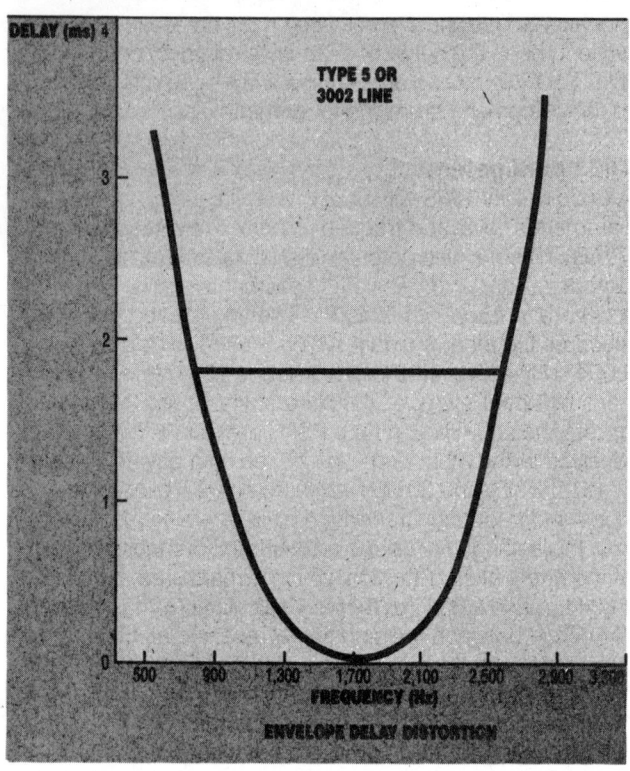

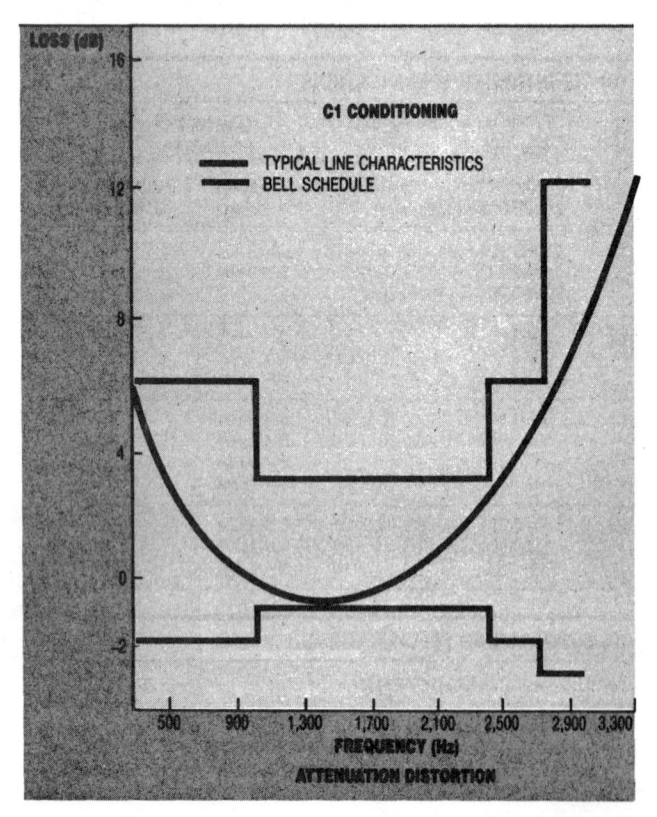

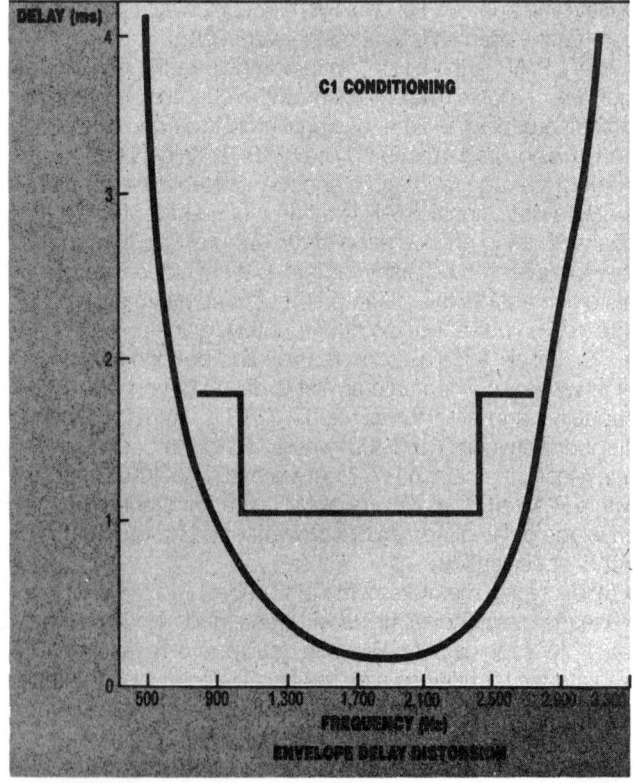

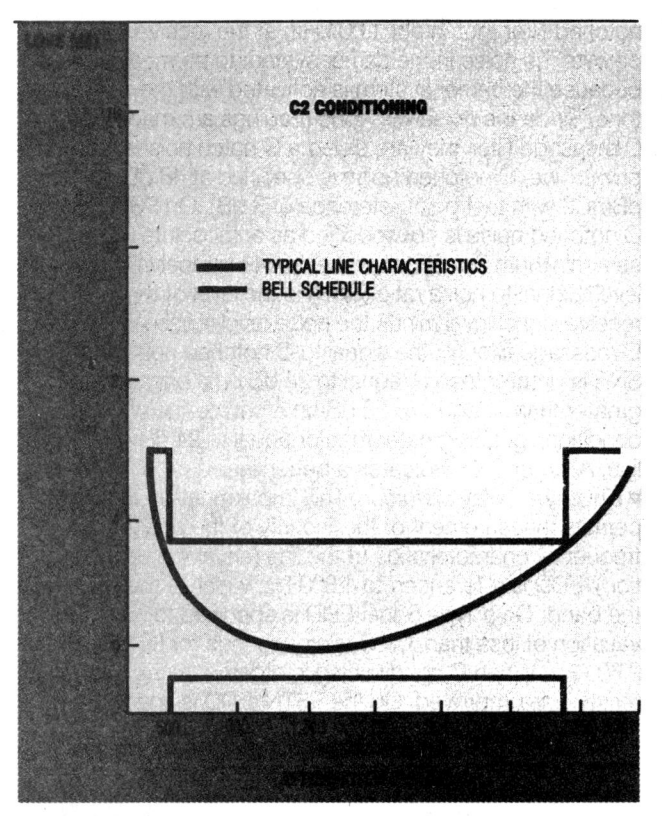

C2 CONDITIONING

— TYPICAL LINE CHARACTERISTICS
— BELL SCHEDULE

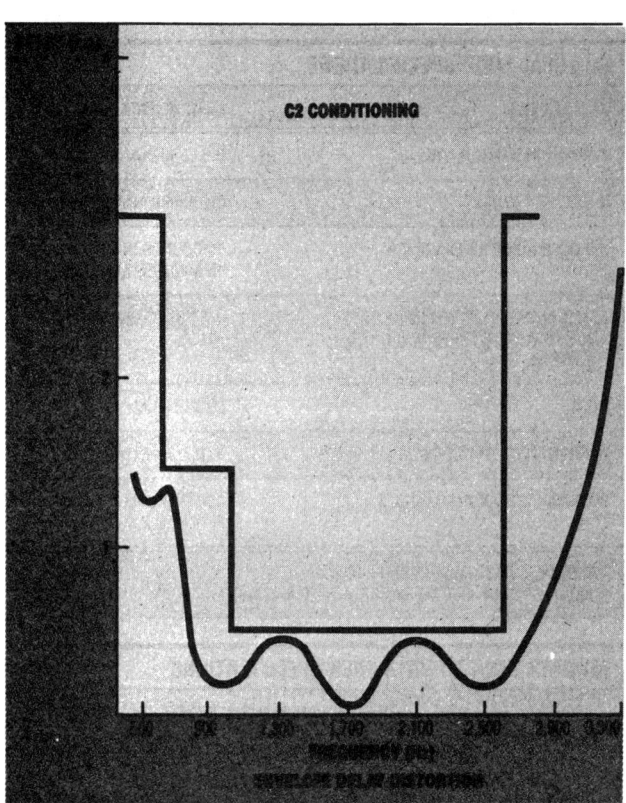

ATTENUATION DISTORTION

C2 CONDITIONING

ENVELOPE DELAY DISTORTION

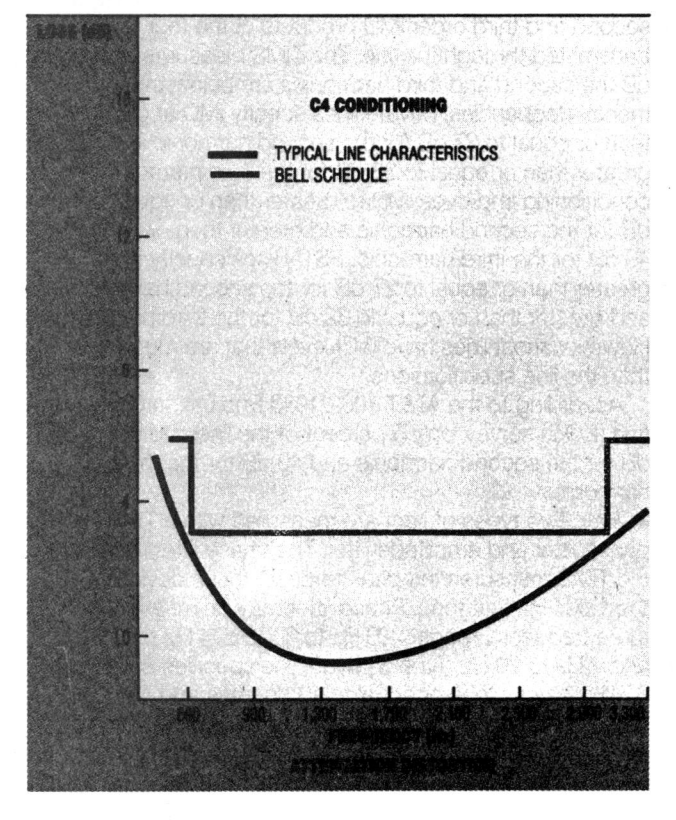

C4 CONDITIONING

— TYPICAL LINE CHARACTERISTICS
— BELL SCHEDULE

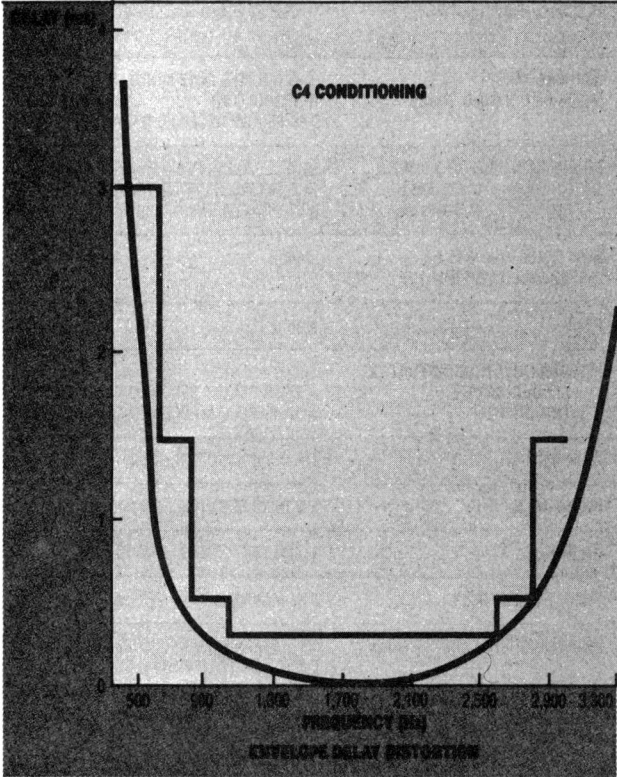

ATTENUATION DISTORTION

C4 CONDITIONING

ENVELOPE DELAY DISTORTION

12. Local loops and end-to-end. *Typical line characteristics followed by most BOCs for the PSTN, when data jacks with "improved data service" are used.*

(A) LOCAL LOOP SPECIFICATIONS

PARAMETER	LIMIT AT DATA JACK
1,004-Hz INSERTION LOSS	8.5 dB MAXIMUM
C-NOTCHED NOISE*	28 dBrnC0 MAXIMUM
IMPULSE NOISE AT 59 dBrnC0	15 COUNTS IN 15 MINUTES MAXIMUM
ATTENUATION DISTORTION (SLOPE) 404 TO 2,804 Hz REFERENCED TO 1,004 Hz	−1 TO +3 dB MAXIMUM
P/AR	90 MINIMUM
TRANSMITTED DATA POWER (AT SERVING CO)	−12 dBm MAXIMUM
ENVELOPE DELAY DISTORTION†	100 MICROSECONDS (1,004 TO 2,804 Hz)

*ASSUMES −13 dBm0 HOLDING TONE.
†REQUIRED ONLY IF P/AR REQUIREMENTS ARE NOT MET.

(B) DATA JACK TO DATA JACK SPECIFICATIONS

PARAMETER	REQUIREMENTS (DATA JACK TO DATA JACK)
1,004-Hz INSERTION LOSS	30 dB MAXIMUM
C-NOTCHED NOISE (1,004-Hz HOLDING TONE)	AT LEAST 24 dB BELOW RECEIVED POWER OF 1,004-Hz TEST TONE AT DATA LEVEL
IMPULSE NOISE (1,004-Hz HOLDING TONE)	≤ 15 COUNTS IN 15 MINUTES, THRESHOLD AT 6 dB BELOW RECEIVED DATA LEVEL
PHASE JITTER* (20 TO 300 Hz) (4 TO 300 Hz) (4 TO 20 Hz)	≤ 10 DEGREES, PEAK-TO-PEAK ≤ 15 DEGREES, PEAK-TO-PEAK ≤ 5 DEGREES, PEAK-TO-PEAK
SLOPE, 404 TO 2,804 Hz (REFERENCED TO 1,004 Hz)	≤ 14dB
P/AR	≥ 48
INTERMODULATION DISTORTION SECOND ORDER THIRD ORDER	≥ 27 dB BELOW RECEIVED FUNDAMENTAL ≥ 32 dB BELOW RECEIVED FUNDAMENTAL
GAIN HITS	≤ 8 IN 15 MINUTES ≥ 3 dB
PHASE HITS	≤ 8 IN 15 MINUTES ≥ 20° dB
DROPOUTS	≤ 2 IN 15 MINUTES ≥ 12 dB
FREQUENCY OFFSET	5 Hz MAXIMUM
ENVELOPE DELAY DISTORTION†	800 µs MAXIMUM (1,004 TO 2,404 Hz) 2,600 µs (604 TO 2,804 Hz)

*TWO OF THREE PHASE JITTER MEASUREMENTS REQUIRED (4 TO 20, 20 TO 300, 4 TO 300 Hz)
†REQUIRED ONLY IF P/AR REQUIREMENTS ARE NOT MET

sage circuit noise is expressed in terms of dBrn. It is not specified for private line or PSTN lines, but may be used as an aid in isolating problems. Noise with tone is measured with a 1,004-Hz tone transmitted through the line and with a notched filter (notch-out 1,004 Hz) at the receive end. This permits the noise in the carrier system to be measured because the carrier system is activated with the 1,004-Hz tone. Since the noise-with-tone readings are made using a C-message filter, they are called a C-notch noises. On a private line, C-notched noise is specified at 48 dBrnc (51 dBrnC0 with test point reference of 3 dB). On PSTN lines, C-notched noise is not specified as an absolute level but as a minimum 24 dB below the 1,004-Hz receive signal level. Signal-to-noise ratio (SNR) is the level of the 1,004-Hz receive signal level minus the noise level measured with a C-message filter (or the signal-to-C-notched-noise ratio). SNR is greater than or equal to 24 dB on a private line, greater than or equal to 28 dB on a private line with D conditioning, and greater than or equal to 24 dB on a PSTN line. A larger SNR indicates a better line.

■ *Envelope delay distortion.* This impairment on the TIMS permits measurement of the linearity of the phase versus frequency characteristics of the line (envelope delay distortion). EDD is referenced to 1,800 Hz, which is the center of the band. On a Type 5 line, EDD is specified to have a variation of less than 1,750 microseconds for 804 Hz and 2,604 Hz. When C conditioning is ordered, these characteristics are improved. On the PSTN, EDD is specified at 800 microseconds at 1,004 Hz and 2,404 Hz, and 2,600 microseconds at 604 Hz and 2,804 Hz.

■ *Intermodulation distortion.* The intermodulation distortion (IMD) mode on the TIMS permits measurements of the second and third order IMD products of the four tones transmitted through the line. The TIMS measures how many dB the second and third harmonics are below the fundamental frequencies. Private lines specify IMD at greater than or equal to 27 dB for the second harmonic and greater than or equal to 32 dB for the third harmonic. D conditioning improves IMD to greater than or equal to 35 dB for the second harmonic and greater than or equal to 40 dB for the third harmonic. PSTN lines specify IMD at greater than or equal to 27 dB for the second harmonic and greater than or equal to 32 dB for the third harmonic. However, most lines have IMD levels that are much better than the line specifications.

According to the AT&T 1982/1983 End Office Connection (EOC) survey, only 5 percent of the lines fall below 38 dB for the second harmonic and 40 dB for the third harmonic.

■ *Jitter.* Two types of jitter are measured with a TIMS: phase jitter and amplitude jitter. The phase jitter mode on the TIMS measures the peak-to-peak phase deviation of the 1,004-Hz test tone. Phase jitter may be measured at three frequency ranges: 20 Hz to 300 Hz, 4 Hz to 300 Hz, and 4 Hz to 20 Hz. Type 5 private line specifies 20 Hz to 300 Hz at less than or equal to 10 degrees and 4 Hz to 300 Hz at less than or equal to 15 degrees. The specs for a PSTN line are 20 Hz to 300 Hz at less than or equal to 10 degrees, 4 Hz to 300 Hz at less than or equal to 15 degrees, and 4 Hz to 20 Hz at less than or equal to 5 degrees.

Amplitude jitter is the summation of incidental amplitude modulation and the effects of interference and noise. Amplitude jitter is measured at the same frequency ranges as phase jitter. There are no specifications for amplitude jitter on the private line or on the PSTN, but it is usually less than 5 percent.

- *Transient impairments.* The transient impairment mode on a TIMS measures impulse noise, phase hits, gain hits, and dropouts. Impulse noise is usually measured at three thresholds: 62 dBrn, 64 dBrn, and 68 dBrn. The private line specifies 15 counts in 15 minutes at 68 dBrn (71 dbrnC0 with a TLP0 of 3 dB). The PSTN specifies 15 counts in 15 minutes at a threshold of 6 dB below received data level, although most LECs follow the 68 dBrn threshold. Phase hits are measured at a threshold of greater than 20 degrees and are specified at less than 8 counts in 15 minutes for private and dial-up lines. The threshold for a gain hit is 3 dB and is specified at less than 8 counts in 15 minutes for private and PSTN lines. Dropouts are measured at a threshold of 12 dB and are specified at less than 2 counts in 15 minutes for private and PSTN lines.

Pinning down the telco

Measuring the telephone-line characteristics, in most cases, requires two people and two TIMS—one at each end of the line. On a private leased line, one person may measure the line characteristics by looping back the remote NCTE. This is done by placing a 2,713-Hz signal on the line. When measuring the line characteristics this way, one is measuring the characteristics of the line in both directions simultaneously. This means that the line impairments in both directions are combined and that it is very difficult to determine if the characteristics are very good in one direction and very poor in the other. Ideally, two TIMS should be used. When testing over the PSTN, two TIMS are a must.

Frequencies in the range from 2,504 Hz to 2,750 Hz should be avoided. If you have looped back the NCTE, the 2,713-Hz signal will take it out of loopback. If the NCTE is not in loopback, sending 2,713 Hz will put it in loopback. When testing on the PSTN, sending 2,600 Hz (the billing tone) will disconnect the call. Most TIMS have a skip option that, when enabled, automatically skips these frequencies. When sweeping the line, ensure that the modem is disconnected and that the TIMS is set in the terminated rather than bridged mode.

A table for recording measured characteristics should be prepared. It should contain the telephone circuit number, its location (address), and each of the parameters to be measured (see sample table). All the parameters should be measured to give a complete picture of the line characteristics. It is also important to use the aural monitor, which allows you to hear the test signals while testing the line. This will often reveal the source of the problem.

Once all the parameters are recorded and it has been determined which characteristics appear to be out of specification, call the local telephone company repair service listed in the phone directory or contained on a label associated with the phone-line connection. Give the technical support person the circuit number, its location, the type of problem that is occurring, the type of equipment being used (modem and TIMS), the value of the measured parameters, and the ones believed to be out of specification. Also mention any abnormal sounds (loud humming sounds, clicks, pops, unusual tones) that may have been heard during testing of the line or during data transfer.

Make sure that sounds being heard are not from the modem or the TIMS, since this gear generates unusual sounds. Also, be sure to get the name of the phone company's technical support person and a telephone number where he or she can be reached. This avoids having to speak to a different person and re-explaining the problem each time you call in.

The technical support people may ask a lot of questions in an effort to determine credibility of the test results. Being courteous will help bring a quick solution to the problem. If the test results are accurate, be firm about the findings. The phone company will always question the test results and their relation to the specification. The support personnel may even say that the specifications are being misinterpreted when they are not. They may say that this type of line will only support very low-speed (1.2-kbit/s or 2.4-kbit/s) modems and won't support the higher-speed data rates used in the application. This is not normally true. If you tell the phone company that it is having line problems because the modems have a higher error rate than normal, the company will usually say that it doesn't guarantee any specific error rate. This is true; the phone company only guarantees line specifications, not modem performance. Specify the parameters that are out of specification rather than modem performance specifications.

Retest the telephone line after the phone company says that the trouble situation is fixed. Often, there are multiple line problems, or the phone company may think it has resolved the problem but it may not have. The trouble situation may go away after the phone company has tested the line, but the problem may reappear within a few hours or days, depending on the type of problem. One may have to work the same problem several times before finally getting it resolved.

Unfortunately, some problems may be intermittent or may only occur during certain times of the day. When this happens, the phone company may call back and say that the line is fine because the trouble situation was not occurring during the testing. Request that it leave the trouble report ticket open and that they be on standby so that when the problem occurs again support persons can quickly get on the line and run tests. Some problems may last for only 10 or 15 minutes every three or four hours, or the problem may be there one day and not the next. These kinds of problems are very difficult for the phone company to resolve.

When working on a PSTN data trouble situation, it may be more difficult to resolve the problem. Most PSTN telephone-line problems are associated with the local loop. Since long-distance calls are routed through different paths

Transmission line test report

COMPANY _____ CONTACTS _____
COMPANY PHONE NUMBER _____
Location From _____ To _____
PHONE OR CIRCUIT NUMBERS _____
DATE _____ TESTED BY _____
Phone Co. _____ Phone # _____
Contacts: _____

P/AR _____

1,004 Hz LINE LOSS
TX. LEVEL _____ dBm
RCV. LEVEL _____ dBm
LINE LOSS _____ dBm

FREQUENCY TRANSLATION
FREQ. TX. _____ Hz. RCV. _____ Hz.

NOISE

	C	3K	15K	
MESSAGE	___	___	___	dBrn
NOISE W/TONE	___	___	___	dBrn
S/N	___	___	___	dB

JITTER
20-300 Hz Amp _____ %
         Phase _____ Deg.
 4-300 Hz Amp _____ %
         Phase _____ Deg.
  4-20 Hz Amp _____ %
         Phase _____ Deg.

INTERMODULATION DISTORTION
(NOISE CORRECTED)
2nd _____ dB   3rd _____ dB

TRANSIENTS
Test Time _____ min.
Impulse Noise
Low   62 dBrn _____ Cnts.
Mid   64 dBrn _____ Cnts.
High 68 dBrn _____ Cnts.
Phase Hits ±20 Deg. _____ Cnts.
Gain Hits ±3dB _____ Cnts.
Dropouts 12dB _____ Cnts.

ATTENUATION ENVELOPE DELAY
         (dB)   (μsec)
204 _____
304 _____
404 _____
504 _____
604 _____
704 _____
804 _____
904 _____
1,004 _____
1,104 _____
1,204 _____
1,304 _____
1,404 _____
1,504 _____
1,604 _____
1,704 _____
1,804 _____
1,904 _____
2,004 _____
2,104 _____
2,204 _____
2,304 _____
2,404 _____
2,504 * _____
2,604 * _____
2,704 * _____
2,804 _____
2,904 _____
3,004 _____
3,104 _____
3,204 _____
3,304 _____
3,404 _____
3,504 _____
3,604 _____
3,704 _____
3,804 _____

*SF Skip—skip these frequencies to avoid NCTE loopback and billing tone disconnection.

each time a call is placed, it is unlikely that the same path will be reached on consecutive calls. Therefore, a problem between central offices is less likely to occur.

You will have to isolate which local loop is at fault. This may be determined by placing the call from an alternate location, such as another telephone line within the same building or in another building. This should be tried on both ends of the circuit. If the problem goes away when placing the call from the alternate location, the problem is in that local loop. The problem is likely to follow one local loop or the other. Problems may also occur when placing the call in one direction but not the other. The technical support person should be informed of this situation. Also, the problem may follow a particular local exchange carrier (LEC) or interexchange carrier (IC) such as AT&T, MCI, or Sprint. If the IC or LEC is suspected, use another. If the problem goes away when the alternate IC or LEC is used, the problem is associated with that particular IC or LEC. The technical support person should be advised of this situation and the problem IC or LEC should also be contacted.

The ICs and LECs have agreed via the Network Operations Forum (NOF) Installation and Maintenance Document that the IC or LEC that is giving the trouble report will follow the problem through until its completion—provided that data access service has been purchased.

Often, the solution to phone-line problems lies in the correlation of several test parameters that appear to be out of specification. Certain out-of-specification parameters can indicate a certain type of problem. Relating the correlation of various parameters to a particular problem is beyond the scope of this article. A very difficult telephone-line problem may have to be referred to an experienced troubleshooter.

A consulting service for resolving telephone line problems is offered by some modem companies and telephone companies. These organizations have the equipment and experience necessaryto resolve the problems fully and quickly. A large company with many modems and telephone lines may find it well worth the time and expense to develop these skills, because the amount and severity of telephone line problems is expected to get worse in this post-divestiture world of telecommunications. ■

Jack Douglass is a senior manager at Universal Data Systems and chairman of the EIA TR30.3 technical subcommittee. He also serves on three Federal Communications Commission working groups. He has authored two books on data communications and teaches courses on that subject at the University of Alabama in Huntsville and at Athens State College, Athens, Ala. Douglass received his B. S. E. E. from the University of Alabama in Huntsville.

Kevin R. Sharp, Burr-Brown Corp., Tucson, Ariz.

Protecting networks from power transients

Mother Nature is a meanie, and lightning has a particularly shocking effect on communications gear. Forewarned is forearmed.

Fireballs rolling along bare conductors, electrical transformers blown to smithereens by a lightning strike. These and other kinds of electrical equipment hazards are the products of electrical storms—a kind of destruction that is as old as the nation's power grid.

Over the years the communications industry has amassed an enviable record in meeting the threat of outages and spikes caused by the weather. But as communications gear becomes more sophisticated, it becomes more susceptible than ever to "transient" voltage damage, especially the extremes induced by the weather.

In the face of increasing vulnerability, communications managers should understand how such "spikes" are generated—and what steps can be taken to protect computers and networks against them.

Unlike machinery and lighting, communications gear reacts much more quickly to changes in electrical conditions. Large electric motors continue to rotate by inertia for many tenths of a second if power is temporarily disturbed. Likewise, the human eye cannot detect light failures shorter than several hundredths of a second. But when communications equipment and computers encounter an outage of even just one millionth of a second—the kind of disturbances that would go completely unnoticed in motor circuits and lighting applications—the result can be real problems, especially in the high-speed digital circuitry that now is ubiquitous in communications networks.

Since computers and communications facilities consume only about 1 percent of the commercial electrical power generated in the United States, users should not count on the power utility to protect their networks. It is inevitably up to communications equipment users to protect their equipment from power-supply transients. And unless the user takes steps to achieve this protection, the result can be a pattern of equipment damage—and data errors—that may be difficult to trace.

How widespread is this problem? Too often, damage to electronic equipment is not attributed to the spikes and surges that plague the commercial power grid. If a piece of electrical machinery is damaged by power-line surges or voltage spikes, the damage is obvious and sometimes spectacular. In the power-supply circuits of electrical machinery, the total electrical energy that is available is often hundreds of horsepower—even if the actual consumption is less than a fraction of one horsepower. Once the insulation of these circuits is damaged, all of the available power can be released, causing melted wiring, burned insulation, and hazardous fires.

In the digital electronics used in communications networks, however, a combination of deliberate circuit design and fortuitous component characteristics limits the available power inside the equipment to a few tenths or hundredths of a watt, which is less than a tenth of a horsepower. Still, this available energy is more than enough to damage the sensitive semiconductors and integrated circuits that comprise communications equipment, even though it is far less power than is needed to cause the spectacularly obvious damage often associated with electric motor failure. Therefore, tracing communications component failures to power-supply transients is often difficult.

If a pattern of equipment damage or failure emerges over time, electrical transients could be the problem. Users should be particularly sensitive to patterns of failure in power supplies and transmitter/receiver circuits in equipment. The pattern will usually be time-dependent; maybe a company experiences a lot of transmitter/receiver failures in the fall of each year (when thunderstorms are most frequent in many parts of the country). Or maybe most of the communications equipment's power-supply damage occurs on Monday mornings (when heating and air-conditioning systems are most active).

Another suspicious sign is a sudden change in the failure

rate, such as an industrial park installation that had no hardware failures for two years and then had four power-supply failures in two weeks. (Maybe a welding contractor just rented the shop next door.) If the user detects any of the previous patterns, he or she should first try to determine where the problem is coming from, and then take measures to protect against it.

How new a problem?
Communications equipment is susceptible to damage and data errors from power sources, communications lines, even the telephone network itself. The telephone industry was the first to protect data and power lines from the influences of electrical transients. But today, semiconductor-based equipment is more transient sensitive than older vacuum tube equipment. And the low-power CMOS (complementary metal oxide semiconductor) circuits are more sensitive than the bipolar semiconductors that were ubiquitous just a couple of years ago.

Because components used in communications equipment are now much more susceptible to transients, what used to be a "pop" during a phone conversation can today cause a funds transfer to be routed into the wrong account or a purchase of 10,000 shares of the wrong stock. It is up to the data communications network installer to protect his or her own equipment and data from a power source designed to work lighting and machinery, and to ensure that data communications lines subject to lightning surges do not damage equipment.

Prudent location of communications lines is the easiest and most economical way to minimize the network's exposure to damage. Some areas, like overhead communications lines, are much more susceptible to lightning-induced spikes than buried conductors. Also, since transients are by nature propagated in either electrical or magnetic conductors, the use of fiber optic cables wherever possible will go a long way toward avoiding the problem altogether. The guiding rule is always to keep a transient from getting into the communications network in the first place rather than rely on protective devices on each piece of equipment to protect the user's investment in expensive communications hardware. After the user has taken reasonable steps to keep transients out of the network, the next tasks are to understand what circuits and devices will protect the equipment at risk and to select commercially available equipment that uses these techniques to greatest advantage.

The first step in protecting equipment is to understand where the damaging transient spikes come from. Most spikes are caused by one of four phenomena: lightning, switched inductive loads, electrostatic discharge (ESD), and nuclear electromagnetic pulse (NEMP). This article will deal only with the first three causes, since hopefully these are the only sources a communications network will need to survive. However, for critical military communications networks the effect of high-altitude nuclear device detonation must be considered.

Whatever their source, transients can enter a communications network three ways: from the power grid before entering the communications installation, from other electrical or electronic equipment attached to the power network inside the installation, and through data lines.

Lightning may be the most studied of the transient generators, but it is also the toughest to guard against because the energy released during a lightning stroke is enormous. Direct strikes may contain voltages of 1,000,000 V and currents of 200,000 A. According to a paper presented to the Institute of Electrical and Electronic Engineers power conversion conference in 1976, this energy would be sufficient to lift the Queen Elizabeth 2 luxury liner 2 feet! It is virtually impossible and definitely not economical to protect delicate communications equipment from these primary effects of lightning if the energy gets into the communications network. The guiding rule must be to not allow these high energy spikes into conductors in the first place.

The best solution for protecting outdoor communications lines in high-lightning areas is to use fiber optic cables with nonmetallic sheaths. These cables will not attract a lightning strike and will be mostly immune to the effects of nearby lightning flashes. If running fiber optic cable is not practical then a lightning-protected zone should be created with lightning rods, lightning conductors, and grounding equipment. The single conductor on the top of most standard electrical utility poles is one example of a lightning conductor. A communications conductor suspended under the power lines on a transmission tower will usually be protected from lightning. If a communications conductor is stretched here, however, the user should watch out for electrical/magnetic interference from the power line and protect equipment and personnel from the possible hazard of a broken power cable resting on a communications conductor.

Secondary effects of lightning contain much less energy than primary effects, so they can be controlled with available products even after the energy gets into communications conductors. When lightning strikes the ground (actually lightning current streams from the ground to the cloud), three effects take place that can cause problems for data communications equipment: induction, bound charge release, and noise radiation.

Large earth currents must flow in order to neutralize the charge deposited by the stroke. These currents can induce voltages in nearby conductors, particularly buried electrical lines (but not fiber optic cables).

Just before the lightning strike, electrostatic fields can charge elevated conductors to more than 30 kV for every meter the cable is suspended above ground. This bound charge is no hazard to communications equipment since the air around the conductor is also "charged" to the same potential.

This electrostatic field of 30 kV per meter will rapidly collapse to about 150 V per meter after a lightning strike. This field change will leave the overhead conductor with a net potential of about 30,000 V for every meter above the ground, effectively generating a voltage spike of over 100,000 V on a power line with 10-meter-high towers. This high voltage is manageable by reasonably sized and priced transient protectors because there is not much energy stored in the charge.

The final secondary lightning effect to be considered is magnetic induction, or noise radiation. A lightning bolt will act as a vertical antenna, radiating high-frequency interference. This is what causes radio and TV static during

1. Thunderstorm days. *The frequency with which lightning will strike close enough to damage communications equipment varies widely across the country. The isoceraunic map shows the average number of days per year that a person standing at a data communications site would be able to hear a thunderstorm.*

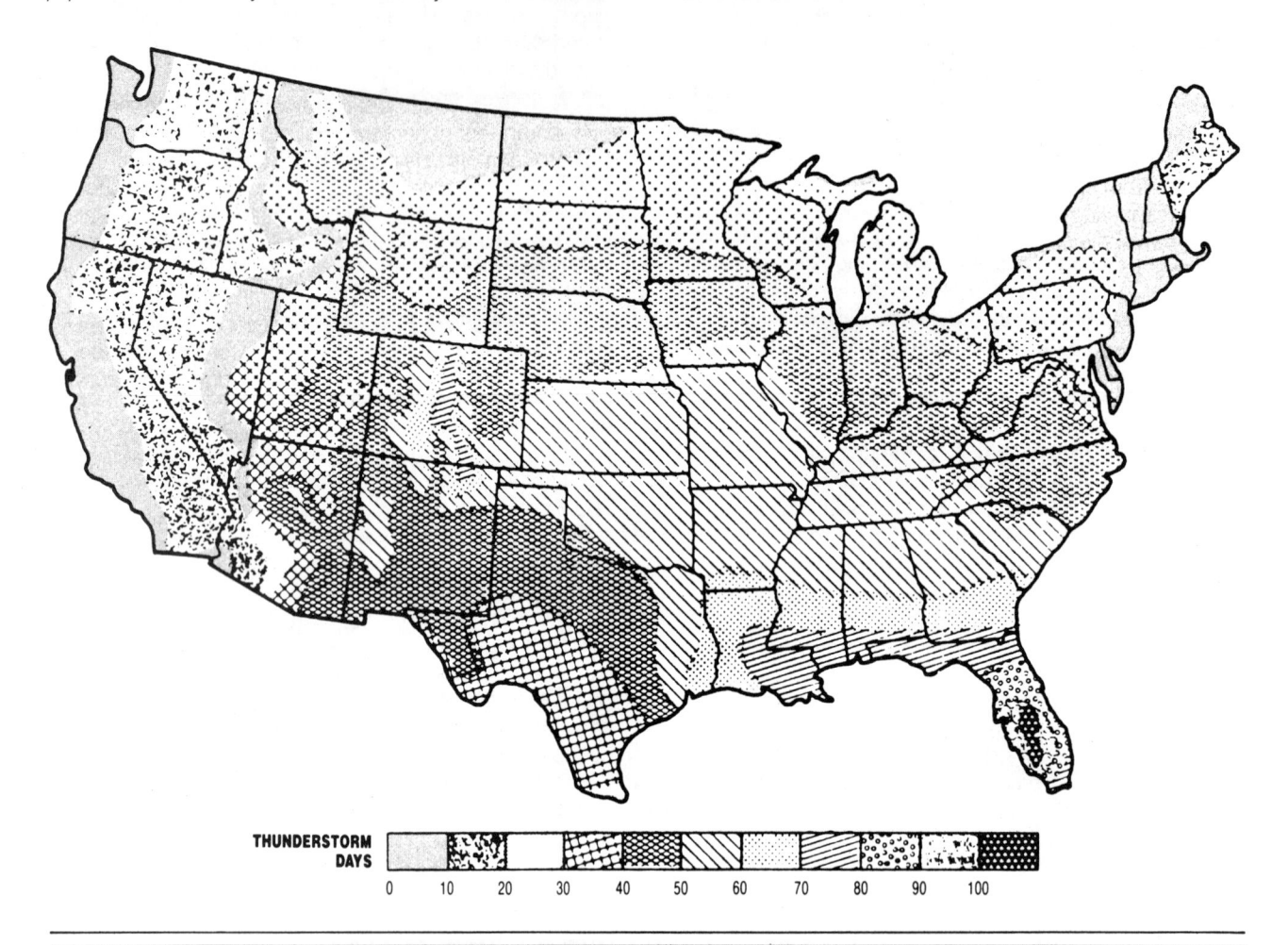

Table 1: Ground lightning strikes vs. thunderstorm days

THUNDERSTORM DAYS PER YEAR	GROUND FLASHES/SQ. KM./YEAR		GROUND FLASHES/SQ. MI./YEAR	
	NOMINAL	RANGE	NOMINAL	RANGE
5	0.2	0.1-0.5	0.5	0.26-1.3
10	0.5	0.15-1	1.3	0.39-2.6
20	1.1	0.3-3	2.8	0.78-7.8
30	1.9	0.6-5	4.9	1.6-12.9
40	2.8	0.8-8	7.3	2.1-20.7
50	3.7	1.2-10	9.6	3.1-25.9
60	4.7	1.8-12	12.2	4.7-31.1
80	6.9	3-17	17.9	7.8-44
100	9.2	4-20	23.8	10.3-51.8

thunderstorms, and it can cause data loss and control errors if it gets into communications networks. Power lines and communications conductors will act as receiving antennas, conducting this interference right into an unprotected piece of equipment. Many commercially available transient suppressors contain filters that help control this problem.

Lightning-induced transients are not the only threat to communications hardware; other damaging transients may originate from inside and outside the building. Switching loads, resonating circuits associated with switching devices, power circuits requiring the action of fuses or circuit breakers, and arcing faults all contribute to an electrical environment that can be damaging to the electronic devices used in communications equipment and the computers processing the data. All of these sources produce transient voltages directly proportional to the rate of current change and contain energy directly proportional to the square of the current (a particular problem during power-supply faults, when the current can be very high before a fuse or circuit breaker opens).

Assessing the threat
After the communications professional knows what can happen to equipment and what causes the damage, it is necessary to estimate the magnitude of the threat to each node in the network. This is done by considering the likelihood of a nearby lightning strike and the frequency of spikes caused by other sources.

The frequency with which lightning will strike close enough to damage communications equipment varies widely, from hundreds of times per year in the southeastern United States to less than 10 times per year on the West Coast. To determine how often lightning will strike near a proposed installation, refer to Figure 1, a map of thunderstorm days per year (isoceraunic map). Find the location on the map and read off the isoceraunic number. This number is the average number of days per year that a person standing at that site will be able to hear thunder at least once during the day (meaning lightning has struck within about 14 miles). To convert this number of thunderstorm days per year to an average number of lightning strikes per year refer to Table 1. The number of expected lightning strikes per year per land area ranges from 1/2 strikes per square mile for an isoceraunic level of 5 to 24 strikes per square mile for an isoceraunic level of 100.

Besides lightning, transients may be generated by the switching of inductive loads, particularly rotating machinery and large relays. When current flows through an inductor, energy is stored in a magnetic field. If the current is removed, the stored energy will be released, often quite suddenly if the current is cut off by a switch or circuit breaker. While load-switching transients are much smaller than lightning-induced ones, they occur much more often. Instead of hitting equipment with one knockout punch like lightning, load-switching transients can take out equipment with a long series of body blows.

Because switching transients and lightning transients account for the majority of the damaging transients in an electrical installation, the user should add to the lightning-threat evaluation done with isoceraunic maps a switching-transient evaluation made much more intuitively; there is no easy way to determine exactly how bad a particular installation will be. Industrial areas present the greatest possibility for switching transients, so the user should be particularly alert for problems if heavy electrical equipment, such as a crane, is in use nearby. Arc welders are another bad transient source.

Even though heavy industrial areas contain the most obvious transient generators, just because an installation is in a nice clean office is no reason to ignore transient problems. A residential air-conditioning unit can produce 6 kV spikes when it shuts off. Residential power circuits also generally have lower impedances because fewer large loads are connected to a circuit at one time. Because the voltage that can be generated by a transient with fixed energy is inversely proportional to impedance (Voltage energy2/impedance), a transient generator can produce larger voltage spikes in a residential setting than in an industrial circuit.

An analysis of switching-transient sources usually shows that most installations are vulnerable. If two or more large switching sources are present at an installation the user should protect the equipment as though a moderate lightning threat was present—even if the location would indicate a low lightning incidence.

Possibly the most brutal transient environments occur in vehicles, both spark-ignited and electrically driven ones. Spark-ignited engines produce problems in several ways. In order to burn fuel most efficiently, high voltages must be applied to the spark plugs at precise times. This means that extremely high transient voltages are purposely generated by the ignition circuitry. These transients produce radio-frequency interference and induce transient voltages in the power supply and in any conductors close to the ignition cables.

If a manager thinks he can get away from the vehicle transient problem by going to a nice clean battery-operated lift truck, he should think again. If anything, these vehicles make it even harder for electronic equipment to survive. The biggest problem with electric trucks is the fact that the electric motors draw large DC currents through highly inductive motors. Often, particulary in dirty factories or humid conditions, the battery cables will not make good contact with the battery posts. When a cable vibrates loose the current to the motor is abruptly cut off, suddenly releasing the energy stored in the motor's magnetic field. The failing battery cable presents an open circuit to the energy released by this field decay, producing voltages high enough to generate an arc between the battery terminal and the battery cable. This arc establishes a conductive path, re-energizing the motor and allowing the transient voltage to decay until a vibration again momentarily jars the troublesome battery cable loose. This process happens so fast that the operator will normally be unaware that it is occurring. Literally thousands of spikes can be generated every operating shift for weeks until the cable finally fails altogether, forcing a repair.

Because of the transient environment and the fact that power-supply voltages in vehicles vary greatly according to the state of the battery and the charging circuit, the survival of any electronic device in a car or on a forklift is a very special design case. Do not expect success if you take a 12-volt DC radio-operated modem and use it on a vehicle unless it was specifically designed for that use.

With so many possible sources of power problems, how can a communications network possibly be protected from all of them? Actually it cannot. The user must gain an insight into what the transients look like, the energy contained in most of them, and then make some rational decisions about what level of protection to provide for the different components in the communications network. Transient protection, like the transients themselves, is statistical in nature. No criterion is worst case and no design is foolproof.

Disturbances that cause equipment problems are divided according to their duration into surges and transients. Transients are generally considered to be less than about 8.4 milliseconds (ms) in duration (one-half cycle of 60-Hz power), surges are longer than a half cycle. Power-line transients normally arise from some electrical disturbance outside of the power grid, a surge is usually the result of a mechanical reaction by the utility power supply to a sudden load change. The designer of protective circuits must consider surges and transients separately since extremely short transients generally only require the ability to conduct large currents with low voltage drops without regard to heating, while dealing with longer transients requires the ability to dissipate heat to avoid damage to the protective device.

Semiconductors are particularly prone to heat dissipation failure from surges since their active region is the atomic junction of two crystalline regions buried inside a silicon block. If the transient endures for too long the heat at this junction can actually vaporize a portion of the crystal, destroying the protective device and exposing equipment to damage. Therefore, just because a device is specified to protect a multiplexer from 3,000 V transients, a failed transmitter that applies 120 VAC to an input for a few seconds may still damage it. In communications lines almost all voltage disturbances will be transients. The only major surge source is a failed transmitter that applies its power-source voltage to its output.

Because transients are sudden releases of stored electrical energy they are almost always unipolar, exponentially decaying current or voltage spikes. They result from a redistribution of electromagnetic energy, either from a sudden shift of charge (as in lightning) or a rapid collapse of a magnetic field (as in an inductive load switch). Quantifying the transient environment is difficult at best since oscillograms of actual transients look like short, high-energy bursts of white noise.

Instead of trying to actually describe the transients occurring, standards have evolved that describe repeatable transient conditions against which equipment can be tested. As the installed base of equipment tested according to a particular standard grows and studies are made about the equipment's ability to survive real-world transient conditions, the standard will be refined and give birth to new revisions or new standards. More than 20 transient standards have been written in the United States and Europe since the science began, and the evolution continues as electrical transmission techniques change and the requirements of the connected equipment develop.

The best course of action for the user is to specify that protective equipment comply with the current most-

2. Protecting formula. *The IEEE-587 standard describes two unipolar impulse waves, one voltage and one current, that approximate the effects of transient conditions.*

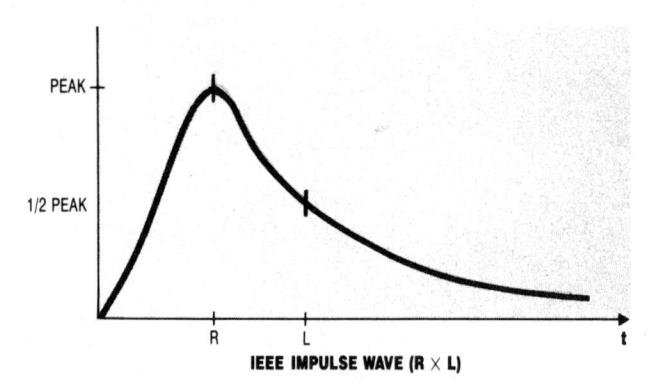

LOCATION CATEGORY	R	L	PEAK
B	1.2 μS	50 μS	6 kV
B	8 μS	20 μS	3 kA

accepted standards and monitor the equipment's ability to protect the gear in the required transient environments. Currently the most widely accepted transient standard in the United States is IEEE-587, which describes two unipolar impulse waves, one voltage and one current, as the best approximation of conditions likely to be experienced outdoors in overhead lines and indoors within 30 feet (10 m) of the electrical service entrance (Fig. 2). The voltage wave rises to a peak in 1.2 microseconds and decays to half that value in 50 microseconds. The peak voltage is dependent on the location, but is commonly 10 kV or greater. The wave is slower-rising and shorter-lasting based on years of observation. One explanation is that characteristic inductance (tending to slow current impulses) in transmission lines is greater than characteristic capacitance (tending to slow voltage changes).

Two things happen as an electrical transient travels through a building's power wiring. First, the unidirectional shape becomes oscillatory because of resonance in the wiring and loads. Second, an installation gets the first level of transient protection—flashover in the wiring devices—for free. Somewhere in every circuit, air is used as an electrical insulator. Overhead power lines are not insulated at all, relying on their distance from the ground to protect people from the thousands of volts applied to the power line.

There is, however, a limit to this air insulation. Given enough voltage, air will eventually break down and the ionized atmosphere left is a very good conductor. This arcing action is what happens during a lightning strike. The amount of voltage required to start this arcing action is proportional to the air-gap distance; the smaller the gap, the lower the voltage required to create an arc. Outdoor 120 V power lines are usually spaced so that the breakdown voltage is about 10 kV, while indoors the flashover voltage is closer to 6 kV. Therefore, just moving a communications device inside reduces by 40 percent the magnitude of the voltage spikes to which it may be subjected.

Unlike power circuits, communications-line transients are

dominated by unidirectional impulse waves indoors and out. These waves are less well defined than those in power lines because fewer studies have been done, but in general they are one-fourth to one-third longer and slower rising, due mostly to the wave "smearing" effects of buried coaxial cable. Older data on communications-line transients are not representative of the problem today, since they were mostly gathered from overhead telecom lines, and show rise times and durations one-fourth to one-third the figures expected with buried coaxial cable.

Older transient protector designs may not work in new coaxial circuits since the coordination of different elements in a protective circuit is often dependent on some assumptions about the rise times of the transient. Designs that use gas tubes or other spark-gap devices as part of the protection circuit are particularly sensitive to the speed with which the transient voltage rises, clamping at voltages that are partially proportional to the incoming transient rise time. The moral of the story when protecting communications lines is to make sure that a protector bought for use in a coaxial circuit was designed for use with the specific coaxial cable type.

Unlike voltage transients, voltage surges normally arise because of some electromechanical action, so they are much longer in duration than transients. If a large load is suddenly removed from a utility grid, a temporary surge may result. Even though surges take much longer to pass than transients they are much smaller in magnitude. Ninety percent of surges will be less than twice the normal voltage, 99 percent less than three times normal.

Preparing a defense
Once the user understands how surges and spikes effect the network, the next step is to protect against them. Most equipment is sold without any specified immunity to transients. It's up to the installer to protect the equipment. The best approach is a combination of good installation, strategic protection, and calculated retrofit.

Good installation means determining where the worst transients will occur and not installing equipment there. Outdoors, whether aboveground or buried, is the worst place to have communications equipment during an electrical storm. Indoors, with as many feet of conductor between the equipment and the outdoors as possible, is the best place to install equipment to avoid lightning transients. Therefore, whenever planning an installation, the user should select a location with at least 100 feet of wiring between it and the electrical service entrance if possible.

When it is not practical to install a device away from transient exposure, then it must either be protected or the user should cross his fingers. Frankly, sometimes it is wisest to cross your fingers. From the isoceraunic map and Table 1, see if a location would be expected to have more than about 12 lightning strikes per year within about a half mile. If so, then it's probably best to protect all equipment. Also, if any local conditions or equipment make a location a moderate to high risk, protect all equipment (Table 2).

What components and circuits are available to protect communications gear against transients and how should they be used? Two transient entry points must be guarded for an installation to be protected: communications lines and power lines.

Table 2: High risk factors

HIGH LIGHTNING ACTIVITY

OVERHEAD ELECTRICAL COMMUNICATION CABLES

LARGE ELECTRICAL MOTORS

ARC FURNACES

WELDERS

Most of the transients on communications lines will come from secondary effects of lightning strokes, and therefore will contain considerably more energy than the average power-line transient found inside buildings. Communication-line transients contain so much energy they can cause spikes in nearby cables through induction. Protect data lines at the building entrance to avoid this kind of transient coupling. If it is not practical to protect communications cables exactly at the building entrance then use magnetically shielded cable from the entrance to the protectors, and keep a good distance between the communications cables and any unprotected data lines or power circuits.

Good distance here varies somewhat with installation circumstance. It is important to remember that the goal is to avoid magnetic induction between two conductors and that magnetic induction is most effective between two conductors that are parallel and close together for a long distance. Therefore, never run unprotected cables in the same cable tray or conduit that contains the unprotected communications cable. If the two cables are parallel for more than 10 feet they should be separated by at least 10 feet, if parallel at all they should be separated by at least 3 feet, and if they cross each other at right angles they should be at least 1 foot apart. If the cables are in a grounded conduit system, all the distances may be halved.

After protecting the data lines in an installation, protecting the communications equipment's power supply is the next priority. One approach to power-supply protection is to run a dedicated line, or separate circuit, all the way from the building's electrical service entrance to the computer

3. Transient protection. *The first widely accepted transient-protection standard, was IEEE-472, the test wave used for data and signal lines not exposed to lightning threats.*

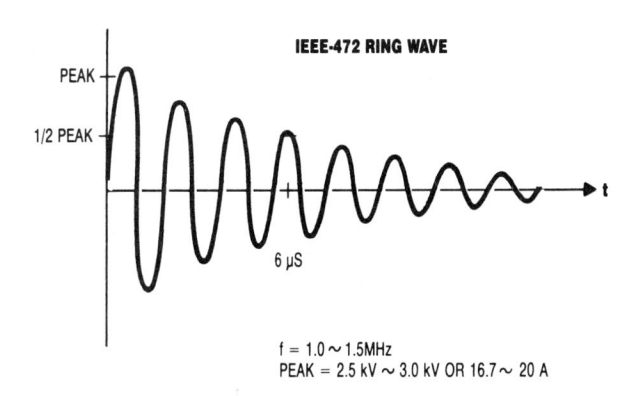

IEEE-472 RING WAVE

6 µS

f = 1.0 ~ 1.5MHz
PEAK = 2.5 kV ~ 3.0 kV OR 16.7 ~ 20 A

Table 3: Partial list of transient protection devices

POWER CONDITIONING DEVICES

MANUFACTURER	MODEL/SERIES	FILTER	IEEE-587 RATED	PRICE (US $)	PHONE
PILGRIM ELECTRIC	SMART STRIP	YES	YES	175	1-516-420-8990
PILGRIM ELECTRIC	VOLTECTOR	YES	YES	174	1-516-420-8990
PLAINVIEW, N.Y.					
TII INDUSTRIES	TII 428 MKII	NO	YES	42	1-516-789-5020
TII INDUSTRIES	TII 439	YES	YES	58	1-516-789-5020
COPIAGUE, N.Y.					
TOPAZ	SURGEBUSTER	YES	NO	60	1-619-279-0831
SAN DIEGO, CALIF.					
TRIPP LITE	ISOBAR	YES	NO	48-110	1-312-329-1777
TRIPP LITE	SPIKE BARS	YES	NO	40-50	1-312-329-1777
CHICAGO, ILL.					
S. L. WABER	DATAGARD	NO	NO	16-36	1-800-257-8384
S. L. WABER	DATAGARD	YES	NO	45-160	1-800-257-8384
WESTVILLE, N.J.					
LEA DYNATECH	SE	NO	NO	97 UP	1-213-944-0916
LEA DYNATECH	KLEANLINE	YES	NO	209 UP	1-213-944-0916
FOUNTAIN VALLEY, CALIF.					
EFI	DPI	YES	YES	119-129	1-800-221-1174
SALT LAKE CITY, UTAH					
TRANSTECTOR	VARIOUS	NO	NO	145 UP	1-800-635-2537
HAYDEN LAKE, IDAHO					
ACCO	50671-50676	OPTION	NO	30-100	1-800-222-6462
WHELLING, ILL.					
MCG	VARIOUS	OPTION	YES	87 UP	1-516-586-5125
DEER PARK, N.Y.					
ELECTRONIC SPECIALISTS	ISOLATOR	OPTION	YES	90-425	1-800-225-4876
NATICK, MASS.					
CONTROL CONCEPTS	VARIOUS	OPTION	YES	32 UP	1-607-724-2484
BINGHAMTON, N.Y.					

NOTE: IEEE-587 RATING REFERS TO WHETHER OR NOT THE MANUFACTURER INDICATES THE IEEE-587 CATEGORY ON THE DATA SHEET. THOSE PRODUCTS SHOWN AS NOT IEEE-587 RATED ARE NOT NECESSARILY LESS RUGGED THAN THOSE CARRYING THE RATING, JUST HARDER TO COMPARE.

DATA LINE PROTECTION

MANUFACTURER	MODEL/SERIES	COMPATIBILITY	PHONE
TRIPP LITE CHICAGO, ILL.	SPIKE BARS	RJ-11	1-312-329-1777
LEA DYNATECH FOUNTAIN VALLEY, CALIF.	TRANSIENT ELIMINATORS	BARRIER STRIPS, RJ-11 COAX, RS-232	1-213-944-0916
POLYPHASER GARDNERVILLE, NEV.	IS	75/50 OHM COAX BARRIER STRIPS	1-800-325-7170
EFI SALT LAKE CITY, UTAH	DPI	RJ-11	1-800-221-1174
TRANSTECTOR HAYDEN LAKE, IDAHO	DLP, LMP, TSJ, FSP	RJ-11, RJ-45, RS-232	1-800-635-2537
MCG DEER PARK, N.Y.	DLP	BARRIER STRIP, BNC, RS-232, 50 PIN RIBBON, RJ-11, RJ-45	1-516-586-5125

or communications room. This approach, although required by some mainframe computer companies, is not really much help by itself. At best it will somewhat decrease the communications equipment's exposure to load-switching spikes originating in the building, at worst it may lead to the false impression that the best location for a communications/computer room is right next to the service entrance.

A more effective protection technique is to create safe islands of protected power where needed by installing commercially available surge suppressors between sensitive communications gear and the power source. Literally hundreds of companies manufacture transient-suppression equipment, ranging in price from less than $50 to more than $1,000, depending on features. For communications protocols and networks that are intolerant of noise these devices can be purchased with built-in electromagnetic/radio-frequency interference filters. Some equipment will automatically turn on the user's printer, CRT, and modem in the right order when a desktop computer's power is turned on. Since some computer systems expect all the peripherals to be energized and ready to talk when power is applied to the central processing unit, these fancy power-protection strips are quite convenient for unskilled operators to use.

Determine what level of protection a piece of equipment or group of devices require, install some sort of protection device between that equipment and the rest of the power wiring, and prominently label the protected outlets as off limits to any equipment other than authorized equipment. Make sure that the building's wiring is connected to the input side of the suppressor and the protected island is wired to the output side, because some products use circuits that are unidirectional protectors and won't protect equipment well if installed backwards.

How much is enough?

A good place to start in determining the level of protection requires a device to analyze the location in which the equipment will be installed. Two protection standards will help in this analysis: the Institute of Electrical and Electronic Engineer's IEEE-472, and IEEE-587. Both standards define the testing waveforms appropriate for devices to be installed in particular locations. The standards don't dictate the protective device operation, just the transient waves to be expected. When evaluating a product for suitability in an application, find out what the output from the protector will be if it is subjected to the proper standard transient wave, and determine if the communications equipment will survive that voltage.

The first widely accepted transient protection standard was IEEE-472, adopted by the IEEE in 1974. It was designed as a standard transient environment for electrical substation apparatus subjected to transients due to the switching of large inductive loads. The standard is widely accepted as the specified test wave for data lines and signal lines not exposed to lightning threats.

The IEEE-472 standard test wave is an exponentially decaying oscilliatory wave with an original peak of 3,000 V through 150 Ohms source impedance (Fig. 3). The bottom line for protective equipment is that it must survive 20 A spikes, positive and negative, for all signal lines.

Because of increased data and some misinterpretation of the scope of IEEE-472, a new standard was issued in 1980. This standard is IEEE-587, which is now referred to as American National Standards Institute/IEEE C62.41-1980. It is meant to deal with power wiring subjected to lightning influences as well as load-switching spikes. This standard, like IEEE-472, only defines the transient waves to be expected in particular locations, not how to protect against them. This standard is the best one to specify for transient protectors on communications lines and for communications equipment power lines.

IEEE-587 defines three classes of locations. These locations are the starting point in defining the protection requirements of all electronic equipment. The first step in transient protection is to install equipment in the location of lowest possible exposure. If this is cannot be done then make sure the equipment can survive repeated exposure to the test waves defined by the standard.

The harshest environment defined by IEEE-587 is outdoors (location category C). In outdoor locations equipment will be exposed to much higher peak transient voltages because wiring flashover will occur at about 10,000 V instead of the 6,000 V level common for indoor power circuits. The standard transient defined by IEEE-587 for outdoor environments and service entrances is a unipolar exponential spike.

As the power line enters a building the environmental rating decreases and becomes much more definable. The open circuit voltage and short circuit current impulse waves have the same shape as for category C locations, but they now have specific maximum values, 6 kV for the voltage wave and 500 A for the current wave. Any device that includes a crowbar device must be able to instantaneously switch between the voltage and current impulse without damage when the crowbar operates. This location is defined as category B, major feeders and short branch feeders. Devices in these locations also need to handle an oscilliatory wave defined in the standard.

After the power wiring travels far enough inside the building the cumulative wiring impedance limits the short circuit current available to damage protectve equipment. Therefore if the wiring length is at least 10 meters (30 feet) from a category B area and at least 20 meters (60 feet) from a category C area then the current wave peak is defined as 200 A. The voltage wave remains the same.

In general, IEEE-587 allows users to specify the transient protection requirement of their communications equipment by knowing where the equipment is installed. If it is outside, it's category C; indoors but within 60 feet (cable length) of the service entrance, then it's category B, farther than 60 feet from the service entrance, it's category A.

Table 3 lists a few of the more than one hundred manufacturers of power conditioning and data line protection devices, many of whom categorize their equipment according to which IEEE-587 standard wave they are designed to suppress. The products are here rated as neither good nor bad; the suitability of a particular product is dependent on the exact requirements at each location. It is up to the user to determine which products offer the best price/performance combination. ∎

Kevin Sharp, a design engineer with Burr-Brown Data Acquisition and Control Division, received his B.S.E.E. from the University of Missouri-Rolla in 1981.

Arielle Emmett and David Gabel, Special to DATA COMMUNICATIONS

Cases in direct microcomputer connections: Nuts and bolts

In this exclusive excerpt from an upcoming book, three case studies discuss the hazards of hardwired links between microcomputers.

Editor's note: *The last few years' microcomputer revolution has dramatically altered the communications landscape. "Distributed processing" is no longer the concern only of analysts trying to sell their pronostications. And users, finding that, indeed, there are enough physically diverse computers to take a hard look at where applications should best be run. In addition, microcomputers have played a major role in helping the local area networking industry fulfill promises made years and years ago.*

It is the microcomputer's versatility that makes the industry move toward increasingly efficient connections from microcomputers to value-added networks, mainframe and minicomputer environments, and videotex equipment. But it cannot be forgotten that there are times when users want to make very "simple" connections: directly from one microcomputer to another, or even to a less intelligent device. In this realm, the innovation that has produced a wealth of microcomputer choices comes back to haunt: the lack of standardized hardware causes problems. As the cases studied below indicate, these difficulties can be thorny, but not intractable.

The case studies were taken from an upcoming book, Direct Connections: Making Your Personal Computer Communicate. *Copyright (c) 1986 by Arielle Emmett and David Gabel. Published by New American Library. All rights reserved. Because of the long production cycles in book publishing, the authors discuss some computers that are no longer major forces in the microcomputer market. Still, the principles that the case studies embody should serve very instructive for any user concerned with direct links between microcomputers.* —DWC

CASE NO. 1: MY BUFFER RUNNETH OVER

In Oxnard, Calif., Charlie Leighton and the Public Works Department were experiencing major difficulties getting an automated fuel-dispensing terminal to talk successfully to an Apple II+ belonging to the street division.

The terminal, a Fuel Master System, manufactured by Engineering Systems Inc. of Tempe, Ariz., and marketed by the Veederoot Fuel Co. of Hartford, Conn., had been installed in an Oxnard equipment maintenance garage. The terminal recorded vehicle identification by reading codes from a plastic credit card-like device that a driver inserted when purchasing fuel. Once the truck's current mileage was recorded, the terminal automatically activated one of several fuel pumps (diesel, gasoline, propane, and so on), dispensed fuel, and recorded the total number of gallons, the date, and time of day.

Leighton, a general supervisor in the Street Division, was assigned to download this data to his division's Apple II+ microcomputer. As many as 1,000 transactions, each of which took up 58 bytes of memory, would be transferred from the terminal to the Apple during a single transmission. At the end of the month, Leighton merged the weekly records into a database program and presented a monthly report on fuel consumption. He kept track of 360 city vehicles.

First results

Leighton's initial transmission setup included an Apple II+ (48 kbytes of random access memory), a Racal-Vadic modem, a 16-kbyte memory card, two floppy disk drives (5.25 inch), an Apple Super Serial Card, and Data Capture 4.0 communications software (Southeastern Software, New Orleans) equipped with 30-kbyte memory buffer (Fig. 1a).

The data-entry terminal and Fuel Master System, equipped with a 300-bit/s auto-answer modem, was connected to a dial-up telephone line. The communications software for the fuel control unit resided in the machine's read-only memory.

When Leighton attempted the transmission by using

his Apple II+ and modem to dial up the fuel terminal, he established a clear physical connection and was able to download data successfully. But because of the limited memory space of his Data Capture 4.0 buffer, the communications program was able to record only 20 kbytes of information—344 fuel transactions at a time—before automatically writing that data to a file, called Overflow-1 on disk.

During disk access, the light on the disk drive turned on, indicating the communications program was emptying its memory buffer. Meanwhile, the Fuel Master System continued to transmit data, but Data Capture, busy with disk access, ignored the new data coming in. When Leighton surveyed the saved fuel transaction files on his Apple disks, he found that he had lost roughly 40 fuel transactions during each disk access. The total amount of data that was lost during any one transmission was approximately 4.6 kbytes.

Analysis and correction

What had caused the problem? Leighton's immediate analysis pointed to an insufficient memory in the Apple II+. With 48 kbytes of available memory space, and only 20 kbytes of capture buffer memory when equipped with Data Capture 4.0 software, the Apple II+ could not capture the full 58 kbytes of fuel transaction data sent by the Veederoot Fuel Master System. The situation was exacerbated by the fact that the Veederoot terminal continued to transmit during each disk access. The new incoming characters were flushed from Leighton's small modem-input buffer before Data Capture knew they had come in.

Leighton's investigations of the problem indicated he could correct it in part by expanding Apple's available memory space to capture more data from the fuel terminal. A second approach, however, appeared more advantageous: finding out why the Veederoot gear continued to transmit when Data Capture accessed the disk drive. For some reason, the Veederoot terminal was not monitoring the status of Data Capture during disk access, and data was being lost.

A broader diagnostic

This proved, in fact, to be the crux of the matter. According to George McClelland, president of Southeastern Software, the fuel terminal was failing to acknowledge a message flow-control protocol that Data Capture used. This protocol, known as X/ON, X/OFF, allows Data Capture to automatically signal the other computer that its capture buffer is full. Under normal circumstances, the receiving computer would get the X/OFF signal (a CTRL-S command) and temporarily halt transmission during disk access. It would once again resume transmission after it got an X/ON signal (a CTRL-Q) indicating Data Capture had cleared its buffer and was ready to receive more data. This simple method of data pacing would have prevented any loss of fuel transactions during the transmission.

Unfortunately, Veederoot is among many communicating devices that do not understand X/ON, X/OFF. In terms of the seven-layer OSI communications model, the unit lacked a simple data-link layer protocol.

At first, Leighton opted to get around the problem by ignoring the protocol altogether and working exclusively

1. More. *A telephone line linked the fuel terminal and the Apple (a). Moving the operating system to the language card effectively expanded the Apple's memory.*

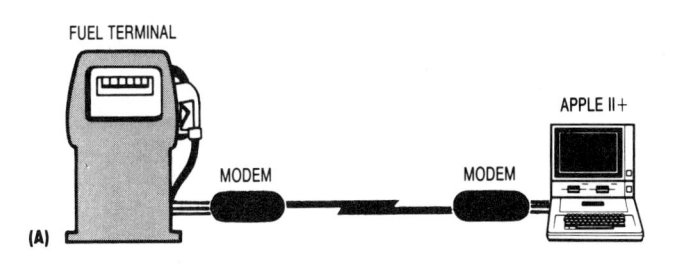

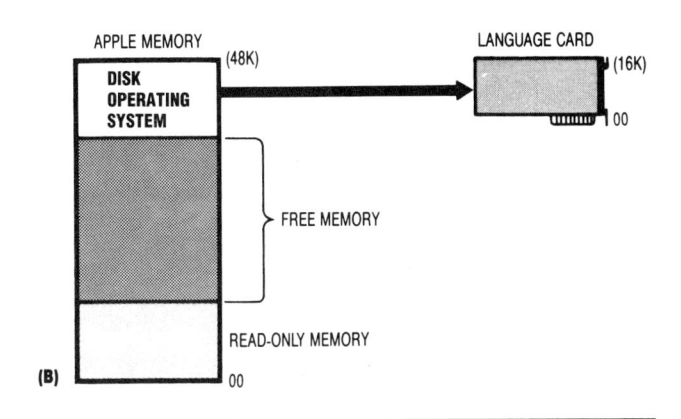

from the Apple side of the link. He decided to expand the Apple's memory, for example, in order to capture larger chunks of data. The manual for Data Capture 4.0 recommended one way of doing this: by using a small programming routine, called DOS MOVE. The routine transports the DOS operating system from its normal location in memory to yet another location—a RAM extension that is also called the Apple language card. This maneuver frees up an additional 10 kbytes of available memory, bringing the total capture buffer memory to 30 kbytes (Fig. 1b). The additional space allowed the Apple to save an extra 200 transactions during each transmission. Although this might have partially solved the problem, Leighton knew he would still have to go back and pick up the missing fuel data in separate transmission sequences.

Eureka

The incompleteness of the strategy, though, prompted him to investigate other options. After much searching and discussion, he learned that an independent company had already written an Apple software program that would communicate directly with the Veederoot Terminal. The program, called Automated Fueling System, by Cork Control, Inc. of Missoula, Mont., automatically dials up any number of fuel terminals and polls them for fuel transaction data. It then uses a sequence of commands that "packs" the data into a shortened form and dumps it to the Apple memory. When data is sent, the flow is controlled through a simple control-character protocol, ACK/NAK.

In this protocol, the Apple sends a control character, CTRL-F to Veederoot indicating it has acknowledged a particular data transaction. Apple sends a "NAK" control character (Control U) when it fails to read a transaction.

That solves the problem of disk access if transmissions are exceptionally long. If, for example, the Apple must write the contents of its buffer to a disk, it flashes a "NAK" signal to the fuel terminal; and the terminal will keep transmitting the same data until Apple is finished writing out its memory buffer. Thus, the Apple does not lose any of the transmitted data.

Like the X/ON-X/OFF protocol, ACK/NAK is essentially a software handshaking protocol, a simple protocol designed to control message flow in the data link layer. Moreover, it is the one protocol that the Veederoot Fuel Master system understands. To fulfill his application's requirements, Leighton had to find a piece of Apple software that could match that protocol. Luckily, Leighton was able to find a company that had already invented it.

This points up a moral of sorts that very sophisticated users sometimes forget: If you can identify the problem, you may be able to find someone who has either written a program to solve it. You do not always have to write a program yourself. User groups and vast public domain libraries offer a wealth of software that may help you solve connection problems, if there is not an off-the-shelf product easily available.

Of course, it is entirely possible that you cannot completely solve the problem with software from another source. Then, of course, the challenge to the user is greater. The first step, as this case illustrates, is clearly diagnosing and identifying the problem.

CASE NO. 2: A SPEED-MATCHING PROBLEM
In Aurora, Colo., Ernest Mau, a writer, was trying to implement communications between his Morrow Decision I, an S-100 bus CP/M computer, and an Apple II+. He had a specific goal in mind for the connection: Mau had written profitable word-find puzzles on the Morrow, and he wished to merge these with the excellent graphics capabilities of the Apple. He decided to generate the puzzles on the Morrow and transfer them in ASCII text file format across the RS-232-C serial ports of each computer. Apple DOS's Toolkit graphics program could then be used to illustrate the puzzles.

Because of his extensive experience in direct connecting dissimilar computers, Mau had little trouble modifying a cable to connect to each computer's serial port. In his initial configuration he used a California Computer Systems 7710a Asynchronous Serial Interface card (RS-232-C) on the Apple and the serial printer port on the Morrow.

The cable was a 100-foot-long direct-connect cable he had modified, with two DB-25 connectors bolted back to back (male to female). He short-circuited the pins that carried the hardware handshaking signals (4,5,6,8, and 20). This solved the problem of hardware signal control across the RS-232-C interface (Fig. 2). As Mau explains it, "It just eliminates the handshaking capabilities from the interfaces by making each computer think each handshaking line is present at all times." Mau thought this cable configuration to be "an almost universal connector for intercomputer communications among several different machines."

Once the physical link had been completed, Mau expected to be able to send standard files at a speed of 1.2 kbit/s without a modem. That equalled the speed of most of the fastest modems in the microcomputer market at the time, and also saved him the hassle of tying up his telephone lines.

Mau, however, had no communications software to handle the transmission. Consequently, he had to modify a BASIC program on the Apple slightly so that it would accept incoming data directly from the RS-232-C serial port, then buffer it into memory and write it out a disk file when the process was completed. Mau did this by modifying a MAKE TEXT program provided on the Apple DOS 3.3 diskette. He was able to make simple changes that would allow the Apple to accept characters from the port rather than from the keyboard. In a sense, he was fooling the Apple into thinking the text was being generated from the keyboard.

With these changes in place, Mau thought he was set for the data transfer. To keep things simple, he stored the files as plain Ascii text. Even with this precaution, Mau got "nothing but garbage" on the Apple screen. "The Apple was misinterpreting the ASCII codes from the Morrow," he said. What was the cause?

Analysis and correction
Mau retraced his steps. Since he was knowledgeable about communications and boasted a programming background, he had already made sure that his Apple knew where to look for incoming data. He did not think there was anything wrong with his modification of the MAKE TEXT program or with his cable connection.

"I knew what I was sending to the Apple was clean material," he said, "but it wasn't being received clearly." Mau remembered that the Apple screen display had a quirk: It could be "overtyped" or "overwritten" if Mau typed too rapidly. He contemplated that the screen was being "overtyped" by characters coming in too rapidly from the RS-232-C port.

Mau checked the transmission speeds of each computer. Both the Morrow's and the Apple's communications port were set to send and receive data at 1.2 kbit/s. Yet the Morrow indeed seemed to be "typing in data" faster than the Apple screen display could handle it.

A broader diagnostic
There's no question that Mau's computers were suffering from a speed-matching problem. Despite the overt "match" between transmission rates, data was still arriving too quickly given the Apple's peculiar screen display. A definite hardware limitation—the Apple's screen speed (rate at which it turned data into visible characters on the screen)—had turned good data arriving at the port into

2. Custom built. *The Apple II and the Morrow computer were linked by a direct connection. Implementing the link required a specially rewired RS-232-C connector.*

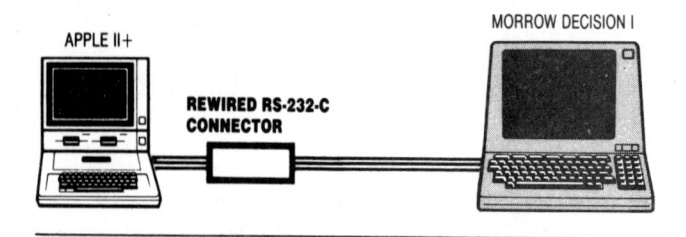

garbage on the screen. Mau had only two alternatives to fix the problem: Either speed up the Apple screen or slow down the Morrow. By far, the latter was the more feasible approach.

Practical solutions
It was a relatively simple matter to write a program in Basic to slow down the data transfer. Delays could be inserted after each line of text. "I put in a delay loop," he said. "There would be a delay after the Morrow would send a line of data, which simply allowed the Apple to catch up." Though Mau had to write a small program that sent data line by line and inserted pauses after each line, he noted that this is often a built-in capability of communications software packages. Simply by accessing a menu, an operator can elect to send text on a character-by-character or a line-by-line basis. That solves a great number of speed-matching problems generated by microcomputer hardware.

Indeed, speed matching is a common problem in microcomputer communications, especially when the computers connect directly through serial ports. On one level, simple peculiarities in one computer's hardware (a screen speed display is an example) will affect data transport in the physical layer. Garbage characters will appear in the data stream because of hardware distortion. Protocols, then, are needed to control speed and to match speed. These protocols provide flow-control, and thus primarily affect the data-link layer. Using a delay after a line is a common trick for getting one side to slow down.

CASE NO. 3: HANDSHAKING, CODES, AND OTHER MYSTERIES

In Briarcliff Manor, N. Y., software consultant George Heidenrich was attempting to implement a direct data transfer between his portable Radio Shack Model 100 and an Osborne I computer. Heidenrich, who did a great deal of writing on the Radio Shack while traveling, wished to transfer files easily back and forth to the Osborne, and also to a Xerox MemoryWriter printer. This would let him format data files and programs using the most appropriate software and output equipment available (Fig. 3).

First tests
A preliminary test of the Osborne's telecommunications capability indicated the machine could communicate. Heidenrich, relying on documentation provided by a client, used a standard modem connection (the Osborne was equipped with a built-in modem) to access Telemail, an electronic-mail offering of GTE Telenet. Having first gotten a screenful of mixed garbage and legible characters, Heidenrich realized that communications parameters in his software program, AMCALL (from MicroCall Services), were not set correctly. He experimented with parity checking until he settled on seven bits, even parity, which completely cleared the problem.

Following early telecommunications with public databases, Heidenrich began his direct-connect experiments in earnest. He first attempted a direct transfer of data from his Radio Shack Model 100 to the Osborne using a modem-connecting cable, which plugs into each machine's modem port. Heidenrich's modem connection simulated an actual communications data transfer through a telephone.

The initial transfer set up was as follows: The Radio Shack's TELCOM (telecommunications software program) was set to answer a call. In accord with the user manual, the machine's communications parameters were set at 300 bit/s, 8 bit bytes, no parity, one stop bit, X/ON-X/OFF enabled. (The code appears on the Radio Shack screen as M8N1E, which translates to Modem, 8 Bits, No parity, 1 Stop bit, X/ON-X/OFF enabled.) The Osborne's AMCALL communications program was set for identical parameters, so that physical- and data-link protocol would match. Heidenrich also specified "O" in the AMCALL menu for originating the call. By entering an "@" command and pressing the RETURN key, he enabled AMCALL to send a carrier signal to the Radio Shack unit. The Model 100, recognizing the signal, buzzed. Heidenrich then pressed F4 on the Radio Shack, allowing it to enter terminal mode. The Osborne flashed a message showing the connection was established.

First results
At first, there were no problems. Heidenrich could type back and forth on either the Radio Shack or the Osborne, and the characters appeared on the other computer. No line feeds could be sent, however, so he had to enter line feeds separately by using a Control J command, which enabled the computers to space the entry of each line.

When Heidenrich decided to send a Radio Shack file to the Osborne, he used the same communications parameters. Pressing an ESC R keystroke command on the Osborne, which prepared it to receive a file, he pressed an F3 key (File Upload) on the Radio Shack, specified a file name and a column width, then pressed a RETURN keystroke to enable Radio Shack to send the file. The "upload" light on the Radio Shack turned on, indicating the file was being sent. Characters streamed across the bottom of the Osborne screen. No extra line feeds or carriage returns had been added.

After checking the Osborne disk file directory, Heidenrich discovered that the file had not been recorded. After much experimentation and reading of the Radio Shack manual, he typed in a separate Control Z keystroke on the Radio Shack keyboard. This closed the file and enabled Osborne to write it to disk.

Analysis and correction
"Evidently, Osborne never recognized the end-of-file character from Radio Shack," Heidenrich observed. The Osborne was apparently missing, or failing to properly interpret, some of the Radio Shack's automatic control characters sent in the datastream. The control characters, non-printed characters generated by the communications software, are generally used by each computer to control the formatting of files. The fact that line feeds were missing during the connection indicated that some control characters were being screened out. The problem could be solved easily, however, by entering separate control characters (such as CTRL-Z) from the keyboard once the transmission was complete.

Sending data from the Osborne machine to the Radio Shack unit proved to be a still greater problem. The

3. Elegant hardcopy. *These two links would allow files created on the Radio Shack machine to be massaged on the Osborne and output to the Memorywriter printer.*

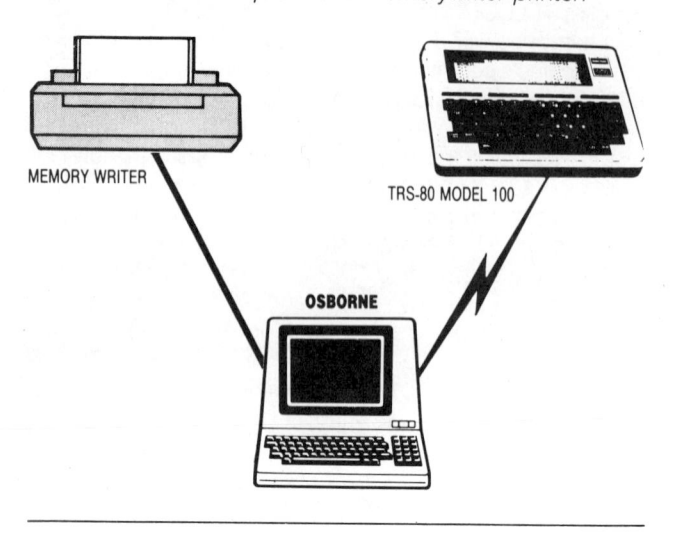

MEMORY WRITER

TRS-80 MODEL 100

OSBORNE

Osborne would send text only line by line, waiting for a CTRL-Q command from the Radio Shack to enable it to continue sending. The Radio Shack never sent the command. In addition, it could not be sent manually from the Radio Shack keyboard. If Heidenrich entered separate Control Q keystrokes on the Osborne keyboard, though, text could be sent. But this method proved rather cumbersome.

A second, direct cable connection
Heidenrich decided to attempt a fast, serial transfer of data by hardwiring the RS-232-C ports of each computer. To do this, he built his own adaptor cable. Transmit and receive lines ran straight through from Radio Shack to Osborne without a crossover. The Osborne is configured differently from most computers; its transmit and receive signal lines are configured as DCE (data communications equipment), which means they "look" like a modem to another computer wired as a DTE (data terminal equipment). The #7 ground wires from each machine were mated directly. The lines that concerned handshaking were more of a problem.

Following guidelines specified by an Osborne computer user's group, Heidenrich nullified (short-circuited) pins 4 and 5 on the Radio Shack, as well as pins 6, 8, and 20. He left all the corresponding pins on Osborne unconnected. This allowed each computer to think that the other had cleared it for data transmission or reception.

Finding a software connection that would work was still a problem. Heidenrich could not use the AMCALL program because it was designed only to work with modem connections, not with RS-232-C serial ports. He had to find some other means for getting the Osborne to accept data and control codes from its serial port.

Internal program
The answer Heidenrich found was a program called PIP (Peripheral Interface Processor) that resides in the Osborne's CP/M operating system. This program, says Heidenrich, "talks to the physical device [the RS-232-C port] directly from the operating system. That enables the operating system to process the control characters embedded in the Radio Shack Text."

To set-up for communications, Heidenrich needed to use another program in CP/M called Stat, which told PIP exactly how to talk directly to the RS-232-C serial port. The STAT commands established a basic physical connection. Radio Shack TELCOM parameters were set to send and receive data at 1.2 kbit/s, 8 bits, no parity, one stop bit, X/ON enabled. Heidenrich entered a terminal mode command to allow the Radio Shack to communicate with the Osborne. He pressed the "Upload" key, specified a file name, a column width, and pressed carriage returns on both the Radio Shack and the Osborne.

Once again, a CTRL-Z keystroke was needed on the Radio Shack to send an end-of-file instruction to the Osborne. Line feeds, however, were not sent, only carriage returns. Separate commands were entered on both Osborne and Radio Shack to close the file and write it on the disk. In the reverse direction, Radio Shack was able to receive data, but with errors. PIP continued not to recognize end-of-transmission control codes.

Diagnostic
The problem with the Osborne and Radio Shack machines proved extremely complex. Even after the PIP program was modified to accept data from the serial port, Heidenrich found that control characters from the Radio Shack were still being screened out during transmission. To solve this problem, he had to find exactly what control characters PIP was looking for and then embed those characters in the text in order to save the Radio Shack file. A similar strategy would be needed to get files transferred in the reverse direction, from the Osborne machine to the Radio Shack computer.

Heidenrich has not found the complete answer and is still looking for a better solution. He suspects that his direct-connect cable is responsible for at least some of his problems. Without the correct hardware handshaking signals, neither computer can properly monitor the status of the other. This affects the physical link protocol, including the establishment and termination of a connection. That problem is compounded by a hardware or software screening of control characters in the data stream. Heidenrich is working on this by changing communications parameters affecting the PIP program. He is experimenting with setting the PIP parameters to accept non-ASCII files. This trick may allow the Osborne to accept many of the Radio Shack's control codes. ∎

(This is the first part of a two-part article excerpted from the upcoming book Direct Connections: Making Your Personal Computers Communicate. *Next month's excerpt from the book will focus on microcomputer direct connections that entail modems.)*

Arielle Emmett, a freelance writer with an extensive list of articles about the computer industry, has a master's degree in advance writing from the University of Washington. Her work has appeared in the New York Times, Omni, Personal Computing, Newsweek, *and other publications. David Gabel, also a freelance writer, is a graduate of West Point. Mr. Gabel also attained a master's degree in electrical engineering from Stanford University.*

Arielle Emmett and David Gabel,
Special to DATA COMMUNICATIONS

Modem connections: Practical, quick check

In this, the second part of a two-part article, the authors offer 11 points to aid in sending data between micros.

*I*mplementing modem communications between microcomputers no longer requires the specialized training of a network operator, but the task can still be quite complex and fraught with errors. This article, the second of two parts, provides a quick checklist for modem connections.

1. Check pins, protocols, and control characters, in that order.

Before attempting to transmit, check hardware, communications protocols available for use in software, and special control codes your computer may use to perform transmission functions or formatting. Even if standard Bell-compatible modems are used (both modems must implement the same hardware protocol), you must assure yourself that you've chosen the correct RS-232-C cable.

Check your cable selection with a dealer and have him try it out for you before buying the cable. Otherwise you may get a garbled transmission or no transmission at all. Problems with hardware handshaking may also destroy the tail end of transmission buffers.

Communications settings or parameters are also crucial. If you are transmitting one-on-one to another computer, choose the highest-level protocol common to sender and receiver. If it doesn't work, proceed downward on the ladder until you find a common protocol that does work. For example, buffered terminal mode will enable virtually all dissimilar computers to communicate ASCII text files, as long as communications settings match and hardware handshaking is working properly. However, buffered terminal mode does not do error checking.

Control characters are used differently in different computers. They let either the computer or the user control some transmission tasks and formatting. Review your list of control characters in your documentation or software. Learn the idiosyncracies of your communicating computers: It may be necessary not only to rely on the control codes automatically sent back and forth by the software, but also to separately enter control characters from the keyboard to open and close files.

2. Files are best converted into as simple a format as possible.

Start with ASCII text files and the simplest communications settings possible: for example, seven bits, even parity, one stop bit, 300 bit/s. Ignore the parity bit, if necessary. Avoid using an eight-bit setting because eight bits correspond to ASCII codes above 128. These are nonstandard, control, formatting, and graphics characters.

3. Type back and forth in terminal mode before beginning a file transfer.

Once you are hooked up, access terminal mode and type a few words to test the accuracy of the data bits coming across the line. Never attempt a file transfer until you have ironed out garbles or nonmatched communications settings in your software.

4. Choose the highest-level error-checking protocol implemented in both sender and receiver communications software.

Always try a protected or error-free protocol before you resort to straight, unprotected, buffered terminal transmission. Protected transfers are vital if you're sending computer programs, numerical data, or binary files. But be forewarned: Some protocols are actually subsets or reinterpretations of standard protocols.

Also, dissimilar computers running packages implementing the same protocol may nevertheless misread incoming characters. The only way to know for sure is to experiment; you can always crank down to a simple X-On/X-Off (or no protocol) if the other schemes don't work.

5. Try modem communications first, direct connect second.

Modem communications are almost always easier to set up and troubleshoot than a direct serial transfer. By contrast, serial and null modem cables pose the problem of hard-wire connection, a complex matter. Take our advice, try a modem connection first. It's comparatively easy.

6. Pay attention to parity bits if you use them.

A screenful of mixed garbage and legible characters often signals a discrepancy in parity checking. Make sure parity is matched before pulling the panic button. Try each parity setting methodically (even, odd, ignore, no parity) on both sending and receiving ends and record the results.

7. Learn how to open and close data files.

Some telecommunications packages don't help an operator call up and survey a file that has just been transmitted. A case in point is PC to Mac and Back (Dilithium Press)—otherwise an excellent telecommunications program. Its conventions demand that the user first store a file on disk, then call it up with the MacWrite word processing program. Other programs don't tell a user exactly how to save a file once it's been stored in the capture buffer. Just to play safe, familiarize yourself with file saving and loading operations before you attempt a transmission.

8. Read your manuals.

Most contain troubleshooting checklists breaking out characteristic symptoms, possible causes, and cures. Modems generally come with checklists, as do programs. Often solutions are buried in the back of the manual under a heading like "Advanced Topics." You may also get some help by purchasing additional books geared toward your particular computer and its operating system.

9. Experiment with file conversion formats.

Some telecommunications software, as well as spreadsheets, database, and word processing programs, offer special file conversion utilities that enable you to convert data files into a neutral or virtual format. These files are then suitable for transmission to other computers. Programs such as VisiCalc and 1-2-3 offer a file format called DIF (Data Interchange Format) enabling the receiving computer to read the data and reconvert it to a form that its own version of the program can use. Other neutral file formats are also available. Some telecommunications programs geared toward specific machines (PC to Mac and Back, for instance) offer conversion utilities for data files from WordStar and Multiplan.

10. Transmit in half duplex when possible.

Remember, half duplex affects local echo settings. Full-duplex settings can cause echo-back problems. Sometimes an operator may transmit to another computer in full-duplex terminal mode, finding that his own words, entered from the keyboard or from a disk file, don't appear on his own screen. The remedy is almost invariably a switch to half-duplex setting. Half duplex echoes characters both to the screen and the communications line; full duplex sends characters out the communications line, then waits for the receiving computer to echo back the characters. In some cases, though, the echoed characters are misinterpreted as a control code.

11. If your files are overtyped...

Some communications programs don't send line feeds after carriage returns. Some computers' screen controllers will send line feeds, while others will screen out the linefeed codes so that the type is overwritten on the receiving end. The ASCII codes for line feeds may be stored in the receiving computer's memory. Off-line, the receiver's own word processing program may be able to read these codes and format the document accordingly. If that fails, the operator may need to write a small program to insert line feeds in the transmitted text when needed. ■

(This is the second part of a two-part article excerpted from the upcoming book Direct Connections: Making your Personal Computer Communicate. *Copyright © 1986 by Arielle Emmett and David Gabel. Published by New American Library.)*

Nathan J. Muller, Telecom Planning & Analysis, Huntsville, Ala.

ADPCM offers practical method for doubling T1 capacity

Network managers who have long wrestled with balancing cost and quality in private T1 networks now have a solution.

Escalating equipment costs and the frustratingly long lead times needed to order, install, and cut over new T1 facilities are forcing communications managers to turn to adaptive differential pulse code modulation, or ADPCM. When pressure builds to upgrade the transmission capabilities of private voice and data networks, ADPCM gear can double the number of voice conversations that can be carried over T1 facilities.

By implementing ADPCM gear on T1 channel banks, substantial network economies can be realized with only a modest increase in hardware costs—and at virtually no sacrifice in transmission quality. Besides being economically attractive, ADPCM adds a high degree of flexibility to network planners since it limits reliance on the local carriers.

Until recently, the easiest way to keep pace with increasing voice and data traffic was by ordering more line termination equipment and leasing additional T1 lines from local carriers—all at substantial expense. In T1 equipment, voice signals are converted to digital pulses for transmission at 1.544 Mbit/s. At this speed, a single T1 line usually accommodates up to 24 channels or as many as 24 simultaneous voice conversations.

ADPCM halves the number of bits required to encode a voice signal accurately, so T1 transmission capacity is doubled from the original 24 channels, to 48. This provides users with a 2-for-1 cost savings on monthly charges for leased T1 lines, as well as reducing the capital outlay for line termination equipment. And since many ADPCM devices handle network management signaling inband, all 48 channels may be used for voice or data transmission.

The conventional encoding technique used in T1 lines is called pulse code modulation. In PCM line equipment the voice signals are sampled at the minimum rate of twice the highest frequency level. This translates to a rate of 8,000 samples per second since the telephone industry's standard voice signals range from 200 to 4,000 cycles per second (200 Hz to 4 kHz). The amplitudes of the samples are then encoded to binary form using enough bits per sample to keep the quantizing noise low while still maintaining an adequate signal-to-noise ratio.

In a PCM-based application, this means eight binary bits per sample are required, which allows up to 256 discrete amplitude values (255 amplitude values are used in North America), or frequency levels. The conversion of a voice signal to digital pulses is performed by the coder-decoder, or codec, which is a key component of D4 channel banks. The codec then multiplexes 24 channels together to form a 1.544-Mbit/s signal suitable for transmission over digital facilities, like the T1 leased line.

ADPCM does not shortcut the 8,000-sample-per-second requirement for encoding 4-kHz voice signals. Instead, the ADPCM coding device, called the transcoder, accepts the sampling rate, then applies a special algorithm to reduce the 8-bit samples to 4-bit words using only 15 quantizing levels. These 4-bit words no longer fully represent sample amplitudes; instead, they contain only enough information to reconstruct the amplitudes at the distant end.

A crucial element of the transcoder circuitry is its adaptive predictor feature, which predicts the value of the next signal based only on the level of the previously sampled signal. Since the human voice changes little from one sample interval to the next, prediction accuracy for voice tends to be very high.

A feedback loop built into the predictor circuitry ensures that voice variations are followed with minimal deviation. The deviation of the predicted value measured against the actual signal value tends to be very small and can be encoded with only four bits, rather than the eight bits used in PCM. In the unlikely event that successive samples vary widely, the algorithm adapts by increasing the range represented by the four bits though at a slight increase in the noise level over normal signals.

At the other end of the T1 line, another transcoder performs the process in reverse. Predictor circuitry reinserts the deleted bits and restores the original 8-bit code. Since the receiver's decoder must be able to track the transmitter's encoded signal, both must utilize the same algorithm. This locks the user into a brand of transcoder.

Since voice and data sampling patterns differ greatly, separate adaptive predictors are dedicated to voice and data applications. A speech-data detector is used in the transcoder to decide which prediction algorithm to employ.

Other schemes

Other circuit multiplication schemes are used over T1 facilities, such as Continuously Variable Slope Delta Modulation (CVSD) and Time Assigned Speech Interpolation (TASI). But the encoding schemes employed in these techniques are effective only within a relatively narrow range of T1 applications.

CVSD modulation uses a sampling rate as high as 32,000 samples per second. Since the difference between each CVSD sample tends to be very small, a single bit can be used to represent the change in the slope of the analog curve. The big advantage of CVSD is that it can be used to encode voice signals at a lower bandwidth than ADPCM. CVSD will support voice data rates of 16, 24, 32, and 64 kbit/s. The drawback is that the quality of the CVSD-modulated speech is not as good as an ADPCM-encoded signal at 32 kbit/s.

TASI takes advantage of the pauses in human speech to interleave several conversations together over the same channel. Since most speakers cannot talk and listen simultaneously, the effective utilization of the network in most voice conversations is typically somewhat less than 50 percent—and the natural pauses between utterances drops the efficiency an additional 10 percent. TASI-based schemes seek out and detect the active speech on a line and assign only active talkers to the T1 facility. Thus, TASI makes more efficient utilization of time to double T1 capacity.

Although TASI increases T1 capacity, it also may cause significant delay. TASI equipment has also been found to cause "clipping" in small tie line configurations. Clipping occurs when speech signals are deformed by the cutting off of initial or final syllables.

Relative merits

PCM, ADPCM, and CVSD encoding schemes each have advantages and disadvantages depending on their application (see table). PCM-encoded voice quality is good and relatively simple to implement; its drawback is that it delivers only enough bandwidth for 24 channels.

ADPCM also delivers toll-quality voice, and it doubles T1 transmission capacity for voice. Though it passes modem traffic at just 4.8 kbit/s or less, this limitation concerns only those users with a very large installed base of modems.

Businesses frustrated by having to lease separate private-line circuits for voice and data can garner substantial cost savings by incorporating ADPCM technology into their networks and integrating their voice and data traffic. For example, in channels that carry data at speeds greater than 4.8 kbit/s, the ADPCM function can be disabled locally at a front control panel or remotely via an administrative terminal connected to an RS-232-C/V.24 supervisory port. Either arrangement allows noncompressible signals to be passed at their normal rate. Since these instructions are typically saved in nonvolatile electronically programmable read-only memory, there is no need to reset or reprogram them after power outages or network failures. Though ADPCM is slightly more complex to implement than PCM or CVSD, its benefits override its limitations.

CVSD falls between PCM and ADPCM in terms of implementation complexity, but it does not exhibit toll-quality voice at 32 kbit/s and will not reliably carry even 4.8-kbit/s modem traffic. CVSD is highly susceptible to noise interference, which results in a relatively poor-quality signal. Thus it performs best in point-to-point applications, where low cost is the overriding factor. Unlike many ADPCM devices, most CVSD devices do not offer the option of selecting dedicated signaling channels. Not only is CVSD unsuitable for multinode applications, but because

	BENEFITS	DRAWBACKS
PULSE CODE MODULATION	INTEGRATES VOICE AND DATA AT 1.544 MBIT/S	LIMITED TO 24 CHANNELS
	SINGLE CIRCUIT IS MORE EFFICIENT THAN 24 STANDARD VOICE-GRADE CIRCUITS	INSTALLATION AND CUTOVER MAY TAKE AS LONG AS 18 MONTHS
	MORE ECONOMICAL THAN EQUIVALENT NUMBER OF VOICE CHANNELS	
	MAINTAINS TOLL QUALITY VOICE, SUITABLE FOR TANDEM APPLICATIONS	
	SIMPLE TO IMPLEMENT	
CONTINUOUSLY VARIABLE SLOPE DELTA MODULATION	DOUBLES TRANSMISSION CAPACITY OF T1 CIRCUIT	DOES NOT EXHIBIT TOLL-QUALITY VOICE AT 32 KBIT/S
	INEXPENSIVE AND RELATIVELY SIMPLE TO IMPLEMENT	DOES NOT RELIABLY PASS 4.8-KBIT/S MODEM TRAFFIC
	SUPPORTS VOICE DATA AT 16, 24, 32, AND 64 KBIT/S	HIGHLY SUSCEPTIBLE TO NOISE INTERFERENCE
		LIMITED TO POINT-TO-POINT APPLICATIONS
ADAPTIVE DIFFERENTIAL PULSE-CODE MODULATION	DOUBLES TRANSMISSION CAPACITY OF T1 CIRCUIT	MORE COMPLEX, MORE EXPENSIVE TO IMPLEMENT THAN CVSD
	EXHIBITS TOLL-QUALITY VOICE AT 32 KBIT/S; RELIABLY PASSES 4.8-KBIT/S MODEM TRAFFIC	LIMITED TO SUPPORTING 32 KBIT/S
	INCORPORATES EXTENSIVE TEST FEATURES; OPTIONALLY PROVIDES IN-BAND SIGNALING	LIMITED TO PASSING 4.8-KBIT/S TRAFFIC
	PROVIDES NETWORK PLANNING FLEXIBILITY AND COST CONTROL	

CVSD implementations are vendor-specific, CVSD does not work with all AT&T carrier facilities.

Considering the high monthly cost of T1 lines, ADPCM devices provide substantial savings to businesses operating private networks. For example, the current charge for a single 712-mile Accunet circuit from New York to Chicago runs about $23,000 per month, with an additional charge of about $4,000 for installation. Some circuits between New York and Los Angeles can cost close to $1 million a year. Compare these costs with the one-time charge of about $16,500 for a complete ADPCM network, which can double the T1 channel capacity between these cities.

Bottom-line benefits

Further savings can be won by using higher order digital multiplexers between ADPCM devices (Fig. 1). For example, the output of two ADPCM devices can be multiplexed together over a single T1C carrier (3.152 Mbit/s), increasing channel capacity by four times. With a T2 microwave link (6.312 Mbit/s), channel capacity may be increased eightfold to 192 channels and, over a T3 satellite link (44.738 Mbit/s), may be increased 58 times to provide 1,344 channels.

ADPCM transcoders do not require special repeaters to regenerate signals over long distances nor do they require ancillary test equipment, so benefits also come in the form of direct hardware savings. And when ADPCM gear is added to the network, it does not complicate the testing of T1 facilities.

Determining whether the source of a fault lies in the line itself or with the added equipment is simplified by the "loopback" points found in most ADPCM circuitry. Loopbacks allow operational verification of individual T1 channels or the entire T1 link (Fig. 2).

For example, using a specialized test mode, the user may verify that the entire near-end ADPCM scheme and individual channels are operational. In another test mode, the user may verify near-end operation as well as the operation of the entire transmission link.

Still another test mode may allow verification of both near and distant transcoders and the entire link. End-to-end voice quality may be verified through an analog-digital-analog voice port.

Another feature of most transcoders is an automatic internal bypass, which ensures that the original 24 channels of a T1 line remain available for use in the event of a network failure. This feature is especially important when considering the revenues and productive working hours that are lost during downtime and the confusion that often results when the transmission of critical information is disrupted.

Cost savings aside, ADPCM devices are easy to order and install, as well as to operate and maintain. Some T1 circuits may take as long as 18 months to order and put into service, compared with 30-day off-the-shelf delivery for most ADPCM devices.

Installation of the ADPCM device may be as simple as mounting an additional shelf onto the line termination equipment rack, inserting the required ADPCM modules, and wiring these modules to the channel bank assembly—an easy task for an experienced technician. For an extra charge, some vendors will pre-wire an equipment rack

1. Savers. Using higher-order multiplexers, ADPCM devices increase capacity of T1C to 96 channels, T2 microwave to 192 channels, and T3 satellite to 1,344 channels.

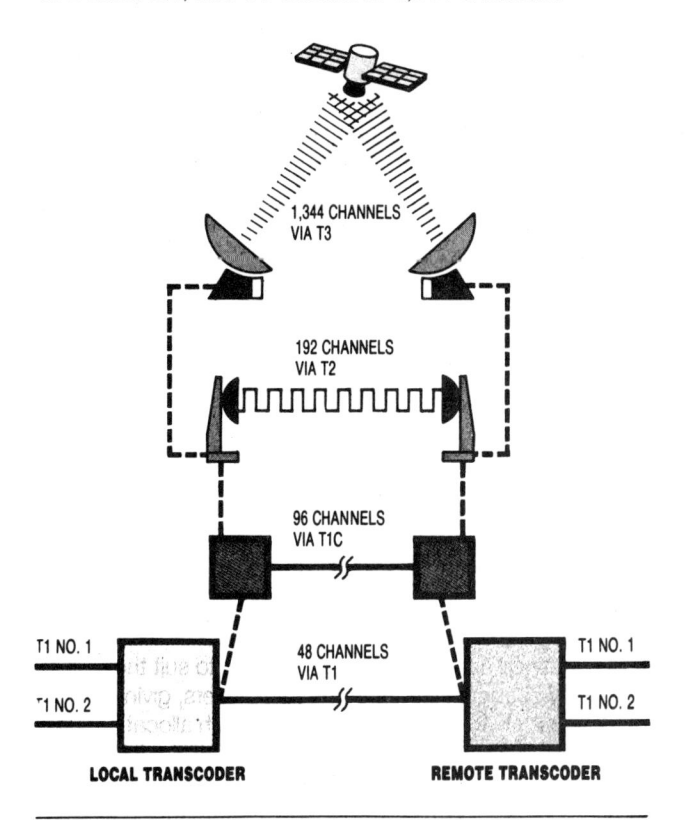

when customers order both the D4 line termination equipment and the transcoders, and then pre-test the entire configuration before shipment.

The use of ADPCM devices also permits greater latitude in designing or expanding T1 facilities. Because most ADPCM networks are modular, T1 capacity can be increased as needed simply by adding modules. This eliminates the long lead times required to order T1 circuits to meet forecast requirements.

If future transmission requirements fail to materialize as forecast, ADPCM cushions the impact. T1 tarrifs allow the carrier to levy a penalty charge if lines are canceled prior to the start of service. ADPCM gives the user the ability to increase the traffic-carrying capability of the network without central office assistance.

Questions that may arise during the purchase of ADPCM gear are what will happen to the investment when an Integrated Systems Digital Network becomes available, and will the bandwidth glut created by fiber optic networks negate the need for circuit multiplication techniques? ISDN promises intelligent, end-to-end digital connectivity on a network that will support simultaneous voice and data. Bell operating company field trials are scheduled through 1988. Various manufacturers have announced the availability of so-called ISDN chips so that off-the-shelf products may be on the market by the end of the decade.

Under AT&T's concept of nodal architecture, ISDN primary rate PBX-oriented services (23 BD) will be available to users through its No. 4 ESS toll switching centers accessible via T1 links. Each of the 24 channels can be defined

2. Maintenance mode. *Loopback features in most ADPCM transcoders simplify device and network test procedures. Tests include the near-end ADPCM scheme and individual channels, the entire transmission link, and both near and distant transcoders. End-to-end voice quality may be verified through an analog-digital-analog voice port.*

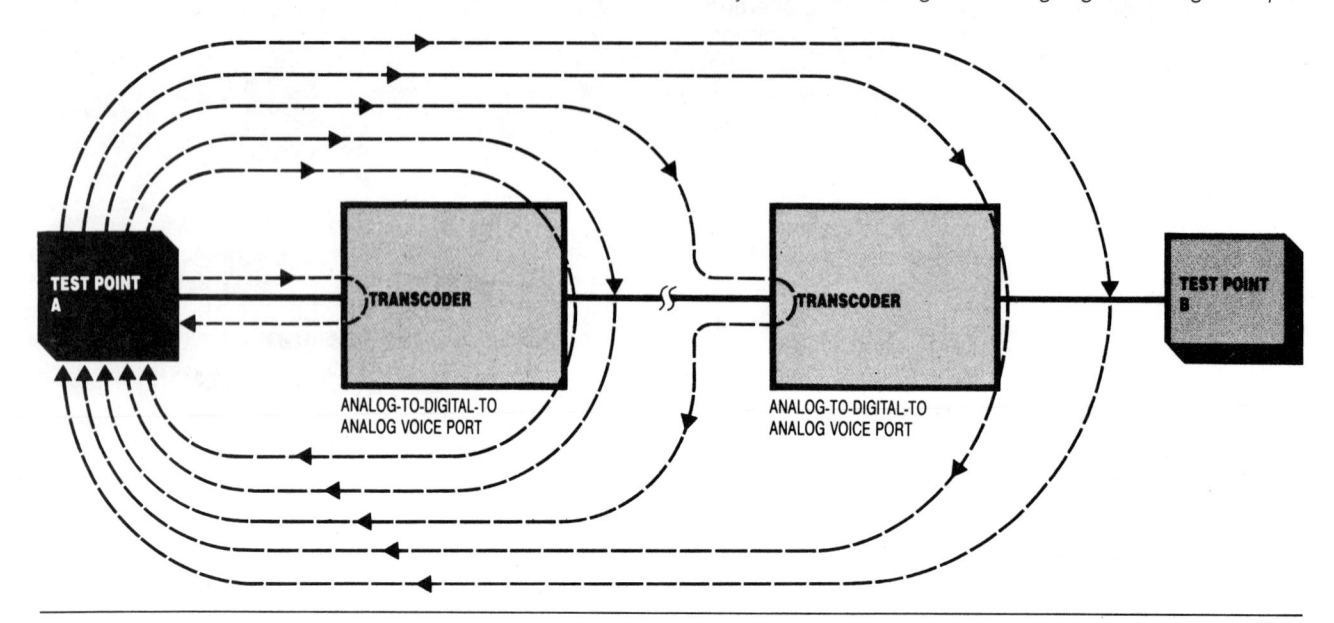

as a special type of circuit to suit the constantly changing needs of individual users, giving customers not only total control over bandwidth allocation, but also service definition—all with minimal reliance on the telephone company. Thus some channels may be defined on demand as AT&T Megacom 800 circuits, while others may be defined as Accunet switched 56-kbit/s, Accunet 1.544-Mbit/s, or Dataphone digital service.

The Bell operating companies plan to offer ISDN services initially through their Centrex exchanges once field trials prove that there is a genuine demand. These ISDN services will be brought up on switched facilities under the carrier's control.

T1 already allows private network users to allocate bandwidth any way they choose—and ADPCM enhances the economic flexibility of network planning. So while ISDN will become a powerful tool for managing corporate voice and data communications, it should be viewed, at least initially, as just another option with which to design, manage, and maintain a high-volume digital backbone network. The initial rollout of ISDN services is in the future. In the beginning, ISDN will exist only as a pilot technology and probably will remain a limited offering at least until the mid-1990s. It may also involve high up-front costs.

Although ISDN promises eventually to become economical, it may force users to give up some of their freedom. ISDN is a service provided largely by telephone companies. In using ISDN, T1 users may have to give up some of the operational latitude that they have grown accustomed to with T1 and be at the mercy of AT&T once again for timely and reliable installation, repair, and maintenance services, as well as features and network options.

Users opting for ISDN services may find themselves locked into a single-vendor solution and lose the bargaining power they now have with private networks. As with T1 circuits, corporations would then be at the mercy of both AT&T and the telephone companies for priorities and schedules for ISDN circuit installation and cutover.

Becoming dependent once again on the telephone company is a prospect few T1 users would welcome. It would not be the wisest decision, therefore, to suddenly abandon T1 in favor of ISDN, even if that were to become possible tomorrow. The reality of ISDN is that such services will evolve gradually, taking into consideration the available capital investments of AT&T and the telephone companies.

Although AT&T could conceivably make ISDN so attractive that it makes T1 less affordable, the emergence of fiber optic networks makes this highly unlikely. As fiber optic networks continue to evolve and become operational, the number of T1 circuits sending voice, data, and video around the country will skyrocket. This portends lower rates for long-haul interLATA T1 circuits and may lengthen the payback period of circuit multiplication networks that were put into service along high-density routes. But the fiber optic networks, as currently laid out, are only backbone networks linking major cities. Such networks may not coincide with the backbone facilities of private networks; not even fiber is economical for reaching into every nook and cranny of the country. Circuit multiplication schemes such as ADPCM will continue to be cost-justifiable for far-flung private networks for the foreseeable future and may play an expanded role in providing economical short-haul access to fiber facilities.

For businesses burdened with the escalating costs of operating their own private networks, the technology embodied in ADPCM represents a viable, economical alternative for increasing transmission capacity. What's more, ADPCM technology adds a high degree of flexibility to network planning—with only minimal reliance on the telephone company. ∎

Nathan Muller, who specializes in hardware and software evaluation and selection, is an independent consultant in Huntsville, Ala. He holds a graduate degree in management from George Washington University.

Section 8
Standards

Uyless Black, Information Engineering Institute Inc., Falls Church, Va.

A user's guide to the CCITT's V-series modem recommendations

It's true. ISDN is coming. But until then, the rich and growing repertoire of international modem standards will rule the stage.

The Integrated Services Digital Network (ISDN) will eventually lead to the changing of the familiar physical connectors and interfaces now found in many user devices and data communications equipment. For the foreseeable future, however, most data transmissions will continue to use the analog telephone lines or other lines engineered to similar specifications.

During the past decade, the CCITT V-series recommendations have become prominent specifications for defining physical level interfaces. The V series defines the interfaces and signaling procedures between user equipment (DTEs, or data terminal equipment) and modems, multiplexers, and digital service units (DCEs, or data circuit-terminating equipment).

Specifications for the physical level operations of modems, digital service units, and other DCE-type components with DTE devices are also published by the Electronic Industries Association (EIA), the Institute of Electrical and Electronic Engineers (IEEE), and others. In addition, the International Standards Organizaton (ISO) publishes standards for the dimensions of the mechanical connectors that join the DCEs with DTEs. In North America, Bell specifications have become de facto standards; in the past few years, Hayes modems have taken the lion's share of the market with their microcomputer-based modem product line. It is noteworthy that most vendors have aligned their products, including the recent Bell modems and the Hayes modem family, with the V series.

Although the CCITT V-series conventions are used worldwide, the reader is cautioned that some vendors' "CCITT-aligned" products may be at variance with a specific recommendation. For example, the European and North American products sometimes use different originate and answer signals on certain modems. When in doubt, as the saying goes, read the directions.

The V series is published as part of the 1984 Red Book, Volume VIII-Fascicle VIII.1: "Data Communication over the Telephone Network." The 1984 document is intended to be a reference, not a tutorial. As such, it assumes the reader's familiarity with the many terms and concepts used therein. (Several key changes to the V-series specifications were made in the latest round of CCITT standards activity. For highlights of these changes see "Latest changes to V series.")

The V-series recommendations can be somewhat confusing to the uninitiated because a V-series specification may describe a specific type of modem or, alternatively, a convention that is used within the modem. For purposes of compatibility and simplicity, the V modems include a set of foundation V-series specifications and then use specific techniques unique to the modem itself to achieve the actual data encoding and modulation.

The entire V-series recommendations are broadly classified as:
- The foundation recommendations
- Voiceband modems
- Wideband modems
- Error-control and transmission-quality conventions
- Internetworking with other networks.

The foundation V series

These recommendations are used in many of the V-series voiceband and wideband modems (see "V-series recommendations"). They provide conventions for the electrical interfaces, the signaling rates in bits per second, definitions of the interchange circuits (pins), and procedures for dial-and-answer operations.

The V.28 and V.24 recommendations are examples of two foundation specifications that are used extensively in North America. They are found in the RS-232-C and EIA-

232-D standards. Most modem and multiplexer manufacturers stipulate the use of V.28 and a subset of V.24 in their specification sheets and marketing material.

V.28 is applied to almost all interchange circuits operating below the limit of 20 kbit/s. On a general level, the signals must conform to the following characteristics. For data interchange circuits, the signal is in the binary 1 condition when the voltage on the circuit is more negative than −3 volts. The signal is in the binary 0 condition when the voltage is more positive than +3 volts. For control and timing interchange circuits, the circuit is on when the voltage on the interchange circuit is more positive than +3 volts and is off when the voltage is more negative than −3 volts.

V.24 defines the functions of the connecting interchange circuits (pins) between the DTE and DCE. Many devices also use V.24 for direct DTE-to-DTE or DCE-to-DCE interfaces. The V-series voiceband and wideband modems typically use V.24, as do standards such as RS-232-C and EIA-232-D, although the EIA standards use different designations for the circuits.

The reader should be aware that a device may use V.24 and be incompatible with another device that also uses V.24. One reason is that V.24 is what might be called a superset standard. That is to say, V.24 provides descriptions of the functions of 43 pins, and most of the modem manufacturers then choose the appropriate circuits for their interface.

The voiceband modems
The presence of the V series may be no more noticeable than in the area of voiceband modems. A modem vendor's specification for medium (2.4-kbit/s) to high-speed (9.6-kbit/s) data transfer rates, for example, may say something like ". . . compatible with V.22*bis*, V.32 . . .," and so on.

Unless one is tenacious enough to read through myriad detailed V specifications, it is quite difficult to gain an overall understanding of these protocols. The principal characteristics of the V-series voiceband modems are summarized in Table 1, and each column entry is briefly explained below.

A V-series modem type shown in Column 1 may be listed in the table more than once. For example, V.29 has three entries. These multiple entries do not mean the series is published in more than one recommendation. Rather, it means that the modem type has more than one possible option for its implementation (usually, but not always, variations in speed).

The modems operate either with alternate two-way transmission (half duplex) or simultaneous two-way transmission (full duplex), as shown in Column 3. To achieve this, the V modem uses one of three techniques, shown in Column 4, to achieve channel separation:
- Frequency division
- Four-wire circuit
- Echo cancellation.

With frequency division, at least two signals are used, one for each direction of transmission. For example, a signal of 1,080 hertz (Hz) can be used to carry the data in one direction of transmission and a 1,750-Hz signal is used for the other direction. These carrier signals are listed in Column 5.

Another approach for achieving channel separation is through the use of a four-wire circuit. The two pairs of wires are used for the signals, a signal in each direction on each of the wire pairs. The newer V-series recommendations stipulate the use of echo cancellation, which uses the modem's receiver circuitry to cancel the transmitted signal. This provides full-duplex operations (see "V.32 modems are breaking through the echo barrier, DATA COMMUNICATIONS, April 1988, p. 187).

The chart also notes the modulation technique of each modem. The following methods are employed:
- Frequency shift
- Frequency modulation
- Phase shift
- Quadrature amplitude modulation
- Trellis-coded modulation.

The earlier recommendations stipulate the use of frequency shifting, where a carrier signal is modulated by the binary data stream by shifting a basic carrier signal by +100 Hz to represent a binary 1 or −100 Hz to represent a binary 0. For example, consider the V.21 modem. Its

---

Latest changes to V series

The 1989 CCITT Blue Books, to be released later this year, contain several changes and additions to the V-series recommendations published in the 1984 Red Books. Perhaps the most interest has focused on the addition of V.42, which specifies the use of error-correcting modems. These modems also perform asynchronous-to-synchronous conversion between the host machine (data terminal equipment, or DTE) and the modem (data circuit-terminating equipment, or DCE). Consequently, the DTE can operate with conventional asynchronous protocols (as found in most personal computers).

The V.42 modem converts the transmission to a synchronous stream for transmission over the communications circuit. It also contains a link-level protocol, called Link Access Procedure for Modems (LAPM) for error correction, which is derived from high-level data link control.

Another new recommendation of interest is V.33, which describes the operations for 14.4-bit/s modems over four-wire leased circuits.

The Blue Books also include other V-series recommendations on simulated carrier control (V.13), asynchronous-to-synchronous conversion (V.14), ISDN, and V-series interfaces (V.120 and V.230).

The major modifications to existing V-series recommendations have occurred to V.25*bis* (automatic calling/answering modems), and another ISDN-to-V series interface (V.110). Both recommendations contain enhancements to the 1984 versions, and have been edited to improve their clarity.

Table 1: Summary of V-series voiceband modems

1 SERIES NUMBER	2 USER DATA RATE (BIT/S)	3 FULL DUPLEX OR HALF DUPLEX[2]	4 CHANNEL SEPARATION	5 CARRIER FREQUENCY	6 MODULATION TECHNIQUE	7 MODULATION RATE (BAUD)	8 BITS ENCODED	9 SYNCHRONOUS OR ASYNCHRONOUS
V.21	300	FULL DUPLEX	FREQUENCY DIVISION	1,080 & 1,750	FREQUENCY SHIFT	300	1:1	EITHER
V.22	1,200	FULL DUPLEX	FREQUENCY DIVISION	1,200 & 2,400	PHASE SHIFT	600	2:1	EITHER
V.22	600	FULL DUPLEX	FREQUENCY DIVISION	1,200 & 2,400	PHASE SHIFT	600	1:1	EITHER
V.22bis	2,400	FULL DUPLEX	FREQUENCY DIVISION	1,200 & 2,400	QUADRATURE-AMPLITUDE MODULATION	600	4:1	EITHER
V.22bis	1,200	FULL DUPLEX	FREQUENCY DIVISION	1,200 & 2,400	QUADRATURE-AMPLITUDE MODULATION	600	2:1	EITHER
V.23	600[1]	HALF DUPLEX	NA	1,300 & 1,700	FREQUENCY MODULATION	600	NA	EITHER
V.23	1,200[1]	HALF DUPLEX	NA	1,300 & 2,100	FREQUENCY MODULATION	1,200	NA	EITHER
V.26	2,400	FULL DUPLEX	4 WIRE	1,800	PHASE SHIFT	1,200	2:1	SYNCHRONOUS
V.26bis	2,400	HALF DUPLEX	NA	1,800	PHASE SHIFT	1,200	2:1	SYNCHRONOUS
V.26bis	1,200	HALF DUPLEX	NA	1,800	PHASE SHIFT	1,200	1:1	SYNCHRONOUS
V.26ter	2,400	EITHER	ECHO CANCELLATION	1,800	PHASE SHIFT	1,200	2:1	EITHER
V.26ter	1,200	EITHER	ECHO CANCELLATION	1,800	PHASE SHIFT	1,200	1:1	EITHER
V.27	4,800	EITHER	ND[3]	1,800	PHASE SHIFT	1,600	3:1	SYNCHRONOUS
V.27bis	4,800	EITHER	4 WIRE[4]	1,800	PHASE SHIFT	1,600	3:1	SYNCHRONOUS
V.27bis	2,400	EITHER	4 WIRE[4]	1,800	PHASE SHIFT	1,200	2:1	SYNCHRONOUS
V.27ter	4,800	HALF DUPLEX	NONE	1,800	PHASE SHIFT	1,600	3:1	SYNCHRONOUS
V.27ter	2,400	HALF DUPLEX	NONE	1,800	PHASE SHIFT	1,200	2:1	SYNCHRONOUS
V.29	9,600	EITHER	4 WIRE	1,700	QUADRATURE-AMPLITUDE MODULATION	2,400	4:1	SYNCHRONOUS
V.29	7,200	EITHER	4 WIRE	1,700	PHASE SHIFT[5]	2,400	3:1	SYNCHRONOUS
V.29	4,800	EITHER	4 WIRE	1,700	PHASE SHIFT[5]	2,400	2:1	SYNCHRONOUS
V.32	9,600	FULL DUPLEX	ECHO CANCELLATION	1,800	QUADRATURE-AMPLITUDE MODULATION	2,400	4:1	SYNCHRONOUS
V.32	9,600	FULL DUPLEX	ECHO CANCELLATION	1,800	TRELLIS-CODED MODULATION	2,400	5:1	SYNCHRONOUS
V.32	4,800	FULL DUPLEX	ECHO CANCELLATION	1,800	QUADRATURE-AMPLITUDE MODULATION	2,400	2:1	SYNCHRONOUS

1. BIT/S NOT USED IN SPECIFICATION; RATE STATED IN BAUD
2. HALF DUPLEX MAY STILL USE A BACKWARD CHANNEL
3. MAKES NO MENTION OF 4 WIRE (MUST BE ASSUMED)
4. FOR HALF DUPLEX, 2 WIRE USED
5. AMPLITUDE IS CONSTANT ON A RELATIVE BASIS

10	11	12	13	14	15	16	17
BACKWARD CHANNEL	SWITCHED LINES	LEASED LINES	USE OF V.28	ISO PIN CONNECTOR	EQUALIZATION	SCRAMBLER	USE OF V.54
ND	YES	NO	YES	2110	ND	ND	ND
ND	YES	POINT-TO-POINT, 2 WIRE	YES	2110	FIXED	YES	YES
ND	YES	POINT-TO-POINT, 2 WIRE	YES	2110	FIXED	YES	YES
ND	YES	POINT-TO-POINT, 2 WIRE	YES	2110	FIXED/ADAPTIVE	YES	YES
ND	YES	POINT-TO-POINT, 2 WIRE	YES	2110	FIXED/ADAPTIVE	YES	YES
YES	YES	NO	YES	2110	ND	ND	ND
YES	YES	NO	YES	2110	ND	ND	ND
YES	NO	POINT-TO-POINT, MULTIPOINT, 4 WIRE	YES	2110	ND	ND	ND
YES	YES	NO	YES	2110	FIXED	ND	ND
YES	YES	NO	YES	2110	FIXED	ND	ND
ND	YES	POINT-TO-POINT, 2 WIRE	YES	2110	EITHER	YES	YES
ND	YES	POINT-TO-POINT, 2 WIRE	YES	2110	EITHER	YES	YES
YES	NO	YES[3]	YES	2110	MANUAL	YES	ND
YES	NO	2 WIRE, 4 WIRE	YES	2110	ADAPTIVE	YES	ND
YES	NO	2 WIRE, 4 WIRE	YES	2110	ADAPTIVE	YES	ND
YES	YES	NO	YES	2110	ADAPTIVE	YES	ND
YES	YES	NO	YES	2110	ADAPTIVE	YES	ND
NO	NO	POINT-TO-POINT, 4 WIRE	YES	2110	ADAPTIVE	YES	ND
ND	NO	POINT-TO-POINT, 4 WIRE	YES	2110	ADAPTIVE	YES	ND
ND	NO	POINT-TO-POINT, 4 WIRE	YES	2110	ADAPTIVE	YES	ND
ND	YES	POINT-TO-POINT, 2 WIRE	YES	2110	ADAPTIVE	YES	YES
ND	YES	POINT-TO-POINT, 2 WIRE	YES	2110	ADAPTIVE	YES	YES
ND	YES	POINT-TO-POINT, 2 WIRE	YES	2110	ADAPTIVE	YES	YES

KBIT/S = KILOBITS PER SECOND (THOUSAND BITS PER SECOND)
KHz = KILOHERTZ (THOUSAND CYCLES PER SECOND)
NA = NOT APPLICABLE
ND = NOT DEFINED (I.E., NOT SPECIFIED IN THE RECOMMENDATION)

carriers of 1,080 Hz and 1,750 Hz are shifted by 100 Hz to represent binary 0s and 1s.

Phase-shift modulation is used on several of the medium-speed modems. This technique alters the carrier's signal by shifting its phase at precise degree markings. Table 2 provides more detail for the interested reader.

Quadrature amplitude modulation (QAM) is stipulated for the higher-speed modems (9.6 kbit/s) and the widely used V.22*bis* recommendation. QAM allows the carrier amplitude values and phase markings to be changed to represent the binary data stream.

The V-series modems that use combined amplitude modulation (AM) and phase-shift (PS) modulation still differ in the bit-encoding structure they use:

- V.22*bis*, operating at 2.4 kbit/s, encodes four consecutive bits (quadbits); the first two bits are encoded relative to the quadrant of the previous signal element, the last two bits are associated with the new quadrant.
- V.22*bis*, operating at 1.2 kbit/s, encodes two consecutive bits (dibits); the dibits are encoded as a change relative to the previous signal element.
- V.29, operating at 9.6 kbit/s, encodes four consecutive bits (quadbits); the first bit determines the amplitude, the last three bits use the encoding scheme of V.27.
- V.29, operating at 7.2 kbit/s, encodes three consecutive bits (tribits); the three bits are determined as in V.29 operation at 9.6 kbit/s.
- V.29, operating at 4.8 kbit/s, encodes two consecutive bits (dibits); amplitude is constant and phase changes are the same as V.26.
- V.32, operating at 9.6 kbit/s, encodes four consecutive bits (quadbits); the bits are mapped to a QAM signal.
- V.32, operating at 9.6 kbit/s with Trellis-coded modulation (TCM), encodes four consecutive bits, two of which are used to generate a fifth bit; the bits are mapped to a QAM signal.
- V.32, operating at 4.8 kbit/s, encodes two consecutive bits (dibits), which are mapped to a QAM signal.

Trellis-coded modulation is employed as one option of the V.32 modem for the purposes of forward error correction (see "Trellis Coded Modulation: What it is and how it affects data transmission," DATA COMMUNICATIONS, May 1985, p. 143). TCM actually uses QAM modulation techniques, but adds 1 bit to every 4 bits to aid in the error-correcting process at the receiving modem.

The modulation rate, shown in Column 7, is the rate of signaling change of the carrier(s). It is measured in the number of changes per second and is more commonly known as baud. Thus, the modulation rate of the V.29 modem is 2,400 baud. In the case of lower-speed modems, the line speed (in bits per second) is the same as the modulation rate (in baud). In the case of the medium- and higher-speed modems, bit/s and baud are not the same. Unfortunately, many people use these terms as if they were synonymous.

To analyze this seeming discrepancy, look at Column 8. The values there express the number of bits encoded per one signal change (that is, per baud). It is possible to encode multiple bits per baud. As an example, the V.26 modem encodes two bits per baud. The reader need only multiply the value in Column 8 by the value in Column 7 (modulation rate) to reveal the value in Column 2 (speed).

This simple equation holds true for all the entries except the V.32 TCM. It uses a 5:1 encoding ratio but achieves a bit rate of 9.6 kbit/s. Its actual throughput is 12,000 bits (5 × 2,400 = 12,000) but 2,400 bits are extra (redundant) bits used for forward error correction and do not contribute to the syntax of the user data stream.

V series recommendations

V.1—Definitions of key terms for binary symbol notation, such as binary 0 = space, binary 1 = mark.

V.2 (1)—Specification of power levels for data transmission over telephone line.

V.4—Definition of the order of bit transmission, the use of a parity bit, and the use of start/stop bits for asynchronous transmission.

V.5—Specification of data-signaling rates (bit/s) for synchronous transmission in the switched telephone network.

V.6—Specification of data signaling rates (bit/s) for synchronous transmission on leased telephone circuits.

V.7—Definitions of other key terms used in the V-series recommendations.

V.10—Description of an unbalanced physical level interchange circuit (unbalanced means one active wire between transmitter and receiver with ground providing the return).

V.11—Description of a balanced physical level interchange circuit (balanced means two wires between the transmitter and receiver with both wires' signals constant with respect to Earth).

V.15—Description of use of acoustic couplers for data transmission.

V.16—Description of the transmission of ECG (electrocardiogram) signals on the telephone channel.

V.19—Description of one-way parallel transmission modems using push-button telephone sets.

V.20—Description of one-way parallel transmission modems, excluding push-button telephone sets.

V.24—Definition of the interchange circuit pins between DTEs (data terminal equipment) and DCEs (data circuit-terminating equipment).

V.25 (2)—Specifications for automatic-answering equipment.

V.25*bis* (2)—Specifications for automatic-answering equipment.

V.28—Description of unbalanced interchange circuits operating below 20 kbit/s.

V.31—Description of low-speed interchange circuits (up to 75 bit/s).

V.31*bis*—Description of low-speed interchange circuits (up to 1.2 kbit/s).

Note: In the United States, EIA RS-496 specifies these measurements and RS-366 specifies these procedures.

Table 2: Modems using phase-shift modulation
(Entries represent bit(s) encoded with the phase changes)

SERIES NUMBER	SPEED (BIT/S)	PHASE CHANGE							
		0°	45°	90°	135°	180°	225°	270°	315°
V.22	1,200	01		00		10		11	
V.22	600			0				1	
V.26	2,400	00		01		11		10	
V.26bis	2,400		00		01		11		10
V.26bis	1,200			0				1	
V.26ter	2,400	00		01		11		10	
V.26ter	1,200	0				1			
V.27	4,800	001	000	010	011	111	110	100	101
V.27bis	4,800	001	000	010	011	111	110	100	101
V.27bis	2,400	00		01		11		10	
V.27ter	4,800	001	000	010	011	111	110	100	101
V.27ter	2,400	00		01		11		10	

NOTE: A FEW OTHER ENCODING OPTIONS ARE AVAILABLE FOR SEVERAL OF THE MODEMS.

Column 9 states whether the modem supports asynchronous or synchronous transmission. Several of the V-series modems can be configured to support either convention. The new recommendations specify only synchronous transmission. The asynchronous modems use timing signals between the modem and user device called start/stop bits. They are placed around each character. Synchronous transmission requires the use of a timing circuit between the devices to achieve synchronization (interchange circuit numbers 113, 114, and 128).

Column 10 indicates whether the V series uses a backward channel (also known as reverse channel). Several of the medium-speed V-series modems provide this channel. It is of limited capacity (typically, 75 baud with 390 Hz representing a 1 and 450 Hz representing a 0).

The channel is often used to obtain a return channel for diagnostic data or acknowledgments of the data transmitted over the primary circuit. It can also be used to send a limited amount of data. The use of a reverse channel does not preclude the simultaneous use of two primary full-duplex channels, but the V series defines this channel only for half-duplex modems using two-wire circuits or full-duplex modems using four-wire circuits.

The V-series modems provide several options for the use of switched or leased lines. These options are shown in Columns 11 and 12 of Table 1.

The inclusion of Columns 13 and 14 may seem somewhat superfluous since all the V-series voiceband modems use the V.28 electrical specification and the ISO 2110 mechanical connector. They are included to emphasize how certain foundation standards are used in the other standards.

Column 15 shows whether the modem uses equalization techniques. (Equalization is used to compensate for the attenuation associated with certain frequencies.)

Column 16 notes whether the modem uses a scrambler and descrambler to create self-sychronizing signals between the two modems' transmitters and receivers.

If the modem uses the V.54 loopback procedures, it is listed in Column 17. Fault location can be facilitated with the use of a looping procedure. In its simplest form, signals are generated at the transmitter and returned (looped back) to the transmitter to be checked for accuracy.

The wideband modems

The V-series recommendations also include specifications for wideband modems (Table 3). V.35 is widely used in North America. However, the North American implementation does not use the 48-kbit/s speed. The majority of implementations use the familiar 56-kbit/s digital data rate known to data communications users.

The V-series wideband modems operate within the 60- to 180-kHz bandwidth. They can be used for the transmission of data at rates from 58 kbit/s to 168 kbit/s. They also have options for the transmission of voice pulse-code modulation signals.

In January 1987, the EIA revised the RS-232-C standard and renamed it EIA-232-D. EIA-232-D includes:
- Specification for the 25-pin interface connector
- Addition of local loopback (pin 18), remote loopback (pin 21, which was named Signal Quality Detector in RS-232-C), and test-mode (pin 25) interchange circuits
- Addition of shield
- Redefinition of Protective Ground
- Terms of data communications equipment and data set defined as DCE
- Driver renamed Generator
- Terminator renamed Receiver.

The changes bring the standard into conformance with the following CCITT and ISO standards:
- Electrical: CCITT V.28
- Circuit definitions: CCITT V.24
- Mechanical connector: ISO 2110.

Bell modems (data sets) are widely used throughout the

Table 3: Wideband modems

SERIES NUMBER	LINE SPEED (KBIT/S)	FULL DUPLEX OR HALF DUPLEX	CARRIER FREQUENCY (KHz)	MODULATION TECHNIQUE	USE OF V.28	USE OF V.24	SCRAMBLER	BANDWIDTH (KHz)	LEASED LINES
V.35	48	FULL DUPLEX	100	SINGLE-SIDEBAND AMPLITUDE MODULATION	YES[3]	YES	YES	60-108	YES
V.36	48[1]	FULL DUPLEX	100	SINGLE-SIDEBAND AMPLITUDE MODULATION	NO[4,5]	YES	YES	60-108	YES
V.37	72[2]	FULL DUPLEX	100	SINGLE-SIDEBAND AMPLITUDE MODULATION	NO[4]	YES	YES	60-108	YES

1. RATE MAY ALSO BE 56, 64, AND 72 KBIT/S.
2. RECOMMENDED RATES ARE 96, 112, 128, 144, 168 KBIT/S.
3. EXCEPT THE DATA CIRCUITS (V.24 103, AND 104) AND TIMING CIRCUITS (V.24 114, AND 115) ARE BALANCED.
4. INTERCHANGE CIRCUITS USE A MIX OF V.10 AND V.11 RECOMMENDATIONS
5. FOR AN INTERIM PERIOD, V.35 INTERFACE AND ISO 2593 (34-PIN CONNECTION) CAN BE USED. 4902 IS A 37- OR 9-PIN CONNECTOR.

United States and other parts of the world. The physical level interfaces in North America have been largely dictated by the former Bell System specifications. For example, the vast majority of vendors base their automatic dial-and-answer DCEs on the Bell 103/212A specifications, and the Bell 103, 113, 201C, 208A/B, 212A specifications are used by many vendors as a basis for their modem designs.

The Bell modems
The term "Bell modem" has been associated with those modems manufactured by AT&T/Bell/Western Electric before divestiture. For convenience, the term is still widely used. The newer CCITT V-series modem specifications are increasingly used in North America, especially since divestiture, when AT&T relinquished its role as North American modem-specification writer and standards setter.

As noted in this section, the Bell modems and the self-styled CCITT counterparts are not always compatible.

Generally speaking, the Bell modems use the RS-232-C recommendation as it is defined by the EIA. However, exceptions exist. For example, the Bell 212A DCE defines pin 12 differently than does the EIA. A careful review of the vendors' specifications is quite important.

The Bell modems are categorized as follows:
- 100 series: Narrowband
- 200 series: Voiceband
- 300 series: Broadband
- 400 series: Voiceband parallel.

The more recent Bell modems use microprocessor-based synchronous protocols. These modems also provide adaptive equalizers and extensive diagnostic capabilities. They continuously monitor themselves and analyze the quality of the received signal. If necessary, they identify problems and report them to diagnostic control devices. Generally, the trouble reporting is provided over the reverse channel.

As with most modems today, the Bell modems provide the user with test menus and command menus, which allow the isolation and diagnosis of problems.

Recognizing that existing installed devices will need an interface to ISDN (probably for a considerable period of time), the CCITT has defined the physical level interface between the ISDN terminal adapter (TA) and a V-series device. This information is available in CCITT V.110.

V series interfaces with an ISDN
The TA provides the electrical/mechanical interface signal conversion and bit-rate adaptation between the non-ISDN user device, TE2 (terminal equipment 2). The TA also provides synchronization and automatic dial-and-answer functions as well as manual call-control functions for either voice or data circuit-switched services.

One principal task for the TA is to adapt the V-series bit rate to the ISDN 64-kbit/s, B-channel rate. This function is performed by 2-bit rate adapters (RA) located inside the TA. The first adapter, RA1 converts the V-series voiceband bit rate to an intermediate rate of either 8 kbit/s, 16 kbit/s, or 32 kbit/s. RA2 takes the intermediate rate or the V-series wideband modem rate and converts this rate to 64 kbit/s. The TA also provides adaptation of an incoming 64-kbit/s B channel to the appropriate V-series interface.

The CCITT V-series recommendations have provided a cohesive foundation for vendors to build compatible products. The user is the winner with this approach. It is anticipated that the ISDN physical level standards will provide a similar foundation for the emerging all-digital communications facility. ∎

Uyless Black is president of Information Engineering Institute Inc., a consulting firm in Falls Church, Va. The author of numerous articles, he has just completed two books: Physical Level Interfaces and Protocols, IEEE Computer Society Press (Washington D.C., 1988), and Data Networks: Concepts, Theory and Practice, Prentice-Hall Inc. (Englewood Cliffs, N.J., 1988). He holds a BS in industrial psychology from the University of New Mexico, Albuquerque, an MS in Computer Systems from American University, Washington, D.C., and a graduate degree in banking and finance from Stonier Graduate School of Banking at Rutgers University, New Brunswick, N.J.

Daniel R. Ruffalo, Rotelcom, Fairport, N.Y.

Understanding T1 basics: Primer offers picture of networking future

By becoming more familiar with T1, managers can anticipate change in the network before it happens.

Rapid development of digital technology in the early 1960s gave telephone companies the long-sought opportunity to relieve heavy loading on interexchange cables. The foundation of what's turned out to be a great leap forward was pulse code modulation equipment, a new class of central-office gear that converted analog voice signals into a digital format and, in the process, improved network performance.

A cornerstone of the digital revolution in telephony is the channel bank, a device that transmits 24 independent channels over copper cable that had before carried only one voice call. The early channel banks, which acted as multiplexers, were also called T-carriers. The T-carrier is built around two or more channel banks, or D banks, which convert analog signals into a digital format and multiplex them into one digital signal for transmission over a digital trunk facility. The multiplexed digital signal is called the T1 bit stream or the DS-1 signal.

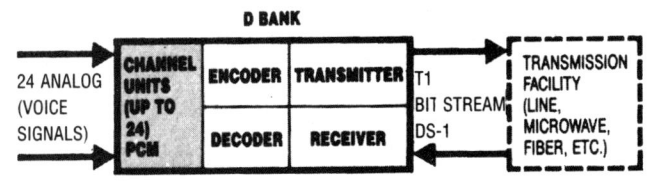

PCM = PULSE CODE MODULATION

Over the years specifications for the performance of a number of PCM channel banks have evolved. They are generally referred to by the designations first used at Western Electric Co.: D1, D2, D3, and D4. Although D1 and D2 channel banks are no longer being manufactured, many are still used in the telephone network. The D3 and D4 banks are state of the art.

D3 and D4 banks are very similar. The D4 bank is basically two D3 banks in a single chassis; the two share common equipment. The D3 and D4 banks continue to use the T1 bit stream for each set of 24 channels. The D3 bank has a 24-channel capacity using one T1 bit stream, while the D4 bank uses two T1 bit streams for a total capacity of 48 channels.

The T1, or DS-1, bit stream encoded by the D banks in today's time-division multiplexer (TDM) equipment is a high-speed digital stream of ones and zeros that runs at a rate of 1.544 Mbit/s. PCM, or pulse code modulation, is the technique used to transmit analog (voice) signals on D banks. Bipolar, also called AMI, or alternate mark inversion, is the digital form the T1 signal takes once it is passed to the digital trunk facility.

An analog signal is first sampled at preselected, equally distributed time intervals. The resulting analog samples are referred to as pulse amplitude modulation (PAM). Each analog PAM sample is quantized and coded as a digital eight-bit PCM byte. The eight-bit byte can be transmitted on a digital facility to another location where the PCM process is reversed and the information is reconstructed or decoded into its original analog form.

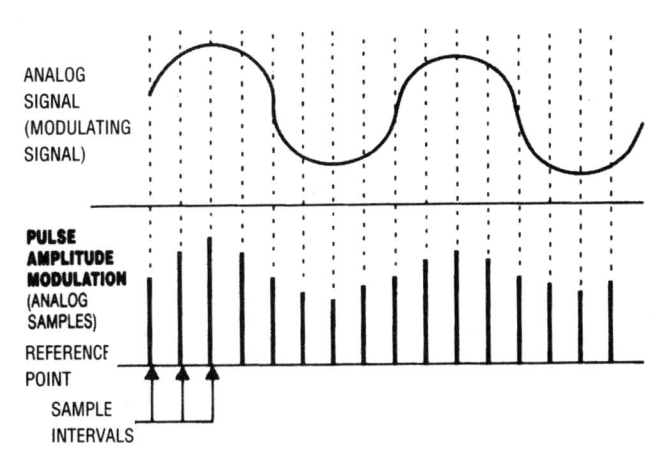

The T1 rate evolves from the sampling rate applied to the analog signal. The Nyquist theorem of information theory states that to encode an analog signal it must be sampled at twice its bandwidth. The telephone industry's voice-grade band runs at about 300 Hz to 3,000 Hz. For various reasons, the upper limit of frequencies on a voice-grade facility is taken as 4,000 Hz. Hence, twice the bandwidth (2 × 4,000 Hz) is 8,000 samples per second. This sampling rate allows reconstruction of the analog signal.

This is an example of a bipolar signal used in a T1 bit stream (DS-1):

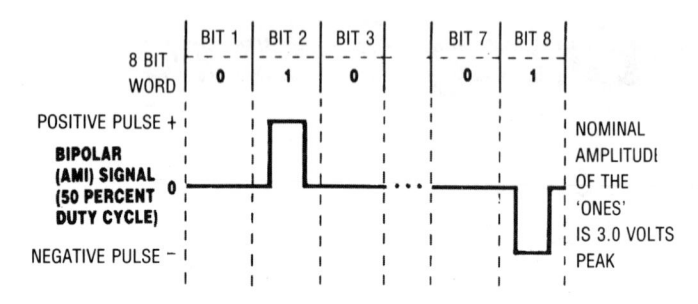

```
                BIT 1   BIT 2   BIT 3         BIT 7   BIT 8
8 BIT             0       1       0             0       1
WORD
POSITIVE PULSE +                                              NOMINAL
BIPOLAR                   ___                                 AMPLITUDE
(AMI) SIGNAL     _____|   |_____  ...  _____         OF THE
(50 PERCENT    0                                              'ONES'
DUTY CYCLE)                                        |___|      IS 3.0 VOLTS
NEGATIVE PULSE -                                              PEAK
```

The 0s are at a 0.0 voltage potential, while 1s are produced by a nominal 3.0 volt peak positive or negative going pulse. The 1s pulses have an alternating polarity. If the first 1 is represented by a positive going pulse, the next 1 will be a negative pulse and vice versa. These alternating pulses are called bipolar, or alternate mark inversion. A violation of the bipolar signaling scheme would have occurred if bit 4 had been a positive pulse in relation to bit 2 or if bit 5 had been a negative going pulse in relation to bit 4.

As a fundamental representation of the T1, or DS-1, bit stream transmitted from a D bank or TDM equipment, the 1.544-Mbit/s stream must meet certain basic requirements:

```
T1
BIT STREAM    |        1.544 MBIT/S         |
DS-1
```

- It is a bipolar AMI, non-return-to-zero signal.
- Each pulse has a 50 percent duty cycle with a nominal voltage of 3.0 volts.
- There can be no more than 15 consecutive "0s" present in the stream.

A D4 framing pattern has been added to the T1 specification. D4 framing has traditionally been used in D banks, although it did not become a requirement in network TDM equipment until early 1985. Prior to that time, suppliers of TDM equipment were required only to comply with the DS-1 specifications.

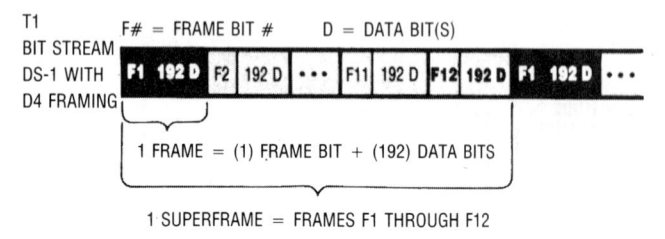

```
T1            F# = FRAME BIT #    D = DATA BIT(S)
BIT STREAM
DS-1 WITH     | F1 | 192 D | F2 | 192 D | ... | F11 | 192 D | F12 | 192 D | F1 | 192 D | ...
D4 FRAMING
              _____/
                   1 FRAME = (1) FRAME BIT + (192) DATA BITS

                   1 SUPERFRAME = FRAMES F1 THROUGH F12
```

D4 framing in a T1 bit stream begins with a single frame bit (F1) followed by 192 data bits. The F1 is followed by frame bit 2 (F2) and another 192 data bits. Next comes frame bit 3 (F3) followed by its 192 data bits. The sequence continues up through frame bit 12 (F12); each frame bit is followed by 192 data bits. Then the 12-bit frame pattern repeats itself with each frame bit followed by 192 data bits. The 12-bit frame pattern is precise and repeats itself the same each time. This repetition enables the transmission equipment to keep the bit stream in synchronization.

Here a D4 framing pattern is used:

D4 FRAMING PATTERN (FRAME BITS)	F1	F2	F3	F4	F5	F6	F7	F8	F9	F10	F11	F12
	1	0	0	0	1	1	0	1	1	1	0	0

1 FRAME = (1) FRAME BIT + (192) DATA BITS
1 SUPERFRAME = FRAMES F1 THROUGH F12

F1 includes one frame bit followed by 192 data bits for a total of 193 bits in a frame. A superframe includes 12 frame bits, each followed by 192 data bits.

New telephony requirements are being developed for customer equipment. Once again, a new requirement will necessitate that TDM manufacturers upgrade their equipment. Besides having to meet the DS-1 specification and the D4 framing requirement, in the future they will have to meet the D4 formatting requirement as well.

The D4 format consists of 24 consecutive eight-bit words, or "channels," following a framing bit. Much as the D bank transmits and receives 24 voice channels, the D4 framing and formatting will enable customer premises TDM equipment to mimic the separation requirement of the central-office equipment.

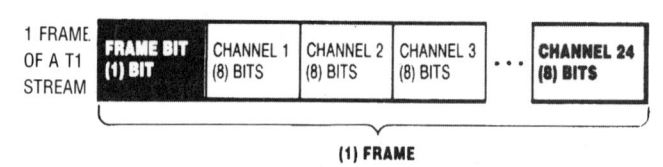

```
1 FRAME   | FRAME BIT | CHANNEL 1 | CHANNEL 2 | CHANNEL 3 |     | CHANNEL 24 |
OF A T1   |  (1) BIT  | (8) BITS  | (8) BITS  | (8) BITS  | ... |  (8) BITS  |
STREAM
          _____/
                                    (1) FRAME
```

1 FRAME = (1) FRAME BIT + [8 BITS PER CHANNEL × 24 CHANNELS]
1 FRAME = (1) FRAME BIT + [192 CHANNEL BITS OR DATA BITS]
1 FRAME = (193) BITS [FRAME AND DATA]

To summarize: 8,000 samples per second are required to reproduce an analog signal using PCM with each sample represented by an eight-bit byte (channel). There are 24 eight-bit channels following each frame bit in a T1 stream that uses D4 framing and D4 formatting. The frame bit is followed by 24 eight-bit channels yielding 193 bits per frame. These frames are being produced at a rate of 8,000 per second.

1 FRAME INTERVAL (time) = 1/8,000 OF A SECOND (BY VIRTUE OF THE SAMPLING THEOREM) OR

THERE ARE 8,000 FRAME INTERVALS A SECOND IN A T1 BIT STREAM (8,000 FRAMES/SECOND)

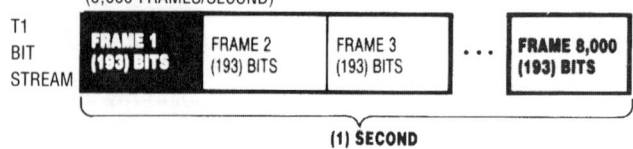

```
T1        | FRAME 1   | FRAME 2   | FRAME 3   |     | FRAME 8,000 |
BIT       | (193) BITS| (193) BITS| (193) BITS| ... | (193) BITS  |
STREAM
          _____/
                                (1) SECOND
```

T1 BIT STREAM = 8,000 FRAMES/SECOND
T1 BIT STREAM = 8,000 × (193) BITS/SECOND
T1 BIT STREAM = 1.544 MBIT/S

Thus a total of 1.544 Mbit/s is derived from the 193 bits at a sampling rate of 8,000 bit/s.

SOME BASIC T1 MATH MANIPULATION:
T1 BIT STREAM = 8,000 FRAMES/SECOND
T1 BIT STREAM = 8,000 × 193 BITS/S (FRAME AND DATA)
T1 BIT STREAM = 8,000 × (1 FRAME BIT + [192 DATA BITS])/SECOND
T1 BIT STREAM = 8,000 × (1 FRAME BIT + [8 DATA BITS PER CHANNEL × 24 CHANNELS])/SECOND
T1 BIT STREAM = 8,000 FRAME BITS/SECOND + 8,000 [8 DATA BITS PER CHANNEL × 24 CHANNELS]/SECOND
T1 BIT STREAM = 8,000 FRAME BITS/SECOND + [64,000 DATA BITS PER CHANNEL × 24 CHANNELS]/SECOND
T1 BIT STREAM = 8,000 FRAME BITS/SECOND + 1,536,000 DATA BITS/S
T1 BIT STREAM = 1.544 MBIT/S

Some basic mathematics will demonstrate that the eight data bits from one of the 24 channels, sampled 8,000 times each second, yields 64,000 bits per second. A single channel from a T1 bit stream yields 64,000 bits per second (64 kbit/s). A channel from the T1 bit stream is referred to as a DS-0. Therefore, there are 24 DS-0s in a T1 bit stream with the D4 format.

Within a DS-0, the eight bits are being sampled 8,000 times a second, thus producing the 64,000 bit/s.

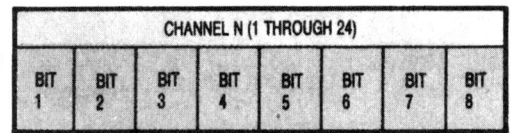

(1) T1 DS-0 CHANNEL

CHANNEL N (1 THROUGH 24)							
BIT 1	BIT 2	BIT 3	BIT 4	BIT 5	BIT 6	BIT 7	BIT 8

1 CHANNEL = 8 DATA BITS
1 CHANNEL IS SAMPLED 8,000 TIMES A SECOND IN A T1 STREAM
1 CHANNEL IN A T1 STREAM = 8,000/SECOND × 8 BITS
1 CHANNEL IN A T1 STREAM = 64,000 BITS/SECOND
1 CHANNEL IN A T1 STREAM IS ALSO KNOWN AS A DS-0
DS-0 = 64 KBIT/S

Some restrictions on transmission apply to the T1 bit stream. In voice transmissions, there is a need to transmit not only the voice signal, but also the mechanical signaling information. The D bank at each end must know when the line is "on-hook" or "off-hook," or if there is a battery reversal, and so forth.

Every 6th and 12th frame is used to transmit and receive voice channel signaling information.

T1 BIT STREAM DS-1 WITH D4 FRAMING AND D4 FORMAT: F1 192 D ... **F6 192 D** ... **F12 192 D** F1 192 D ... F6 192 D
SUPERFRAME

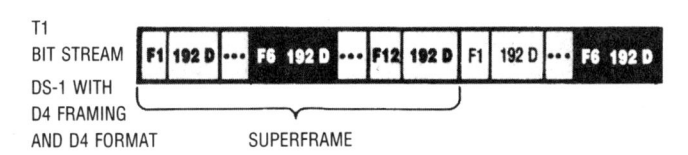

In the 6th and 12th frames, every 8th bit in a voice channel (DS-0) is used for signaling.

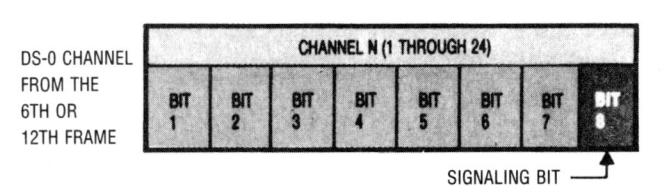

DS-0 CHANNEL FROM THE 6TH OR 12TH FRAME

CHANNEL N (1 THROUGH 24)							
BIT 1	BIT 2	BIT 3	BIT 4	BIT 5	BIT 6	BIT 7	BIT 8

SIGNALING BIT ↑

If all 24 DS-0s are used for voice transmission, then there will be 24 signaling bits in every 6th and 12th frame (one bit per channel per signaling frame). This technique is known as bit robbing. The theft of the signaling bits does not interfere with the PCM voice signal.

Those bits taken from the DS-0s during the 6th frame are referred to as the "A" bits, while those taken from the channels during the 12th frame are referred to as the "B" bits. From every superframe there will be one A-and-B bit pair per DS-0 (voice channel). Each pair of A and B bits is used to relay the signaling information for its respective channel between D banks: for example, loop closures, battery reversals, on-hook, off-hook, and so on. Not surprisingly, bit robbing affects data transmissions in the T1 bit stream.

Another T1 requirement that affects the volume of data transmitted in the T1 bit stream is the "1s density" requirement. To keep the telephone company T1 line, repeaters, and channel service units (CSUs) in synchronization, the DS-1 specification calls for no more than 15 consecutive zeros in the bit stream at any one time. This is referred to as 1s density. The telephone company repeaters and CSUs use the 1s pulses like a clock signal to maintain synchronization. Too many 0s (no pulses), and the repeaters and CSUs will drift and lose sync. Though today's equipment may actually be able to handle more than 15 zeros, the standard is set. Private facilities using microwave, fiber optic, and so on may not have a 1s density requirement.

To ensure 1s density in the T1 Bit Stream, the telephone company uses B7 zero code suppression.

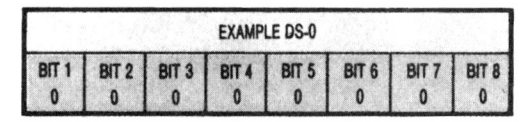

EXAMPLE DS-0							
BIT 1	BIT 2	BIT 3	BIT 4	BIT 5	BIT 6	BIT 7	BIT 8
0	0	0	0	0	0	0	0

IF THIS BYTE OCCURS ....

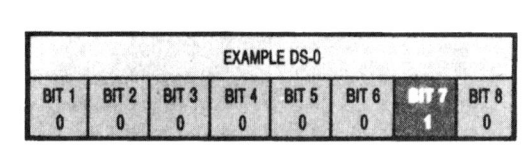

EXAMPLE DS-0							
BIT 1	BIT 2	BIT 3	BIT 4	BIT 5	BIT 6	BIT 7	BIT 8
0	0	0	0	0	0	1	0

THIS WILL BE SUBSTITUTED FOR IT

The B7 ensures that if all eight-bit positions in a DS-0 are 0s, than a 1 will be substituted in the Bit 7 position.

Here is a worst-case scenario:

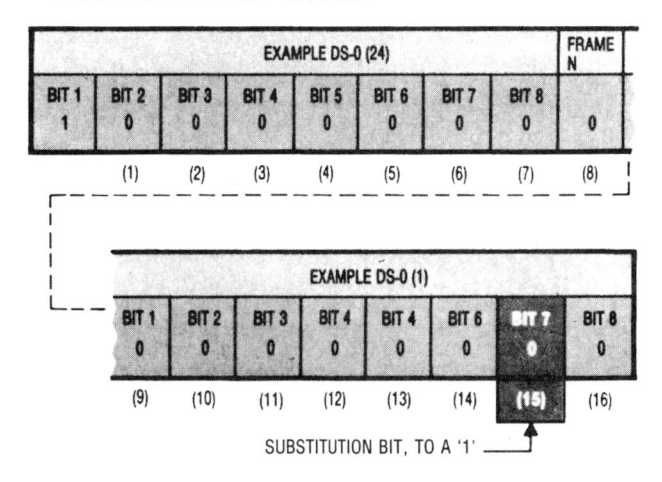

EXAMPLE DS-0 (24)								FRAME N
BIT 1	BIT 2	BIT 3	BIT 4	BIT 5	BIT 6	BIT 7	BIT 8	
1	0	0	0	0	0	0	0	
(1)	(2)	(3)	(4)	(5)	(6)	(7)	(8)	

EXAMPLE DS-0 (1)							
BIT 1	BIT 2	BIT 3	BIT 4	BIT 5	BIT 6	BIT 7	BIT 8
0	0	0	0	0	0	0	0
(9)	(10)	(11)	(12)	(13)	(14)	(15)	(16)

SUBSTITUTION BIT, TO A '1' ↑

It shows the longest possible string of 0s with B7. Within the T1 bit stream, if Channel 24 were followed by a frame bit "0" and then Channel 1 were all 0s, there would be a total of 16 consecutive 0s. B7 cuts the number of 0s to 14, maintaining the integrity of the DS-1 specification.

How does B7 and bit robbing affect both a voice and data channel at the DS-0 level? Here we have an example of a voice channel (DS-0) in which either the 6th or the 12th frame contains all 0s:

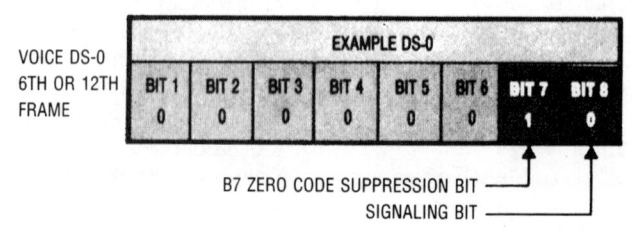

VOICE DS-0 6TH OR 12TH FRAME	EXAMPLE DS-0							
	BIT 1	BIT 2	BIT 3	BIT 4	BIT 5	BIT 6	BIT 7	BIT 8
	0	0	0	0	0	0	1	0

BIT 7 — B7 ZERO CODE SUPPRESSION BIT
BIT 8 — SIGNALING BIT

In this example, the original voice channel is losing its Bit 8 to a 0A or 0B signaling bit. A PCM channel can tolerate the loss of the 8th bit to signaling as well as the loss of Bit 7 to the B7 zero code suppression.

There is no need to rob bits in a data channel (DS-0) since no signaling is required. However, having all 0s in the data channel is a possibility. If this occurs, data is corrupted by the B7 zero code suppression. While a voice channel can tolerate this, a data channel cannot. To compensate for this situation, a data channel generally contains only seven usable data bits. One of the eight data bits in the data channel (DS-0) is made a 1. This prevents the data channel from being corrupted by B7 zero code suppression.

This type of arrangement is called a nonclear channel. A nonclear channel is a data channel (DS-0) with seven usable and one unusable data bit.

NON-CLEAR CHANNEL

NON-CLEAR CHANNEL = 7 USABLE DATA BITS (INSTEAD OF 8 BITS) × 8,000 SAMPLES/SECOND IN A T1 STREAM
NON-CLEAR CHANNEL = 7 USABLE DATA BITS × 8,000/SECOND
NON-CLEAR CHANNEL = 56,000 BITS/SECOND (USABLE DATA BITS)
{THERE ARE 8 BITS PER CHANNEL IN A NON-CLEAR CHANNEL (DS-0). ONLY 7 ARE USABLE FOR DATA}

EXAMPLE OF HOW A NON-CLEAR CHANNEL MIGHT LOOK	DATA CHANNEL (DS-0)							
	BIT 1	BIT 2	BIT 3	BIT 4	BIT 5	BIT 6	BIT 7	BIT 8
	1			USABLE DATA BITS				

The seven usable data bits yield 56,000 usable bit/s and 8,000 unusable bits. The 56,000 bit/s on a nonclear channel is also referred to as a DS-A.

MORE BASIC T1 MATH MANIPULATION:

IF ALL 24 CHANNELS IN THE BIT STREAM ARE 'NON-CLEAR CHANNELS' THEN:
T1 BIT STREAM = 8,000 FRAME BITS + [64,000 DATA BITS PER CHANNEL × 24 CHANNELS]/SECOND
T1 BIT STREAM = 8,000 FRAME BITS + [(56,000 USABLE DATA BITS + 8,000 UNUSABLE DATA BITS) × 24 CHANNELS]/SECOND
T1 BIT STREAM = 8,000 FRAME BITS + [(1,344,000 USABLE DATA BITS + 192,000 UNUSABLE DATA BITS)]/SECOND
T1 BIT STREAM = 8,000 FRAME BITS + 1,536,000 USABLE AND UNUSABLE DATA BITS/SECOND
T1 BIT STREAM = 1.544 MBIT/S (FRAME AND DATA, BOTH USABLE AND UNUSABLE)

The mathematics shows that in a T1 bit stream in which all channels are considered nonclear, there will be only 1.344 Mbit/s available for data transmission. We have 8,000 frame bits and 192,000 usable data bits that hold to the 1s density requirement in the T1 bit stream. Thus in a T1 bit stream (1.544 Mbit/s) with nonclear channels, fully 200,000 bit/s are needed for framing and 1s density.

Clear channels are available. A clear channel is one in which all 64,000 bits are usable. A medium such as microwave can support clear channels; private microwave links do not require B7 zero code suppression nor do they need 1s insertion. Though there is always a question of losing synchronization if too many consecutive 0s appear on the link, with today's technology the quantity of consecutive 0s can generally run in excess of 15. And just because there are eight consecutive 0s in a particular DS-0 does not mean you will have 15 consecutive 0s in the T1 bit stream.

Clear channel capability can also be obtained on DS-1 telephone company equipment by using bipolar transmission with Binary 8 zero substitution (B8ZS) coding in the T1 bit stream (DS-1). With B8ZS coding each eight consecutive 0s in a byte are removed and the B8ZS code is substituted.

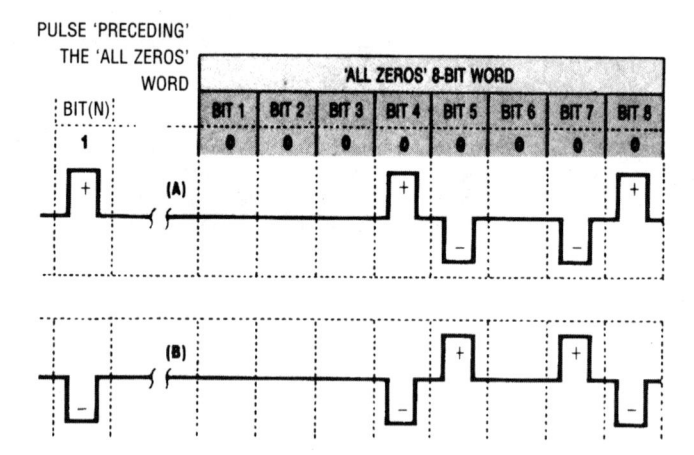

PULSE 'PRECEDING' THE 'ALL ZEROS' WORD	'ALL ZEROS' 8-BIT WORD							
BIT(N)	BIT 1	BIT 2	BIT 3	BIT 4	BIT 5	BIT 6	BIT 7	BIT 8
1	0	0	0	0	0	0	0	0

(A): + pulse, then 0 0 0 + − 0 − +
(B): − pulse, then 0 0 0 − + 0 + − 0

If the pulse preceding the inserted code is transmitted as a positive (+) pulse, the inserted code is 0 0 0 + − 0 − + (for example, A). If the pulse preceding the inserted code is a negative (−) pulse, the inserted code is 0 0 0 − + 0 + − 0 (for example, B). In the only two possible examples (A and B), bipolar violations occur in the fourth and seventh bit position. For this operation to work, all the equipment (telephone company and customer) used to transmit the T1 bit stream in the bipolar format must be able to recognize these codes as legitimate signals and not as bipolar violations or errors. Through normal evolution, significant integration of equipment with clear channel capability into the telephone company network is expected in the 1990s. The integrated services digital network will make extensive use of clear channel capability to transmit voice and data and will use a separate out-of-band channel for signaling information.

Another change coming to the network is the Extended Superframe format (ESF), also called the F_e format. ESF redefines the D4 framing pattern. Instead of looking for the resident 12 consecutive bits in the D4 framing, 24 consecutive frame bits are being processed.

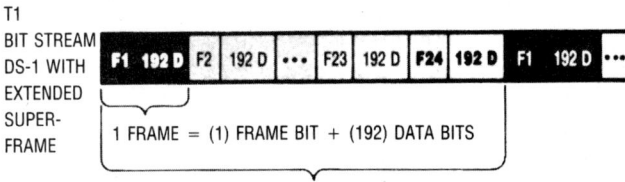

T1 BIT STREAM DS-1 WITH EXTENDED SUPERFRAME

| F1 | 192 D | F2 | 192 D | ... | F23 | 192 D | F24 | 192 D | F1 | 192 D | ... |

1 FRAME = (1) FRAME BIT + (192) DATA BITS

1 EXTENDED SUPERFRAME (ESF) — FRAMES F1 THROUGH F24

A single ESF frame contains 24 frame bits. Unlike D4 framing, in which the 12 framing bits follow a specific pattern, the ESF is not entirely a specific repeating pattern. The ESF framing pattern always keeps the same format, yet the actual frame bits are broken down into three types of frame bits.

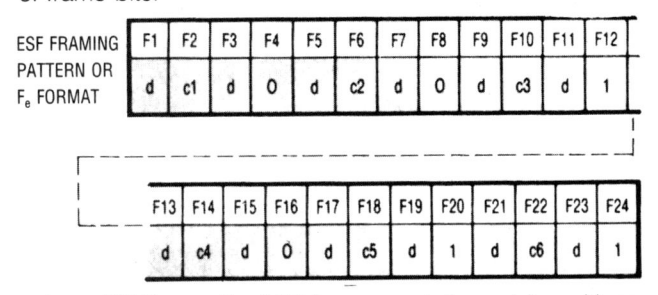

ESF FRAMING PATTERN OR F_e FORMAT

F1	F2	F3	F4	F5	F6	F7	F8	F9	F10	F11	F12
d	c1	d	0	d	c2	d	0	d	c3	d	1

F13	F14	F15	F16	F17	F18	F19	F20	F21	F22	F23	F24
d	c4	d	0	d	c5	d	1	d	c6	d	1

In an ESF frame, the "d" bits appear in frame bit positions 1, 3, 5, 7, 9, 11, 13, 15, 17, 19, 21, and 23. Of the 24 bit positions, the "d" bits use 12 positions or half of the available frame bits. Even though there are now 24 frame bits as opposed to 12, there are still only 8,000 frame bits per second in the T1 stream. Since the "d" bits are using half of the available frame bits, the "d" bits total 4,000 bit/s. The "d" bits will be used by the telephone company to perform network monitoring, alarms, reconfiguration, and so forth.

The remaining bits are split. Frame bit 2, 6, 10, 14, 18, and 22 will be used for a Cyclic Redundancy Check code consuming 2,000 bit/s. The remaining 2,000 bit/s constitute the basic frame pattern. This part of the F_e format is very specific, with a pattern of 0 0 1 0 1 1. The pattern will always appear in frame bits 4, 8, 12, 16, 20, and 24. The ESF, like B8ZS, will be applicable only when the equipment to recognize it is deployed in the network.

Wide implementation of ESF is expected to bring about several improvements in overall network performance. Not the least of these will be the use of the ESF to monitor network performance. With the ESF it is possible to provide continuous performance checking without inhibiting traffic performance. Overall network control and performance measurement will also benefit from the ESF. The ESF makes it possible to use a 4-kbit/s channel to control and report on performance. Another important advantage that will flow from networkwide implementation of the ESF is the elimination of false framing patterns. False framing can lead to serious error conditions going unreported, such as instances when a NAK is mistaken for a network crash. ■

Daniel R. Ruffalo has spent the last eight of his 28 years as a system application engineer at Rotelcom, a subsidiary of Rochester Telephone Corp., Fairport, N.Y. He is a graduate of Auburn Community College in Auburn, N.Y., where he earned an A.A.S. in electronics.

Frank Bradley, Bradley Telcom Inc., Leonia, N.J.

The hidden treasures of ESF

Although some users have heard of the extended superframe format, few appreciate its advantages.

The extended superframe format, or ESF, is the latest in a long line of improvements to digital transmission. One well-known advantage of ESF is its ability to provide continuous data link performance checking without causing traffic interference. ESF also provides a 4-kbit/s data link for network report and control. In addition, this format completely solves the problem of false framing, which can make the difference between a "NAK" and a network crash.

To fully appreciate the advantages of the extended superframe format, it is important to have a general understanding of the technical progress of T1 links. The concept of digital carrier was introduced to the U. S. telecommunications network in the early 1960s. Equipment operating at 1.544 Mbit/s placed 24 voice frequency (VF) channels on a two-wire pair. To identify each of the 24 channels, a framing pattern consisting of alternate ones and zeros was used in every 193rd bit position. The other 192 bits (divided into 24 eight-bit bytes) were used for customer traffic and signaling. A sampling rate of 64 kbit/s was used. Since that initial release, pulse code modulation (PCM) techniques have evolved, and the framing pattern has changed. Still, the basic DS-1 PCM signal used by telephone companies in the United States is made up of 8,000 frames per second with a frame length of 193 bits.

The first PCM techniques used D1 channel banks. ("Channel bank" is typically a carrier term for what users often call a multiplexer.) The framing pattern was alternate ones and zeros in bit position 193. The eighth bit of every byte was reserved by the carrier for transmission of signaling information. Customer traffic was thus confined to seven bits.

To provide the amplitude resolution required to ensure voice intelligibility over the wide range of signal levels, analog-to-digital signal conversion was logarithmically weighted. (The signal level ranges widely because of the variation in the signal loss between the central office and the customer site, and because of the variation in the volume of the speaker's voice.) This weighting was accomplished by compandors, devices that convert between linear and logarithmic signals before and after the signal conversion. Compandors are of no interest in all-digital transmission paths, but they are of considerable interest when analog modem signals pass through a digital facility.

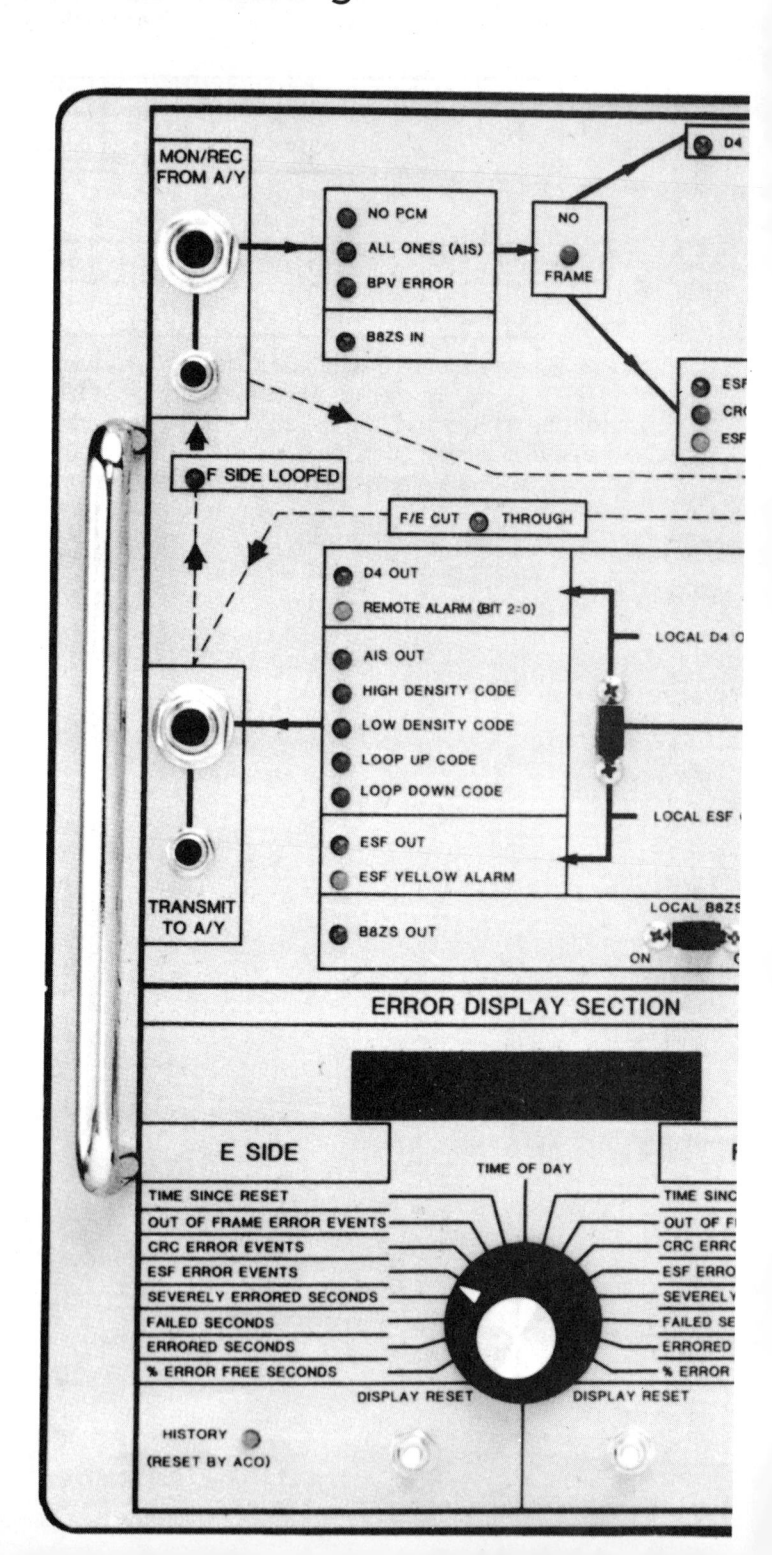

The D1 banks proved to be susceptible to loss of frame in the presence of a 1,000-Hz test tone because, at exact submultiples of the 8,000-frame-per-second sampling frequency, the digitally encoded result contained ones and zeros in the same bit position in successive frames—exactly 193 bits apart. This, then, resulted in false framing, meaning that the signal mimicked the framing pattern and confused the circuitry of channel bank framing. False framing slows down or stops the resynchronization process required after the occasional loss-of-frame conditions that occur in communications channels due to such typical occurrences as noise, line hits, circuit interruptions, and protection switching. The effect of this on a communications channel is to convert a short line hit into to a long error burst that can sometimes disrupt a communications environment. Carriers have thus embarked on, and nearly completed, the conversion of all test oscillators and digital milliwatt sources from 1,000 Hz to 1,004 Hz.

D1 channel banks were eventually migrated to D2 channel banks. In these, the analog (nonlinear circuit element) compandor was replaced with a logarithmically weighted analog-to-digital converter. In addition, a superframe consisting of 12 frames was defined by a unique 193-bit sequence repeated once every 12 frames. This superframe accomplished two tasks. Since the frame pattern was more complex, its susceptibility to traffic was reduced. Also, D2's capability of identifying frames permitted the introduction of robbed-bit signaling. With this technique, each customer byte was eight bits except for frames 6 and 12. In those frames the eighth (least significant) bit of each byte carries the signaling information: the "A" bit in frame 6 and the "B" bit in frame 12. Voice traffic fidelity was thereby upgraded, and analog modem performance on PCM equipment was improved. D2 was the first PCM having toll quality. The PCM ap-

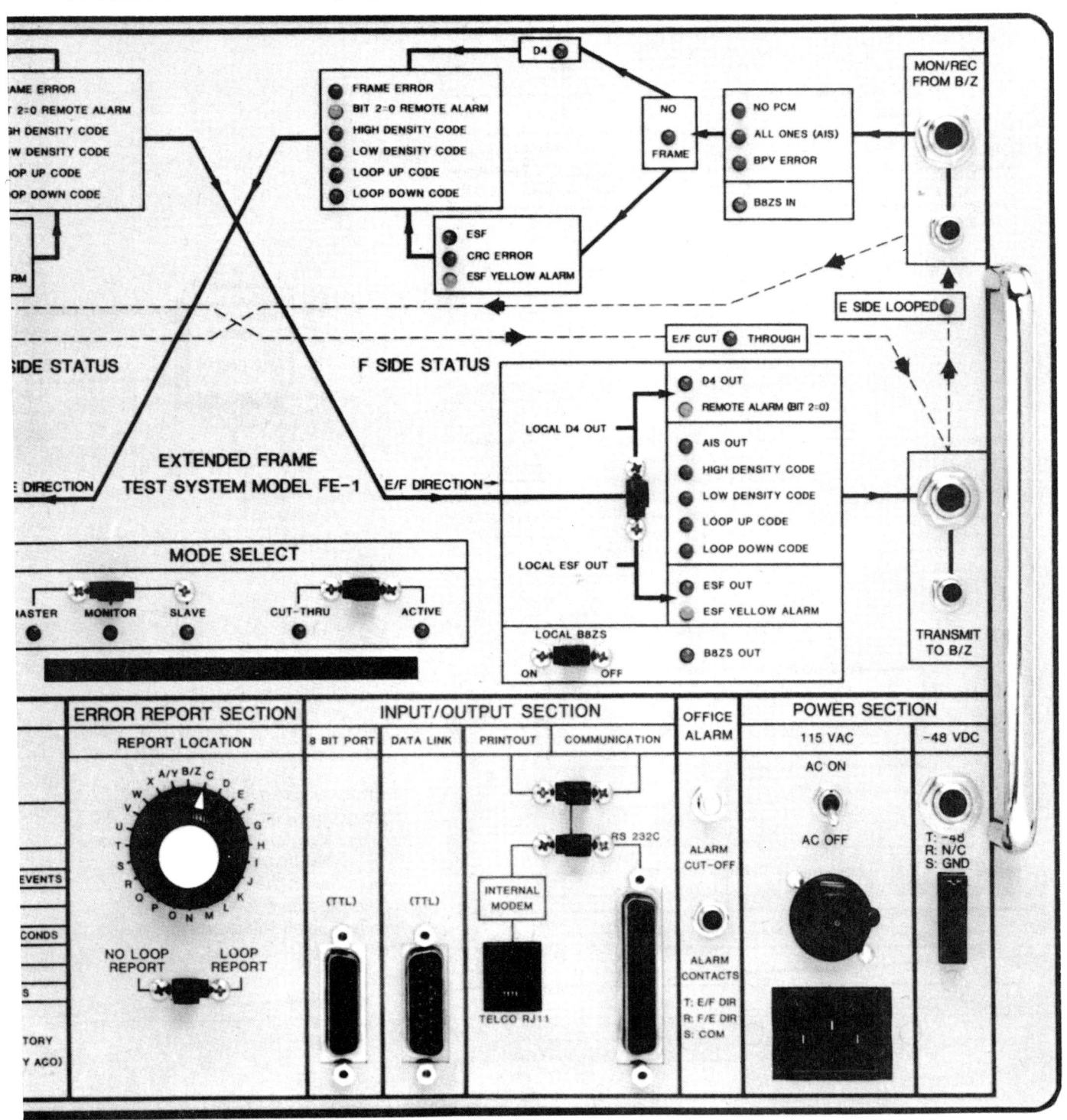

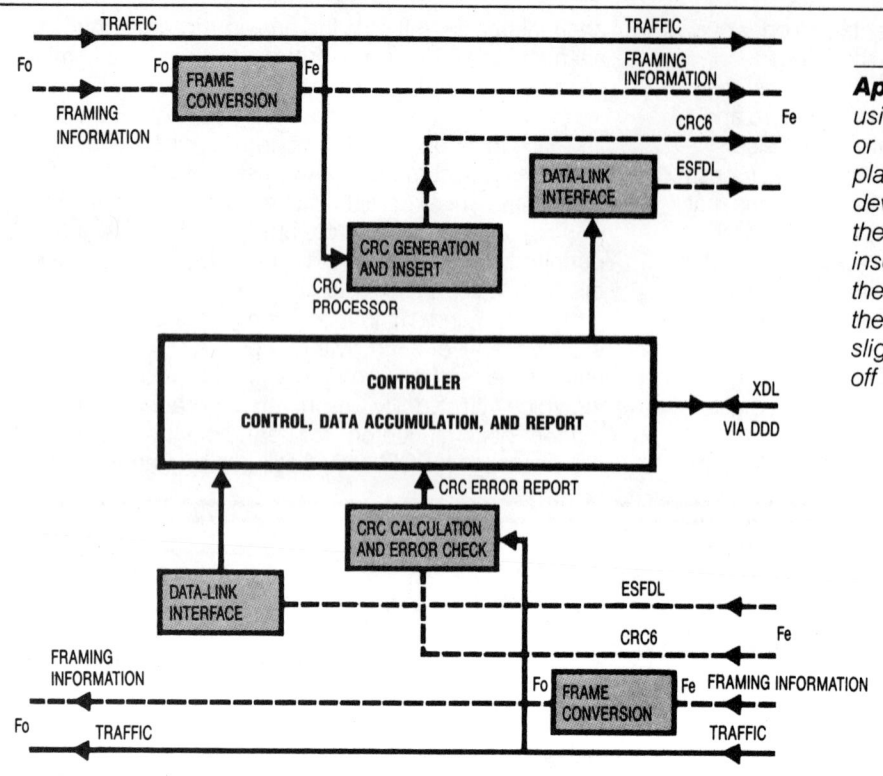

Applying ESF. One practical way of using the extended superframe format, or ESF, on the existing digital service plant is to insert temporarily a special device into the T1 line, shown here with the designation DS-1. The unit can be inserted in two ways: (A) at the end of the link and (B) at a mid point along the link. It can also be used, with a slight alteration explained below (C), off line as a monitor.

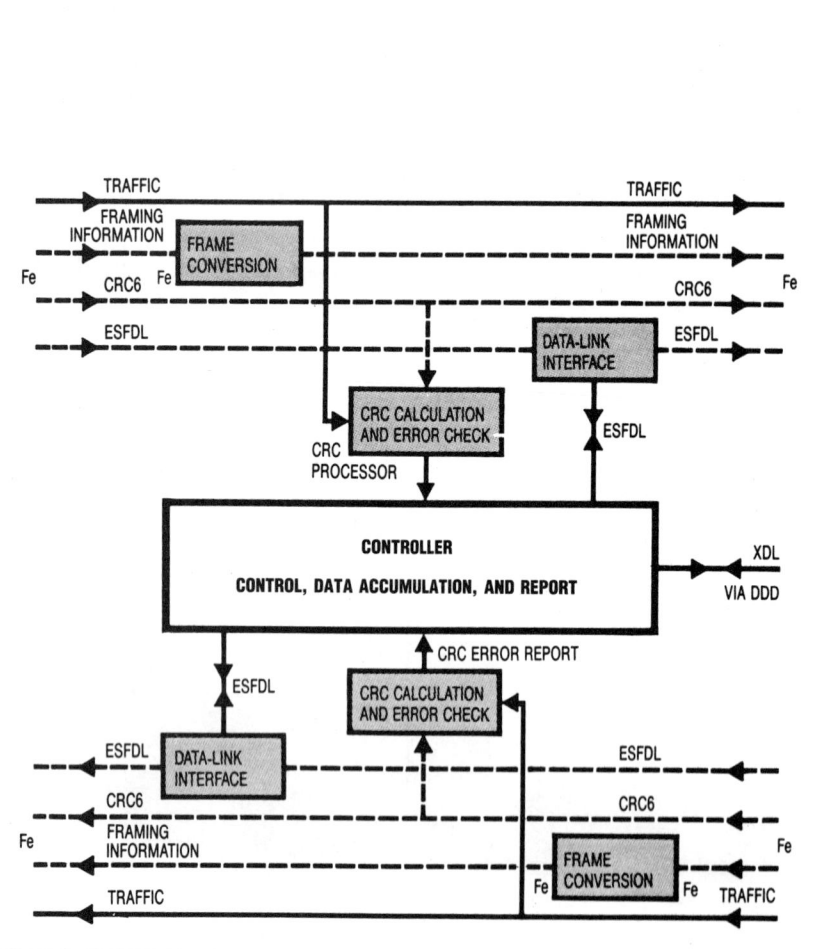

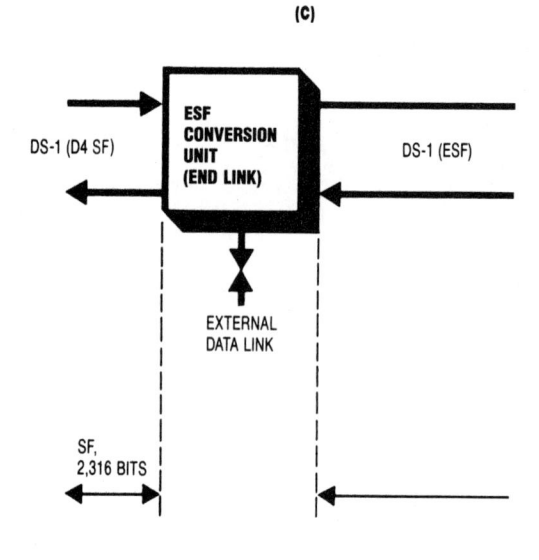

Part B. As a mid-link unit, the ESF device doesn't perform conversion. The dotted lines represent 24 bits out of the 4,632-bit superframe. While they are embedded in the data, these bits are broken out here to illustrate that they are flagged and handled separately by the device.

Part A. *As an end-link unit, the ESF device converts D4 framing between terminals while the intermediate traffic is in the ESF format. The blocks labeled "frame conversion" are transparent to the format. They convert bidirectionally between ESF and D4.*

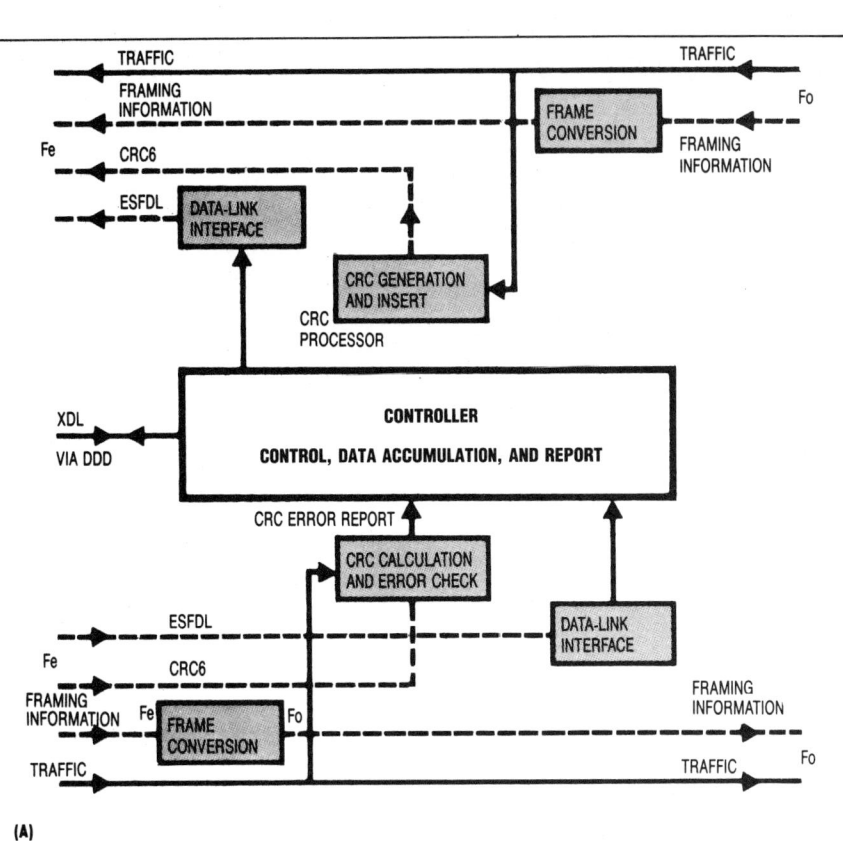

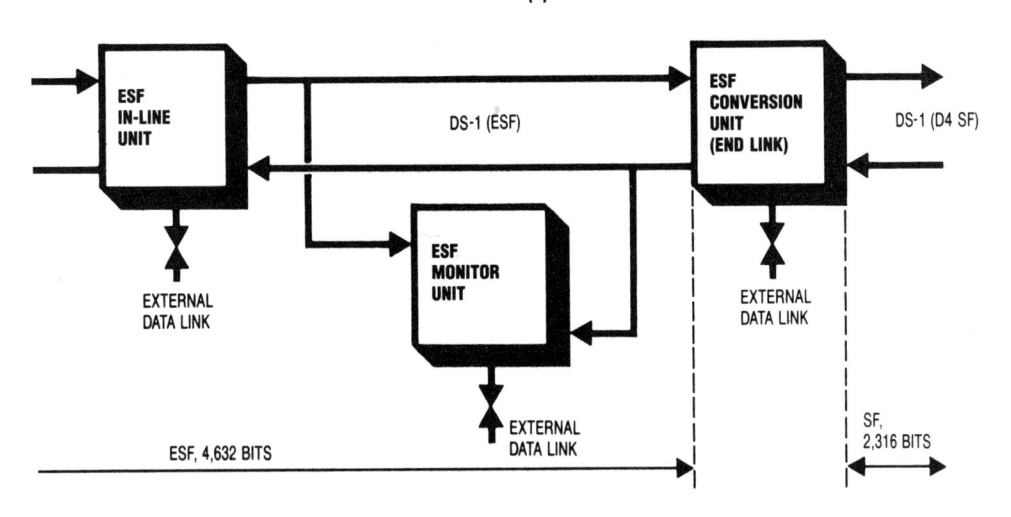

(A)

CRC = CYCLIC REDUNDANCY CHECK
DDD = DIRECT DISTANCE DIALING
Fe = AT&T TERM FOR 24-BIT SUPERFRAME, ESF TYPE
Fo = AT&T TERM FOR 12-BIT SUPERFRAME, ESF TYPE

SF = SUPERFRAME
ESF = EXTENDED SUPERFRAME

Part C. *The ESF unit may be controlled over an external data link (XDL) from a maintenance control unit, or MCU. The MCU can be an MS-DOS-compatible microcomputer running special ESF software. The MCU need only communicate with one of the locations on a circuit in order to have access to the ESF data links and to collect information from equipment at the other locations.*

plication was, therefore, no longer limited to end-link applications but could be used in the switched network for interoffice trunking.

Various improvements were made in channel banks D3 and D4. Other than improving codec performance, these changes did not affect the customer voice channel; they primarily concerned administrative issues, such as the accommodation of special services, the adaptation to DDS (Dataphone digital service), and the adaptation to higher-order T1 multiplexed links. (These include T1C with 48 channels, T2 with 96 channels, and fiber optics.)

DDS has the lowest error rate of the data links furnished by carriers. To meet the DDS performance objectives, a higher level of backup is provided. In addition, for high-density DDS applications, where as many as 460 customers may be sharing a single DS-1 channel, channel 24 was removed from customer service and assigned to overhead: A fixed data word and a maintenance supervision channel were placed in channel 24. The fixed data word permits rapid reframe in DDS multiplexer equipment and may be monitored for bit errors. The occurrence of errors is reported locally by test equipment and remotely via a maintenance supervision channel. This supervision channel permits the continuous monitoring of network performance, thereby identifying incipient failures. More recently, error correction capability and a secondary channel capability have been offered.

Other encoding techniques, such as ADPCM (adaptive differential pulse code modulation), have been used to increase intelligibility at lower data rates; other hardware, notably Subscriber Loop Carrier (SLC) 96, have used the 193rd bit for signaling and control. But extended superframe is the first technique to provide error detection and reporting capability without affecting traffic. At this time, D5 channel banks, which support ESF, are in the early stages of use.

Superframe layout

In ESF the superframe is extended to 24 frames. The organization and use of these frame bits provides a remarkably efficient mechanism for continuous maintenance supervision of DS-1 PCM equipment. Of perhaps greater significance, interference between the signal content and the framing pattern is eliminated. In ESF six bits are assigned to framing, six to cyclic redundancy checking (CRC), and 12 to a maintenance data channel. Note also that a sequence of four signaling frames is defined (A, B, C, and D) instead of the two-frame sequence (A and B) for the 12-frame ESF format. There are a negligible number of ESF channel banks actually in use today, although there are tens of millions of D1, D2, D3, and D4 format channel banks in service.

Signal interference with framing was significantly reduced by the shift from D1 to D2 banks, but it was not completely eliminated. In D2 and in subsequent channel banks, frames are delineated by alternate ones and zeros in every 386th bit position. In the case of ESF, if a channel bank frame is on an alias of the framing bits, the frame interval will be incorrectly identified, and the CRC will indicate an error in every superframe. This fact is used to debug the "in-frame" declaration, and the channel bank seeks a new position in the data stream, where the frame bits match. The channel bank will continue to seek until it finally seizes the correct framing pattern, in which case the frequency of CRC errors will then return to its normal low level.

One way of applying ESF to the existing digital service plant is to change the millions of existing channel banks. But for users a more practical approach is to temporarily insert, during maintenance, conversion devices into the T1 line (see figure). Conversion hardware, placed at each end of a transmission facility, permits D4 (or previous generation) framing communications between terminals while the intermediate traffic is in the ESF format as shown in part A in the upper right and upper left portions of the figure. CRC error detection techniques can be used to monitor the transmission facility both end-to-end and at intermediate points (such as the maintenance interfaces the telephone company or carrier uses for sectionalization).

Error detection

Because of its low overhead, CRC has become the generally preferred method of error checking, usually CRC16. This means that an n th degree polynomial representing the data (where n is the number of bits in the data block) is divided by a specific 16th-degree "check" polynomial; the 16 remainder bits are the CRC bits. These check bits, generated at the data origination source, are transmitted along with the data as the transmitted data CRC bits.

At the termination point, the same calculation is repeated on the received data to generate receive CRC bits. The received data CRC bits are compared with the transmitted data CRC bits. If there is a discrepancy, a CRC error is declared. Regardless of the block length, CRC16 level detects more than 99.998 percent of the block errors in transmission.

In ESF, the CRC function provides protection against false framing and permits evaluation of facility performance. It is not meant to replace customer use of error checking procedures, but it may be used by both customers and carriers for continuous monitoring of data link performance without interfering with traffic. ESF uses CRC6 for error detection. The block length is one ESF superframe, or 4,632 bits. At 1.544 Mbit/s this block length corresponds to 3 milliseconds. Thus the ESF scheme examines data in approximately 333 windows per second. CRC6 level detects more than 98.5 percent of transmission block errors, which is a sufficient level of transmission monitoring. This is even more comprehensive and several orders of magnitude faster than existing techniques, which, during live traffic, are limited to monitoring frame bits, bipolar violations, and some of the bits in maintenance channel 24. Furthermore, the ESF technique can be employed directly by the user, which is otherwise difficult because bipolar violation monitoring and channel 24 error monitoring are limited to telephone company application.

Overview of ESF capability

One practical way of describing the variety of capabilities of ESF is to discuss a sample design of a device that a user might use to implement it. Such an instrument must encompass several functions, including D4-to-ESF conversion, which provides the basic link (see figure, part A); CRC checking, providing circuit error performance monitoring without interruption of traffic; and in-channel data link capability, providing error report and remote operating control (see part B of the figure). A single DDD circuit can be used to implement supervision, control, and error reporting on the D4 link.

The instrument must convert the framing format between D4 and ESF, insert and remove CRC information, handle the information in the maintenance data channel, monitor equipment and circuit status, and accumulate error performance history. The device could reside either close to or far from network operations personnel. Equipment and circuit status, as well as error history, could thus be presented locally or remote via data link. The reports should contain information for each of up to 24 instrument locations in the bidirectional path.

To facilitate remote operation, control of the device should be possible in three modes: from the unit itself, via the 4-kbit/s ESF data link (ESFDL) embedded in the ESF framing, and from an external data link (XDL) from a maintenance control unit, or MCU, which could be an off-the-shelf MS-DOS-compatible microcomputer (see part C of the figure).

Note that an MCU need only communicate with one of the locations on a circuit in order to have access to the ESFDLs and to collect information from, or control, equipment at any of the other locations.

Parts A and B of the figure show the functional information distribution of framing, CRC, and data link information for the sample device in two operating modes: in-line and end link. The dotted lines represent 24 bits out of a total of 4,632 bits in the superframe. These bits are embedded in the data but are shown broken out separately for tutorial purposes, just as they are flagged and handled separately in the sample device's hardware.

The blocks labeled "frame conversion" are transparent to the format or convert bidirectionally between D4 and ESF framing. The frame conversion function is controlled from either the device, from the ESFDL, or from the XDL. For the remainder of this discussion, Fo refers to a 12-bit superframe of the D4 (or lower) type, and Fe refers to a 24-bit superframe of the ESF type. (This terminology is taken from AT&T's technical literature.)

When receiving data in the Fe format, the blocks labeled data link interface drop and/or insert information into the ESFDL as specified by the controller.

When receiving Fe data, the blocks labeled "CRC" processor calculate the CRC for the currently received traffic frame and compare it with the CRC that is calculated at the origin and transmitted during the previous traffic frame. Any difference between the two is a CRC error occurrence and is communicated to the controller. The controller processes this information to define error statistics, such as errored seconds and failed seconds. In addition, the controller accumulates the number of each of the above in each 15-minute interval for 24 hours. When requested, it reports the individual interval figures and the totals. The report should include a figure for errored seconds (of interest in digital data services) as well as failed seconds, which is more relevant to VF service.

It is worth noting again that ESF is concerned with bit 193. Other than for operating mode commands, the 192 traffic bits remain unaffected by this flurry of activity in bit 193. The 12-bits-per-superframe ESFDLs comprise a full-duplex 4-kbit/s data channel. In addition, each unit has a full-duplex 2.4-kbit/s external data link (212-type modem), which may be DDD (direct distance dialing), private line, or directly accessed by an MCU. When not in the monitor-only mode, such conversion devices as previously described are capable of drop and/or insertion of data on the 4-kbit/s ESFDL in each direction. The 2.4-kbit/s XDL is capable of dialog with the ESFDL in such a way that the operating status of any or all locations may be monitored or controlled via XDL access at a single location. Additionally the declared CRC6 errors at each location (in each direction), as accumulated and processed, may be collected via a single XDL.

DS-1 customer service

Since January 1985, AT&T Communications, when installing initial services, has required a framed format (either Fo or Fe) in order to provide maintenance support on 1.544-Mbit/s end-to-end channels. If the multiplex is Fo (D4), format conversion is required as described above for the end link application. If the multiplex is in Fe format, no conversion is required, as in the mid-link or monitor application. In either case, the data is transmitted with the extended superframe.

There is one other limitation on traffic imposed by the carriers. Specifically, a maximum of 15 successive zeros can appear in the DS-1 data stream. This limitation is required because the clock recovery circuitry in repeaters and in terminal equipment must be periodically refreshed by a transition, that is, a "1."

To provide clear channel capability, which means an absence of restrictions on the number of successive zeros but not an absence of restrictions on framing, a technique known as bit 8 zero substitution, or B8ZS, is gradually being deployed. (This deployment is happening independently of ESF.)

B8ZS involves the insertion of an artificial combination of ones and bipolar violations when eight zeros occur in sequence. This substitution affects all traffic, including bit 193. At the receive end this artificial combination is recognized and the code group replaced by eight zeros. The duplication of this encoding combination as a result of line problems is extremely rare, so the information transfer is reliable. A problem exists, however, because terminal equipment has, since the beginning of PCM, been designed to clean up (remove bipolar violations) received data before retransmitting it. Retrofitting an existing terminal to recognize B8ZS received data and retransmit is just as unfeasible as changing existing channel banks to secure ESF operation. Both of these strategies are far too expensive.

Terminal equipment that includes this capability is beginning to be deployed. Because of this, frame conversion hardware must automatically recognize B8ZS code groups on its inputs and optionally insert B8ZS code groups on its outputs. B8ZS capability is in addition to the ESF scheme and, hence, not shown in the figure. ∎

Frank Bradley is president and founder of Bradley Telcom Inc., a company that has been in business since 1970. He holds a B. A. in mechanical engineering, from Brooklyn Polytechnic Institute.

Michael Lefkowitz, Larse Corp., Santa Clara, Calif.

A tale of two standards—the T1 ESF (r)evolution

Nondisruptive monitoring via ESF is critical to the management of T1 networks. However, ESF comes two ways: an AT&T version and a recently adopted ANSI standard.

The growth of T1-based networks has been a startling phenomenon of the data communications industry and user community. The proliferation of these networks reflects a growing corporate dependence on fast, reliable information transfer. But any disruption of a corporation's T1 (1.544-Mbit/s) network can severely restrict its ability to do business. Efficient network management is more critical here than with lower-speed networks.

As a measure of T1's network popularity, from a start of less than $100 million in 1984, the T1 equipment market is forecast to grow beyond $2 *billion* by 1993. Efforts to keep the resultant networks fully operational has fostered the development and deployment of the extended superframe format. As a monitoring and diagnostic aid, ESF has major ramifications for network management (see "The hidden treasures of ESF," DATA COMMUNICATIONS, September 1986, p. 204).

Now, a sea change in ESF standards is significantly affecting how T1 networks are being planned and implemented. Network managers must understand the impact of this change and know the right questions to ask their service and equipment vendors.

The ESF standard is a critical one since it provides, for the first time on digital facilities, a method of nondisruptive full-time monitoring for both logic and format errors (see "T1 network management"). This capability provides for more rapid trouble isolation, resulting in reduced downtime. Considering how much of a typical corporation's success is riding on its digital backbone network, taking advantage of ESF is a must for any network manager.

Similar, but not the same
The two ESF standards, AT&T's PUB 54016 and ANSI's T1.403-1989 (T1E1), have many similarities. They also have several important differences. Both can be seen in an examination of salient aspects of the standards (see table).

Monitored parameters. PUB 54016 calls for two parameters to be monitored: CRC-6 errors, where the calculated CRC-6 does not equal the received CRC-6; and Out-of-Frame (OOF), defined as two out of four or five consecutive framing bits in error.

The T1E1 standard specifies five error events, two mandatory and three optional. Error events that *must* be detected—called Severely Errored Framing in T1E1—are the same as in 54016: CRC-6 errors and OOF. Error events whose detection is optional are Controlled Slip (duplication or deletion of an entire frame), Framing Error (a single framing bit in error), and Bipolar Violation (BPV, where a mark or space has the same—not opposite—polarity as the previous mark or space).

Derived parameters. PUB 54016 specifies three types of problem seconds:
- Errored Second (ES): a second having one or more CRC-6 errors and/or an OOF state.
- Severely Errored Second (SES): a second having 320 or more CRC-6 errors and/or an OOF state. (A total of 320 CRC-6 errors corresponds to a bit error rate of one in 10^3, a good-quality threshold for voice lines but not for data. Some carriers have contracted to provide T1 service with SES defined to correspond to more stringent bit error rates, such as one in 10^5.)
- Failed Second (FS): a second during which a failed signal state is in effect. A failed signal state is declared after 10 consecutive SESs and cleared after 10 consecutive non-SESs. (FS is so defined to distinguish between error bursts—which are typical of digital facilities—and failure states.)

These derived parameters are organized into performance registers that may be accessed over the data link by monitoring equipment in the central office.

The T1E1 standard does not call for any processed parameters. Instead, a performance report is transmitted

T1

over the data link every second. No historical data is kept beyond three seconds.

Performance Reports. In PUB 54016, derived parameters are organized into 24-hour and one-hour registers of Errored Seconds and Failed Seconds. Each register is organized into 15-minute increments. In addition, all ESF errors (CRC-6 and OOF) are counted and stored in the ESF Error Counter. The four registers and the ESF Error Counter are accessed by data link commands using the Telemetry Asynchronous Block Serial (TABS) protocol, a modified X.25 Level 2 AT&T standard.

Typically, registers are read once a day and then reset.

Central office equipment stores this information and processes it to create other performance reports used by the carrier.

In contrast, the T1E1 standard specifies a single performance report formatted to conform to the Q.921/LAPD (Link Access Procedure-D) protocol and broadcast via the data link. (Other message-oriented signals and reports may be added to the standard in the future.) The performance report, consisting of 112 bits, contains performance information about the current second and the three previous seconds. The report is transmitted every second by equipment (such as a channel service unit, or CSU) located on the

T1 network management

There are several factors that contribute to the difficulty of T1 network management:
- The high volume of traffic carried by a single T1 line means that line degradations and failures have a much greater impact on the network.
- The complexity of services and equipment increases the ways in which things can go wrong, making troubleshooting more complicated.
- The multivendor networks make rapid isolation and restoral more difficult.
- Last, but certainly not least, there is a shortage of trained personnel to manage this T1 complexity.

With the extended superframe format, real-time performance data is gathered at various network sites and promptly made available at a central location. With this data, the management team rapidly pinpoints, diagnoses, and corrects a problem, thus keeping downtime to a minimum. Degradations are identified and dealt with before they seriously affect operation. Historical data is used for trend analysis and performance documenting. And because the carrier and user have access to the same performance data, finger-pointing is greatly reduced.

■ Historical perspective. In 1981, driven by the need to provide better maintenance for the Dataphone Digital Service network and the then-planned High Capacity Terrestrial Service (the precursor of Accunet T1.5), AT&T developed the ESF format. ESF is basically an enhancement of the D4, or superframe, format. In both D4 and ESF, the digital bit stream is organized into frames consisting of 192 information bits and one framing bit. The 1.544-Mbit/s bit stream is thus divided into 1.536 Mbit/s of data and 8 kbit/s of overhead.

The D4 format employs a superframe of 12 frames, with all 12 framing bits providing a specified pattern for framing synchronization. ESF employs an extended superframe of 24 frames, with six of the framing bits used for framing synchronization and 18 bits available for other monitoring and maintenance functions. Specifically, the ESF format divides the 8 kbit/s of framing information into three data streams as follows:
- 2 kbit/s for framing;
- 2 kbit/s for a CRC-6 logic check (CRC-6 is a cyclic redundancy check that uses six frame bits, those in frames 2, 6, 10, 14, 18, and 22); and
- 4 kbit/s for a data link, used for transmission of performance information and control signals.

When AT&T published the ESF Technical Reference, PUB 54016, in late 1984, the only unresolved issue was if and how users could access the data link for their own applications. In early 1985, AT&T started testing ESF equipment for the central office, and also encouraging manufacturers to design and market ESF equipment for the customer premises.

At the same time, AT&T submitted PUB 54016 to the newly created Exchange Carriers Standards Association committee T1C1.

Things were sailing along smoothly in T1C1.2, the working group responsible for the DS-1 interface standard, until August 1985, when Bellcore introduced a new proposal. Under this scheme, the 4-kbit/s data link would be split into four channels so that each stakeholder (the user, local exchange carrier, interexchange carrier, and equipment vendor) would have its own link for maintenance purposes. This proposal, considered at Bell Labs prior to 1981, had some interesting merits, but was rejected by AT&T. (The merits included: notification to the sending end of an error detected at the receiving end and a designated channel portion for each carrier involved and for the user.)

After many long and sometimes heated debates, a compromise was reached. It was agreed to retain the data link as a single 4-kbit/s channel and to use a message-oriented (Q.921/LAPD [Link Access Procedure-D]) protocol for performance information. A number of bit-oriented data link maintenance messages were defined, such as Yellow Signal (indicating loss of synchronization), loopback commands, and protection switching commands that can activate standby circuits.

In early 1988, the T1 standards committees were reorganized and T1E1 was charged with the DS-1 interface standard. This standard was recently issued by ANSI as T1.403-1989.

During the deliberation and approval processes, AT&T continued to deploy central office equipment compatible with the PUB 54016 version of ESF. In addition, many users deployed customer premises equipment compatible with PUB 54016, creating something of a dilemma. To what extent are the two standards compatible? And how do we make the transition from one to the other? —*M.L.*

customer premises at the network interface. Transmitting data four times for each second helps ensure the accuracy of the performance reports to the receiving network devices.

The following information is provided for each second:
- Range of CRC-6 errors: one, two to five, six to 10, 11 to 100, 101 to 319, 320+;
- Severely Errored Framing (same as OOF), occurrence equal to or greater than one;
- Frame bit errors, equal to or greater than one;
- BPVs equal to or greater than one;
- Slip event equal to or greater than one; and
- Payload loopback (where only information bits are looped) activated.

There are three bits reserved for future applications, such as synchronization.

Maintenance messages. In addition to performance reports, the data link transmits maintenance messages that, in the D4 (superframe) format, are transmitted in-band. Three maintenance messages are defined in both PUB 54016 and T1E1: Yellow Signal, Line Loopback, and Payload Loopback. The maintenance messages are either identical or very similar in the two standards.

Data link operation. The main difference between the two standards is in the operation of the data link. Besides using different protocols (TABS versus Q.921/LAPD), the standards differ in basic maintenance philosophy (see the figure).

As specified in PUB 54016, the data link operates on an inquiry-response basis, depending on the premises equipment (CSU) to store 24 hours of performance data. On receipt of a valid command from the network's central office, the CSU transmits the contents of the appropriate performance register(s).

Under the T1E1 standard, performance messages are broadcast every second on the data link. These performance reports apply to the direction opposite to that in which they are transmitted. For example, performance data for the link from A to B is broadcast from B toward A. T1E1 performance reports can be monitored anywhere along the T1 network.

Bridged performance monitors, located in the central office, monitor the data stream for performance parameters such as CRC-6 errors and OOF conditions. In addition, they extract performance data for the direction of transmission opposite from the data link's. Collected data is organized into reports and forwarded to an Operations Support System (OSS), which is used to isolate network problems and provide historical performance information for ongoing studies, such as trend analysis. (As shown in the figure, as many as three OSS units may be present on a single T1 configuration.)

From the carrier's point of view, T1E1 is more efficient to implement. First, T1E1 is less expensive because the performance monitor in the central office is bridged—that is, it reads the data link but does not write on it as required under PUB 54016. Second, a bridged monitor is not a potential point of failure in the T1 network, as a 54016 in-line performance monitor would be.

From the user's point of view, access to historical performance data is the critical issue. Currently, where only AT&T PUB 54016 has been implemented, users have access to the same 24-hour performance registers as the carrier. In addition, some CSU manufacturers build in more extensive, user-accessible performance registers. Under T1E1, users would have to add performance data storage external to the CSU or be able to access information from the carrier's OSS. In fact, some carriers are planning to allow customers to access their own performance data; others are evaluating the possibility of doing so.

The good news

At first glance, things look pretty bleak for the user in the ESF world. There are key differences between the two ESF standards. On one hand, AT&T has made a big investment

Summary of features, AT&T PUB 54016 versus T1E1

ATTRIBUTE	AT&T PUB 54016	T1E1 (ANSI T1.403)
ALLOCATION OF 8 KBIT/S OF OVERHEAD	2 KBIT/S FRAMING 2 KBIT/S CRC-6 ERROR CHECKING 4 KBIT/S DATA LINK (DL)	SAME AS PUB 54016
MONITORED PARAMETERS	CRC-6 ERRORS OUT OF FRAME (OOF)	CRC-6 ERRORS SEVERELY ERRORED FRAMING (= OOF) CONTROL SLIP (OPTIONAL) FRAMING BIT ERROR (OPTIONAL) BIPOLAR VIOLATION (OPTIONAL)
DERIVED PARAMETERS	ERRORED SECOND (ES) SEVERELY ERRORED SECOND (SES) FAILED SECOND (FS)	RANGE OF CRC-6 ERRORS
MONITORING EQUIPMENT (CARRIER)	READ AND WRITE ON DATA LINK	READ DATA LINK
DATA LINK PROTOCOL	TABS	Q921/LAPD
MAINTENANCE PHILOSOPHY	IN-LINE INQUIRY-RESPONSE	BROADCAST TO BRIDGED MONITORS
MAINTENANCE MESSAGES	YELLOW SIGNAL PAYLOAD LOOPBACK LINE LOOPBACK	YELLOW SIGNAL PAYLOAD LOOPBACK LINE LOOPBACK PROTECTION SWITCHING (RESERVED) SYNCHRONIZATION (RESERVED)
HISTORICAL PERFORMANCE DATA	24 HOURS	NONE

CRC = CYCLIC REDUNDANCY CHECK
LAPD = LINK ACCESS PROCEDURE-D

T1

Data link operation. *The two ESF standards differ in basic maintenance philosophy. Under AT&T PUB 54016, the data link operates on an inquiry-response basis, where the network retrieves 24 hours of performance data from the T1 CPE. Under the T1E1 standard, performance messages are broadcast to the network once every second.*

AT&T PUB 54016: Inquiry/response

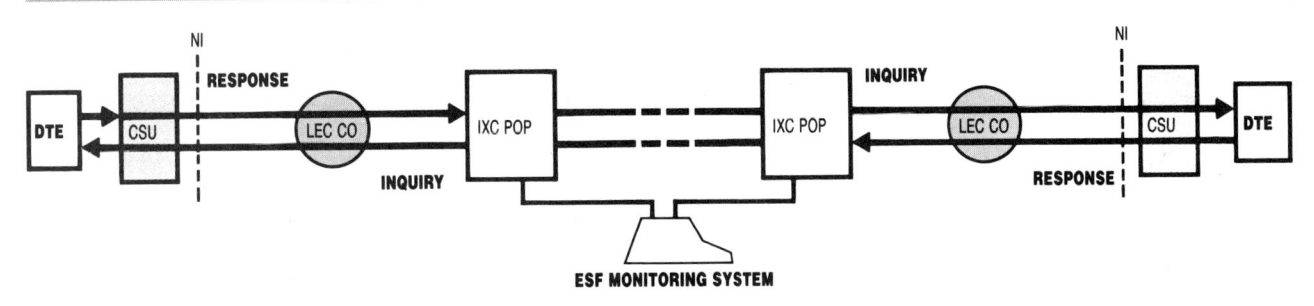

T1E1: Broadcast

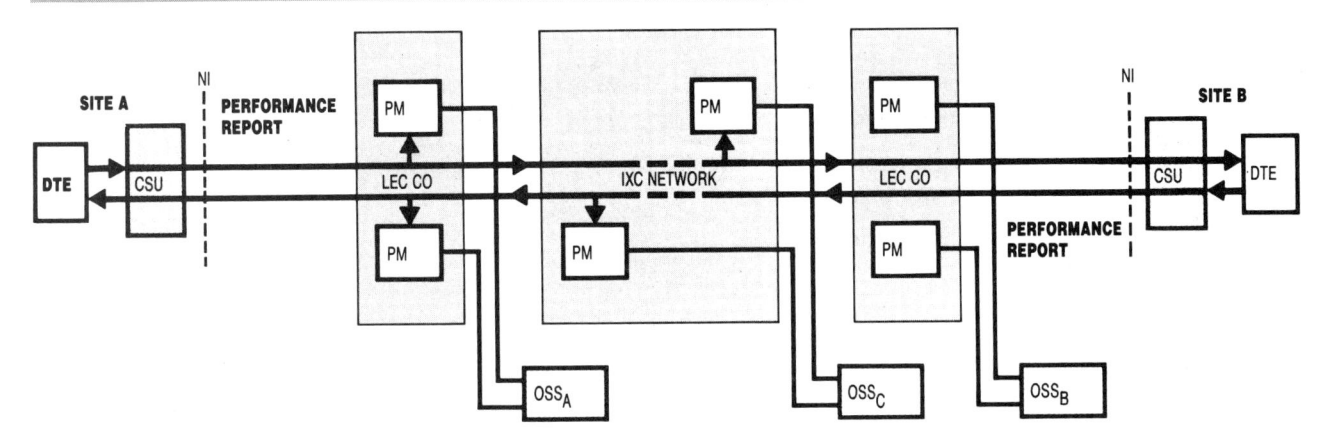

CO = CENTRAL OFFICE
CSU = CHANNEL SERVICE UNIT
DTE = DATA TERMINAL EQUIPMENT
ESF = EXTENDED SUPERFRAME FORMAT
IXC = INTERLATA CARRIER
LEC = LOCAL EXCHANGE CARRIER
NI = NETWORK INTERFACE
OSS = OPERATIONS SUPPORT SYSTEM
PM = PERFORMANCE MONITOR
POP = POINT OF PRESENCE

in deploying equipment based on PUB 54016. And on the other, most of the regional BOCs and other interLATA carriers are either planning or are likely to implement T1E1. What's the user to do today?

In spite of the fact that some observers are calling the two standards completely incompatible, the good news for users is that the two standards can coexist. The main factor making this possible is the brevity of the T1E1 performance report, which takes only 112 bit/s of the 4-kbit/s data link (or only 28 milliseconds of each second on the data link). With proper flow control, this leaves more than enough bandwidth for PUB 54016 messages. Furthermore, since maintenance messages such as Yellow Signal and loopback commands take priority over other messages, a CSU or other ESF terminating device can wait until these preemptive messages are transmitted over the network. The devices can then resume responding to and generating the proper messages for both standards. The CSU can even store historical performance data for access by the user.

The possibility of coexistence is good news because the transition between PUB 54016 and T1E1 standards will take time. While AT&T is the only carrier that invested heavily in PUB 54016 ESF equipment, most vendors of T1 customer premises equipment have also implemented PUB 54016, either directly or through separate CSU equipment.

There is a substantial amount of ESF equipment on customer premises today that is compatible with PUB 54016. Once the RBOCs and other local exchange carriers begin to implement T1E1, this equipment will, in all likelihood, have to be upgraded. If AT&T is the interLATA carrier, the equipment may have to meet both standards.

The transition can be accomplished with minimum disruption to the corporate network if the CSU or other ESF terminating device can add T1E1 capability through downline-loadable software. Otherwise, CSUs or PROMs (programmable ROMs) must be physically swapped at every network site, a process both disruptive and expensive.

The key to a smooth transition is planning. Users should be made aware of the likely evolution to T1E1 by their network carriers. To respond to evolving conditions, users should choose CSUs and other network equipment that meet both standards or that can be readily upgraded through downline-loadable software.

The not-so-good news

From a user's point of view, no discussion of ESF is complete without considering its limitations. First of all, both ESF standards are carrier-oriented; they provide one-way information from the customer premises to the network. Neither has a provision for user access to the performance data residing in the carrier's network or at the far end of the user's network.

The second limitation is that use of the data link is restricted to the carrier. Currently, there is no provision for user applications such as reconfiguration and far-end performance-data retrieval. Responsibility for this shortcoming thus far rests—at least in part—with the users. As stakeholders, users need to take an active role in the standards process. Since T1E1.2 has an open project to define alternative applications of the data link, there is still time for users to become involved in setting the standards for their applications.

The third limitation of the current ESF standards is that neither supports the capturing of all major events at the customer premises. For example, Loss of Signal, Yellow Signal, Alarm Indication Signal, and other performance problems are not captured. Bipolar Violations are a good indicator of performance degradations on metallic circuits (they are not a factor with other media), yet neither standard makes use of BPV rates.

Finally, neither standard—except for one item in PUB 54016—defines user-oriented performance thresholds. The lone exception is the Severely Errored Second in PUB 54016, which corresponds to a bit error rate of one in 10^3 bits. This is considered a good threshold for voice circuits, but it is much too poor for data or integrated voice/data T1 circuits. ESF standards need to define performance thresholds that more accurately indicate line availability. Optimally, thresholds should not be set solely by the carrier but jointly with the user. This is another area of standards development in which users should get involved—for their own protection. ∎

Michael Lefkowitz earned a BSEE from Cooper Union (New York City) and an MSEE from New York University. He spent six years at AT&T Bell Laboratories designing data communications networks and nine years at AT&T in a variety of technical and marketing positions. He joined Larse in 1984, where he is director of business development.

Kenneth J. Thurber, PhD, Architecture Technology Corp., Minneapolis, Minn.

Getting a handle on FDDI

There's no place to hide when LAN end users suddenly demand high-bandwidth applications. It's coming, and so are cheaper FDDI nodes.

Like most new technologies, FDDI (the 100-Mbit/s fiber distributed data interface) faces the skepticism that greets any novelty. Right now many potential FDDI users are asking: How could my network conceivably have need for 100 Mbit/s?

That's the wrong question. The best way to look at future bandwidth requirements is to see that networks must be able to carry applications, and there will eventually be applications that make even 100 Mbit/s seem slow. For example, with the advent of Reduced Instruction Set Computing and, in time, workstations that do their processing at the speed of 100 million instructions per second, the bandwidth of any communications network to which such a workstation is attached must be dramatically increased.

A number of factors drive up the performance requirements of a communications network: the introduction of new technologies, the improvement and innovative use of existing technologies (including their use in previously untried combinations), and the development of increased user expectations for performance.

One major cause of bottlenecks in future networks will be the expanded use of high-powered microcomputers and workstations. Engineering workstations and computer-aided design/computer-aided engineering devices already incorporate multiple processors, accelerators, smart communications controllers, and Ethernet LANs to increase information throughput. Yet, while the internal backplane of a typical workstation transfers data at approximately 160 Mbit/s for a VME system and 300 Mbit/s (burst rate) for a Multi Bus II processor, Ethernets transfer data at 10 Mbit/s, only a fraction of the internal backplane speed.

FDDI offers the throughput required to fulfill the high-bandwidth demands of: backplane networks for high-speed communications between mainframes and to link processors with high speed storage devices; backbones to other LANs; and front-end networks used to link workstations.

The FDDI standard is in the process of being drafted by the X3T9 Committee of the Computer and Business Equipment Manufacturers Association, which is an accredited American National Standards Institute (ANSI) committee. In the past, the X3T9 committee has defined only communications schemes and standards for computer channel interfaces. But FDDI supports a variety of front-end, back-end, and backbone networks configured into a variety of topologies.

Beyond FDDI, FDDI-II is being developed to satisfy diverse needs. FDDI-II is intended primarily for voice/data/video capabilities. It is set up to divide the available network bandwidth between voice and data with a time-division multiplexed approach that can create up to 16 separate and equal channels, each using a maximum of 98.304 Mbit/s and each being full duplex.

FDDI Description

The FDDI network is based on dual counter-rotating 100-Mbit/s token rings. The physical layout is two strands of optical fiber powered by light emitting diodes at 1,300 nanometers. FDDI uses the token-passing algorithm to pass packets (which may be no larger than 4,500 bytes) from one active station to the next. Each station generally regenerates and repeats each symbol and serves as the means for attaching one or more devices to the network for the purpose of communicating with other devices on the network.

The method of physical attachment to the FDDI network may vary and is dependent on specific applications. A physical connection consists of the physical layers of two stations that are connected over the transmission medium by both a primary link and a secondary link. Two classes of stations are defined, dual attachment and single attachment. Physical FDDI rings may only be composed of dual stations and these must have two PHY (the physical layer protocol) entitites to accommodate each of the two counter-rotating rings. Concentrators provide additional PHY entities. Because several devices can be hooked to each concentrator—in contrast to a station—it is a relatively inexpensive way to make a number of attachments to the network.

There is, however, a limit on the number of connections. The FDDI standard sets a maximum of 1,000 physical connections, which could be as many as 500 stations.

There is also a relationship between the number of stations and the network's size. According to the formula, fewer connections to the network mean a larger geographic distance that the FDDI LAN can cover. The maximum total perimeter is 200 kilometers, but that's with 500 stations. The maximum distance between two adjacent devices on the FDDI ring can be no more than 2 kilometers. But devices need not be directly attached to the network: They can be connected through fiber optic spurs to the concentrators discussed earlier. Fiber allows a significant increase in their distance from the ring.

Standards status
How close are standard FDDI networks to implementation? How close is a final standard? The answer in both cases is: very close.

Work on the first of the FDDI layers, the Media Access Control, was unanimously approved by X3T9 in February 1986. In the previous year, the FDDI physical layer had been divided into two parts. The lower of these two, the Physical Medium Dependent (see figure), has had a contentious course.

Though a February 1987 X3T9 meeting unanimously approved Physical Media Dependent (PMD) for forwarding to X3, comments received during the public review process raised a bitter dispute over the fiber connector and required some refinements to other specifications, such as a reduction in the loss permitted by the optical bypass switch. The refinements were fairly easy to make, but the connector issue proved difficult. It was finally resolved in a roll call vote in June 1988, with the selection of the fixed-shroud duplex connector footprint. X3T9 has subsequently moved the PMD document to higher committees for further processing, and it is virtually impossible to change it at this time.

PHY was unanimously approved by an X3T9 meeting in August 1987 and has now become an ANSI standard. Thus, three of the four FDDI standards are solid. The only standard that remains to be completed is Station Management (SMT), which may even be a more involved standards effort than PMD because of the complexities of multilayer station management. However, there is a feeling that this task must be accomplished, and I believe that it can be wound up in six to 12 months.

After some initial difficulties with implementing the technology, the early versions of standard FDDI chips are being shipped by Advanced Micro Devices (AMD). Indeed, these

One of four. Three of the four FDDI protocols are virtually standards. The complex SMT is outstanding, but the X3T9 committee seems committed to swift action.

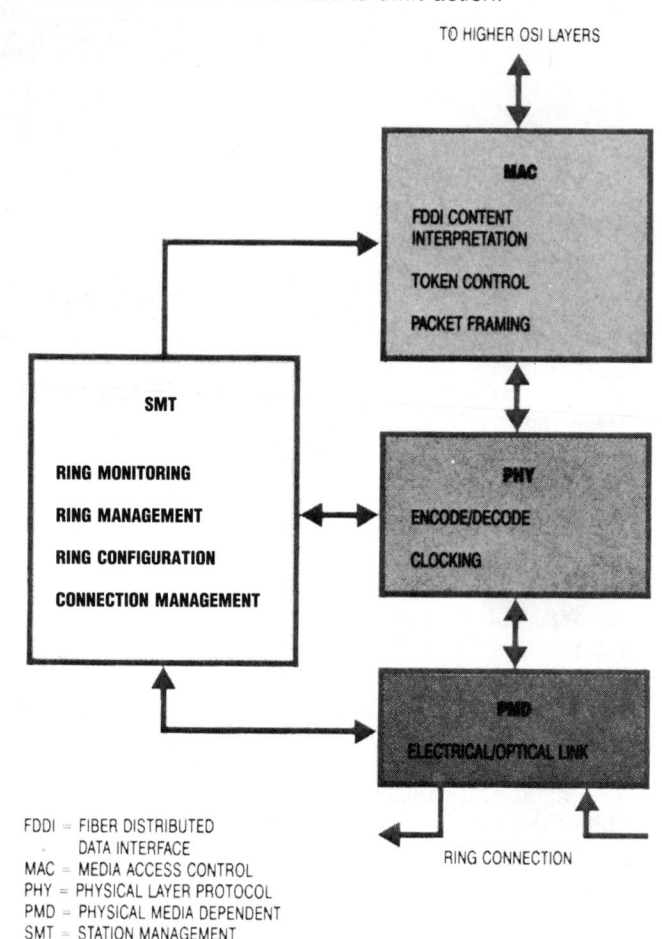

chips are likely to be shipped in volume by the end of this year. When these chip sets become generally available, the price of FDDI is likely to plunge. Other chip manufacturers, including National Semiconductor, are working on chip sets.

Costs and availability
Even at a substantial cost, FDDI—the highest performance, standard LAN technology yet available—will find an immediate application niche. In some ways, FDDI is a bargain even at its current high cost. The highest price for an FDDI node is in the $20,000 range for one of the FX family of FDDI nodes from Fibronics International (Hyannis, Mass.). These FDDI products, for example the IBM-Mainframe-to-FDDI Channel-Attached Unit, can be used to replace similar high-speed LAN nodes from Network Systems (the 50-Mbit/s Hyperchannel), which cost around $40,000.

Because of the availability of the AMD chip sets, which are likely to sell for around $800 each, I estimate, based on soundings of the vendors, that the price of FDDI nodes next year will be in the $5,000–$10,000 range. Virtually all

In the long run, FDDI is likely to prove lacking in adequate bandwidth.

the major players have stated—or at least hinted—that they will come into the market. Ungermann-Bass has just announced, and INNET showed FDDI-to-IBM host interfaces at Comnet.

Other board-level products promised or available are from Artel, BICC, Develcon, Ferranti, Fibronics, Network Systems, Raycom, Simple Net Systems, and Siemens. Fibercom and CrossComm have announced FDDI learning bridges, and AT&T, Hewlett-Packard, and ITT have all announced or alluded to other products. I expect IBM to have its FDDI LAN available within 18 months.

In the long run, FDDI, like other LAN technologies, is likely to prove lacking in adequate bandwidth (and already research is being conducted on considerably faster LANs). LAN designers have consistently underestimated the application needs of users and the progress of applications. The designers of FDDI will fare no better than other LAN designers: They too will be criticized for not taking a large enough step.

Also, and importantly, based FDDI's cost, I see room for another increment of performance before 100 Mbit/s. The difference in price between the 16-Mbit/s token ring LAN and FDDI leaves space for a 50-Mbit/s or 64-Mbit/s alternative. I expect some people will move into this market. Finally, it is essential that those who are considering FDDI networks avoid making a decision based on a single technical aspect of a network. If a user focuses on only one part of a configuration—handling links to terminals, for example—an Ethernet may seem like a large available bandwidth. But Ethernet's bandwidth no longer seems high when one considers the requirements of high-performance workstations. In fact, FDDI's 100 Mbit/s may be nowhere near enough bandwidth for some of the applications that are proposed for its use. ■

Kenneth J. Thurber is president of Minneapolis-based Architecture Technology Corporation (ATC), a consulting firm that specializes in LANs. The present article is derived in part from ATC's new FDDI Technology Report.

William Stallings, Comp-Comm Consulting, London, England

Digital signaling: Which techniques are best—and why it matters to you

The NRZ codes common to DP equipment interfaces are not appropriate for LANs and ISDN. But bipolar techniques are.

The emergence of local area networks (LANs) and the ongoing evolution of public and private wide-area telecommunications networks toward digital technology and services have led to a confrontation of sorts over digital signaling techniques. The past—the way computer communications has traditionally functioned—seems on a collision course with the future. And informed users, caught in the middle as usual, may ultimately name the winner: Soon, the choice of transmission equipment may well depend on the digital signaling technique incorporated in that equipment.

Digital signaling may be illustrated by considering the case of digital data being generated by a source, such as a data processing device or a voice digitizer. In either case, the data is typically represented as discrete voltage pulses, using one voltage level for binary 0 and another for binary 1. This traditional encoding technique is known as non-return-to-zero (NRZ) and is common in physical interfaces such as RS-232-C.

A common means of transmitting digital data is to pass it through a modem, then transmit it as analog signals. There are a number of cases where this is not done. For example:
■ Baseband local area networks, such as Ethernet and Token Ring.
■ Digital PBX connections for terminals, hosts, and digital telephones.
■ Digital access to public telecommunications networks over a digital local loop.

In all of these cases, the digital data is transmitted using voltage pulses—called digital signaling. Although it is possible to use NRZ signaling directly, NRZ's form is not compatible with the data rates and/or distances of LANs and digital long-haul networks (including ISDN—Integrated Services Digital Network). Instead, the NRZ signal is encoded in such a way as to optimize performance with these applications (more on NRZ's limitations later).

The data communicator's increasing reliance on digital communications and the multitude of implemented networking applications require a variety of solutions for the problems associated with digital signaling.

Described and compared here are the various encoding approaches used in LANs, long-haul networks, and ISDN. Two of the major issues are signaling-rate requirements and quality and performance.

There are two important tasks in interpreting digital signals at the receiver. First, the receiver must know the timing of each bit. That is, the receiver must know when a bit begins and ends, so that the receiver may sample the incoming signal once per bit time to recognize the value of each bit. Second, the receiver must determine whether the signal level for each voltage pulse is high or low.

A number of factors determine how successful the receiver will be in interpreting the incoming signal: the signal-to-noise ratio (S/N), the data rate, and the bandwidth of the signal. With other factors, such as type and length of transmission medium, held constant:
■ an increase in data rate increases bit error rate—that is, increases the probability that a bit is received in error.
■ an increase in S/N decreases bit error rate.
■ increased bandwidth allows increased data rate.

There is another factor that can be used to improve performance: the encoding scheme. This is simply the mapping from data bits to signal elements. A variety of approaches have been tried. Before describing some of them, let us consider the ways of evaluating and comparing the various techniques. Among the important factors are signal spectrum, signal synchronization capability, error-detection capability, cost, and complexity.

As to the signal spectrum, a lack of high-frequency (high relative to the data rate) components means that less bandwidth is required for transmission. In addition, lack of a direct-current (d.c.) component is also desirable. If the signal has a d.c. component, there must be direct physical attachment of transmission components; with no d.c. component, transformer coupling is possible. This provides excellent electrical isolation, reducing interference.

Finally, the magnitude of the effects of signal distortion and interference depends on the spectral properties of the transmitted signal. In practice, the transmission fidelity of a channel is usually worse near the band edges. Therefore, a good signal design should concentrate the transmitted power in the middle of the transmission bandwidth. This results in lower distortion in the received signal. To meet this objective, codes can be designed to shape the spectrum of the transmitted signal.

For successful reception of digital data, there must be some signal synchronization capability between transmitter and receiver. Some drift is inevitable between the clocks of the transmitter and receiver, so some separate synchronization mechanism is needed. One approach is to provide a separate clock lead to synchronize the transmitter and receiver. This approach is rather expensive since it requires an extra line, plus an extra transmitter and receiver. The alternative is to provide some synchronization mechanism that is based on the transmitted signal. This can be achieved with suitable encoding.

Error detection is the responsibility of a data link protocol that is executed on top of the physical signaling level. However, it is useful to have some error detection capability built into the physical signaling scheme. This permits errors to be detected more quickly. Many signaling schemes have such an inherent error-detection capability.

Finally, although digital logic continues to drop in price, the cost and complexity of the signaling scheme is a factor that should not be ignored.

The most common way to transmit digital signals is to use two different voltage levels for the two binary digits. For example, the absence of voltage can represent binary 0, with a positive voltage level representing binary 1. More commonly, a negative voltage represents one binary value and a positive voltage represents the other (Fig. 1). This latter code, as noted earlier, is known as NRZ. NRZ is generally the code used to generate or interpret digital data by terminals and other EDP devices. If a different code is to be used for transmission, it is typically generated from an NRZ signal by the transmitting device.

A variation of NRZ is known as NRZI (nonreturn-to-zero-inverted [inverted on ones]). As with NRZ, NRZI maintains a constant voltage pulse for the duration of a bit time. The data itself is encoded as the presence or absence of a signal transition at the beginning of the bit time. A transition (low to high or high to low) at the beginning of a bit time denotes a binary 1 for that bit time; no transition, binary 0.

NRZI is an example of differential encoding. In differential encoding, the signal is decoded by comparing the polarity of adjacent signal elements rather than determining the absolute value of a signal element. One benefit of this scheme is that it is usually more reliable to detect a transition in the presence of noise than to compare an absolute value to a threshold value.

Differential encoding is also beneficial in a complex transmission environment, where it is easy to lose the sense of the signal's polarity. For example, on a multidrop line, if the leads from an attached device to the twisted pair are accidentally reversed, all 1s and 0s for NRZ will be inverted. This cannot happen with differential encoding.

The NRZ codes are readily engineered and make efficient use of bandwidth. This latter property is illustrated in Figure 2, which compares the spectra of various encoding schemes. In the figure, frequency is normalized to the data rate. As can be seen, most of the energy in NRZ and NRZI signals is between d.c. and half the bit rate. For example, if an NRZ code is used to generate a signal with a data rate of 9.6 kbit/s, most of the energy in the signal is concentrated between d.c. and 4.8 kHz. (The other codes mentioned are discussed later.)

The main limitations of NRZ signals are the presence of a d.c. component and the lack of synchronization capability. For the latter, consider that, with a long string of 1s or 0s (10 or more) for NRZ, or a long string of 0s for NRZI, the output is a constant voltage over a long period of time (10 or more bit times). Under these circumstances, any drift between the timing of transmitter and receiver will result in the loss of synchronization between the two.

Because of their simplicity and relatively low frequency response characteristics (Fig. 2), NRZ codes are commonly used for digital magnetic recording. But their limitations make these codes unattractive for signal transmission.

---

1. The formats. *The most common way to transmit digital signals is to use two different voltage levels. For example, a negative voltage represents one binary value, and a positive voltage represents the other.*

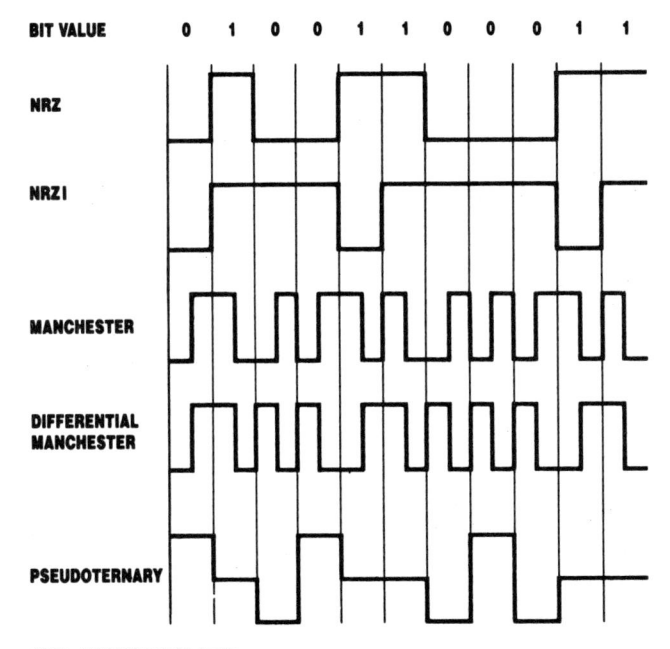

NRZ = NONRETURN TO ZERO
NRZI = NONRETURN TO ZERO INVERTED

2. The spectra. *Most of the energy in NRZ and NRZI is between d.c. and half the bit rate. Most of the energy in biphase is between one-half and one times the bit rate. Thus, in biphase—such as Manchester encoding—the bandwidth is reasonably narrow (there are no high-frequency components) and contains no d.c. component.*

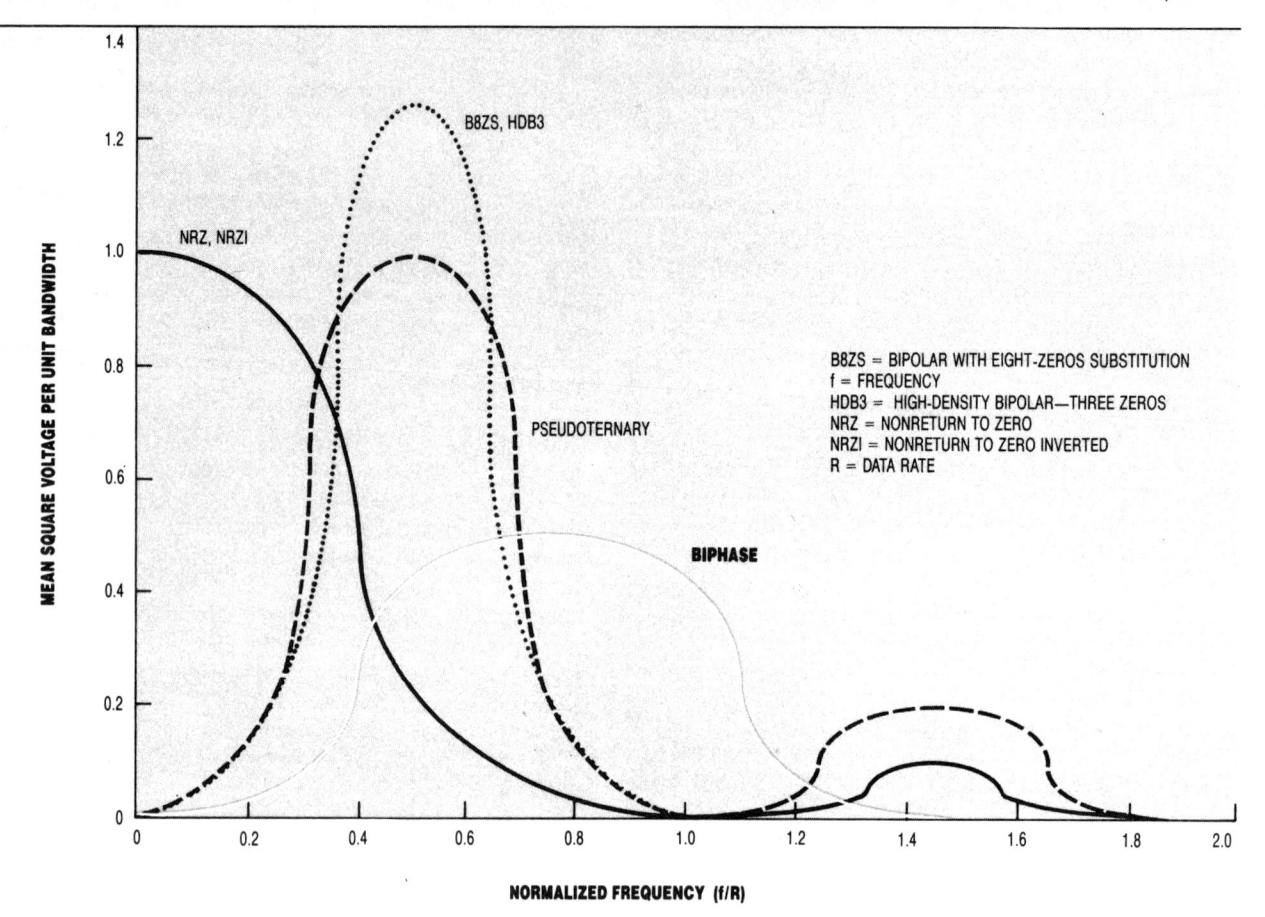

B8ZS = BIPOLAR WITH EIGHT-ZEROS SUBSTITUTION
f = FREQUENCY
HDB3 = HIGH-DENSITY BIPOLAR—THREE ZEROS
NRZ = NONRETURN TO ZERO
NRZI = NONRETURN TO ZERO INVERTED
R = DATA RATE

There is a set of alternative coding techniques, called biphase, which overcomes the limitations of NRZ codes. Two of these techniques, Manchester and Differential Manchester (Fig. 1), are in common use in LANs.

In the Manchester code, there is a transition at the middle of each bit period. The mid-bit transition serves as a clocking mechanism and also as data: A high-to-low transition represents a 1, and a low-to-high transition represents a 0. In Differential Manchester, the mid-bit transition is used only to provide clocking. The encoding of a 0 is represented by the presence of a transition at the beginning of a bit period, and a 1 is represented by the absence of a transition at the beginning of a bit period. Differential Manchester has the added advantage of employing differential encoding (described earlier).

All of the biphase techniques require at least one transition per bit time (transition rate) and may have as many as two (Table 1). Thus, the maximum modulation (digitization) rate—equal to the transition rate—is twice that for NRZ; this means that the bandwidth required is correspondingly greater. To compensate for this, the biphase schemes have several distinct advantages:
- *Synchronization.* Because there is a predictable transition during each bit time, the receiver can synchronize on that transition. For this reason, the biphase codes are known as self-clocking codes.
- *d.c.* Biphase codes have no d.c. component.
- *Error detection.* The absence of an expected transition can be used to detect errors. Noise on the line would have to invert both the signal before and after the expected transition to cause an undetected error (Fig. 1).

The bulk of the energy in biphase codes is between one-half and one times the bit rate (Fig. 2). Thus, the bandwidth is reasonably narrow (no high-frequency components) and contains no d.c. component.

Biphase codes are popular techniques for data transmission. The more common Manchester code has been specified for the IEEE 802.3 standard for baseband coaxial cable and twisted-pair CSMA/CD (carrier-sense multiple access with collision detection) bus LANs. It has also been used for MIL-STD-1553B, which is a shielded twisted-pair bus LAN designed for high-noise environments. Differential

Table 1: Signal transition rate

	MINIMUM	101010...	MAXIMUM
NRZ	0 (ALL 0s OR 1s)	1.0	1.0 (1010...)
NRZI	0 (ALL 0s)	0.5	1.0 (ALL 1s)
MANCHESTER	1.0 (1010...)	1.0	2.0 (ALL 0s OR 1s)
DIFFERENTIAL MANCHESTER	1.0 (ALL 1s)	1.5	2.0 (ALL 0s)
PSEUDOTERNARY	0 (ALL 1s)	1.0	1.0

NRZ = NONRETURN TO ZERO
NRZI = NONRETURN TO ZERO INVERTED

Manchester has been specified for the IEEE 802.5 Token Ring LAN, using shielded twisted-pair wire.

The biphase codes are well-suited for digital signaling on baseband IEEE 802 LANs. In principle, they could also be adapted for the most recent LAN standard, the Fiber Distributed Data Interface (FDDI), which specifies a 100-Mbit/s optical-fiber ring.

Synchronous, but inefficient

For example, for Manchester encoding, a pulse of light would comprise the first or second half of the bit time to represent 1 or 0, respectively, with the absence of light in the other half of the bit time. This would provide the Manchester synchronization benefit. The disadvantage of this approach is that the efficiency is only 50 percent. That is, because there can be as many as two transitions per bit time, a signaling rate of 200 million signaling elements per second (200 Mbaud) is needed to achieve a data rate of 100 Mbit/s. At FDDI's data rate, this approach represents an unnecessary cost and technical burden.

To overcome the data rate burden imposed by Manchester, the FDDI standard specifies a code referred to as 4B/5B. In this scheme, encoding is done four bits at a time; each four data bits are mapped into a five-bit code. Each bit of the code is transmitted as a single signal element (presence or absence of a light pulse). The efficiency is thus raised to 80 percent: FDDI's 100 Mbit/s, for example, is achieved with 125 Mbaud. The resulting cost savings are substantial: A 200-Mbaud optical transmitter/receiver can cost from five to 10 times that of a 125-Mbaud pair.

In order to achieve synchronization, there is actually a second stage of encoding for FDDI. Each element of the 4B/5B stream is treated as a binary value and encoded using NRZI. The use of NRZI, which is differential encoding, aids the ultimate decoding of the signal after it has been converted back from optical to the electrical realm.

Table 2 shows the symbol encoding used in FDDI. There are 32 five-bit codes; 16 are used to encode all of the possible four-bit blocks of data. The codes selected to represent the 16 four-bit data groups are such that a transition is present at least twice for each five-bit code pattern on the medium. Since NRZI is being used, this is equivalent to requiring that there be at least two ones in each five-bit code (recall that in NRZI, a one is encoded by a transition). As can be seen (Table 2), all 16 of the codes that represent data contain at least two ones.

To summarize the FDDI encoding scheme:
- A simple on/off encoding is rejected because it does not provide synchronization; a string of 1s or 0s would have no transitions with which to synchronize.
- The 4B/5B code is chosen over Manchester because it is more efficient.
- The 4B/5B coded data is further encoded using the NRZI technique. This enables the resulting differential encoding

Table 2: 4B/5B Code

CODE GROUP	ASSIGNMENT	
LINE STATE SYMBOLS		
00000	QUIET	
11111	IDLE	
00100	HALT	
STARTING DELIMITER (SD)		
11000	1ST OF SEQUENTIAL SD PAIR	
10001	2ND OF SEQUENTIAL SD PAIR	
DATA SYMBOLS		
	HEX	BINARY
11110	0	0000
01001	1	0001
10100	2	0010
10101	3	0011
01010	4	0100
01011	5	0101
01110	6	0110
01111	7	0111
10010	8	1000
10011	9	1001
10110	A	1010
10111	B	1011
11010	C	1100
11011	D	1101
11100	E	1110
11101	F	1111
ENDING DELIMITER		
01101	USED TO TERMINATE THE DATA STREAM	
CONTROL INDICATORS		
00111	DENOTING LOGICAL ZERO (RESET)	
11001	DENOTING LOGICAL ONE (SET)	
INVALID CODE ASSIGNMENTS		
00001* 00010* 00011 00101 00110 01000* 01100 10000*	THESE CODE PATTERNS SHALL NOT BE TRANSMITTED BECAUSE THEY VIOLATE CONSECUTIVE CODE-BIT ZEROS OR DUTY-CYCLE REQUIREMENTS. CODES MARKED WITH AN ASTERISK, HOWEVER, SHALL BE INTERPRETED AS HALT WHEN RECEIVED.	

3. Two techniques. *For the 1.544-Mbit/s primary-rate interface, the coding scheme is known as bipolar with eight-zeros substitution (B8ZS). For the 2.048 Mbit/s interface, the coding scheme is known as high-density bipolar-three zeros (HDB3) code (Table 3). In each case, the fourth zero is replaced with a code violation.*

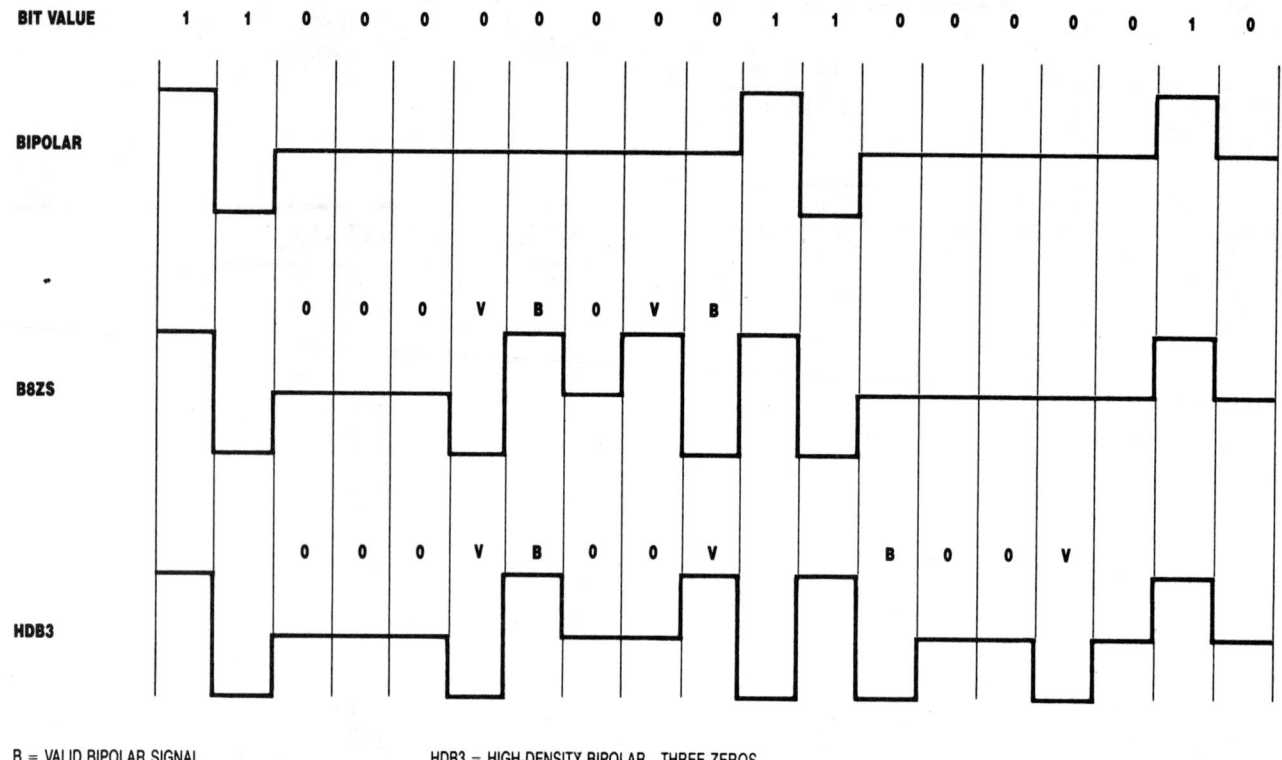

B = VALID BIPOLAR SIGNAL
B8ZS = BIPOLAR WITH EIGHT-ZEROS SUBSTITUTION
HDB3 = HIGH-DENSITY BIPOLAR—THREE ZEROS
V = BIPOLAR VIOLATION

to significantly improve reception reliability.
- The specific codes chosen for encoding the 16 four-bit data groups guarantee at least two ones—hence, at least two transitions; this provides adequate synchronization.

Only 16 of the 32 possible code patterns are required to represent the input data. The remaining symbols are either declared invalid or assigned special meaning as control symbols. For example, two of the patterns (codes 11000 and 10001) always occur in pairs and act as start delimiters for a frame.

Undesirable
For ISDN, two forms of access are specified: basic and primary. The basic rate provides two user channels and a control-signaling channel at a total data rate—including overhead bits—of 192 kbit/s. The primary interface offers rates of 1.544 and 2.048 Mbit/s.

As with the interface to a LAN, the use of NRZ codes is undesirable for the ISDN basic access interface because of the lack of synchronization and the presence of a d.c. component. To overcome these problems, the encoding chosen for the basic-rate interface is pseudoternary coding. In this scheme, a binary 1 is represented by no line signal; a binary 0, by a positive or negative pulse. The binary 0 pulses must alternate in polarity. The term pseudoternary arises from the use of three encoded signal levels (positive, negative, and zero) to represent two-level (binary) data.

There are several advantages to this approach. First, there will be no loss of synchronization if a long string of 0s occurs. Each 0 introduces a transition, and the receiver can resynchronize on that transition. A long string of 1s would still be a problem, but the basic interface-framing structure includes extra 0s to avoid this problem. Second, since the 0 signals alternate in voltage from positive to negative, there is no net d.c. component. Also, the bandwidth of the resulting signal is considerably less than the bandwidth for NRZ. Finally, the pulse alternation property provides a simple means of error detection. Any isolated error, whether it deletes a pulse or adds a pulse, causes a violation of this property.

Thus, pseudoternary coding has a significant advantage over NRZ. Of course, as with any engineering design decision, there is a trade-off. With pseudoternary coding, the line signal may take on one of three levels. But each signal element, which could represent $\log_2 3 = 1.58$ bits of information, bears only one bit of information. Thus, pseudoternary is not as efficient as NRZ coding.

Another way to state this is that the receiver of pseudoternary signals has to distinguish between three levels ($+A$, $-A$, 0) instead of just two levels in the other signaling formats previously discussed. Because of this, the pseudoternary signal requires approximately 3 db more signal power than a two-valued signal for the same probability of bit error.

A second disadvantage of pseudoternary coding is that it lacks a synchronization capability. If there is a long string of ones, there are no transitions, and it is easy for the receiver to get out of synchronization with the transmitter. As mentioned, this is overcome in the basic interface with the use of special framing bits that guarantee a minimum number of transitions. These bits add overhead, of course, so that the full data rate of the interface is not available for user data.

Primary-access interface

As stated earlier, to overcome this lack-of-transition problem in the basic interface, the framing structure includes some zeros. In the primary interface, to make maximum efficient use of the high data rates provided, there are no bits available for such balancing, so another approach is needed. A biphase approach is not desirable because this will raise the signal transition rate. At the data rates of the primary interface, this is an expensive alternative.

Another approach is to make use of some sort of scrambling scheme. The idea behind this is simple: Sequences that would result in a constant voltage level on the line are replaced by "filling" sequences that provide sufficient transitions for the receiver's clock to maintain synchronization. The filling sequence must be recognized by the receiver and replaced with the original data sequence. The filling sequence is the same length as the original sequence, so there is no data rate increase. The design goals for this approach can be summarized as:
- No d.c. component.
- No long sequences of zero-level line signals.
- No reduction in data rate.
- Error detection capability.

Two techniques are specified for the primary-rate interface (Fig. 3), depending on the data rate used (1.544 or 2.048 Mbit/s). The coding scheme used with the 1.544-Mbit/s interface is known as bipolar with eight zeros substitution (B8ZS). As with the basic interface, the coding scheme is based on a pseudoternary code. In this case, the code, referred to as bipolar, is as follows: Binary 0 is represented by no line signal; binary 1, by a positive or negative pulse. The binary 1 pulses must alternate in polarity. Note that the assignment of codes to binary 0 and 1 is the reverse of that for the basic interface. The drawback of the bipolar code is that a long string of zeros may result in loss of synchronization.

To overcome this problem, the bipolar encoding is amended with the following rules (Fig. 4):
- If an octet of all zeros occurs and the last voltage pulse preceding this octet was positive, then the eight 0s of the octet are encoded as $000+-0-+$.
- If an octet of all zeros occurs and the last voltage pulse preceding this octet was negative, then the eight 0s of the octet are encoded as $000-+0+-$.

This technique forces two code violations of the bipolar code, an event unlikely to be caused by noise or other transmission impairment. The receiver recognizes the pattern and interprets the octet as consisting of all zeros.

The coding scheme used with the 2.048-Mbit/s interface is known as the high-density bipolar-three-0s (HDB3) code (Table 3). As before, the approach is based on the use of bipolar encoding. In this case, the scheme replaces strings of four 0s with sequences containing one or two pulses. In each case, the fourth zero is replaced with a code violation. In addition, a rule is needed to ensure that successive violations are of alternate polarity so that no d.c. component is introduced. Thus, if the last violation was positive, this violation must be negative, and vice versa. Table 3 shows that this condition is tested by knowing whether the number of pulses (ones) since the last violation is even or odd and knowing the polarity of the last pulse before the occurrence of the four 0s.

Figure 2 shows the spectral properties of the B8ZS and HDB3 codes. Neither has a d.c. component. Most of the energy is concentrated in a relatively sharp spectrum around a frequency equal to one-half the data rate. Thus, these codes are well-suited to the high-data-rate transmission of the primary ISDN interface. ∎

William Stallings is a consultant and president of Comp-Comm Consulting, London, England. This article is based on material from his Data and Computer Communications, *Second Edition (Macmillan, 1988) and from the recently published* ISDN: An Introduction *(Macmillan, 1989). Stallings holds a Ph. D. in computer science from M. I. T.*

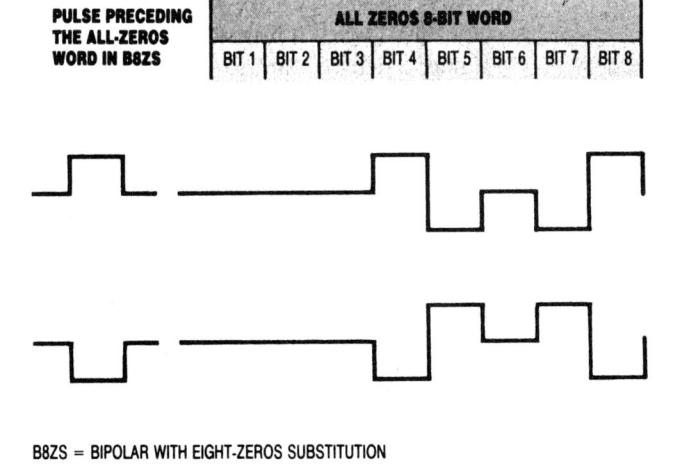

Table 3: HDB3 substitution rules

POLARITY OF PRECEDING PULSE	NUMBER OF BIPOLAR PULSES (ONES) SINCE LAST SUBSTITUTION	
	ODD	EVEN
−	000−	+00+
+	000+	−00−

4. B8ZS. *If a bipolar code has a long string of zeros, a loss of synchronization may result. To overcome this in B8ZS, two otherwise unlikely code violations are forced.*

B8ZS = BIPOLAR WITH EIGHT-ZEROS SUBSTITUTION

Section 9
Questions and Answers

Hal B. Becker, Consultant, Phoenix, Ariz.

Can users really absorb data at today's rates? Tomorrow's?

Some say no, that many have reached their limit, fostering faulty judgment. But new tools promise to relieve the overload.

In 1775, news of the "shot heard 'round the world" took four days to travel the 180 miles from Lexington, Mass., to New York City, and another 11 days to reach Charleston, S. C. Today, news of a significant event circles the globe in less than a minute, and the impact is observed in the stock and commodities markets no more than 30 seconds later. The average speed of transmission in the first case was approximately 2.25 miles per hour. Now it is about 1.5 million miles per hour.

Data communications and related computer technologies present people with so much information so fast that the number of decisions being made often becomes a substitute for their quality. Gone forever are the days when there was time for contemplation and reflection concerning information received and the course of action it might dictate.

Symptoms of this transition can be seen in the record number of post-Depression bank failures that occurred in 1984, and the continuing increase in the failure rate of other corporations. Another new post-Depression record was set in early 1985 when seven banks in four states failed in a single day.

Computer and data communications technologies, however, have evolved far more rapidly than the comprehension abilities of the people who use them. The bad decisions that led to the recent bank failures may be tied to the inability of people to assimilate exponentially increasing volumes of information presented to them in rapidly diminishing time periods, to sort through it and separate the useful from the "noise," and to make quality decisions. While the symptoms of the ailment are troubling, there is a positive prognosis. But first, let us explore some of the background.

The speed at which news could be transmitted progressed slowly and erratically over the centuries. In 490 B. C., the Greek runner Pheidippides ran 22 miles in just over three hours to bring news of the Greek victory over the Persians at the town of Marathon. He then fell dead of exhaustion. His average speed was slightly over seven miles per hour. For several centuries, communications transmission rates were limited to the speed at which a person could run.

The decision-making speed of humans may be related to their maximum running speed. Evolving over millennia, human data acquisition and decision-making processes may have been genetically selected, derived from the skills necessary both to avoid capture by predators and to capture prey. Human decision-making speed may reach a peak during chases of this type, as constantly changing information, received by the senses, is processed and decisions are made either to avoid or achieve capture. It is questionable how much this decision-making speed has increased in the 15,000 years since the last major Ice Age receded.

Data by foot

In 1690 A. D., almost 22 centuries after Pheidippides, express runners were maintained by armies to carry news from battlefields to command posts. These runners could travel a maximum of 20 leagues (about 60 miles) in 24 hours, averaging 2.5 miles per hour.

In 1775, the aforementioned news of the shot heard 'round the world was carried on horseback at an average rate of about 2.25 miles per hour. Under ideal conditions, a horse could carry information at a maximum of 300 miles in approximately 52 hours, for an average speed of 5.77 miles per hour.

By 1795, mechanical semaphore signaling was being tested. In one instance, a message was transmitted—in relays—the 500 miles between London and Plymouth, England, in three minutes. The average speed for this distance was 10,000 miles per hour. The cost of building, staffing, and maintaining such mechanisms precluded their wide use.

In 1815, bankers in London, England, made a killing in the stock markets using the news of Napoleon's defeat at Waterloo by the Duke of Wellington. They received the news by carrier pigeon and thus had it before the public did. Another of the Duke's pigeons held a record for long-distance communications, traveling 7,000 miles from West Africa to England in 55 days, averaging 5.3 miles per hour. In the long-established tradition of great communications feats, the pigeon died after delivering its message. [In 1941, a pigeon traveled 803 miles in 24 hours for an average speed of 33.46 miles per hour.]

In 1844, Samuel F. B. Morse invented the telegraph and the Morse code. The first message, "What hath God wrought?" was carried on a line between Washington, D. C., and Baltimore, Md. Soon, a skilled telegraph operator could achieve transmission speeds of 50 words per minute. By 1866, the many small telegraph companies that sprang up were consolidated into the Western Union Telegraph Co., which owned over 2,000 offices and 10,000 miles of lines.

At this time, news could travel rapidly around the United States. Overseas communications still relied on ships, which took many days to travel the Atlantic Ocean to Europe. Thus an event occurring on one continent would be old news by the time the message was received on the other.

In 1866, the first transatlantic telegraph line was laid by the then-largest steamship in the world, the *Great Eastern.* Not counting the propagation delay involved, a message could be sent across the Atlantic in the time it took an expert telegrapher to tap it out on the key. A 50-word message could be sent and received in one minute. News was now much more current when received, and an immediate response was possible.

On March 3, 1876, the patent for what would become the telephone was issued to Alexander Graham Bell. The telephone quickly began to replace the telegraph in the United States. People did not have to be skilled telegraphers. They simply picked up the instrument, spoke into it, and listened. By 1928, the first transatlantic telephone line had been laid. Thus did the world's shrinking accelerate.

Chatter speed

A rapid, easy-to-use instrument of communications was available to the masses. News of an event traveled quickly. Issues could be discussed and questions answered promptly. The ease of use quickly made the telephone an indispensable element of every culture that adopted it. The place of the telephone in American culture was best summarized by Marshall McLuhan, who said: "The telephone began as a novelty, became a necessity, and is now regarded as an absolute right" (from *The Telephone Book,* by H. M. Boettinger, Riverwood, 1977).

By the mid-1970s, the AT&T Long Lines Department had coaxial cables between Pittsburgh, Pa., and St. Louis, Mo., capable of handling in excess of 100,000 simultaneous conversations. During the same period, Americans placed an average of 12 million interstate telephone calls per day. Later, waveguide technology was capable of handling 500,000 simultaneous conversations.

The invention of the vacuum tube produced a similarly dramatic advance in communications. Starting with simple crystal radios, powerful receivers evolved that were built around the new invention. By the mid-1930s, an estimated 13.5 million radio sets were in use in the United States. While not cheap (over $100 each), they fulfilled the growing desire to obtain increased amounts of information in shorter time periods and, hence, were purchased in large numbers.

Television produced an even greater impact on an information- and entertainment-hungry public. From the earliest public demonstration by Bell Laboratories in 1927 to the first antenna installed on New York's Empire State Building in 1931, the industry has, to date, produced millions of high-quality, relatively inexpensive sets.

The early telegraph, slow as it was, had one significant advantage over the telephone, radio, and television that followed: The sender presented the telegrapher with a copy of the message to be sent. The telegrapher at the other end presented the recipient with a copy of the message received. Thus both sender and recipient had a reasonable facsimile of the message, which could be examined and retained for future reference. For several decades, subsequent technologies lacked this feature.

Few people can write nearly as fast as most people can talk. And recording gear was not yet available for the masses. As communications speeds increased, therefore, the relative amount of information retained decreased. Continuing progress in computer and printer technologies, despite accelerating communications speeds (both discussed below), offered a method of coping with this problem.

Figure 1 represents the increasing communications rates provided by continuing advances in technology. The example used is the time required to send 250 words 3,000 miles.

Notable events

Concurrent with the advances in communications speeds, three major revolutions occurred that produced profound and long-lasting changes in cultures exposed to them: the Agricultural Revolution, begun about 14,000 years ago, probably resisted by few; the Industrial Revolution, begun in the mid-eighteenth century, not readily beneficial to all (particularly those who lost their jobs to automation); and the Information Revolution, begun in the mid-twentieth century and still accelerating.

Several generations of information elements have come and gone: vacuum tubes, replaced with transistors, replaced, in turn, with third-generation integrated circuits. The current fourth-generation elements, consisting of very-large-scale integrated (VLSI) circuits, will be replaced by a fifth generation that has yet to be defined but is clearly on the horizon.

Computer and communications technologies are providing exponentially increasing volumes of information to exponentially increasing numbers of users in exponentially decreasing time periods. It is not yet clear whether this is a blessing, a nightmare, or a mix of the two. Are human assimilation and comprehension abilities evolving at the same rate as information production and transmission rates? The answer appears to be no.

1. Increasingly rapid transit. *Shown is the time required—through the ages—to send 250 words 3,000 miles. Printers help to cope with the mass of data.*

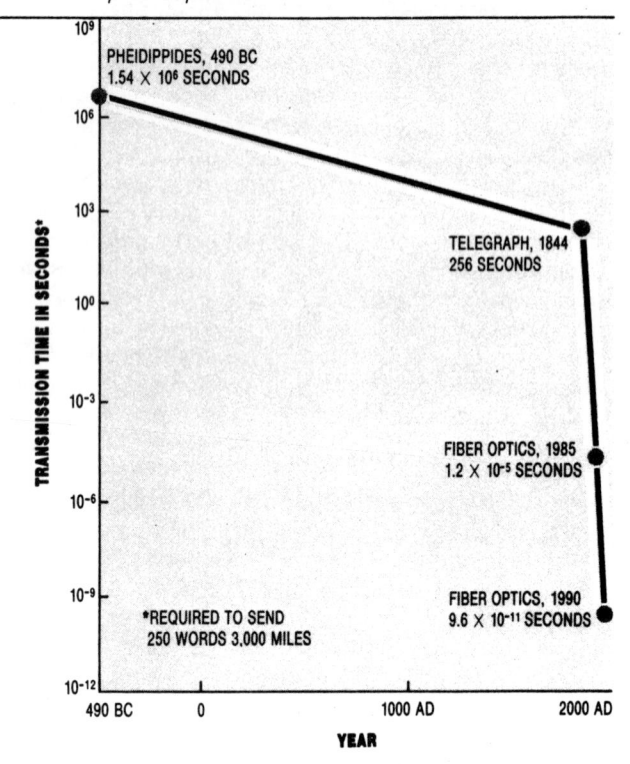

Figure showing transmission time in seconds vs. year:
- PHEIDIPPIDES, 490 BC: 1.54×10^6 SECONDS
- TELEGRAPH, 1844: 256 SECONDS
- FIBER OPTICS, 1985: 1.2×10^{-5} SECONDS
- FIBER OPTICS, 1990: 9.6×10^{-11} SECONDS

Required to send 250 words 3,000 miles.

In the Sumerian era, 4,000 B. C., information was recorded by using sharpened sticks on wet clay tablets to write cuneiform symbols representing the desired message. After they were dried, the tablets provided a relatively permanent record, which could be stored or carried as needed. They contained approximately one symbol per cubic inch of clay. Thus a person could convey to others as much information as could be lifted. Since writing in clay tablets took so long, it can be assumed that literate people could read and acquire knowledge much faster than it could be produced and transmitted. This situation was to prevail for several thousand years.

The Egyptian invention of papyrus—later to be known as paper—produced another dramatic change in the recording density of communications media. A single sheet of paper could contain considerably more information than could a clay tablet, and, of course, it was more convenient to carry. Early documents were prepared one at a time; if more were required, they were laboriously copied. People could still read and acquire knowledge faster than it could be prepared and transmitted.

The invention of devices for printing multiple copies of information, while known for centuries, did not greatly accelerate the production rate until the mid-fifteenth century, when Johannes Gutenberg invented a printing press that used movable type. The rate at which information could be produced, copied, and transmitted began to soar to the exponential heights observed today, while the human ability to assimilate and comprehend such volumes continued at its relatively linear and leisurely rate.

The recording density achieved by Gutenberg was approximately 500 symbols (characters) per cubic inch—500 times the density of the earlier clay tablets. Figure 2 illustrates the increasing recording density of various media. By the year 2000, semiconductor random access memory should be storing 1.2510^{11} bytes per cubic inch.

In Europe at about 1501, the incunabula (total number of books printed before that year) equaled about 20 million, and the population was approximately 70 million. Thus there was an average of slightly more than one book for every three people. By 1600, just 150 years following the introduction of Gutenberg's press, an estimated 140 million to 200 million books (representing 140 thousand to 200 thousand titles) were in print. By this time, the population of Europe was up to 100 million, which meant there were approximately two books per person. Considering the literacy rates of the time, the information-production curve had already soared well beyond the comprehension rate of the masses.

Modern computers equipped with laser printers can produce information at the rate of 20,000 lines per minute, well beyond the human reading rate (Fig. 3). Fiber optic data communications facilities will soon be transmitting information at the rate of one billion bits per second. Consider the following, possibly absurd, example:

Twenty thousand lines per minute produce 9.6 million lines of print in a single eight-hour shift. Assuming 55 lines per page (60 characters per line), this rate produces 349 books of 500 pages each, which totals almost 576 million bytes of information. A fiber optic data communications link, transmitting one billion bits per second will require just 4.6 seconds to transmit the entire eight-hour production of the single laser printer.

Assuming an average of 550 words per page, and a reading rate of five words per second (a slower rate usually equates to a higher comprehension and retention), a total

2. Package compaction. *Recording density continues to increase. Gutenberg achieved about 500 symbols per cubic inch—500 times that of the earlier clay tablets.*

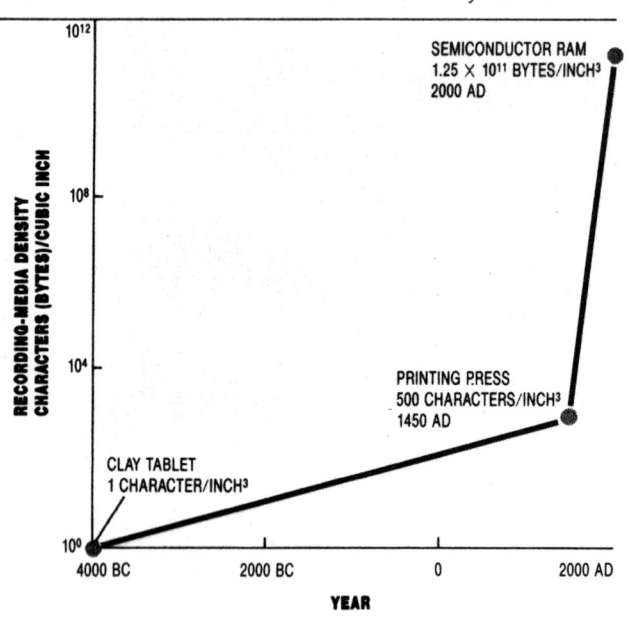

Figure showing recording-media density (characters (bytes)/cubic inch) vs. year:
- CLAY TABLET: 1 CHARACTER/INCH³, 4000 BC
- PRINTING PRESS: 500 CHARACTERS/INCH³, 1450 AD
- SEMICONDUCTOR RAM: 1.25×10^{11} BYTES/INCH³, 2000 AD

RAM = RANDOM ACCESS MEMORY

of almost 5,332 hours are required for one person to read a single night-shift's production from a single laser printer. Since the printer will produce another 349 volumes the next night, one can assume that each company owning such a device employs enough people to read and act on each day's production before the next batch arrives. This requires a total of 666 people reading steadily for eight hours.

Furthermore, companies will soon be equipped with the aforementioned billion-bit-per-second fiber optic communications links. Thus they could send an entire copy—several, if desired—of each night's production to their outlying regions and divisions. With little imagination, it is clear that this technology, used effectively, can immobilize an entire army of people every 24 hours. What is being done with all this information?

As the Information Revolution continues, and computer and communications technologies spread among the business, professional, and work environments, a growing number of people are beginning to exhibit several common symptoms of information overload. So much information is being presented in such a short time that people are incapable of assimilating it all before the next batch appears. In many instances, the rush to get the current task finished is accelerated before the next batch of information arrives in the in-basket or pops up on the terminal screen, demanding attention. As a result, the number of decisions made has, in many cases, become a substitute for their quality.

Faster than desired?
The "float" time associated with information is diminishing, perhaps at a faster rate than that associated with checking accounts and credit cards. A trip of two weeks or more will often result in the bill with the current credit card charges beating the traveler home. When news of a major event reached a neighboring town 200 years ago, it was often too late to act. Today, news of an invasion or a new war is flashed around the globe in a minute or less, and the reaction can be seen 30 seconds later in the price of gold on the world market. Communications media of all types have reduced the information float time to the point that reactions taken to new information are often driven more by the emotion of the moment than by reasoning, logic, and contemplation.

Stock market investors appear to be driven more by mob psychology than by the worth of either a particular company or its products. How much thought and deliberation have occurred when the recommendation of one analyst, flashed through an investor network, causes thousands of people to call their brokers and issue frantic "sell everything" orders?

Or what happens when instant communications indicates that the market has plunged seven points—or soared 11 points—in the first trading hour. This causes a number of investors to leap to get in on the action. Seven points on a base of 1,800 points is about four-tenths of 1 percent. Before the days of instant communications, moves of this nature took considerably longer; today, they are commonplace. If the market is not plunging or soaring, it is stagnating (meaning no change), which apparently invokes other investor reactions.

One of the basic tenets of the Information Revolution is: "Next to people, information is an organization's most valuable resource." To many computer vendors and users alike, this apparently means: "If a little information is good, more is better." Coupled with the adage, "Time is money," the two concepts have produced some interesting results.

Since time is a constant resource and information appears to be unlimited, many users are impatiently awaiting the next generation of computer and data communications technology. They will use it to produce even greater volumes of information in a given time period. For many of these users, the most visible result will be their ability to make even larger mistakes faster (see "Two disasters").

Computer-generated and -transmitted information acquires an aura of authenticity that most people do not question. The explosive proliferation of microcomputers has added considerably to the confusion. Newspaper articles relate stories of analysts who have programmed their latest sure-fire algorithms into their microcomputers. They become entranced by the output and continually recommend the purchase of losing stocks, while regularly passing over winners. Perhaps, in the market vernacular, a "technical adjustment" is necessary.

Employees in corporations of all sizes are victims of the same myth of omniscience. Having finally been sold—after many long and trying years—on the value of computers and their work-saving attributes, many employees do not question the accuracy and value of the output data.

The anonymity of computers perhaps offers a partial explanation for the employees' indifference. A report or set of figures prepared by a human can usually be traced, in a few easy steps, to the originating individual. Questioning elements of the report is thus perceived as questioning the individual or group that prepared it.

But questioning a computer-prepared report appears to be another matter. The swift, anonymous, electronic device

3. Outpacing comprehension. *Computers and lasers are producing 20,000 printed lines per minute. Optical fiber will soon transmit one billion bits per second.*

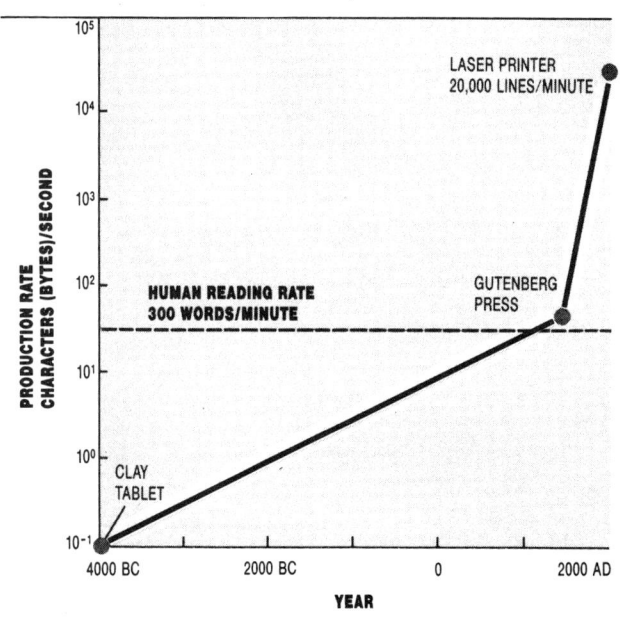

> **Two disasters**
>
> The availability of increasing volumes of information raises some critical questions. How often do fatal flaws in computer-generated and -transmitted designs remain undetected until too late? How many engineering projects fail because the simulator models were faulty? Or the appropriate questions were not asked? Or the answers were incorrectly interpreted? Furthermore, how many decisions to proceed are based on a lack of any negative response transmitted from the computers?
>
> **Substitute for humans?**
>
> Have computer outputs been ignored in some areas where they could help? Have they become a premature substitute for human intelligence in other areas? The collapse of a Kansas City hotel skywalk in 1981 and the recent space shuttle disaster may be two very visible examples of these phenomena. In the former, design changes made in the skywalk suspension were, apparently, not properly evaluated—the right questions were not asked. In the latter, the computers had not detected any reason to halt the countdown, so the launch proceeded. (Only later were factors publicly revealed—such as low temperature and its effects—that were not part of the automatic-halt process.) In both cases, early clues—part of the masses of available data—apparently were not brought to a high enough decision level or were ignored.

can sort through huge local and remote databases in minutes, extract selected information, manipulate it in a variety of ways, and present it simultaneously to several people in widely separated locations. The workings and the outputs of such mechanisms are beyond the comprehension and questioning ability of most users.

Computers are not often treated with the same anthropomorphic tenderness given other inert devices, such as ships, aircraft, and automobiles. The reluctance to accord computers this status may be attributable to the anonymity discussed earlier. "Blame-the-computer" is another aspect of this perceived anonymity. Examples include: "We're sorry the check didn't get mailed last week; our computer was down." Sales banners advertising: "Gigantic overstocked inventory clearance—our computer goofed!" "I'm sorry your order wasn't shipped; our computer was down." It is somehow easy to place the blame for these actions on an inanimate computer, whether or not it was involved in the problem. Many people presented with these excuses accept them readily.

The situation is slowly changing for the better. But current application development methodologies are horribly slow. A large, complex program can take 12 to 18 months to design, debug, and implement. All too often, by the time the application is up and running, the problem has changed so much that it is time to start modifying the program—or to scrap it entirely and start over. The "vanishing-problem" syndrome is alive and well. In many situations, the user opts to live with the less-than-adequate solution that is no longer completely applicable and tries to recover some of the investment. Thus users today are often forced to fit their problems to the solution.

Another possible effect of the Information Revolution: Both newly formed and well-established corporations are failing in increasing numbers. Many new ones are "high technology" companies that enjoy a wild ride as the darling of the investor community—only to discover, usually too late, that the ride was a short one. The scenario is now familiar: Information obtained from the many research and analysis firms indicates that the market that their product addresses will be $8.1 billion, say, in another year. Using their spreadsheet programs, these firms calculate that with only one-tenth of 1 percent of that market, the company will have gross sales of $8.1 million.

The lure is often irresistible, and a number of now-classic traps await. Two of the biggest: an overestimation of the ability to produce and successfully market the product in the face of intense competition, and an underestimation of the complexities and dynamics of the user environment.

Banks represent another visible effect of the Information Revolution: More banks—65 of them—failed in the first 10 months of 1984 than during any full year since the Depression. By mid-1984, the Federal Deposit Insurance Corp. (FDIC) had covered bank losses of $2.4 billion—more than four times the amount paid in the preceding 47 years. In 1985, another record was set as 120 banks failed. And FDIC Chairman L. William Seidman does not foresee any decline in the bank-failure rate this year.

Bankers are obviously making a lot of bad loans, bad decisions, or both. What role do computers play in this scenario? A few bankers will admit, off the record, that they are impressed with a loan applicant who presents a well-thought-out, computer-generated financial plan when requesting a loan. So long as the cash-flow projections, anticipated operating figures, selected ratios (such as debt-to-equity), and trends meet their requirements, bankers find it hard to question the proposal. A few are aware of just how easy it is to prepare such a proposal using a microcomputer and a spreadsheet program; many are not.

Are the bankers to blame? Partially. Are the loan applicants to blame? Partially. Are the computer and software vendors to blame? Partially. Each contributes a piece of the problem. Bankers will have to learn to look beyond the slick, computer-generated proposals and question applicants in more depth. Applicants will have to learn that the one-tenth of 1 percent projections and a business plan based on them are risky business. They should also learn to scrutinize the role that computer and data communications technologies play in their decision-making process. Many entrepreneurs appear to be so myopically entranced with their microcomputers, spreadsheets, and remote databases that they begin accepting them as "givens." Finally, vendors have been selling computers and related hardware and software as nothing short of magic for years—this will likely never change.

The recent breakup of AT&T and the deregulation that followed contribute another twist to the communications environment. A comparison with the computer industry illustrates this complication. For 25 years, computer vendors fought to retain their individual, incompatible postures. The goal was simple: If my terminals are incompatible with every other vendor's terminals, my users will have to buy my terminals. For several years it worked.

The efforts to change this thesis moved slowly, until the recent microcomputer explosion. Suddenly, everyone had to be compatible with IBM, and the race was on. Most successful look-alike microcomputers *are* compatible. A number of vendors who tried to remain independent have failed. At least at the mainframe, terminal, and microcomputer level, compatibility seems to be the watchword. The data communications world is another matter.

Deviations
At least six international organizations are hard at work trying to derive a workable set of data communications standards. It has not been easy. Every time a new standard, or piece of an existing one, is announced, it is often a matter of weeks before some vendor announces: "Yes, we are 90 percent compatible with the new standard. However, we chose to implement a certain feature of it slightly differently." The scope of the world's data communications networks and the multiplicity of vested interests will likely keep this problem recurring. While there is admitted progress in many standards areas, new applications continue to appear that are as yet without standards of any kind.

Back to deregulation: Perhaps the earliest and most visible indication of things to come is represented by the telephones provided in airports for travelers. During predivestiture, to make a telephone call from an airport—be it voice, or data via acoustic coupler—was only a matter of finding an instrument and picking it up. They all worked the same, and it was a simple matter to drop in a coin and make the call. If so desired, the call could be charged to a home or office number.

Today, placing a telephone call from an airport is considerably more complicated. The instruments are more easily located, however, because there are so many of them. Arranged neatly in a row, in little soundproof enclosures, can be found:
- A telephone with no dial or pushbuttons, to be used only to answer airport paging.
- Another telephone with a set of pushbuttons, but no place to insert a coin. The instructions indicate that this phone is to be used only for calls on specified, non-Bell (or is it AT&T?) carriers, which require an access code to use.
- Another telephone with pushbuttons but no place to insert coins. The instructions indicate that this phone is to be used for credit card calls only, which will be charged through AT&T (or is it Bell?), providing you have an acceptable code number.
- Another telephone that looks more like a computer terminal with a small CRT screen. It takes several minutes to decipher just what can be done with this instrument. Kids like to play with it. Adults like to ignore it.
- Finally, with the user having received a short, on-the-spot lesson in the advantages of deregulation, a small, "plain-vanilla" telephone with pushbuttons and a slot for coins. It is usually the busy one. This is the instrument that must be used to place a simple local call.

Communications implies a two-way exchange of information. Successful communications occurs when the sender's information or knowledge, after being prepared and readily transmitted, is acquired and understood by the recipient. Now that computer companies are making an effort to allow computers to interact freely, telephone companies seem determined to revert to the posture maintained by the computer vendors 25 years ago. George Santayana was right: "Those who cannot remember the past are condemned to repeat it" (from *The Life of Reason,* volume 1, 1905-1906).

The problem goes far beyond airport telephones. The good news is the countless inexpensive, computer-driven telephones available today presenting truly staggering arrays of features and options. The bad news is that no two of them work alike. The pleasures of the money saved by switching to the new equipment and by the use of the new features are often quickly replaced with the frustration of lost or misrouted calls.

A hopeful sign
The existing incompatibilities in computer, data communications, and voice facilities appear to be contributing to another phenomenon: the increasing entropy of the information with which these mechanisms deal. (Entropy may be defined here as a measure of the randomness or disorder within information.) Viewed globally, from the perspective of the rapidly expanding national and international communications networks and their inconsistencies and incompatibilities, it appears that entropy is increasing. There is hope, though: Standards bodies have several efforts under way (Integrated Services Digital Network and Open Systems Interconnection are two) that are intended to eventually ease the situation.

If the growing number of decisions discussed earlier are based on information that is unverified, received late, or inaccurate, the confidence level in these decisions must also decrease. While difficult to quantify, this aspect of the information issue makes for interesting speculation.

The three revolutions discussed earlier occurred over progressively shrinking time periods. In both of the first two revolutions (Agricultural and Industrial), the benefits were achieved over considerable time periods, with succeeding generations becoming familiar with the new technologies and adapting to them. The changes in any one lifetime were so gradual that they could usually be accepted with proper motivation and training.

The Information Revolution has been evolving within considerably less than one lifetime. The changes in the last 25 years have been—and promise to continue to be—dramatic. But the benefits provided by this revolution remain a mystery to many.

A candidate for a fourth revolution has recently appeared: artificial intelligence. While still in its relative infancy, and considered by some to be poorly named, artificial intelligence may, in time, provide the means to cope with the vast amounts of information produced and transmitted by the computers of the third revolution. The first 10 years of the revolution will likely provide dramatic insight to the process called intelligence, whether exhibited by a human or a machine. (Figure 4 presents the shrinking time frames associated with major technology revolutions.)

To date, in spite of news articles to the contrary, artificial intelligence is not very intelligent. Clever, yes. Brilliant, occasionally. Intelligent, not yet. In many cases, the harder the goal of artificial intelligence is pursued, the more willing the machines become to display genuine ignorance.

Small companies are springing up rapidly and presenting products labeled, in one way or another, artificial intelligence. Articles and books abound describing "thinking machines," and seminars and conferences on the subject are rapidly increasing.

One fundamental problem continues to defy solution: an acceptable definition of the term "intelligence." Describing intelligence is not necessarily the same as defining it. The resolution of this problem may be a long time in coming.

Meanwhile, efforts in two areas related to artificial intelligence bear watching: human-to-machine interfaces and expert systems. They may offer the initial means to cope with increasing amounts of computer-generated and computer-transmitted information.

Visible progress

Human-to-machine interfaces are improving steadily. Although natural-language interfaces are not here yet, progress in that direction is visible. Major remaining obstacles include: content and context analysis, the resolution of ambiguities inherent in natural languages, and the derivation of directions or instructions contained in a statement that can be presented several ways.

Expert systems are developing rapidly in a number of disciplines, including medical diagnosis, failure analysis, and geophysical exploration. These systems are being developed in two areas that will have a significant impact on the Information Revolution: operating systems and data communications network control.

Operating systems, which control computer resources, are becoming increasingly complex. The problems of efficiently scheduling and allocating these resources in response to rapidly changing user demands are starting to exceed the capacity of human operators.

In the days of large, centrally located configurations connected to a network of remote terminals, the operator's problems were much simpler. Today, commonplace distributed configurations contain many sizable processing centers that are interconnected through megabit-per-second networks that span continents and oceans. Further, these installations maintain databases in the gigabyte range that are accessible 24 hours a day.

Operating systems are being developed that increasingly resemble evolving expert systems. The goal is to achieve the most efficient scheduling and allocation of resources in response to increasingly dynamic user demands. Ultimately, combinations of three basic procedures (see below) will be applied, and all three are totally dependent on the rapidly increasing bandwidth available in communications networks.

In some situations, with one procedure the process (application software) will be transmitted for execution to the location of the relevant database. In a second procedure, the database, or portions thereof, will be moved to the process. In other situations, the process and the database will be moved to a third location (the third procedure), where processing hardware is idle, or where excess capacity exists.

Another use of the third option will be to reconfigure around device or network failures. Fault-tolerant proces-

4. Shrinking time periods. *Major technology revolutions are occurring more frequently, and their durations are growing progressively smaller.*

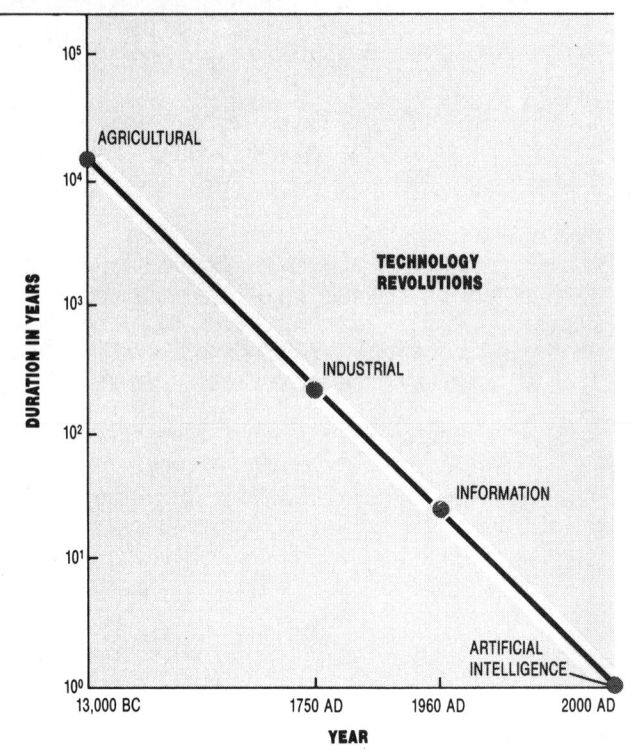

sors, previously limited to somewhat specialized applications (such as airline-reservation and process-control networks), will become increasingly common. Computer users of all types will recognize how dependent they have become on information processing technologies and will demand higher availability and reliability.

The control of network communications is also exceeding the capacity of human operators. As voice becomes digitized and integrated within networks already handling a variety of other types of traffic, the dynamic allocation of bandwidth requires decision-making at rates beyond human abilities. This level of control, exercised when all resources are functioning properly, is one of several communications areas requiring attention.

A second area involves the selection of the least-expensive route through a network. Considerations include the urgency levels of traffic, the load on the network, and, possibly, the time of day. The ultimate goal is the shortest propagation delay at the lowest possible cost. Computer-driven private branch exchanges are already exhibiting primitive versions of this logic.

A third area involves the diagnosis of network-component failures, followed by dynamically reconfiguring around them to maintain the desired throughput and availability levels. Many failures today result in an interruption of service to users, followed by manual location and diagnosis of the fault by human operators using sophisticated equipment at network control centers. User demand for continuous, trouble-free service coupled with the desire to keep control-center-personnel costs down will result in the application of expert systems to the task.

The major problems involved in applying expert systems to these three examples include: extracting the decision-making rules from "expert" human operators and controllers and building them into the "inference engines" that drive the expert systems; designing and implementing the data-acquisition logic required to build and maintain the necessary databases; building in the equivalent of human, intuitive tests of reasonableness; and testing the developing expert systems in realistic environments to raise the confidence in them to acceptable levels.

Speed it up
The use of expert systems to develop application software is another area receiving considerable attention. The major goal is to shorten the current development time such that applications can be developed and modified more readily, in response to the increasing rate of change observed in the user environment. In addition to the major problems discussed above, this development task includes the evaluation of techniques for verifying deterministic answers to questions while using probabilistic procedures.

Beyond these areas lies the enticing realm of applying expert and intelligence-emulating mechanisms that will be largely self-programming. At the core of this research, again, is the question of the definition of intelligence. The search for this definition appears similar to that of particle physicists seeking to understand the fundamental nature of matter. In spite of several centuries of speculation, intelligence researchers are still seeking the identity of their "atom": intelligence itself.

Considerable progress has been made in understanding and emulating the sensory mechanisms that contribute to the development of intelligence in humans. Visual, aural, tactile, and olfactory mechanisms are being produced that begin to approximate their human models. Speech synthesis is commonplace in a variety of devices. While these sensory and speech schemes are clearly a part of the quest for artificial intelligence, they do not yet provide much of an insight to intelligence itself. They are, in a sense, clues to a still unsolved puzzle.

Stated simply, the goal of intelligence may be the survival of a species. If that is true, then the question of the origin of the survival goal must be asked. Why is it necessary for a species, any species, to survive? Where did the survival goal originate, and why?

Consider bacterial or viral species. As soon as humans develop a drug that is effective, these species often evolve to a different, resistant form. Is this behavior perhaps a form of intelligence applied to the survival goal? Much research activity in the field of artificial intelligence is centered around the task of "teaching" computers knowledge, as if they have already acquired the ability to "learn." Without first instilling a goal (perhaps survival) in computers, thus motivating them to learn, it is doubtful that they will ever exhibit true intelligence, regardless of the amount of knowledge they have acquired.

Within the next few years, it may be possible to produce a rough approximation of the human brain with semi-conductor technology. When equipped with the sensory mechanisms discussed earlier, it could then be exposed to a variety of external stimuli. Without a survival goal, the behavior of such a device is questionable.

Instilling a survival goal in such a device poses a number of interesting questions. How long would it take for the rudiments of survival, or any other goal, to appear? Could the process be accelerated, or would it take as long to develop as it did in humans (tens or hundreds of thousands of years)? Should it appear, what end would it serve? What form of natural selection would appear that would retain useful characteristics and discard the rest?

It may be that many of the questions being asked about creating artificial intelligence in computers are the wrong ones. Time will tell. If artificial intelligence should become a fourth revolution, it may be accelerated out of the necessity to cope with the computers of the Information Revolution. Two outcomes appear to exist: The problems of the Information Revolution will be solved, or simply moved to an even more abstract, incomprehensible realm. Given the current headlong rush into the artificial intelligence environment observed in the industry, the latter seems, for the moment, more likely.

Social and cultural implications
The Western World's fascination with computers and related technologies presents an interesting contrast to what is observed in Japan, now several years into its well-publicized fifth-generation project. In the Western World, new technologies are often rushed through development, placed in production, and introduced to the market at an ever-increasing rate. Before the social and cultural impact of one revolution (computers) is identified and evaluated, most researchers appear to be on to the next one without so much as an occasional backward glance.

The Japanese have approached the problem from a considerably different perspective. They began with an evaluation of the social and cultural needs of their society. Then they asked: "How can technology help us in meeting these needs?" A number of these needs were evaluated in approaching their fifth-generation project, including:
- The successful integration of 100 million people—in a country about the size of California—with an increasingly information-oriented culture.
- Culturally acceptable methods of adapting to a society that is becoming highly educated and older.
- Greater efficiencies in managing scarce natural resources and energy.
- Enhancing Japan's ability to become an internationalized culture.
- Improvements in fields currently exhibiting low productivity.

These are, by any standards, ambitious goals. It is significant that the Japanese started with the social and cultural goals and then asked how technology could help. The Japanese also evaluated the current fourth-generation computer technologies. The conclusion: that generation would not take them where they wanted to go.

Stated another way, much of the Western World appears determined to seek change for the sake of change alone. As a rule, the Japanese, on the other hand, choose to select desired social and cultural enhancements and then apply technology to achieving them. Most Western cultures continue to surround themselves with increasingly sophisticated examples of technology, without first evaluating their cultural and social impacts. With current production techniques, the products of a relatively few are made available, at affordable prices, to the many. Are the data acquisition and processing skills of the many — as facilitated by today's increasingly ubiquitous microcomputers — up to the challenges represented by these devices' copious outputs?

Automobiles and telephones are necessities. It is not clear that computers fall into the same category. While many organizations are entirely dependent on computers for their survival in competitive environments, their overall impact on society has yet to be determined.

The computer industry continues its shakeout. IBM retains its dominant position while hundreds of others, including the telephone companies, pursue a niche in the market. The recently observed sluggishness in the computer industry and the closely related semiconductor industry is attributed to many things, including the shakeout process itself. The slowdown may reflect the initial stages of a general misunderstanding by the masses. Surveys abound suggesting that 40 percent of all microcomputers delivered to date are gathering dust or are used for inconsequential tasks, having failed to provide the benefits promised when purchased. Many first-time users have discovered that they do not possess anything approaching the computer literacy required to apply the machines to their tasks, in spite of vendor assurances that it would not be required.

What role will computer and data communications technologies play in coming years? Stafford Beer, in his book *Brain of the Firm* (John Wiley & Sons Ltd., 1981) poses the question elegantly: "The question which asks how to use the computer in the enterprise, is, in short, the wrong question. A better formulation is to ask how the enterprise should be run given that computers exist. The best version of all is the question asking what, given computers, the enterprise now is."

Many — perhaps most — organizations can be observed pursuing answers to the first two versions of the above question. Few, if any, are seeking answers to the third version. The third question cannot be answered until a sufficiently high level of computer literacy exists in a sufficiently large number of people. Herein lies the problem.

A majority of middle- and senior-level managers in companies of all sizes are people in the 35-to-65 age bracket. Many management techniques they use were developed long before computers and data communications technologies began their explosive evolution. While surrounded by examples of these technologies on all sides, they have little understanding of how the technology works and claim: "I am not computer literate."

The computer-user community supports a growing number of consultants who can apply computer and communications technology to business problems, thus relieving the user of the task. Many of these consultants, like their counterparts employed by the users, have become specialists in narrowly defined areas like operating systems, database architectures, data communications, and specialized application package development. While providing quality work in their chosen specialty areas, many lack the "renaissance" perspective required to step back, view the enterprise as a whole, and ask: "What is the nature of the enterprise I am dealing with, now that computers play such an integral role in it. How is it changing? What is the rate of change observed?"

5. Convergence salvation. *While humans are becoming more computer literate, computers — through "artificial intelligence" — are becoming more human literate.*

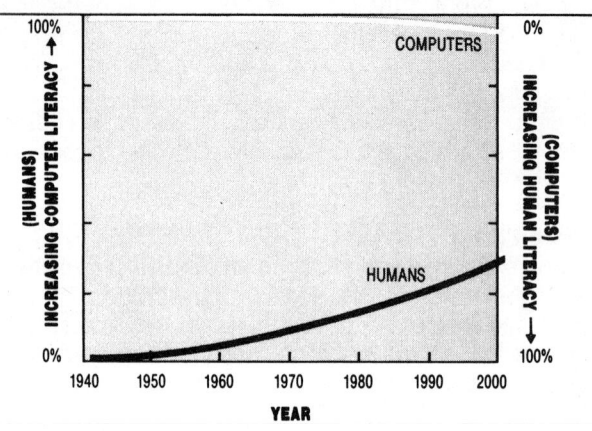

From another perspective, the computer industry continues to pursue the goal of "user friendly" equipment. Like the definition of artificial intelligence, the harder it is pursued, the farther away it seems to be. Much of this activity has obscured the fact that the first generation of "friendly users" is already here, and their average age is about 12 to 15. (It is estimated that 92 percent of U. S. public schools now have computers for student use; this compares with just 30 percent three years ago. And at the public schools of at least one state — Texas — computer literacy is a graduation requirement.)

Those friendly users (noted above), introduced to information technology at an early age, have no inhibitions about approaching a keyboard, pressing a key, observing a response, and pressing another key. Soon a dialogue is established, and they are launched effortlessly and painlessly into a realm largely unknown to those just one generation removed. When these people assume the middle and senior management positions in their chosen fields, computer literacy will be an integral element of their management skills. Many of them will look back and wonder: "What was it like back in the old B. C. [Before Computer] days?"

These new managers will inherit the legacy left by the present generation. They will bring a Renaissance perspective to the problems that the earlier generation failed to develop and apply. They will be able to answer the third of Stafford Beer's questions and proceed accordingly.

While the next few decades pass and the friendly users achieve their management goals and increase their computer literacy, another evolutionary process will be occurring: Computers, through their enhanced capabilities and, possibly, intelligence, will become increasingly human literate. Figure 5 presents this convergence. Just when the two will converge remains to be seen. ∎

Following 20 years with GE and Honeywell, Hal Becker started a career as an information management consultant. He has authored two books as well as many articles and makes presentations at major industry conferences.

John T. Mulqueen, DATA COMMUNICATIONS

Consultants: For better or worse, business is booming

Consultants call the tune in many communications sales. But what song are they singing? Sorting the charlatans from the pros.

For three days early last month, AT&T played host at a very upscale Florida resort to 25 people that it considers among the most influential in the industry. These were not politicians whose votes could sway the outcome of telecommunications legislation. Nor were they judges whose cases set the industry ground rules. They were not rate-setting regulators, and neither were they AT&T customers—chief information officers or telecommunications directors who buy AT&T's products.

The fortunate group, dubbed the Top 25, were members of AT&T's National Consultants Council, a body that the telephone company first called together in November 1987 at Quail Lodge, a posh resort in Carmel, Calif. This year's meeting was on Captiva Island, on Florida's Gulf Coast (see "AT&T wines and dines the cream of the crop").

Courting consultants
The council is interesting not because it is unique to the industry (that won't last long), but as a sign of the mounting attention that equipment and service suppliers are paying to consultants.

MCI Communications Corp. (Washington, D. C.) has money in its 1989 budget for a council of 50. And Northern Telecom Inc. (Nashville, Tenn.) is cogitating a similar move while it steps up the number of seminars it holds for consultants. Even Digital Equipment Corp. (Maynard, Mass.), not previously known for its marketing acumen, has 19 persons working full time and another 30 devoting part of their time to consultant liaison.

MCI did not even have a full-scale, consultant-liaison program until 1987, when it took a pilot program run in its Pacific region and expanded it nationwide. It now includes an electronic-mail service, complete with bulletin board and software packages, as part of its information service for consultants. Curtis Abrue, manager of consultant services for MCI, says he hopes to expand his database from 1,200 to 5,000 consultants, to include both communications and computer experts.

Smaller companies have also caught the bug. General DataComm Inc. (Middlebury, Conn.) hired a consultant to feed GDC product information to his former colleagues. Timeplex Inc. (Woodcliff Lake, N. J.) pulled a sales person out of the field to set up a sophisticated consultant-liaison program. And both Digital Communications Associates Inc. (Alpharetta, Ga.) and Network Equipment Technologies Inc. (Redwood City, Calif.) are in the process of getting similar programs going.

The reason for all the attention? Consultants have clout. They have a lot to say when it comes to purchasing communications equipment or services.

Nynex Corp. cites studies that consultants in 1984 influenced 24 percent of all communications system purchases. That percentage is expected to grow to 52 percent by 1990 and to 65 percent by the year 2000.

Fred Bartl, vice president of TMC Inc. (Boston), one of AT&T's Top 25, says he has seen estimates that 70 percent or more of communications sales involve consultants in some form or another. "If you take a look at what goes on in the university, health care, and government markets," he adds, "virtually [every project] has a consultant."

Others say that perhaps 90 percent of all the PBXs sold in the United States first have to pass inspection by a customer's consultant.

Tales from the Darkside
But how well are these experts serving their customers? Are they in fact experts? How competent are most consultants to implement the projects customers entrust to them? Do the consulting arms of the Big Eight accounting firms

inflate their bills by stretching out projects needlessly? Do they staff their projects with fresh-faced college graduates who have too little practical technological experience?

Can clients trust consultant experts to give them fair, objective evaluations and recommendations? What about the suspicions of many that consultants are tied too closely to certain suppliers? Do suppliers buy recommendations with design fees, implementation fees, or by buying market research reports?

Obviously, when talking about so multifaceted an industry, no pat answer will do. But a survey of the members of AT&T's council, independent consultants, and users turns up enough mistakes and botched jobs to give one pause. For instance:

- The Evangelical Lutheran Church of America earlier this year had to pull 120,000 feet of RS-232 cabling out of its new headquarters in north Chicago because it would not support an IBM Token Ring local area network. The builder had installed the wiring on the advice of a telecommunications consultant, according to James Carlini, president of Carlini Associates, a Chicago consultant the church called on for help. The cabling was replaced with twisted-pair wiring, Carlini says. Church officials back his story.

Carlos Santiago, principal of the Harbinger Group (Norwalk, Conn.), agrees with Carlini that many real developers know little about the way the buildings should be wired and that few modern buildings, let alone older ones, are adequately wired for today's communications needs.

- I. M. S. International Inc. (Plymouth Meeting, Pa.), a pharmaceutical research house, on the advice of a consultant, switched its corporate network from AT&T to MCI, only to have a near-disastrous collapse in service. The consultant, who had been hired by the corporation's administrative services office, tried to make the switch over one weekend. When he realized how out of control things were, he "vamoosed," says Robert Sarracino, manager of telecommunications, leaving I. M. S. with a tangle of long-distance lines that its internal staff had to sort out. It was months before the mess was straightened out, and I. M. S. eventually went back to AT&T as its carrier, he adds.

- Molex Inc., a Chicago connector manufacturer, paid $4,000 a month more in communications costs—10 percent of its bill—because no one had bothered to tell the consultant to check that the company was being billed correctly for a variety of services. Bruce Thatcher, president of TelCon Associates Inc. (Overland Park, Kan.), was able to straighten out the billing. Claude Strass, president of a Molex division, says the company received a refund check for about $50,000 from Illinois Bell (see "From vending machines to PBXs").

- A fiber optic telecommunications network being built now for a New Zealand railroad fell so far behind schedule that the railroad called in Fluor Consulting Co. (Irvine, Calif.) to get the work back on track. The consultant handling the job was an international, world-class firm based outside the United States, says Bill Coplin of Fluor.

- AT&T two years ago successfully sued several consultants who told their clients not to pay a termination fee that AT&T charged customers who canceled equipment leases.

- A major financial services firm bought a PBX that was loaded with features the firm could not use. A consultant specialist recommended the purchase, and a major national consultant reviewed the proposal and "blessed it," says Gerald Mayfield of DMW Group (Stamford, Conn.), who was called in later. The financial firm was billing back users for their share of the PBX. It will never entirely amortize the switch's cost, says Mayfield, and has had to "live with reality."

- Officers of two California consulting firms, former San Diego county officials, and officers of a defunct interconnect company were indicted for rigging bids on a $25 million San Diego County telecommunications network (see "Six years, several guilty pleas later, San Diego gets its network").

- A consultancy helping the New York City Board of Education select a PBX for its headquarters in Brooklyn quit the job without notice when it was bought by another company. Board employees with almost no knowledge of telecommunications had to evaluate bids on equipment they knew nothing about—until Xtend Communications Corp., a Manhattan consultant, loaned a helping hand. Scott Matluck, deputy director of the board's telecommunications department, says Xtend's principals were knowledgeable and available.

- Price Waterhouse built a $6 million computer operation for the New Jersey Department of Motor Vehicles that was termed a fiasco and collapsed the day it went into operation (see "How not to design a network—New Jersey style").

- Price Waterhouse, on the other hand, also helped a dental insurance company whose revenues began to decline after another consultant had designed an automatic call distribution "whose configuration was hopelessly incorrect," says Anne O'Loughlin, a consultant in Price Waterhouse's New York office. The client was losing close to 80 percent of its incoming calls until a Price Waterhouse consultant changed the access tables and reduced the number of lost calls to less than 10 percent, she says.

- William Morgan, a principal of W & J Partnership (Morgan Hill, Calif.), a highly respected consultant, says that his firm has provided data on installed equipment to major research houses only to see his numbers "inflated by up to 500 percent in subsequently published form." Says Morgan: "Most market research firms produce market-size projections aimed at pleasing the most optimistic member of the client's firm. This, when combined with the optimistic base sales provided by the manufacturers themselves, explains the large to very large overestimates of market sizes in computers and telecommunications that have been made by all of the major market research firms during the last few years."

Several things are obvious from this list of disasters. Some of the problems were the work of small consultants who packed up and vanished. In others, major players were at fault.

One of the discoveries made by the New Jersey State Commission of Investigations that looked into the Motor Vehicles fiasco was that state workers entrusted too much

AT&T wines and dines the cream of the crop

They range from a former Bell Laboratories scientist to a former distributor of vending machines, but all of them are equal enough in the eyes of AT&T to be included among the nation's 25 top communications consultants.

The 25 persons listed below attended the first meeting of AT&T's National Consultants Council in November 1987. They were invited back this year for what apparently will be an annual event.

AT&T sent some of its top managers to last year's conference, including Senior Vice President Alexander C. Stark Jr. and Vice President Charles Yates, both of whom were scheduled for this year's session. Vittorio Cassoni, who used to head AT&T's data systems group, was supposed to address the 1987 conference but never appeared. His successor, Robert Kavner, was not on this year's list of speakers.

AT&T does not skimp on these occasions. The 1987 conference was at Quail Lodge in Carmel, Calif., a Mobil five-star resort that is home to a championship golf course.

There were 18 AT&T employees (and 10 spouses), along with 25 consultants (and 20 of their wives), in attendance at the two-and-a-half-day conference. That makes a total of 73 persons. The shindig likely cost the phone company roughly $75,000.

"It must have been very expensive for AT&T," says Bill Coplin of Fluor Consulting (Irvine, Calif.), who referred all questions about who picked up the tab to AT&T. Steven Epner, president of the User Group (St. Louis), says AT&T paid for everything, including airfare.

"Some of the people who were at the meeting did not allow them to pay," said another consultant who attended the meeting. "Obviously they paid for dinners. If we had asked, they would have flown us anywhere. They were willing to pay any of the charges anybody wanted them to pay."

Showing it is not prejudiced in favor of the West Coast, AT&T moved the meeting this year to the equally posh South Seas Plantation on Captiva Island, near Fort Myers on Florida's Gulf Coast.

Several consultants said that AT&T's regional consultant-liaison representatives nominated those candidates they deemed the leading consultants in their areas. AT&T chose 30 names out of a database of 6,000, but five consultants declined to attend, one council member said.

Some are obvious choices: David Rappaport of Arthur Andersen & Co.; Francis Gunther of Booz, Allen & Hamilton; Gerry Mayfield of DMW Group; Eugene Reilly of Ernst & Whinney; and Dennis Conroy of Cooper & Lybrand. Robert Liepold is a former executive vice president for United Telecommunications. But many are not household names. Many did not know each other.

Several consultants said they were told they were picked because they had been advisors on very large contracts within the previous 12 months. One pointed out, however, that Shen Lin is a former Bell Laboratories researcher and could not have affected much in the way of purchases.

The former vending machine distributor is Bruce Thatcher, president of Overland Park, Kan.-based Tel-Con Associates Inc. (see "From vending machines to PBXs").

The session focused heavily on the Business Machines Group and was aimed at the user, not network services that other carriers might use, one source said.

Topics covered seem to have been broad strategic issues rather than specifics about equipment and services. Some attendees say that questions about specific issues were answered during the question-and-answer periods. Mayfield says hard information on AT&T's "underlying costs" were revealed.

Nearly all of the consultants said the Carmel meeting was worthwhile and a good chance to hear AT&T's top management discuss where the company is going. It is also a good marketing ploy to name a National Consultants Council, Rappaport pointed out. A statement by Epner of the User Group indicates his agreement: "Consultants often feel left out in left field," he says. "This was a great opportunity to meet the top executives of AT&T face-to-face and to get to identify contacts."
—J.T.M.

AT&T's National Consultants attendees at November 1987 meeting

ATTENDEE	FIRM	
JOHN ANDERSON	ANDERSON & GLASCOW	GREAT FALLS, VA.
PAUL BROWN	THE USER GROUP	ST. LOUIS, MO.
JACK CALOZ	ELECTRONIC SYSTEM ASSOCIATES	NEW YORK, N.Y.
BROWNELL CHALSTROM	BBN COMMUNICATIONS	CAMBRIDGE, MASS.
FRED BARTL	TMC INC.	NEEDHAM HEIGHTS, MASS.
DENNIS CONROY	COOPERS & LYBRAND	NEW YORK, N.Y.
BILL COPLIN	FLUOR CONSULTING	IRVINE, CALIF.
DAVID EDELHEIT	PRICE WATERHOUSE*	NEW YORK, N.Y.
STEVEN EPNER	THE USER GROUP	ST. LOUIS, MO.
JIM GORDON	TCS MANAGEMENT GROUP	NASHVILLE, TENN.
FRANCIS GUNTHER	BOOZ, ALLEN, & HAMILTON	BETHESDA, MD
GREGORY JACOBSEN	TELECOMMUNICATIONS INTERNATIONAL INC.	LAKEWOOD, COLO.
DOUG KISTLER	M&SD INC.	NEWARK, N.J.
ROBERT LIEPOLD	INDEPENDENT	FAIRWAY, KAN.
SHEN LIN	WANDL INC.	RINGWOOD, N.J.
JOE MASSEY	JTM ASSOCIATES	ATLANTA, GA.
GERRY MAYFIELD	DMW GROUP	STAMFORD, CONN.
JOHN MCQUILLAN	MCQUILLAN ASSOCIATES	CAMBRIDGE, MASS.
DON MONACO	ANDERSEN CONSULTING	CHICAGO, ILL.
BILL MORGAN	W & J PARTNERSHIP	MORGAN HILL, CAL.
DALE MULLEN	MULLEN TELECOMMUNICATIONS SERVICE	ENGLF .JD, COLO.
DAVID RAPPAPORT	ANDERSEN CONSULTING	CHICAGO, ILL.
EUGENE REILLY	ERNST & WHINNEY	PITTSBURGH, PA.
BILL SCHWARTZ	COMPUTOL/XTEND	NEW YORK, N.Y.
BRUCE THATCHER	TELCON ASSOCIATES	OVERLAND PARK, KAN.

*Now with Andersen Consulting

From vending machines to PBXs

Sixteen years ago Bruce Thatcher was comfortably situated as a distribution manager for a vending machine company when a friend talked him into joining his floundering consulting business.

The friend's entry to the business was not auspicious. He had purchased a franchise from an Atlanta, Ga., firm to become a consultant. The idea was to sell contracts for consulting services, determine the clients' needs, and send the information to the Atlanta office for analysis and solutions on the franchiser's computer.

There was no computer, of course, but Thatcher's partner stuck it out, learned something about telecommunications from a telephone company associate, and invited Thatcher to join.

■ **On his own.** The friend left the firm—TelCon Associates Inc. (Overland Park, Kan.)—in 1980. Thatcher today is its president and one of the members of AT&T's National Consultants Council. That is as close as one can come to an unofficial designation as one of the leading telecommunications consultants in the nation.

Robert Liepold, former executive vice president of United Telecommunications Inc. and another member of AT&T's Council, thinks very highly of Thatcher. "I would recommend him to anybody," says Liepold, who is an independent consultant to manufacturers and carriers.

Molex Inc. (Chicago) has retained TelCon for five years to evaluate its telephone operations, order its phones and lines, and study the need for new services. Claude Strass, president of a Molex division, says he has no doubt TelCon has saved the company hundreds of thousands of dollars over that period. "Our telephone bill has gone down even though our volume has gone up six or seven times," Strass says.

■ **Diverse backgrounds.** TelCon does about $1 million a year in revenues from its headquarters and offices in St. Louis and Chicago. It employs 24 persons, 13 of them professional consultants with a variety of backgrounds. The manager of the Chicago office was a systems analyst with Honeywell Corp.; another is a retired Navy telecommunications specialist.

Thatcher says the firm serves about 150 clients a year—almost 1,800 in the past 16 years—drawn largely from medium-size companies with sales below the $400 million mark.

Some have grown beyond that level since TelCon has been working with them, Thatcher says, and some clients are in the *Fortune* 500. Most customers do not have their own telecommunications departments.

The company avoids government work because so much effort is required before a contract is even awarded and because the chances of getting the jobs are so difficult to estimate that it is not cost-efficient.

Again, TelCon's St. Louis office is an exception. Thatcher says the office has developed a cost-efficient way to go after the business and has done consulting work for 20 school districts and half a dozen universities within a 200-mile radius of St. Louis. The track record makes it easier to get more work.

TelCon's geographic market is the entire United States and Canada. It does not sell any equipment or act as a systems integrator. Most of its work has been in voice, but data communications is becoming a more important segment—especially the combination of voice and data over T1 facilities.

Thatcher says a rule of thumb used to be that a company should have its own telecommunications department if it spent $1 million a year for telecommunications services. Today, because of the variety and complexity of service offerings and their potential impact on operations, that number might be as low as $500,000.

Most of TelCon's work deals with reducing expenditures or getting the most use out of existing equipment or services—cost reduction and cost optimization in industry jargon—areas that Thatcher says most consultants do not want to touch. They would rather be designing and installing new networks or equipment.

—*J. T. M.*

---

to Price Waterhouse's reputation and left undue responsibility with the consultant.

Another not so obvious point is that the mistakes detailed above are likely only the tip of the proverbial iceberg. No one likes to talk about mistakes, least of all (as one consultant points out) the client who is too embarrassed to admit he hired the wrong person in the first place.

Consultants admit they do not like cleaning up a mess made by another consultant. "We do it on occasion, but we tend to be reluctant to do it," says Bartl of TMC. "It is always sticky. It is seldom a win-win business, and you have to get past a lot of emotional content. We'd rather start at the front and be accountable."

Thatcher of TelCon Associates agrees. Most consultants do not want to be involved with existing installations, he says. They prefer to work on new assignments. Thatcher himself, however, makes his living helping clients get the most out of what they already have, including patching up errors his colleagues and vendors have made.

Still, virtually every consultant interviewed, including 15 of AT&T's Top 25, say they have done this type of cleanup work, however distasteful.

Finding a good consultant

As dismaying as some of those stories are, they are not the whole picture of how consultants routinely perform. Arthur Andersen & Co. (Chicago), for example, has not built a $1 billion consulting business by being incompetent. (The firm last month changed the name of its U. S.

Six years, several guilty pleas later, San Diego gets its network

By next year, California's San Diego County should finally have a data, voice, and video communications network that it began work on six years ago. The final pieces of the long-delayed project—PBXs connected to microwave links that will provide T1 connections to sites spread over a 4,300-square-mile area—are being installed now.

The price will be steep—at least $20 million—only slightly less than the $24.5 million the county agreed to pay in June 1982 when it awarded a contract to Telink Inc. (Anaheim, Calif.). But the final network will be considerably larger than that envisioned in 1982.

Telink will not be there to see the final installation. The pact with the now defunct company called for cutting over the network by the end of 1984. Before that happened, San Diego County had fired several officials involved in selecting Telink and canceled the contract.

■ **Indictments.** Then a federal grand jury dropped a bombshell in October 1984 by indicting 13 individuals and two companies on charges that bidding for the contract had been rigged. Among those indicted were several former county communications officials, Telink, several of its officers, its parent company—Burnup & Sims Inc. (Fort Lauderdale, Fla.)—and officers of two consultancies that had worked on the project for the county—Telecommunications Design Inc. (TDC) and Telecomm Consultants Inc. (TCI). A sensational story was made more so by the charges that in addition to cash bribes, cocaine and prostitutes had been used to fix the contract.

It was the largest scheme to defraud San Diego County in history, according to the local district attorney. It was certainly one of the most notorious cases on record charging wrongdoing by communications consultants. But Lantz Lewis, the federal prosecutor handling the case, says that the practice of suppliers paying consultants to win contracts was common at the time.

In addition to San Diego County, the indictment said that Telink, between 1978 and 1982, paid officers of TDC to recommend Telink for almost $5 million worth of contracts with five corporations in California.

Further, the indictment charged that between 1980 and 1982 Univeral Communication Systems, a Roanoke, Va.-based interconnect company, paid TDC for recommending it to install networks for the St. Francis Hotel (San Francisco) and the Westin Plaza Hotel (Seattle, Wash.). Universal lost the San Diego bid in 1982 to Telink. (BellSouth Corp. of Atlanta, Ga., bought Universal in 1987. As of January 1, 1989, its name will be changed to BellSouth Communication Systems.)

Lewis says that under California state law secret payments by a contractor to a consultant to obtain a contract—"commercial bribery"—were not clearly illegal. Nor are they illegal in many states, he adds.

Such activities do, however, fall under federal prohibitions against mail fraud, and that is one of the reasons the case is being tried in federal court, Lewis adds. When government contracts are involved, he says, the payments are clearly prohibited by state law.

Lewis charges that Universal Communications paid $500,000 to be the consultants' "backup" choice for the San Diego contract in case Telink did not get it. Universal denies that.

Telink's former controller, John Bostwick, pleaded guilty to one count of mail fraud in February 1985 and is now a witness for the prosecution. In June 1986, Telink and Burnup & Sims pleaded no contest to the accusations and Burnup & Sims paid $4.85 million in fines and penalties to various government agencies.

Under the settlement, San Diego County also kept $2.5 million worth of equipment—including two SL1 switches—that Telink had already installed when the charges were filed.

■ **Civil penalties.** Before the June 1986 settlement was reached, Burnup & Sims had paid more than $3 million in penalties and court costs to Northern Telecom Inc. (Nashville, Tenn.) to settle a suit that the equipment manufacturer brought against Telink after Northern Telecom lost the San Diego contract and a $4 million Fresno County contract. Telink had been a Northern Telecom distributor and allegedly caused its supplier to lose the contract by scheming with other defendants to misrepresent Northern's bids. Northern said it bid $5.6 million less for the San Diego job than Telink. The indictment charges that Telink charged Fresno County $600,000 more for an SL1 PBX than Northern's bid.

In November 1986, Robert St. Pierre, a TDC vice president, pleaded guilty to mail fraud and agreed to testify for the government in the trial. A used car salesman now, he awaits sentencing after the trial.

That trial began in March 1987 but was delayed in July 1987 when U. S. District Court Judge Earl Gilliam declared a mistrial. Gilliam later overturned his own ruling, says Lewis, and rescheduled the trial for October 4, 1988.

Among those in the dock are Hilario Gonzales, former San Diego County director of general services; Abraham Stein, former county communications director; and top officers of TCI and TDC.

The county awarded Contel Page Systems Inc. (now part of Contel Customer Support) a $12.6 million contract late in February 1986. Michael James, director of support services for Contel Customer Support, says the project was expanded by 25 percent, bringing the total cost up to $16 million. That network was cut over September 28, 1987; the county accepted it in March 1988.

The county has signed a maintenance contract with Contel that adds $4.5 million a year to the bill.

Work going on now is for four additional SL1s and more microwave equipment to serve areas not covered by the original contract specifications, James says. That work will probably have to go for bid and will take at least until 1989, he estimates. —*J. T. M.*

Management Information Consulting division to Andersen Consulting.)

Nor should the poor performance of some consultants overshadow the job that Joseph T. Massey of JTM Associates Inc. (Atlanta, Ga.) has done for such clients as the Oregon State Higher Education System, Fairfax Hospital System, or National Broadcasting System (see "Georgian consults for 'love of it' ").

The miscues of some do not reflect the $1 million that James Hynes, vice president of voice and data communications at Chase Manhattan Bank (New York, N. Y.), says that Coopers & Lybrand saved his bank with its analysis and recommendations for using a packet-switching network. Coopers & Lybrand was also able to draw on personnel who were familiar with banking operations to make useful recommendations to the bank, Hynes adds.

Nor does the incompetence of some taint the trust that Harper & Row, the New York City-based publishing house, has in Xtend Communications. Eugene Clarke, Harper & Row's vice president of manufacturing, virtually defers to Xtend when communications questions arise. "I am not technical," Clarke says when asked about his telephone facilities. "You have to go to my consultant for that." Xtend has been a facilities manager for the publishing company, which lacks its own technical staff.

All consultants, then, clearly are not incompetent, but it is not always clear who the competent, or even the honest ones, are.

Stuart Tuchband, president of Communication Sciences Inc. (Edison, N. J.), who admits that his firm has committed its share of boners, says flatly: "Any consultant who tells you that he has not made mistakes is a liar." CSI is a medium-size independent consulting firm with almost 20 years' experience and a list of references that includes PaineWebber Group and Oppenheimer & Co. It helped move PaineWebber into its new headquarters in Manhattan and has been a consultant for Oppenheimer for 15 years.

"The big problem," says Gregory Jacobsen, president of Lakewood, Colo.-based Telecommunications International Inc. (TII), "is that industry is not ready to pay for professional consulting services. There are a lot of charlatans who don't charge much but can make money elsewhere, or they are mom and pop operations that don't need much to get by. You can buy consulting services for $20 an hour or $400 an hour, and the $400-an-hour consultant has no more credentials than the $20-an-hour one."

Robert Liepold, a former executive vice president of United Telecommunications Inc. (Westwood, Kan.) echoes that thought. "A lot of customers are not used to paying for that kind of help [that they received before divestiture]," he says, "and some consultants are really more beholden to manufacturers than they are to users because they work so closely with the manufacturers."

The golden fleece
That raises the sensitive issue of some vendors buying consultants' recommendations to get contracts—in a word, commercial bribery.

Most consultants and many consultant liaison people say that the soliciting and paying of fees is largely a thing of the past. The industry, as one consultant ironically put it, has cleaned itself up since the "good old days of the '70s." But there is evidence that the practice continues.

David Rappaport, who leads Andersen's communications consultancy, says it is "widely known in the industry that that happens, particularly among smaller consulting firms."

Considering Andersen's position as the biggest consultant, Rappaport might be considered a biased witness against small firms.

But Nathan Muller, the ex-consultant who heads General DataComm's liaison effort, says that consultants have asked that company's personnel for fees in exchange for favorable recommendations. "It's only happened twice in the 10 months I have been here," Muller says.

Culprits are most often retirees who do not understand consulting's mores and think that such fees are part of the business, Muller says. Sales representatives tend to be impressed with such directness, he says, but he stresses that he warned them about the legal and ethical problems inevitably attached to such payments.

A Codex Corp. (Canton, Mass.) spokesperson says that consultants tend to ask for assignments to write articles for the company or to address its customers. "There are only so many that you can accommodate," he adds.

Manufacturers are not the only marks. Curtis Abrue, consultant liaison manager with MCI, says requests for fees are "rare," but they do happen. MCI does not pay them for ethical and practical reasons, he says. "If we wanted to be pragmatic, we would, but the problem is we don't get a lot of demand."

Consultants, however, are not the only guilty parties. Vendors are not above trying to buy approval.

Rappaport says that vendors have tried to win his recommendation for their products by threatening to take their auditing business away from Andersen. "It is invariably an empty threat," he adds. "If they brought that before their board of directors, the board would have a fit."

Sal Catania, the partner in charge of Coopers & Lybrand's information technology service, says manufacturers do make "inappropriate suggestions about the way we can jointly bring a product to market."

Coplin, at Fluor Consulting, says the offering of fees or special payments happens but is not "real common. Sometimes it's awfully subtle and if you are not tuned in, you won't hear it. A whole lot more common with larger companies are giveaway programs. . . . They may try to create some sense of codevelopment or comarketing that will bring some profits."

Exposure to bribery and potential conflicts of interest, of course, are not limited to consultants. Nor are the long hard hours and weeks and even months away from home that consultants must put up with. But why do intelligent people who consider themselves professionals put up with this?

Massey of JTM Associates says he does consulting for the love of it. He is well compensated, he says, but stresses that he has studied telephony since childhood.

How not to design a network—New Jersey style

Any manager who wants a casebook study on how not to deal with a consultant should ask the New Jersey State Commission of Investigation for a copy of its report "On The Price Waterhouse Computer Contract with the N. J. Division of Motor Vehicles."

The 76-page document describes in rich detail how the DMV abdicated to its consultant almost total control of the design and implementation of a computer processing network that is vital to the public, the courts, and law enforcement agencies.

"When the new computer system went on line in June 1985, DMV operations all but collapsed because the system could not process hundreds of thousands of transactions or otherwise function at an acceptable level of effectiveness," the SCI noted.

SCI said DMV was guilty of mismanagment of the project and Price Waterhouse (PW) of "professional misjudgment."

■ **Expensive fix-up.** One result of the collapse was that PW had to spend at least $2 million just in the first year after the network broke down to clean up the mess. The state had to spend an additional $1 million.

The last chapter has not been written yet. According to the state Attorney General's office, negotiations are still going on with PW to settle the matter.

The accounting firm was awarded the $6.5 million contract to supply software and training to DMV in June 1983 after it had done a master plan on modernizing DMV's computer and other operations.

Among the findings of the SCI included in the report were:

■ DMV ignored the recommendations of its own master plan—the one prepared by PW—against using one consultant. PW said relying on one consultant would multiply final costs by three or four times.

■ DMV bypassed experienced state personnel who normally oversaw such projects and turned complete control of the project over to PW, which itself had no experience in building a data processing operation of that size.

■ Then-Deputy Director of Motor Vehicles Robert Kline was project manager, but he was an attorney "with no computer or technical experience." He delegated day-to-day supervision to a senior assistant director, whom the SCI called "another data processing novice."

■ DMV accepted Price Waterhouse's policy for billing expenses without ever reviewing it, did not adequately monitor tasks PW claims were done or the expenses that were billed.

■ For its part, Price Waterhouse did not adequately document and track employees' time for which it sought reimbursement. The SCI "questioned PW's judgment in charging numerous inappropriate expense items to the state." PW's own policy that professionals participate in determining how their work should be billed was ignored.

■ Competitive bidding on the contract was improperly waived, and no other firms were contacted. Even Price Waterhouse was surprised by the decision to make it the sole source supplier.

■ Price Waterhouse's contribution of $35,000 to three Republican fund-raisers during that period "tainted the public's perception that its performance would be judged without favortism."

■ Price Waterhouse risked the success of the project by using Ideal, then a new and virtually untested fourth-generation computer programming language from Applied Data Research (Princeton, N. J.).

■ The accounting firm used a large percentage of recently hired, inexperienced programmers on the job, had a very high turnover in personnel, misrepresented its ability to maintain staff continuity, and failed to adequately manage its staff.

■ If the database went down, "the entire DMV computer system would have been inactive" for at least 60 hours because PW's design did not ease the impact of a failure by segmenting files over separate computers.

The SCI report says one of the reasons Price Waterhouse was selected without public bidding was that the DMV wanted to rush the project so it would be completed before the November 1985 gubernatorial election.

William Driscoll, PW's partner in charge of the project, said in an internal PW memo that Kline told him the political contributions, solicited days after Price Waterhouse won the $6.5 million contract, would not affect the award but would be "good business" on the firm's part.

Kline, who is back in private practice, denied saying that. Driscoll said in another internal memo to PW's Policy Board that he and another partner decided that contributions in 1984 would "perhaps buy some insurance on the DMV job." Driscoll testified before a New Jersey State Assembly committee that the phrase was a poor choice of words meant to be synonymous only with maintaining good relations with the state.

■ **Not ideal.** Among the problems with the Ideal programming language was that even if there were only 200 terminals in the network, there would be serious response delays. The DMV planned to have at least 400 terminals at the beginning of the installation and 569 by the end of 1986. Kline testified that PW knew that. SCI said that ADR, Ideal's creator, had no data indicating that even 400 terminals could be supported by Ideal.

PW tried unsuccessfully to bill the state for 2,500 hours work spent fixing Ideal.

"When PW belatedly realized that it could not rely on the Ideal programming language alone for the new DMV system, which by then was fragmenting, it sought to evade full blame for its software misjudgment in an apparent effort to avoid the cost of correcting the problems its misjudgment had caused," the SCI report states.

—J. T. M.

Georgian consults for 'love of it'

Ask Joseph T. Massey to describe his background in telecommunications, and the president of JTM Associates Inc. (Atlanta, Ga.) replies: "I started when I was nine years old by dismantling a telephone in my father's motel. I spent most of my formative years studying AT&T and the Bell System. It was a great hobby."

The claim sounds almost comical, but Massey, whom a client describes as a "class act with a style all his own," means it. Telecommunications is his love.

He began consulting 19 years ago when, as a junior at the Georgia Institute of Technology, he designed a telephone system for a local hospital. It led to other jobs and the formation of JTM Associates in 1970. "I have never done anything but consulting," says Massey.

He hired two partners five years ago, one for his business management skills, the other for his marketing expertise. "It's not that I pay the most," he says. "I wanted people for whom this is fun, who love it."

The 42-year-old Massey is one of the leading consultants to higher-education institutions and a member of AT&T's National Consultant's Council. Massey says he is a consultant on projects worth $40 million in equipment and services. He also is the object of lavish praise from his clients.

David Stubbs, telecommunications project manager for the Oregon State System of Higher Education, says that a $19 million telecommunications project to link eight state campuses could never have been done without Massey and his partners.

"We have an extremely clean procurement without any serious obstacles, and that is almost entirely because the consultant guided us through it in a very well organized and planned way," Stubbs says.

Cost of the network originally had been projected at $35 million to $40 million by in-house staff and a cabling consultant, Stubbs says. Not all of the lower price was due to JTM Associates, Stubbs adds, but "some part is. The RFP [request for proposal] was so clear and so well defined that it was like going down a list of do this or don't do this."

AT&T won as the low bidder, with eight System 85s with 28,000 telephone lines and equipped for Integrated Services Digital Network (ISDN). The network will integrate both voice and data. Local area networks, predominately on twisted-pair wiring, are included. AT&T beat Denver, Colo.-based U S West Inc. for the contract.

The style is definitely hands on, and the word that clients use to describe Massey is flamboyant. "He's a real character," says Frederick Wenzell, business administrator of the Marshfield Clinic (Marshfield, Wis.). "He would tell vendors it is not because you can't do it. It's because you won't do it. He cajoles, praises, pushes until they do it."

Massey points out that his organization is independent of any supplier. He was the consultant for the Fairfax Hospital System (Springfield, Va.), in which seven Northern Telecom Inc. SL1 switches, with one AT&T Dimension and one General Dynamics Focus PBX, were installed. Rolm and other equipment has been selected for other clients.

Robert Hager, director of management systems at Fairfax Hospital, says the holding company for nine medical facilities, saved almost $500,000 on a project that cost about $1.5 million by using JTM.

"They would not short the work under client pressure," Hager says. He explains that David Douglass, one of JTM's partners, insisted on the need for thorough training of hospital personnel in use of the telecommunications equipment, even though the hospital did not like having to incur the expense of taking personnel off working shifts to receive the training.

Much of JTM's work has been with schools and institutions in the South, but customers also turn up in show business. Ted O'Karma, director of communications for National Broadcasting Co. in Burbank, Calif., hired Massey on a recommendation from MCA Universal Studios.

O'Karma credits Massey with the successful installation of a System 85 PBX and says Massey's outgoing personality was an asset: "His down-home style with people fits. He does not come across as a pain in the ass the way some people in television do."

—*J. T. M.*

Others undoubtedly like the independence of the consultant, even if they have to work seven days a week to earn relatively modest amounts of money—typically $50,000 to $70,000—in the bargain. At the bigger consulting houses, the compensation is considerably more—$200,000 and up for principals. Some consultants, obviously, are between jobs.

Sizing up the market

Whatever motivates them and whatever individual consultants are paid, the industry is huge. Worldwide consulting revenues for the Big Eight in 1987 were $3.3 billion (see table). But that includes a lot more than just communications, or even just information technology, consulting.

Allan Kamman, director of telecommunications marketing for KPMG/Peat Marwick (Lexington, Mass.), guesses that communications consultants in the United States pull in $1 billion annually in fees. Coplin of Fluor Consulting says the Big Eight accounting firms and other major consultants may be taking in that much when software sales are included. He says that the Big Eight have been responsible for much of the demand for consultants by their heavy marketing efforts. Andersen will spend $10 million next year advertising its services. Other consultants cite divestiture, the shortage of skilled personnel, especially in designing and installing networks, the complexity of rapidly changing technology, and the emphasis on communications and information sharing as competitive tools.

Coplin says that when revenues to independents are added, total revenue for the industry goes well over $1 billion. That does not include construction costs, a strong point of Fluor's, which Coplin says can call on 140,000 persons—most of them construction workers but including professionals—around the world. Fluor has 170 communications consultants, he adds.

Peter Meade, editor of Communications Consultant, a magazine for the consulting industry, says no one really knows how many communications consultants there are. It is a highly fragmented business that is easy to get into, and it is not shrinking. Last year, Andersen had 9,600 consultants worldwide, most of them in information technology. It now has about 13,000 and plans to have 18,000 by 1991. About 200 of those 13,000 are dedicated to communications.

The rest of the Big Eight accounting firms are increasing their technology practices as fast or faster than Andersen, which claims to be the largest independent technology consulting business in the world.

Many of the accounting firms are forming alliances or buying other consultancies, as Peat Marwick did when it acquired Nolan and Norton (Boston), a firm that even competitor Coplin says is first rate. Ernst and Whinney last month bought Network Strategies (Fairfax, Va.), a telecommunications specialist.

Kamman says that Peat Marwick's communications consulting business is growing by 52 percent annually, and that a lot of it is coming from international customers. Peat Marwick has committed $1.1 million for a study of global networking needs that it will sell to major corporations for $50,000—$30,000 to early subscribers.

Rappaport says that Andersen's international business is growing faster than its domestic end. Domestic demand, he adds, is not slowing down but is a "mature" market. There is a greater shortage of technically skilled personnel overseers where new networks are just being built, Rappaport says.

The accounting firms, especially Arthur Andersen and Arthur Young & Co. (New York, N. Y.), have been rocked in the last year by defections and lawsuits involving dissatisfied consultants. Andersen earlier this year dismissed Gresham Brebach, its leading consultant in the United States, for allegedly trying to lure business away.

The company renamed and reshaped its consulting business reportedly to settle some of the unrest. Consultants feel they can make more when they are not wrapped up in the rules of traditionally bureaucratic accounting partnerships.

Arthur Young is suing five of its former consultants in Chicago, trying to prevent them from hiring former co-workers away from the firm. The former partners tried unsuccessfully to buy Arthur Young's midwestern consulting business for $50 million. They in turn are suing Arthur Young for trying to cripple their new business.

The business is certainly attracting a lot of players. Computer Sciences Corp. (El Segundo, Calif.) has purchased Index Group, a Cambridge, Mass.-based computer consultancy to speed its entry into the commercial systems integration market. Telephone companies have bought consulting firms, and Saatchi & Saatchi, the United Kingdom-based advertising company, has snapped up the Gartner Group (Stamford, Conn.), among others, on the way to building a $1 billion advisory business. Saatchi also is backing a new venture headed by Brebach and four of Andersen's former top consultants.

How to select a consultant

Where does all this movement and countermovement among the experts leave the user? What should a communications director or MIS manager do when selecting a consulting firm? Thatcher of TelCon Associates publishes a handy booklet called "How to select a telecommunications consultant" that lists six steps a client should follow. They are:

1. Articulate your concerns.
2. Narrow the field of consultants down by specialty, size of organization, the need for a big name to make recommendations that others must approve, and location.
3. Identify the candidates from reference materials.
4. Screen the ones who seem to fit the requirements.
5. Interview them, giving information about your company and obtaining information about theirs while sizing up their personalities.
6. Obtain a written proposal.

Users and consultants give similar advice in interviews. They stress the need for communications and the ability for a consultant to work easily in the customer's environment.

Neil Sachnoff, director of information services at Columbia University (New York, N. Y.), says that Tom Ashworth, a consultant from Jacobsen's firm, worked on the university's new $16 million network for almost four years. Not every consultant could have fit into a university scene, he adds, and Ashworth became more valuable the longer he stayed on the project.

A user should be precise in describing what the consultant is expected to produce. John Compitello, a vice president at Irving Bank (New York, N. Y.), says he usually requires a contract. He spells out specifically what is required and the exact number of billable hours anticipated, with full explanations of any overages. Some allowance obviously has to be made for unforeseen events.

Thatcher warns that too narrow a definition may often leave a project undone. That was one cause of Molex's billing problems, he says. The company had not asked its first consultant to do it, and he was content to walk away from a half-finished job. Mayfield at DMW warns that high-level strategic consulting generally does not work within precisely spelled out deadlines and objectives.

Control of the project must be kept in the customer's hands. That may seem obvious, but the New Jersey Commission of Investigation castigated state officials for turning control of the Motor Vehicle Division's new computer network over to Price Waterhouse. "A private party, Price Waterhouse, made the decisions on whether the state should take technological risks, and technically informed state representatives had little or no input," the commission said.

Compitello hired a consultant to supply telephone management software to run over a local area network because his own staff could not do it. Still, the bank kept the source code, just in case the consultant should "fade away."

Jody McCann, Wisconsin's telecommunications officer, says that several consultants were called in to plan its $45 million voice and data network, but the state staff was always involved in decisions. "You have to manage them and make sure they are doing their assignment," he says. McCann says he received reports at least weekly.

Clients should check references carefully to see if the company, and especially the consultant who will be assigned to the job, has experience doing the kind of work the project calls for.

Price Waterhouse, for instance, had never handled a project similar to the New Jersey Motor Vehicle Division's when it agreed to do the work. "Some of the Price Waterhouse staff on the DMV project were only recently hired and some had only limited experience on a large-scale implementation project," the state found later.

David Stubbs, director of telecommunications projects for the Oregon State System of Higher Education, says he had written into his contract with JTM Associates a requirement specifying exactly who would be on the job. Since JTM is a three-man shop, that was not too hard to do. Columbia University did not do that when it hired Jacobsen's firm, and it had no problems. But Sachnoff says a well-run consultantcy should know when its people will be available for different jobs. If it does not, he adds, that is cause for concern.

A client should not take the consulting firm's word for anything. Roberta White, director of telecommunications systems for National Broadcasting Company Inc. (New York, N. Y.) and a former consultant, says that the firm she once worked for always promised it could do anything. Now on the receiving end of consultant services, she says she would want references.

A customer should decide what qualifications his consultant should have and whether they match the price he is willing to pay. Hynes at Chase Manhattan Bank, for instance, says he prefers to use engineers from specialist firms for implementation projects to Big Eight consultants. "The Big Eight do not do implementation frequently, and their fees for certain types of work might be higher than you want to spend," he says. "For large projects," Hynes adds, "they [the Big Eight] bring better organizing and project management skills."

Working through the details

Coplin and Benedict Occhiogrosso at DVI Communications Inc. (New York, N. Y.) point out that, despite all the talk about technical specifications in the press, actual implementation skills are probably more crucial to a project.

Consultants like to say that a prime requirement of the job is to understand a client's business. The Big Eight

1987 consulting revenues for top accounting and management firms

	U.S.	WORLDWIDE	NUMBER OF CONSULTANTS*
ANDERSEN CONSULTING	$522 MILLION	$838 MILLION	9,639
COOPERS & LYBRAND	187 MILLION	381 MILLION	4,712
DELOITTE HASKINS & SELLS	91 MILLION	209 MILLION	N/A
ERNST & WHINNEY	228 MILLION	374 MILLION	3,255
KPMG/PEAT MARWICK	244 MILLION	438 MILION	4,700
PRICE WATERHOUSE	153 MILLION	345 MILLION	4,300
TOUCHE ROSS	157 MILLION	248 MILLION	2,142
ARTHUR YOUNG	111 MILLION	204 MILLION	N/A
GRANT THORNTON	25 MILLION	60 MILLION	N/A
BOOZE, ALLEN & HAMILTON	N/A	412 MILLION	2,075

*Total consultants in all fields.
Source: Consultants News (Fitzwilliam, N.H.) and Bowman's Accounting Report Atlanta, Ga.

particularly like to emphasize the depth and breadth of their consultants' skills.

It is true that a consultant should be familiar with a customer's operation, says Marie Dobson, president of Hilton Reservation Services (Dallas, Tex.), "but no one understands your business as well as you do."

Coplin agrees. "It is inane to think that someone can out-produce your own business plan," he says, adding: "A consultant can help people implement a vision or help them get something done on time."

If the consultant uses subcontractors, their qualifications—and their fees—should be made clear.

If it is important, the client should ask if the consultant carries "errors and omissions" insurance to cover any mistakes. Most consultants, it seems, do not. The policies are too expensive, they say. Some of the risk can be eliminated by passing responsibility for equipment and services on to suppliers, but any such warranty is probably going to add to the user's cost.

How consultant expenses are to be paid should be specified. That may seem obvious, but New Jersey's Motor Vehicle officials trusted Price Waterhouse completely in this matter, to their dismay. If the attorney general had not finally stepped in and ordered a halt, the DMV would have paid Price Waterhouse more than its contract called for. The firm charged the state for television sets it bought young programmers and for a $109 lunch for two partners in Manhattan, for example.

Stubbs says Oregon decided what "reasonable expenses" for its project would be and then included them in the project fee it agreed to in the contract with JTM. It was easier than trying to reconcile expenses, especially when the state sets limits and a consultant likes to fly first class, he says.

Robert Hager, director of management systems at Fairfax Hospital, says JTM Associates provided detailed reports that documented every trip—with receipts for all travel expenses, the hours of service, and what had been accomplished during those hours.

The relationship of consultants to vendors should be checked. Independents complain that the Big Eight use their consulting arm to hawk their software or software from vendors with whom they have relationships.

For example, Andersen and Telxon Corp. (Akron, Ohio) are comarketing Telxon's hand-held terminals and Andersen's software for manufacturing applications.

Many independents see potential conflicts between the auditing side of the Big Eight's business and their application of information technology as consultants. Auditors might be forced to overlook shortcomings in a software package or in computer installations that their firms' consultants implemented, critics say. That may have happened, but no cases could be corroborated for this article.

Some consultants do, however, sell their own software. Logica PLC, the British software house that bought an American financial software supplier last year, sells market research, software, and consulting services.

Xtend Communications gets almost one-third of its revenues from selling a telecommunications management package of its own. It is also an agent for reselling New York Telephone services. It is apparently the only consultant in the country with such an arrangement. Bill Schwartz, an Xtend vice president, says the relationships are fully disclosed to clients, but that the company may cease its membership in the Society of Telecommunications Consultants to eliminate any confusion.

The society, the industry's New York-based association, is hotly debating whether its members should be allowed to sell products.

Some consultants also invest in or are connected to companies, which is something clients may want to ask about and may consider important. Dixon Doll, president of DMW Inc., the parent of DMW Group, is a director of Network Equipment Technologies, for example.

Doll and two other members of his firm, Jim Swartz and Arthur Patersen, are also general partners in Accel Venture, a venture capital fund. Mayfield and Robert Follett, also a DMW partner, are special limited partners. The interests are not secret, and Mayfield says clients are told about them. The Yankee Group (Cambridge, Mass.) has had similar connections to venture capital funds that invest in communications companies.

Caveat emptor

A client's relationship with a consultant is a delicate one. It is built on personalities and the ability of different individuals to work together under what are often extremely trying circumstances. Consultants may have to work seven days a week in order to meet, say, a cut-over date.

Undoubtedly, the vast majority of consultants are dedicated, honest professionals who give their clients more than a full day's work for their dollar. Even though only a minority is incompetent, inexperienced, poorly supervised, or downright dishonest, it can do serious damage when the demand for equipment and services is so huge.

The relationship is basically a business one and should be handled as such. After all, the client's, not the consultant's, operations are at risk. ■

Industry Watch

Leasing becomes a user's paradise

IBM, AT&T, and RBOCs help drive prices down in a tough market

Competition inevitably means lower prices and more services for the customer. In computer- and communications-equipment-related leasing, the struggle to lock in users is driving some weaker leasing companies to the wall and forcing them into bankruptcy or mergers.

For an insight into how tough the leasing business is becoming, consider the experience of Roy Adams, who is director of data processing for Wilson Sporting Goods in River Grove, Ill. Adams recently decided to ask computer leasing companies for prices on an upgrade of Wilson's IBM 4381 mainframe and costs to replace other older processors with an IBM 9370. He used a tactic that had mixed success in the past.

Adams called in his IBM representative and asked him to get a bid from Stamford, Conn—based IBM Credit Corp. (ICC), the leasing arm of the computer giant.

In the past, Adams would take the number ICC came up with and use it to start negotiations with other companies that also lease IBM gear.

With the independent lessors' numbers in hand, he would then go back to IBM to wheedle a better price out of ICC. Years ago even the IBM rep had a hard time getting a follow-up bid from ICC, recalls Adams. So the third-party lessors got much of Wilson's business.

■ **New ICC.** This time it was different. ICC responded with such an aggressive package that it aced the competition and landed the $3 million-plus deal. Not only were ICC's lease rates for the 9370 the cheapest available, it was also willing to take risks that other lessors avoided—such as upgrading Wilson's older 4381/P2 model to a new 4381/T92 and giving Wilson the right to terminate the lease on the 4381 without penalty when the 4391 mainframe that will replace it is released sometime in 1991.

On top of that, ICC threw in some additional inducements that Adams does not want to discuss, but which apparently included free or discounted servicing and, perhaps, even free software.

Whatever the factors behind ICC's competitive spirit, Adams offers a common explanation of why he favors leasing over purchase.

Leasing eliminates the risk of obsolescence and the financial risk of owning unwanted equipment. Many lessors will allow a customer to end a lease ahead of schedule without penalty if the customer upgrades his equipment.

"The most significant advantage," Adams stresses, "is that I avoid getting caught by changes in technology. I am responsible for providing data processing services for Wilson. What would I do with equipment that I purchased if I needed more capacity or if the technology changes?

"I am not an equipment broker and I don't know what the equipment's value would be," continues Adams. "I don't want to have to remarket it. And I don't want to have to go to my management a few years after buying something and tell them that I want to get rid of it."

Adam's experience illustrates some of the benefits that users can get from the fierce competition that has the leasing industry in a tumult (see "Tax breaks for leasing").

■ **RBOCs too.** Causing a fair share of this commotion, leasing industry executives say, are ICC and other finance arms of major corporations. Included are AT&T Credit Corp. (Morristown, N.J.), and Dataserve Inc. (Hopkins, Minn.), an arm of BellSouth Corp. (Atlanta). AT&T Credit has purchased one leasing company and is close to buying another. Bell Atlantic has purchased four leasing companies since divestiture in 1984.

Harvey Kinzelberg, chairman of the Meridian Group (Deerfield, Ill.), is especially critical of the RBOC's leasing subsidiaries and says that many lessors have been "stupid" in their pricing. Adams, at Wilson, which does business with Meridian, says Meridian has become very conservative recently and backed away from the deal that ICC won.

Bell Atlantic Financial Services executives deny they are buying market share with excessively low lease rates. Indeed, some leasing executives claim that the company has pulled back recently in biddings.

Guy Arvia is senior vice president of Forsythe & McArthur Associates (Skokie, Ill.), a lessor that lost out on the Wilson deal to IBM. Arvia says that he knows of cases where IBM has given free software and system personnel support to win deals. Concessions are beyond normal volume discounts, he contends.

Jack Durliat, president of Capital

Industry Watch

Tax breaks for leasing

The benefits of leasing can often transcend technology. With a lease, of course, a corporation does not sink its money into a piece of equipment for years. If a company borrows to buy equipment, it must list the purchase as an asset and the debt as a liability.

With an operating lease, there is no debt or asset listed since the customer does not own the goods. Thus, a company's debt-to-equity ratio looks better, making it easier to borrow funds.

Moreover, the managers' bonuses are often tied to returns on assets, which will look better if there are not a lot of assets on the books.

Leases can be tailored to departmental or overall budget needs. A department within a company may need a piece of equipment immediately but not have funds available to begin payments on the lease until a new fiscal year begins.

Some lessors will install the equipment and delay payments until the new budget year begins. Lessors will also offer short-term leases so a customer can test a piece of equipment.

■ **Other taxes.** New incentives for leasing were created by the Tax Reform Act of 1986, which mandated a new Alternative Minimum Tax (AMT) for corporations that pay little or no taxes. Under the new tax code a business whose federal income taxes were reduced by heavy depreciation expenses could be subject to AMT because depreciation credits became taxable items. One way to avoid the levies is to lease rather than buy gear.

There are some disadvantages, of course. With operating leases the lessee is not able to take depreciation charges that could reduce a tax bite. A leasing company can go bankrupt, as Continental Informations Systems Inc. (Syracuse, N.Y.) did in February. That opens a can of worms, an industry spokesman pointed out, about the mutual responsibilities of lessee and lessor.

Leases can also be "hell-or-highwater" obligations, which means exactly what it sounds like. The lessee has to pay the monthly charge for the entire term of the lease—no matter what happens to the equipment. Damages to equipment are covered by insurance, of course, but with this type of lease the customer must pay for the equipment even if his operations change and he wants to change the gear.

Timeplex Inc. (Woodcliff Lake, N.J.) for instance will lease its products to customers only on a hell-or-high-water basis.

■ **Selling paper.** Leases are often sold to other financial institutions or to private investors by equipment suppliers or leasing companies. Users obviously should know who is responsible for servicing equipment that they have leased.

Tax credits used to be an attraction of both buying and leasing, but what the government gives the government can tax back. Business relearned that sorrowful lesson in 1986 when the revised tax code eliminated the 10 percent investment tax credit that used to go with new equipment purchases and with capital leases, sometimes called a finance lease, which in effect is a purchase of equipment.

Some corporations needed that 10 percent credit and kept it to reduce their federal taxes. Others whose tax bills were not so pressing did not need the ITC and gave it back to the lessor who in turn lowered the monthly lease charge. Congress eliminated the credit because of widespread trafficking in ITCs by tax-dodging corporations.

■ **No breaks.** Excising the ITC from the tax code was supposed to increase lease rates. If lessors could not take back the credit from the customer, they theoretically would have to raise their rates.

That has not happened, however, and the experience of Roy Adams, at Wilson Sporting Goods, with ICC is one example of why. The leasing arms of large corporations such as ICC, AT&T Credit, and the regional Bell operating companies, especially Bell Atlantic Financial Services and other lessors, have been very aggressive in their pricing. —J.T.M.

Associates, Inc. (Colorado Springs, Colo.), says ICC tends to get very competitive toward the end of financial quarters in which IBM sales have been slow in order to help IBM move product. An ICC spokesman says the company is competitive in pricing but disputes Durliat's statement.

Ken Bouldin, president of the Computer Dealers & Lessors Association (Washington, D.C.), says that ICC is quoting prices 10 percent below what the market would require. ICC has become so competitive in the leasing of used equipment that it is driving CDLA members out of the business of leasing IBM gear, he contends. Bouldin claims that IBM is also restricting users' and lessors' ability to change microcode, which limits remarketing of IBM equipment.

IBM denies that the limitations on changing microcode seriously affect lessors.

ICC is making excessively high estimates of the residual values of 4300 and higher series processors, 3080X equipment and 3380 disk drives, Bouldin claims.

(Residual value is what the lessor thinks he can sell the equipment for when it comes off lease. The higher the value, the lower the lease payments. ICC had to take a $25 million writedown largely on storage devices in 1988's fourth quarter, apparently because it overestimated the gear's residual values.)

When that willingness to risk higher residual value is added to ICC's ability to borrow at the lowest rates possible because of IBM's AAA credit rating, it is not surprising that ICC can offer the cheapest lease rates possible.

■ **Kudos for AT&T.** Whatever ICC's

Industry Watch

alleged sins, IBM did not get a chance to use the tactics that worked so well with Wilson with Red Devil Inc. (Union, N.J.), which is replacing an IBM 4361 processor.

Instead of staying with IBM, Red Devil MIS director John Coff opted to lease three 3B2 minicomputers from AT&T Credit, which is also financing an installment purchase of relational database management and applications software. Coff can buy the software for the minis in four years for $1. A leased 10-Mbit/s StarLAN to tie the CPUs together may be installed later this year.

"That company [Red Devil] has a history of buying equipment," Coff says. "Some of this equipment has been around here from the 1970s. I don't want to have to keep that stuff that long."

Coff says that while AT&T's Credit's lease terms might have been a "couple of tenths of a percent" cheaper than the competition, that was not the only reason he chose AT&T. He also leaned toward AT&T because he wanted a mini that runs Unix application as does the 3B2. He also wanted the ability to upgrade to newer equipment without penalty, and he wanted to deal with only one vendor. IBM had simply "dropped the ball" by ignoring the account, he adds.

Compounding this competition among lessors has been the slowdown in the computer industry, forcing more lessors to chase a limited number of deals. To pick up a portion of the slack, some lessors have tried branching out in telecommunications, but that market has not grown as rapidly as expected, says Durliat.

The most commonly leased data communications equipment are PBXs, modems, satellites, and very small aperture terminals. There is almost no third-party leasing of T1, packet-switching, or statistical multiplexing equipment (see figure).

This is largely because these are relatively new types of products, with a small installed base compared to PBXs. Communications equipment tends to stay on lease longer than computers so there are not as many newer data communications products available for the secondary markets. Some of the lack of interest also has to do with lessors' unfamiliarity with equipment and the difficulty of predicting its residual value.

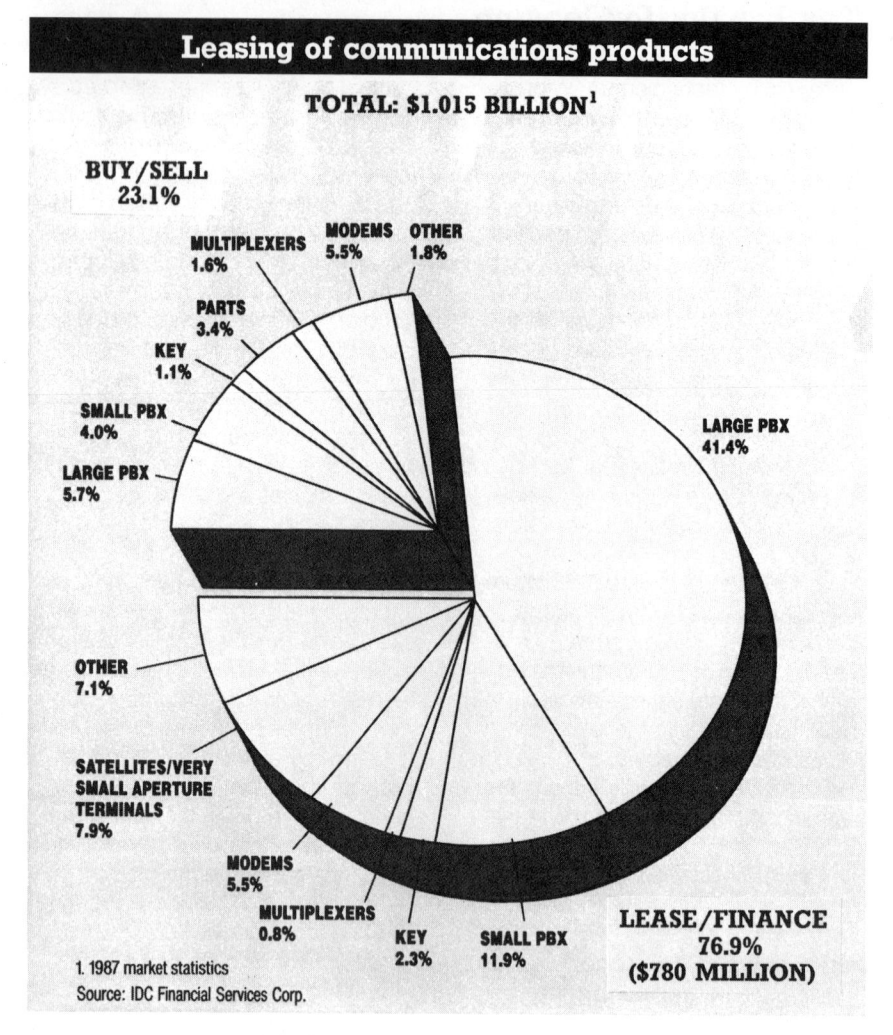

But independent lessors are also reluctant to handle data communications equipment because, some lessors say, manufacturers do not support the aftermarket.

Tom Donovan is director in investment banking services for Technology Investment Corp., a division of IDC Financial Service Corp. (Framingham, Mass.). Donovan says that NCR Corp. charges $25,000 to reconfigure its front-end processors when they come off lease. That kills any third-party leasing market for that product.

Big lessors seem to shy away from LANs because they are such commodity products and so tailored to individual customers. On the other hand, distributors such as Leasemetric Data Communications Inc. (Foster City, Calif.) will lease or rent LAN hardware.

George Newman, manager of leasing planning services for IDC Financial Services Corp., says with the advent of T3 multiplexing, T1 multiplexers might work their way onto the secondary market for installation in remote sites before users and lessors place them in headquarters sites. "That's the way it works in this business," Newman says.

Competition in leasing communications gear is also tough, and AT&T Credit is obviously a major player.

■ **Good interest.** Scallion Controls (Beaumont, Tex.) last February leased from AT&T Credit a System 25 PBX

Leasing of communications products

TOTAL: $1.015 BILLION[1]

- BUY/SELL 23.1%
  - MULTIPLEXERS 1.6%
  - MODEMS 5.5%
  - OTHER 1.8%
  - PARTS 3.4%
  - KEY 1.1%
  - SMALL PBX 4.0%
  - LARGE PBX 5.7%
- LEASE/FINANCE 76.9% ($780 MILLION)
  - LARGE PBX 41.4%
  - OTHER 7.1%
  - SATELLITES/VERY SMALL APERTURE TERMINALS 7.9%
  - MODEMS 5.5%
  - MULTIPLEXERS 0.8%
  - KEY 2.3%
  - SMALL PBX 11.9%

1. 1987 market statistics
Source: IDC Financial Services Corp.

Industry Watch

with voice mail and other features. "It was an awfully good interest rate—close to zero, maybe 1 or 2 percent," says Scallion President Glen Nieman.

The System 25 replaced a 10-year-old key telephone. Scallion put the System 25 on a three-year operating lease because it can recoup the cost faster than it could by buying it and depreciating the gear over the normal five years, Nieman says.

Florida National Banks (Jacksonville) leased System 85 PBXs and cluster controllers from AT&T Credit because AT&T was able to give a better rate than the bank could have earned by lending the money out, says Dale Quigg, senior vice president of central services at Florida National.

"It was probably a full basis point [one hundredth of one percent] better", says Quigg. But in another case, he adds, AT&T lost out to the leasing arm of Pitney-Bowes Inc. (Stamford, Conn,) for another System 85 lease. Pitney-Bowes undercut AT&T's offer by a quarter of a basis point.

Quigg disputes independents who contend that captive lessors such as AT&T Credit are rigid in their policies. AT&T Credit "was refreshingly flexible and upfront," he says. "Major organizations understand other major organizations better than little guys." He deals only with the likes of Pitney-Bowes or AT&T. Florida National Bank was affected by the Alternative Minimum Tax, which was one reason for putting some of the System 75s and 85s it uses on leases, he says.

If a customer has trouble leasing data communications from third-party lessors, some of the smaller equipment vendors may offer the service.

■ **Other players.** General DataComm Inc. (Middlebury, Conn.), for instance, established DataComm Leasing Corp. in 1979. Around 20 percent of GDC's sales are put on leases through DataComm Leasing, says Vice President Dennis Nessler. GDC sells off financial interests in about 35 percent of its leases to nonbanking financial institutions. But GDC retains ownership of the equipment, which it services and eventually remarkets for the investors in the leases for a fee.

DataComm Leasing will allow customers to cancel leases on any anniversary date without penalty: otherwise the customer pays a percent of the lease fees left to terminate a lease.

Jeff Seiloff, senior product manager at Codex, Inc. (Canton, Mass.), says that about 40 percent of that company's domestic sales have been leases, but that percentage has been falling, probably a reflection of the slowdown in modem sales.

Infotron Systems Inc. (Cherry Hill, N.J.) attempts to put at least 10 percent of its domestic sales on leases, says Mike Weiner, finance manager for the company. Last year the rate rose to about 14 percent because more networks were sold, he says.

Infotron administers all the leases itself, but last year sold a long-term contract worth more than $1 million with a federal agency. The agency mandated that the lease be renewed annually because it could only get annual funding. Infotron still services the equipment, but the lease contract was sold to a bank.

■ **Reselling is tough.** Weiner says that Infotron also remarkets equipment that comes off lease, but it is considering looking for another way of doing that. It uses historical precedent to determine residual values.

"Remarketing can be very tough for Timeplex to be involved in," says Ted Thayer, the Woodcliff Lake, N.J., firm's assistant vice president for business policy management. "Systems are uniquely configured for a customer's requirements and the probability of finding a user who needs that same configuration is probably zero."

While Timeplex has written leases for 10 years, it has not pushed them and they involve only 5 percent of sales, Thayer says. He adds that Comdisco Inc. (Rosemont, Ill.), Chrysler Capital Corp. (Stamford, Conn.), and other leasing operations have written leases on some Timeplex sales.

Thayer says because of growing customer interest in leasing, Timeplex may create this summer a financing arm called Timeplex Finance Corp. It would use the computer facilities and borrowing power of Unisys Corp. (Blue Bell, Pa.) to reduce the financial and administrative costs of running a leasing business, he says. Timeplex has sold some leases to Unisys Credit.

—*John T. Mulqueen*

Nathan J. Muller, Special to DATA COMMUNICATIONS

Minimize risk: Pick the right product—plus the right vendor

Product reliability is important, of course, but so is the stability of the vendor. Here are seven points to consider while shopping.

New pitfalls—ranging from dubious business practices to standards noncompliance—have combined to magnify the potential risk to today's equipment buyer in the data communications industry.

No matter how impressive a vendor's financial statements look, it's not uncommon today for companies to inadvertently buy nonexistent products, to find themselves boxed into proprietary technologies, or to discover they are stranded without ongoing vendor support. Business conditions are changing, and this is throwing new variables into the already complicated purchase-decision equation. A few examples follow:

■ The deregulated communications industry, which is now crowded with start-up companies that are compelled to compete on price to break into high-end markets (see Table, part a).

■ The emergence of small, aggressive start-up companies that are funded by equally aggressive venture-capital firms whose overriding concern is to bail out of the toddler company with windfall profits within three to five years (see Table, part b).

■ The so-called yuppie philosophy, which is becoming much admired among young sales and marketing professionals. In their quest for instant wealth and recognition, the yuppies see nothing wrong with promoting the reliability and performance of products that are still in the design stage.

■ The ease with which bankruptcy statutes can be invoked by financially strapped vendors to protect themselves from creditors—and customers who have put up money to ensure timely customization or product delivery.

Communications managers who recommend, specify, or approve product purchases cannot afford to ignore the potentially harmful impact these variables can have on their networks, organization, or career. It takes more time and is becoming more difficult to reconcile the differing claims of vendors. Technological innovations, rapid product obsolescence, and the ever-increasing number of suppliers not only make easy comparisons impossible, but also increase the chance that an unwary buyer will make the wrong decision.

The ripple effect throughout the organization of the wrong purchasing decision is sobering to contemplate. In addition to risking the loss of capital, taking the time and effort to remedy adverse situations diverts valuable human resources from other productive pursuits. Beyond that, degraded network performance may be severe enough to jeopardize the company's competitive position.

An uninformed purchasing decision can create an irreversible credibility gap that may limit a manager's advancement opportunities. And if the mistake is serious enough, it can cost a network manager his job.

Recognizing these risks, many network managers require credit references before they will consider proposals from vendors. This "snapshot" approach may or may not be effective in identifying and disqualifying undercapitalized firms. But creditworthiness does not, by itself, indicate a vendor's organizational stability, nor can it be used to determine the reliability of a company's products.

A vendor with a promising but unproven product can make itself look good on paper. For example, loans may be secured against order backlog instead of capital assets. This might lead the unwary customer to conclude that the vendor is solidly "in the black." At the other end of the spectrum is the vendor that is genuinely cash rich, but product deficient.

A systematic evaluation of a vendor's organizational structure, operating philosophy, and performance record in a variety of categories will improve the quality of purchase decisions. The following seven-point plan is offered as the core for such a risk-avoidance strategy. Also offered is a decision-making model highlighting the risk avoidance strategy that network managers can use during the overall decision-making process (see chart).

Product development

Probing the vendor's research and development efforts helps to determine its track record. How well has it translated research and innovative thinking into production prototypes, then into finished, marketable goods? Look for a formal, budgeted program with dedicated staff. Without it, there will be no basis for predicting the product's long-term reliability or for being reasonably assured that enhancements will be developed to extend the useful life of an investment.

To validate vendor claims of offering "innovative" products, find out what unique features the product development group is responsible for. Inquire about the performance record of products already deployed in networks similar to yours. If the product has undergone design changes since its introduction, find out how many changes were made and the vendor's rationale for each change. The answers may help you determine product quality, levels of customer satisfaction, and the vendor's responsiveness to changing customer requirements.

To determine the vendor's commitment to the product, check its research and development budget, as well as the percentage of product development costs relative to annual revenues. Make sure the staffing level for the product is adequate to accomplish its objectives within a reasonable time. Determine what kind of enhancements are planned or are being developed, their time frames for release, how they will be offered to customers when they become available, and at what cost.

Find out to what extent future enhancements will affect the product's basic design. For example, will the enhancement require factory modification of the existing product, or will it be accomplished on the customer's premises with a replacement of chips, boards, or software? The answers may reveal the extent to which the vendor has examined the life cycle and growth path of its products.

Determine how effective the vendor is in planning new products and enhancements by checking into the number of completed-versus-canceled projects. If the vendor's record of canceled projects strikes you as high, it may indicate that money is being thrown at projects to establish instant market position. If so, keep in mind that this strategy is very risky, even for an industry giant.

Compare the vendor's present product-development budget with budgets of previous years. If the current budget is significantly lower than past budgets, find out the reason. If the vendor has recently instituted layoffs and other cost-cutting measures, find out to what extent product development is affected. You must walk away convinced that the vendor is not shortchanging long-term development efforts in the hope of improving short-term revenues. If this appears to be the case, the enhancements promised at the time of purchase or the level of technical support required in the future may not be forthcoming.

Another way to check the vendor's record in product planning is to compare product announcement dates with their release dates. Ask for an explanation of discrepancies. Such questions may uncover serious problems. Some red flags include software problems, personnel turnover, and budget cuts.

A vendor's product development plans can be evaluated during a discussion of what the product will look like in two to three years: the levels of functional control it will have, what features it will provide, and what technology might be used to achieve design goals. Details may be viewed as proprietary, of course, but a general idea of the vendor's plans, if any, can be gleaned.

Find out if the vendor is taking advantage of any new components in its prototypes. If so, it indicates that the product may be endowed with operating efficiencies that could substantially improve the price/performance ratio of the existing line. But be on the alert if the vendor is "sole-sourcing" critical components to leapfrog the competition. To minimize risk, check into the availability of production quantities of these components to ensure that delivery will not be delayed by their initial scarcity. For some components, it may take six months or more for the vendor's supplier to fulfill pent-up demand. Of course, the vendor can get around critical component shortages by engineering around them and using parts that are available. The disadvantage of doing this is that the price/performance ratio of the product may suffer.

Also, ensure that the vendor's product development effort includes compliance with industry standards. Avoid one-of-a-kind products that are not compatible with the offerings of other manufacturers. Letting a single vendor's technology overshadow compliance with industry standards may require investing more time and money later just to get the network operating as smoothly as before. However, regaining lost credibility among top management may not be quite so simple.

Beta test arrangement aside, steer clear of start-up companies using proprietary technology. Over the years, relatively few entrepreneurs have been lucky enough to achieve success with proprietary technology—mostly with such products as T1 multiplexers and modems where, until recently, features and performance were more highly valued than standards. But implementing a proprietary local area network (LAN) operating system, for example, may be unwise if only because the industry is rapidly coalescing around standards that promise greater connectivity among competing devices.

The International Consultative Committee for Telephone and Telegraph (CCITT) has established standards to ensure the compatibility of like devices. Choosing modems, for example, without regard for standards could result in the accumulation of devices that can't communicate with each other on the same network.

Of course, for every rule there's an exception. In the area of engineering workstations, for example, some companies that once touted their adherence to standards are becoming spectacularly successful by deviating from the norm.

Typical start-up company

A. NO VENTURE-CAPITAL FINANCING

PRODUCT DEVELOPMENT	TECHNICALLY ORIENTED FOUNDER(S) FINALIZING PROTOTYPE OF THE FIRST PRODUCT. DISORGANIZED ADMINISTRATIVELY, BUT ENTIRELY PRODUCT FOCUSED. ONE OR TWO OTHER PRODUCTS ARE IN THE DISCUSSION STAGE. SELF-FINANCED AT THE START; LIMITED BANK CREDIT; OVERLY OPTIMISTIC ABOUT MARKET DEMAND AND REVENUE PROJECTIONS. WILL PROBABLY NEED INFUSION OF CAPITAL TO FINISH DEVELOPMENT, MARKET THE PRODUCT, AND START PRODUCTION.
INTEGRATION SERVICES	FOUNDER(S) INSTALL THE PRODUCT TO SUIT CUSTOMER'S APPLICATION AND CONFIGURATION. THEY WILL WORK CLOSELY WITH SMALL NUMBER OF KEY CUSTOMERS WHO WILL "TRIAL" THE PRODUCT AND PROVIDE FEEDBACK FOR POSSIBLE DESIGN MODIFICATIONS. OTHERWISE, NO DEDICATED FIELD SERVICE STAFF.
QUALITY CONTROL	QUALITY CONTROL PROCEDURES EVOLVE WITH THE PRODUCT, MOSTLY THROUGH TRIAL AND ERROR.
CUSTOMER SUPPORT	FOUNDER(S) INTERFACE WITH KEY CUSTOMERS TO MONITOR PRODUCT PERFORMANCE AND TO PROVIDE ADVICE ON FEATURE IMPLEMENTATION.
DOCUMENTATION	LITTLE OR NO DOCUMENTATION AVAILABLE; FOUNDER(S) WILL "HAND HOLD" CUSTOMERS UNTIL THEY CAN AFFORD TO DEVELOP DOCUMENTATION.
SCOPE OF BUSINESS	SINGLE-PRODUCT ORIENTED UNTIL SALES REVENUES JUSTIFY THE DEVELOPMENT OF NEW PRODUCTS.
ESCROW ACCOUNTS	FOUNDER(S) MAY BE PERSUADED TO OPEN AN ESCROW ACCOUNT IF IT WILL RESULT IN A SIZABLE SALE; OTHERWISE WILL RESIST THE CONCEPT AS NOT WORTH BOTHERING WITH.
RISK FACTOR	**VERY HIGH**

B. WITH VENTURE-CAPITAL FINANCING

PRODUCT DEVELOPMENT	TECHNICALLY ORIENTED FOUNDER(S) FINALIZING PROTOTYPE OF THE FIRST PRODUCT, BUT RUN OUT OF CAPITAL AND CREDIT TO BRING IT TO MARKET. FIRST-ROUND VENTURE-CAPITAL FINANCING PROVIDES INFUSION OF CAPITAL TO FINISH DEVELOPMENT, MARKET THE PRODUCT, AND START PRODUCTION. FOUNDER(S) MAY HAVE TO GIVE UP MAJORITY STAKE IN THEIR COMPANY AND ACCEPT PROFESSIONAL MANAGEMENT TO OVERSEE OPERATIONS. THIS MAY BECOME A SOURCE OF DISILLUSIONMENT ON THE PART OF THE FOUNDER(S).
INTEGRATION SERVICES	UNDER SUPERVISION OF THE FOUNDER(S), NEW EMPLOYEES ASSUME RESPONSIBILITY FOR INSTALLING THE PRODUCT TO SUIT CUSTOMER'S APPLICATION AND CONFIGURATION.
QUALITY CONTROL	QUALITY CONTROL PROCEDURES THAT HAVE EVOLVED WITH THE PRODUCT ARE REFINED BY PROFESSIONAL MANAGEMENT BROUGHT INTO THE COMPANY BY THE VENTURE-CAPITAL FIRM.
CUSTOMER SUPPORT	EXPERIENCED TECHNICAL HELP REPLACES THE FOUNDER(S) AS THE PRINCIPAL POINT OF CONTACT FOR CUSTOMERS EXPERIENCING PROBLEMS.
DOCUMENTATION	CRUDE DOCUMENTATION IS PUT TOGETHER TO SATISFY CUSTOMERS UNTIL THE COMPREHENSIVE REFERENCE PACKAGE IS READY FOR RELEASE.
SCOPE OF BUSINESS	FIRST PRODUCT INTO PRODUCTION; SECOND PRODUCT IN PROTOTYPE; THIRD PRODUCT IN THE DESIGN STAGE.
ESCROW ACCOUNTS	COMPANY IS OPEN TO THE CONCEPT OF ESCROW ACCOUNTS.
RISK FACTOR	**HIGH**

Companies like Apollo Computer Inc. (Chelmsford, Mass.) and Hewlett-Packard Co. (Palo Alto, Calif.) are building their products around proprietary RISC (Reduced Instruction Set Computer) architectures. Right now, the features of these products count more than standards or even the ability to port software across incompatible RISC architectures. Currently, the only way to minimize the risk associated with such products is to buy from an established company until the standards issue sorts itself out. If current trends continue, the products of one or two companies capturing the greatest market share in the shortest time will become de facto standards, similar to the way Netware, from Novell Inc. (Provo, Utah), became a de facto standard for LAN operating systems.

Integration services
Because of the technical sophistication of today's product offerings, the vendor usually must help integrate the product into the customer's network. In this regard, don't rely on vague statements in the vendor's proposal or accept a sales representative's verbal assurances that the vendor will provide this kind of support after the sale. All vendor promises should be spelled out on paper, including a "weasel" clause that gets you out of the contract with no penalty if the vendor cannot deliver the product on time or make it work on the network at an agreed upon performance level by the cutover date. Whenever possible, pay only a fraction of the product's price in advance—your objective is to provide the vendor with maximum incentive to finish the job. If you must pay 20 percent or more to ensure timely delivery, insist on a clause that penalizes the vendor for missing the cutover date. The penalty may consist of discounting the outstanding balance 1 or 2 percent for every week that cutover is delayed.

Specify penalties for delays, even when dealing with the most reputable vendor who has been servicing your company for years—as protection against potentially disruptive corporate mergers, hostile takeovers, or industry shakeouts.

Unnecessary risk can be averted by talking directly with the vendor's operations staff to get an accurate picture of what can and can't be done within a specified period. The marketing staff is not always up to date on the schedules of the operations people, the whereabouts of technical crews, or what is actually involved in a product's installation. Yet, the accuracy of such information is very important, especially during a major network upgrade that involves multiple carriers and vendors. The failure of a hardware vendor to deliver channel banks on time, for instance, can have a ripple effect on the cutover schedules of T1 circuits, which may entail penalties being imposed by the carrier. The last thing you want to hear later from the hardware vendor is: "Sorry, our salesperson wasn't authorized to offer that delivery date."

The problem of integrating products with an existing network is especially pronounced when dealing with vendors who have only suddenly realized the marketing wisdom of selling "connectivity" rather than proprietary products. Whether mere marketing savvy or a genuine reversal in operating philosophy, the connectivity orientation brings with it new responsibilities that the vendor must be able to handle. LAN vendors, for example, must extend service and support to an entirely new level because there are now more products that must be pulled together, each with its own communications protocol, some of which may be steeped in vendor secrecy. When dealing with a vendor who offers "connectivity solutions," thoroughly explore its track record to separate reality from marketing hype.

Don't forget to check on the availability of local support. The shrinking demand for some products has forced many companies to pull back local field service staff into larger regional centers. If the price includes local support with a response time of one or two hours, make sure that the purchase agreement includes a rebate if the vendor decides later to centralize support operations and prolong response times to three or four hours.

A program of quality control is generally a good indicator that the product is as reliable as the vendor says it is. A good quality control program includes multiple inspections, starting with the receipt of batch components and other raw materials at the receiving dock. While touring the vendor's manufacturing facilities, look for several inspection points at various stages of the assembly process, including automated testing stations and visual inspections by operators.

How much testing is enough? The answer depends on the product and its intended application. If the item is a plug-on option module that inserts into a product's motherboard and is designed for on-site replacement and disposal after being diagnosed as faulty, simple economics dictates that a final functional test is all that is required. However, if the product is a digital cross-connect, a final functional test is woefully inadequate. In this case, multi-level testing is required—the more, the better. It's much easier and less costly for the manufacturer to test during the assembly than to continually rip apart finished products to identify and correct problems. But in the face of order backlogs, even the largest companies may not be able to resist the temptation to skimp on testing to keep up production levels. In such cases, delivering the product on time to avoid penalties may take piority over final testing.

In questioning plant personnel, don't be surprised to discover printed circuit board failure rates as high as 25 percent or more. There may be a variety of reasons for this, such as shorts due to solder splashes, or mistakes in the placement of oversized components that do not lend themselves to automatic insertion. High failure rates may also be attributable to the vendor purchasing components in bulk quantities that have undergone little or no testing by the manufacturer. Such components may be purchased at a substantial discount. If this is the case, make sure the vendor uses automated tests and multiple inspections to ensure proper performance of all board components. Further, make sure that all boards are tested at the finished-product level. With high failure rates, statistical sampling methods at this juncture should be viewed as unacceptable.

When considering the purchase of new products with no

The role of risk avoidance in the purchasing process

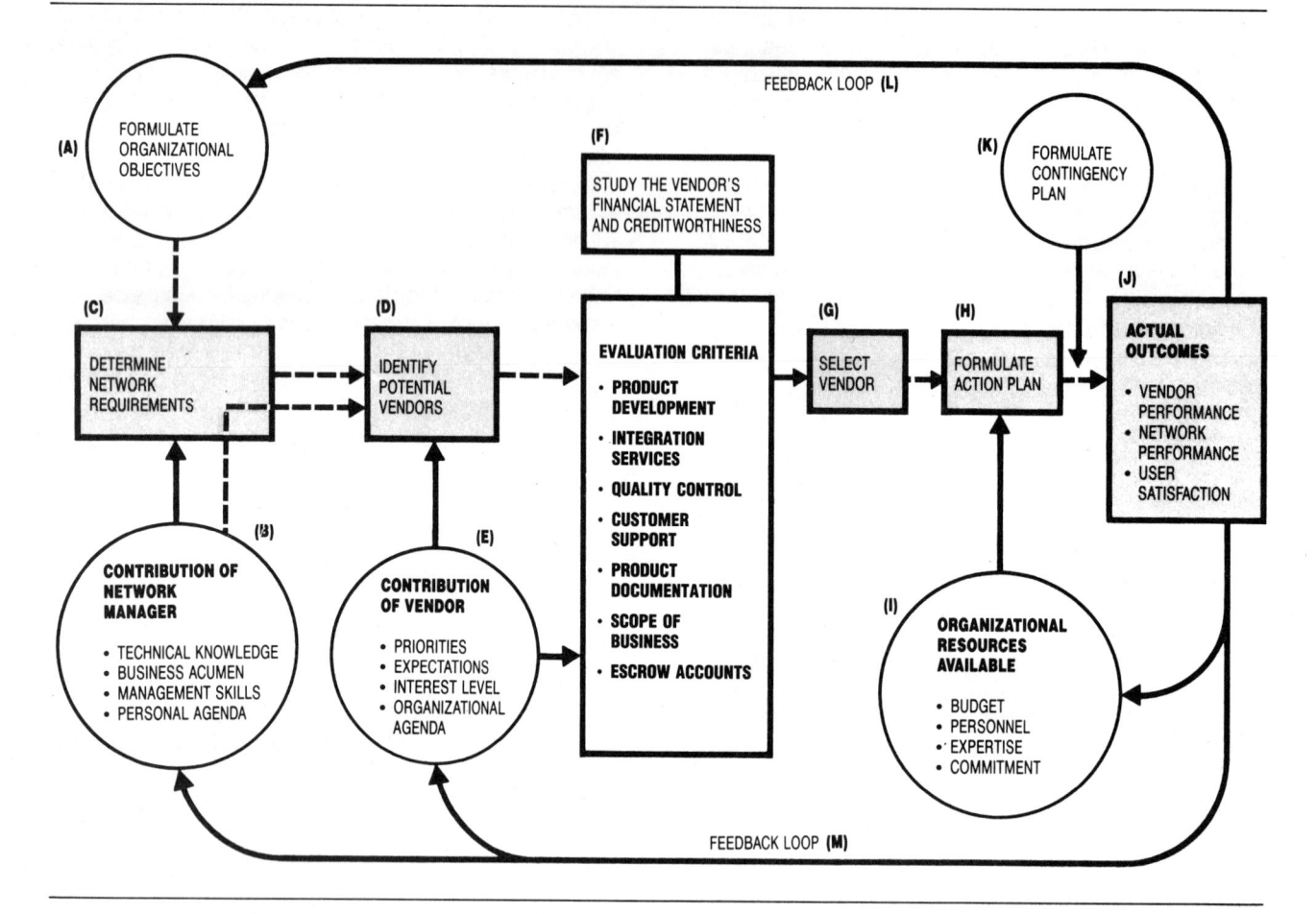

(A) FORMULATE ORGANIZATIONAL OBJECTIVES

(C) DETERMINE NETWORK REQUIREMENTS

(D) IDENTIFY POTENTIAL VENDORS

(F) STUDY THE VENDOR'S FINANCIAL STATEMENT AND CREDITWORTHINESS

(G) SELECT VENDOR

(H) FORMULATE ACTION PLAN

(K) FORMULATE CONTINGENCY PLAN

(J) ACTUAL OUTCOMES
- VENDOR PERFORMANCE
- NETWORK PERFORMANCE
- USER SATISFACTION

(B) CONTRIBUTION OF NETWORK MANAGER
- TECHNICAL KNOWLEDGE
- BUSINESS ACUMEN
- MANAGEMENT SKILLS
- PERSONAL AGENDA

(E) CONTRIBUTION OF VENDOR
- PRIORITIES
- EXPECTATIONS
- INTEREST LEVEL
- ORGANIZATIONAL AGENDA

Evaluation criteria:
- PRODUCT DEVELOPMENT
- INTEGRATION SERVICES
- QUALITY CONTROL
- CUSTOMER SUPPORT
- PRODUCT DOCUMENTATION
- SCOPE OF BUSINESS
- ESCROW ACCOUNTS

(I) ORGANIZATIONAL RESOURCES AVAILABLE
- BUDGET
- PERSONNEL
- EXPERTISE
- COMMITMENT

FEEDBACK LOOP **(L)**

FEEDBACK LOOP **(M)**

---

performance history, obtain the location and key contact of the beta site. Make sure the results of those tests come from a customer site and not the vendor's own laboratory. Find out what benchmark tests are being used and why they were chosen.

When a variety of benchmarks are available, you must ensure that you are basing your purchase decision on the right one for your application. Bigger computers, such as the VAX 11/780, from Digital Equipment Corp. (Maynard, Mass.), or the Sun 4/260, from Sun Microsystems Inc. (Mountain View, Calif.), measure raw CPU power in terms of millions of instructions per second (MIPS). With these or similar midrange computers, make sure the vendor is using commonly accepted benchmarks like the Dhrystone, Whetstone, and Linpack tests. If your MIS/data processing group uses high-level language C to develop its applications programs, for example, then you should find out how various midrange computers fare in the Dhrystone benchmark, which simulates the C programming environment. The Dhrystone benchmark contains 100 statements, of which 53 are assignments, 32 are control statements, and 15 are function calls. As it turns out, the Sun computer comes out the winner by executing 13 times as many Dhrystones per second as the VAX.

The Dhrystone benchmark is not adequate for comparing the performance of computers that will be used primarily for scientific applications like data collection, statistical analysis, and analytical graphics. In this case, the Linpack benchmark is more appropriate. It solves very dense sets of linear equations to arrive at a measure of floating-point performance. As measured against the single-precision Linpack benchmark, the Sun 4/280 is only eight times faster than the VAX 11/780.

While comparisons of raw CPU performance are useful, remember that choosing one product over another based only on its MIPS number makes for a poor purchasing decision because it trivializes the need to evaluate products based on their fit with specific applications, the availability of appropriate software, features that facilitate rather than complicate management, and the commitment of the vendor to a unified product line.

Some products, such as modems, do not lend themselves to easy benchmark comparisons because there are no standard tests. Many of the product comparisons issued by vendors are biased: Most vendors release test results on only those features that beat the competition. To add "credibility," they might list a feature that didn't perform so well—but by a narrow margin.

The "independent" benchmark testing conducted by trade magazines—although well-intentioned—further confuses buyers because of inadequate test designs. For example, when devising a benchmark test to compare the performance of error-controlled modems, it is a common mistake to simulate line impairments on the receive side of the data path, whereas a valid test must induce impairments on the send side as well. Also, most tests do not include the most common transient line impairments like impulse, phase, and gain hits, which tend to degrade the throughput of high-speed modems.

Customer support

A vendor's commitment to customer support should go far beyond merely having a 24-hour hot line to technicians who can resolve problems over the phone. The customer support unit should be staffed with people who will "own" the problem until it is resolved. Find out the budget for this operation and inquire about the qualifications of the customer support people, including the number of years they've been in the industry.

A vendor who stresses the quality of customer support will have measured response times to service calls and performed surveys to assess the level of customer satisfaction—all this with the goal of maintaining a continuing relationship with its customers. This kind of information is especially important for products being considered for a multinode network that is dispersed over a large geographical area. The vendor's ability to provide prompt service to any node may be a critical factor in your purchasing decision. In times of economic uncertainty, corporate budget trimmers usually don't think twice about cutting back service staff; on paper they look like liabilities rather than assets.

If you want to survive in the multivendor environment, check the vendor's commitment to standards as well as its track record in supporting the products of other manufacturers. Check references to ensure that the vendor's performance record in this area has not been exaggerated.

Ask the vendor to justify the price of customer support. You will typically find that prices bear an inverse relationship to product reliability or performance—the higher the quality, the lower the price for support; the lower the quality, the higher the price for support. In fact, many vendors confide that pricing customer support is merely a question of finding out what the market will bear.

It's always a good idea to compare the service agreements of the product vendor and a third-party maintenance provider before entering into any purchase agreement. Third-party service vendors are becoming more competitive in both terms and pricing, offering two-hour response times and up to 35 percent cost savings. Since they typically service the gear of multiple manufacturers, they may provide added flexibility in terms of product choices.

Product documentation

Until recently product documentation typically received scant attention from vendors. As products moved from the design stage to the production stage, rudimentary documentation was hastily thrown together in the hope of placating customers who were not really accustomed to expecting anything more. Although this is changing, many vendors still do not appreciate the customer's need for quality documentation. They try to smooth things over by delivering production drawings, circuit schematics, photocopied internal memoranda, and parts lists that are of little or no use to customers. Today's complex computer and telecommunications technologies require that vendors view documentation as an integral part of the product, inseparable from the hardware or software.

Review the vendor's product documentation to validate the claims of salespeople. Check it for comprehensive installation procedures, initialization/set-up instructions, and a complete explanation of the product's features. In addition to appendices that amplify aspects of the product's operation, look for a detailed index. A good documentation package will also include a troubleshooting guide to help the network manager determine the nature and scope of problems before requesting customer support.

Products typically evolve over time as a result of enhancements. Unfortunately, many vendors do not keep their documentation up to date. Find out how the product documentation will be maintained and distributed to customers.

When buying products from an OEM (original equipment manufacturer) or VAR (value-added reseller), find out to what extent the original product's technical references have been substituted with the OEM/VAR's own manuals. Sometimes the original references are deliberately trashed with the idea of increasing the level of customer dependence on the OEM/VAR. With this ploy, the OEM/VAR can recover costs or even turn a profit over the life of the product when its "free" short-term maintenance agreement expires, or by charging for services not specifically covered in the service agreement. Keep in mind that when vendors get away with inadequate documentation, it encourages poor performance, which may spill over into other areas—like customer support.

Scope of business

Find out if the product being considered for purchase is a major or minor part of the vendor's business—a sideline or only a means to gain entree into more lucrative markets. An effective way to determine long-term commitment to the product is to look into the vendor's product development efforts, described earlier in this article.

> Product choices based on MIPS alone overlook many other variables.

Be skeptical of small companies that want to become a "single-source supplier." In today's competitive environment even large vendors are becoming more responsive to customer needs to better serve specific territories and market niches. The very idea that a small vendor can step in as a single-source supplier is ludicrous.

But as customer needs become more diverse and sophisticated, even small vendors may seek alternative means to deliver the products and services their customers want. One way is to repackage an existing product to make it more appealing to the customer. Some vendors of matrix switches, such as Data Switch Corp. (Shelton, Conn.) and Dynatech Data Systems (Springfield, Va.), have decided to offer scaled-down versions of their products, enabling customers to install them at the departmental or work-group level rather than in the computer room for company-wide access. In addition to saving valuable space in the computer room, these distributed matrix switches permit more efficient configurations, which result in substantial savings in cabling costs. The distributed approach also enhances departmental control over network operations, relieving the MIS/data processing group of day-to-day management responsibilities.

Mergers constitute another approach to meeting customer needs, as illustrated by the marriage of two LAN vendors: 3Com Corp. (Santa Clara, Calif.) and Bridge Communications Inc. (Mountain View, Calif.). But if the product being considered is essentially the result of a VAR/OEM arrangement, look into the vendor's relationship with its main supplier. Find out if the supplier views the vendor as a "preferred" account. If not, components or products in critical demand will go to those who are. Manufacturer support of VARs/OEMs has never been consistently good because these types of vendors are viewed as direct competitors of the manufacturer's own sales force. Other times, manufacturers neglect their VARs/OEMs because they are more concerned about what they can supply through direct sales than what VARs/OEMs need to fulfill customer requirements.

Acquisitions is another method vendors use to plug holes in their product lines. One company that recognized its deficiency in the area of networking is Unisys Corp. (Blue Bell, Pa.). Appreciating the increasing importance of networking in the mainframe environment, it recently acquired Timeplex Inc. (Woodcliff Lake, N. J.), which is a leading supplier of T1 multiplexers. With the networking know-how of Timeplex, Unisys hopes to develop products that can compete—and perhaps link up with—IBM's Netview, a host-based network management product. For Timeplex, the deal means that it can expand and enhance its maintenance and support capabilities. Whether such plans will prove successful remains to be seen.

Any inkling that the vendor is either engaged in or pursuing such relationships indicates that they are serious about staying close to customers for a long time to come. But do not discount vendors whose network offerings are so complete as to make strategic arrangements unnecessary. It may be the case that some low-profile firms are just not as skilled in blowing their own horn as they are in developing a comprehensive product line.

If you're buying a software product, find out if you are entitled to the program's source code in the event the vendor goes out of business or closes out the product. The source code, which reveals details of the operating system's architecture, should be deliverable automatically from an escrow account or from a third party specializing in such services. These arrangements require the assistance of an attorney who is experienced in matters of software protection because it's too easy to overturn

If the vendor goes out of business, could you get the source code to a program?

such agreements in court. Additionally, make certain that when the product is updated the source code in escrow is also updated.

For hardware, find out how much of the product's technology is proprietary and what provisions have been made to provide customers with continuing support if the vendor should go out of business or discontinue the product. Find out if the circuit schematics, parts lists, and production drawings can be deposited in escrow.

Conclusion

Obviously, not every purchase decision requires a rigorous risk-avoidance strategy. Sometimes there is no significant risk. Even when this risk-avoidance strategy is justified, few vendors will score an acceptable grade in every one of these categories. The network manager must evaluate each factor in terms of its relevance to your organization's circumstances.

Effective purchasing decisions require business acumen as well as technical knowledge. In today's competitive arena, network managers cannot become so focused on technology that they forsake logic and practical business considerations. The overriding objective in any major purchase should be to minimize uncertainty, while endeavoring to increase planning flexibility and reduce costs over the long term. There's really no room for wishful thinking or the attitude that everything will somehow fall into place. Nor can you afford to delegate purchase decisions to others. Top management has a low tolerance for excuses that blame subordinates for costly mistakes. ∎

Since writing this article as an independent consultant, Nathan Muller has joined General DataComm Inc. as manager of consultant relations. His 17 years in the computer and telecommunications industry include positions in engineering, operations, field service, and sales/marketing. He has an M. A. in social and organizational behavior from George Washington University (Washington, D. C.).

Thomas B. Cross, Cross Information Co., Boulder, Colo.

What makes a building intelligent?

Primarily, the answer lies in the structure's networking of communications technologies that make possible the automation and sharing of tenant services.

Users are increasingly aware of the intelligent-building concept. It is achieved by fully using and integrating—via communications networks—available technologies so that the building is made to adapt to the occupants' needs, rather than the other way around.

Buildings have traditionally been described by how they are designed from the outside. Intelligent buildings, however, are described by the way they are used on the inside. Intelligence quotients may well emerge to better describe how much information technology is being used in a building.

The technologies of an intelligent building must be managed efficiently to provide the owner with bottom-line performance. There have been many cases where intelligent buildings have failed. In nearly all of these situations, no business plan had been developed. Many regulatory barriers and uncertainties about the sharing of local communications circuits are yet unresolved. In addition, there remain many questions regarding the marketing and pricing of enhanced telecommunications (voice and data) services and long-term operations management.

Another crucial management issue is the managing of the intelligent services. In a number of cases where these services have failed or were marginally successful, there was a lack of proper management by either the building owner, the building manager, or the equipment supplier. For example, one multitenant building failed because the PBX (private branch exchange) vendor and the building owner both thought the other was working with the tenants. As a result, the PBX vendor concluded that the shared telephone network was a complete failure and subsequently declined to bid on other multitenant telecommunications. Without a business plan and a professional management team, there are only questions, few answers, and no profit. Many developers wonder whether the intelligent building is another "roach motel" concept, where money goes in, but nothing comes out.

While information technology makes intelligent buildings possible, the driving forces behind their development are:

■ *Regulatory change.* The new regulatory environment is driving many developers into the telecommunications business. Building owners may have no choice but to be in the telecommunications service business, if they want to keep existing tenants and attract new ones.

■ *Economic advantages.* The efficiency of new technologies, such as office automation and energy management, provide economic advantages by lowering energy, labor, and operating costs. According to vendor Anthony D. Autorino, head of Parsippany, N. J.-based ShareTech (affiliated with AT&T and United Technologies), shared services can "save a tenant, on average, 24 percent on telecommunications costs and 35 percent on office automation costs."

■ *Maintaining a technological edge.* Equipment that provides office automation and energy management services plus the support personnel that such gear requires are too costly for most individual tenants who occupy fewer than 100,000 square feet. A multitenant intelligent building provides these services to such firms at the savings cited above.

■ *Holding a competitive edge.* In a recent survey, 78 percent of the developers contacted stated that they had plans to build intelligent buildings. It was concluded that a building without intelligence would be at a serious competitive disadvantage.

■ *Providing suitable office environments.* As competition increases for staff personnel who are familiar with new technologies, the quality of the work environment becomes critical. While presenting the office model as a technologically advanced concept, Lawrence Lerner, chairman of New York City-based Environetics International, one of the nation's largest office design and space planning firms, stresses the importance of human resources planning in designing offices: "The clear and overriding reason for automating has always been, and still is, to give the right technology to employees in order to boost overall productivity. The latter is directly linked to worker satisfaction with the environment.... When it comes to making workers happy, fiber optics play a second fiddle to sunshine, air, and comfort. The most sophisticated information processing tool of the future is the human brain. No matter how automated we become, we will always design for people as well as for equipment."

- *Greater investment opportunities.* Building owners can realize revenues that are directly attributable to the proper installation and management of information technologies. Such revenue can run as high as an estimated $5 per square foot per year.
- *Improved building management performance.* Pressure from building owners, who constantly stress the need to reduce costs and manage building facilities (air, space, energy) more effectively, will force the issue of incorporating new information technology into the building to gain and maintain a competitive edge.
- *Providing new jobs.* Intelligent buildings have the potential to attract start-up companies that grow with the information-technology installation and to provide jobs for the community.

Intelligent strategies

Building management, tenant issues, tenant technologies, and intelligent products and services are key factors in the viability of a structure. Their interaction could be complex. For example, employees working at home via communications networks will change a building's heating, security, and management requirements—all of which are ongoing processes.

All buildings are somewhat intelligent—for example, in their energy management and fire safety provisions. The pace of building-intelligence development is rapidly increasing. Developers and managers must anticipate the consequences of this development rather than be trampled by them.

The intelligent building is becoming an economic necessity for a company's survival in terms of land development. Twenty-five years ago, most offices had individual window air-conditioning units. These have been replaced by centralized, multitenant installations that provide better, personalized service at a lower unit cost. The intelligent building continues this evolutionary sharing trend.

The anatomy

The telephone equipment of an intelligent building is commonly referred to as its heart. Similarly, the other components play roles comparable to various parts of the body. For example, local area networks (LANs) are very similar to the body's neurological design, while the command-and-control center functions as the brain.

Telecommunications is the nervous system of the multitenant intelligent building. Two basic switching schemes may be used to perform its networking: the PBX or Centrex. The choice depends on individual building needs and the preferences of owners and managers. The advanced models of both include capabilities such as call accounting (station message detail recording, or SMDR), least-cost routing (also known as automatic route selection), and support of office automation equipment.

In its communications operations, the intelligent building functions in much the same manner as a telephone company's local exchange central office (CO). A PBX provides a multitenant building with the benefits of a star network. By switching at the building site rather than at the CO, wire pairs from individual network devices can be connected directly to the PBX.

With a PBX, when one trunk is not in use, a call can be placed via the common or shared pool of trunks from any of several different devices. In this way, fewer access lines to the CO are needed—the reduction in lines can be as much as 90 percent. In addition, the total tariff charges are reduced.

Take, for example, New York City's World Trade Center, which possesses 44,324 access lines. In comparison, Cheyenne—the largest city in Wyoming, served by Mountain Bell—has 33,260 access lines. PBX aggregation of communicating devices in the World Trade Center, if it were to become an intelligent building, would sharply reduce access-line costs.

On a more sophisticated level are the tenant benefits that result from a voice/data integrated switch. Most corporations have expensive separate voice and data networks. When most of the telephones and computers were originally acquired, the integration of voice and data was not generally available and, therefore, was of little concern. However, advances in technology have made this integration feasible.

One underlying factor to consider when promoting integration development was the need for microcomputers, word processors, and other office-automation devices to be connected to on-site or distant time-sharing and other computers; what was sought was more-complete, prompter service to the user. Another consideration was the prospect of more readily controlling wiring costs.

It should be noted that business productivity and profits depend increasingly on communications. One way to effectively employ today's profusion of microcomputers, terminals, and other data devices and links is by using a central switch having adequate processing power. Data devices are generally most cost-effective when shared—via a PBX—rather than dedicated to individual users. A building's energy and security gear may be linked to sensors using a PBX.

The latest PBXs transport and switch both voice and data completely in digital form on twisted-pair telephone cable. Once a digital PBX is installed, it is relatively easy to add data devices to the network, as needed, thus simplifying the planning and managing of data traffic. As more data lines are installed, more processing and memory capacity often must be added to the switch to keep pace with network growth.

If the average daily use of a network is low—under 50 percent utilization—then the cost of a minimally configured PBX is also low (about $500 to $1,000 per line). The PBX solution may therefore be particularly useful in an office environment where terminal use is low—that is, in an environment that enables per-terminal operation by three to five people. It is estimated that the average office worker uses an assigned terminal for fewer than 30 minutes per day. Because its services make up the majority of expected intelligent-building tenant functions, the PBX is well-suited to be considered for the role of hub of intelligent traffic.

The features and capabilities inherent to PBX-network switching provide numerous management benefits, including simplified billing (one bill for all services used), centralized control, less dependence on a carrier for PBX services, and more readily applied maintenance and administration.

The PBX acts as an information network's node or central switching point. Each PBX can be programmed to serve individual network locations. PBXs can, in most cases, provide custom features in a configuration designed specifically to meet the needs of an organization. More importantly, these switches can be readily reconfigured to adapt to changing conditions and needs. This makes the PBX attractive to developers of multitenant intelligent buildings who are faced with the special demands of many organizations.

Need software, too

Designs that support both voice and data communications for multilocation applications provide the features, capabilities, and management control necessary to maintain and operate a voice/data network. During the process of procuring switching nodes, careful consideration should be given to ensure that compatible network software packages are included. In evaluating networking and telecommunications management for an intelligent building, the following features should be included: automatic route selection, automatic data rate identification, optional format and protocol conversion, network accessibility software, four-wire switching, network control center, authorization codes, digital interconnection of remote peripheral equipment, network alternate route selection, traffic measurements, and queuing.

Automatic route selection (ARS) is a feature that uses many variables to determine the most efficient route for completing calls placed across the network. Route selection incorporates many factors for completion of a network call, such as access codes, automatic least-cost routing, and time-of-day routing. ARS enables route selection to be totally transparent to the network user.

PBXs are now being developed specifically for the multitenant intelligent building. Among the offerings of these switches are a variety of network management software functions plus the following:

■ *Tenant partitioning.* Partitioning provides separate calling privileges and processing for each department or tenant. Up to 512 or more tenant partitions can be defined in some switches, with each tenant retaining access to the many resources of the switch.

■ *Advanced networking features.* Tenants may share long-distance services and additional amenities, such as modem pooling, protocol conversion, integrated voice and data, text message centers, and videoconferencing. Instead of sharing, if required, these enhanced services can be configured solely for a single tenant. Queuing and contention are other advanced network management features that enable tenants to benefit from the services with minimum delays.

■ *Optional tenant-to-tenant access.* This software package permits internal calling between tenants within the network.

The other switch

Centrex is a service offered by all Bell operating companies and by some independent telephone companies. The two types of Centrex are Centrex-CO and Centrex-CU. The major difference between them lies in the location of the switch.

Centrex-CO has been the standard service offered. It links each of an organization's devices to a central-office switch located at the telephone company's site. In contrast, Centrex-CU combines basic central-office

Table 1: Centrex vs. private branch exchange

ISSUE	CENTREX-CO	PRIVATE BRANCH EXCHANGE
ON PREMISES	NO	YES
INITIAL COST	—	HIGHER
ONGOING COST	UNCERTAIN	RISING
MAINTENANCE		
RESPONSE TIME	IMMEDIATE	2-4 HOURS
COST	INCLUDED	$3-5/PORT DEVICE/MONTH
BACKUP COSTS	INCLUDED	OPTIONAL
SPACE REQUIREMENTS	MINIMAL	CABINETRY FLOOR SPACE
POWER REQUIREMENTS	NONE	FOR CIRCUITRY
MULTISITE CAPABILITY NO ADDITIONAL EQUIPMENT	YES	NO
FEATURES		
NOW	ABOUT 20	MORE THAN 200
FUTURE	ABOUT 50	ABOUT 300
DATA TRANSMISSION		
NOW	TO 9.6 KBIT/S	ABOVE 9.6 KBIT/S
FUTURE	ABOVE 9.6 KBIT/S	ABOVE 9.6 KBIT/S
SMDR	PER STATION	PER PRIVATE BRANCH EXCHANGE
LEAST-COST ROUTING	**	YES
OFFICE AUTOMATION	NO*	YES
MOVES AND CHANGES CUSTOMER CONTROLLED	NO*	YES

*PRESENTLY RESTRICTED BY STATE REGULATORY AUTHORITY.
**AVAILABLE IN ADVANCED UNITS, BUT PRESENTLY RESTRICTED BY FEDERAL REGULATION.
CO = CENTRAL OFFICE
SMDR = STATION MESSAGE DETAIL RECORDING

ISDN and the intelligent building

The digital voice/data switch is the heart of the intelligent building. This function may be provided in a number of different ways: on-site (PBX), centralized (CO), or distributed multinode (multisite, multicity combinations of PBXs and COs). The Integrated Services Digital Network (ISDN) embodies present efforts to provide a wide range of network services over common set of digital network facilities, including voice, data, image, music, and video.

The ISDN is characterized as an end-to-end digital network capable of providing a range of digital services from very low-speed telemetry (such as 10-bit/s) to 56-kbit/s digital facsimile to, perhaps, the very high T1 speed (1.544 Mbit/s) needed for videoconferencing. Fundamental to ISDN is the concept that the subscriber will gain access to it via a standardized interface or group of interfaces. The subscriber will be able to combine voice and data traffic and to present it to the interface, where it will be multiplexed onto a digital bit stream and sent to its prescribed destination.

In the United States, the public switched telephone network has been evolving toward an ISDN. Originally, the impetus was the cost savings of substituting electronics for copper wire and duct space in the metropolitan area interoffice trunk environment. Digital multiplexing was initially introduced into the telephone network to reduce the costs of interoffice trunks in metropolitan area networks. The original T1 offering allowed 24 digitized voice conversations to be multiplexed. In this application, the analog-to-digital conversion occurs in the equipment (channel banks) located in each switching office, and repeaters are employed at regular intervals along the cable route. By installing T1 equipment, telephone companies were able to avoid the costs of installing expensive copper pairs for each interoffice trunk.

What T1 hath wrought

This economic advantage is accentuated in intelligent buildings and office parks to maximize transmission while minimizing the cable plant required. The development of the T1 configuration utilizing cable pairs was followed by the development of comparable schemes using other transmission media, such as coaxial cable and microwave radio. T1 data transmission became possible because certain of these media allow such transmission speeds. This in turn led to the increased demand for combined voice/data communications.

The basic building blocks of an ISDN network are the digital multiplexers and digital switches. The technical advantages of ISDN networks are:
- Ease of multiplexing.
- Ease of signaling.
- Integration of transmission and switching.
- Signal regeneration.
- Accommodation to other services (see below).
- Performance monitoring with digital gear.
- Ease of encryption.

The most important advantage, from the aspect of an evolving ISDN, is the accommodation to other services. This allows for data, video, and practically all other forms of communications. (The exceptions require rates higher than T1.) Actually, due to competitive policies, several ISDNs are likely to evolve in the United States, depending on a number of factors, including the adoption of standards, competitive techniques, and the regulatory environment. ISDN is the next evolution and realization of the advantages of digital technology, typified by simple end-to-end connectivity.

The demand for many of the services that an ISDN would support is still speculative. One such service is videotex. The potential applications range from government services to banking, games, training, and news services. The bulk of ISDN business usage may be in the transport of large amounts of data traffic from computer-to-computer at T1 speed, on demand.

One major advantage of the ISDN concept is that it is not service specific. It could be used for telemetry, interactive data, image, voice, and video traffic, although the switching technique used (such as circuit, message, or packet) would vary depending on the statistical characteristics of the traffic.

With an ISDN, intelligent buildings will communicate among themselves, to other buildings, and to home telecommuters. ISDN will also play a critical role in the development of teleports. The PBX or central office will provide local processing and switching, connected by ISDN and local area network to a teleport or other network gateway. The latter would provide access to other ISDN networks.

---

service with additional on-premises switching. The same switches found in a BOC's CO can be installed as Centrex-CU, similar to a PBX.

Most advanced digital services can be made available at the CO equipped with the 5ESS (Number 5 Electronic Switching System). In terms of the features it offers, Centrex is becoming more and more competitive with PBXs. Moreover, the manufacturers of the 5ESS—such as AT&T, Northern Telecom, and Siemens—are developing the next generation Centrex to allow for energy management, security, fire safety, and other attributes of an intelligent building.

With tenant turnover, the demands placed on the telecommunications and other information functions will change. Centrex is attractive to building developers because of its capacity (up to hundreds of thousands of lines, compared with the maximum 5,000 to 10,000 lines of most PBXs) and its dynamic volume-swing capability (from 10 users to thousands).

The BOCs charge Centrex users per line. Traditionally, Centrex has been tailored for large customers (those with more than 100 lines), for which the switch has been proven cost-effective (Table 1) — especially in intelligent buildings. Combined with Centrex's superiority over the PBX in mean time between failures (MTBF) — discussed below — activities to market Centrex more vigorously have resulted in additional advantages (especially for Centrex-CO) over the PBX. These include no space needed, no capital investment financing, and a tenant service that encompasses future enhanced-service offerings, such as those of ISDN (Integrated Services Digital Network) — see "ISDN and the intelligent building."

For those building developers who choose the Centrex-CO option to avoid doing their own maintenance, there is an installation fee and monthly charge per station, adjusted by the add-on features requested. Total shutdown is avoided since each station is individually linked to the central-office switch (with its approximate 100-year MTBF rate). For those developers who choose Centrex-CU service (on-premises), the greatest benefit is in gaining the same dependability as that of its central-office equivalent.

Dedicating data

In a multitenant environment, it is not always cost-effective to connect all terminal users to an integrated voice/data PBX, which typically dedicates only 10 percent of its capacity to data switching. In cases where the data traffic exceeds this, a dedicated data switch or PBX handles data switching needs in a more cost-effective manner.

In the past, data PBXs were called port selectors, private automatic computer exchanges, data switches, intelligent switches, and smart switches, among other labels. Since integrated voice/data PBXs came on the scene, data communications vendors have adopted the name data PBX almost universally. Since data PBXs tie computers and terminals together in the same manner that PBXs originally tied together telephones — and offer many of the same features that the original PBXs offered — the name appears appropriate.

A data PBX allows terminal users to select different computers or other destinations from their keyboards. Access requests are queued by priority or by order of arrival. Since most terminal operators do not use their terminals all day, every day, the number of terminals hooked up to a data PBX can be more than the number of ports. If the network is properly designed, users seldom need to wait for a line — as is the case with an integrated voice/data PBX.

Data PBXs have been around for about 12 years, having started with the popularity of minicomputers that used dumb, asynchronous terminals. The evolution to microcomputers has fueled the data PBX growth.

The LAN solution

Local area networks serve as the major means of transmitting information among the various devices indigenous to an intelligent building, such as workstations, microcomputers, electronic files, databases, and graphics terminals. In the office environment, LANs provide a relatively simple means of transmitting text, data, voice, image, and sensor signals. By emphasizing a network rather than a component-by-component approach, LANs can accommodate the changing goals and structure of a multitenant environment. LANs act as an intelligent building's major arteries.

One misconception about LANs is that once a network is wired, an organization or building has to live with it. On the contrary, there are a variety of LANs and similar networks that include the option to mix and match topologies (Fig. 1).

There is also growing acceptance of the "mixed media" approach to LANs. With this approach, an organization designs the LAN that suits its needs, and all of the building's other networks and subnetworks are joined to a central backbone. For example, in the

---

1. Spine signals. Local area networks (LANs) serve as the major means of transmitting information among the various devices indigenous to an intelligent building. One misconception about a LAN is that once it is wired, an organization has to live with it. But the market supports the option to mix and match topologies.

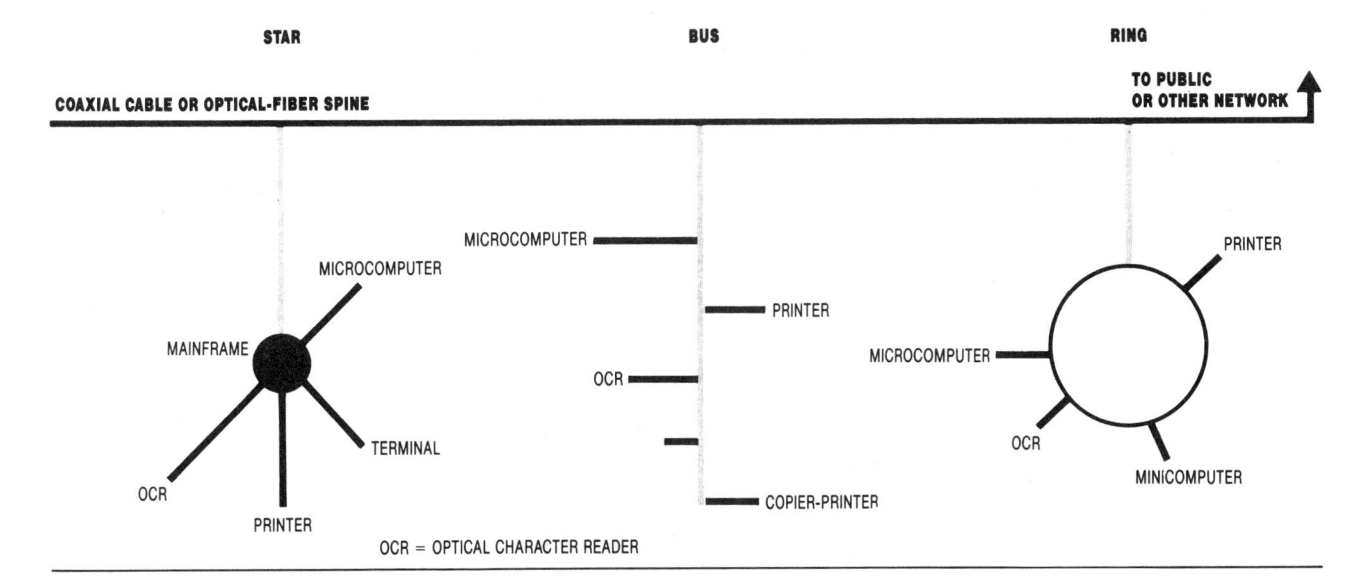

network from Milwaukee-based Johnson Controls, a complete range of devices—from fire safety to HVAC (heating, ventilating, and air conditioning) equipment—can be connected to computers via transmission media (Fig. 2). In this way, each tenant maintains its autonomy, yet access to central databases and intertenant communications is assured. The best technical approach to a mixed-media LAN is to use broadband coaxial cable or optical fiber as the backbone medium throughout the building and baseband twisted-pair to function as the "ribs" for serving individual groups of user-tenants.

An integrated voice/data network can use many alternative transmission media. Factors such as right-of-way, line-of-sight locations, distances, transmission speeds, and costs determine the most effective solution. Among the approaches that a corporation should evaluate—particularly for data transmission in an intelligent building environment—are twisted pair, coaxial cable, optical fiber, microwave, RF (radio frequency) transmission, and light link (such as laser or infrared). Table 2 compares the features and costs of each.

Managing cable can be a major problem, especially in existing buildings. One microcomputer typically has five or more interfaces to peripheral equipment. Local area networks may reduce the number of cables, but such a technology highlights the general management problem of keeping cable layouts rational by routing and labeling and by removing unused cables. Wire-management software is one method of coping with this problem. For example, there are microcomputer-based wire-management software packages that have the following functions:
- Graphic layout of building cabling.
- Calculation of cable and accessory requirements.
- Estimate of hardware and installation costs.
- Preparation of cable labels and location charts.
- Creation and maintenance of a building cabling database.

Caring for the environment

Energy management and control system (EMCS), as commonly used, is applied to a computer-based monitoring, management, and control network designed

2. The building network. *Shown here is a typical wiring plan that integrates building-automation devices with those of office automation and voice/data communications. The backbone's hub is the PBX and its main distribution frame. Each tenant firm maintains its autonomy yet can access others and central databases.*

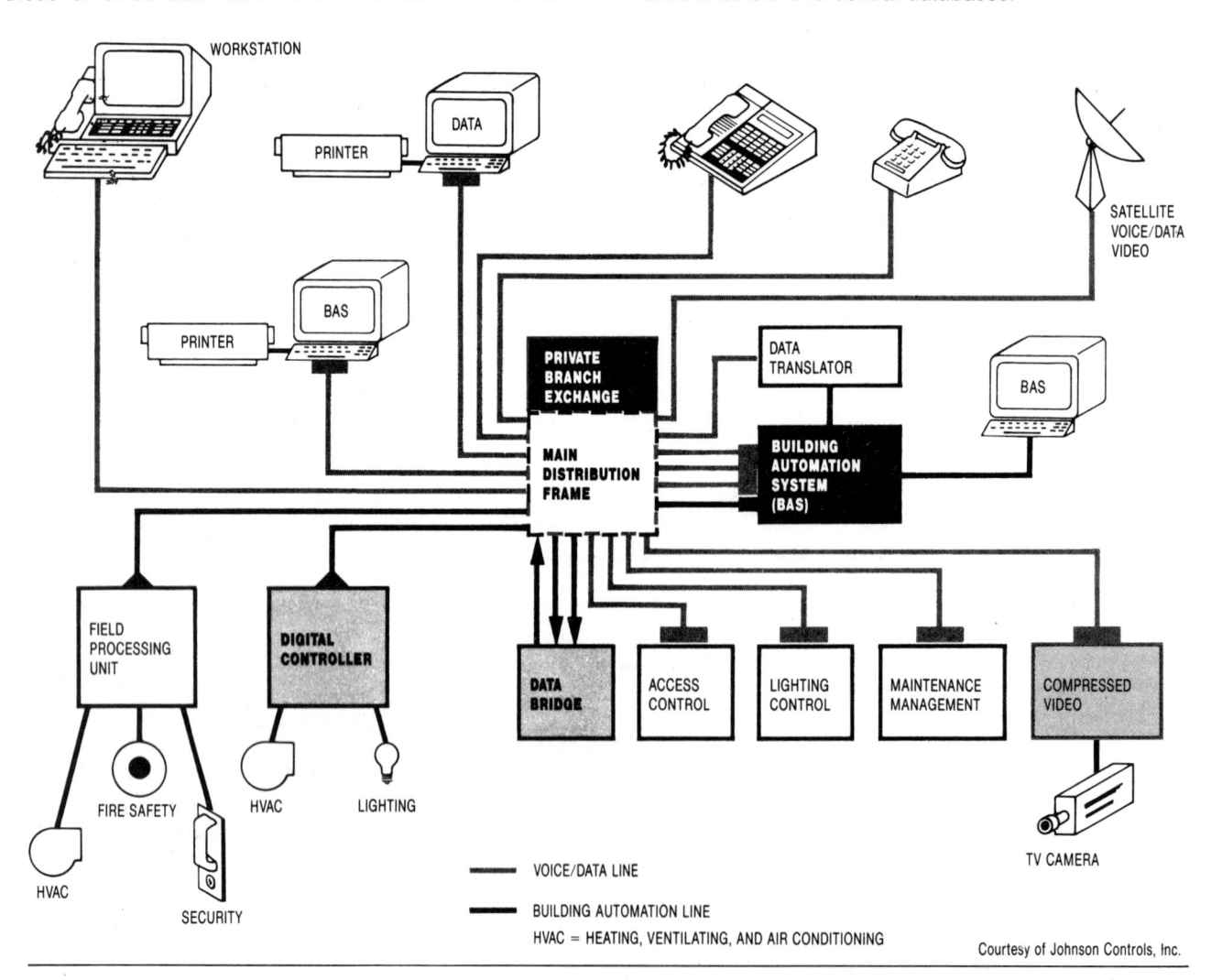

Courtesy of Johnson Controls, Inc.

and installed for the primary purpose of managing energy use and cost in a building. This includes HVAC equipment and computerized building automation.

Energy management and other building operations are controllable costs. Energy costs represent over one-third of overall operating expenses. Also, the efficiency and reliability of a building's mechanical and electrical mechanisms affect both costs and the ability to provide workable conditions. As the costs of energy and labor rise, the importance of optimum selection, design, and construction of building operations equipment increases.

Intelligent buildings can simplify these management functions. In addition, the life of mechanical and electrical equipment as well as the return on investment of the existing physical plant are increased in an intelligent environment.

EMCS makes use of a computer programmed to override local controls under specific conditions, thus conserving more energy than the controls would in unassisted operations. "Local" in this instance refers to those controls that directly relate and are usually contiguous to an HVAC mechanism.

As an office approaches a one-to-one ratio of people to terminals, more peripherals will be used. The addition of such units as printers, copiers, and storage devices results in additional power consumption and heat generation. Terminals produce as much heat as 1 to 1½ people doing work while sitting still. Therefore, the expected ratio of people-to-terminals means the equivalent of a more than doubled building occupancy. The HVAC equipment must be expandable to handle this extra load.

Today's interior planning calls for a mix between open and enclosed spaces. HVAC zoning can handle these variations. Also to be recognized is the possible concentration of electronic hardware in one location. Cooling in only that area will need to be increased, but if equipment is distributed evenly over all areas, all cooling must be increased. An EMCS can handle these necessary variations of temperature.

An EMCS can be as simple as a switch-clock, or as complex as a computer-based device with elaborate monitoring and control hardware and software. It is the

Table 2: Media alternatives

	TWISTED PAIR	COAX	OPTICAL FIBER	MICROWAVE	RADIO FREQUENCY	LIGHT LINK*
PROVEN TECHNOLOGY	YES	YES	YES	YES	YES	YES
TECHNOLOGY						
TWO-WAY	YES	YES	YES	NO	NO	YES
AVAILABILITY	YES	YES	LIMITED	YES	YES	YES
IMMUNITY TO:						
RADIO FREQUENCY INTERFERENCE	NO	NO	YES	NO	NO	YES
POWER LINE INTERFERENCE	NO	NO	YES	NO	NO	YES
ELECTROMAGNETIC STATIC	NO	NO	YES	NO	NO	YES
CROSSTALK	NO	NO	YES	NO	NO	YES
BANDWIDTH						
UP TO 24 CHANNELS OF 64 KBIT/S EACH	YES	YES	YES	YES	NO	YES
UP TO 50 VIDEO CHANNELS	NO	YES	YES	NO	NO	NO
BEYOND 50 VIDEO CHANNELS	NO	YES	YES	NO	NO	NO
ABILITY TO USE FOR POWER	YES	YES	NO	NO	NO	NO
CONSTRUCTION COSTS PER MILE						
AERIAL	$13,000	$15,000	$20,000	$40,000	NA	$30,000
UNDERGROUND	$23,000	$25,000	$40,000	$40,000	NA	$30,000
INSTALLATION CYCLE IN DAYS	90	120	120	120	120	90
SUBJECT TO THIRD-PARTY DISRUPTION	YES	YES	YES	NO	NO	NO
FCC REGULATION	YES	YES	NO	YES	YES	NO

*SUCH AS LASER AND INFRARED.
NA = NOT APPLICABLE
FCC = FEDERAL COMMUNICATIONS COMMISSION

latter that an intelligent building uses for energy management. Other functions may be included, such as maintenance scheduling, fire and smoke control, security, and the reporting associated with all of these.

Management specifics
Among the many functions that EMCS manufacturers offer, the most important are:
- *Monitoring.* Those items to be monitored must be identified from the onset. They include ambient and critical-area (such as a computer room) temperatures, boiler operation, pump status, and sump pump levels. Monitoring for optimal building operation and working conditions include comfort and energy management, amount of outdoor air permitted, zone temperatures, electrical demand, and water temperatures and flows.
- *Equipment programming.* Equipment may be programmed to turn on or off automatically, as needed. The key is to determine when and for how long a machine can be in the off condition without adversely affecting tenants or building equipment operations. A properly programmed EMCS, with sufficient sensors and functions (such as optimum start—which entails preventing excessive cooling or heating while monitoring outside conditions), provides this type of time-cycle and load-demand control.
- *Intervention.* Direct control of, or intervention into, local controls is necessary for the EMCS. Intervention due to fluctuations outside normal parameters helps to return the environment to optimum efficiency. Intervention control primarily includes start/stop of motors and reset of controller settings.
- *Graphics.* Graphic representations of air-handling mechanisms, pumping loops, mechanical processors, building outlines, smoke and fire alarm zones, and site plans are available with most EMCS installations. Graphic displays of measured variables aid the operator in understanding the building's intelligence and are particularly valuable in training new operators.
- *Alarms.* Critical points should be connected to an alarm program. Most monitors provide easily set high and low alarm limits for each point. If the measured value exceeds a limit in either direction, the operator is alerted to correct the situation. This function often includes fire, smoke, and security alarms.
- *Printouts.* The ability to print a record of variables and alarms is a feature of an increasing number of EMCSs. Printers can be programmed to print out certain variables at specified times, alarm indications whenever they occur, the time conditions return to normal, or any variation of these. Preventive-maintenance work orders and reports may also be printed if a suitable program is incorporated into the building's intelligence. Historical data and analyses are useful for improving the building's operation.

The function of the EMCS is to improve existing or new operations by analyzing all the interacting factors of building use and environmental needs. The benefit of an EMCS is usually stated as that of conserving energy use while maintaining satisfactory building environment control. The ultimate benefit is, of course, lowered energy costs. While money may be saved if energy is conserved, an EMCS can also contribute to cost reduction in other ways, such as life safety and ease of maintenance.

An EMCS adjusts the building's mechanisms for optimal operation. For example, heating and air-conditioning devices have sensors that pick up environmental changes (such as the sun shining on one part of a building) and adjust temperatures automatically. Sensors on each floor monitor, and computers adjust, air flow and temperature. In addition to energy savings, labor and maintenance costs can be reduced. Failures and excessive wear of plant equipment can be reduced with automated maintenance scheduling.

To ensure smooth working of the network once it has been fully configured and is operational, a network "life support" is needed. When this is tied into the building information network, it provides the power and controls that guarantee the continual functioning of the network.

Expensive outage
The need for this backup stems from the functional nature of the PBX and all the other elements of an intelligent building's information network. In case of a PBX shutdown due to a power outage, costs can range as high as tens of thousands of dollars per hour in lost business, besides obviously angry tenants. The developer of an intelligent building cannot afford to ignore the need for a reliable and secure information network environment for the tenants and equipment. Although initial investments are large (hundreds of thousands of dollars), backup and monitoring devices would cost less than a single disaster might cost.

The elements of a network's life support are an uninterrupted power supply (UPS) and power conditioners. The UPS is designed to feed emergency electricity to the elements of an information network and its air conditioners in the event of a municipal power failure. In the critical first moments of a blackout, UPS batteries automatically send power to the network. The power span of these batteries is from two to eight hours—enough time to save existing data and either to shut down the network or to verify that a backup diesel generator is ready to supply the needed power.

Besides its initial capital investment and ongoing maintenance, UPS costs include those of storage and related battery needs. Since battery fumes are toxic, and fuel for the diesel generator is volatile, the practical issue of safely housing the batteries and diesel generator must be addressed.

The batteries and fuel tanks must be stored in a protected and secure area, such as an isolated structure in the suburbs or the basement of a city high-rise building. Because few people need physical access to the UPS, inconvenient locations are quite adequate. To ensure proper operation when needed, the generator should be started at least once a week.

Adjust that flow
Power conditioners are to the UPS what pacemakers are to the human heart. They constantly adjust the energy flow, keeping the voltage within 3 or 4 percent

of a specified level. This conditioning is critical, since fluctuations of municipal power often average about 5 to 7 percent. Even greater variances occur in midsummer, when demands for air conditioning play havoc with utility power. Note that fluctuations shorten the life of the switch and computers and can interrupt and distort the flow of data.

Power line disturbances (blackouts) occur less frequently than do sags (decreases in power line voltage), impulses (brief overvoltages), or line surges. However, these line impairments actually cause more damage in the long run than power failures can cause, since they can result in ghosts (partial or undetectable erasures in tapes and disks) and premature equipment burnout. Therefore, any building equipped with computer devices—especially an intelligent building—has a critical need for power conditioning.

Most UPS equipment does not address sharp voltage peaks (spikes). These may require additional filtering. This filtering may be achieved with a power conditioner, which protects hardware and generally resides in the computer room, where operators can use the device's monitoring and self-test features.

Computers are as sensitive to changes in temperature and humidity as they are to power variations. Their needs outstrip the capacity and parameters of standard air-conditioners for the following reasons:
- Some mainframes operate within a plus or minus 10-degree temperature range with a relative humidity (RH) range of plus or minus 5 percent (generally centered around 72 degrees Fahrenheit and 50 percent RH). Many standard air conditioners cannot maintain an environment within these limits.
- Air conditioning of the average building is controlled seasonally—depending on the geographic location—and by the daily working hours. Computers, however, operate 24 hours a day, year round, continually generating heat and creating the need for constant cooling.
- Since the same utility power that is prone to outages also drives air conditioners, consideration should be given to linking the air conditioners to a UPS.

Air-conditioning compressors may be located outside the computer room, since only maintenance personnel need access to them. But, because the proper air conditioner functions constantly and is a mechanical device, it must occasionally be shut down for repairs. Computers cannot tolerate this loss, so standby air conditioning must be made available.

Computer rooms should be located in the interior of a building so the air conditioning does not have to battle heat from the summer sun through windows or the roof. This means that the space people find the least desirable is perfectly appropriate for computers.

Air conditioning is usually distributed under the same raised floor that accommodates computer wiring. The facilities manager needs to examine all new and changed wiring plans to confirm that cables will not block air flow in the 12- or 18-inch space below the raised floor.

Many mainframe computers require a super-cooled environment far beyond simple air conditioning, including schemes such as internal water cooling. If developers expect to keep up with the changing work environment, they need to look ahead and prepare for the technical problems that come with advances. One way of protecting equipment is through the use of automated power management, which protects not only the building information network, but also the individual computing devices of the automated office.

Gaining protection

Automated building security, like energy management, has been used for some time. Its utility within the intelligent building lies in its degree of automation. In addition, the integration of security mechanisms with other building services is also critical (see below).

Security equipment monitors sensors to provide protection of the perimeter, the area, and specific objects. Security devices are used to control access to a building or restricted area. In access-control, personnel with authorized access to restricted locations are identified through the use of magnetic card readers, card keys, or other identification devices. Then, a security mechanism opens the proper door to allow entry to, or exit from, the restricted area.

Should unauthorized entrance be obtained, some equipment not only provide printed reports and visual displays of break-ins, but also follow the intruder's progress throughout the building on a color graphics monitor or via closed-circuit TV. This function is included in only the most sophisticated security gear and requires extensive wiring to support the necessary sensors. Installation of such equipment is simplified by an abundantly wired intelligent building.

The supervisory post

An intelligent command and control center is a central location from which the performance of each branch and node of an information network can be monitored. From this site, an organization can readily obtain data on the performance of each network element. A network cannot function effectively without this centralized control, especially a network of the functionally separate entities of an intelligent building.

The functions of an intelligent command and control center include:
- Life support and comfort.
- Wire management (networks, power, computer, and telephone).
- Power management (UPS, power generation, and energy management).
- Building control (remote administration and simulations).
- Maintenance (repair and diagnostics).
- Traffic monitoring (for flow, accounting, and control).

To perform these functions, an intelligent command and control center must monitor, diagnose, and—when possible—repair problems.

Centralized monitoring offers distinct network control advantages over a decentralized configuration, such as economies in the administrative tasks associated with control-center development and maintenance, and improved productivity of control center personnel. This improved productivity is due to the concentration of

3. Conference transmission. *Intelligent buildings, linked via satellite, provide a shared videoconferencing environment on a reservation or time-available basis to those tenants who cannot afford their own installations. Typical cost is $100 to $8,000 per meeting, depending on duration and distances.*

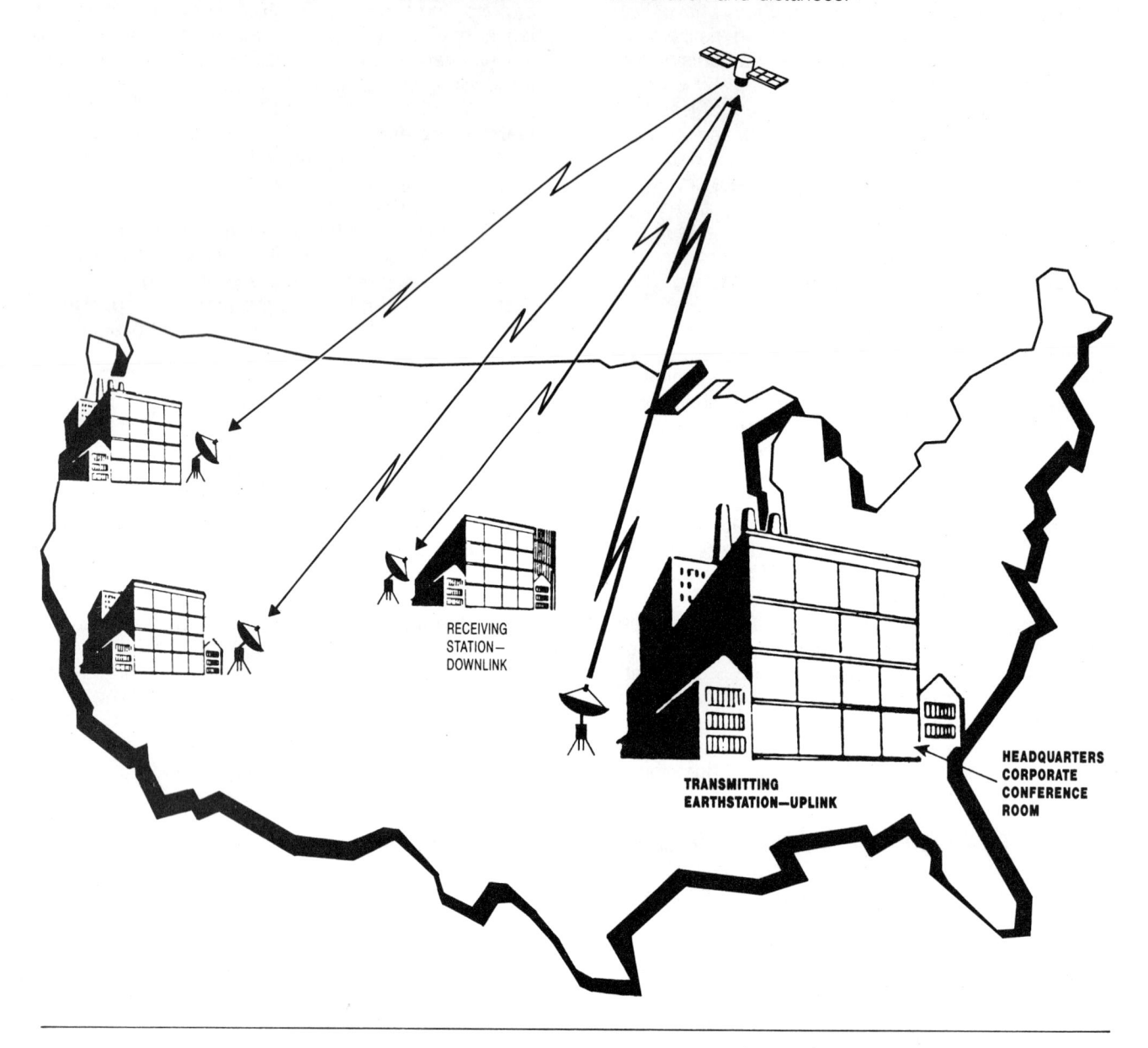

expertise at the network control center.

The control center provides the means for monitoring the performance of network elements. These elements include the transmission channels of the LAN, switching equipment, computers, terminals, and any other devices that are sources or destinations for transmission. In addition, the ability to test the elements and detect, diagnose, and repair defects is also provided. Monitoring can be performed as needed by the control-center operators or periodically on an automatic basis. The automatic monitoring should inform the operators of any deterioration in the performance of an element before it actually begins to malfunction enough to cause a problem.

The effectiveness of the control center is directly related to the degree to which its functions are automated, and it can be measured in terms of costs saved. It is difficult to give a strict dollars-and-cents accounting of the cost benefits of installing and operating a control center. Nevertheless, an analysis will show, at least on a qualitative basis, why such a center is a worthwhile investment for any organization that maintains its own communications network.

Each organization must determine the costs it will incur during each phase of a problem as well as the various impacts of one element on another. The life of a problem is marked by five phases: occurrence, detection, isolation, correction, and return to normal operation. To reduce the total incurred cost, efforts can be concentrated on reducing the time from problem occurrence through detection to isolation. A tangible benefit is improved network service.

Implementation of a fully developed, highly automated control center is a major undertaking. It can cost hundreds of thousands of dollars and requires meticulous planning. However, the rewards—as noted above—are commensurate with the effort.

Another way to go

For those unwilling to take the plunge into automating their offices, intelligent buildings offer an attractive alternative: the use of office automation equipment and information services supplied through a building information center (BIC). In some cases, tenant needs do not justify the rent, lease, or purchase of automation equipment. A BIC can provide tenants with shared equipment to meet their limited needs. Tenants can purchase and use those services needed regularly and then use the BIC to meet less frequent needs.

Services available through such a center might include network interfaces (both carrier and bypass), videoconferencing, a message center, facsimile, Telex, word and text processing, paging services, and training. In addition to the information network services, many intelligent buildings are offering other intelligent resources, such as the concierge-type services in which some hotels specialize.

A note on videoconferencing: This service is a valuable business tool that could be prohibitively expensive if acquired on an individual-tenant basis. Intelligent buildings, linked together through satellite and fiber optic transmission media, provide an affordable environment on a reservation or time-available basis to those tenants who cannot afford their own installations. Videoconferencing used on a shared basis in an intelligent building requires a specially equipped room and a microwave link or satellite uplink (Fig. 3). Typical use of videoconferencing is for six to 10 people per location at $100 to $8,000 per meeting, depending on duration and distance.

For those who are unwilling to pay such usage costs, intelligent buildings can provide audio teleconferencing. The same room that provides videoconferencing can be equipped with speakerphones and used for this order-of-magnitude less expensive form of teleconferencing. When numerous sites must be connected, however, an audio bridge is required—this interconnects 48 to 72 callers without degradation.

Audio teleconferencing can be augmented visually through the use of facsimile machines as well as interconnected computers. Microcomputers can add the extra visual dimension of graphics.

Message centers can provide services as simple as telephone answering or as complex as the networking of electronic mail. Most message center equipment is capable of storing answer phrases, organizational and personnel directories, and temporary status information so that the message center operators can answer each extension as if they were the secretary for the party being called. They can also activate message-waiting indicator lamps similar to the message lights in hotels. If the organization uses electronic mail, the message center operator can key telephone messages to have them delivered electronically.

Voice mail can be made available to tenants through the BIC in conjunction with an operator-based CRT message center. Busy or unanswered calls are first routed to the message center for an operator to answer. After it is determined that the party wants to leave a message, the operator can either record the message or key it into the CRT message terminal, depending on how the called party wants the calls delivered. Voice mail increases the productivity of the operators, extends the operating hours for delivery of messages, and assures that messages are delivered exactly the way they are left by the caller.

Another service provided to tenants of the intelligent building is access to remote information sources (databases) on an as-used basis. The requisite equipment is integral to the intelligent building, available to the tenant through the BIC.

Information central

Accessing of databases is also one application of videotex in an intelligent building. Videotex may be used as an information dispersal medium from building managers to tenants, among tenants, and from tenants to visitors. For example, a visitor could receive information on services offered by the building and/or tenants without the time-consuming process of having the visitor sent to this or that department for information. The lobby of the building could contain a readily accessible terminal with a menu of all services and businesses contained in the building.

Videotex can offer a welcome departure from the traditional static lobby directories. In place of a large amount of wall space required by the old method, the directory needs only enough space to put a monitor and a keypad. In fact, the electronic directory allows the listing of more information than previously possible due to its expandable storage capability. An added benefit is that updates may be made instantly, without building personnel ever leaving the management office.

The intelligent building provides archival storage, which includes both the traditional vault's hard-copy storage of paper or microfilm and on-line storage and retrieval of information to and from computer files. Many vendors think that paper will continue to be a key element in business because people are more comfortable with storing and retrieving hard copy. In fact, office automation is actually responsible for the growth in paper files. The cost of compact copiers and microcomputers is decreasing, encouraging more purchases of these devices, which tends to generate more paper. Paper has been—and, in many cases, remains—the primary information-storage medium for most businesses. Renting excess storage capacity through a BIC provides a valuable service to space-conscious tenants and revenues to building managers. ∎

Thomas B. Cross is managing director of the Cross Information Co., which sponsors conferences on intelligent buildings, teleconferencing, and telecommuting. This article is adapted from his book, Intelligent Buildings: Strategies for Technology & Architecture, *to be published in 1986 by Dow Jones-Irwin, Homewood, Ill.*

Timothy G. Zerbiec and Rosemary M. Cochran, Vertical Systems Group, Dedham, Mass.

Is a private T1 network the right *business* decision?

The bottom line: Cost is an issue, but only after you've screened the multiplexer vendors who can best satisfy your T1 network needs.

You've heard about the cost economies and benefits of private T1 networks. But before you go any further, you must ensure that such an investment would yield sound business benefits for your particular networking environment. First, evaluate your business requirements. Second, thoroughly understand the T1 (1.544-Mbit/s) multiplexer technology that will support these requirements.

Evaluate your business requirements by defining and measuring your risks. Decide if the network is a strategic necessity or a cost-saving tactic. For example, if you lost your voice and data networks right now, how long could your company operate? If your business is processing stock transactions or airline reservations, the answer is obvious.

Competitive business demands have created a trend toward T1 networks that enable companies to strategically leverage communications for their businesses. These networks enable companies to respond quickly to competitive pressures and customer needs.

As an example, let us look at two competing retail banks, First National Bank and Last National Bank, each with a branch office at a busy shopping mall. Each bank has two automatic teller machines (ATMs) that are constantly busy. Customers must often wait up to five minutes (it only *seems* longer) to use each machine. To alleviate customer complaints, Last National Bank decides to install a third ATM. The telecommunications manager places an order with the local telephone company for a new line and is quoted 45 days for installation.

Meanwhile, First National Bank has also decided to install another ATM. When it is ready to be connected to the ATM network, the bank's network operations manager simply provides a 4.8-kbit/s channel from First National's existing T1 network. This is accomplished from the bank's central operations center in minutes using interactive commands from a network management console. The result is that First National Bank has improved service to its existing customers and may even attract new customers from among those standing across the mall in the ATM lines at Last National Bank.

Increased user control has resulted in a trend toward the strategic use of T1 networks. At the beginning of this year, 871 of the largest 1,750 user organizations in the United States had installed T1 networks, a 22 percent increase over 1987. Of these 871 organizations, 362 have implemented backbone T1 networks, while the rest have point-to-point T1s.

'End' versus 'networking' muxes
Your business requirements determine the type of network capability you need. For relatively static configurations that provide the transport of applications between two or three locations, point-to-point networks can be implemented using less-featured, lower-cost "end" multiplexers. In contrast, "networking" multiplexers are used to build backbone networks that interconnect multiple locations and support multiple voice and data applications. The backbones have capabilities such as intelligent switching, automatic rerouting, and operations control.

More than 40 vendors offer end multiplexers. The leading vendors, based on worldwide market share—directly sold and through distributors—are Amdahl, Coastcom, Datatel, and Granger. Others are Aydin Monitor, Bayly, Dynatech, Fujitsu, Gandalf, Integrated Telecom, Megaring, NEC, Newbridge, Pulsecom, Scitec, Tau-tron, and Telco Systems. (Note: Addresses, telephone numbers, and contacts can be found in the DATA COMMUNICATIONS *Buyers' Guide*.)

Table 1 outlines a decision profile for each T1 multiplexer category. Based on an average cost of $26,390 per end multiplexer, the payback period for a point-to-point network

Table 1: T1 multiplexer decision profile

PARAMETER	END MULTIPLEXERS	NETWORKING MULTIPLEXERS
NETWORK TYPE	POINT-TO-POINT	BACKBONE
DECISION CRITERIA	COST, PRODUCT FEATURES	RELIABILITY, PRODUCT FEATURES, VENDOR SUPPORT, COST
DECISION MAKER	DEPARTMENT MANAGER, PURCHASING	CORPORATE COMMITTEE
DECISION CYCLE	LESS THAN 6 MONTHS	6 MONTHS +
AVERAGE PAYBACK PERIOD	LESS THAN 6 MONTHS	LESS THAN 1 YEAR
AVERAGE $/UNIT	$26,390	$80,420
CONFIGURATION OPTIONS	LIMITED	MANY, DESIGN REQUIRED
MODULARITY	LIMITED	SUBSTANTIAL
VENDOR EXPERTISE	EQUIPMENT	APPLICATIONS, EQUIPMENT
SUPPLIER	MANUFACTURER, MANUFACTURERS' REP., OEM, DISTRIBUTOR, CATALOG	MANUFACTURER, OEM

OEM = ORIGINAL EQUIPMENT MANUFACTURER
REP = REPRESENTATIVE

is typically less than six months. These networks are usually procured at a departmental level to support discrete voice and data applications. Also, many companies operate multiple point-to-point networks.

With the device viewed as a commodity purchase, your primary purchase-decision criteria for point-to-point networks are price and product features. End-multiplexer manufacturers such as Amdahl, Coastcom, Granger, and Tau-tron sell through direct sales organizations and manufacturers' representatives. End multiplexers are also available through distributors such as AT&T and the Bell operating companies and through catalogs such as that of Glasgal Communications of Northvale, N. J.

With the average cost of a networking multiplexer at about three times the cost of an end multiplexer—$80,420—backbone networks represent a comparatively major capital expenditure. Based on the latest tariffs, the average payback period for these networks has been cut to less than one year, half the period required as recently as two years ago. Because backbone networks support applications that affect multiple departments, a buy decision will most likely involve a management-level committee.

Backbone networks are typically deployed in three phases and planned for an average "locked-in" life of five to seven years. (In point-to-point networks, with the end multiplexer viewed as a commodity, it is readily replaced—typically when requirements change.) The pilot phase occurs during the first year, when networking multiplexers are deployed in four to six major locations and the functionality of the network is tested. The following year to 18 months is a "rollout" phase, when multiplexers are added to extend the network's capabilities to other company locations. At this point, the network is mature and enters a growth phase. New multiplexers are added more gradually, and existing equipment is upgraded with new features and additional capacities to support new applications.

Evaluate! Evaluate!

Because implementing a backbone network is a long-term commitment, consider your selection of a vendor as carefully as your selection of the multiplexer. In addition to equipment costs, carefully evaluate the vendor's financial stability, long-term product strategy, and the depth and experience of the support and service organizations. Before making your final decision, insist on customer references. Visit prospective vendors' headquarters to meet the executive management and tour the manufacturing and development facilities.

Based on market share, Timeplex, Network Equipment Technologies, and Digital Communications Associates are the leading networking multiplexer manufacturers. Avanti, General DataComm, Infotron, Micom Digital, Stratacom, and Tellabs have also developed networking multiplexers to target the backbone network market. The Vertical Systems Group projects a 54 percent increase in shipments of networking multiplexers for 1988, while shipments of end multiplexers will remain flat.

Computer and PBX manufacturers are also beginning to recognize the strategic importance of being the private-transport network vendor for major companies. These companies view T1 backbone networks as a platform on which corporate information movement resides, using network management as the cornerstone.

This private-transport strategy, which may be called vertically integrated rollout, has resulted in a number of recent acquisitions and strategic alliances. These include Unisys's acquisition of Timeplex, IBM's OEM (original equipment manufacturer) agreement with Network Equipment Technologies, and Digital Communications Associates' OEM agreement with Northern Telecom. There will be more of these relationships within the next year as other vendors plan their strategies.

Increased competition among the networking multiplexer vendors has also enlarged the task of analyzing product functionality and feature availability. No single feature will determine which product is best. And, unfortunately, you cannot rely on vendor brochures to make product comparisons or evaluate network capabilities. There are actually more than 100 elements that can be used to analyze the functionality of networking multiplexers. These elements can be categorized under five headings: Capacity, Capability, Configuration, Control, and Cost. Table 2 shows how the five headings can be used to map your business requirements to T1 multiplexer functionality.

■ *Capacity.* Ensure that the multiplexer has enough capacity to support the number of locations and applications,

Table 2: Matching requirements to functionality

	BUSINESS REQUIREMENTS	MULTIPLEXER FUNCTIONALITY
CAPACITY	• NUMBER OF LOCATIONS (CURRENT & PLANNED) • NUMBER OF USERS (CURRENT & PLANNED) • RELIABILITY • RESPONSE TIME OBJECTIVES	• NUMBER OF NODES PER NETWORK • NUMBER OF T1 AGGREGATES • NUMBER OF CIRCUITS PER AGGREGATE • THROUGHPUT • NODAL DELAY • BUS DESIGN • BUS SPEED
CAPABILITY	• APPLICATIONS AVAILABILITY • COMPETITIVE RESPONSE • USER CONNECTIVITY • DISASTER PLANNING	• NODAL INTELLIGENCE • AUTOMATED BANDWIDTH PROVISIONING • NETWORK SYNCHRONIZATION • CLASS OF SERVICE • INTEGRAL CHANNEL SERVICE UNIT (CSU) • EXTENDED SUPERFRAME FORMAT (ESF) SUPPORT • BINARY EIGHT ZERO SUBSTITUTION (B8ZS) SUPPORT • T3 INTERFACE
CONFIGURATION	• APPLICATIONS AVAILABILITY E.G.–ORDER PROCESSING –OFFICE AUTOMATION –RESERVATION SYSTEMS –TELEMARKETING –CAD/CAM –VIDEOCONFERENCING	• APPLICATIONS INTERFACES –VOICE (E.G. ANALOG, DS-1) –DATA (E.G. V.35, RS-232-C) • BANDWIDTH COMPRESSION • CHANNEL SYNCHRONIZATION • CONTROL-LEAD SUPPORT
CONTROL	• MANAGEMENT REPORTS • SECURITY • EQUIPMENT INVENTORY • VENDOR-SERVICE TRACKING	• NETWORK ADMINISTRATION • TECHNICAL-CONTROL FEATURES • ANALYSIS TOOLS
COST	• BUDGET –EQUIPMENT –OPERATIONS –TRANSMISSION FACILITIES	• NETWORK EQUIPMENT • NETWORK MANAGEMENT • INSTALLATION • TRAINING • MAINTENANCE • OTHER EQUIPMENT (E.G. CSUs, CHANNEL BANKS, ECHO CANCELLERS)

CAD = COMPUTER-AIDED DESIGN
CAM = COMPUTER-AIDED MANUFACTURING

---

both current and planned. Bigger is not always better. Variables such as the number of T1-aggregate ports, number of channel interfaces, and number of nodes (multiplexers) can all be used as measures of capacity. A multiplexer may be bigger in one category and lacking in another.

The number of nodes that can be configured as a single logical network is important to operations issues and will become even more important as your network grows. The numbers that appear in product literature can be misleading. Statements such as "There is no limit to the number of nodes in a network" suggest the vendor's assumption that the architecture it has implemented for initial networks will work for growing ones.

Investigate those assumptions; ask for an explanation of how the architecture works; get references of other customers who have already implemented large networks. Calculate the actual time required to perform tasks such as multiplexer reconfigurations (which include port re-assignments) and the time to reroute traffic from a failed transmission facility for both your current and planned topologies. These times may be acceptable for your five-node network today but unacceptable (rerouting time may be greater) when you expand the network to 20 nodes in the future.

Another variable for evaluating multiplexer capacity is the number of slots available for application channels (synchronous or asynchronous ports), common logic (logic common to other slots), and aggregate modules. The maximum number of input channels typically overstates real-world multiplexer-configuration capacities. Evaluate the node-site configuration, including its aggregates, channel interfaces, and redundancy. Too often, users find themselves buying another node because they forgot to consider the slot capacity required for logic redundancy or internodal links.

Real-world configurations for T1 multiplexers usually include redundancy for common logic and some—if not all—of the aggregates. Redundancy implementations that use one spare for N active modules will use fewer slots than implementations that use one-for-one protection. And do not forget future environmental requirements, such as power, air conditioning, and floor space.

If the number of module slots is at a premium, is it necessary to back up aggregate modules? Many network designers think multiple internodal links on a node will provide protection from individual link failure. The theory is that the transmission link is the more likely element to fail. Moreover, the bandwidth available on other aggregates will permit a redundant path to provide substitute connectivity. However, use this shortcut with care; weigh the use of a slot against the effects of the loss of internodal bandwidth caused by an aggregate-module failure.

The maximum number of circuits a multiplexer can carry on an aggregate link affects decisions on topological design. The actual number of circuits carried is a function of the application-circuit bandwidth, channel-framing technique, and overhead used by that vendor. Verify that the mix of circuits you need can be supported on a single aggregate. Errors in calculation may result in requiring additional T1 lines.

Circuit propagation times of 20 milliseconds or more introduce a noticeable echo on voice circuits or cause throughput delays for data. Delay is imposed by a multiplexer as it switches a circuit from a channel interface to an internodal link or when bypassing a circuit from one internodal link to another. Even geographically small networks—such as in campus environments or those with as few as five nodes—may route applications through many nodes to complete a transmission path, resulting in unacceptable circuit delay. To compensate for such a delay requires the installation of echo cancellers or other corrective equipment.

Variables such as throughput capacity (in Mbit/s) and internal bus design and speed influence the aggregate and channel-interface capacity and availability. A good bus design—recognized as such by being redundant and by how many functions it can handle—provides protection from bus failure and provides for the higher bandwidth necessary for future applications. Bus speed measures the capacity of a single switching shelf. (A shelf contains mux cards. A switching shelf is dedicated to T1 aggregate terminations and switching.) It also gives an indication of the maximum bandwidth that can be switched as a single channel or aggregate. Most network managers expect a five-to-seven-year life from their T1 networks. Therefore, a multiplexer design that provides no growth path could be disastrous.

■ *Capability.* The operations of a T1 backbone network show why users have embraced "do-it-yourself" common-carrier transport services. The single aspect that has made networking T1 multiplexers so revolutionary is the addition of nodal intelligence to a formerly manually controlled environment. The combination of software-controllable multiplexers and vendors' network-operations experience results in the automation of tedious network operations tasks. The benefits to the user include transmission-facilities usage optimization, automatic recovery of failed facilities, real-time arbitration for access to resources, and audit trails of anomalous network events.

Multiplexer intelligence is not a single feature but an integration of multiplexer capabilities. If there is a single area where multiplexer intelligence can be observed, it is in networking support. While you may be interested in the specific vendor implementation of networking support, focus instead on the vendor's understanding of user-operations issues. When evaluating functionality, you must measure the benefit to your organization of the substitution of nodal capability for personnel. Experience has shown that users of T1 networking-multiplexer backbone networks have the same or smaller staffing levels while increasing network services.

A large number (typically 10 to 15) of locations and complex intersite connectivity (such as a "mesh") are common with T1 backbone networks. Network-operations personnel usually require assistance in planning the utilization of transmission facilities. A circuit "router" function (part of the T1 mux), which examines potential paths for a circuit, must take into account many variables. These include permissible path length, call priority, status of network transmission facilities, and such special considerations as permissible delay, encryption, and transmission security. The goal is to let the network automatically arbitrate bandwidth management as much as possible. It is not practical to have a network operator manually interconnecting circuits.

Decide how much automation you're willing to buy. Use this checklist as an analysis aid to measure nodal intelligence:

■ *How much manual intervention is required to define a circuit? Do you specify only circuit endpoints, or all intermediary nodes as well?*
■ *Does the router automatically adapt to changes in the network topology?*
■ *Is there vulnerability because router intelligence is concentrated in only one node?*
■ *Try "what-if" scenarios to examine what it will take to run your network on either a normal or an exceptional (failure-mode) basis for currently planned functions.*
■ *How long does it take to reconnect all of the circuits on a failed internodal link? (Note: Use specific examples when comparing this parameter for networking multiplexers. The truly high-end [multifeatured] products jump off the page at you; their milliseconds reroute times are one to two orders of magnitude lower than less powerful competition.)*
■ *How is contention for internodal link resources (aggregates) handled? for channel resources (ports)?*

As networks expand in size, precautions must be taken to ensure that all transmission facilities work together. This is especially true if a number of different common carriers or a combination of public and private carriers (such as bypass microwave and fiber) are used.

The method the multiplexer employs to maintain synchronization with its neighbors is called network synchronization. This parameter must be addressed during the network's design phase, prior to transmission-facilities engineering, or the result may prove inadequate.

T1 multiplexers provide an economic division of T1 transmission bandwidth into multiple application services. Before the advent of networking multiplexers, the predominant method for multiplexing applications on T1 facilities constrained the minimum controllable circuit-bandwidth size to 24 DS-0 channels (64 kbit/s each) per T1.

This generation of networking T1 multiplexers permits as many as 573 individually controllable circuits of 2.4 kbit/s each per aggregate. While this has improved T1 line utilization, it has some disadvantages. To gain this level of efficiency, vendors have developed proprietary link communications formats—especially for an aggregate of fewer than 64 circuits—that are not compatible with those of other vendors at the internodal link level. This situation is similar to that of statistical multiplexers.

"Open" network T1 architectures (such as what Avanti is proposing) are on the horizon, but they address only the potential synergy between T1 multiplexers and carrier

> **Don't settle for 'Yes, we support T3' or you'll be left trying to plug it in.**

services. An "open-network gateway" could be used to connect two different vendors' networks. But this may incur a penalty of decreased T1 line efficiency—gateway overhead may reduce the usable bandwidth—and decreased network management functionality (different vendors usually have different, incompatible network management approaches). Therefore, carefully assess your long-term relationship with your vendor, because you will probably be relying exclusively on this vendor for the life of your network.

There has been considerable interest in a T1 line-framing technique, called extended superframe format (ESF), which increases the level of technical control capability on a T1 line (see "The hidden treasures of ESF," DATA COMMUNICATIONS, September 1986, p. 204). Line-quality statistics as well as a communications channel for messaging are its most promising features. While ESF is not yet universally available on carrier-provided T1 lines, ensure that your multiplexer will be compatible with ESF. Specifically, find out what it will be able to do with the ESF technical-control features.

Mentioned almost synonymously with ESF is binary eight zeros substitution (B8ZS). B8ZS is a T1 coding method that ensures sufficient signal transitions on a T1 line to maintain line-repeater synchronization, even when there are more than 15 consecutive zeros in the T1 data stream. Like ESF, it is not yet supported on all common carrier circuits. Ensure that your T1 multiplexer vendor has implemented this capability or a similar one.

Now that T1 networks have gained acceptance, users and vendors already want to up the ante with T3 (44.736 Mbit/s—commonly, 45 Mbit/s) internodal links. Today, T3 common carrier services are at the point of development that T1 service was in 1983, with users trying to decide how to apply all that bandwidth. Most T1 users cannot cost-justify T3 links yet. For those who can, the issue is how to compartmentalize its use.

T3 is available as M28 tariffed service—where the T3 channel is formatted as 28 T1s—or a single, large bit pipe running at 44.736 Mbit/s. For those who want it as M28, an external separate M13 (industry terminology for T3) multiplexer can take up to 28 T1 multiplexer interfaces and combine them into a single T3.

Some T1 mux vendors integrate M13 multiplexers into their T1 nodes. If a multiplexer's switching bus can handle T3, then the multiplexer has the potential of operating at T3.

Another way of incorporating T3 operation is by using multiple T1 interfaces. For users seeking to support individual application channels running at greater than T1 rates (such as bridging local area networks), they should determine if the multiplexer can accommodate T3 as a single 45-Mbit/s pipe. Vendors with a definitive T3 strategy will be able to explain their specific T3-support plans. Do not settle for a simple "Yes, we support T3" response, or you'll be left trying to figure out how to plug it in.

■ *Configuration.* Business applications for T1 networks include order processing, factory automation, office automation, reservation networks, telemarketing, and video-conferencing. The T1 network represents a bandwidth utility for implementing these applications.

Vocal support

T1 networks heralded the first practical method for toll-quality voice channels to be multiplexed with other voice and data channels on a single transmission facility. The applications include the support of inter-PBX trunks, tie lines, and foreign exchanges. The number of ports at a site may vary considerably. The interface may be analog—one circuit per line—or digital, per AT&T Technical Publication 62411, with a format of 24 circuits per line.

Look at product descriptions to see how voice is interfaced to the multiplexer. On a networking T1 multiplexer, the use of a digital-PBX interface reduces hardware clutter and supports a large number of channels—24 per T1, typically. These multiplexed interfaces allow direct connection to PBXs with a T1 interface or to channel banks that provide adaptation to analog facilities. Multiplexed interfaces have inconsistent technical-control functions. Features like channel loopbacks or level-check and -adjust may be lacking. T1 voice interfaces may not be cost effective at sites where the support of only a few voice channels is required. This cost may not help determine vendor selection, but it will, of course, affect the overall network cost.

Voice channels use large amounts of bandwidth: 64 kbit/s in a standard toll-quality channel using pulse code modulation (PCM). The advent of integrated-circuit digital signal processors has enabled voice compression to reduce this bandwidth requirement to 32 kbit/s—in some cases to 16 kbit/s. Adaptive differential pulse code modulation (ADPCM) is a widely accepted compression method, with vendors moving toward a common ANSI standard: T1.301. When evaluating a product, find out if it has ADPCM, the data rates it supports, and the level of quality it provides. A good measure of ADPCM quality is the group type of facsimile machine that can be supported (at least

Group 2—analog 3-minute transmission over the public telephone network) and the modem data rate supported (in the range of 2.4 to 4.8 kbit/s).

Other low-bit-rate voice digitization methods offer variable results and/or introduce other operational considerations, such as additional circuit delay. However, do not believe that ADPCM is a panacea. The issue is not the compatibility of your private network's ADPCM coding with that of other networks. (Chances are, your ADPCM codes will never leave the network.) ADPCM standards are important to ensure that a channel meets minimum service objectives.

Digital speech interpolation and packetized voice are growing in popularity. Bandwidth-compression methods offer from 2:1 to 10:1 gain in the number of channels on a T1 line. They provide adequate-quality speech but do not provide bandwidth compression for facsimile transmission and for modem traffic. Applications like voice order-entry are well suited to this type of transmission.

The term "integral transcoder" appears on many product descriptions. Transcoding refers to the ability to change PCM coding to ADPCM and vice versa. This is particularly important if T1 voice interfaces are used to access the network. These interfaces use PCM at 64 kbit/s, which would be costly for backbone transport at that low a data rate. Determine if the transcoder performs its function on a "per port" or "bundle" (a group of 11 channels) basis. Find out what the options are for converting PCM to some lower-bit-rate method. This capability will affect the flexibility and economy with which you will be able to route voice calls through the network.

Compatible interfaces

Besides voice, the network configuration is, of course, affected by data support. Care must be taken to ensure that the interfaces between the application and the network are compatible.

On a T1 network, a data channel looks like a private-line data link. The same channel-service objectives—such as availability, signal integrity, and acceptable delay—must be met by the multiplexer network for an application to work as before. When evaluating the adequacy of the data support on a networking mux, consider these items: bandwidth efficiency, channel transmission control, physical interface type, and circuit availability.

Data-interface specifications for multiplexers are generic. They all contain descriptions that address the rates they will support, types of electrical interfaces, and number of ports per [printed-circuit] card. Evaluate these items to ensure that your applications can be connected to the network at the physical level—Open Systems Interconnection (OSI) Layer 1. Although this issue may seem obvious, vendors often use adapters external to the multiplexer to accommodate different logical, physical, or mechanical configurations. This issue may interest your operations staff, which must inventory, install, and maintain the connecting cables.

Channel-control leads are important to data link level (OSI Layer 2) channel support. Determine how the multiplexer supports control-lead signaling. Some applications use control leads for ascertaining channel status or for flow control. Know how many leads you need per channel and how quickly a change in status must be recognized relative to the data. Vendors differ widely on the number of control leads supported and the amount of overhead required to support them.

Perhaps the most important aspect of data-channel support concerns how the multiplexer supports channels that cannot be synchronized to the network reference clock—which normally results in transmission errors. While many data applications incorporate protocols to ensure end-to-end data integrity, poor channel performance results in frequent retransmissions and, therefore, reduced throughput. Methods like "positive justification" use a small amount of additional bandwidth per channel to pass the data independent of network-reference timing. Other methods include buffers that provide protection for short-duration, transaction-oriented transmissions—typically less than 15 minutes. Ask vendors what their methods are, and ask them to explain what performance level (parameters such as recovery time and throughput) their methods will give your application. Failure to do so could result in the unavailability of a critical application.

T1 time-division multiplexers are not well suited to asynchronous-circuit support. Asynchronous traffic is better supported by a secondary network of statistical muxes or packet switches, with the aggregates of these network processors then passed as synchronous data channels onto the T1 backbone. For those applications that justify direct connection to the backbone, investigate how the multiplexer combines direct connection with other traffic.

Most T1 multiplexers that do support async convert the async channel to a synchronous one for transit across the backbone. Thus, even when the port is idle, it takes up backbone bandwidth. Some T1 multiplexers incorporate statistical muxes, which reduce this bandwidth penalty. Consider carefully the requirement for asynchronous support on your T1 backbone; there are many other economical and feature-rich methods—such as packet switching and statistical multiplexing—for supporting async.

■ *Control.* Beyond the cost economies of buying bandwidth at "wholesale" prices, T1 networks opened the doors to user control of the bandwidth resource. Communications-wise corporations use T1 networks to reduce the connectivity time between sites, thereby improving their responsiveness to business conditions. Similarly, they use the technical control capabilities of these networks to reduce the MTTR (mean time to repair). This reduction is accomplished by pinpointing network problems and involving the appropriate parties sooner to affect restoral of service. Automation in network management is blossoming as the cost of processor MIPS (million instructions per second) comes down and artificial intelligence and graphic presentations become prevalent.

It is incumbent on a corporate network designer to work with operations staff to develop an operations philosophy for ensuring the availability of services across the network. Each vendor has different experience, wisdom, and network control methods.

Table 3: Features of T1 networking multiplexers

	AT&T 740/745	AVANTI ONC/ONX	DCA SYSTEM 9000	GDC MEGA-SWITCH	INFOTRON NX4600	MICOM DX-500	NET IDNX/70	STRATACOM IPX	TIMEPLEX LINK/2
NUMBER OF AGGREGATES	1/16	1/16	36	16	21	8	96	16	6
AGGREGATE REDUNDANCY	1:1/1:N	1:1/1:N	1:1	1:1	1:1	1:1	1:1	M:N	1:1
THROUGHPUT CAPACITY	1.5 M/ 25 MBIT/S	2 M/ 25 MBIT/S	55.3 MBIT/S	24.6 MBIT/S	20.2 MBIT/S	12 MBIT/S	1,966 MBIT/S	160,000 PPS	12.3 MBIT/S
MAXIMUM NUMBER OF NODES IN NETWORK	250	100	80	128	64	125	250	63	160
SOURCE CHANNEL CAPACITY (PORTS)	128	128	136	512	4000	508	384	384	208
BYPASS DELAY (MICROSECONDS)	N.A./250	N.A./250	375V, 3,000D	250	2,000	500	5,000	2,750	2,000
MULTIPLEXING ORIENTATION	BIT/BYTE	BIT/BYTE	BYTE	BIT	BYTE	BIT	BYTE	PACKET	BYTE
ROUTER INTELLIGENCE	DISTRIBUTED	DISTRIBUTED	CENTRAL	DISTRIBUTED	DISTRIBUTED	DISTRIBUTED	DISTRIBUTED	DISTRIBUTED	DISTRIBUTED
ROUTER TYPE	TABLE	ALGORITHM	ALGORITHM	TABLE	TABLE	ALGORITHM	ALGORITHM	ALGORITHM	TABLE
ROUTE GENERATION	AUTOMATIC	AUTOMATIC	AUTOMATIC	MANUAL	MANUAL	AUTOMATIC	AUTOMATIC	AUTOMATIC	MANUAL
TIME TO REROUTE (SECONDS)	#	10	20	#	86	#	10	2	#
PARAMETERIZED ROUTING	NO	YES	YES	NO	NO	NO	YES	YES	NO
MAXIMUM NUMBER OF HOPS	N.A.	16	10	N.A.	N.A.	N.A.	12	10	7
PRIORITY LEVELS	3	16	16	NONE	NONE	64	4	NONE	16
PRIORITY BUMPING	YES (3)	NO	NO	NO	NO	NO	YES (4)	NO	NO
TRAFFIC BALANCING	NO	NO	NO	NO	NO	NO	NO	YES	NO
BANDWIDTH CONTENTION	NO	NO	NO	NO	YES	NO	YES	YES	YES
LOWEST BYPASS CHANNEL	N.A./ 64 KBIT/S	N.A./ 64 KBIT/S	2,667 BIT/S	75 BIT/S	300 BIT/S	400 BIT/S	1.2 KBIT/S	N.A.	50 BIT/S

D = DATA
N.A. = NOT APPLICABLE
PPS = PACKETS PER SECOND
V = VOICE
# = NOT DETERMINED

Source: VERTICAL SYSTEMS GROUP

The product descriptions and options have only enough depth to suggest which issues the vendors address. The nature of the capabilities offered by state-of-the-art network management requires an evaluation in itself.

Consider these questions when evaluating network management:

■ How robust (feature-rich) is the telemetry for both node-to-node as well as node-to-network-management communications? The bandwidth must be adequate to propagate control messages with acceptable delay and be sufficient for current and future requirements.

■ Do technical control features allow for timely and accurate problem diagnosis?

■ Can you inventory network components as well as circuits currently in use?

■ Is there a software administration program to help maintain down-loadable multiplexer code?

■ How do you control network management access?

■ Can you track trouble tickets, dispatch of repair personnel, and other maintenance activity?

■ What is the capability to produce such management reports as on-line utilization and line-failure analysis?

- *Can the vendor produce working evidence of product claims (with user references)?*
- *Cost.* T1 multiplexer costs are as difficult to compare as T1 multiplexer features. Since the ultimate test of a multiplexer's functionality is how well it supports user applications, costs really can only be compared on a network-implementation level.

When considering costs, obtain itemized prices for each network node, all network management options, and any other equipment required to support your applications (such as channel service units, echo cancellers, channel banks, and satellite-transmission buffers). In addition to equipment costs, closely evaluate the costs of installing and maintaining the network and training your network operations staff.

To analyze and compare total network costs, nine networking multiplexer manufacturers were asked to propose implementations of a sample four-node network (see the figure). The nine were Avanti, Digital Communications Associates, General DataComm, Infotron, Micom, Network Equipment Technologies, Stratacom, Tellabs (represented by AT&T), and Timeplex. They also answered technical questions concerning applications support (see "Product analysis"). Network costs varied considerably from vendor to vendor. The total network list price, including basic network management, ranged from under $300,000 to over $500,000. Most of the vendors also offer sophisticated network management, which ranges from PC-based software packages at $1,000 to workstations with color graphics priced up to $80,000.

Check the extras

There was also a wide range in the cost proposed for installation, maintenance, and training. Installation costs for the sample network ranged to over $30,000. Monthly maintenance costs ranged from $2,200 to $5,800, based on standard business-day coverage (eight hours per day, Monday through Friday). These maintenance costs also assume that the network locations are all in major cities. If you have remote locations to support, check for vendor surcharges for nonmetropolitan areas. On a per-trainee basis, training costs ranged up to $1,300, not including travel, living, and other incidental expenses.

With this much variation in the costs for a small network configuration, it is no surprise that all of these vendors offer discounts. Expect a 20 to 30 percent discount on the total network price, plus other special offers on services such as training and project management. Also, do not forget to evaluate the costs of upgrades (such as additional port cards) and announced new product features. The bottom line is that cost is only an issue after you have qualified the vendors that can satisfy your T1 network requirements.

Once you've mapped your business requirements to T1 multiplexer functionality, the next step is to determine which product is best suited to your company's needs.

Products and product features shown in Table 3 (also see "Product analysis") are currently operable in user network environments. The units represent the top offerings available from these nine vendors as of March 15, 1988.

Many vendors have aggressive development plans, but planned products and features should not be compared to deliverable capabilities. The information for the matrix was compiled based on discussions with users and vendors, coupled with independent technical evaluations. A number of the products listed are also sold by other vendors under OEM agreements.

Although all of these multiplexers support backbone-network configurations, their networking architectures vary. Two of the products (described below) have an architecture that combines an end multiplexer and a cross-connect under common network management software. This is done to achieve networking-multiplexer functionality. A cross-connect assigns and redistributes 64-kbit/s channels among the internodal links in a T1 multiplexer network (see "The digital cross-connect: Cornerstone of future networks?" DATA COMMUNICATIONS, August 1987, p. 165).

AT&T's Acculink 740/745—consisting of the 740 end multiplexer and the 745 cross-connect—is manufactured by Tellabs and is an enhanced version of Tellabs's own Crossnet product.

The Avanti ONC/ONX is a combination of the Open Network Concentrator (formerly called Ultramux) and the Open Network Exchange cross-connect. These products are being delivered in this configuration until the ONX has channel interface support. Although other companies market separate end multiplexer and cross-connect combinations as a single solution, AT&T and Avanti are the market leaders.

The Timeplex Link/2 is included in the Table 3 comparison rather than the Link/100 because the latter was not deliverable by the March 15 cutoff date.

Routing intelligence

Networking multiplexers have automated capabilities that assist in the operation of T1 networks. One of the most important capabilities is that of having the network build circuits to support applications

Business requirements mandate maximum network availability. The loss of a circuit—even for as little as 30 seconds—could result in a critical loss of revenue. Loss of a circuit for less critical networks may only present an inconvenience, and therefore recovery delays can be more readily tolerated.

A company's business requirements also reflect how much automation will be necessary in order to satisfy circuit requirements. The complexity of the network and the expertise of the operations staff necessitate a particular level of routing automation.

Network complexity and staff expertise lead to specific requirements for the multiplexer's routing intelligence. The network should be totally self-healing within a specified time frame, or it may be flexible enough to allow time for operator intervention. Circuit requirements that change on a daily basis mandate automatic route generation.

The networking multiplexers available today utilize various techniques to satisfy circuit-routing objectives. All of the multiplexers profiled in this article can automatically reroute around a failed transmission facility. The key issues

The alternatives. *To analyze and compare total network costs, nine networking multiplexer manufacturers were asked to propose implementations of this four-node network. They also answered application-support questions. Network costs, including basic network management, ranged from under $300,000 to over $500,000.*

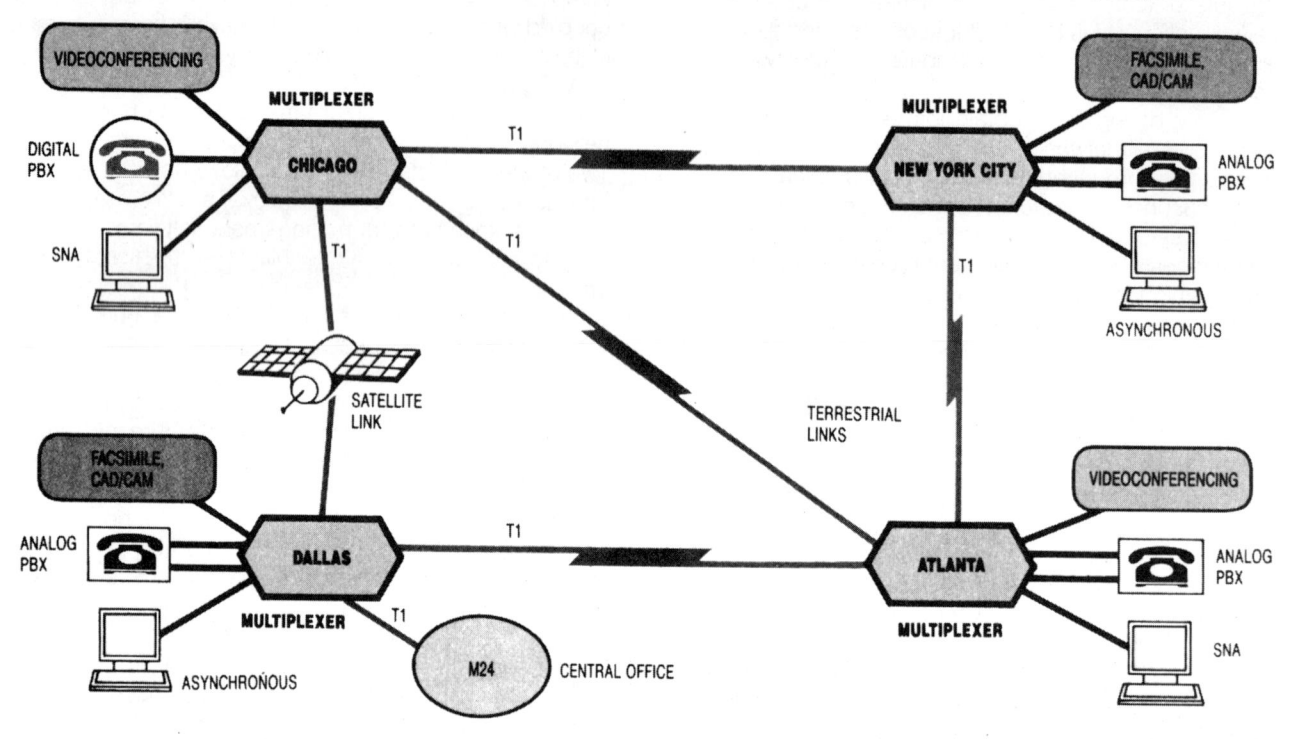

CAD/CAM = COMPUTER-AIDED DESIGN/COMPUTER-AIDED MANUFACTURING
M24 = AT&T SERVICE THAT SUPPLIES 24 VOICE CHANNELS FROM A T1 LINE
SNA = SYSTEMS NETWORK ARCHITECTURE

are the ease of implementing changes to the network and the speed at which the multiplexer restores circuits affected by an outage. The goal for circuit restoral in a data environment is typically 22 to 30 seconds, which is the time after which an SNA session will time-out. (SNA is IBM's Systems Network Architecture.) In a voice environment, the circuit-restoral requirements are dependent on service objectives. Some users may tolerate circuit drops and call again. Others may wish to keep calls in progress if connectivity can be reestablished in 10 seconds or less.

Circuit reroute times are determined by multiplexer factors such as the number of routes that can be calculated per second, the time to send circuit setup messages, and the time needed to reframe (time-align) an internodal trunk when adding a new circuit. For example, NET's IDNX can reroute four circuits per second; DCA's System 9000 can reroute two circuits per second. Reroute times will vary depending on the number of circuits affected and how many intermediate nodes must be traversed to restore the connection. In Table 3 (under "Time to reroute"), the amount of time to restore 40 affected circuits rerouted over an average of three intermediate links each is shown.

These numbers do not reflect the time necessary to determine that a facility is actually out of service. Many of these products allow the user to program this wait time before declaring transmission-facility failures; this time would be added to the times shown. Table 3 shows that only Avanti's ONX, DCA's System 9000, NET's IDNX, and Stratacom's IPX could satisfy a reconnect time of under 30 seconds for this example.

There are two philosophies for routing intelligence: distributed and centralized. Each can satisfy sophisticated network requirements but with varying levels of functionality. Distributed router intelligence specifies that each node in the network has routing responsibilities. A benefit of this implementation is a decrease in the network's vulnerability to node or trunk failures by not depending on a single site for circuit-routing functions.

Pluses and minuses
Typically, the origin end node is responsible for getting a circuit to its destination. Each node has either a table or algorithm that determines the route path for the circuit. An additional benefit of distributed intelligence is the ability to have multiple call-request queues, which decreases the time to reconnect circuits after a transmission facility or node failure. A disadvantage is that each node requires some additional processing capability, which drives up the cost per node by about 15 to 30 percent.

Centralized router intelligence can be based in a node or in host-based network management. In a centralized scheme, a single control point maintains current informa-

Product analysis

A comparison was made of the extent of networking support inherent in networking multiplexers supplied by nine different vendors. In four areas, the nine products have the same properties:

- *Redundant switching*. There is no traffic disruption with automatic cutover to backup logic. This is called "hot" redundant switching.
- *Nondisruptive capability*. The node's logical and/or physical configuration can be changed without disruption to circuits terminating or passing through that node.
- *Automatic rerouting*. No manual operator intervention is required to reconnect a circuit that has been disrupted by a node or line failure; connection is reestablished automatically.
- *Time-of-day switching*. Sometimes called bandwidth reservation, this network management feature allows the user to predefine circuit connectivity in order to ensure bandwidth availability when an application is to be run. The feature is most useful in networks where connectivity requirements are different for regular business hours than for nonprime time.

Where they differ. Table 3 compares the nine networking multiplexers in 18 other areas:

- *Number of aggregates* is the maximum number of non-redundant internodal physical interfaces supported by a single addressable node. The product's largest possible configuration is assumed. (For the AT&T and Avanti units with separate access and cross-connect elements, the number for each element is given: access/cross-connect.)
- *Aggregate redundancy* indicates the implementation of the redundant internodal aggregates. 1:1 means one backup card for each card protected. 1:N means one backup card can protect multiple cards. M:N means "M" cards can protect "N" cards on an as-needed basis. For products that employ separate access and cross-connect elements, two numbers are given: access/cross-connect.
- *Throughput capacity* is the total (input plus output) full-duplex switching capacity for a maximum configuration. The figures include source-channel-to-aggregate connections and aggregate-channel-to-aggregate-channel connections.
- *Maximum number of nodes in network* is the maximum number of individually addressable nodes that can be managed as a single network.
- *Source-channel capacity* is the maximum number of nonmultiplexed channels using a single physical interface per port that can be housed in a single addressable node.
- *Bypass delay* is the additional circuit propagation delay that occurs when a circuit is passed through a node from one internodal link to another. For those units where this delay varies depending on circuit transmission rate, a value for a 32-kbit/s circuit was calculated.
- *Multiplexing orientation* indicates the type of internodal aggregate multiplexing method used: bit-, byte-, or packet-interleaving.
- *Router intelligence* indicates the processing-information design required to route/build circuits for applications carried by the network. DISTRIBUTED means that responsibility for circuit routing may be handled by one of several network nodes. CENTRAL (or centralized) is where a single node has the routing responsibility.
- *Router type* indicates the method for selecting the internodal links that provide an end-to-end network connection. TABLE means a predefined list at the origin-end node or at the network control point. ALGORITHM means that a formula in a program running in the origin node or at the network control point determines the best network path at the time the circuit is requested.
- *Route generation* indicates whether path routes are op-

tion about network-resource utilization. One advantage of this is the ability to easily arbitrate bandwidth utilization on a network-wide basis. Updates to the central router affect the entire network, which guarantees consistency of routing decisions throughout the network. An additional benefit of centralized routing is a lower-cost implementation. (Distributed routing costs 15 to 30 percent more, as cited above.)

The disadvantages of centralized routing are its single-site vulnerability and the delay that can occur when many circuit paths are requested at the same time. In the case of the System 9000, a sophisticated centralized routing scheme allows a single node to select circuit paths for all circuits in the network. This central node can be any of the nodes in the network. If that node should be lost, a new node is automatically chosen to take over the routing responsibilities. Centralized router intelligence located in the network management host is being developed by GDC for the Megaswitch and by Newbridge for their 3600 series. (This is a low-end multiplexer—with fewer features—not included in Table 3.)

Two methods are used for the selection of circuit paths: either tables or algorithms. An algorithm calculates the circuit path based on current topology and user-defined parameters. Algorithmic implementations simplify route selection. For example, the operator of an algorithm-based multiplexer, such as the IDNX, System 9000, or IPX, need only specify the end points of a circuit and the path will automatically be determined. Topology and resource changes are automatically taken into consideration for subsequent path selections.

Global and neighbor

Algorithmic routing implementations vary. Those in the IDNX, IPX, System 9000, and ONX decide the best route for a circuit based on global knowledge of the network topology. Alternatively, Micom's DX-500 uses "nearest-neighbor" algorithms, where each node knows the inter-

erator initiated or are automatically generated and maintained by the network.

■ *Time to reroute* is the time required to reconnect 40 circuits (representative of traffic on an internodal link) that have just been disrupted by a T1 outage. This measurement takes into account the time to select the new route and to send the appropriate circuit-setup messages. It does *not* include the time that the nodes wait to ensure that the outage is "hard." Since the time calculation may depend on the length of the new path selected, an average value of three links was chosen. The time values listed were calculated with vendor-supplied reroute factors. The latter included the time to establish a frame on an internodal link and the time to "look up" a new path. (# denotes that no calculable or credible reroute time could be ascertained for those units so indicated. Vertical Systems estimates these reroute times to be 30 seconds to minutes for the 40-circuit-reconnection example.)

■ *Parameterized routing* indicates the ability to define and route circuits using path-selection variables. Typical variables are: media (such as copper wire, microwave, optical fiber, and satellite), security requirements (encrypted or unencrypted), and delay tolerance (such as a circuit not to exceed a certain delay threshold). Units with algorithmic routers take these parameters into account in the selection of circuit paths. Parameterized routing is most important in complex-topology networks, to gain efficient use of internodal transmission facilities while ensuring that basic applications support objectives are met.

■ *Maximum number of hops* indicates the maximum number of internodal links that a circuit can traverse to complete an end-to-end connection. This number becomes an issue when the total of internodal links becomes large (exceeds 10), since end-to-end connectivity is achieved by completing connections as a continuous series of internodal line segments between endpoint nodes. Even geographically small networks (such as in campus environments or those with as few as five nodes) may involve a large number of internodal links. (Where "not applicable" is listed, vendor-supplied information states that the multiplexer imposes no restrictions on the maximum number of hops. Units with N. A. have not had sufficient field exposure to provide verifiable numbers.)

■ *Priority levels* indicates the ability to specify, as part of the circuit definition, a priority to arbitrate contention for multiple-circuit router requests. One example: When an internodal link fails and the multiple circuits that had been traversing that link must be rerouted. This feature determines who will get reconnected first when a node or link fails. (Four priority levels is a practical maximum.)

■ *Priority bumping* indicates the ability to override existing circuits on an internodal link when a new circuit needs that internodal bandwidth to complete its connection. (The number next to the Yes listings is the number of priority-bumping levels.)

■ *Traffic balancing* is a traffic-distribution ability for load-leveling in internodal trunk utilization. For time-division multiplexed internodal trunks, traffic balancing does not affect throughput. Its benefit: It reduces the number of circuits that may be affected by an internodal link failure.*Bandwidth contention* is the ability to oversubscribe a transmission facility by configuring multiple ports with a total bandwidth exceeding that of the transmission facility. With all available bandwidth in use, any subsequent active ports would receive a busy signal until the session of one of the busy ports is completed.

■ *Lowest bypass channel* is the lowest data rate (smallest bandwidth) that can be transferred from one internodal link to another. The smaller the number, the greater the potential for internodal link and nodal multiplexing-bus efficiency.

connections of only those nodes directly connected to it. Routing algorithms that are based on global network topology result in lower reroute times than neighbor-node algorithms, since the end-to-end route is known immediately. Neighbor-node algorithms seek the best possible route from neighbors on a link-by-link basis. This may result in multiple connection attempts. The disadvantage of global algorithm methods is the large amount of messaging necessary to keep all nodes current on network conditions.

The table-driven multiplexer is less flexible in a frequently changing network. Table-driven multiplexers use predefined paths for routing circuits to other nodes. Tables that determine a circuit's path are stored either in each node or in central network management. These tables must be updated when nodes or lines are added or deleted. Route selection must be defined manually by the network operator or by an automated process under operator control. Complex networks that require many alternate-route scenarios and daily table updates become difficult to manage.

The number of alternate routes that can be stored is important. Timeplex's Link/2 can store up to eight alternate routes—this is typical. For example, a network connecting three sites in a triangle would require a maximum of four routes in each node—one directly to each adjacent node, and one alternate for each. As the complexity of the network increases, the number of possible alternate routes also increases. A limited number of alternate routes may require the network operator to manually configure new table entries during a node or line outage. Table-driven multiplexers, such as the Link/2, GDC's Megaswitch, and Infotron's NX4600 are best suited to networks with infrequent topology or circuit changes.

Networking boons

All of the products represented in Table 3 have basic features such as time-of-day switching. This feature allows the network to automatically reallocate bandwidth and circuit connectivity based on the time of day.

The more advanced features that have emerged include: parameterized routing, priority levels, priority bumping, traffic balancing, and bandwidth contention (all defined in "Product analysis"). These features allow users to gain greater control over a circuit's initial and fallback routing.

For example, the IDNX allows the user to specify class-of-service parameters for each circuit. These parameters can be used to specify that a particular circuit travel only over optical-fiber, encrypted links. If the network topology cannot support the circuit request, the IDNX automatically responds with an alert.

In another example, an IPX network uses each fast packet to carry information that specifies the maximum permissible circuit delay. (In fast packet switching—analogous to statistical multiplexing—there is no time alignment among transmissions [while providing internodal transport]. This constrasts with TDM [time-division multiplexing], where the transmissions are all time-aligned.) The intermediate nodes will adjust fast packet queuing to control this delay.

A priority-level example: The Link/2 allows the user to specify one of 16 priority levels for each circuit. The user may place important data applications higher in the queue than voice to avoid time-out restrictions and maintain data circuit availability. Without this feature, the user has no control over the order in which circuits are placed back in service.

Priority bumping enhances the user's control during facility outages. This feature allows a higher-priority circuit to override or "bump" a lower-priority circuit when its bandwidth is required. For example, with the 740/745, three levels of bumping are available. When a facility failure decreases the available bandwidth, the multiplexer automatically arbitrates which circuits stay up and which get bumped. Four levels is the practicable, usable number for priority bumping.

Priority levels are often confused with priority bumping levels. While a circuit may have a priority level of one and get reconnected first, it may eventually be bumped by a circuit from another node with a higher bumping priority.

As for the traffic-balancing feature, it is supported only by the IPX as part of its fast-packet architecture.

Nodal architectures

"Multiplexing orientation" is how the product interleaves information on its internodal aggregate links. Almost all the multiplexers in Table 3 utilize TDM; the one exception: Stratacom's IPX, which uses a fast-packet architecture. The TDM units are either bit- or byte-oriented. This means that the multiplexer puts individual channels in either one-bit-oriented or eight-bit (byte)-oriented time slots.

Bit multiplexing is more efficient, but it is implemented using vendor-proprietary formats. This limits flexibility for trunk interconnection to carrier services (such as CCR, AT&T's Customer Controlled Reconfiguration, and M24, AT&T's multiplexed voice interface) or to other vendors' equipment (PBXs, channel banks, other T1 multiplexers). It is possible to be bit-oriented and still be DACS (Digital Access and Cross-connect System)-compatible at the DS-0 level, as is the case with the 740 and the ONC. These products bit-interleave within DS-0 boundaries, but they do not interface to channelized services such as M24 and subrate (below DS-0) digital multiplexing.

Compared to the TDM approach of the other vendors, Stratacom's IPX fast-packet architecture is a unique multiplexing technique. It assembles a T1 transmission stream into fast packets, using a standard T1 frame (193 bits), with one bit used for framing. Each 192-bit fast packet contains a destination address as well as the T1 channel's data or voice information. The fast-packet architecture permits faster reroute times than are found with circuit-switched products (see Table 3, "Time to reroute"). It also provides bandwidth efficiency (more channels per given bandwidth, accomplished more efficiently than with TDM) for low-speed channels (9.6 kbit/s and below). A disadvantage of this architecture is its relatively long (about 2.7 milliseconds) intermediate-node circuit delays and lengthy (also about 2.7 milliseconds) processing delays for low-speed channels at the origin node.

Network delays can impose restrictions on applications support. Circuit-delay time is based on the combination of propagation time across transmission facilities and the bypass delay imposed by intermediate multiplexers. Some data applications, such as CAD/CAM (computer-aided design/computer-aided manufacturing), are delay-sensitive. A round-trip delay of 20 milliseconds on a voice circuit can produce echo that is annoying during a phone conversation. This delay corresponds to that of a terrestrial circuit of about 1,800 miles and results in a need for echo cancellers as additional equipment on voice channels.

For some multiplexers, this problem manifests itself at shorter (less than 1,800 miles) distances. On a 32-kbit/s voice circuit, an IDNX imposes a bypass delay of 5 milliseconds per intermediate node, and the IPX imposes a delay of 2.75 milliseconds. These intermediate-node delays are high enough to warrant the use of echo cancellation equipment at shorter internodal distances (the equivalent of 450 miles shorter for each IDNX and 250 miles shorter for each IPX).

A different way

The System 9000 employs an approach that does not impose, on voice-signal information, the delays that are incurred when multiplexing low-speed data (see Table 3, "Bypass delay"). Voice samples are placed in the multiplexer's internodal transmission frame so that an intermediate node can recognize them and pass them immediately. In order to achieve the granularity (the ability to divide the T1 "pipe" into lower-data-rate channels) necessary for low-speed data, the data is buffered and placed in a subframe. The result is an intermediate delay of 0.375 millisecond for voice circuits, compared with 3 milliseconds for data circuits.

The lowest allowable bypass channel reveals another aspect of a multiplexer's flexibility. The lowest bypass channel is the bandwidth of the envelope carrying a single circuit. A large envelope (such as 64 kbit/s in the ONX and the 740/745) could create bandwidth inefficiency when a single low-speed circuit needs its own path. A small envelope, like 50 bit/s in the Link/2, creates a flexible and efficient bandwidth utilization.

Most network applications mandate redundancy of internodal link modules. The total number of aggregates supported is affected by the redundancy scheme employed (see *Aggregate redundancy* in "Product analysis"). The 1:N scheme is not only more flexible but more cost-effective. For example, the IDNX can support 96 non-redundant internodal links and employs a 1:1 redundancy scheme. Therefore, a fully redundant IDNX could support 48 aggregates (with 48 backups). The 1:N redundancy scheme utilized in the 745 and the ONX allows the user to create a backup arrangement where one module can back up as many as 15 aggregates (15 backed up by one).

The maximum number of aggregates and the maximum number of channels a multiplexer can hold does not necessarily reflect the multiplexer's true capacity (see *Throughput capacity* in "Product analysis"). The throughput capacity values in Table 3 give a relative measure of the real "work" potential of each multiplexer. These values can be used in network planning to determine the number of nodes required to support a given location. Other elements that can affect actual capacity are physical slot restrictions and the logical number of circuits that can be managed by the node.

After determining individual nodal requirements, you should determine the maximum number of nodes that will be required in the network. Restrictions may be imposed by the network management scheme or by the multiplexer's addressing capabilities. Circuits will be required to traverse a number of intermediate links to get to the destination. Under normal conditions, the number of hops should be kept to a minimum, but alternative reroute scenarios could cause the circuit to be routed over many more links than intended. Most corporate backbone networks require support of at least five intermediate hops. ∎

Tim Zerbiec is a principal and vice president for technology at the Vertical Systems Group, a consulting and market research firm. He is responsible for managing technology-related offerings. Zerbiec has over 17 years of telecommunications engineering, research, and management experience.

Rosemary Cochran, also a principal of Vertical Systems, is responsible for managing the firm's marketing-related offerings. She has 14 years of experience in data services and telecommunications.

This article is based on material abstracted from the report, "T1 Multiplexer Industry Analysis: 1988," available from Vertical Systems Group, One Dedham Place, Dedham, Mass. 02026; telephone: (617) 329-0900.

John R. Curran, Curran Communications Laboratory, Colorado Springs, Colo.

Using testing to pick the right multiplexer

Stat mux performance can vary. Here are some secrets from a test lab to help you select the right multiplexer.

Until the appearance of the statistical multiplexer, there was little need to test multiplexers. Time-division and frequency-division multiplexers are relatively simple devices, and as long as they are properly designed, their performance is completely predictable. The data put into one end comes out the other end, with propagation causing the only delay.

But the statistical multiplexer does pose problems. The device is essentially a time-division multiplexer with no fixed bit assignments in the composite data stream. The sum of the input or aggregate data rate can exceed the composite data rate. Data delay is now much more of a possibility. In addition, the input data is broken up into unpredictable patterns and reconstructed at the other end. The information that goes into one end may not be sequentially identical to what comes out at the remote multiplexer.

Performance of statistical multiplexers cannot be predicted empirically; many factors are involved. Testing of statistical multiplexers can be a complicated and time-consuming operation, yet it is the only sure way of predicting performance.

Performance factors

Before addressing multiplexer testing, we must better understand the factors contributing to multiplexer performance:

■ *Composite protocol.* All statistical multiplexers superimpose a composite protocol on the data transmitted between the multiplexers. This protocol provides a means of verifying proper receipt of data. It also provides information on the destination channel for the data, and information on the status of the multiplexer and the channels connected to the multiplexer. Any composite protocol degrades the throughput capacity of the multiplexer because it takes valuable composite bandwidth away from the actual data transmission. Some protocols use greater numbers of bits to accomplish their tasks, but proper design can minimize the effect of the protocol on multiplexer capacity.

Another important aspect of the protocol is retransmission handling. If a multiplexer requires an acknowledgment for each block before sending the next block, the network will be needlessly delayed waiting for block acknowledgments. However, acknowledgment on a block-by-block basis reduces the number of blocks that need to be retransmitted in case of an error.

More commonly, multiplexers allow a certain number of outstanding unacknowledged blocks (typically seven). This method increases the requirement for buffers in the multiplexer because all unacknowledged blocks must be stored. With multiple unacknowledged blocks, the multiplexer may employ a retransmission of the bad block and all subsequent blocks, or it may use a Go-Back-N method whereby only the block in error is retransmitted (see "Here is one way to get a close estimate of a data link's efficiency," DATA COMMUNICATIONS, October 1986 for a discussion of protocol retransmission methods). The retransmission of all unacknowledged blocks is a simpler and more common method of composite protocol retransmission.

■ *Overhead recovery.* The sophisticated capabilities of a statistical multiplexer are costly. The composite protocol adds overhead to the composite block, reducing the multiplexer's throughput. Most multiplexers employ some variation of the high-level data link control (HDLC) protocol because they vary the meaning of the address bytes in the header. In some cases, they have an additional byte for multiplexer operations. HDLC by itself adds four bytes of overhead to each block, while some multiplexers add another byte for control purposes.

Some multiplexers allow data from only one terminal

1. Composite blocks. *In A, a composite block with one channel per block consists of two bytes of control characters, and 1-to-N bytes of data, framed with leading and trailing flag bytes. In B, a block with multiple channels contains successive control characters and data for each additional channel, identifying a change in channel destination.*

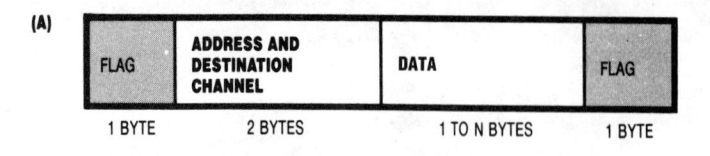

(A) | FLAG (1 BYTE) | ADDRESS AND DESTINATION CHANNEL (2 BYTES) | DATA (1 TO N BYTES) | FLAG (1 BYTE) |

(B) | FLAG (1 BYTE) | ADDRESS AND DESTINATION CHANNEL (2 BYTES) | DATA (1 TO N BYTES) | DESTINATION CHANNEL (1 BYTE) | DATA (1 TO N BYTES) | DESTINATION CHANNEL (1 BYTE) | DATA (1 TO N BYTES) | FLAG (1 BYTE) |

channel within a composite block; however, more sophisticated multiplexers mix data from multiple channels within a composite block. The mixing of channels adds more overhead to the block because some control information must be added to indicate the channel where the data is destined. Figure 1 shows a typical composite block for a multiplexer that allows only one channel per block (A) and one that allows multiple channels per block (B).

To recover the protocol overhead, most multiplexers employ one or more methods of reducing the number of data bits being sent. For example, most multiplexers use synchronous composite transmission. On an asynchronous multiplexer, the channel start and stop bits can be stripped from the incoming data and added back on the distant end. Therefore, the multiplexer recovers two bit times on every character. If the multiplexer adds four bytes (32 bits) to each block, then the composite block must be at least 16 data bytes long to recover the 32 bits of protocol overhead. This method only works on asynchronous multiplexers; synchronous multiplexers receive only eight data bits from the terminal.

Another trick to save composite bit times can be used if we know that the attached terminals will be sending only text characters (rather than control or graphics characters, which go beyond the ASCII set). The information content of text characters can be transmitted in seven data bits, with the eighth bit being used as a check, or parity, bit. Since the composite already uses an error-checking protocol, the parity bit does not need to be transmitted. The parity bit can be added to the outgoing data stream at the distant end. Again, this method only works on asynchronous channels. Synchronous channels may use the eighth bit for protocol control or addressing information.

Finally, some multiplexers use a data compression algorithm to further reduce the amount of information transmitted in the composite. The simplest data compression algorithm compresses repetitive blanks or spaces. To be truly effective, data compression algorithms must have existing knowledge of the type of data to be compressed; general-purpose multiplexers cannot know ahead of time the type of data they will be receiving. In addition, data compression algorithms usually require a significant amount of firmware, making them more expensive. Consequently, data compression algorithms are usually found only in synchronous multiplexers, because asynchronous multiplexers already reduce information content by 20 to 30 percent (20 percent for start and stop bits and an additional 10 percent for the parity bit). Any additional reduction is not really worth the development effort and processing time.

■ *Composite block size.* All multiplexers have built-in rules for determining the size of the composite block to be sent. This rules-setting constitutes the real art in the design of a general-purpose multiplexer. If the block becomes too long, then any characters arriving just after the block is closed must wait for the transmission of the current block and the building of a new block. Depending on the multiplexer's traffic activity, the quality of the composite line (indicated by the number of retransmissions required), and the block size, this delay could become significant. Yet if the block is too short, the protocol overhead will add a considerable percentage to the composite line. On a multiplexer heavily loaded with short blocks, the protocol overhead could add enough bits to the composite that delays in channel-data transmission could become onerous.

Most multiplexer manufacturers close a block when there is no more channel data to send or when a block reaches a predetermined size. However, if a character arrives just after closing a block, the character may experience a significant delay. The alternative is to wait for a period of time to see if any more data will arrive on a channel: The question then becomes how long to wait. If no more data comes in during the wait period, then all data has been needlessly delayed. Empirical evidence indicates the optimum block size to be 64 bytes.

■ *Unit synchronization.* Periodically, multiplexers must exchange information about the status of channel interface leads and the status of the multiplexers themselves. Most multiplexers exchange this information in separate composite blocks, between data blocks, or as extra bytes within the data block. Normally, this operation is transparent to the user. The constant exchange of status can be a problem when the composite is being routed through another (intermediate) multiplexer. The intermediate multiplexer, receiving composites from other multiplexers, can become saturated as a result.

■ *Buffer pool organization.* In simplest terms, a statistical multiplexer is nothing more than a special-purpose computer with a series of transmission queues. A statistical multiplexer's memory controls the amount of data that can be buffered. Multiplexer designers determine how this memory is apportioned among buffers. For example, some

Using a minicomputer or or mainframe is costly. The microcomputer is the ideal way to test muxes.

multiplexers have one large memory pool in which the composite and all the channels compete for buffer space on an equal basis. Other multiplexers assign a fixed amount of buffering to the composite. This ensures that there will always be space to transmit and receive data on the composite. Then a fixed amount of buffer space is allotted and all channels compete for it.

Still other multiplexers assign a fixed amount of buffer space to the composite and to each channel. Channel assignments may be based on priority or may be changed dynamically based on channel activity. In any case, many vendors make a major sales pitch out of how their unit allocates buffer space. In reality, it is impossible to predict how well a multiplexer will perform in a particular network solely by looking at its buffer allocation method.

■ *Flow-control methods.* At some point, data will come into a multiplexer faster than it can be transmitted. When the channel buffers fill, the multiplexer must be able to tell the terminal to stop sending data. This operation is called flow control. The most common types of flow control on asynchronous multiplexers are dropping the Data Set Ready lead on the interface, sending an X-OFF character (DC3) to the terminal, or dropping the Clear To Send lead on the interface. But there may be proprietary methods of flow control that require attention. For example, Wang terminals use unique flow-control characters that are not supported on all multiplexers.

In some cases, multiplexers may be ready to send data to a terminal when the terminal is not ready. In this case, the terminal must be able to control the flow of information from the multiplexer. However, not all multiplexers accept flow control. Therefore, users must know what types of flow control their terminals use and must consider their own need for this feature when comparing multiplexers.

Many multiplexers can improve their performance by "playing" with flow control. Under certain protocols, terminals send 80 characters and wait for an acknowledgment (ACK) from the remote end before sending another 80 characters. To improve performance, when a local terminal sends 80 characters, the local multiplexer returns the ACK immediately. The local multiplexer then sends data to the distant end in the normal sequence. When the terminal at the distant end returns its ACK, the remote multiplexer discards it, since the local terminal already has received an ACK for the data. Multiplexer manufacturers have found that they can significantly improve terminal data throughput with this method. Further, local multiplexers can withhold acknowledgment from the local terminal as a flow-control method, or the distant terminal can withhold its ACK until it is ready to receive more data.

It is important to know if all channels have to be configured for a particular kind of terminal. Some multiplexers require that all or none of the channels be configured for a particular protocol. Other multiplexers can support particular protocols on each channel independently.

Flow control on synchronous multiplexers poses a complex problem. Synchronous terminals require a definite send/receive sequence of allowable messages for all situations. Any departure from this sequence results in an error notice. In addition, message blocks are numbered and must be accounted for within a specified time period, so an active device cannot be inserted between two synchronous terminals. An effective method of synchronous flow control varies clock rates. Typically, the multiplexer provides the clock by which the terminal transmits data (transmit clock) and the clock by which the terminal receives data (receive clock). The multiplexer can reduce the rate at which data comes in by slowing the clock as the buffers begin to fill. Most synchronous terminals can handle a reduced clock rate as long as the clock doesn't stop completely. However, a few terminals cannot tolerate a variable clock rate: They may drop the channel connection, terminating the session because they are programmed to assume that something is malfunctioning. The only way to be sure of the effect of a variable clock rate on a terminal is to test the multiplexer with the terminal under a traffic-stressed condition, so that the multiplexer reduces the clock rate.

■ *Aggregate vs. composite data rate.* The aggregate data rate is the sum of the data rates on all of the individual channels. As a general rule, on an asynchronous statistical multiplexer, the aggregate data rate is about four times the composite rate.

For example, if a statistical multiplexer has a 9.6-kbit/s composite and its terminals have average activity, four 9.6-kbit/s terminals can be connected to the multiplexer. If the terminals have light activity, as many as eight 9.6-kbit/s terminals could be attached to the multiplexer. However, if the terminals have heavy activity—such as in interactive program development—only two or three 9.6-kbit/s terminals could be connected to the multiplexer. More terminals can be connected to the multiplexer in each case if the data rates of the terminals are reduced, thereby keeping the aggregate data rate the same.

■ *Channel priority.* Some manufacturers allow assignment of channel priorities (high/low or 1 to n) when the unit is configured. This assignment allows time-critical or high-priority data to preempt normal data. However, if a high-priority channel is heavily loaded, it can monopolize the network and effectively lock out lightly loaded, low-priority

2. Daisy-chain. *One terminal generates data for all channels. Characters put into channel 1 go through both muxes and are looped back to end up at the inputting terminal.*

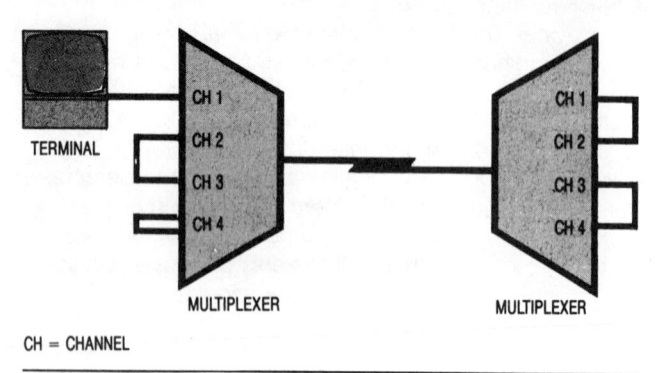

channels. While the total throughput of data is the same, delays experienced on a locked-out channel would be excessive.

Methods of testing multiplexers

Most multiplexer vendors will lend a couple of evaluation units for a period of time. So the best method of evaluating multiplexers—putting them into an actual network where they can run live traffic—can be performed. However, since poor performance or a malfunction could seriously affect the network, this is a very risky operation. If asynchronous terminals are being used, there is no reliable way to detect missing or garbled data. Most users will not put units into a production network until they have some confidence in the multiplexers. Rather, users test multiplexers on a test link until they feel secure about the unit. The problem here is determining how to simulate a production network to stress the multiplexer.

One stressing method is to connect one terminal to multiple channels with a "split" cable and send the same data on all channels simultaneously. However, if the multiplexer flow-controls the terminal on one channel, the terminal stops sending on all channels. Also, the received data from multiple channels is intermixed (identical messages all addressed the same), so it is impossible to tell if the data is received correctly.

Another method of stressing a multiplexer is to daisy-chain (loop back) the channels (Fig. 2). Thus, a character sent from the terminal is received on remote channel 1 and immediately sent back on channel 2. The character is received on channel 2 of the local multiplexer and immediately sent out on channel 3. This operation continues until the character reaches the last channel, where it is sent back through the same path. Eventually it is received back at the originating terminal.

The loopback method requires only one terminal and can easily stress the network. However, it also requires a multiplexer that can give as well as receive flow control. For example, if remote channel 3 has full buffers, it sends back a flow-control message. However, the message does not go to a terminal but to remote channel 2. Remote channel 2 is required to recognize flow control from its simulated terminal; otherwise, data will be lost. In addition, all channels must operate at the same data rate.

In the third method, a separate terminal is connected to each channel. To truly simulate traffic, operators must be operating all terminals. As an alternative, a multiport computer connected to the multiplexer can simulate multiple operators. The advantage of this method is that the computer can rapidly compare the received data to the transmitted data and identify errors. However, using a minicomputer or mainframe is costly, requires time-consuming programming, and few computers have the required number of ports to test the multiplexer.

In recent years, the microcomputer has become an ideal way to test multiplexers. The microcomputer is relatively inexpensive, easy to program, and has interface cards to simulate most terminal types. Also, there are many microcomputer interface cards that support multiple asynchronous ports.

The most important aspect of multiplexer performance is its efficiency in moving data. That determines the overall multiplexer throughput, each channel's throughput, and the end-to-end delay on each channel. For example, a multiplexer with four fully loaded channels may transmit 60 characters from each, in turn. A character arriving on the fourth channel precisely when the first character arrives on channel 1 could be delayed by as much as 180 characters. If the terminals are operating interactively with a computer, and the host echoes the characters, the 180-character time delay could be extremely disconcerting for the terminal operator.

A second important aspect of multiplexer performance is data integrity. Multiplexers can lose data by inappropriate operation of the composite protocol or by inappropriate operation of the channel flow-control feature.

A third important aspect of statistical multiplexer performance is the possibility that one channel could monopolize a network.

Statistical multiplexer testing

Four procedures can be run to test the performance of multiplexers. The basic test setup consists of connecting two multiplexers back-to-back, with an error injector and recording protocol analyzer in the composite link (Fig. 3). A microcomputer simulates terminals by sending typical text data. The number of terminals simulated by one computer depends on the speed of the terminals to be simulated. Typically, an IBM PC/AT-class computer can handle 150 kbit/s; an IBM PC/XT-class, 75 kbit/s. If multiple computers are used, the same computer connects to the corresponding channels at both ends of the link. This arrangement provides a common time base upon which to measure file-transmission time and end-to-end delay.

■ *Error-free unstressed test.* This test consists of dividing the composite equally among all channels (that is, not stressing the multiplexer) and not injecting any errors onto the composite. For this test, a four-channel multiplexer, operating a 9.6-kbit/s composite, would activate all channels at 2.4 kbit/s. If the same multiplexer had eight channels, the channels would be run at 1.2 kbit/s. The same test

3. Test setup. *The basic multiplexer-test configuration has an error injector, one or more PCs, and a recording protocol analyzer in the composite path.*

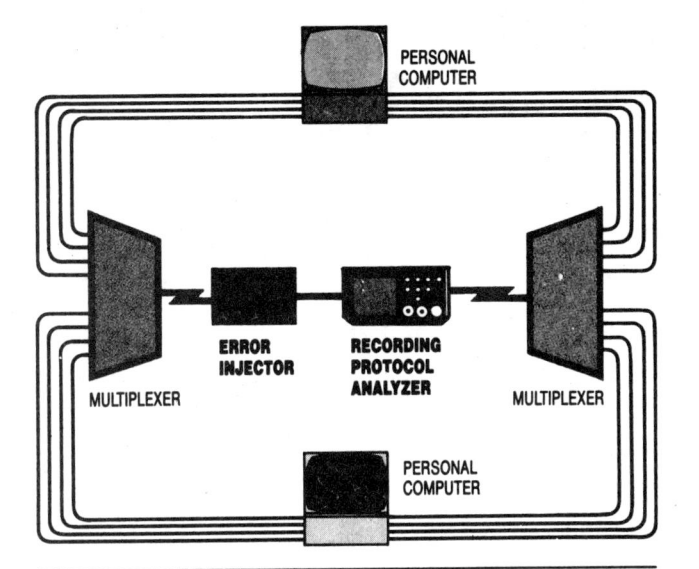

file is sent on all channels simultaneously.

The end-to-end delay is measured for random characters on each channel, along with the total file-transfer time for each channel. The random end-to-end delay measurement provides average delay time for each channel. The total file-transfer time measures the efficiency of the protocol and bit-stripping techniques.

If there were no protocol operation and no bit stripping involved, the transmission rate would equal the channel rate. In the example of a 2.4-kbit/s channel, the channel transfer rate should equal 2.4 kbit/s. In fact, the transfer rate is somewhat less; however, the better the multiplexer design, the closer the transfer rate approaches the channel rate. In addition, the transmitted file is compared with the received file on each channel. The results of this comparison prove whether the multiplexer routes data to the proper channel. There are cases where a multiplexer routes data entered on one channel only to have it appear at a different channel on the output end. Multiplexers with this bug are essentially worthless.

■ *Error-free stress test.* Next, repeat the above test but stress the multiplexer by providing data on the channels faster than the multiplexer can handle it. Increase all of the channels' data rates until the aggregate data rate is four times the composite rate. In the case of a four-channel multiplexer, with a 9.6-kbit/s composite, each channel is operated at 9.6 kbit/s. If testing an eight-channel multiplexer, each channel is operated at 4.8 kbit/s. The multiplexer must invoke flow control or it will lose data. Each channel should invoke a different type of flow control—if more than one type is provided—in order to test all methods of flow control available to the multiplexer.

The same parameters that were measured in the error-free unstressed test are measured in this test. If the average end-to-end delay or the total throughput time varies appreciably from the previous test, it indicates that the multiplexer has trouble handling data in a stressed condition. If the multiplexer is properly designed, the measurements should not differ dramatically.

The comparison of the transmitted file to the received file verifies the proper flow of data in a stressed multiplexer and proper operation of the channel flow-control methods. If the received data does not match the transmitted data, then the channel flow controls are not operating properly. A multiplexer can issue flow control in the middle of sending a character, and then expect the terminal to stop immediately. The multiplexer discards the character in progress, but the terminal assumes reception of that character and resumes with the following character when it is turned back on. Therefore, one character is lost each time the multiplexer flow-controls the terminal.

■ *Stress test with errors.* Next, repeat the error-free stress test but with errors on the composite link. In this test, record the composite link on the recording protocol analyzer. A multiplexer with a properly operating composite protocol and proper operation of the channel flow control will get the data through to the remote end with no errors.

Compare the received data with the transmitted data to ensure that all data was received error-free. This validates the proper operation of the channel flow-control and correcting-error recovery of the composite protocol. If data is not received correctly, review the recordings of the composite to determine the malfunction in the error recovery of the composite protocol.

■ *Channel monopoly test.* In this test, repeat the error-free unstressed test, but change channel utilization. Data is generated on channel 1 (or a high-priority channel) at the operating data rate; however, two characters per second are generated on the other channels—and at the operating data rate. In the example of the four-channel multiplexer in the error-free unstressed test, channel 1 would be receiving 240 characters per second (2.4 kbit/s and 10 bits per character) at 2.4 kbit/s. Meanwhile, the other three channels would be receiving two characters per second at 2.4 kbit/s. Randomly measure end-to-end delay. If one channel is allowed to monopolize the network, the end-to-end delay will significantly exceed the end-to-end delay measured in the error-free, unstressed text. However, in a properly designed multiplexer, the end-to-end delays will not differ noticeably.

Upon completion of the four multiplexer tests, multiplexer performance and data reliability should be fairly well established. However, these tests do not measure the performance in a particular application. Multiplexer performance can only be determined conclusively in a specific network with a specific application. ■

John Curran holds a BS in mathematics from the College of William and Mary (Williamsburg, Va.) and a master's degree in operations research, engineering from Tulane University (New Orleans). He has been active in the data communications industry for more than 25 years, developing and designing modems and multiplexers. He now owns Curran Communications Laboratory, an independent testing laboratory.

Gilbert Held, 4-Degree Consulting, Macon, Ga.

Is ISDN an obsolete data network?

Amid all the hoopla, what's getting lost? Here's a comparison of eight applications: How are they served by ISDN versus other data transmission methods?

Although the demand for information about ISDN continues to escalate—and vendors, service providers, and users march to the ISDN cadence—the technology's data transport capabilities are not necessarily better than those of other existing and emerging transmission methods. While it may seem like heresy, developments in other areas of data communications may be rendering ISDN obsolete.

How, for example, does ISDN transmission capacity compare with the transmission rates offered by recent advances in such fields as local and wide area networking, PC video graphics, and voice digitization techniques?

ISDN notwithstanding, a wide variety of technologies exists to satisfy end-user communications requirements. These options yield a range of transmission rates: from fewer than 100 bit/s to millions of bits per second. There are 17 popular categories of such transport mechanisms (see Table 1). Several are specific to particular industry segments. The continuous slope variable delta modulation digitization technique, for example, was originally developed for military applications. This technique encodes each analog voice sample into a single bit based on a comparison of the height of the sample with the height of the previous sample—thus increasing the sampling rate with respect to the data rate. Although voice quality at 8 and 16 kbit/s is marginal, with an increased sampling rate the encoding of 1 bit per sample produces a reasonably acceptable voice quality at 32 kbit/s.

Another digitized voice technology, linear predictive coding (LPC), synthesizes a voice conversation by encoding pitch, energy level, and other voice parameters. Although LPC digitizes a voice conversation into an extremely low data rate, it is very expensive to implement and not suitable for general use.

Two video transmission methods are readily available: Full-motion video, which can be transmitted at about 700 kbit/s, and freeze-frame, which can be transmitted at 64 kbit/s using commercially available equipment that compresses digitized video signals. Although both types of video have been successfully compressed at lower data rates, the current cost of equipment precludes widespread use. A small-band ISDN videophone terminal, according to the Netherlands Foreign Investment Agency, a unit of the Dutch Ministry of Economic Affairs (North American headquarters in New York City), is expected to be available for home and office use in Holland in 1992. The agency says this videophone is expected to provide high-quality moving pictures accompanied by high-quality voice at 64 kbit/s by using a "hybrid method of data compression that combines DPCM [differential pulse code modulation] and transform coding."

Communications applications

Although there are many existing and evolving non-ISDN communications applications, a small subset can be used as a representative base to compare against the data transportation capabilities provided by ISDN (for details of the ISDN architecture, see "ISDN overview"). Eight current and potential communications-related applications that can be expected to occur on an ISDN B channel are listed in Table 2.

Currently, electronic-mail applications are most often satisfied by dial-up access via the switched telephone network at data rates ranging from 110 bit/s to 9.6 kbit/s. Thus, an ISDN B channel should be more than sufficient to serve text-based messaging with this application. If the transmission of graphics images is required as part of an electronic-mail application or as a standalone application, then the type of graphics image, as well as what one considers a reasonable transmission time, will govern whether or not a B channel provides an acceptable level of service.

As for whether ISDN will benefit file transfer operations, at the 64-kbit/s data rate of a B channel, this application is

ISDN

Table 1: Popular transmission options

TRANSMISSION TECHNOLOGY	DATA TRANS-PORTATION RATE
ANALOG MODEMS	
SWITCHED NETWORK USE	110 BIT/S–9.6 KBIT/S
LEASED LINE USE	1.2–19.2 KBIT/S
DATAPHONE DIGITAL SERVICE	
SWITCHED NETWORK	56 KBIT/S
LEASED LINE	2.4–56 KBIT/S
DIGITIZED VOICE	
PULSE-CODE MODULATION	64 KBIT/S
ADAPTIVE PULSE-CODE MODULATION	32 KBIT/S
CONTINUOUS SLOPE VARIABLE DELTA MODULATION	8–64 KBIT/S
LINEAR PREDICTIVE CODING	2.4–4.8 KBIT/S
LOCAL AREA NETWORKING	
APPLETALK	.25 MBIT/S
ARCNET	2.5 MBIT/S
ETHERNET	10.0 MBIT/S
TOKEN RING	4/16 MBIT/S
IBM 3270 TWISTED WIRE	2.38 MBIT/S
T1	
NORTH AMERICA	1.544 MBIT/S
EUROPE	2.048 MBIT/S
VIDEO	
FULL MOTION	700 KBIT/S
FREEZE FRAME	64 KBIT/S

served 3.33 times faster than it is with 19.2-kbit/s modems. The number of 8-bit characters that could be transmitted at the ISDN B-channel rate, at 19.2 kbit/s on a high-speed conditioned analog leased line, and at 2.4 kbit/s using a V.22*bis* modem on the switched telephone networkare compared in Table 3.

Applying this data to typical interactive file transfer operations indicates that an ISDN B channel should provide satisfactory performance. For example, consider the standard 360-Kbyte 5.25-inch and 1.44-Mbyte 3.5-inch diskettes commonly used in PCs. Using an ISDN B channel, it would take about six seconds to transfer the contents of a 360-Kbyte diskette and 23 seconds to transfer the contents of a 1.44-Mbyte diskette. Since interactive users rarely transfer the contents of an entire diskette, it appears that a 64-kbit/s data transfer rate should provide an acceptable level of service for interactive file transfer operations.

For distributed computer systems requiring the transfer of large databases, the ISDN 64-kbit/s B channel, however, may not prove satisfactory. As an example of this situation, consider the transfer of a 100-Mbyte file. At 64 kbit/s, the file transfer would require almost four hours!

Text versus graphics
How well ISDN will serve applications involving graphics image transmission is less easily determined than its suitability for electronic-mail and file transfer operations. The time required for the transmission of screen images on PCs varies, as can be seen in an examination of three popular video display modes.

When an IBM PC or compatible is in its text video mode, each ASCII character is displayed in a box defined by a number of vertical and horizontal pixels. The pixels that represent the character are generated by the video circuitry, which interprets the ASCII character. In the computer, each character of the text video image requires 2 bytes of storage. The first byte is the ASCII code that defines the character; the second byte is known as the character attribute and defines such parameters as whether the character is blinking, underlined, highlighted, and so on. Thus, the transmission of a full text screen image would require sending 32,000 bits of data (80-character column by 25 lines by 2 bytes per character—for storage—by 8 bits per character). When transmitted using a V.22*bis* modem operating at 2.4 kbit/s, the screen transfer time is 13.3 seconds. Using an ISDN B channel, the time required to transfer a full text screen image is reduced to 0.5 seconds.

The introduction of IBM's Presentation Manager and the growth in other window-oriented machines—including the Apple Macintosh series, Atari STs, and Sun workstations—will result in an increasing need to transmit and receive computer screens in their graphics mode. In fact, remote computer control has grown in use over the past few years from a single product offering to software marketed by about a dozen vendors, one of which (Norton-Lambert) claimed sales of more than 100,000 units during 1988.

The time required to transmit a graphics screen image depends first on the video graphics mode that is being used. Second, transmission time depends on whether the communications software is capable of performing data compression and/or transmitting only screen changes with respect to a prior transmitted image. In examining the transmission of a graphics screen image, first consider the time required to transmit the screen without compression.

If a PC has the Enhanced Graphics Adapter (EGA) display capability, it can display a window with a resolution of 640-by-350 pixels and one of four possible colors. Such a display requires 224 kbits to transmit a black-and-white image, each bit carrying the pixel image and its color composition: black or white. If an image using any color other than black or white is transmitted, an additional 2 bits per pixel would be used to represent one of the four possible colors, increasing the transmission requirements for a full-screen image to 448 kbits. If a V.22*bis* modem operating at 2.4 kbit/s is used to transmit an EGA screen image, a total of about 187 seconds, or more than three minutes, would be required. Even with the use of an ISDN B channel, seven seconds would be required to transmit an EGA screen.

For a PC with the Video Graphics Adapter (VGA), the higher resolution of the VGA display results in a corresponding increase in the time required to transmit a screen of data. In the VGA graphics mode a resolution of 640-by-480 pixels results in a minimum of 307,200 bits to represent a black-and-white image. Since VGA permits up to 16 possible colors, using 4 bits per pixel to represent color yields a total of 1,228,800 bits. A V.22*bis* modem at 2.4 kbit/s would take about 8.5 minutes to transmit a screen image. Using an ISDN B channel would reduce transmission time to 19.2 seconds.

The preceding computations of transmission time are for a graphics screen without compression, but what effect can

ISDN

be expected through the use of a sophisticated remote-control software package? In the advertising literature for Co/Session 3.0, Triton Technologies Inc. (Islin, N.J.) claims to offer the fastest text and graphics screen updates of any remote-control package. The vendor specifies that the time needed to display a large directory in a window at 2.4 kbit/s is 43 seconds. Since this is approximately a quarter of the time computed for the transmission of a screen under the EGA mode, an interpolation would suggest that transmitting the screen image over an ISDN B channel would require less than two seconds. A similar interpolation for the use of a VGA video mode would reduce the computed transmission time of 19.2 seconds to less than five seconds for transmitting a large directory in a windows environment.

Since late 1988, numerous vendors have introduced register-level superextended VGAs. Downward compatible with conventional VGAs, these cards support the emerging 1,024-by-768 pixel superextended VGA resolution. That resolution requires 786,432 bits to represent a black-and-white screen image. In its color mode, where 4 bits per pixel can be used to represent 16 colors, the transfer of a full screen would require transmitting a total of 3,145,728 bits. At the ISDN B-channel data rate of 64 kbit/s, it would take about 49 seconds to transmit an extended VGA screen. Even if one assumes that remote-control software provides an approximate 4:1 reduction in transmission time (which is what the author experienced using the previously mentioned Co/Session package), the transmission of an extended VGA screen can be expected to take more than 10 seconds on an ISDN B channel. While 10 seconds does not seem particularly long by itself, for a repeating process—such as dialing into a network management system and scrolling through screens—this delay could be irritating at the least and would be unacceptable to organizations that aim to obtain a three- to five-second response time.

Voice versus graphics

There is one communications application that may well be over-served by ISDN: human voice transmission. Since toll-quality voice can be transmitted at 32 kbit/s, the 64-kbit/s transmission rate of an ISDN B channel may actually be excessive. In contrast, graphics applications may pose some difficulty. Although the author is not well versed in the economics of adaptive PCM voice digitization versus conventional PCM, it would appear that having variable-rate channels instead of fixed-rate channels provides a higher level of capability that could alleviate some of the problems associated with transmitting graphics images. As an example, consider the figure, which illustrates two possible modifications that can be made to the data transporting capability of the B channel under a variable-rate channel creation scheme.

The first variable-rate channelization illustrated in the figure could assign 96 kbit/s to a B channel and 32 kbit/s to a B1 channel. This would permit higher data transfers on the B channel and simultaneous transmission of voice, digitized at 32 kbit/s, on the B1 channel. The second variable-rate channelization scheme could merge the transportation capability of two B channels, providing subscribers with the ability to transmit data-intensive applications, such as ex-

---

ISDN overview

Under the evolving ISDN architecture, access to the network is possible via one of two major connection methods: basic access and primary accesss. Basic access defines a multiple channel connection derived by multiplexing data on twisted-pair wiring. This connection method consists of two bearer (B) channels, each operating at 64 kbit/s, and a data (D) channel operating at 16 kbit/s. The ISDN basic access channel format is illustrated in the figure. Because of the composition of the basic access format, it is commonly referred to as a 2B + D service.

The bandwidth of each B channel is structured to carry either one pulse code modulation voice conversation or one 64-kbit/s data transmission. Together, the two B channels permit users to transmit data and, at the same time, conduct a voice conversation using a single telephone line; to converse with one person and to receive a second call; or to place one person on hold while answering a second call.

The D channel provides a transport mechanism for signaling information. Signals on the D channel are designed to control the B channels or to supplement their use by providing subscribers with information not readily available with conventional telephone service. Examples of the former include the carrying of off-hook and dial numbers, while examples of the latter include presenting

B1 CHANNEL	D	B2 CHANNEL

B CHANNELS OPERATE AT 64 KBIT/S EACH
D CHANNEL OPERATES AT 16 KBIT/S
2B + D SERVICE OPERATES AT 144 KBIT/S

the calling party or carrying information for home alarm systems or utility meters.

Primary access can be considered a multiplexing arrangement whereby a group of users having basic access share a common line facility. This type of access permits a private automated branch exchange to be directly connected to the ISDN network. In North America, primary access consists of a grouping of 23 B channels and one D channel, with each channel operating at 64 kbit/s. This structure enables the T1 (1.544-Mbit/s) carrier to serve as the transport mechanism for ISDN primary access.

Included in the specifications for ISDN is a provision for packet-switched channels that are designed to carry streams of user information at varying data rates. An H channel is designed to operate at 384 kbit/s, while H11 and H12 channels operate at 1.536 and 1.92 Mbit/s, respectively. Although H channel primary-rate interface provisions exist within ISDN, vendors have not yet designed equipment to operate on H channels. —G.H.

ISDN

tended VGA screens, in half the time possible with a single B channel.

The Q.931 recommended standard ("ISDN User-Network Interface Layer 3 Specification for Basic Call") includes a provision for the concatenation of two B channels to obtain a 128-kbit/s data transfer capability. In addition, under CCITT I.460 ("Multiplexing, Rate Adaption, and Support of Existing Interfaces") there is a provision that permits a B channel to be split into 8-kbit/s intervals. Unfortunately, neither standard has, to the author's knowledge, been adopted by switch vendors; nor have manufacturers begun work to develop equipment that operates with concatenated or interval B channels. Clearly, variable-rate B channel capability would provide consumers options that are not available under the present ISDN structure.

Videophone and videotex

As previously mentioned, videophones are expected to be commercially available by 1992. The key to the operation of a videophone is the videocodec, which effectively compresses full-motion video images to approximately 1/1,500 of their original information content. Since the videocodecs that are currently marketed sell for around $15,000, it is reasonable to question vendor expectations that mass production will result in economical videophones by 1992. One only has to look at the relatively stable retail price of CD-ROM players between 1986 and 1988 to question expected price declines in high-technology equipment.

One wonders, though, what effect a 128-kbit/s B channel—obtained by merging two B channels—would have on videophone developments. Since the complexity of a compression scheme is proportional to the required compression ratio, the cost of videocodecs that operate at 128 kbit/s could be less than that of videocodecs operating at 64 kbit/s. Although the degree of cost reduction is a matter of

Table 3: Transfer of 8-bit characters

TIME	64 KBIT/S (ISDN B CHANNEL)	19.2 KBIT/S*	2.4 KBIT/S**
1 SECOND	8,000	2,400	300
30 SECONDS	240,000	72,000	9,000
1 MINUTE	480,000	144,000	18,000
1 HOUR	28,800,000	8,640,000	1,080,000

*VIA CONDITIONED ANALOG LEASED LINE.
**VIA V.22bis MODEM ON SWITCHED PHONE NETWORK.

conjecture, its existence provides another rationale for the implementation of a variable-rate set of B channels.

Current videotex implementations create screen images by transmitting character codes that form cells, or blocks, of characters on the screen. Although videotex pictures are rather crude compared with EGA and VGA images, videotex data transmission requirements are relatively modest. Thus, 2.4-kbit/s transmission used on analog facilities will be substantially improved through the use of an ISDN B channel.

If videotex should eventually use pixel graphics, the same problems mentioned for remote-control PC software can be expected. That is, the time it takes to update screen images on an ISDN B channel would increase from a fraction of a second to more than 10 seconds for videotex using pixel graphics.

Interconnecting LANs and WANs

A network curiosity in the 1970s, local area networks have become an important communications mechanism for most organizations. Since the data rates of most LANs are in the megabits-per-second range, the delay encountered when connecting geographically dispersed LANs or connecting LANs to WANs via an ISDN B channel could severely tax a user's ability to do real-time work. This is because interconnection through Direct Distance Dialing or the ISDN B channel would be at 56 kbit/s or 64 kbit/s, compared with a megabits-per-second transfer on a LAN, resulting in delays when moving data between networks.

If data is in the form of high-resolution screen images, using the ISDN B channel will result in a slight bottleneck compared with the data transfer rate that can be achieved on a LAN. For other LAN operations, such as downloading a file contained on the server of one LAN to a workstation on a second LAN, the B channel will probably provide a sufficient data transfer capability. In fact, for many LAN-to-LAN data transfer operations, the key to whether a B channel is sufficient or acts as a bottleneck will be the number of users simultaneously requesting cross-LAN data transfers and the type of data transfer involved. Although broadband ISDN (BISDN) can be expected to provide a much higher data transporta-

Table 2: Applications versus capacity for ISDN B channel utilization

APPLICATION	CAPACITY
ELECTRONIC MAIL TRANSMISSION	MORE THAN SUFFICIENT
FILE TRANSFER OPERATIONS	VERY GOOD FOR INTERACTIVE WORK; INAPPROPRIATE FOR LARGE DATABASE TRANSFER
GRAPHIC IMAGE TRANSMISSION	REASONABLE NOW BUT LIKELY TO BE UNACCEPTABLE FOR SUPEREXTENDED VGA AND OTHER EVOLVING HIGHER-RESOLUTION SCREEN IMAGES
VOICE CONVERSATION	EXCESSIVE
REMOTE-CONTROL PC SOFTWARE	NOT ACCEPTABLE FOR GRAPHICS IMAGES
VIDEOPHONE TRANSMISSION	TOO SOON TO TELL
VIDEOTEX	ACCEPTABLE FOR TEXT; UNACCEPTABLE WITH HIGHER-RESOLUTION SCREEN-BASED GRAPHICS
INTERCONNECTING LANS AND WANS	BOTTLENECK IN SOME APPLICATIONS

ISDN

tion capability than is currently available in ISDN field trials, its implementation is probably five or more years distant. Because of this, ISDN as it now exists will probably be a bottleneck to some LAN and WAN interconnections.

ISDN problem areas

Besides the question of whether ISDN serves current and evolving applications as well as or better than other transmission technologies, there are problem areas that could delay the implementation of ISDN. One of the key features associated with digital ISDN telephone sets is the capability of displaying call progress and calling information. The telephone sets' ISDN capabilities can only be used when both the calling party and the called party are served by ISDN-compatible central office switches that can communicate with one another. This stumbling block may affect how long it takes to get ISDN telephone sets into the marketplace.

The communications between ISDN switches—known as Signaling System Number 7 (SS7)—is also both a key component of ISDN and a major bottleneck to universal ISDN services. When this communications method sets up telephone calls it uses circuits that are separate from those actually used for conducting the calls. Also known as out-of-band signaling, this technique permits the network database to be accessed as part of the call setup process, providing communications carriers with the ability to offer a variety of enhanced services to subscribers. Unfortunately, without a widespread deployment of SS7, ISDN will resemble a series of isolated islands. Thus, users implementing ISDN have no guarantee that they will obtain all or a portion of the advantages associated with its use.

Another area of concern is the data transmission rate between non-ISDN and ISDN devices. Until pre-ISDN equipment is replaced, access to most ISDN facilities will be through the use of terminal adapters, which convert 19.2 kbit/s to 64 kbit/s by appending null bits. Functioning as sophisticated speed converters, these expensive devices will use a rate-adaption process to enable non-ISDN equipment to function at the ISDN data rate. But since the device does not make the data come out of the PC faster, a PC with a serial port would still be limited to an effective data rate of 19.2 kbit/s when attached to an ISDN B channel through a terminal adapter.

Summary

Is ISDN an obsolete data network? In general, an ISDN B channel provides a transmission capacity that is sufficient for most current and emerging applications when viewed from the perspective of data rate capability. For some applications, such as extensive file transfer operations, high-resolution screen image transmission and interactive remote control involving window-oriented screens will result in the ISDN B channel being a data transfer bottleneck. For other applications, such as transmitting data between distant LANs, the bottleneck potential of the ISDN B channel will depend on the number of users simultaneously requesting remote access to another LAN and the applications they intend to perform.

Although BISDN can be expected to alleviate bottlenecks of data transfer on the B channel, its implementation is far too distant to overcome current and pending transmission problems. Bottlenecks at the B channels could be eliminated, in the near term, by using packet-switched H channels and variable-rate B channels. Unfortunately, the use of both H channels and variable-rate B channels requires actions by communications vendors—out of the hands of the user.

Although the capability for high-speed data transfer exists, vendors have not begun developing equipment to use these facilities. Thus, for the near future, the use of an H channel does not appear to be a reasonable way to alleviate B-channel bottlenecks. With respect to variable B channels, the implementation of Q.931 and I.460 also appears to be in the distant rather than the near future. Owing to the preceding, this author expects vendors to come to the rescue, probably developing a device equivalent to a conventional limited-function multiplexer for a 2B + D channel. If this occurs, the ability to combine two 64-kbit/s B channels into a 128-kbit/s data pipe (for applications that do not require voice coordination when simply performing file transfers, sending screen images, or accessing a distant LAN) can be expected to alleviate many of the data transfer problems foreseen in this article. Eventually, with the implementation of equipment supporting I.460, the author expects the splitting of a B channel into 8-kbit/s intervals; voice digitization advances that simultaneously permit quality voice transmission at 16 kbit/s with data transfer occurring at 112 kbit/s; and full data transfers at 128 kbit/s, which will provide considerably more user flexibility and eliminate most B-channel bottlenecks. ■

Gilbert Held, director of Macon, Ga.-based 4-Degree Consulting, is an internationally recognized author and lecturer on data communications subjects.

References

Frost & Sullivan Inc., Report E1095, Digital Telecommunications/Europe

Netherlands Foreign Investment Agency, Telecommunications Industry Update, 11/15/88

Modifying the B channel. *Using variable-rate channelization can result in a higher level of transmission capability. Two methods are shown.*

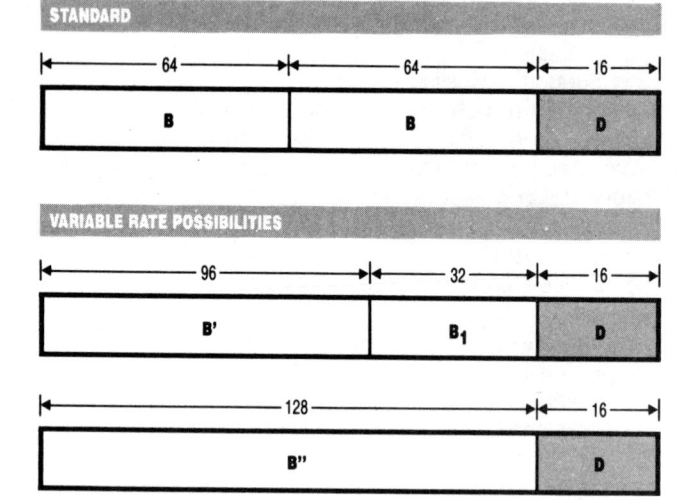

STANDARD: B (64) | B (64) | D (16)

VARIABLE RATE POSSIBILITIES:
- B' (96) | B_1 (32) | D (16)
- B'' (128) | D (16)

Donald J. Ryan, CAP International Inc., Marshfield, Mass.

Making sense of today's image communications alternatives

Facsimile, a well-established way to exchange information, is taking on new dimensions and offering new capabilities.

Millions of documents and messages are sent each day by a variety of means. The U. S. Postal Service, express delivery companies, and computer-based electronic mail services like MCI Mail handle the bulk of the traffic. The first two rely on delivery of the original document; the third transmits character information.

A fourth way to send information is to electronically transmit a visual image of the original. A bit-map representation is created of the image, which can include text, graphics, or pictures. When the bit map is transmitted, the result is image communications (see "How facsimile works").

The image communications market is led by fast-growing facsimile installations, which, it is estimated, will grow from 185,000 placements in 1986 to approximately 425,000 by 1990. Users also are integrating digital scanners, nonimpact printers, microcomputers, and mass storage media for image communications.

A standalone facsimile machine; a standalone microcomputer with a facsimile communications board; or a fully configured workstation consisting of a microcomputer, image scanner, laser printer, and facsimile board can be used to communicate image data (see figure). (For an earlier discussion of the technology, see "Facsimile: An old technology with a fresh digital look," DATA COMMUNICATIONS, January 1982, p. 65.)

As with most growth areas, the image communications market has rapid product obsolescence. Most vendors are introducing a new line of facsimile machines at least every 12 months. In addition, there are many new vendors in the market—the past 12 months have seen a doubling of the number of companies selling or announcing their intention to sell image communications hardware. Finally, there are significant price declines, which allow an increasing number of users to participate in the market.

More and more U. S. businesses will take part in the image communications market during the next five years. Roughly 10 percent of business locations have a facsimile machine today. That figure is expected to increase to over 30 percent by 1990. In addition, new products will not only handle image communications but also incorporate such peripheral features as laser printing and document scanning for computer publishing and document storage and retrieval applications.

By grouping competitive products, matching technology to market segments, and highlighting growth areas, a segmentation model will help end users understand the image communications marketplace.

Market segmentation
Image communications requires the capability for document input, document output, communications interfacing with a wide area or local area network, and communications software, which may include data compression and expansion algorithms. Three main classes of equipment have these functions: facsimile terminals; digital scanners, nonimpact printers, and microcomputers when integrated through software for communications; and document storage and retrieval workstations.

Primary market research indicates that two parameters are particularly useful in analyzing the market for image communications: operating environment and major application area. Image communications occurs in three major operating environments: hub, cluster, and standalone. These environments vary in terms of transmission volume, communications features, network size, and number of user departments or work groups (Table 1).

There are two application areas in which image communications is used: dedicated and multi-use. The dedicated application category defines communications-only uses and includes most facsimile currently marketed today. The multi-use application category defines communications uses but also includes input, output, or data processing functions. Equipment having these functions encompasses plain-paper facsimile machines such as the Fujitsu 7800 and the NEC Bit IV and microcomputers/scanners such as the DataCopy 730 when used with communications hardware and software.

Operating environments

The hub environment is the focal communications point for multiple departments and is part of an established communications network. This environment sends and receives the majority of traffic in a network comprising at least 10 locations regularly. Multiple departments often share equipment in this environment, driving up volume usage and increasing the variety of documents. Typically at least five departments make up a hub location.

A hub environment has at least one well-defined use, such as sales order entry or loan application processing. These applications are highly automated, programmable, and are capable of multi-use image communications applications like plain-paper printing, document editing, or document storage. High-bandwidth networking using full-duplex analog circuits or digital service at speeds of 9.6 to 56 kbit/s is needed to handle peak-hour traffic.

Store-and-forward memory, auto-dialing, and broadcast are some of the communications features required, and optical document storage and transmission will appear in the future. Equipment used in hub environments transmits 1,500 pages per month, generally range in price from

---

How facsimile works

There are seven basic steps in the digital facsimile process. First, a scanner looks at a document and creates a simple electronic representation of its image, called a "bit map" (step 1). This electronic representation describes the blackness of each dot on the page in a "raster scan" pattern—left to right and top to bottom. For a typical facsimile with a resolution of 200 dots/inch, there are 3.7 million dots on a 8.5-by-11-inch page, with 1 bit per dot. Because this number of bits takes too long to transmit, a processor redescribes the image in such a way that fewer bits are required, creating a compressed electronic representation (step 2).

Eighty-five percent of the dots in typical copy are white. If the boundaries of the black dots are specified, the image can be described with fewer bits. Also, successive rows of dots (scan lines) are often similar, so that further compression is possible by describing only how each row differs from the last row. This last technique is known as two-dimensional coding, which involves comparing each line of a scan to a reference line, with new reference lines determined at programmable intervals.

Digital to analog

The sequence of bits must then be "packaged" by a modulator to provide a signal that the telephone system can carry (step 3). The digital facsimile signal is converted into an analog telephone signal that can be carried over the public switched telephone network. The telephone call is then placed either manually or automatically and the modulated signal is delivered to the addressee's facsimile terminal (step 4). Steps 1, 2, and 3 are performed in the transmitter part of the facsimile terminal. Step 4, transmission of the signal, is traditionally performed by telephone companies.

At the receiving terminal the reverse process takes place. The telephone signal is demodulated (converted from analog into digital form) and the compressed electronic representation is restored (step 5). Next, an expander, or decompressor, restores the simple electronic representation of the image (step 6). Finally, the bit map is printed on a sheet of paper (step 7), and the delivery of a copy is complete.

The CCITT, an organ of the International Telecommunications Union within the United Nations, is the universally recognized organization for recommending standards within the facsimile industry. The CCITT has defined four levels, or "groups," of facsimile service (see table). The Group 4 standard, which is just beginning to be used in advanced facsimile equipment in the United States, is subdivided into three classes, according to resolution and features. All three classes specify automatic conversion of resolution in the receiver, the use of the International Standards Organizations seven-level Open Systems Interconnection reference model, and the CCITT data network interface.

CCITT facsimile standards

	SIGNAL	COMPRESSION	SPEED	NETWORK
GROUP 1	ANALOG	NONE	6 MIN.	PSTN
GROUP 2	ANALOG	LIMITED	3 MIN.	PSTN
GROUP 3	DIGITAL	COMPLEX	<1 MIN.	PSTN
GROUP 4	DIGITAL	COMPLEX	<10 s	ISDN, DATAPHONE DIGITAL SERVICE (DDS)

GROUP 4 CLASSES	CLASS 1	CLASS 2	CLASS 3
MANDATORY RESOLUTION (BITS/INCH)	200	300	300
OPTIONAL RESOLUTIONS (BITS/INCH)	300, 400	200, 240, 400	200, 240, 400
FEATURES	EASE OF COMPATIBILITY WITH GROUP 3; 5-YEAR GRANDFATHERING OF 203 × 196 BITS AS EQUIVALENT TO 200 BITS/INCH; MODIFIED READ II COMPRESSION CODE	MUST RECEIVE FROM TELETEX; FONT STORED; MODIFIED READ II COMPRESSION CODE	MUST RECEIVE FROM AND SEND TO TELETEX; TELEX FONT STORED; MUST DO OCR; MUST USE MIXED-MODE COMPRESSION CODE

Table 1: Operating environment characteristics

	VOLUME (PAGES/MONTH)	COMMUNICATIONS	USER DEPARTMENTS	NETWORK LOCATIONS	PRICING	VENDOR EQUIPMENT
HUB	1,500+	9.6-56 KBIT/S	1-5+	10+	$4,500-$25,000	RICOH 610 NETEXPRESS 2100 FUJITSU 7800
CLUSTER	500-1,500	9.6-19.2 KBIT/S	1-4	5-10	$2,500-$4,500	PANAFLEX 600 AT XEROX 7020 PITNEY BOWES 8200
STANDALONE	0-500	4.8-9.6 KBIT/S	1-2	2-4	$1,000-$2,500	CANON 110 DATACOPY MICROFAX SHARP 200

$4,500 to $20,000, and includes facsimile gear, such as the Toshiba TF-341M and the Pitney Bowes 8200 with 10 megabytes of memory.

Two to five departments, usually similar, make up a cluster environment. About half the time, a well-defined application is present. Equipment in a cluster environment transmits to and receives documents from about four to 10 locations, all similar in size and functions. These machines send and receive 500 to 1,500 pages per month, cost generally $2,500 to $4,500, and include fax machines like

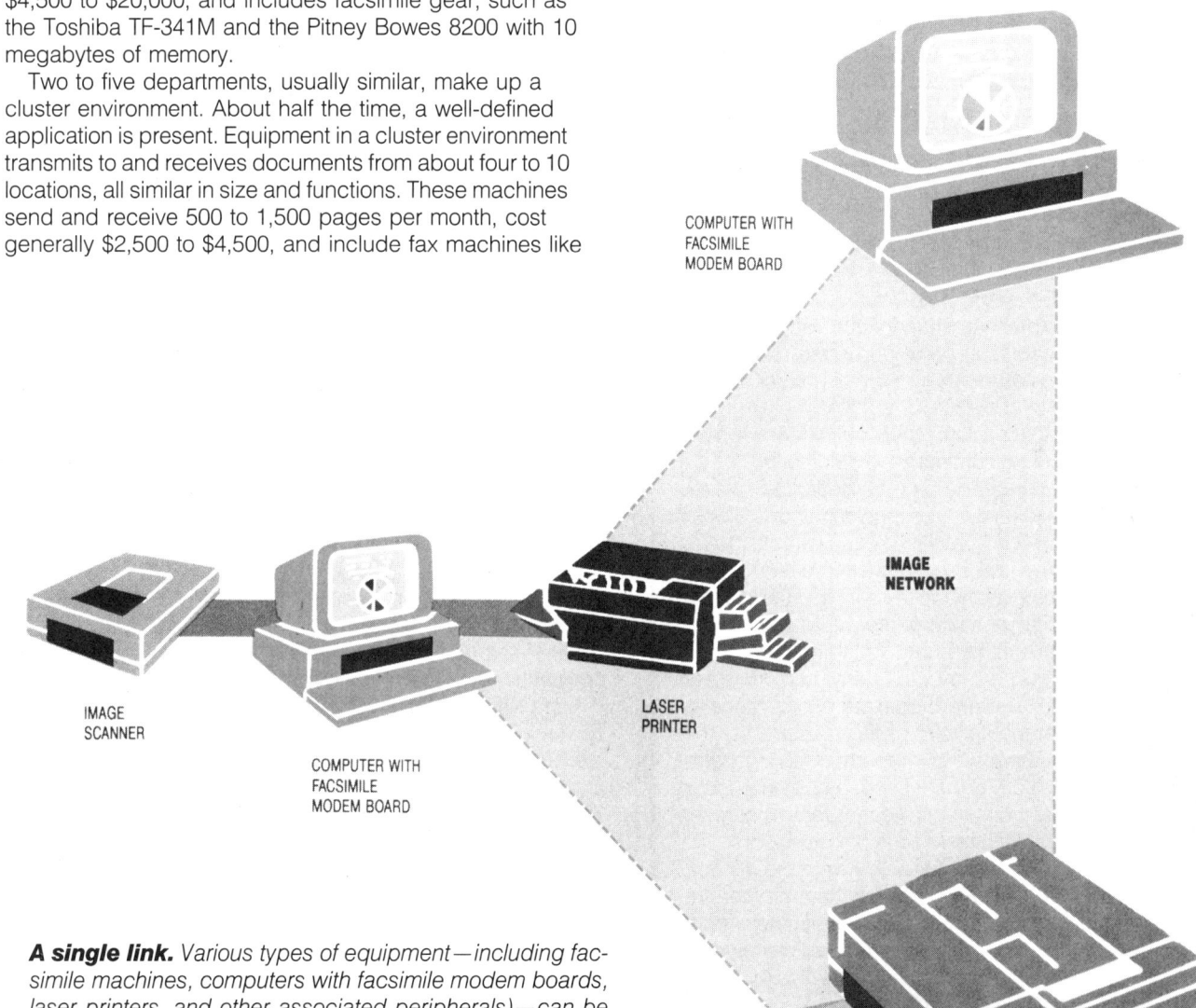

A single link. Various types of equipment—including facsimile machines, computers with facsimile modem boards, laser printers, and other associated peripherals)—can be used for image communications, and all can be linked in a single network. Most vendors are introducing a new line of facsimile machines at least every 12 months.

Table 2: Application feature requirements

	MULTI-USE	DEDICATED
NETWORK	WIDE AREA AND LOCAL AREA	WIDE AREA
PRICE	TO $25,000+	TO $10,000
LOCAL SCANNING	YES	NO
LOCAL PRINTING	YES	NO
COMPUTER PROCESSING	YES	NO
PLAIN PAPER	ALWAYS	SELDOM
LOCAL STORAGE ACCESS	YES	NO

the Canon 610 and the Konica Konimail 200. Transmission is primarily half-duplex at 9.6 kbit/s, although analog circuits with speeds of up to 14.4 kbit/s are used.

The standalone environment consists of one or two departments that primarily send to and receive images from two or three other locations on a regular basis. Specific standalone environment uses are not usually well-defined and often include the transmission of general business correspondence as the main function. Generally the equipment used in stand-alone environments sends and receives fewer than 500 pages per month and costs between $1,500 and $2,500. These machines are characterized by compactness, easy-to-use operations, and limited automation, and transmission is either at 4.8 or 9.6 kbit/s on analog two-wire lines. Increasingly, the standalone environment will be populated by facsimile machines for personal use, such as the Xerox 7010, the Sharp FO-200, and the Minolta MF250.

In the standalone environment, facsimile to facsimile is the main pairing for transmission. This environment includes communications board upgrade products that allow personal computers to act like facsimile machines. An example is Panasonic's FX-BM88 facsimile communications board and software product. The standalone environment also includes digitizing scanners, like the Canon IX-12, that have a local area network (LAN) link for transmitting image data. Personal computers and scanners equipped to communicate using facsimile modems or LAN cards are examples of computer-based image communications. Applications for computer-based image communications include the distribution of files generated by electronic publishing equipment or remote input of image files into a centralized database.

Application areas

As noted, the image communications market can be further segmented by application use and required functions: dedicated and multi-use (Table 2). To reiterate, the dedicated application for image communications involves solely the transmission of image data between two or more locations. This application involves primarily wide area (long-distance) communications using facsimile for intra- and intercompany communications. Transmission is either digital or analog; however, analog predominates, using the public switched telephone network.

The urgency to transmit the document is the primary driver of volume. Manufacturers with widespread locations are users in this application area. Most standard facsimile machines with the scanner and printer included in the same unit are examples of equipment in this area. In multi-use applications, the user requires input scanning, output printing, storage, or local computer processing, as well as communications. The requirement is to produce, distribute, or communicate image data through image capture, storage, and printing.

Multi-use capability is appearing in high-end plain-paper facsimile equipment. Most machines can be used as digital plain-paper copiers and can be modified through the addition of printer drivers and controllers to act as laser printers. Their speed and print quality approximate that of many of today's standalone laser printers. These machines cost between $7,000 and $12,000.

Multi-use image communications also encompasses computer-based communications applications. Whereas present-day facsimile is used for wide area communications, computer-based applications have both requirements: wide area and local area connectivity. The growth in computer-based multi-use image communications will be driven by the ability of LANs to handle the transmission

---

No zap to ZapMail

Though multi-use communications may dominate the future, the current road for vendors is mined with peril. In 1984, Federal Express started ZapMail, an electronic document delivery service that used machines which approximated the Group 4 standard (see Panel 2: How facsimile works). Two years and $200 million later, Federal Express abandoned the service.

The ZapMail terminal combined state-of-the-art features for image communications — plain-paper printing using laser electrophotography, a 10-page-per-minute scanner and printer, high-speed digital communications interfaces, and connection to a private X.25 data network. Federal Express set up a dedicated service force, as well as a network operations and customer help center. However, ZapMail was never able to generate the volume needed to make it profitable.

Three reasons explain the failure. First, Federal Express charged a premium for the ZapMail service, primarily because of high-quality plain-paper printing and fast transmission speed. To many customers and prospects, the availability of plain paper was not a critical feature; the content of the message and the reliability of delivery were more important than what the output looked like. As for speed, ZapMail, though faster than overnight or traditional facsimile, wasn't considerably faster in the minds of many users.

Second, the ZapMail terminals were not Group 3-compatible. As with any network, the greater the number of sending and receiving points, the greater the amount of traffic. By making the ZapMail network proprietary, Federal Express significantly limited the rate at which volume could grow.

Finally, moving large amounts of image data over an X.25 network proved to be more difficult than originally anticipated. Bottlenecks developed in the network that slowed transmission time and in some cases entirely blocked the transmission of documents.

Table 3: Image communications market matrix

OPERATING ENVIRONMENT	MAJOR APPLICATION AREA	
	MULTI-USE	DEDICATED
HUB	CANON L-910 FEDERAL EXPRESS ZAPMAILER FUJITSU DEX 7800 IBM SCANMASTER NEC BIT I NETEXPRESS 2100 RICOH R830 SHARP PLAIN PAPER FACSIMILE	ADLER ROYAL 940 ATT 3530D FUJITSU DEX 6500 HARRIS/3M 2167 KONICA KONIMAIL 400 MITSUBISHI 4570 MURATA IMAGEMASTER NEC BIT II PANAFAX 600SF, UF-450 PITNEY BOWES 8900, 8200 (MEMORY) RICOH R230, R610 SHARP FO-3200 TELAUTOGRAPH 9S, G10 (MEMORY) TOSHIBA 341M
CLUSTER		ADLER ROYAL 920 CANON 220, 520, 620 FUJITSU DEX 6100, 6200, 6300 HARRIS/3M 2110, 2123 HITACHI 35 KONICA KONIMAIL 200 MINOLTA MF 750 MITSUBISHI 3160 MURATA IMAGEMATE PANAFAX 600AT NEC BIT I, BIT III, BIT V PITNEY BOWES 8150, 8200 RICOH R210, R205, R510 SANYO SF515 SHARP FO-620 TOSHIBA 221, 341 TELAUTOGRAPH G38, G10 XEROX 495, 7020
STANDALONE	ADVANCED VISION RESEARCH MEGAFAX AT&T IMAGE DIRECTOR CABLE & WIRELESS DATAFAX COMPUSCAN 240 DATACOPY 730, MICROFAX EIT PC-FAX GAMMALINK GAMMAFAX GULFSTREAM MICRO EZ-FAX IOC READER MICROTEK MS-200, MFAX PANASONIC FX-BM88 FAX BOARD PITNEY BOWES PATH 3 SPECTRAFAX 200 TALUS T20/20 TITN FAXWARE	ATT 3510D CANNON 110 HITACHI 495 IMAGE DATA PHOTOPHONE MINOLTA MF 110 MURATA IMAGEMATE II, VIEWFAX NEC PF-I, PF-2 RICOH R120, R200 SANYO SF615 SHARP FO-200, UX-80 TEC PN-3000 TELAUTOGRAPH G36 XEROX 295, 7010

of image data, the availability of low-cost mass storage for document images, and continued price decreases for scanners and personal computer communications hardware and software. Other major driving factors include the availability of hardware and software products that allow personal computers to transmit image data in facsimile format, and the growth in desktop computer publishing that uses graphics formats extensively.

Multi-use communications today is handled by plain-paper facsimile machines like the NEC Bit IV, by document processing and transmission systems like the NetExpress 2100, and by personal computer/scanners like the AT&T Image Director. In addition, it is expected that a new class of equipment will be available in 1987 that will combine document storage using optical media with transmission capability over local area and wide area networks. These are storage computers, which will be available for under $25,000 and will be the new hubs for image communications networks. Panafax and Ricoh are developing such computer workstations, which will provide mass storage, database access, and communications all in one device (for a case study of one service vendor's abortive efforts, see "No zap to ZapMail").

Market segmentation matrix
The combination of the three operating environments and two application areas creates an image communications market matrix (Table 3). Within each cell of the matrix are examples of currently available or publicly shown image communications products. The number of products listed is an indication of the diverse and expanding need for image communications. At the present time, the matrix shows, the standalone and cluster environments are the most active in terms of usage in the dedicated application category. This trend is expected to continue as the traditional requirement for low-cost facsimile products continues to dominate the market. The hub environment will also grow because of automation of heavily paper-intensive industries such as banking and insurance.

In the multi-use application area in 1987 and 1988, the standalone environment will see the most user activity. The reason is that multi-use capabilities will be required in environments that already make heavy use of microcomputer-based processing. Microcomputers today are operated at the departmental level, and multi-use products that combine communication hardware and software, scanners, and personal computers will be used at the departmental level, as well as by individuals.

Users of image communications have a variety of product and service choices geared to specific applications. (See references such as the "DATA COMMUNICATIONS Buyers' Guide" for information on contacting companies mentioned in this article.) With the future holding the prospect of declining equipment prices, the availability of integrated service digital networks, and multi-use equipment, the use of image communications will increase significantly into the 1990s. ■

Donald J. Ryan is director of the Image Communication Systems Market Requirements Service at CAP International. Ryan received a B. A. in economics from Wesleyan University and an M. B. A. from the Wharton School of Finance at the University of Pennsylvania.

Section 10
Glossary

Data Communications Glossary

A ready reference for finding what you need to know. Compiled by the staff of Data Communications

A

A and B signaling Procedure used in most T1 transmission facilities operated by telephone companies, where bits, "robbed" from each of the subchannels, are used for carrying dial and control information; a type of in-band signaling used in T1 transmission

Abbreviated dialing A feature of some telephone switches that permits users to establish calls by entering fewer digits than would otherwise be required; speed-dialing directories are predefined, though usually changeable by the user; also, speed dialing

ABM Asynchronous Balanced Mode (ADCCP)

Access charges FCC-specified tariffs levied for access to a local exchange carrier (LEC), either for private-line access by users or for access to the LEC by interexchange carriers (IECs)

Access line That portion of a leased telephone line that permanently connects the user with the serving central office or wire center

Accunet Data-oriented digital services from AT&T Communications, including: Accunet T1.5, terrestrial wideband at 1.544 Mbit/s; Accunet Reserved T1.5, satellite-based channels at 1.544 Mbit/s primarily for video teleconferencing applications; Accunet Packet Services, packet-switching services; Accunet Dataphone digital service (DDS), private-line digital circuits at 2.4, 4.8, 9.6, and 56 kbit/s; Accunet Switched 56

ACF Advanced Communications Function; family of IBM communications software products that add to other systems (nonapplications) software the functions of SNA network operation, control, and management; with IBM's Network Control Program (NCP), the software load for front-end and remote communications processors (370X/3725), generated in the host and downloaded; performs critical control functions for IBM SNA networks; ACF/NCP/VS (ACF/Network Control Program/Virtual Storage); also, ACF/TCAM, ACF/VTAM, ACF/VTAME

ACK Control code or designation for a positive acknowledgment; sent from a receiver to a transmitter to indicate that a transmission, or sequence of transmissions, has been received correctly

ACM Association for Computing Machinery

Acoustic coupler A device that allows a telephone handset to be used for access to the switched telephone network for data transmission; digital signals are modulated as sound waves; data rates are typically limited to about 300 bit/s, some up to 1.2 kbit/s

A/D Analog-to-digital (conversion)

ADCCP Advanced Data Communications Control Procedure

ADCU Association of Data Communications Users

Address A sequence of bits, a character, or a group of characters that identifies a network station, user, or application; used mainly for routing purposes; in telephony, the number entered by the caller that identifies the party called

ADPCM Adaptive differential pulse code modulation; encoding technique, standardized by the CCITT, that allows an analog voice conversation to be carried within a 32-kbit/s digital channel; 3 or 4 bits are used to describe each sample, which represents the difference between two adjacent samples; sampling is done 8,000 times a second

AFIPS American Federation of Information Processing Societies

Alternate routing A feature of network switches, especially PBXs, where a call is completed over other circuit routes when first-choice routes are unavailable (not in service or occupied)

AM See Amplitude modulation

Ameritech One of seven regional Bell operating companies (RBOCs) resulting from divestiture, covering the Midwestern United States, based in Chicago, Ill.

Amplifier Any electronic component that boosts the strength or amplitude of a transmitted—usually analog—signal; functionally equivalent to a repeater in digital transmissions

Amplitude modulation (AM) Transmission method in which variations in the voltage or current waveform of a carrier signal determine encoded information

Analog In communications, transmission employing variable and continuous waveforms to represent information values, where interpretation by the receiver is an approximation (quantization) of the encoded value; compare with digital

Analog loopback Technique for testing transmission equipment and devices that isolates faults to the analog signal receiving or transmitting circuitry; where a device, such as a modem, echoes back a received (test) signal that is then compared with the original signal; see Loopback; compare with digital loopback

ANSI American National Standards Institute

Answerback The response of a terminal or other communications device to remotely transmitted control signals; typically part of handshaking between devices

APD Avalanche photodiode; a diode that, when light strikes it, increases its electrical conductivity by a multiplication effect; popular technology employed in receivers for lightwave transmission due to its sensitivity to weakened light signals

APPC Advanced Program-to-Program Communications; also called Logical Unit 6.2, an IBM-specified network node definition featuring high-level program interaction capabilities on a peer-to-peer basis

Application layer A logical entity of the OSI model; the top of the seven-layer structure, generally regarded as offering an interface to, and largely defined by, the network user; in IBM's SNA, the end-user layer

Application Program Interface (API) A set of formalized software calls and routines that can be referenced by an application program to access underlying network services

ARPA Advanced Research Projects Agency; operates within the U. S. Department of Defense

ARQ Automatic request for repeat or retransmission; communications feature whereby the receiver asks the transmitter to resend a block or frame, generally because of errors detected by the receiver

ASCII American National Standard Code for Information Interchange; the standard, and predominant, seven-bit (eight bits, with parity) character code used for data communications and data processing

ASR Automatic send/receive; describes a type of operation, typically of a teleprinter terminal, and especially of older ones equipped with paper tape punches and readers

Asymmetrical A term applied to certain modems that use the majority of the bandwidth on a dial-up link for data transmission in one direction, and a small portion of the bandwidth for control information traveling in the opposite direction

Asynchronous Transmission that is not related to a specific frequency, or to the timing, of the transmission facility; describing transmission characterized by individual characters, or bytes, encapsulated with start and stop bits, from which a receiver derives the necessary timing for sampling bits; also, start/stop transmission

Asynchronous balanced mode (ABM) Used in the IBM Token Ring's logical link control (LLC), ABM operates at the SNA data link control level and allows devices on a Token Ring to send data link commands at any time and to initiate responses independently of each other

AT Command set The de facto autodialing command-set standard for most Bell 212A full-duplex dial-up modems. The command set refers to a specific set of ASCII characters that may be sent to the modem for control purposes. The command set, developed by Hayes Microcomputer Products Inc., can be used by any computer or intelligent terminal to tell the modem to perform such functions as "go off-hook," "hang up," "enable carrier," "disable carrier," "use dial tone," "use pulse dialing," "echo characters," "nonecho characters." An ASCII "A" and "T" must precede each command

ATM Automated teller machine

Attenuation Reduction or loss of signal strength, measured in decibels; opposite of gain

Audiotex A service that allows a database host to pass data to a voice-mail computer, where it is interpreted and delivered over the telephone as a natural, spoken-voice message

Authentication In security, ensuring that the message is genuine, that it has arrived exactly as it was sent, and that it comes from the stated source

Auto-answer Automatic answering; capability of a terminal, modem, computer, or similar device to respond to an incoming call on a dial-up telephone line and to establish a data connection with a remote device without operator intervention; unattended operation for incoming dial-up calls

Autodial Automatic dialing; capability of a terminal, modem, computer, or similar device to place a call over the switched telephone network and establish a connection without operator intervention; also, autocall

Automatic fallback A modem's ability to negotiate an appropriate data rate with the modem on the other end of the link, depending on line quality. For example, if two 1.2-kbit/s modems could not pass data at 1.2 kbit/s, each might "fall back" to 300 bit/s automatically in order to transmit data without excessive errors

Automatic Route Selection (ARS) The capability of a switch, typically a private branch exchange (PBX), to automatically determine an optimal route establishing a circuit; also called least-cost routing (LCR)

Auxiliary network address In ACF/VTAM, any network address, except the main network address, assigned to a logical unit capable of having parallel sessions (IBM)

AVD Alternate voice/data

B

Backbone network A transmission facility designed to interconnect lower-speed distribution channels or clusters of dispersed user devices

Balanced-to-ground With a two-wire circuit, where the impedance-to-ground on one wire equals the impedance-to-ground on the other wire; compare with unbalanced-to-ground, which in most cases is a preferable condition for data transmission

Glossary

Balun Balanced/unbalanced, in the IBM cabling system, refers to an impedance-matching device used to connect balanced twisted-pair cabling with unbalanced coaxial cable

Bandwidth The difference, expressed in Hertz (Hz), between the highest and lowest frequencies of a transmission channel

Baseband Describing a signal frequency that is below the point that the signal is modulated as an analog carrier frequency; in modulation, the frequency band occupied by the aggregate of the transmitted signals when first used to modulate the carrier (IBM)

Basic Beginners All-purpose Symbolic Instruction Code; the most common end-user programming language used with personal computers

Basic rate In ISDN, two 64-kbit/s information-carrying B channels and one 16-kbit/s signaling D channel (2BD)

Basic (vs. enhanced) services As defined by the FCC, basic service refers to transport-level services provided by the BOCs and AT&T. However, the lines drawn are unclear

Batch processing A type of data processing operation and data communications transmission where related transactions are grouped together and transmitted for processing, usually by the same computer and under the same application; generally regarded as nonreal-time data traffic consisting of large files; type of data traffic where network response time is not critical; compare with interactive (processing)

Baud A measurement of the signaling speed of a data transmission device; equivalent to the maximum number of signaling elements, or symbols, per second that are generated; may be different from bit/s rate, however, especially at higher speeds, as several bits may be encoded per symbol, or baud, with advanced encoding techniques such as phase-shift keying

Baudot code An aging data transmission code using five bits for character representation, usually with one start and one or two stop bits added

BCC Block check character; control character appended to blocks in character-oriented protocols used for determining if the block was received in error; used in longitudinal and cyclic redundancy checking

BCD Binary-coded decimal; aging, numeric-based character code set, where numbers zero through nine have a unique 4-bit binary representation

B channel In Integrated Services Digital Network, a 64-kbit/s information-carrying channel

Beam splitter A device for dividing an optical beam into two or more separate beams; often a partially reflecting mirror

B8ZS Binary 8 zero substitution; a technique used to accommodate the ones density requirements of digital T-carrier facilities in the public network, while allowing 64 kbit/s clear data per channel. Rather than inserting a one for every seven consecutive zeroes (see Ones density), B8ZS inserts two violations of the bipolar line encoding technique used for digital transmission links.

Bell Atlantic One of seven regional Bell operating companies (RBOCs) resulting from divestiture, encompassing the Midatlantic region of the United States

Bellcore Bell Communications Research; organization established by the AT&T divestiture, representing and funded by the BOCs and RBOCs, for the purposes of establishing telephone-network standards and interfaces; includes much of what had been Bell Laboratories

BER See Bit error rate

BERT Bit error rate test, or tester

Beta test, site Testing of product prototypes and early releases at client locations prior to general public marketing. Contrast with alpha tests, which are performed in-house by a vendor

Bipolar The predominant signaling method used for digital transmission services, such as DDS and T1, in which the signal carrying the binary value successively alternates between positive and negative polarities; zero and one values are represented by the signal amplitude at either polarity, while no-value "spaces" are at zero amplitude; also, polar transmission; also, a type of integrated circuit (IC, or semiconductor) that uses both positively and negatively charged currents, characterized by high operational speed and cost

Bisync Binary synchronous communications (BSC); character-oriented data communications protocol developed by IBM; oriented toward half-duplex link operation; still widely employed, though replaced in current IBM data communications products by the bit-oriented synchronous data link control (SDLC)

Bit A binary digit; the representation of a signal, wave, or state as either a binary zero or a one

Bit duration The time it takes one encoded bit to pass a point on the transmission medium; in serial communications, a relative unit of time measurement, used for comparison of delay times (e.g., propagation delay, access latency) where the data rate of a (typically high-speed) transmission channel can vary

Bit error The case where the value of an encoded bit is changed in transmission and interpreted incorrectly by the receiver

Bit error rate (BER) The ratio of received bits that are in error (relative to a specific amount of bits received); usually expressed as a number referenced to a power of 10; e.g., 1 error in 10^{-5} bits—also referred to as a BER of 10^5

Bit-oriented Describing a communications protocol or transmission procedure where control information is encoded in fields of one or more bits; oriented toward full-duplex link operation; uses less overhead—and is therefore more efficient—than character- or byte-oriented protocols

Bit/s Bits per second; basic unit of measure for serial data transmission capacity; kbit/s, or kilobit/s, for thousands of bits per second; Mbit/s, or megabit/s, for millions of bits per second; Gbit/s, or gigabit/s for billions of bits per second; Tbit/s, or terabit/s, for trillions of bits per second

Bit stuffing Process, in bit-oriented data communications protocols, where, for example, a string of "one" bits is broken by an inserted zero, added by the sender and removed by the receiver; adding of zero bits is done to prevent user data containing a series of one bits from being interpreted as a flag control character

BLAST Blocked asynchronous transmission

BLERT Block error rate test

Block A quantity of transmitted information regarded as a discrete entity by size; more commonly, a discrete entity by its own starting- and ending-control delimiters, usually with its own self-contained control, routing, and error-checking information; in (primarily) Bisync, that portion of a message terminated by an EOB or ETB line-control character or, if the last block in a message, by an EOT or ETX line-control character; a block may contain one or more records, or a record one or more blocks

Blocking The inability of a network, switch, or access node to grant service to a requesting user due to the unavailability of a transmission channel; said mainly of PBX and central-office switches that lack the ability to provide circuits for all potential users all of the time

Block multiplexer channel An IBM mainframe input/output (I/O) channel that allows interleaving of data blocks

BOC Bell operating company; one of 22 local telephone companies spun off from AT&T as a result of divestiture, reorganized into seven regional Bell holding companies; among the largest of the 1,600 independent local U. S. telephone companies

Boundary node In IBM's SNA, a subarea node that can provide certain protocol support for adjacent subarea nodes, including transforming network addresses to local addresses, and vice versa, and performing session-level sequencing and flow control for less intelligent peripheral nodes

BPSK Binary phase-shift keying

Bridge A device that connects local area networks at the data link layer

Bridge tap An undetermined length of wire attached between the normal endpoints of a circuit that introduces unwanted impedance imbalances for data transmission; compare with terminated line; also, bridging tap, bridged tap

Broadband Describing transmission equipment and media that can support a wide range of electromagnetic frequencies; typically, the technology of CATV transmission, as applied to data communications, that employs coaxial cable as the transmission medium and radio-frequency carrier signals in the 50-to-500-MHz range; any communications channel having a bandwidth greater than a voice-grade telecommunications channel, sometimes used synonymously with wideband

Broadcast Delivery of a transmission to two or more stations at the same time, such as over a bus-type local area network or by satellite; protocol mechanism whereby group and universal addressing is supported

BSC See Bisync

Glossary

BTAM Basic Telecommunications Access Method; one of IBM's early host-based control programs for managing the remote data communications interface to host applications; supportive of pre-SNA protocols

Buffering Process of temporarily storing data in a register or in RAM, which allows transmission devices to accommodate differences in data rates and to perform error checking and retransmission of data received in error

Buffer storage Electronic circuitry where data is kept during buffering

Bus A transmission path or channel; typically, an electrical connection, with one or more conductors, wherein all attached devices receive all transmissions at the same time; a local area network topology, such as used in Ethernet and the token bus, where all network nodes "listen" to all transmissions, selecting certain ones based on address identification; involves some sort of contention-control mechanism for accessing the bus transmission medium

Bypass Generally refers to any private networking scheme used to access long-distance transmission facilities without going through the local exchange carrier (LEC) to do so

Byte Generally, an 8-bit quantity of information, used mainly in referring to parallel data transfer, semiconductor capacity, and data storage; also generally referred to in data communications as an octet or character

Byte multiplexer channel An IBM mainframe input/output channel that allows for the interleaving, or multiplexing, of data in bytes; compare with block multiplexer channel

C

CAD Computer-aided design

CAE Computer-aided engineering

CAI Computer-aided instruction

Callback modem A modem that must be password-activated by the caller. It will then typically hang up and call back the caller's predefined telephone number to establish a communications session

Call-detail recording (CDR) A feature of private branch exchanges where each telephone call is logged, typically by time and charges, and retrievable by the network operator for cost charging by department; also called station message detail recording (SMDR)

Call forwarding A PBX feature that lets a user direct calls to another extension

Call pickup A PBX feature that lets a user answer an incoming call from any station other than the called destination

Call waiting A PBX feature that informs a station user of an

Glossary

incoming call when another call is already in progress

CAM Computer-aided manufacturing

Carrier A continuous frequency capable of being modulated or impressed with a second data-carrying signal

Carrier band A band of continuous frequencies that can be modulated with a signal

CATV Community Antenna Television (formal) or Cable Television (colloquial); data communications based on radio frequency (RF) transmission, generally using 75-ohm coaxial cable as the transmission medium; communications via coaxial cable where multiple frequency-divided channels allow mixed transmissions to be carried simultaneously; broadband

C band Portion of the electromagnetic spectrum heavily used for satellite and microwave transmission; frequencies of approximately 4 to 6 GHz

CBEMA Computer Business Equipment Manufacturers Association

CCIA Computer and Communications Industry Association

CCIS Common channel interoffice signaling; AT&T method of separate-channel signaling by which control and signaling for a group of (typically digital) trunks between telephone central offices is carried in a separate dedicated channel; being upgraded in the United States to Signaling System No. 7

CCITT International Telegraph and Telephone Consultative Committee (from the French, *Comité Consultatif International Télégraphique et Téléphonique*); see CCITT V.XX and X.XX specifications under appropriate alphabetical listings

ccs Hundred call seconds; unit of traffic measurement in telephony; a circuit, connection, or port where usage of 36 ccs, or one Erlang, is continuous; typical usage for most voice communications ranges from about 3 to 10 ccs per user station, while data circuits generally involve longer holding times ranging from 12 to 20 ccs per station when busy; also used to compare relative nonblocking throughput capacity of a switch, PBX, or network

CDMA Call-division multiple access

CDR Call data recording (port)

Cell The geographic area served by a single transmitter in a cellular radio network

Cellular radio Technology employing low-power radio transmission as an alternative to local loops for accessing the switched telephone network; users may be stationary or mobile—in the latter case, they are passed, under control of a central site, from one cell's transmitter to an adjoining one's with minimal switchover delay

Central office (CO) In telephony, the telephone-company switching facility or center, usually a Class 5 end office, at which subscribers' local loops terminate; handles a specific geographic area, identified by the first three digits of the local telephone number; since divestiture, these are invariably the facilities of the local Bell operating company (see Class X office)

Centrex A widespread telephone-company switching service that uses (typically digital) central-office switching equipment and to which customers connect via individual-extension access lines; telephone features typically supplied include direct inward dialing (DID), direct distance dialing (DDD), and attendant switchboards

CEPT Conference of European Postal and Telecommunications administrations

Channel In communications, a physical or logical path allowing the transmission of information; the path connecting a data source and a data "sink" (receiver)

Channel-attached Describing the attachment of devices directly to the input/output channels of a (mainframe) computer; devices attached to a controlling unit by cables, rather than by telecommunications circuits; same as locally attached (IBM)

Channel bank Equipment, typically in a telephone central office, that performs multiplexing of lower-speed, generally digital, channels into a higher-speed composite channel; the channel bank also detects and transmits signaling information for each channel and transmits framing information so that time slots allocated to each channel can be identified by the receiver

Character Standard bit representation of a symbol, letter, number, or punctuation mark; generally means the same as byte

Character code One of several standard sets of binary representations for the alphabet, numerals, and common symbols, such as ASCII, EBCDIC, BCD

Characteristic impedance The impedance termination of an electrically uniform (approximately) transmission line that minimizes reflections from the end of the line

Character-oriented Describing a communications protocol or transmission procedure that carries control information encoded in fields of one or more bytes; compare with bit-oriented; also, byte-oriented

Checksum The sum of a group of data items, associated with the group, for checking purposes

CICS Customer Information Control System; an IBM program product and mainframe operating environment, designed to enable transactions entered at remote terminals to be processed concurrently by user-written application programs; includes facilities for building and maintaining databases

CIM Computer-integrated manufacturing

Circuit Generally, a transmission medium interconnecting two or more electronic devices

Circuit switching The process of establishing and maintaining a circuit between two or more users on demand and giving them exclusive use of the circuit until the connection is released

Class Custom local area signaling services; based on the availability of common channel interoffice signaling, Class consists of number-translation services, such as call-forwarding and caller

Glossary

identification, available within a local exchange or Local Access and Transport Area (LATA)

Class of Service (COS) Designation for one of several variable network-connection services available to the user of a network, usually distinguished by security offered (such as encryption), transmission priority, and bandwidth; the network user designates class of service at connection establishment, typically using a symbolic name mapped into a list of potential routes, any of which may provide the requested service

Class X office Designation of a telephone-company switching facility in the telephone hierarchy, where Class 5 is an end office, Class 4 is a toll center, Class 3 is a primary center, Class 2 a sectional center, and Class 1 a regional center

Clear channel Characteristic of a transmission path wherein the full bandwidth is available to the user; said primarily of telephone-company digital circuits that do not require that some portion of the channel be reserved for carrier framing or control bits

Clock An oscillator-generated signal that provides a timing reference for a transmission link; used to control the timing of functions such as sampling interval, signaling rate, and duration of signal elements; an "enclosed" digital network typically has only one "master" clock

Closed user group In communications, a subgroup of users assigned to a network facility that restricts communications from any member of that subgroup to members of other subgroups; typically, however, a data terminal equipment (DTE) device may be accessed by more than one closed user group

Cluster controller A device that handles the remote communications processing for multiple (usually dumb) terminals or workstations; generally considered to be an IBM 3270-family controller, such as the IBM 3274 or a compatible device

CMA Communications Managers Association

CMOS Complementary metal oxide semiconductor

Coaxial cable A popular transmission medium consisting of, usually, one central wire conductor (two in the case of twinaxial cable) surrounded by a dielectric insulator and encased in either a wire mesh or an extruded metal sheathing; coaxial cable exists in many varieties, depending on the degree of EMI shielding afforded and voltages and frequencies accommodated; common Community Antenna Television (CATV) transmission cable, typically supporting RF frequencies from 50 to about 500 MHz; also called coax

Codec Coder/decoder; an integrated circuit (IC), or series of ICs, that performs a specific analog-to-digital conversion (e.g., conversion of an analog voice signal to a 64-kbit/s digital bit stream, or an analog television signal to a digital format)

Code conversion The process of changing the bit grouping for a character in one code into the corresponding bit grouping for the character in another

CO-LAN Central office local area network; a Centrex-like service offered by several Bell operating companies (BOCs), in which LAN capabilities are provided to customers within a common local telephone serving area using the capabilities of the BOC's central-office switch

Colocation With regard to the public network, the practice of installing another organization's (either customer's, service provider's, or interexchange carrier's) equipment on the central-office premises of a BOC or an interexchange carrier (IEC). Equipment is usually colocated so the BOC or IEC can provide maintenance service or enhanced network service for the organization that is colocating

Combined station In the high-level data link control (HDLC) protocol, a data station capable of assuming either the role of a primary or a secondary station; also, a balanced station

Common carrier In the United States, any supplier of transmission facilities or services to the general public that is authorized to provide such facilities or services by the appropriate regulatory authority and bound to adhere to the applicable operating rules, such as making services available at a common price (tariff) and on a nondiscriminatory basis

Communications server An intelligent device providing communications functions; usually, an intelligent, specially configured node on a local network designed to enable remote communications access to, and egress from, LAN users

Companding Compressing/expanding; the process of reducing the bandwidth required for representation of an analog waveform for transmission and then reconstructing (most of) the original waveform at the receiving end; performed by electronic circuitry that applies a compression algorithm; generally, the compression/expansion of analog voice or video signals

Compression Any of several techniques that reduce the number of bits required to represent information in data transmission or storage, therefore conserving bandwidth and/or memory, wherein the original form of the information can be reconstructed; also called compaction

Computer Inquiry II (CI II) Formally known as the Second Computer Inquiry, FCC Docket No. 20828. The final decision, in 1980, articulated a policy toward competition and deregulation for all participants in the telecommunications industry, including major long-distance carriers

Computer Inquiry III (CI III) Adopted by the Federal Communications Commission in May 1986, Computer Inquiry III removed the structural separation requirement between basic and enhanced services, for the Bell operating companies (BOCs) and for AT&T; CI III replaced that requirement with "nonstructural safeguards;" this action resulted in the imposition of such concepts as "comparably efficient interconnection (CEI)" and Open Network Architecture (ONA)

COMSAT Communications Satellite Corp.; private U. S. satellite carrier, established by Congress in 1962 for the coordination and construction of satellite communications and facilities for international voice and data communications

Concatenation The linking of transmission channels (telephone lines, coaxial cable, and optical fiber) end to end

Concentrator Any communications device that allows a shared

Glossary

transmission medium to accommodate more data sources than there are channels currently available within the transmission medium

Conditioning Extra-cost options that users may apply to leased, or dedicated, voice-grade telephone-company data circuits, wherein line impedances are carefully balanced; will generally allow for higher-quality and/or higher-speed data transmission; in increasing order of resultant line quality and cost, conditioning may be C1, C2, C4, or D1; allows improved line performance with regard to frequency response and delay distortion

Connector A physical interface, such as RJ-11C or EIA RS-232-C, typically with male and female components

Connect time The time that a circuit, typically in a circuit-switched telephone-like environment, is in use; also, holding time

Contention in communications, the situation when multiple users vie for access to a transmission channel, whether a PBX circuit, a computer port, or a time slot, within a multiplexed digital facility

Control characters In communications, any extra transmitted characters used to control or facilitate data transmission between data terminal equipment (DTE) devices; characters transmitted over a circuit that are not message or user data but cause certain control functions to be performed when encountered; also, extra characters associated with addressing, polling, message delimiting and blocking, framing, synchronization, error checking, and other control functions

Conversational Time-dependent data transmissions, during which an operator, upon initiating a transmission, waits for a response from a destination before continuing; also, interactive

Core The central region of an optical waveguide through which light is transmitted; typically 8 to 12 microns in diameter for single-mode fiber, and 50 to 100 microns for multimode fiber

Corporation for Open Systems (COS) A nonprofit organization of networking vendors and users designed to promote OSI and ISDN standards in the United States and to advance interoperability certification

COS Corporation for Open Systems

CPE Customer premises equipment; in telephony, equipment that interfaces to the telephone network and physically resides at the user's location; includes most, but not all, gear referred to as network channel terminating equipment (NCTE)

CPI Computer-to-PBX Interface (Digital Equipment Corp. and Northern Telecom Co.)

CR Carriage return; teletypewriter, or TTY, code for start of new line of message

CRC Cyclic redundancy check; a basic error-checking mechanism for link-level data transmissions; a characteristic link-level feature of (typically) bit-oriented data communications protocols, wherein the data integrity of a received frame, or a packet, is checked by the use of a polynomial algorithm based on the content of the frame and then matched with the result that is performed by the sender and included in a (most often 16-bit) field appended to the frame

Crossbar switch An early form of the matrix switch; an electromechanical switch that uses moving electronic relays to connect multiple circuits to other multiple circuits via vertical and horizontal leads and mechanisms; an aging switching machine still employed in many telephone central offices

Crosstalk Unwanted transference of electrical energy from one transmission medium to another, usually adjacent, medium; generally in—but not restricted to—the voice-grade frequency range and typical of unshielded twisted-pair wires in telephony and, more recently, data applications

CRT Cathode-ray tube

CSDC Circuit-Switched Digital Capability; AT&T-designed service, implemented within the BOCs, that offers users a 56-kbit/s digital channel on a user-switchable basis; uses same local loop as for analog voice but without loading coils; user first sets up analog circuit, then switches to digital mode; employs time-compression multiplexing over local loop; see PSDS

CSMA/CD Carrier-sense multiple access with collision detection; a leading local area network access-control technique, by which all devices attached to the network "listen" for transmissions in progress before attempting to transmit and, if two or more begin transmitting at the same time, each backs off (defers) for a variable period of time (determined by a preset algorithm) before again attempting to transmit

CSU Channel service unit; a component of customer premises equipment (CPE) used to terminate a digital circuit, such as DDS or T1, at the customer site; performs certain line-conditioning functions, ensures network compliance per FCC rules, and responds to loopback commands from the central office; also, ensures proper ones density in transmitted bit stream and performs bipolar-violation correction (also see DSU)

CTS Clear to send; modem control code

Current The amount of electrical charge flowing past a specified circuit point per unit of time, measured in amperes

Customer-controlled reconfigurability (CCR) An AT&T service that lets users make changes in their digital-access and cross-connect network configurations either in real time or according to a preplanned schedule

CVSD Continuous variable-slope delta modulation; speech encoding and digitizing technique that uses a one-bit sample to encode the difference between two successive signal levels; sampling usually done at 32,000 times a second, though some implementations employ lower sampling rates

Cyclic redundancy check See CRC

D

DACS Digital Access and Cross-connect System; this is a new generation of central-office switching equipment manufactured by AT&T and other switch vendors; DACS allows T1 carrier facilities, or any of the subchannels (nominally at 64 kbit/s), to be switched

Glossary

or cross-connected to another T1 carrier

DASD Direct-access storage device (often pronounced "dazzdee")

Data Digitally represented information, which includes voice, text, facsimile, and video

Data access arrangement (DAA) Device or circuitry that is required to allow attachment of privately owned data terminal equipment (DTE) and communications equipment to the telephone network; now generally integrated into such directly attached devices

Data communications The transmission, reception, and validation of data (IBM); data transfer between data source (originating node) and data sink (destination node) via one or more data links according to appropriate protocols (ISO)

Data Encryption Standard (DES) Cryptographic algorithm designed by the National Bureau of Standards to encipher and decipher data using a 64-bit key; specified in Federal Information Processing Standard Publication 46, dated January 15, 1977

Datagram A finite-length packet with sufficient information to be independently routed from source to destination without reliance on previous transmissions; datagram transmission typically does not involve end-to-end session establishment and may or may not entail delivery-confirmation acknowledgment

Data link Any serial data communications transmission path, generally between two adjacent nodes or devices and without any intermediate switching nodes

Data link layer Layer 2 in the OSI model; the network processing entity that establishes, maintains, and releases data link connections between (adjacent) elements in a network

Data Network Identification Code (DNIC) A four-digit number assigned to public data networks and to specific services within those networks

Data PBX A switch that allows a user on an attached circuit to select from among other circuits, usually one at a time and on a contention basis, for the purpose of establishing a through connection; distinguished from a PBX in that only digital transmission, and not analog voice, is supported

Dataphone A service and trademark of AT&T; refers to the transmission of data over the telephone network (Dataphone digital service, or DDS) or to equipment furnished by the telephone company for data transmission

Data set A software term for a certain type of data file; infrequently used today for a modem, except among telephone carriers

Data transfer rate The average number of bits, characters, or blocks per unit of time transferred from a data source to a data sink

dB Decibel; a unit of measurement used to express the ratio of two values, usually the power of electrical or electromagnetic signals; equal to 10 times the logarithm of the ratio of the two power levels, which are expressed in watts; the relative gain or loss of a signal when the measured signal value is compared in a logarithmic ratio to another—usually its input—value

D-bit The delivery confirmation bit in an X.25 packet that is used to indicate whether or not the DTE wishes to receive an end-to-end acknowledgment of delivery

dBm Decibel referenced to one milliwatt; relative strength of a signal, calculated in decibels, when the signal is compared in a ratio to a value of one milliwatt; used mainly in telephony to refer to relative strength of a signal (e.g., at 0 dBm, a signal delivers 1 milliwatt to a line load, while at 30 dBm a signal delivers .001 milliwatt to a load)

DBMS Database management system

DCE Data circuit-terminating equipment (also, incorrectly, data communications equipment); in a communications link, equipment that is either part of the network, an access point to the network, a network node, or equipment at which a network circuit terminates; in the case of an RS-232-C connection, the modem is usually regarded as DCE, while the user device is DTE, or data terminal equipment; in a CCITT X.25 connection, the network access and packet-switching node is viewed as the DCE

D channel In Integrated Services Digital Network, a 16-kbit/s signaling channel for basic-rate access, or a 64-kbit/s signaling channel within primary-rate access

DCM Digital circuit multiplication; a means of increasing the effective capacity of primary-rate, and higher-level PCM hierarchies, based upon speech coding at 64 kbit/s

DDCMP Digital Data Communications Message Protocol (Digital Equipment Corp.)

DDD Direct distance dialing; referring to the conventional long-distance-switched telephone network, dial-up calls placed over the network, or dial-up long-distance circuits; see MTS

DDN Defense Data Network (DOD)

DDP See Distributed data processing

DDS Dataphone digital service (AT&T); private-line digital service offered intraLATA by BOCs and interLATA by AT&T Communications, with data rates typically at 2.4, 4.8, 9.6, and 56 kbit/s; now a part of the services listed by AT&T under the Accunet family of offerings

DDS-SC Dataphone digital service with secondary channel (also often referred to as DDS II); a tariffed private-line service offered by AT&T and certain BOCs that allows 64-kbit/s clear-channel data with a secondary channel that provides end-to-end supervisory, diagnostic, and control functions

Decnet Digital Equipment Corp.'s proprietary network architecture that works across all of the company's machines; endowed with a peer-to-peer methodology

Dedicated line A dedicated circuit, a nonswitched channel; also

Glossary

called a private line; see Leased line

Delay In communications, the wait time between two events, such as from when a signal is sent until it is received; see Propagation delay, Response time

Demarcation point The point defined under the terms of AT&T divestiture that marks the end of a customer's premises and the beginning of the public network

Demodulation The extraction of transmitted information from a modulated carrier signal

DES See Data Encryption Standard

Destination field A field in a message header that contains the address of the station to which a message is being directed

D4 framing T1 12-frame format in which the 193rd bit is used for framing and signaling information; ESF is an equivalent but newer 24-frame technology

DIA/DCA Document Interchange Architecture/Document Content Architecture; IBM-promulgated architectures, part of SNA, for transmission and storage of documents over networks, whether text, data, voice, or video; becoming industry standards by default

Dial backup A network scheme using two dial-up lines to effect data transmisson as a temporary replacement for a failed dedicated line; in this configuration, one dial-up link is used to transmit data and the other to receive data

Dial-up Describing the process of, or the equipment or facilities involved in, establishing a temporary connection via the switched telephone network

Digital Referring to communications procedures, techniques, and equipment by which information is encoded as either a binary "1" or "0"; the representation of information in discrete binary form, discontinuous in time, as opposed to the analog representation of information in variable, but continuous, waveforms

Digital Access and Cross-connect System See DACS

Digital circuit multiplexing (DCM) A proprietary speech-compression technique, developed by ECI Telecom Inc., to boost voice capacity over the TAT-8 transatlantic cable from 10,000 to 50,000 voice channels

Digital loopback Technique for testing the digital processing circuitry of a communications device; may be initiated locally or remotely via a telecommunications circuit; device being tested will echo back a received test message after first decoding and then re-encoding it, the results of which are compared with the original message (compare with analog loopback)

Digital speech interpolation (DSI) A voice-compression technique that takes advantage of the pauses inherent in human speech to multiplex other voice conversations onto the same transmission link

Digital switching The process of establishing and maintaining a connection, under stored program control, by which binary-encoded information is routed between an input and an output port; generally, a "virtual" through circuit is derived from a series of time slots (time-division multiplexing), which is more efficient than requiring dedicated circuits for the period of time that connections are set up

Direct inward dialing (DID) Feature of some telephone switches and PBXs that allows an external caller to call an extension without going through an operator

Direct outward dialing Feature of some telephone switches and PBXs allowing an internal caller at an extension to dial an external number without requiring an operator to intercede in the function

Disk/file server A mass storage device that can be accessed by several computers

Disoss Distributed Office Support System (IBM)

Distortion The corruption of a signal; quantitatively, the difference between values of two measured parameters of a signal or between the transmitted and received characteristics of the same signal; the measured variation, for example, of frequency (frequency response), of time (delay distortion), or of harmonics

Distributed data processing (DDP) Describing a network of geographically dispersed, though logically interconnected, data processing nodes; generally configured so that nodes can share common resources, such as a file server, a print server, host applications, or a database; communications between DDP nodes may be sporadic or intensive, interactive or batch; also, distributed processing

Distribution frame A typically wall-mounted structure for terminating telephone wiring, usually the permanent wires from, or at, the telephone central office, where cross-connections are readily made to extensions; also, distribution block

Divestiture The breakup of AT&T mandated by the federal courts, based on an antitrust accord reached between AT&T and the U. S. Department of Justice, effective January 1, 1984; most notable effects include the separation of 22 AT&T-owned local Bell operating companies (BOCs) into seven independent regional Bell holding companies, the requirement that AT&T manufacture and market customer premises equipment through a separate subsidiary, and use of the Bell name and logo only by the divested BOCs (RBOCs)

DLC Data link control; data line card

DMA Direct memory access

DMI Digital Multiplexed Interface (AT&T)

DNA Digital Network Architecture (Digital Equipment Corp.)

DOD Department of Defense (United States)

Domain In IBM's Systems Network Architecture, a host-based Systems Services Control Point (SSCP) and the physical units (PUs), logical units (LUs), links, link stations, and all the associated resources that the host (SSCP) has the ability to control

DOS Disk operating system

DOV Data over voice; technology used primarily with local Centrex services or special customer premises PBXs for transmitting data and voice simultaneously over twisted-pair copper wiring; typical data rates for DOV applications with Centrex are 19.2 kbit/s, although speeds of up to 1 Mbit/s have been achieved with certain PBX-based networks

Down-link Complement of up-link

Downtime The period during which computer or network resources are unavailable to users due to a failure

Draft proposal An ISO standards document that has been registered and numbered but not yet given final approval

Driver Usually a software module that, under control of the processor, manages an I/O port to an external device, such as a serial RS-232-C port to a modem

Drop-and-insert A term applied to a multiplexer that can add data (insert) to a T1 data stream, or act as a terminating node (drop) to other multiplexers connected to it

Drop cable In local area networks, a cable that connects perpendicularly to the main network cable, or bus, and attaches to data terminal equipment (DTE)

Dropouts Cause of errors and loss of synchronization with telephone-line data transmission; defined as incidents when signal level unexpectedly drops at least 12 dB for more than 4 milliseconds; Bell standard allows no more than two dropouts per 15-minute period

Dry T1 T1 with an unpowered interface

DS-0 Digital signal Level 0; telephony term for a 64-kbit/s standard digital telecommunications signal or channel

DS-1 Digital signal Level 1; telephony term describing the 1.544-Mbit/s digital signal carried on a T1 facility

DS-1C Digital signal Level 1C; telephony term describing a 3.152-Mbit/s digital signal

DS-3 Equivalent of 28 T1 channels, communications access operating at 44.736 Mbit/s; effectively synonymous with T3

DSU Data service unit; component of customer premises equipment (CPE) used to interface to a digital circuit (say, DDS or T1); combined with a channel service unit (CSU); performs conversion of customer's data stream to bipolar format for transmission

DSX-1 Digital signal cross-connect Level 1; telephony term for the set of parameters used where DS-1 digital signal paths are cross-connected

DTE Data terminal equipment; generally, user devices, such as terminals and computers, that connect to data circuit-terminating equipment (DCE); they either generate or receive the data carried by the network; in RS-232-C connections, designation as either DTE or DCE determines the signaling role in handshaking; in a CCITT X.25 interface, the device or equipment that manages the interface at the user premises; see DCE

DTMF Dual tone multifrequency; in telephony, the push-button, or Touch-Tone, signaling method by which each depressed key generates two audio output tones, the combination of which is unique for each of the 12 keys; in contrast to the older pulse dialing of rotary telephones

DTS Digital Termination Systems; microwave-based transmission technology designed for bypass functions for short-hop, line-of-sight applications; never converts to analog; useful in high-volume, pure-data applications in urban settings where line costs are high; requires FCC license; referred to formally by FCC as Digital Electronic Message Service, or DEMS

Dynamic bandwidth allocation A feature available on certain high-end T1 multiplexers that allows the total bit rate of the multiplexer's tail circuits to exceed the bandwidth of the network trunk; this is allowable since the multiplexer only assigns channels on the network trunk to tail circuits that are transmitting

E

Earth station In satellite communications, a terrestrial communications center that maintains direct links with a satellite. See Ground station

EBCDIC Extended Binary Coded Decimal Interchange Code; 8-bit character code set developed and promulgated by IBM

Echo In communications, the reflection back to the sender of transmitted signal energy; length of delay in an echo depends on the distance from the transmitter to the point of reflection

Echo cancellation Technique used in higher-speed modems that allows for the isolation and filtering out of unwanted signal energy caused by echoes from the main transmitted signal

ECMA European Computer Manufacturers Association

ECSA Exchange Carriers Standards Association; an accredited standards group under ANSI that was in existence before the AT&T divestiture; consists of RBOCs and independent telephone companies

EFT Electronic funds transfer

EHF Extremely high frequency; portion of the electromagnetic spectrum; frequencies in the microwave range of approximately 30 to 300 GHz

EIA Electronic Industries Association; see EIA RS-XX specifications under appropriate alphabetical listings

EMI Electromagnetic interference; a device's radiation leakage that is coupled onto a transmission medium, resulting (mainly) from the use of high-frequency wave energy and signal modulation; reduced by shielding; minimum acceptable levels are detailed by the FCC, based on type of device and operating frequency

Glossary

Emulation The imitation of all or part of one device, terminal, or computer by another, so that the imitating device accepts the same data, performs the same functions, and appears to other network devices as the imitated device

Encoding/decoding The process of reforming information into a format suitable for transmission, and then reconverting it after transmission; for pulse-code-modulated voice transmission, the generation of digital signals to represent quantized samples and the subsequent reverse process

Encryption In security, the ciphering of data by applying an algorithm to plaintext in order to convert it to ciphertext

End office A Class 5 telephone central office, at which subscribers' local loops terminate

EOA End of address; header code

EOB End of block; a control character or code that marks the end of a block of data

EOM End of message; for single-message transmission, equivalent to EOT

EOT End of transmission; a control code in character-oriented protocols, or a bit field set to "one" in bit-oriented protocols, that tells the receiver that all user data (text) has been sent

EPROM Erasable programmable read-only memory

Equal access Mandated by divestiture of AT&T, equal access requires that the Bell operating companies (BOCs) provide interexchange carriers (IECs), other than AT&T, the same convenient access to the BOCs' central-office switches as that provided for AT&T. Hence, under equal access, customers could dial long distance over their preferred IEC without having to dial extra digits

Equalization In the telephone network, the spacing and operation of amplifiers so that the gain provided by the amplifier, per transmission frequency, coincides with the signal loss at the same frequency; within communications devices, equalization is achieved by circuitry that compensates for the differences in attenuation at different frequencies, usually a combination of adjustable coils, capacitors, and resistors

Erasable storage A storage device whose contents can be modified (e.g., random access memory, or RAM), as contrasted with read-only storage (e.g., read-only memory, or ROM)

EREP Environmental Recording, Editing, and Printing (IBM)

Erlang Standard unit of measurement of telecommunications traffic capacity and usage demand; for throughput and capacity planning, an Erlang equals 36 ccs, which represents full-time use of a conventional telecommunications traffic path

Error burst A sequence of transmitted signals containing one or more errors but regarded as a unit in error in accordance with a predefined measure; enough consecutive transmitted bits that are in error to cause a loss of synchronization between sending and receiving stations, and to necessitate resynchronization

Error-correction code In computers, rules of code construction that facilitate reconstruction of part or all of a message received with errors

ESF Extended superframe format; an AT&T-proposed T1-framing standard that provides frame synchronization, cyclic redundancy checking, and data link bits; frames consist of 24 bits instead of the previous standard 12 bits; the standard allows error information to be stored and retrieved easily, facilitating network performance monitoring and maintenance

Esprit European strategic program for research and development in information technology; a $1.7-billion research and development program funded by the European Community

ESS Electronic Switching System; one of a family of AT&T-manufactured, stored-program-control, central-office switches; most prevalent are the Nos. 1, 1A, 4, and 5 switches

ETB End of transmitted block; see EOB

Ethernet A popular local area network design and the trademarked product of Xerox Corp., characterized by 10-Mbit/s baseband transmission over a shielded coaxial cable and employing CSMA/CD as the access-control mechanism; standardized by the IEEE as specification IEEE 802.3; referring to the Ethernet design or compatible with Ethernet

ETS Electronic tandem switch

ETX End of text; control code that notifies the receiver that the end of the message text has been reached

Exchange Referring to the local telephone central office, or to the local area in which a caller may place a call without incurring an extra charge (toll)

Extended addressing In many bit-oriented protocols, a facility allowing larger addresses than normal to be used; may be required in extensive networks; in IBM's SNA, the addition of two high-order bits to the basic addressing scheme

External modem A standalone modem, as opposed to a plug-in "board" modem integrated within a computer or terminal

F

Facsimile The communications process in which graphics and text documents are scanned, transmitted via a (typically dial-up) telephone line, and reconstructed by a receiver; facsimile-device operation typically follows one of the CCITT standards for information representation and transmission (Group 1 analog, with page transmission in four or six minutes; Group 2 analog, with page transmission in two or three minutes; Group 3 digital, with page transmission in less than one minute; and Group 4 digital, with page transmission in less than 10 seconds); also, often called fax

Fading A phenomenon, generally of microwave or radio transmission, whereby atmospheric, electromagnetic, or gravitational influences cause a signal to be attenuated, deflected, or diverted away from the target receiver

Glossary

Far-end crosstalk Crosstalk that travels along a circuit in the same direction as the signals in that circuit; compare with near-end crosstalk

Fast packet switching (also called wideband packet switching); packet switching that supports both voice and data

Fax See Facsimile

FCC Federal Communications Commission; board of commissioners appointed by the President under the Communcations Act of 1934, with the authority to regulate all interstate telecommunications originating in the United States

FDM See Frequency-division multiplexing

FDX See Full duplex; sometimes called duplex or "dux"

FEC See Forward error correction

FED-STD-1001 Synchronous high-speed data signaling rate between data terminal equipment and data circuit-terminating equipment

FED-STD-1002 Time and frequency reference information in telecommunications "systems"

FED-STD-1003-A Synchronous bit-oriented data link control procedures (Advanced Data Communications Control Procedures)

FED-STD-1005 Coding and modulation requirements for non-diversity 2.4-kbit/s modems

FED-STD-1006 Coding and modulation requirements for 4.8-kbit/s modems

FED-STD-1007 Coding and modulation requirements for duplex 9.6-kbit/s modems

FED-STD-1008 Coding and modulation requirements for duplex 600-bit/s and 1.2-kbit/s modems

FEP Front-end processor; a dedicated computer linked to one or more host computers or multiuser minicomputers that performs data communications functions and serves to offload the attached computers of network processing; in IBM SNA networks, an IBM 3704, 3705, 3725, or 3745 communications controller

Fiber Distributed Data Interface (FDDI) An American National Standards Institute (ANSI)-specified standard for fiber optic links with data rates up to 100 Mbit/s. The standard specifies: multimode fiber; 50/125, 62.5/125, or 85/125 core-cladding specification; an LED or laser light source; and 2 kilometers for unrepeated data transmission at 40 Mbit/s

Fiber loss Attenuation of the light signal in optical-fiber transmission

Fiber optics Transmission technology by which modulated lightwave signals, generated by a laser or LED, are propagated along a (typically) glass or plastic medium, and then typically demodulated back into electrical signals by a light-sensitive receiver

File server In local area networks, a station dedicated to providing file and mass data storage services to the other stations on the network

File Transfer, Access, and Management (FTAM) An ISO application-layer standard for network file transfer and remote file access

Filter Electronic circuitry that removes energy in unwanted frequencies, such as noise, from a transmission channel; may be analog or digital in operation

Final-form document An electronic document that is only suitable for printing or displaying but not for modifying

FIPS Federal Information Processing Standard

FIPS PUB 1-1 Code for information interchange

FIPS PUB 7 Implementation of the code for information interchange and related standards

FIPS PUB 15 Subsets of the standard code for information interchange

FIPS PUB 16-1 Bit sequencing of the code for information interchange in serial-by-bit data transmission

FIPS PUB 17-1 Character structure and character parity sense for serial-by-bit data communications in the code for information interchange

FIPS PUB 22-1 Specifies synchronous signaling rates between data terminal equipment (DTE) and data circuit-terminating equipment (DCE)

FIPS PUB 37 Synchronous high-speed data signaling rates between data terminal equipment and data circuit-terminating equipment

FIPS PUB 46 See Data Encryption Standard

FIPS PUB 71 Advanced Data Communications Control Procedures (ADCCP)

FIPS PUB 78 Guideline for implementing Advanced Data Communication Control Procedures (ADCCP)

Flag In communications, a bit pattern of six consecutive "1" bits (character representation is 01111110) used in many bit-oriented protocols to mark the beginning (and often also the end) of a frame

Flow control Capability of network nodes to manage buffering schemes while handling devices operating at different data rates, enabling them to talk with each other

FM See Frequency modulation

FM subcarrier One-way data transmission using signals modulated in unused portions of the FM radio-broadcast frequency band

Fortran Formula translator (computer programming language)

Glossary

Forward channel The communications path carrying data or voice from the call initiator to the called party; opposite of reverse channel; the main communications channel

Forward error correction (FEC) Technique used by a receiver for correcting errors incurred in transmission over a communications channel without requiring the retransmission of any information by the transmitter; typically involves a convolution of the transmitted bits and the appending of extra bits by both receiver and transmitter using a common algorithm

Four-wire Refers to a transmission path that allows for physically separate transmit and receive channels; at one time, four-wire was the only method for implementing full-duplex transmission

Frame A group of bits sent serially over a communications channel; generally, a logical transmission unit sent between data link layer entities that contains its own control information for addressing and error checking; the basic data transmission unit employed with bit-oriented protocols, similar to blocks; also, in video transmission, a set of electron scan lines (usually 525 in the United States) that comprise a television picture

Frame-check sequence (FCS) In bit-oriented protocols, a 16-bit field that contains transmission error-checking information, usually appended at the end of a frame

Framing A control procedure used with multiplexed digital channels, such as T1 carriers, whereby bits are inserted so that the receiver can identify the time slots that are allocated to each subchannel; framing bits may also carry alarm signals indicating specific alarm conditions

Freeze frame Type of digital television transmission whereby screen images are replenished, or "painted," every few seconds at the receiver set; images are sent in real time, and motion is not continuous; in video teleconferencing applications, allows a smaller-bandwidth transmission facility to be used than with full motion

Frequency The number of repetitions per time unit of a complete waveform; typically, the number of complete cycles per second, usually expressed in Hertz (Hz)

Frequency band Portion of the electromagnetic spectrum within a specified upper- and lower-frequency limit; also, frequency range

Frequency-division multiplexing (FDM) Technique for sharing a transmission channel wherein carrier signals of different frequencies are transmitted simultaneously

Frequency hopping A spread-spectrum technique by which the information is hopped between several communications channels. See Spread spectrum

Frequency modulation (FM) Method of encoding a carrier wave by varying the frequency of the transmitted signal

Frequency response The variation in relative strength (measured in decibels) between frequencies in a given frequency band, usually of the voice-frequency range of an analog telephone line

FSK Frequency-shift keying; modulation technique whereby two different tones represent either the "0" or the "1" state of binary information

Full duplex (FDX) Operation of a data communications link where transmissions are possible in both directions at the same time between devices at both ends

Full-motion video Television transmission by which images are sent and displayed in real time and motion is continuous; compare with freeze frame

Fully connected network A network topology in which each node is directly connected by branches to all other nodes; impractical as the number of nodes in the network increases

FX Foreign exchange; special telephone-company line arrangement whereby calls placed into the switched telephone network from a customer location enter the network through a central office other than the one normally serving the customer location

G

G Giga; prefix meaning one billion (e.g., Gbit/s)

Gain Increased signal power, usually the result of amplification; measured in decibels for the ratio of an output signal level to an input signal level; opposite of loss, or attenuation (negative gain)

Gain hits Cause of errors with telephone-line data transmission, usually where the signal surges more than 3 dB and lasts for more than 4 milliseconds; Bell standard calls for eight or fewer gain hits in a 15-minute period

Gateway A conceptual or logical network station that serves to interconnect two otherwise incompatible networks, network nodes, subnetworks, or devices; performs a protocol-conversion operation across numerous communications layers

Gaussian noise Undesirable, random electrical energy that is introduced into a transmission channel from the environment; generally of low amplitude, but it may still occasionally interfere with a carrier signal; background electrical noise

Geosynchronous orbit The orbit where communications satellites will remain stationary over the same earth location, about 23,300 miles above the earth's equator

Ground An electrical connection or common conductor that, at some point, connects to the earth

Ground station An assemblage of communications equipment, including signal generator, transmitter, receiver, and antenna, that receives (and usually also transmits) signals to/from a communications satellite; also, earth station

Group addressing In transmission, the use of an address that is common to two or more stations; on a multipoint line, where all stations recognize addressing characters, but only one station responds

Glossary

H

Half duplex (HDX) Operational mode of a communications line whereby transmission occurs in both directions but only in one direction at a time; transmission directions may be alternately switched to accommodate two-way data flow

Handshake protocol A predefined exchange of signals or control characters between two devices or nodes that sets up the conditions for data transfer; also, handshaking

Hard-wired A link (remote telephone line or local cable) that permanently connects two nodes, stations, or devices; describes electronic circuitry that performs fixed logical operations by virtue of fixed circuit layout, not under computer or stored-program control

Harmonic distortion Communications interference resulting from generated harmonic signals; measured in decibels as compared with the power of the input signal at the base (fundamental) frequency

HASP Houston Automatic Spooling Program; a control protocol adopted by IBM for transmitting data processing files and jobs to IBM 360 and 370 computers; an early job-control language

HDLC See High-level data link control

HDX See Half duplex

Head end A passive component in a broadband transmission network that translates one range of frequencies (transmit) to a different frequency band (receive); allows devices on a single-cable network to send and receive without the signals interfering with each other

Header Control information and codes that are appended to the front of a block of user data for control, synchronization, routing, and sequencing of a transmitted data frame or packet

Hertz (Hz) Measurement that distinguishes electromagnetic waveform energy; number of cycles, or complete waves, that pass a reference point per second; measurement of frequency, by which one Hertz equals one cycle per second

High-capacity service Generally refers to tariffed, digital-data transmission service equal to, or in excess of, T1 data rates (1.544 Mbit/s)

High frequency (HF) Portion of the electromagnetic spectrum, typically used in short-wave radio applications; frequencies approximately in the 3-to-30-MHz range

High-level data link control (HDLC) CCITT-specified, bit-oriented, data link control protocol; any related control of data links by a specified series of bits, rather than by control characters; the model on which most other bit-oriented protocols are based

High pass A specific frequency level above which a filter will allow all frequencies to be passed; opposite of low pass

Hz See Hertz

I

IATA International Air Transport Association

ICA International Communication Association (academic); International Communications Association (users)

IDCMA Independent Data Communications Manufacturers Association

IEC Interexchange carrier; since divestiture, any carrier registered with the FCC that is authorized to carry customer transmissions between LATAs interstate or, if approved by a state public utility commission, intrastate; includes carriers such as AT&T Communications (formerly AT&T Long Lines), Satellite Business Systems, Telenet, U S Sprint, and MCI

IEEE Institute of Electrical and Electronics Engineers

IFIPS International Federation of Information Processing Societies

Impedance The effect on a transmitted signal, which varies at different frequencies, of resistance, inductance, and capacitance

Impulse hits Cause of errors in telephone-line data transmission; voltage surges lasting from 1/3 to 4 milliseconds that come to within 6 dB of the normal signal level; Bell standard allows no more than 15 impulse hits per 15-minute period; also, spikes

IMS/VS Information Management System/Virtual Storage; a common IBM host operating environment, usually under the MVS operating system, oriented toward batch processing and telecommunications-based transaction processing

Infrared Portion of the electromagnetic spectrum used for optical-fiber transmission and also for short-haul, open-air data transmission; transmission wavelengths longer than about 0.7 microns

Inside wiring In telephone deregulation, the customer premises wiring

Intelligent terminal A programmable terminal

Interactive Describing time-dependent (real-time) data communications, typically one in which a user enters data and then awaits a response message from the destination before continuing; also, conversational; contrast with batch (processing)

Interface A shared boundary; a physical point of demarcation between two devices, where the electrical signals, connectors, timing, and handshaking are defined; the procedures, codes, and protocols that enable two entities to interact for a meaningful exchange of information

International standard An ISO standards document that has been approved in final balloting

Glossary

Internet protocol Used in gateways to connect networks at OSI network Level 3 and above

Interoffice trunk A direct circuit between telephone central offices

Intug International Telecommunications Users' Group

I/O Input/output

IP Internet protocol

IPARS International Passenger Airline Reservation System (IBM)

IPL Initial program load

IRC International record carrier; one of a group of common carriers that until a few years ago exclusively carried data and text (record) traffic from gateway cities in the United States to locations abroad and overseas; with recent FCC rulings, there no longer is a rigid IRC monopoly, and several new carriers have entered the international arena, just as the IRCs have been allowed to service points domestically

ISDN Integrated Services Digital Network; project under way within the CCITT for the standardization of operating parameters and interfaces for a network that will allow a variety of mixed digital transmission services to be accommodated; access channels under definition include basic rate (144 kbit/s) and primary rate (nominally, 1.544 and 2.048 Mbit/s)

I-series recommendations A group of CCITT recommendations concerning digital networks in general and ISDN in particular

ISO International Organization for Standardization

ISO 646 7-bit character set for information processing interchange

ISO 2022 Code-extension techniques for use with ISO 7-bit coded-character set

ISO 2110 25-pin DTE/DCE interface connector and pin assignments

ISO 2593 Connector pin allocations for use with high-speed data terminal equipment

ISO 3309 High-level data link procedures; frame structure

ISO 4902 HDLC unbalanced classes of procedures

ISO 4903 15-pin DTE/DCE interface connector and pin assignments

ITU International Telecommunications Union

IVDT Integrated voice/data terminal; one of a family of devices that features a terminal keyboard/display and telephone instrument; many contain varying degrees of local processing power, ranging from directory storage for automatic dialing to full microcomputer capacity; may be designed to work with a specific customer premises PBX or may be PBX independent

J

Jamming The intentional interference of (typically) open-air radio-frequency transmission to prevent communications between a transmitter and a receiver

JCL Job Control Language

JES Job Entry Subsystem; control protocol and procedure for directing host processing of a task in an IBM host environment; the specific IBM software release, host-based, that performs job-control functions

Jitter The slight movement of a transmission signal in time or phase that can introduce errors and loss of synchronization in high-speed synchronous communications; see Phase jitter

Job A large file, typically transmitted in batch mode; specifically, a set of data, including programs, files, and instructions to a computer, that collectively constitutes a unit of work to be done by a computer

Jumper A patch cable or wire used to establish a circuit, often temporarily, for testing or diagnostics

K

k Kilo; notation for one thousand (e.g., kbit/s)

K Expression for 1,024, or 2^{10}; standard quantity measurement for disk and diskette storage and semiconductor circuit capacity; e.g., one K of memory equals 1,024 bytes, or 8-bit characters, of computer memory; slightly more than a thousand

Ka band Portion of the electromagnetic spectrum; frequencies approximately in the 18-to-30-GHz range

kbit/s Kilobits per second; standard measure of data rate and transmission capacity

Kermit Asynchronous file transfer protocol designed for academic computing at Columbia University

Keying Modulation of a carrier signal, usually by frequency or phase, to encode binary information; also, interruption of a DC circuit for the purpose of signaling information

Key management The management of the cryptographic keys or algorithms used to cipher data

Key telephone system (KTS) Key station, key equipment; describing multiline telephone CPE that offers limited PBX-type features; generally with line capacities ranging from 2 to 12 trunk lines, and from 4 to 40 extensions (e.g., 1A KTS)

KSR Keyboard send/receive; operational characteristic describing some terminals, typically teleprinters

Ku band Portion of the electromagnetic spectrum, being used increasingly for satellite communications; frequencies approximately in the 10-to-12-GHz range

L

LAN See Local area network

LAP Link access procedure; the data link-level protocol specified in the CCITT X.25 interface standard; original LAP has been supplemented with LAPB (LAP-Balanced) and LAPD

LAPD Link Access Procedure-D; link-level protocol devised for ISDN connections, differing from LAPB (LAP-Balanced) in its framing sequence. Likely to be used as basis for LAPM, the proposed CCITT modem error-control standard

Laser Light amplification through the stimulated emission of radiation; a major light-signal source for optical-fiber transmission; produces a generally more coherent single-wavelength light signal than an LED and is also, typically, more expensive and shorter-lived; used mainly with single-mode optical fiber

LATA Local Access and Transport Area; one of 161 local telephone serving areas in the United States, generally encompassing the largest standard statistical metropolitan areas; subdivisions established as a result of the Bell divestiture that now distinguish local from long-distance service; circuits with both end-points within the LATA (intraLATA) are generally the sole responsibility of the local telephone company, while circuits that cross outside the LATA (interLATA) are passed on to an interexchange carrier

Latency The time interval between when a network station seeks access to a transmission channel and when access is granted or received; equivalent to waiting time

Layer In the OSI reference model (seven basic layers), referring to a collection of related network-processing functions that comprises one level of a hierarchy of functions

L band Portion of the electromagnetic spectrum commonly used in satellite and microwave applications, with frequencies approximately in the 1 GHz region

LDM See Limited-distance modem

Leased line A dedicated circuit, typically supplied by the telephone company, that permanently interconnects two or more user locations; generally voice-grade in capacity and in range of frequencies supported; typically analog, though sometimes it refers to DDS subrate digital channels (2.4 to 9.6 kbit/s); used for voice (2000 Series leased line) or data (3002-type); could be point-to-point or multipoint; may be enhanced with line conditioning; also, private line

Least-cost routing see Automatic Route Selection

LEC Local exchange carrier

LED Light-emitting diode; device that accepts electrical signals and converts the energy to a light signal; with lasers, the main light source for optical-fiber transmission; used mainly with multimode fiber

Lightwave Referring to electromagnetic wavelengths in the region of visible light; wavelengths of approximately 0.8 to 1.6 microns; referring to the technology of fiber optic transmission

Limited-distance modem (LDM) A comparatively low-cost modem used on customer premises for transmitting data within or between buildings to a maximum distance of a few miles

Line hit An incident of electrical interference causing unwanted signals to be introduced onto a transmission circuit

Line of sight Characteristic of some open-air transmission technologies where the area between a transmitter and a receiver must be clear and unobstructed; said of microwave, infrared, and open-air, laser-type transmissions; a clear, open-air, direct transmission path free of obstructions such as buildings but in some cases impeded by adverse weather or environmental conditions

Line turnaround The action in a (typically half-duplex) communications link that, for example, a device takes after receiving a block of data to prepare sending its own block; in RS-232-C connections, the delay after request to send has been signaled and a clear to send indication is received; see Turnaround time

Link-attached Describing devices that are connected to a network, a communications data link, or telecommunications circuit; compare with channel-attached

Loading Adding inductance to a transmission line to minimize amplitude distortion; generally accomplished with loading coils; also, adding a program to a computer

Loading coil An induction device employed in telephone-company local loops, generally those exceeding 18,000 feet in length, that compensates for the wire capacitance and serves to boost voice-grade frequencies; removed for LDM circuits; often removed in the new generation of high-speed, local-loop data services, such as CSDC, because they may distort data signals at higher frequencies than those used for voice

Local area network (LAN) A type of high-speed (typically in the Mbit/s range) data communications arrangement wherein all segments of the transmission medium (typically coaxial cable, twisted-pair wire, or optical fiber) are in an office or campus environment under the control of the network operator

Local loop In telephony, the wire pair that connects a subscriber to a telephone-company end office; typically containing two wires, though four-wire local loops are common, especially with leased voice-grade circuits

Logical Link Control (LLC) A protocol developed by the IEEE 802 committee, common to all of its LAN standards, for data link-level transmission control; the upper sublayer of the IEEE Layer 2 (OSI) protocol that complements the MAC protocol; IEEE standard 802.2; includes end-system addressing and error checking

Logical unit (LU) In IBM's SNA, a port through which a user gains access to the services of a network; an LU can support two

Glossary

two types of sessions: with the host-based System Services Control Point (SSCP) and with other LUs

Long-haul Long-distance, describing (primarily) telephone circuits that cross out of the local exchange, or serving, area; now generally applied to any interLATA circuits, whether intrastate or interstate; said of a modem to distinguish it from an LDM

Loopback Diagnostic procedure used for transmission devices; a test message is sent to a device being tested, which is then sent back to the originator and compared with the original transmission; loopback testing may be within a locally attached device or conducted remotely over a communications circuit

Loop start Most commonly used method of signaling an off-hook condition between an analog telephone set and a switch, where picking up the receiver closes a wire loop, allowing direct current to flow, which is detected by a PBX or central-office switch and interpreted as a request for service

Loosely coupled Describing processors connected by means of channel-to-channel adapters that are used to pass control information between each other (IBM); compare with tightly coupled

Loss Reduction in signal strength, expressed in decibels; also, attenuation; opposite of gain

Low Entry Networking (LEN) A peer-oriented extension to SNA, first implemented on the System/36, that allows networks to be more easily built and managed by means of such techniques as topology database exchange and dynamic route selection

Low frequency (LF) A portion of the electromagnetic spectrum; frequencies approximately in the 30-to-300-kHz range

Low pass A specific frequency level, below which a filter will allow all frequencies to pass; opposite of high pass

LRC Longitudinal redundancy check

LSI Large-scale integration, as in LSI circuit

LU See Logical unit

LU 6.2 In Systems Network Architecture, a set of protocols that provides peer-to-peer communications between applications

M

m Milli; designation for one-thousandth

M Mega; designation for one million (e.g., Mbit/s)

MAC Media Access Control; media-specific access control protocol within IEEE 802 specifications; currently includes variations for the token ring, token bus, and CSMA/CD; the lower sublayer of the IEEE's link layer (OSI), which complements the Logical Link Control (LLC)

Macintosh A family of Apple microcomputers that represents the first wide-scale PC deployment of icons, windows, "mice," and a consistent user interface

Magnetic medium Any data-storage medium, and related technology, including disks, diskettes, and tapes, in which different patterns of magnetization are used to represent bit values

Magnetic stripe A strip of magnetic material, similar to a piece of magnetic tape, affixed to a credit card, ID badge, or other portable item, on which data is recorded and from which data can be read

Main PBX or Centrex switch into which other PBXs or remote concentration of switching modules are homed; a PBX or Centrex connected directly to an electronic tandem switch (ETS); also, a power source

Main distribution frame In telephony, a structure where telephone-subscriber lines are terminated; in conjunction with a PBX, the place where central-office telephone lines are connected to on-premises extensions; at a telephone central office, a site where subscriber lines terminate

Main network address In IBM's SNA, the logical unit (LU) network address, within ACF/VTAM, that is used for SSCP-to-LU sessions and for certain LU-to-LU sessions; compare with auxiliary network address

Maintenance services In IBM's SNA, network services performed between a host SSCP and remote physical units (PUs) that test links and collect and record error information; related facilities include configuration services, management services, and session services

MAN Metropolitan area network; network that extends to 50-kilometer range, operates at speeds from 1 Mbit/s to 200 Mbit/s, and provides an integrated set of services for real-time data, voice, and image transmission; two standards bodies are involved with work on MANs: IEEE 802.3 and ANSI X3T9.5

Management services In IBM's SNA, network services performed between a host SSCP and remote physical units (PUs) that include the request and retrieval of network statistics

Manchester encoding Digital encoding technique (specified for the IEEE 802.3 Ethernet baseband network standard) in which each bit period is divided into two complementary halves: a negative-to-positive (voltage) transition in the middle of the bit period designates a binary "1," while a positive-to-negative transition represents a "0"; the encoding technique also allows the receiving device to recover the transmitted clock from the incoming data stream (self-clocking)

Manufacturing Automation Protocol (MAP) A General Motors-originated suite of networking protocols, the implementation of which tracks the seven layers of the OSI model

MAP Manufacturing Automation Protocol (General Motors)

Mapping In network operations, the logical association of one set of values, such as addresses on one network, with quantities or values of another set, such as devices on another network (e.g., name-address mapping, internetwork-route mapping, protocol-to-protocol mapping)

Glossary

Maser Microwave amplification by stimulated emission of radiation; a device that generates electromagnetic signals in the microwave range, known for relatively low-noise characteristics

Master clock The source of timing signals—or the signals themselves—that all network stations use for synchronization

Master station A station that controls slave stations; see Primary station

Matrix In switch technology, that portion of the switch architecture where input leads and output leads meet, any pair of which may be connected to establish a through circuit

Matrix switch Device that allows a number of channels, connected via serial interfaces (typically RS-232-C), to connect, under operator control, to designated remote or local analog circuits, as well as to other serial interfaces

MAU Multistation access unit; wiring concentrator used in local area networks

M bit The More Data mark in an X.25 packet that allows the DTE or DCE to indicate a sequence of more than one packet

Mean time between failures (MTBF) A stated, or published, period of time for which a user may reasonably expect a device to operate before an incapacitating failure occurs

Mean time to repair (MTTR) The average time required to perform corrective maintenance on a failed device

Medium Any material substance that can be, or is, used for the propagation of signals, usually in the form of electrons or modulated radio, light, or acoustic waves, from one point to another, such as optical fiber, cable, wire, dielectric slab, water, air, or free space (ISO)

Megabyte (Mbyte or M) 1,048,576 bytes, equal to 1,024 Kbytes; basic unit of measurement of mass storage; also used in describing (primarily parallel) data transfer rates as a function of time (e.g., Mbyte/s)

Message Any information-containing data unit, in an ordered format, sent by means of a communications process to a named network entity or interface; in Bisync, the data between two ETX control characters

Message-Handling System (MHS) The standard defined by CCITT as X.400 and by ISO as Message-Oriented Text Interchange Standard (MOTIS)

Message switching Transmission method by which messages are transmitted to an intermediate point, where they are temporarily stored, and then transmitted later to a final destination in their original form (see Store-and-forward); the destination of the message is typically indicated in an internal address field of the message itself

Message-switching network A public data communications network over which subscribers send primarily textual messages to one another (e.g., TWX, Telex)

Message Telephone Service (MTS) Official designation for tariffed long-distance, or toll, telephone service

Message unit In IBM's SNA, that portion of data within a message that is passed on to, and processed by, a particular network layer (e.g., path information unit, or PIU; request/response unit, or RU)

MICR Magnetic ink character recognition; a process of character recognition in which printed characters, containing particles of magnetic material, are read by a scanner and converted into a computer-readable digital format

Microcode Programmed instructions that typically are unalterable; usually synonymous with firmware and programmable read-only memory (PROM)

Microprocessor An electronic integrated circuit, typically a single-chip package, capable of receiving and executing coded instructions (e.g., Zilog Z80, Intel 8088, Motorola 68000 are popular microprocessors)

Microsecond One-millionth of a second

Microwave Portion of the electromagnetic spectrum above about 890 megahertz; describing high-frequency transmission signals and equipment that employ microwave frequencies, including line-of-sight, open-air microwave transmission and, increasingly, satellite communications

Millisecond One-thousandth of a second

Mini-MAP (Mini-Manufacturing Automation Protocol) A version of MAP consisting of only physical, link, and application layers intended for lower-cost process-control networks. With Mini-MAP, a device with a token can request a response from an addressed device; but, unlike a standard MAP protocol, the addressed mini-MAP device need not wait for the token to respond

Minimum Internetworking Functionality (MIF) A general principle within the ISO that calls for minimum local area network station complexity when interconnecting with resources outside the local area network

MIPS Million instructions per second; a general comparison gauge of a computer's raw processing power

MNP Microcom Networking Protocol; proprietary error-correcting protocol for modems operating at speeds from 2.4 kbit/s to 9.6 kbit/s; commercially licensed to more than 50 vendors, the protocol has been proposed as an adjunct to the CCITT LAP (link access procedure) family; operates only point-to-point and does not have easy connections to X.25 and ISDN technology

Modem Modulator/demodulator; electronic device that enables digital data to be sent over analog transmission facilities; the most prevalent modem types include the following Bell models:
- 103/113 Series: 300 bit/s, full-duplex, dial-up, asynchronous; originate-only (113C), answer-only (113D), or originate-and-answer (103J)
- 201 Series: 2.4 kbit/s, synchronous; dial-up (201C-L1C) or via 3002-type, unconditioned, two- or four-wire circuits (201C-L1D)
- 208 Series: 4.8 kbit/s, synchronous; full-duplex over 3002-type leased line (208A) or dial-up (208B)
- 212A: 0-300 bit/s or 1.2 kbit/s, dial-up, full-duplex

Glossary

■ 209A: 9.6 kbit/s, synchronous, via four-wire, 3002-type leased line with D1 conditioning

Modem eliminator (also known as a null modem) Device that reverses certain serial interface leads so that two DTEs can talk to each other over RS-232 cabling lengths without the need for a modem; for example, a null modem will hard-wire the request to send/clear to send pins and transmit/receive data pins so that data can be transmitted between two devices

Modem-7 Microcomputer communications software program supporting the public-domain, X-modem, error-correcting file transfer protocol

Modulation Systematic changing of properties (e.g., amplitude, frequency, phase) of an analog signal to encode and convey (typically digital) information

Modulo N In communications, refers to a quantity, such as of messages or frames, that can be counted before the counter resets to zero, or, (typically) the number of messages (N-1) that can be outstanding from a transmitter before an acknowledgment is required from the receiver (e.g., Modulo 8, Modulo 128)

MOS Metal-oxide semiconductor

MOSFET MOS field-effect transistor

MPG Microwave pulse generator; a device that generates electrical pulses at microwave frequencies

MS-DOS (Microsoft Disk Operating System) Microcomputer operating system developed for the IBM PC and, hence, a de facto industry standard; also referred to as PC-DOS, primarily by IBM

MTA Message transfer agent

MTBF See Mean time between failures

MTS Message transfer system; also, Message telephone service

MTTR See Mean time to repair

Multidomain network In IBM's SNA, a network consisting of two or more host-based System Services Control Points; typically, a network with more than one host mainframe

Multidrop A communications arrangement in which multiple devices share a common transmission channel, though only one may transmit at a time; see Multipoint line

Multileaving In communications, the transmission (usually via Bisync facilities and protocols) of a variable number of data streams between user devices and a computer

Multimode In fiber optics, describing an optical-fiber light guide, the core of which is capable of propagating light signals of two or more wavelengths or phases; essentially, an optical fiber designed to carry multiple signals, distinguished by frequency or phase, at the same time; compare with single-mode

Multiple routing The process of sending a message to more than one recipient, usually when all destinations are specified in the header of the message

Multiplexed channel A communications channel capable of servicing a number of devices, or users, at a time

Multiplexer (mux) A device that does multiplexing

Multiplexing The combining of multiple data channels onto a single transmission medium; any process through which a circuit normally dedicated to a single user can be shared by multiple users; typically, user data streams are interleaved on a bit or byte basis (time division) or separated by different carrier frequencies (frequency division)

Multipoint line A single communications channel (typically, a leased telephone circuit) to which more than one station or other device is attached, though only one may transmit at a time upon being polled (see Polling); upon selection, one or more devices on such a line may receive transmissions from the master station; also, a multidrop line

Multisystem Networking Facility (MSNF) An optional feature with certain of IBM's telecommunications access methods that permits more than one host entity (running ACF/TCAM or ACF/VTAM) to jointly control an ACF/NCP network

Multitasking Generically refers to the concurrent execution of two or more tasks, typically applications, by a computer; may also be the concurrent execution of a single program that is used by many tasks

Mux Multiplexer

MVS Multiple Virtual Storage; refers to a common IBM host operating environment; also, OS/VS2, Release 2

N

NAK Negative acknowledgment; in synchronous protocols, a supervisory control-code message sent by the receiver to indicate that the previous data block was received in error and that the receiver is again ready to accept a transmission

Nanosecond One-billionth of a second

NAPLPS North American Presentation-Level Protocol Syntax; a protocol for videotex graphics and screen formats; developed by AT&T and standardized within ANSI; based on Canada's Telidon videotex-graphics protocol

Narrowband Describing sub-voice-grade channels characterized by data speeds typically of from 100 to 200 bit/s

NARUC National Association of Regulatory Utility Commissioners

NBS/ICST National Bureau of Standards/Institute for Computer Sciences and Technology; the NBS directorate, based in Gaithersburg, Md., concerned with developing computer and data communications Federal Information Processing Standards that are used in (non-Department of Defense) government procurements

NCC Network control center; any centralized network diagnostic and management station or site, such as that of a packet-switching network

NCP See Network Control Program

NCTA National Cable Television Association; a leading trade organization representing U. S. cable-television carriers

NCTE Network channel-terminating equipment; equipment considered necessary for terminating a telephone circuit or facility at the customer premises; recent FCC decisions have established that most NCTE is customer premises equipment (CPE) and may therefore be supplied by third-party vendors

Near-end crosstalk (NEXT) Unwanted energy transferred from one circuit usually to an adjoining circuit; occurs at the end of the transmission link where the signal source is located; the absorbed energy is usually propagated in the direction opposite to the absorbing channel's normal current flow; caused by high-frequency or unbalanced signals and insufficient shielding

NECA National Exchange Carrier Association; an association of local exchange carriers, mandated by the FCC upon the divestiture of AT&T

Netview An IBM mainframe network management product that integrated the functions of several earlier IBM network management products

Network An interconnected group of nodes (ISO TC97); a series of points, nodes, or stations connected by communications channels; the assembly of equipment through which connections are made between data stations (IBM)

Network addressable unit (NAU) In IBM's SNA, a host-based logical unit (LU), physical unit (PU), or System Services Control Point (SSCP) that is the origin or destination of information transmitted by the path-control portion of a SNA network

Network architecture A set of design principles, including the organization of functions and the description of data formats and procedures, used as the basis for the design and implementation of a network (ISO)

Network Communications Control Facility (NCCF) A host-based IBM program product through which users and other programs can monitor and control network operation

Network Control Program (NCP) In IBM SNA networks, a host-generated program that controls the operation of a communications controller (such as an IBM 3705 or 3725)

Network layer Layer 3 in the OSI model; the logical network entity that services the transport layer; responsible for ensuring that data passed to it from the transport layer is routed and delivered through the network

Network Problem Determination Application (NPDA) A host-resident IBM program product that aids a network operator in interactively identifying network problems from a central point

Network services In IBM's SNA, the services within network addressable units (NAUs) that control network operations via sessions to and from the host SSCP

Network Terminal Option (NTO) An IBM program product that enables an SNA network to accommodate a select group of non-SNA asynchronous and bisynchronous devices via the NCP-driven communications controller

Network topology The physical and logical relationship of nodes in a network; the schematic arrangement of the links and nodes of a network (IBM); networks are typically of either a star, ring, tree, or bus topology, or some hybrid combination thereof

Network virtual terminal A communications concept wherein a variety of DTEs, with different data rates, protocols, codes, and formats, are accommodated in the same network; this is done as a result of network processing, whereby each device's data is converted into a network standard format and then converted into the format of the receiving device at the destination end

NIC Near instantaneous companding; the essentially real-time process of quantizing an analog signal into digital symbols

Node A point where one or more functional units interconnect transmission lines (ISO); a physical device that allows for the transmission of data within a network; an endpoint of a link or a junction common to two or more links in a network (IBM SNA); typically includes host processors, communications controllers, cluster controllers, and terminals

Node type In IBM's SNA, the classification of a network device based on the protocols it supports and the network addressable units (NAUs) it can contain; Type 1 and Type 2 nodes are peripheral nodes, Type 4 and Type 5 nodes are subarea nodes

Noise Any extraneous and unwanted signal disturbances in a link (electromagnetic interference, or EMI); usually, random variations in signal voltage or current, or interfering signals

Noise suppressor Filtering or digital signal-processing circuitry in a receiver or transmitter that automatically reduces or eliminates noise

Nonblocking Describing a switch where a through traffic path always exists for each attached station; generically, a switch or switching environment designed never to experience a busy condition due to call volume

Nonerasable Describing integrated circuitry or any type of data storage that is unalterable; same as read-only

Nonimpact printer A printing device that does not use mechanical strikes to create characters (e.g., thermal, laser, and electrostatic printers)

Nontransparent mode A transmission environment, mainly Bisync, in which control characters and control-character sequences are recognized through the examination of all transmitted data; compare with transparent mode; also, normal mode

Nonvolatile storage Any storage medium or circuitry, the contents of which are not lost when power is turned off or lost

NPDA See Network Problem Determination Application

NRZ Nonreturn to zero; a binary encoding and transmission scheme in which "ones" and "zeros" are represented by opposite,

Glossary

and alternating, high and low voltages; wherein there is no return to a reference (zero) voltage between encoded bits

NRZI Nonreturn to zero inverted; a binary encoding scheme that inverts the signal on a "one" and leaves the signal unchanged for a "zero"; wherein a change in the voltage state signals a "one" bit, and the absence of a change denotes a "zero" bit value; also, transition coding

NTIA National Telecommunications and Information Administration; agency of the U.S. Department of Commerce concerned with the development of communications standards

NTSC signal National Television System Committee-specified signal; de facto standard governing the format of television transmission signals

NUA Network Users Association

Null characters Control characters that can be inserted into, or removed from, a data stream without affecting the meaning of a sequence; typically added to fill in time slots or unused fields

Nyquist theorem In communications theory, a formula stating that two samples per cycle is sufficient to characterize a band-limited analog signal; in other words, the sampling rate must be twice the highest frequency component of the signal (e.g., sampling at 8 kHz for a 4-kHz analog signal)

O

Object code Executable machine code; programs that have been compiled or assembled; compare with source code

OCR Optical character recognition (reader); the process of reading text characters by light-sensitive devices, which converts them into machine-readable digital codes; a popular method of inputting text or graphics data into a computer, storage device, or transmission device

OEM Original equipment manufacturer; the maker of equipment that is marketed by another vendor, usually under the name of the reseller; the OEM may manufacture certain components, or complete devices, which are then often configured with software and/or other hardware by the reseller

Off-hook In telephony, condition indicating the active state of a subscriber's telephone circuit; a line state that signals a central office that a user requires service; opposite of on-hook

Office class Functional ranking of a telephone-network switching center depending on transmission requirements and hierarchical relationship to other switching centers; see Class X office

Off-line Condition in which a user, terminal, or other device is not connected to a computer or is not actively transmitting via a network; operation of a functional unit without the continual control of a computer; compare with on-line

Ones density The requirement for digital transmission lines in the public switched telephone network that eight consecutive zeros cannot be in a digital data stream; exists because repeaters and clocking devices within the network will lose timing after receiving eight zeros in a row; any number of techniques or algorithms used to insert a one after every seventh-consecutive zero; see Bit stuffing

One-way trunk A trunk between a switch (PBX) and a central office, or between central offices, where traffic originates from only one end

On-hook Deactivated condition of a subscriber's telephone circuit, in which the telephone or circuit is not in use; opposite of off-hook

On-line Condition in which a user, terminal, or other device is actively connected with the facilities of a communications network or computer; pertains to the operation of a functional unit under the continual control of a computer; opposite of off-line

Open-air transmission A transmission type, or associated equipment, that uses no physical communications medium other than (usually line-of-sight) air; used for most radio-frequency communications techniques, including microwave, shortwave and FM radio, and infrared; also, free-space transmission

Operating environment The combination of (usually IBM) host software that includes operating system, telecommunications access method, database software, and user applications; some common operating environments include MVS/CICS and MVS/TSO

Operating system (OS) The software of a computer that controls the execution of programs, typically handling the functions of input/output control, resource scheduling, and data management (e.g., CP/M, MS-DOS, VM/370)

Optical disk A very high-density information-storage medium that uses light to read information

Optical fiber Any filament or fiber, made of dielectric materials, that is used to transmit laser- or LED-generated light signals; optical fiber usually consists of a core, which carries the signal, and cladding, a substance with a slightly higher refractive index than the core, which surrounds the core and serves to reflect the light signal; see also Fiber optics

OS See Operating system

Oscillator An electronic device used to produce repeating signals of a given amplitude or frequency

OSI Open Systems Interconnection; referring to the OSI reference model, a logical structure for network operations standardized within the ISO; a seven-layer network architecture being used for the definition of network protocol standards to enable any OSI-compliant computer or device to communicate with any other OSI-compliant computer or device for a meaningful exchange of information; the layers are named (refer to each one for its specific definition): Physical, Data link, Network, Transport, Session, Presentation, Application

OSInet A test network, sponsored by the National Bureau of Standards (NBS), designed to provide vendors of products based on the OSI model a forum for doing interoperability testing

OS/2 Operating software that will run on the Personal System/2. OS/2 Standard Edition is a joint Microsoft/IBM development, while OS/2 Extended Edition is IBM's proprietary extension to include communications and database managers

Outgoing access The capability of a user in one network to communicate with a user in another network (CCITT)

Overhead In communications, all information, such as control, routing, and error-checking characters, that is in addition to user-transmitted data; includes information that carries network-status or operational instructions, network routing information, as well as retransmissions of user-data messages that are received in error

Overrun Loss of data because a receiving device is unable to accept data at the rate it is transmitted

P

Pacing group In IBM's SNA, the number of data units (path information units, or PIUs) that can be sent before a response is received; IBM term for window

Packet A sequence of data, with associated control information, that is switched and transmitted as a whole; refers mainly to the field structure and format defined within the CCITT X.25 recommendation

Packetized voice Digitized voice technology that lends itself to T1 and ISDN applications

Packet switching A data transmission technique whereby user information is segmented and routed in discrete data envelopes called packets, each with its own appended control information for routing, sequencing, and error checking; allows a communications channel to be shared by many users, each using the circuit only for the time required to transmit a single packet; describing a network that operates in this manner

PAD Packet assembler/disassembler; network interface device that allows multiple asynchronous and/or synchronous terminals or host-computer ports to interface to a packet-switching network; a protocol conversion device that allows user terminals not equipped for packet switching to communicate over an X.25-based channel; PAD operations and functions are fully delineated in CCITT recommendations

Pad characters In (primarily) synchronous transmission, characters that are inserted to ensure that the first and last characters of a packet or block are received correctly; inserted characters that aid in clock synchronization at the receiving end of a synchronous transmission link; also, fill characters

PAM Pulse-amplitude modulation

Paper tape A nearly obsolete recording medium for data, where data characters are encoded on paper as a series of holes; also, punched tape

P/AR Peak to average ratio; a standard analog transmission-line test that involves sending a test signal of varying frequencies and amplitudes, which is then compared with the received signal; composite results are a weighted number from 1 to 100, with 100 being the maximum; used increasingly as a standard quick test of a telecommunications channel's comparative quality; per Bell standard, the minimal acceptable P/AR for "medium-speed" data transmission is 48

Parallel processing Concurrent or simultaneous execution of two or more processes, or programs, within the same processor, as contrasted with serial or sequential processing

Parallel sessions In IBM's SNA, two or more concurrently active sessions between the same two logical units (LUs) using different network addresses; each session can have different transmission parameters

Parallel transmission A type of data transfer in which all bits of a character, or multiple-bit data blocks, are sent simultaneously, either over separate communications lines or circuits, over a single channel using multiple frequencies, or over a multiple-conductor cable

Parity bit An additional noninformation bit appended to a group of bits, typically to a 7- or 8-bit byte, to make the number of ones in the group of bits either an odd or even number; a basic and elementary mechanism for error checking

Parity check Process of error checking using a parity method; varied methods include longitudinal parity check and transverse parity check; see Parity bit

Pass-through Describing the ability to gain access to one network element through another

Path-control layer In IBM's SNA, the network processing layer that handles, primarily, the routing of data units as they travel through the network and manages shared link resources

PBX Private branch exchange; telephone switch located on a customer's premises that primarily establishes circuits over tie-lines between individual users and the switched telephone network; typically also provides switching within a customer's premises and usually offers numerous other enhanced features, such as least-cost routing and call-detail recording; also, PABX, for private automatic branch exchange

PCM Pulse-code modulation; digital transmission technique that involves sampling of an analog information signal at regular time intervals and coding the measured amplitude value into a series of binary values, which are transmitted by modulation of a pulsed, or intermittent, carrier; a common method of speech digitizing using 8-bit code words, or samples, and a sampling rate of (typically) 8 kHz

PDN Public data network; typically, a tariffed packet-switching data carrier

PDU (Protocol Data Unit) ISO term referring to a packet of information exchanged between two network-layer entities

Peripheral device With respect to a particular processing unit, any equipment that provides the processor with outside communications (ISO); any device that is peripheral to the major function of its attached processor or other controlling device

Glossary

Permanent virtual circuit A virtual circuit resembling a leased line in that invariant logical channel numbers allow it to be dedicated to a single user

Personal computer (PC) A generic term for a single-user microcomputer; PC also refers to IBM's Personal Computer, the first microcomputer to be widely accepted in business and still a standard for compatibility

Personal System/2 (PS/2) IBM's current family of microcomputers that, with OS/2, represents a higher level of performance, capacity, and software consistency than the firm's previous microcomputers, the IBM PCs

Phase hit In telephony, the unwanted and significant shifting in phase of an analog signal; as defined by Bell, any instance when the phase of a 1,004-Hz test signal shifts more than 20 degrees; error-causing events more severe than phase jitter, especially for data transmission equipment using PSK modulation

Phase jitter In telephony, the measurement, in degrees out of phase, that an analog signal deviates from the referenced phase of the main data-carrying signal; often caused by alternating current components in a telecommunications network

Phaselock loop In electronics, a circuit that acts as a phase detector by comparing the frequency of a known oscillator with an incoming signal and then feeds back the output of the detector to keep the oscillator in phase with the incoming frequency

Phase modulation A data transmission encoding method by which the phase angle of the carrier wave is varied, usually by 90 or 180 degrees, to represent a different bit value to the receiver; the encoding technique used in phase-shift keying

Phase shift A change in the time that a signal is delayed with respect to a reference signal

Phase-shift keying (PSK) The phase-modulation encoding technique employed by many modems; see Phase modulation

Physical layer Within the OSI model, the lowest level (1) of network processing, below the link layer, that is concerned with the electrical, mechanical, and handshaking procedures over the interface that connects a device to a transmission medium; referring to an electrical interface, such as RS-232-C

Physical unit (PU) In IBM's SNA, the component that manages and monitors the resources of a node, such as attached links and adjacent link stations; PU types follow the same classification as node types; see Node type

Picosecond One-trillionth of a second; one-millionth of a microsecond

PIN Positive, intrinsic, negative; type of photodetector used to sense lightwave energy and then to convert it into electrical signals; also, personal identification number

PIU Path information unit; see Pacing group

Pixel Picture element; smallest unit of a graphics or video display, the light characteristics of which (color and intensity) can be coded into an electrical signal for transmission

Plasma display Type of flat visual display in which selected electrodes, part of a grid of crisscrossed electrodes in a gas filled panel, are energized, causing the gas to be ionized and light to be emitted

PL/1 Programming Language One (IBM)

Plotter A type of computer peripheral printer that displays data in two-dimensional graphics form

Point of presence (POP) Since the AT&T divestiture, the physical-access location within a LATA of a long-distance and/or interLATA common carrier; the point to which the local telephone company terminates subscribers' circuits for long-distance dial-up or leased-line communications

Point-to-point Describing a circuit that connects two points directly, where there are generally no intermediate processing nodes, computers, or branched circuits, although there could be switching facilities; a type of connection, such as a phone-line circuit, that links two, and only two, logical entities; see Multipoint line, Broadcast

Polarity Any condition in which there are two opposing voltage levels or charges, such as positive and negative

Polarization Characteristic of electromagnetic radiation (e.g., lightwave, radio, or microwave) when the electric-field vector of the wave energy is perpendicular to the main direction, or vector, of the electromagnetic beam

Polling Communications control procedure by which a master station or computer systematically invites tributary stations on a multipoint circuit to transmit data; contrast with selection

Polling delay The specified interval at which a tributary device is polled by a master station; often a user-specified parameter

Port A point of access into a computer, a network, or other electronic device; the physical or electrical interface through which one gains access; the interface between a process and a communications or transmission facility

Presentation layer In the OSI model, Layer 6, which provides processing services to the application layer (7), allowing it to interpret the data exchanged, as well as to structure data messages to be transmitted in a specific display and control format

Prestel Videotex offering of British Telecom in the United Kingdom

Primary rate In North American ISDN, twenty-three 64-kbit/s information-carrying D channels and one 64 Kbit/s B channel used for signaling (23B+D)

Primary station A network node that controls the flow of information on a link; the station that, for some period of time, has control of information flow on a communications link (in this case, primary status is temporary)

Primitives Basic units of machine instruction

Print server An intelligent device used to transfer information to a series of printers

Prioritization The process of assigning different values to (network) users, so that a user with a higher priority value will be offered access or service before (or more often than) a user with a lower priority value; increasingly available as an added option with network operation; any procedure with different levels of precedence

Private line A leased line; a nonswitched circuit

Private network A network established and operated by a private organization or corporation for users within that organization or corporation; compare with public network

Programmable terminal A user terminal that has computational capability; also, intelligent terminal

PROM Programmable read-only memory

Propagation delay The time it takes a signal, composed of electromagnetic energy, to travel from one point to another over a transmission channel; usually most noticeable in communicating with satellites; normally, the speed-of-light delay

Protocol Formal set of rules governing the format, timing, sequencing, and error control of exchanged messages on a data network; may be oriented toward data transfer over an interface, between two logical units directly connected, or on an end-to-end basis between two users over a large and complex network

PSDS Public Switched Digital Service; a BOC service; AT&T's Circuit-Switched Digital Capability (CSDC), also known commercially as AT&T's Accunet Switched 56 service; allows full-duplex, dial-up, 56-kbit/s digital circuits on an end-to-end basis

Pseudo-random bit pattern Test message consisting of 511 or 2,047 bits ensuring that all possible bit combinations can pass through a network without error

PSK See Phase shift keying

PSTN Public switched telephone network; acronym for the dial-up telephone network

PTT Postal, Telegraph, and Telephone; government authority or agency that typically operates the public telecommunications network, sets standards and policy, and negotiates communications issues internationally for a particular country; not found in the United States; compare with common carrier

PU See Physical unit

Public network Generically, a network operated by common carriers or telecommunications administrations for the provision of circuit-switched, packet-switched, and leased-line circuits to the public; compare with private network

PUC Public Utility Commission

PWM Pulse-width modulation; the process, in communications, of encoding information based on variations of the duration of carrier pulses; also called pulse-duration modulation

Q

QAM, QSAM Quadrature amplitude modulation, quadrature sideband amplitude modulation; modulation technique, using variations in signal amplitude, that allows data-encoded symbols to be represented as any of 16 or 32 different states

Q bit The qualifier bit in an X.25 packet that allows the DTE to indicate that it wishes to transmit data on more than one level

QPSK Quadrature phase-shift keying

Quality of service (QOS) In network operation, a parameter specifying certain performance characteristics of a service, session, connection, or link

Queue Any group of items, such as computer jobs or messages, waiting for service

Queuing In telephony, a feature that allows calls to be "held" or delayed at the origination switch while waiting for a trunk to become available; sequencing of batch-data sessions

R

RACE In the European Community, research and development for advanced communications in Europe

RAM Random access memory

Raster A scanning pattern used in generating, recording, or reproducing television, facsimile, or graphics images on a screen; raster scanning

Rate center A defined geographic point used by telephone companies in determining distance measurements for interLATA mileage rates

RBOC Regional Bell operating company; one of the seven companies (Ameritech, Nynex, Bell Atlantic, BellSouth, Pacific Telesis, Southwestern Bell, and US West) created to provide local communications service by the Justice Department's breakup of the old Bell System

Read-only memory (ROM) A data-storage device, the contents of which cannot normally be altered; storage in which writing over is prevented; also, permanent storage

Real time A transmission or data processing operating mode by which data is entered in an interactive session; pertaining to an application whereby response to input is fast enough to affect subsequent input, such as a process-control "system" or a computer-aided design "system" (IBM); describing processing in which the results are used to influence an ongoing process

Receive only (RO) Describing operation of a device, usually a page printer, that can receive transmissions but cannot transmit

Glossary

Redundancy In data transmission, that portion of the gross information content of a message that can be eliminated without losing essential information; also, duplicate facilities

Reference noise The level of circuit noise that will produce a measured reading equal to that produced by 1 picowatt (-90 dBm) of electric power at 1,000 Hz

Refresh rate With conventional CRT displays, the rate per unit of time at which a displayed image is renewed in order to appear stable; typically, 50 times per second, or 50 Hz (in Europe), or 60 times per second, or 60 Hz (in the United States)

Relative transmission level The ratio, in decibels, of the test-tone signal power at one point in a transmission circuit to some other circuit point chosen as a reference (usually the transmission switch, which is taken as a zero-level reference point)

Remote job entry (RJE) The submission of data processing jobs via a data link

Remote station Any device that is attached to a controlling unit by a data link; also, a tributary station on a multipoint link

Repeater In digital transmission, equipment that receives a pulse train, amplifies it, retimes it, and then reconstructs the signal for retransmission; in fiber optics, a device that decodes a low-power light signal, converts it to electrical energy, and then retransmits it via an LED or laser light source; also, regenerative repeater

Residual error rate In communications, the remaining error rate after protocol-specified attempts at error correction have been exhausted (ISO)

Response An answer to an inquiry; in IBM's SNA, the control information sent from a secondary station to the primary station under SDLC

Response time For interactive sessions, the elapsed time between the end of an inquiry and the beginning of the response; the interval between a user data entry and the reply from a CPU or destination device

Retransmissive star In optical-fiber transmission, a passive component that permits the light signal on an input fiber to be retransmitted on multiple output fibers; formed by heating together a bundle of fibers to near the melting point; used mainly in fiber-based local area networks; also, star coupler

Retry In the Bisync protocol, the process of resending the current block of data a prescribed number of times or until it is accepted

Return to zero (RZ) Method of transmitting binary information in such a way that after each encoded bit, voltage returns to the zero level

Reverse channel A (typically) small-bandwidth channel used for supervisory or error-control signaling; signals are transmitted in the opposite direction to the one in which data is sent; also, the channel in a dial-up telephone circuit from the called party to the calling party

Reverse interrupt (RVI) With the Bisync protocol, a control-character sequence sent by a receiving station to request premature termination of a transmission in progress

Revisable-form document An electronic document with its formatting information intact, readable, and modifiable

RF Radio frequency; describing transmission at any frequency at which coherent electromagnetic energy radiation is possible, usually above 150 kHz

RFI Request for information; general notification of an intended purchase of communications or computer equipment, sent to potential suppliers to determine interest and solicit product materials; also, radio-frequency interference

RFP Request for proposal; sent to interested vendors to solicit a configuration proposal that meets a user's requirements

Ring network A network topology in which each node is connected to two adjacent nodes

RISC Reduced Instruction Set Computing; internal computing architecture where processor instructions are pared down so that most can be performed in a single processor cycle, theoretically improving computing efficiency

RJE See Remote job entry

ROM See Read-only memory

Routing The process of selecting the correct circuit path for a message

RPG Report Program Generator (computer language)

RPQ Request for price quotation; solicitation for pricing of a specific device, software product, service, or configuration

RS-232-C An EIA-specified physical interface, with associated electrical signaling, between data circuit-terminating equipment (DCE) and data terminal equipment (DTE); the most commonly employed interface between computer devices and modems

RS-422-A Electrical characteristics of balanced-voltage digital interface circuits (EIA)

RS-423-A Electrical characteristics of unbalanced-voltage digital interface circuits (EIA)

RS-449 General-purpose 37-position and 9-position interface for data terminal equipment and data circuit-terminating equipment employing serial binary data interchange (EIA)

RTS Request to send; part of modem handshaking

S

Satellite communications The use of geostationary orbiting satellites to relay transmissions from one earth station to another one or more other earth stations

Scattering Cause of lightwave signal loss in optical fiber transmission; diffusion of a light beam caused by microscopic variations in the material density of the transmission medium

SCS SNA character string; type of transmission data format for IBM devices, consisting of EBCDIC control characters optionally mixed with user data, that is carried within an SNA request/response unit

SDLC Synchronous data link control; bit-oriented IBM version of the HDLC protocol; the mainstay of SNA communications

Secondary station A station or node selected to receive transmission from a primary station; the secondary-station designation is usually temporary and only for the duration of the session or transaction; see Primary station

Selection The process by which a computer contacts a station to send it [the station] a message (IBM); see Polling

Sequencing The process of dividing a user data message into smaller frames, blocks, or packets for transmission, in which each has an integral sequence number for reassembly of the complete message at the destination end

Serial interface Usually, as pertains to computers or terminals, the mechanical and electrical components that allow data to be sent sequentially-by-bit over a transmission medium; in contrast to a parallel interface

Serial transmission The sequential transmission of the bits constituting an entity of data over a data circuit (ISO)

Serving area Region surrounding a broadcasting station where signal strength is at or above a stated minimum; the geographic area handled by a telephone central office

Session A connection between two stations that allows them to communicate (ISO); the time period that a user engages in a dialogue with an interactive computer; in IBM's SNA, the logical connection between two network addressable units (NAUs);

Session layer In the OSI model, the network-processing layer (5) responsible for binding and unbinding logical links between users and maintaining an orderly dialogue between them; also, serves the presentation layer (6)

SHF Super-high frequency; portion of the electromagnetic spectrum in the microwave region, with frequencies ranging from about 2 to 20 GHz

Shielding Protective enclosure surrounding a transmission medium, such as coaxial cable, designed to minimize electromagnetic leakage and interference

Short-haul modem Generally, an LDM with transmission distances of less than a mile; see Limited distance modem

Signal converter An electronic device that takes input signal information and outputs it in another form

Signal-to-noise ratio (SNR) Relationship of the magnitude of a transmission signal to the noise of its channel; measurement of signal strength compared to error-inducing circuit noise; given in decibels

Simplex One-way data transmission, with no capability for changing direction

Single mode Describing an optical waveguide that is designed to propagate light of only a single wavelength and perhaps a single phase; essentially, an optical fiber that allows the transmission of only one light beam, or data-carrying lightwave channel, and is optimized for a particular lightwave frequency; compare with multimode

Single-sideband transmission Type of transmission in which one sideband of the carrier signal is transmitted while the other is suppressed; the main carrier wave itself may be either transmitted or suppressed

Sink Data "receptacle," such as a receiver

SITA *Société Internationale de Télécommunication Aéronautique*; the international data communications network used by many airlines

Skewing The time delay, or offset, between any two signals

Smart terminal Terminal that has local processing facilities as well as communications capabilities

SMDR Station message detail recording (AT&T); see Call-detail recording

SNA See Systems Network Architecture (IBM)

SNADS (Systems Network Architecture Delivery System) Applications-level architecture providing generalized, delayed store-and-forward delivery of documents through components called distribution service units

SNR See Signal-to-noise ratio

Software-defined network Network that gives users flexible, software-driven control over network topology, so that configurations can be reconfigured dynamically; see Virtual private network

SOH Start of header (heading); control character that delimits the beginning of the control section of a data block

SOM See Start of message

Sonet (Synchronous Optical Network) Bellcore-proposed protocol for fiber networks handling DS-3 transmission with some overhead; likely to become an official ANSI standard (T1X1); will be used by the RBOCs with large fiber trunks

Source code The form of a program as produced by a programmer; compare with object code

Space-division switching In telephony, a switching technology whereby a separate physical path through the switch is maintained for each call

SPOOL Simultaneous peripheral operation on line

Spot beam In satellite communications, a narrow and focused down-link transmission, typical of newer satellite designs, that allows the satellite to use different frequencies from, or reuse the

Glossary

same frequencies as in, other down-link beams; covers a much smaller geographic area, or footprint, than older satellite down-link transmissions, which also enhances protection of the down-link from unauthorized reception

Spread spectrum A modulation technique in which the information content is spread over a wider bandwidth than the frequency content of the original information

SSCP See System Services Control Point

Starlan A local area network design and specification within the IEEE 802.3 standards subcommittee, characterized by 1-Mbit/s baseband data transmission over two-pair twisted-pair wiring

Start bit In asynchronous transmission, the first element in each character that prepares the receiving device to recognize the incoming information elements

Start of message (SOM) A control character or group of characters transmitted by a station, which indicates to other stations on the line that what follows are addresses of stations to receive the message

Start of text (STX) A transmission control character that designates the start of a message's text as well as (usually) the end of the message heading

Star topology The point-to-point wiring of network elements to a central node

Start-stop transmission Asynchronous transmission characterized by each byte containing its own start and stop bits of data elements that are preceded by a start and followed by a stop signal; reference employed to designate asynchronous transmission

Station Any DTE that receives or transmits messages on a data link, including network nodes and user devices

Step-index Referring to a type of optical fiber, which exhibits a uniform refractive index at the core and a sharp decrease in the refractive index at the core-cladding interface

Stop bit In asynchronous transmission, the last transmitted element in each character, which informs the receiver to come to an idle condition before accepting another character

Store and forward Describing operation of a data network where packets, messages, or frames are temporarily stored within a network node before being transmitted to the destination

STX See Start of text

SWIFT Society for Worldwide Interbank Financial Telecommunications

Switched line Communications link for which the physical path, established by dialing, may vary with each use (e.g., a dialup telephone circuit)

Switched network backup An option in certain communications links, and with certain communications devices such as modems, by which a switched, or dial-up, line is used as an alternate path if the primary, typically leased-line, path is unavailable

Symbol In data transmission, a discrete waveform, usually representing binary digits, modulated as appropriate to be understood by the receiver; see Baud

Sync bits Synchronizing bits in synchronous transmission; maintains synchronism between transmitter and receiver

Synchronous transmission Data communications in which characters or bits are sent at a fixed rate, with the transmitting and receiving devices synchronized; eliminates the need for start and stop bits basic to asynchronous transmission and significantly increases data throughput rates

Sysgen System generation (or generator); loading of an operating system in a CPU

System A logical collection of computers, peripherals, software, service routines, accounting and control procedures, terminals, and end users; a collection of men, machines, and methods organized to accomplish a set of specific functions (*American National Dictionary for Information Processing*); an assembly of components united by some form of regulated interaction to form an organized whole (IBM); generally, systems may include networks, but only to the limited degree that those networks connect users directly to system resources; see Network

System Services Control Point (SSCP) In IBM's SNA, a host-based network entity that manages the network configuration, coordinates network operator and problem-determination requests, maintains network address and mapping tables, and provides directory support and session services

Systems Network Architecture (SNA) In IBM networks, the layered logical structure, formats, protocols, and procedures that govern information transmission; somewhat analogous to the OSI reference model

T

TA Terminal adaptor; in ISDN, a device that provides conversion between a non-ISDN terminal device and the ISDN user/network interface

Table-driven Describing a logical computer process, widespread in the operation of communications devices and networks, in which a user-entered variable is matched against an array of predefined values; frequently used in network routing, access security, and modem operation; involves a table lookup, that is, reference to that array of predefined values

Tandem data circuit A data channel passing through more than two data circuit-terminating equipment (DCE) devices in series

Tandem office A telephone company's major switching center for the switched telephone network; a high-level switching center in the local exchange, or serving, area; a tandem exchange, or switch, interconnects local central offices as a central office inter-connects individual subscriber lines

Glossary

Tariff The formal process whereby services and rates are established by and for communications common carriers; submitted by carriers for government regulatory approval, reviewed, often amended, and then (usually) approved; the published rate for a specific communications service, equipment, or facility that constitutes a contract between the user and the communications supplier or carrier

TASI Time-assigned speech interpolation; a method that increases the capacity of voice links by using the pauses between utterances to carry additional conversations

TAT-8 The eighth transatlantic telephone cable; the first to use single-mode fiber optic technology

TCAM See Telecommunications Access Method

T-carrier A time-division-multiplexed, typically phone company-supplied, digital transmission facility, usually operating at an aggregate data rate of 1.544 Mbit/s and above

TCM See Time-compression multiplexing

TCP/IP Transmission Control Protocol/Internet Protocol; internetworking software suite originated on the Department of Defense's Arpanet network; IP corresponds to OSI network Level 3, TCP to OSI Layers 4 and 5

T1 AT&T term for a digital carrier facility used to transmit a DS-1 formatted digital signal at 1.544 Mbit/s

T3 A T-carrier with an aggregate rate of 44.736 Mbit/s

TDM See Time-division multiplexing

TDMA Time-division multiple access; a satellite transmission technique in which several earth stations have use of total available transponder power and bandwidth, with each station in sequence transmitting in short bursts

Technical and Office Protocols (TOP) A Boeing version of the MAP protocol suite aimed at office and engineering applications

Telco Telephone central office, in most usages; but also, a generic abbreviation for telephone company

Telecommunications A term encompassing both voice and data communications in the form of coded signals over media

Telecommunications Access Method (TCAM) A widely employed communications-management software package from IBM that runs on IBM 370 and compatible mainframes; depending on version and options, can support either SNA or pre-SNA networking; supplanted by VTAM in recent years, especially where networks are primarily SNA

Telegraphy Aging data transmission technique characterized by maximum data rates of 75 bit/s and signaling where the direction, or polarity, of DC current flow is reversed to indicate bit states

Telephony Generic term describing voice telecommunications

Teleprocessing Remote-access data processing (ISO); the use of data link communications to accomplish a computer-based task; distinguished from distributed data processing (DDP), in which remote communications is not a prerequisite to all processing

Teletex Akin to a higher-speed version of ASCII Telex, intended eventually to replace Telex

Teletext Generically, one-way data transmission designed for widespread broadcasting of graphics and textual information, for display on subscriber television sets or (typically) low-cost video terminals; a data communications technique akin to, but more limited than, two-way videotex, by which users can select from among many pages of information for viewing

Teletypewriter Generic term for a teleprinter terminal; Teletype is a trademark of the former Teletype Corp.

Telex Teleprinter exchange; a worldwide switched message-exchange service, characterized by Baudot-coded data (though numerous conversion facilities are now available)

Terminal A point in a network at which data can either enter or leave; a device, usually equipped with a keyboard, often with a display, capable of sending and receiving data over a communications link (IBM); generically the same as data terminal equipment (DTE)

Terminal node In IBM's SNA, a peripheral node that is not user-programmable, having less intelligence and processing capability than a cluster-controller node

Terminated line A telephone circuit with a resistance at the far end equal to the characteristic impedance of the line, so no reflections or standing waves are present when a signal is entered at the near end; compare with bridge tap

Terrestrial The term commonly applied to long-distance links that use earth-bound transmission facilities such as copper wire, optical fiber, or microwave, as opposed to satellite transmission

Test center A facility for detecting and diagnosing problems with communications lines and the equipment attached to them; a facility where a network manager or technician can gain access to (ideally) any circuit in a network for the purpose of running diagnostic testing; also, network control center

Text In communications, transmitted characters forming the part of a message that carries information to be conveyed; in some protocols, the character sequence between start-of-text (STX) and end-of-text (ETX) control characters; information for human, as opposed to computer, comprehension that is intended for presentation in a two-dimensional form (ISO)

Tie line A leased or private dedicated telephone circuit provided by common carriers that links two points together without using the switched telephone network

Tightly coupled Describing the interrelationship of processing units that share real storage, that are controlled by the same control program, and that communicate directly with each other (IBM); compare with loosely coupled

Time-compression multiplexing (TCM) Technology designed to allow high-speed data transmission over the local loop; essen-

Glossary

tially, TCM involves alternating transmission (in Ping-Pong fashion) of high-speed digital data bursts

Time-division multiplexing (TDM) Interleaving digital data from many users onto one or two serial communications links by dividing channel capacity into time slices; two common techniques are bit interleaving and byte (by character) interleaving

Time-out Expiration of predefined time period, at which time some specified action occurs; in communications, timeouts are employed to avoid unnecessary delays and improve traffic flow; used, for example, to specify maximum response times to polling and addressing before a procedure is automatically reinitiated

Timesharing Describing the interleaved use of time on a computer that enables two or more users to execute computer programs concurrently (IBM); any concurrent use of the same processing resource by multiple users

Token bus A local area network access mechanism and topology in which all stations actively attached to the bus listen for a broadcast token or supervisory frame; stations wishing to transmit must receive the token before doing so; however, the next logical station to receive the token is not necessarily the next physical station on the bus; bus access is controlled by preassigned priority algorithms

Token ring A local area network access mechanism and topology in which a supervisory frame or token is passed from station to adjacent station sequentially; stations wishing to gain access to the network must wait for the token to arrive before transmitting data; in a token ring, the next logical station receiving the token is also the next physical station on the ring; compare with token bus

Toll center A Class 4 telephone central-office circuit-switching facility where time- and distance-based toll-charge information is collected; any Class 4 central office, typically one per metropolitan area

TOP See Technical and Office Protocols (Boeing)

Touch-Tone Registered AT&T trademark for push-button dialing; see DTMF

Transaction In communications, a message destined for an application program; a computer-processed task that accomplishes a particular action or result; in interactive communications, an exchange between two devices, one of which is usually a computer; in batch or remote job entry, a job or job step

Transceiver Generic term describing a device that can both transmit and receive

Transients Intermittent, short-duration signal impairments

Translator In telephony, a central-office device that converts dialed or tone digits into call-processing information

Transmission The dispatching of a signal, message, or other form of intelligence by wire, radio, telegraphy, telephony, facsimile, or other means (ISO); a series of characters, messages, or blocks, including control information and user data; the signaling of data over communications channels

Transparent mode (Typically) binary synchronous communications data transmission in which the recognition of control characters is suppressed; the operation of a (usually) digital transmission facility during which the user has complete and free use of the available bandwidth and is unaware of any intermediate processing; generally implies out-of-band signaling; see Clear channel

Transponder In satellite communications, the circuitry that receives an up-link signal, translates it to another, usually higher, frequency, amplifies it, and then retransmits it as the down-link signal

Transport layer In the OSI model, Layer 4; the network processing entity responsible, in conjunction with the underlying network, data link, and physical layers, for the end-to-end control of transmitted data and the optimized use of network resources; also serves the session layer (5)

Transverse parity check Type of parity error checking performed on a group of bits in a transverse direction for each frame; see Parity check

Tree A network topology, characterized by the existence of only one route between any two network nodes; describing a network that resembles a branching tree, such as most CATV distribution networks

Trellis coding A method of forward-error correction used in certain high-speed modems whereby each signal element (baud) is assigned a coded binary value, which represents that element's phase and amplitude; allows the receiving modem to determine—based on the value of the preceding signal elements—whether or not a given signal element is received in error

Trunk A dedicated aggregate telephone circuit connecting two switching centers, central offices, or data concentration devices

Trunk group Multiple trunk circuits between the same two switching centers that can be accessed by dialing a single trunk number and use the same multiplexing equipment at each end

T-span A telephone circuit or cable through which a T carrier runs

T-tap A passive line interface used for extracting data from a circuit; also, a similar device for extracting optical signals from a fiber cable or electrical signals from a coaxial cable

TTY transmission Teletypewriter communications; generally, basic asynchronous ASCII-coded or Baudot-coded data communications

Turnaround time In communications, the time, measured at either the send or receive end, required to reverse the direction of transmission, from send to receive or vice versa, over a halfduplex channel; also, the elapsed time between submission of a transaction, or job, and the return of processed output; typically, the combined time required for line propagation, modem timing, and computer processing; see Response time

Twinaxial cable A shielded coaxial cable with two central conductors

Twisted pair A pair of insulated copper conductors that are twisted around each other, mainly to cancel the effects of electrical noise; typical of standard telephone wiring; unshielded twisted pair contains no outside wraparound conductor

Glossary

Two-way alternate Synonym for half-duplex communications

Two-way simultaneous Synonym for full-duplex communications

Two-wire Applies to the local-loop transmission path from the customer's premises to the central-office switch of a local exchange carrier (LEC); on a two-wire circuit, data is received and transmitted over the same wire loop; also applies to connections between data terminal equipment (DTE) and a private branch exchange (PBX)

TWX Teletypewriter exchange; a switched message service serving Canada and the United States provided by Western Union; employs ASCII-coded equipment

U

UART Universal asynchronous receiver/transmitter

UHF Ultra high frequency; portion of the electromagnetic spectrum ranging from about 300 MHz to about 3 GHz; the frequency band that includes television channels 14 through 83 and cellular radio frequencies

Unattended mode Describing the operation of any device, such as an auto-answer modem, designed to operate without the manual intervention of an operator

Unbalanced-to-ground Describing a two-wire circuit, where the impedance-to-ground on one wire is measurably different from that on the other; compare with balanced-to-ground

Unix Operating system originally designed for communicating multi-user, 32-bit minicomputers by AT&T Bell Laboratories; has come into wide commercial acceptance due to its predominance in academia and its programming versatility. AT&T Version V.3 and Berkeley System Development Version 4.3 are currently popular

Up-link Describing the earth-station transmission and the carrier signal used to transmit information to a geosynchronous satellite; complement of down-link

Uptime Colloquial expression for the period of time when network or computer resources are accessible and available to a user; the length of time between failures or periods of nonavailability

Upward compatible Describing any device that can be configured to function in either a different operating environment or some enhanced mode; a computer's capability to execute programs written for another computer without major alteration, but not vice versa (IBM)

USART Universal synchronous/asynchronous receiver/transmitter; integrated circuitry common to many data communications devices; converts data in parallel form from the CPU into serial form for transmission

USITA United States Independent Telephone Association

USRT Universal synchronous receiver/transmitter; integrated circuit that performs conversion of parallel data to serial form for transmission over a synchronous data channel

V

Value-added network (VAN) A network that provides services that go beyond the pure switching function

VAN Value-added network

Variable quantizing level (VQL) A type of speech-encoding technique that quantizes and encodes an analog voice conversation for transmission, nominally at 32 kbit/s

Vertical redundancy check (VRC) An odd-parity check performed on each character of an ASCII block as the block is received

VHF Very high frequency; portion of the electromagnetic spectrum with frequencies between about 30 and 300 MHz; operating band for television channels 2 to 13 and most FM radio

Video teleconferencing The real-time, and usually two-way, transmission of digitized video images between two or more locations; requires a wideband transmission facility, for which satellite communications has become a popular choice; transmitted images may be freeze-frame (where a television screen is "repainted" every few seconds) or full-motion; bandwidth requirements for two-way videoconferencing range from 56 kbit/s (freeze-frame) to T1 rates (1.544 Mbit/s)

Videotex An interactive data communications application designed to allow unsophisticated users to converse with a remote database, enter data for transactions, and retrieve textual and graphics information for display on subscriber television sets or (typically) low-cost video terminals

Virtual circuit In packet switching, network facilities that give the appearance to the user of an actual end-to-end circuit; in contrast to a physical circuit, a dynamically variable network connection where sequential user data packets may be routed differently during the course of a "virtual connection"; virtual circuits enable transmission facilities to be shared by many users simultaneously

Virtual Machine Facility VM/370: an IBM control program, essentially an operating system, that controls the concurrent execution of multiple virtual machines on a single System/370 mainframe

Virtual private network A carrier-provided service in which the public switched network provides capabilities similar to those of private lines, such as conditioning, error testing, and higher-speed, full-duplex, four-wire transmission with a line quality adequate for data; see Software-defined network

Virtual storage The concept of storage space that may be viewed as addressable main storage to a computer user, but is actually auxiliary storage (usually peripheral mass storage) mapped into real addresses; amount of virtual storage is limited by the addressing scheme of the computer

Glossary

VLF Very low frequency; that portion of the electromagnetic spectrum having continuous frequencies ranging from about 3 to 30 kHz

VLSI Very large-scale integration

VM Virtual memory; see Virtual storage

Voice digitization The conversion of an analog voice into digital symbols for storage or transmission

Voice frequency (VF) Describing an analog signal within the range of transmitted speech, typically from 300 to 3,400 Hz; any transmission supported by an analog telecommunications circuit

Voice-grade channel A telecommunications circuit used primarily for speech transmission but suitable for the transmission of analog or digital data or facsimile; typically supporting a frequency range of 300 to 3,400 Hz; also, voice band

Volatile storage Any storage device whose contents are lost when power is removed

VS See Virtual storage

VSAT Very small aperture terminal; in satellite communications, small-diameter receiver stations typically operated in the ku band

VTAM Virtual Telecommunications Access Method; IBM mainframe communications-software product, oriented toward managing SNA/SDLC communications and links

VTAME VTAM Entry (IBM)

V-series recommendations CCITT-specified standards dealing mainly with modem operation over an interface with the telephone network, including:

V.21 300-bit/s duplex modem standardized for use in the general switched telephone network

V.22 1.2-kbit/s duplex modem standardized for use in the general switched telephone network and on leased circuits

V.22bis 2.4-kbit/s duplex dial-up modem standard

V.23 600-bit/s and 1.2-kbit/s modem standardized for use in the general switched telephone network

V.24 List of definitions for interchange circuits between data terminal equipment and data circuit-terminating equipment

V.25 Automatic calling and/or answering equipment in the general switched telephone network, including disabling of echo suppressors on manually established calls

V.26 2.4-kbit/s modem standardized for use on four-wire leased circuits

V.26bis 1.2/2.4-kbit/s modem standardized for use in the general switched telephone network

V.26ter A standard for 2.4-kbit/s full-duplex modem that uses echo cancellation techniques suitable for application to the public switched telephone network

V.27 4.8-kbit/s modem with manual equalizer standardized for use on leased telephone-type circuits

V.27bis 2.4/4.8-kbit/s modem with automatic equalizer standardized for use on leased telephone-type circuits

V.27ter 2.4/4.8-kbit/s modem standardized for use in the general switched telephone network

V.29 9.6-kbit/s modem standardized for use on point-to-point leased telephone-type circuits

V.32 9.6-kbit/s two-wire duplex modem standard

W

WATS Wide Area Telephone Service; telephone-company service allowing reduced costs for certain telephone-call arrangements; may be In-WATS, or 800-number service, by which calls can be placed to a location from anywhere at no cost to the calling party, or Out-WATS, by which calls are placed out from a central location; cost is based on hourly usage per WATS circuit and on distance based on zones, or bands, to or from which calls are placed

Waveguide Specially constructed metallic pipe for containing, directing, and focusing microwave electromagnetic radiation for transmission

Wavelength Distance between successive peaks of a sinusoidal wave

Wavelength-division multiplexing (WDM) A technique in fiber optic transmission for using different light wavelengths to send data parallel-by-bit (one discrete wavelength per bit), serial-by-character; hence, one single multimode fiber can act as an 8-bit parallel bus

Wet T1 T1 with a BOC-powered interface

Wideband Generally, a communications channel offering a transmission bandwidth greater than a voice-grade channel; data transmission speeds on wideband facilities are typically in excess of 9.6 kbit/s and often at rates such as 56 kbit/s and 1.544 Mbit/s

Window A flow-control mechanism in data communications, the size of which is equal to the number of frames, packets, or messages that can be sent from a transmitter to a receiver before any reverse acknowledgment is required; called a pacing group in IBM's SNA

Wire center A spatial midpoint at the confluence of several cables

Wiring closet Termination point for customer premises wiring, offering access to service personnel; generally serves a specific area, with multiple wiring closets that are cross-connected

Word length The number of bits or characters in a word, which

Glossary

is usually determined as an optimal or convenient size for processing, storage, or transmission; word lengths are often based on the register size and internal operation of a computer (e.g., IBM System/370 uses 32-bit words; IBM PC employs 16-bit)

Working draft In ISO, the initial stage of a standards document describing the standard as envisioned by a working group of a standards committee or subcommittee

Workstation Input/output equipment at which an operator works; a station at which a user can send data to, or receive data from, a computer or other workstation for the purpose of performing a job

X

X The designation assigned to International Telegraph and Telephone Consultative Committee (CCITT, from the French *Comité Consultatif International Télégraphique et Téléphonique*) recommendations related to data transmission over public data networks, most notably:

X.3 Packet assembly/disassembly facility in a public data network

X.20 Interface between data terminal equipment (DTE) and data circuit-terminating equipment (DCE) for start-stop transmission services on public data networks

X.20bis Used on public data networks of data terminal equipment (DTE) that is designed for interfacing to asynchronous duplex V-series modems

X.21 Interface between data terminal equipment (DTE) and data circuit-terminating equipment (DCE) for synchronous operation on public circuit-switched data networks

X.21bis Used on public data networks of data terminal equipment (DTE) that is designed for interfacing to synchronous V-series modems

X.24 List of definitions for interchange circuits between data terminal equipment (DTE) and data circuit-terminating equipment (DCE) on public data networks

X.25 A CCITT recommendation that specifies the interface between user data terminal equipment (DTE) and packet-switching data circuit-terminating equipment (DCE)

X.28 DTE/DCE interface for start-stop mode data terminal equipment accessing the packet assembly/disassembly facility (PAD) in a public data network situated in the same country

X.29 Procedures for the exchange of control information and user data between a packet assembly/disassembly facility (PAD) and a packet-mode DTE or another PAD

X.32 Interface between data terminal equipment and data circuit-terminating equipment for terminals operating in the packet mode and accessing a packet-switched public data network through a public switched telephone network or a circuit-switched public data network

X.75 Terminal and transit call-control procedures and data transfer mechanisms on (typically) international circuits between packet-switched data networks

X.121 The CCITT's international numbering plan for public data networks

X.400 A series of protocol standards for international electronic-mail interexchange

X3 Sequence of data communications standards promulgated by the American National Standards Institute

X3.15 Bit sequencing of ASCII in serial by-bit data transmission

X3.16 Character structure and character parity sense for serial-by-bit data communications in ASCII

X3.36 Synchronous high-speed data signaling rates between data terminal equipment and data circuit-terminating equipment

X3.79 Determination of the performance of data communications devices that use bit-oriented control procedures

X3.92 Data encryption algorithm

Xenix Microsoft trade name for a 16-bit microcomputer operating system derived from Bell Laboratories' Unix

XNS Xerox Network Systems; local area network protocol suite operating at ISO Network and Transport layers

X-off/X-on Transmitter off/transmitter on; a commonly used peripheral-device flow-control protocol, used extensively for modem control by an attached terminal or processor

X.PC Error-correcting protocol for modems, designed largely by Tymnet providing functions typical of the OSI Network Layer 3

Z

ZBTSI Zero Byte Time Slot Interchange; a technique used with the T-carrier extended superframe format (ESF) in which an area in the ESF frame carries information about the location of all-zero bytes (eight consecutive zeroes) within the data stream

Zero code suppression The insertion of a "one" bit to prevent the transmission of eight or more consecutive "zero" bits; used primarily with T1 and related digital telephone-company facilities, which require a minimum "ones density" in order to keep the individual subchannels of a multiplexed, high-speed facility active; several different schemes are currently employed and are being evaluated to accomplish this; see also Bit stuffing, Ones density

Zero transmission level point (0 TLP) In telephony, a reference point at which a zero dBm signal level is applied for measuring the signal power gain and loss of a telecommunications circuit; usually, though not always, referenced to the output signal level at the transmitting switch in a telephone circuit; the signal level reference unit dBm0

Index

Page references in this index are to the first pages of the articles in which the subjects appear, or to special sections devoted to those subjects.

Access techniques, 2, 4, 8
Accunet Reserved T1.5 service, 102
Adaptive differential pulse-code modulation (ADPCM), 205
Attenuation, 178
Availability, 18, 44, 62, 70
Avoidance, 21

Bell modems, 216
Bipolar signaling, 236
Bridges, 8, 22

Cabling, 62, 164, 168
Carrier sense multiple access with collision detection (CSMA/CD), 8, 59
CCITT, see International Telegraph and Telephone Consultative Committee
CD-ROM (Compact Disk-Read Only Memory), 143
Circuit multiplication, 205
Communications costs, 127
Communications management vendors, 132
Continuously Variable Slope Delta (CVSD) Modulation, 205

Data-link access, 2
Data Link Layer, 8
Dataphone Digital Service (DDS), 25, 106
DCS, see Digital cross-connect systems
DCS vendors, 29
DECnet, 66
Diagnostics, 106, 172, 198
Digital Access and Cross-connect System (DACS), 25
Digital circuits, 22
Digital cross-connect systems (DCSs), 25
Distortion, 180
Diversity, 21, 101

Engineering cycle, 151
Erasable optical disks, 143
Ethernet, 54, 63
Event reports, 89
Extended superframe format, 222, 228

Facsimile, 309
Fast packet, 116

Fiber Distributed Data Interface (FDDI), 70, 233
Fiber optics, 13, 70, 233
Frame relay, 116
Frequency translation, 180

History, 244
Human factors, 78, 244

IBM, 31
IEEE (Institute of Electrical and Electronic Engineers), 8
IEEE 802 standards, 8, 59
Integrated Services Digital Network (ISDN), 33, 205, 278, 299
International Telegraph and Telephone Consultative Committee (CCITT), 210

Lasers, 13
Light-emitting diodes (LEDs), 13
Line conditioning, 22
Line noise, 177
Line test equipment, 182
Line transients, 181

Marketing, 148
Marketing cycle, 150
Mean time between failures (MTBF), 18
Mean time to repair (MTTR), 18
Media alternatives, 281
Modem standards, 210
Multinode teleprocessing, 130
Multiple carrier circuit routing, 21
Multiplexers, 45, 299
Multiplexer vendors, 268

Network control center, 78
NetWare, 67
Nodal architectures, 297
Nondisruptive monitoring, 228

Open Systems Interconnection, 41
Optical storage, 143

Packets, 59
Packet switching, 59, 116
Parallel circuits, 22

Performance, 18, 50
Phase-shift modulation, 215
Printers, 136
Protocols, 59, 62
Productivity, 78
Pulse-amplitude modulation, 45
Pulse-code modulation, 45, 205, 222

Reliability, 18, 43, 62, 70, 133, 268
Risk avoidance, 268
Routing, 293
RS-232 standard, 169

Signaling, 33, 41, 236
Signaling System 7 vendors, 39
Single frequency interference, 181
Spectrum analyzers, 99
Switched network backup, 22
Switched T1 service, 102
Synchronous Optical Network (Sonet), 49

Tax breaks, 265
Time Assigned Speech Interpolation (TASI), 205
Time-division multiplexing, 45
Token bus, 54
Token ring, 54, 64, 70
T1 format, 45
T1 multiplexers, 292
T1 networking, 25, 44, 90, 99, 205, 217, 228, 286
T1 network management, 229
Topology, 18, 62, 70
Traffic partitioning, 8
Transient protection devices, 196
Troubleshooting, 62, 85, 106, 172, 177, 198
T3 format, 46
T3 networking, 44

Vendor selection, 268
Voice mail, 156
V-series recommendations, 210

Wideband modems, 215
Wiring, 164
WORM (write once, read many times) memory, 143